THE SUPERNATURAL OMNIBUS

THE SUPERNATURAL OMNIBUS

BEING
A COLLECTION OF STORIES

of

APPARITIONS, WITCHCRAFT, WEREWOLVES,
DIABOLISM, NECROMANCY, SATANISM,
DIVINATION, SORCERY, GOETY,
VOODOO, POSSESSION, OCCULT
DOOM AND DESTINY

Edited, with an Introduction, by
MONTAGUE SUMMERS

LONDON
VICTOR GOLLANCZ LTD
1982

First published June 1931
Reissued 1949
Second reissue 1961
This edition 1982

British Library Cataloguing in Publication Data
The Supernatural omnibus.
1. Ghost stories, English
I. Summers, Montague
823'.01'08375[FS]   PR1309.G5
ISBN 0-575-03120-4

Printed in Great Britain by
St Edmundsbury Press, Bury St Edmunds, Suffolk

CONTENTS

§1 HAUNTINGS AND HORROR

§ 2 DIABOLISM, WITCHCRAFT, AND EVIL LORE

INTRODUCTION

In the full flush of success during its first London run, Tom Sheridan, who was playing the hero of " wax-work " Brooke's *The Earl of Essex*, was wont to be loud up and down the Town in his praises of the poetry and exalted sentiments of this truly mediocre tragedy. In his fine stage voice *ore rotundo* he would declaim some half a dozen wilting lines and demand applause. On one occasion, in some crowded drawing-room, Sheridan spouts the conclusion of the first Act, ending up with a tremendous—

Who rules o' er freemen should himself be free !

O happy sentiment ! Enraptured silence ; and then enthusiastic applause. The company vastly commend and admire. After a moment or two, all eyes are turned towards where Dr. Johnson sits. They await a polished panegyric, a swelling eulogy. The great man opens his mouth and looks sternly enough at Sheridan from beneath his frowning brow. " Nay, sir," quoth he, " I cannot agree with you. It might as well be said :

" *Who drives fat oxen should himself be fat.*"

Should the writer of the ghost story himself believe in ghosts ? Dr. M. R. James, who is among the greatest—perhaps, indeed, if we except Vernon Lee, the greatest—of modern exponents of the supernatural in fiction, tells us that it is all a question of evidence. " Do I believe in ghosts ? " he writes. " To which I answer that I am prepared to consider evidence and accept it if it satisfies me." This leaves us, I venture to think, very much in the same position as we were before the question was asked and the reply returned. Can an author " call spirits from the vasty deep " if he is very well satisfied that there are, in fact, no spirits to obey his conjurations ? I grant that by some literary *tour de force* he may succeed in duping his readers, but not for long. Presently his wand will snap short, his charms will lose their potency and mystic worth ; he will soon have turned the last page of his grimoire ; he steps all involuntarily out of the circle, the glamour dissipates, and the spell is broken ! This has been the fate of more than one writer who began zestfully and fair, but whose muttered abracadabras have puled and thinned, who has clean forgot the word of power if, indeed, he ever knew it and not merely guessed at those occult syllables.

Dr. James quite admirably lays down that the reader must be put " into the position of saying to himself, ' If I'm not very careful, something of this kind may happen to me !' '' Surely to convey this impression the writer is at least bound to admit the possibility of such happenings. He should believe in a phantom world if he is convincingly, at any rate, to draw the denizens of that state, for let it be granted that locality in the sense we understand it may not have. Yet there will be some kind of laws ; unknown to us and as yet unknowable, but such as should be in part surmised ; such as are reasonable and fitting. A well-reputed writer, whose name I will by your favour omit, gave us some excellent stories at first, but in his eagerness to create horror, to thrill and curdle our blood, latterly he trowels on the paint so thick, he creates such fantastic figures, such outrageous run-riot incidents at noon and in the sunlight, that it is all as topsy-turvy as Munchausen. In contradiction to the postulate of Dr. James we say : " Nothing of this kind could ever happen to anyone ! "

There must be preserved a decorum. Even in imagination such wild flights only serve to defeat their own end.

I conceive that in the ghost stories told by one who believes in and is assured of the reality of apparitions and hauntings, such incidents as do and may occur—all other things, by which I imply literary quality and skill, being equal—will be found to have a sap and savour that the narrative of the writer who is using the supernatural as a mere circumstance to garnish his fiction must inevitably lack and cannot attain, although, as I have pointed out, some extraordinary talent in spinning a yarn may go far to mask the deficiency. Thus, and for this very reason, it seems to me that there are few better stories of this kind than those the late Monsignor Benson has given us in *The Mirror of Shalott* and other of his work. Especially might one instance *Father Meuron's Tale*, *Father Bianchi's Story* and *Father Madox's Tale*. But indeed the whole symposium bears amplest evidence. Very fine tales have, no doubt, been written by authors who regarded the supernatural as just a fantasy and a flam. They topple, however, either on the one side into nightmare indigestion or on the other into vague aridities that are in fine meaningless.

Were I not myself convinced of the sensible reality of apparitions, had I not myself seen a ghost, I could hardly have undertaken to collect and introduce *The Supernatural Omnibus*.

A further important point is made by Dr. James. " Another requisite, in my opinion, is that the ghost should be malevolent or odious : amiable and helpful apparitions are all very well in fairy tales or in local legends, but I have no use for them in a fictitious ghost story." To this I would allow exceptions : I would add the unhappy ghost seeking rest who manifests itself for some purpose, generally that an old wrong may be righted at last, or else the ghost returns to discover a secret necessary for the happiness of descendants or others ; I would include the spectre who is a messenger of calamity, a harbinger of ill. There are also the phantoms who seek a just retribution ; and

" There are spirits that are created for vengeance, and in their fury they lay on grievous torments."—Ecclesiasticus xxxix. 33.

In fiction I concede that the good and kindly ghost has little or no place. And this is because in real life, as it seems to me, we should hardly term such appearances ghosts. When I read that the " ghost " of Sir Thomas More appeared at Baynards, in Surrey, I know that there was a vision of the Beato vouchsafed. There is a striking instance in the life of the mystic Teresa Higginson, who died in 1905. When she was living at the little village of Neston, in Cheshire, the local priest was away and the keys of the church were in her charge. Early one morning a strange priest came to her, and, although he did not speak, intimated he wished to say Mass. She prepared the altar and lighted the candles, noting with some surprise that he seemed strangely familiar with the place. She answered his Mass and received Communion at his hands. When it was finished and she went into the sacristy shortly after him, the vestments were all neatly folded, but the visitant had gone. She made inquiries in the village, yet nobody appeared to have seen him. Upon his return, she reported the matter to the resident priest, who in due course informed the bishop. His Lordship remarked that the description of the stranger was exactly that of a priest who used to serve the church many years before and who lay buried in the graveyard. It is, if I mistake not, on this event that Miss Grace Christmas founded her story *Faithful unto Death* in *What Father Cuthbert Knew.*

But this incident is not fiction, and it is with fiction that we are now concerned. I quote such an example to point out that the ghost story should follow upon the same lines as the veridical accounts. Of course, all kinds of trappings and cerements are not merely allowable, but much to be recommended. This sort of thing must not be overdone, however, and I fear that to-day there is a tendency to be too lavish with the pargeting, too curious with the inlay.

The ghost story should be short, simple and direct. Who told the first ghost story? I do not know, but I am sure that it was simple enough and that it sufficiently thrilled the hearers. Some son of Adam, I suppose, far back in dimmest antiquity, housed in a cave, as he looked up at the vast endless spaces of heaven powdered with nightly stars, as he wondered at the mysterious darkness, the depths of shadow, the remoteness of shapes familiar by day but which took on strange forms at the approach of evening : marvelled and told his children how he seemed to see the shadow of their grandsire who had gone from them so short a while, who had lain stark and motionless and cold. The old hunter had returned, yet he brought terror in his train, for now he had something of the night and the wind, of the great untrammelled forces of Nature with which man contended daily for his right to live. And his brood listened with awe ; they trembled, they scarce knew why, and were afraid.

The Assyrians dreaded those ghosts who were unable to sleep in their graves, but who came forth and perpetually roamed up and down the face of the earth. Especially did these spectres lurk in remote and secret places. Elaborate rituals and magical incantations are preserved to guard the home from pale spectres who peer in through the windows, who mop and mow at the lattice, who lurk behind the lintel of the door.

Egypt the ancient, the mysterious, the wonderful, is the very womb of wizardry, of ghost lore, of ensorcellment, of scarabed spells and runes which (as many believe) have not lost their fearful powers nor abated one jot of their doom and winged weird to-day, as witness the mummy of the Memphian priestess and the fate of those who rifle Royal tombs.

Greek literature is shadowed by the supernatural ; ever in the background man is conscious of those mighty forces who weave his destiny for weal and woe, who rend the veil and send him crazed with some glimpse of apparitions before whom reason reels and life is shaken in its inmost places.

The Nekyuia, the ghost scenes, of Homer and the great tragedians are famous throughout the ages. The weary wanderer Odysseus has been counselled by Circe the witch-woman to evoke the shade of Tiresias, the seer of olden Thebes. He makes his way to the shores of eternal darkness, the home of the Cimmerii who dwell amid noisome fog and the dark scud of heavy cloud, and here he lands where the poplar groves hem the house of Hades. Betwixt earth and gloomy Acheron is a twilight land of ghosts, Erebus. In this haunted spot Odysseus digs deep his ditch wherein must flow the hot reeking blood of black rams whom he sacrifices to Dis and to mystic Proserpine. At the foul stench of the new stream pale shadows swarm forth, a silent company, athirst to quaff the gore ; but with drawn sword he keeps at bay the gibbering crowd, for the prophet and none other must first drink if he is to tell sooth and rede the wanderer well. The phantoms cannot speak to the living man until they have tasted blood, and even then, when he talks with his mother's wraith and would clasp her in his arms, the empty air but mocks his grasp in vain.

No ghost story has ever been better told than this.

There are several first-rate stories of the supernatural in Latin prose writers, two at least of which are so curiously modern in their method that they may well be heard again. One was told at that splendid banquet to which—in spite of our host's plutocratic vulgarity—we have all so often wished we had been invited guests ; the other is written by Pliny in a letter to Sura.

At Trimalchio's table Niceros relates that one evening, planning to visit his mistress Melissa—" and a lovely bit to kiss she was ! (*pulcherrimum bacciballum !*) "—he persuades a young soldier who happens to be staying in the house to bear him company to the farm which lay some five miles out of town. Off they go, jogging along the country road merrily enough, for in the silver moonlight all is as clear as day. In highest fettle, thinking of his dear, Niceros, his head well thrown back, trolls lustily a snatch of comic song, and tries to count the host of stars above. Suddenly he notices his companion is no longer at his side. He looks back, and there, a few yards away by the hedgerow, is the lad stark naked in the moon, his clothes thrown in a muss. His lithe white limbs gleam ivory clear, but his teeth shine whiter than his limbs. There is a fierce,

long-drawn howl, and a huge gaunt wolf leaps into the forest
depths. Trembling and sweating with fear, Niceros somehow
stumbles along until he reaches the lonely grange. Then Melissa
greets him with a story of a wolf which had attacked the folds and
bawns, broken through the wattles and killed several sheep ; " but
he did not get off scot free," she says, " for our man gave him a
good jab with a pike to remember us by for a bit." At earliest dawn
Niceros, faint and ill, hurries back home, and as he passes by the
spot where the soldier had cast off his clothes he notices shudderingly a pool of fresh blood. On reaching the house, he finds the
youth is abed sick, whilst the doctor is busy dressing a deep gash
in his neck. This were-wolf story must necessarily lose not a little
in the translation, since the Latin of Petronius, with its racy
swing, is admirably adapted for a good yarn.

Pliny's tale (*Epistles*, vii. 27) runs :

" There was formerly at Athens a large and handsome house
which none the less had acquired the reputation of being badly
haunted. The folk told how at the dead of night horrid noises
were heard : the clanking of chains which grew louder and
louder until there suddenly appeared the hideous phantom of
an old, old man, who seemed the very picture of abject filth
and misery. His beard was long and matted, his white hairs
dishevelled and unkempt. His thin legs were loaded with a
weight of galling fetters that he dragged wearily along with a
painful moaning ; his wrists were shackled by long cruel links,
whilst ever and anon he raised his arms and shook his gyves
amain in a kind of impotent fury. Some few mocking sceptics,
who once were bold enough to watch all night in the house,
had been well-nigh scared from their senses at a sight of the
apparition ; and, what was worse, disease and even death itself
proved the fate of those who after dusk had ventured within
those accursed walls. The place was shunned. A placard ' To
Let ' was posted, but year succeeded year and the house fell
almost to ruin and decay. It so happened that the philosopher
Athenodorus, whilst on a visit to Athens, passed by the deserted
overgrown garden, and seeing the bill, inquired the rent of the
house, which was just such as he was seeking. Being not a little
surprised at the low figure asked, he put more questions, and
then there came out the whole story. None the less, he signed the
lease and ordered that one room should be furnished for him

with a bed, chairs and a table. At night he took his writing-tablet, style, books and a good lamp and set himself, as his wont, to study in the quiet hours. He had determined to concentrate upon some difficult problems lest if he sat idle and expectant his imagination should play tricks, and he might see what was in reality not there. He was soon absorbed in philosophical calculations, but presently the noise of a rattling chain, at first distant and then growing nearer, broke on his ear. However, Athenodorus, being particularly occupied with his notes, was too intent to interrupt his writing until, as the clanking became more and more continuous, he looked up, and there before him stood the phantom exactly as had been described. The ghastly figure seemed to beckon with its finger, but the philosopher signed with his hand that he was busy, and again bent to his writing. The chains were shaken angrily and with persistence, upon which Athenodorus quietly arose from his seat, and, taking the lamp, motioned the spectre to lead before. With low groans the figure passed heavily through the spacious corridors and empty rooms until they came out into the garden, when it led the philosopher to a distant shrubbery and, with a deep sigh, mingled with the night. Athenodorus, having marked the spot with stones and a broken bough, returned to the house, where he slept soundly until morning. He then repaired to the nearest magistrates, related what he had seen, and advised that the spot where the ghost disappeared should be investigated. This was done, and in digging they found a few feet below the surface a human skeleton, carious, enchained and fettered in gyves of a pattern many centuries old—now rusty and eroded, so that they fell asunder in flakes of desquamating verdigris. The mouldering bones were collected with reverend care and given a decent and seemly burial. The house was purged and cleansed with ritual lustrations, and never afterwards was it troubled by spectre or ill luck."

Pliny vouches for the truth of his narrative. Ludwig Lavater, at any rate, than whom there is no more serious-minded author, reproduced it entire in his *De Spectris, lemuribus, et magnis atque insolitis fragoribus* (*Of Ghostes and Spirites Walking by Nyght*), and the little duodecimo edition of Lavater, published at Gorkum in 1687, give us an illustration of the haggard spectre confronting the philosopher.

In Latin literature the supernatural informs at least one masterpiece of the world's romance, the *Metamorphoses* of Apuleius, a book to which that sadly overworked word " decadent " may be most fittingly and justly applied. From the first sentences to the last these pages are heavy with the mystic and the macabre, as some ornate cortège is palled with velvet trappings and the pomp of solemn habiliments of sacred dignity and reverend awe. Lucius is travelling in Thessaly, earth's very caldron, where voodoo and unclean sciences seethe and stew amain. At the outset he falls in with Aristomenes, who tells how, as it seemed to him, his fellow-companion had been slain by foul hags in the midnight inn, and yet he counted it but some evil dream, and travelled through those early morning hours with a dead man at his side. But when they came to running water the spell was broken, the corpse fell rigid and stiffening fast upon the river's bank with staring eyes long glazed and slackened, gaping jaw. It may be that this suggested Richard Middleton's *On the Brighton Road*, where the tramp plods along and two miles beyond Reigate meets the boy who asks to walk with him a bit, who died in the Crawley hospital twelve hours before.

It has not been possible to give any selection from Apuleius. It were difficult and it were profane to attempt any excerpt from his chapters, which must be read in the fullness of their beauty— a beauty which is that of some still night when the cypress point to heaven like burned-out torches against the dusky sky and the yews darkly splotch the landscape, when the sickle of the harvest moon rides high in heaven, and nightingales are singing amor-ously, and the owl hoots dully ever and anon to remind us that there is death as well as love.

" *Aut indicauit, aut finxit*," wrote the supreme wisdom of S. Augustine as he pondered the tale that Apuleius told.

Throughout the Middle Ages the supernatural played as large a part in literature as in life. Those were the days of the sabbat and the witch. The old chronicles narrate deeds more horrible and facts more grim than any writer of fiction could weave. In the sixteenth century, too, the ghost story had no place when the *Malleus Maleficarum* lay open upon every judge's bench, when Guazzo and later Sinistrari penned their narratives of demon lovers, and Remy wrote his *Demonolatry* " Drawn from the Capital Trials of 900 Persons " executed for sorcery within the space of fifteen years.

There is a little interlude of sheer horror it may not be amiss to quote, *The Three Queens and the Three Dead Men* :

> *1st Queen :* I am afeard.
> *2nd Queen :*   Lo ! what I see ?
> *3rd Queen :* Me thinketh it be devils three !
> *1st Dead Body :* I was well fair.
> *2nd Dead Body :*   Such shalt thou be.
> *3rd Dead Body :* For Gode's love, beware by me !

Boccaccio in the *Decameron*, giornata quinta, novella ottava, relates the story of Nastagio degli Onesti, who one day whilst walking lonely in a wood near Ravenna, sees flying down the glades a wretched woman,

> *Her Face, her Hands, her naked Limbs were torn,*
> *With passing through the Brakes, and prickly Thorn ;*
> *Two Mastiffs, gaunt and grim, her Flight pursu'd,*
> *And oft their fasten'd Fangs in Blood embru'd.*

Mounted on a black charger there follows a grisly knight, and he looes on the two swift hounds of hell. Nastagio already had his hand upon the pommel of his sword, when, as the rider faces him, he realises that he is gazing at a damned soul. The knight reveals that he is no distant ancestor of the Onesti line, who during his life loved, but loved in vain. In despair at the lady's wanton cruelty, he stabbed himself, and now, after death, for her pride she is condemned to be hunted down by her spectre lover,

> *Renew'd to Life, that she might daily die,*
> *I daily doom'd to follow, she to fly ;*
> *No more a Lover but a mortal Foe,*
> *I seek her Life (for Love is none below :)*
> *As often as my Dogs with better speed*
> *Arrest her Flight, is she to Death decreed :*
> *Then with this fatal Sword on which I dy'd,*
> *I pierce her open'd Back or tender Side,*
> *And tear that harden'd Heart from out her Breast,*
> *Which, with her Entrails, makes my hungry Hounds a Feast.*
> *Nor lies she long, but as her Fates ordain,*
> *Springs up to Life, and fresh to second Pain,*
> *Is sav'd to Day, to Morrow to be slain.*
> *This, vers'd in Death, th' infernal Knight relates,*

> *And then for Proof fulfill'd their common Fates ;*
> *Her Heart and Bowels through her Back he drew,*
> *And fed the Hounds that help'd him to pursue.*

The horrid details of the ghostly chase in the haunted forest are admirably related by Boccaccio, and are even better told by our great poet John Dryden in *Theodore and Honoria* (*Fables*, folio 1700), which he has taken from the Italian.

In Chaucer the expression runs quite naturally :

> *He was not pale as a for-pyned goost ;*

and in the Nonne Preestes Tale Chanticleer most appositely relates an excellent ghost story of the two travellers. They sleep at separate inns, and during the night one vainly endeavours, as in a dream, twice to wake his friend and call him to his assistance. A third time he appears covered with wounds and bleeding sore, and reveals that his corpse will be conveyed out of the town gates that morning in a tumbril of filth. The second traveller early hurries to his comrade's hostelry, to learn he has left ere daybreak. Ill content, he makes his way to the western gates ; a cart is jolting through ; at his cries the people come running up ; they search amid the manure, and there they find

> *The dede man, that mordred was al newe.*

At the Reformation, divines and common folk attempted to revise their ideas of the supernatural. And then it was, as Pierre Le Loyer says in his *IIII Livres de Spectres* (1586), which was translated into English by Z. Jones (1605) :

> "Of all the common and familiar subjects of conversation
> that are entered upon in company of things remote from Nature
> and cut off from the senses, there is none so ready to hand, none
> so usual, as that of visions of Spirits, and whether that said of
> them is true. It is the topic that people most readily discuss and
> on which they linger the longest because of the abundance of
> examples, the subject being fine and pleasing and the discussion
> the least tedious that can be found."

Words that are as true to-day as they were when written three centuries and a half ago.

Ludwig Lavater of Zurich, who has been already mentioned, published his treatise *De Spectris, lemuribus, et magnis atque insolitis fragoribus* at Geneva in 1570. This was translated into English in 1572 as *Of Ghostes and Spirites Walking by Nyght and of strange Noyses, Crackes, and Sundry Forewarnynges*, and a year before it had been turned into French as *Trois livres des Apparitions des Spectres, Esprits, Fantasmes*. Lavater, however, was unorthodox and often at fault, and so Pierre Le Loyer in 1586 issued a learned and, it must be confessed, salutary corrective in his *Discours et Histoire des spectres, visions et apparitions des esprits . . . en VIII livres . . . esquels . . . est manifestee la certitude des spectres et visions des esprits*. Le Loyer's book is far more important than that of Lavater, and equally valuable in ghost lore is the *De Apparitionibus . . . et terrificationibus nocturnis (Of Ghosts and of Midnight Terrors)*, by Peter Thyræus, a famous Jesuit professor of Würzburg, which was first published in 1594 and several times reprinted, although it has now become an exceedingly scarce book, the more so inasmuch as it was never translated from the original.

It is not out of place to devote a little attention to these serious and learned treatises of ghosts and apparitions, since they form the background, as it were, to the fiction of the subject, the ghost story. Indeed, a few more well-known English books of this kind may here be mentioned, although it must be always remembered that of very many it is possible only to name some half a dozen, which yet, at any rate, will serve to show how deeply the whole philosophy of ghosts was studied and treated in literature.

The Terrors of the Night, or, A Discourse of Apparitions, 4to, 1594, by Thomas Nashe, is important as an indication of popular interest, for none so quick as Nashe to catch the topics of the hour. In itself this piece is of little value.

In 1681 was published Joseph Glanvil's *Saducismus Triumphatus, or, Full and Plain Evidence Concerning Witches and Apparitions*, a work which caused no small sensation in its day. It is Glanvil who tells of the Drummer of Tedworth, of a Hollander who was strangely psychic, of the ghost of Major George Sydenham, and many more.

It was long thought, and amongst others even Sir Walter Scott gave currency to the error, that Defoe's " A True Relation of the Apparition of one Mrs. *Veal*, the next day after her Death, to one Mrs. *Bargrave*, at *Canterbury*, the 8th of *September*, 1705," which was published for threepence by Bragg of Paternoster Row, and which is often printed with Charles Drelincourt's *The Christian's Defence against the Fears of Death*, translated into English by D'Assigny, was specifically written to help off a number of copies of the Huguenot pastor's treatise which lay heavy on the booksellers' hands. Such is far from the case. Recent research has shown that Mrs. Veal and Mrs. Bargrave were not fictitious characters, but real persons, well known in their proper circles. Mrs. Veal was buried at Canterbury on 10 September, 1705. Mrs. Bargrave was Barbara Smith, a widow, whom Mr. Richard Bargrave, a maltster, married at S. Alphege, Canterbury, on 11 January, 1700. The narrative relates facts, and Defoe is merely a reporter. It is true that in an interview, 21 May, 1714, Mrs. Bargrave stated that a few trifling details were not strictly accurate ; " all things contained in it, however, were true as regards the event itself on matters of importance." Mrs. Bargrave told her story in 1705, and at the time it caused a tremendous sensation.

It is possible but barely to mention Increase Mather's *Remarkable Providences*, and Cotton Mather's *Wonders of the Invisible World*. Andrew Moreton's *The Secrets of the Invisible World Disclos'd : or, An Universal History of Apparitions*, which had run to a third edition in 1738, is a useful and ably argued book.

To come down to the nineteenth century, a very famous work is Mrs. Crowe's *The Night Side of Nature*, 1848, which has been called " one of the best collections of supernatural stories in the English language," and of which I cherish a real yellow-back copy of about 1885. In 1850 the Rev. Henry Christmas, Librarian of Sion College, issued a translation of Dom Augustine Calmet's great work under the title *The Phantom World*. Thomas Brevior, in *The Two Worlds*, has a chapter on apparitions which should not be neglected. That fine scholar and—may I say it ?—romantic ritualist, Dr. F. G. Lee, sometime Vicar of All Saints', Lambeth, left a whole library of ghost lore : *The Other World, or Glimpses of the Supernatural*, 2 vols., 1875 ; *More Glimpses of the World Unseen*, 1878 ; *Glimpses in the Twilight*, 1885 ; and *Sights and Shadows*, 1894. The Christmas and New Year's Numbers of the *Review of Reviews*, 1891-2, supplied a large number of *Real Ghost Stories*, under which title, indeed, they were reprinted in October, 1897. Many of us will remember how people at the time spoke of the review with bated breath : how it was hurried out of the sight of children, and read almost in secret by their elders with blanching cheeks and tingling nerves. I fear we may have become very sophisticated since those happy days. In *True Irish Ghost Stories* (1926), by St.

John D. Seymour and Harry L. Neligan, we have an admirable book. The tales are fascinating and most excellently told. From Ingram's *Haunted Homes of Great Britain*, third edition, 1886, I can always be sure of a shudder. True, the book has been largely superseded by Mr. Charles G. Harper's *Haunted Houses*, first published in 1907 and re-issued in 1924, with some first-rate drawings of haunted mansions by the author. It is a veritable encyclopædia, but I wish Mr. Harper would not try to strip us of our last vestige of Victorian romanticism. He does not succeed—at any rate, in my case—but the bad intent is there. None the less he has, and well deserves, my hearty thanks. In *The White Ghost Book* and *The Grey Ghost Book*, Miss Jessie Adelaide Middleton has given us a series of excellently told accounts of apparitions. Her reports of these hauntings are quite simple and sober ; there is no bravura, there are no artificial situations and long planned climaxes. The result is that *The House of Horror* in *The White Ghost Book* is one of the most terrible, as it is one of the best authenticated, narratives I know.

To go back a little, in 1859 that ardent " old Conservative " Edward Tracy Turnerelli (1813–1896) published *A Night in a Haunted House, A Tale of Facts*, describing his own experiences in an ancient mansion at Kilkenny. It is a narrative of extraordinary interest ; and publicly related, as it originally was told, at a meeting in aid of various charities at Ryde, it created an immense sensation.

Perhaps even more notice was attracted by the same author's *Two Nights in a Haunted House in Russia*, 1873, which ran through many editions, and was very widely discussed during the next decade and longer.

Here should be mentioned *News from the Invisible World*, a little known and older collection, which was (I believe) first published in Manchester, 1835, as by John Tregortha. This name, however, is variously given, and the author is more usually called George Charlton, but of him nothing seems actually to be recorded. Whoever he may have been, he had a wide knowledge of his subject and, in addition to the more familiar, one might say the historical matter, he has drawn on a number of new sources. At least they are new to me, and I have not found them mentioned in similar repertories.

Mr. Elliot O'Donnell has given us a long series of ghost tales and of studies in phantom lore which will be familiar to all who are interested in that misty borderland. Such are his *Ghostly Phenomena* ; *Ghostland* ; *Twenty Years' Experiences as a Ghost Hunter* (in which there is a most creepy chapter : " A Haunted Mine in Wales ") ; *Animal Ghosts* ; *Scottish Ghosts* ; *Byways of Ghostland*. Personally I am inclined to rate his *Some Haunted Houses of England and Wales* (1908) ; *Haunted Houses of London* ; and *More Haunted Houses of London* as among the best of his work. This latter has a horrible tale, *The Door that would never keep Shut* ; and the first relates some fully authenticated narratives of the West Country.

The Ghost of Broughton Hall in Miss Violet Tweedale's *Ghosts I Have Seen*, second edition, 1920, is well within the good old-fashioned, but none the less matter-of-fact, tradition ; whilst the account of the hideous satyr, Prince Valori's familiar, is so incontestably attested, that it should " furiously give to think " those, if any there be, who cling to what Stead justly termed the out-worn superstition of a denial of supernatural agencies.

Very many more collections might be cited ; many admirable, some few a little weak, perhaps ; but it is high time we passed from fact to fiction. It must not be thought that this review " gat-tothed," insufficient and scanty to the last degree as it is, of books relating to the actuality of the supernatural, is in any way impertinent, since it is these veridical narratives which supply the background to romance and fiction self-confessed.

Even although we are to be entirely concerned with prose fiction, the extraordinary popularity of the " Drama of Blood and Horror " evoking whole crowded cemeteries of ghosts upon the Elizabethan stage must not be passed over without a word. The earlier Elizabethan ghosts were copied from the formal phantoms of Seneca and his Italian imitators. The Umbra Tantali and the fury Megæra commence the *Thyestes* with a declamatory duologue of one hundred and twenty lines. Nor did these spectres lose one whit of their loquaciousness when they crossed to English shores. They are, one and all, extremely voluble. Thus Jonson's *Catiline His Conspiracy*, acted in 1611, opens with a monologue of over seventy lines delivered by Sylla's ghost. It must be acknowledged that this is a magnificent speech, but not all spectres in tragedy had such splendid periods. In fact, many of the phantoms were unmercifully parodied, and Kyd's *Spanish Tragedy* in particular (which, it is interesting to note, was attracting audiences as late as 1668) became a very nayword for mockery and burlesque. In that curious yet striking drama, *A Warning for*

Faire Women, 4to, 1599, at the very outset are introduced Tragedy and Comedy, and the latter jeers her august sister in this wise :

> *A Chorus too comes howling in,*
> *And tels us of the worrying of a cat,*
> *Then of a filthie whining ghost,*
> *Lapt in some fowle sheete, or a leather pelch,*
> *Comes skreaming like a pigge halfe stickt,*
> *And cries* Vindicta, *revenge, revenge :*
> *With that a little Rosen flasheth forth,*
> *Like smoke out of a Tabacco pipe, or a boyes squib.*

It may be remarked that the ghost upon the Elizabethan stage was plainly visible to the audience. He presented himself very materially, all blotched with blood, with chalked face and linen shroud. When Kemble at Drury Lane in 1794 let Macbeth gaze upon an empty seat in the scene of royal revelry and apostrophise the vacant air, all this was absolutely alien to Shakespeare's intention and practice. The spectre of Banquo must be to vision clear, " with twenty trenched gashes on his head."

Thus in Webster's great play *The White Devil* we see " Brachiano's *Ghost in his leather cassock and breeches, boots ; a cowl ; a pot of lily-flowers, with a skull in't.*" The minute details of the stage direction, if nothing else, are proof that the ghost was no shadow seen in the mind's eye alone. Moreover, when Flaminio addresses it, " *the Ghost throws earth upon him, and shows him the skull.*"

It has been observed that " tragedy was the main channel of romanticism " in England during the seventeenth century and the earlier part of the eighteenth. Accordingly when Horace Walpole, who if not actually the very first was certainly the most important pioneer of prose romanticism, brought out in 1764 his *Castle of Otranto*, we are not surprised to find that the corridors and chambers of his Castle are haunted indeed, so much so in fact that eventually, like Manfred, we become " inured to the supernatural," and when we enter the chapel and see a figure " in a long woollen weed " are hardly the least surprised as it turns towards us to behold " the fleshless jaws and empty sockets of a skeleton, wrapt in a hermit's cowl."

Nevertheless, with all its faults and furbelows, *The Castle of Otranto* is a romance of extraordinary fascination. It may seem to us nowadays that the raptures—they were no less—with which

Walpole's rococo was received cannot have been other than monstrously unreal, a tribute to the author rather than to his work. Yet such assuredly was not the case. *The Critical Review* was certainly unfriendly at the time, and Hazlitt later damned *Otranto* as " dry, meagre, and without effect." But Byron, writing in 1820, spoke of Walpole as " the father of the first romance and of the last tragedy in our language, and surely worthy of a higher place than any living writer, be he who he may." Sir Walter Scott, too, was lavish in his eulogy of *Otranto* : " This romance has been justly considered not only as the original and model of a peculiar species of composition, attempted and successfully executed by a man of great genius, but as one of the standard works of our lighter literature."

Otranto, at any rate, primarily inspired that notable revival—we might say creation—of romantic fiction which may conveniently be termed the Gothic Novel, and which drinks deep of two springs : the sentimental and the supernatural. The genius of Ann Radcliffe stands out pre-eminent far above all her contemporaries and disciples, but two at least, Matthew Gregory Lewis and Charles Maturin, had something of her quality, and were both writers of fearful if fantastic power. The villains may talk ever and anon in the richest vein of Surrey-side and Coburg melodrama ; their heroines are all peerless, fleckless, graceful, lovelier than nymphs who trip the lawn ; their dungeons may be murmurous with sepulchral groans ; their corridors labyrinthing beyond aught that Dædalus could ever contrive, and a shudder at every turn ; but in spite of crudities, of absurdities if you will, at the very moment when bathos seems irretrievably to have wrecked the situation, genius kindles to a flame and carries them through triumphant to the end.

Lewis and Maturin never shrank before the supernatural. Ghosts, the grislier the better, throng their pages.

Mrs. Radcliffe, however—and this is her one and only fault—could not bring herself frankly to engage the supernatural. At least, only her last and posthumous work, *Gaston de Blondeville*, admits the genuine supernatural, and even here the treatment is almost timid in its reticence. At the close of her romances it is explained that the marvels of the story are due to some natural agency, that we have shuddered all in vain and idly trembled in the shadowed halls of Udolpho, or amid the Black Penitents, what time we paced the cloisters of Paluzzi.

{2}

This is a blemish, and the critic of the *Quarterly Review* for May, 1810, was just, if severe, when he wrote that he heartily disapproved " of the mode introduced by Mrs. Radcliffe, and followed by Mr. Murphy and her other imitators, of winding up their story with a solution, by which all the incidents appearing to partake of the mystic and marvellous are resolved by very simple and natural causes." So we find that even in an ultra-Gothic tale rejoicing in so delightful a title as *The Phantom, or Mysteries of the Castle* when Mowbray cries : " My Matilda, blest shade ! " a moment later Mrs. Mathews dashes us with " Matilda was still mortal," and we have been duly awed by her ghost for a couple of hundred pages ! In *The Spirit of Turrettville* two youths are attracted by the sound of mysterious music to a distant room, where they see a veiled figure softly touching the strings of a harp. As they advance, the apparition turns towards them " a grinning mouldering skull." Eventually it is discovered she is the living wife who thus endeavours to frighten the villain into a confession. Even in *Vesuvia*, where the mysterious incidents are puzzling but hardly supernatural, a very careful and rational explanation is provided.

None the less, I would hasten to add that there are ghosts who haunt Gothic novels. T. J. Horsley-Curties scorned to tamper with the supernatural. *Ancient Records, or, The Abbey of St. Oswyth*, which is generally esteemed his best work, has spectres who shriek and moan and threaten the guilty to great effect. In the Preface to *Ethelwina ; or, The House of Fitz-Auburne* he makes confession of his literary creed, and writes : " The Author of this Work . . . in one circumstance . . . has stepped beyond the modern writers of Romance, by introducing a *Real Ghost*—to many, such a circumstance will not appear unnatural or improbable ; but he neither apologises, nor justifies on that ground—he only pleads the example of the immortal Bard of Avon, who found a spectre necessary for his purpose to heighten his story, or to ' harrow up the soul,' but never thought it necessary to account for the ' unreal mockery.' " In *The Accusing Spirit* a headless and mangled figure glides through the haunted convent, the tortured shade of the sinful Benedicta. The spirit of the old marquis appears in W. C. Proby's *The Spirit of the Castle* ; in *The Priory of St. Clair, or, The Spectre of the Murdered Nun*, the dead Julietta is nightly seen. There are literally dozens of romances in which ghosts play a great part. Thus we have *Phantoms of the Cloyster* ; *The Vindictive Spirit* ; *The*

Spectre of Lamnere Abbey ; *The Spectre Mother* ; *Eleanor, or The Spectre of St. Michel's* ; *The Haunted Tavern* ; *The Haunted Palace* ; *The Haunted Priory* ; *The Haunted Tower* ; and very many more. In fact, Mrs. Rachel Hunter felt constrained to name one of her novels *Letitia : A Castle Without a Spectre*, whilst the author of *The Ghost* and *More Ghosts* merrily dubbed himself Felix Phantom.

Again, we have such popular romances as *The Midnight Groan ; or, The Spectre of the Chapel* (1808), which " presents to view . . . a man spectre " and " a perfect skeleton " ; *The Convent Spectre*, published in the same year ; *The Forest Phantom, or, The Golden Crucifix*, in which a ghost in armour stands " visible on the top of a coffin " and exhibits " features blanched by the hand of death " ; and Isaac Crookenden's *Spectre of the Turret ; or, Guolto Castle*. There is also an amazing collection, *Tales of Terror ! or More Ghosts. Forming a Complete Phantasmagoria*, which has the appropriate motto :

> *Twelve o'clock's the Time of Night*
> *That the Graves, all gaping wide,*
> *Quick send forth the airy Sprite*
> *In the Churchway Path to glide.*

There was even published in 1823 *Ghost Stories, Collected with a Particular View to Counteract the Vulgar Belief in Ghost and Apparitions, and to Promote a Rational Estimate of the Nature of Phenomena commonly considered as Supernatural.* The book, now very rare, was issued by Ackermann, and the six coloured engravings with which it is embellished possess the greatest charm. In fact, they are far too good for their setting, inasmuch as the stories themselves, *The Green Mantle of Venice*, *The Ghost of Larneville*, *The Village Apparition*, and the rest, are extremely tame. Nothing could be more disappointing, since the titles promise most palatable fare. What could be more tempting than *The Haunted Castle, or, The Ghost of Count Walkenried*, or *The Haunted Inn ?* And it all fritters away into accounts of imposture, or somnambulism at the best. I protest this is not playing the game.

In James Hogg's *The Wool-Gatherer* a man of vicious life is haunted by the wraiths of those whom he has wronged, and as he lies in the throes of death he hears the sad voices of women in torment and the pitiful wailing of infants. After he is dead, the cries become so insistent that " the corpse sits up in the bed, pawls wi' its hands and stares round wi' its dead face." Not dissimilar is the adventure of de Montfort in Maturin's *The Albigenses*. As he is passing through the depths of a gloomy wood, there presses round him a throng of those who have fallen in the religious wars, a hideous company with " clattering bones, eyeless sockets, and grinning jaws."

Unfortunately, most novelists preferred to imitate Mrs. Radcliffe in her explanations, and even among her later followers the best are at some pains to throw down the whole edifice they have so adroitly constructed and with such toil. That fine romance of G. P. R. James, *The Castle of Ehrenstein, Its Lords Spiritual and Temporal, its Inhabitants Earthly and Unearthly*, is completely spoiled for me by the last chapter, and I reject the explanation " that the whole of this vast structure, solid as it seems, and solid as it indeed is, in reality is double," so that the phantoms were the Count and his faithful band who dwelt there secretly until such time as he should dispossess his usurping brother. It is they who appear as the Black Huntsman and his demon train. I am satisfied, none the less, that " The Ghost " and " The Black Huntsman " as depicted by Phiz when the first few chapters of *Ehrenstein* appeared in *Ainsworth's Magazine*, 1845, are supernatural. It is a fearsome phantom who terrifies Sickendorf and Bertha ; it is the " wild Jager " himself who careers in awful chase.

There was one professed disciple of that " great mistress of romance " who happily disdained these subterfuges, and he has reaped his reward in that his name is remembered, his works are read, when so many another is forgotten and scarcely to be traced, nay, not even in the pages of Shobert and Watkins, or Upcott, or Allibone. It may, I think, almost undeniably be granted that his sense of the supernatural, and the truly admirable way in which he utilised awe and mystery in his romances, have at least culled one and that not the least green, laurel in the stephane of immortality which crowns Ainsworth's brow.

William Harrison Ainsworth proudly confessed in his earliest, and by no means his least successful romance, *Rookwood* (1834), that he was bold to tread in the footsteps of Ann Radcliffe—she had died but eleven years before, and actually her posthumous romance, *Gaston de Blondeville*, had only preceded *Rookwood* a twelvemonth in publication. I have not the opportunity here to appraise Ainsworth as he deserves ; that has been excellently done by Mr. S. M. Ellis, who well writes that in *The Lancashire Witches*, for example, Ainsworth " achieved a masterpiece . . . for this . . .

is the greatest of all romances dealing with the occult and the combined influences and 'atmosphere' of wild and suggestive scenery." I had wished to include some example of Ainsworth's work in this collection, and I had intended to give *The Legend of Owlarton Grange*, told by old Hazelrigge in *Mervyn Clitheroe* and *The Haunted Room* from *Chetwynd Calverley*, one of the later (1876) and lesser known novels. Both stories are related with singular power and effect, but upon consideration it was plain that in both cases the incidents were so bound up with the thread of the whole romance that they would essentially lose by being read in the form of separate chapters, and any such excerpts would be unfair to the merits of Ainsworth as a writer.

Neither has it been possible to represent Mrs. Shelley, whom I omit with reluctance. *Frankenstein* is a classic of the occult, but it must be read entire. It seemed equally difficult to make any extract, which by itself would not appear inadequate, from her other work ; although she was deeply versed in the art of shudders and fear.

Fortunately Sir Walter Scott has left us stories which may stand apart from their setting. *Wandering Willie's Tale* in *Red gauntlet* (1824) is of consummate artistry ; as also is *The Tapestried Chamber* (1829), but both are too easily accessible to be given here. I have no defence save human limitations of space if I am told that both should be included.

Few books have a greater reputation than the *Ingoldsby Legends*. There are—all power to them—Ingoldsby enthusiasts ; but I question (I hope, sincerely hope, I may be wrong) whether outside this devoted band the Ingoldsby poems are appreciated and loved as they deserve. To the *Ingoldsby Legends* we may safely and literally apply the word " unique." There is nothing like them, not merely in degree but also in kind, in any literature I know. Perhaps the nearest rhymes are the maccaronics of Folengo, which again *sui generis* have never been excelled and hardly approached. Yet Ingoldsby is altogether different, and, when one seeks to compare any juxtaposition eludes and escapes. The witches of the *Maccaronea* are grotesque, evil, ridiculous, just as are old Goody Price and old Goody Jones ; whilst Father Francis, Father Fothergill, Mess Michael, Roger the Monk, can be amply paralleled by Fra Jacopino, the village priest, " Master Adrianus, Constantius atque Jachettus."

Curiously enough, even those who know the poems of the

Ingoldsby Legends well are often somewhat indifferent to Barham's prose, which is, in my opinion at any rate, of a very high quality. Accordingly I have included two of his stories in this collection. I hesitated whether *The Spectre of Tappington* should not make a third, but it belongs to a species of ghost story of which I disapprove : the humorous ; nor is it, indeed, strictly a ghost story ; that is to say, it does not introduce the supernatural, and there are Radcliffian explanations to boot. However, *The Spectre of Tappington* is the exception that proves the rule. The genius of Barham has triumphed and given us a tale of the first order, although it belongs to an illegitimate *genre*. There is only one other humorous ghost story which justifies itself—Oscar Wilde's fantasy *The Canterville Ghost*. This ranks with *The Spectre of Tappington* among the foremost. Yet it will not escape attention that Wilde has mingled with his brilliant wit a touch of pathos, and more than a touch of beauty, that even in his liveliest passages he gives an undercurrent of something running much deeper and touching us more nearly than mere persiflage, however exquisitely wrought and pointed.

" Death must be so beautiful. To lie in the soft brown earth, with the grasses waving above one's head, and listen to silence. To have no yesterday, and no to-morrow. To forget time, to forgive life, to be at peace."

Hardly a disciple, but in his day certainly a rival, and a very formidable rival of Ainsworth, was G. W. M. Reynolds, whose output is equal to, even if it does not o'ertop, those of Defoe or the prolific water-poet himself. The lengthy novels of Reynolds teem with mystery and the supernatural. To name but a few of many, *Faust*, based upon the old legend but almost infinitely varied ; *Wagner, the Wehr-Wolf ; The Necromancer* ; all have as their theme diabolic contracts and the fearful retribution that results therefrom.

A contemporary of Reynolds, who was as prolific indeed as he, but who has been almost entirely forgotten, was Thomas Preskett Prest, the author of *The Skeleton Clutch ; or, The Goblet of Gore ; The Black Monk, or, The Secret of the Grey Turret ; The Rivals, or, The Spectre of the Hall ; Varney the Vampire, or, The Feast of Blood*, and many more. This latter, although of inordinate length, is powerfully told, and has hardly, I think, been excelled even by the famous *Dracula*.

It is impossible to name a tithe of these writers who dealt with the supernatural in its most terrible manifestations. Lengthy bibliographies might be compiled of fiction alone which had the vampire and the werewolf as its themes. Of vampire tales we might instance Le Fanu's *Carmilla* ; Bram Stoker's *Dracula*, mentioned above ; E. F. Benson's *The Room in the Tower* ; Mrs. *Amworth* in *Visible and Invisible* ; F. G. Loring's *The Tomb of Sarah* ; F. Marion Crawford's *For the Blood is the Life* (*Uncanny Tales*) ; Conan Doyle's *The Parasite* ; E. and H. Heron's *The Story of Baelbrow* ; Victor Roman's *Four Wooden Stakes* ; X. L.'s *The Kiss of Judas* ; Eric Count Stenbock's *The True Story of a Vampire* ; and a score beside.

The werewolf boasts an almost richer library. There is Captain Marryat's fine tale from *The Phantom Ship* ; Mrs. Crowe's *A Story of a Weir-Wolf* ; H. Beaugrand's *The Werwolves* ; Saki's *Gabriel* ; Ainskallas' *The Wolf's Bride* ; Fred Whishaw's *The Were-wolf* ; Eric Count Stenbock's *The Other Side* ; Charles Severn's *Were Wolf* ; Ambrose Bierce's *The Eyes of the Panther* ; " cum multis aliis quos nunc perscribere longum est," as the old Latin Grammar has it.

Reynold's *Miscellany* contained not a few well-told tales of the supernatural, and this magazine gave rise to many more which flourished exceedingly for the last half of the nineteenth century. Edwin J. Brett was a wholesale purveyor of these ephemera, and one may remark that latterly he concentrated almost entirely upon boys' books. The history of boys' books, which is of extraordinary interest, has yet to be written. Thus running through *Boys of the Empire*, vol. ix., 1892, I find a really thrilling serial, *Doctor or Demon ?*, a romance of the *Dr. Jekyll and Mr. Hyde* type.

At the same time as Reynolds, Prest and others were writing, one of the supreme masters of English fiction, Charles Dickens, was showing his keen interest in the supernatural, which lurks in the background of, and sensibly informs, some among his finest works. Moreover, as Mr. S. M. Ellis has well said in his essay, *The Ghost Story and its Exponents* (*Mainly Victorian*) :

" In *Household Words* and *All the Year Round*, both under Dickens's editorship, are to be found some of the best ghost stories ever written."

I have not, of course, failed to include in this collection tales by

Amelia B. Edwards, Rosa Mulholland and Charles Collins, who were all contributors to these periodicals.

It was for *All the Year Round* that Dickens asked Bulwer-Lytton to furnish a serial, and this resulted in *A Strange Story* (1861). Andrew Lang was of opinion that " There is no better romance of the supernatural than *A Strange Story* ; and perhaps a kind of sketch for it, *The Haunted and the Haunters*, is at least as good." The only reason I have omitted to give' this latter tale, which I immensely admire, is that it has been very frequently reprinted. It is said to be founded upon the succession of noises and appari- tions that so disturbed the haunted mill at Willington when the Procter family, serious and devout members of the Society of Friends, resided there. This is one of the best known veridical histories in all psychic lore. There were legends of earlier troubles at Willington in 1806, and there were poltergeist vexations in 1823, but it was not until January, 1835, that the actual hauntings at the mill itself assumed serious proportions. In 1847 the Procters moved to Newcastle, but as late as 1867 and 1870 tenants who wished to reside at the mill were driven out by supernatural alarms.

Bulwer-Lytton was a serious and discriminating student of the occult, and that is why he was able to write so well and so con- vincingly of the supernatural. *Glenallan*, an early work, gives evi- dence of this ; and it is made even more clear by *Zanoni*, which he enlarged and completed from his *Zicci*, published in the *Monthly Chronicle* for 1838. When *A Strange Story* appeared, " He beats one on one's own ground ! " cried Wilkie Collins, a generous appraisal, which perhaps must not be pressed to the letter, for there have been few, if any, writers to excel Collins at his best. A master of detective and " mystery " fiction—and one may draw attention to the close connexion between " mystery " fiction and the ghost story—Collins has also left some fine tales of the eerie and the weird. He was a past master of the art of creating an atmosphere of suspense and loneliness, of awe and trembling fear. He even achieved that most difficult of feats, a full-length ghost story. It is, I think, well-nigh essential for success that the ghost story should be short. Only the adroitest skill and talent of no ordinary kind can avail to keep the reader in that state of expectancy bordering on the unpleasant yet never quite overstepping the line which is the true triumph of this *genre*. All too frequently a tale spun in many chapters is apt either, on the one hand, to fall slovenly flat, to become banal and to bore ; or else on the other to sweal into crude physical disgust and end as a mere mixen of horror. *The Haunted Hotel*, however, is wrought with consummate ability.

In 1847 the famous military novelist James Grant published *The Phantom Regiment*, in which, although it be confessed that the main narrative runs rather thin, the episodes—from one of which the book takes its name—are splendidly done. The story tells of a phantom regiment, accursed and banned, doomed on each anniversary of that foul butchery to march from " hell to Culloden." Grant also has two short stories of the macabre, *The Dead Tryst* and *A Haunted Life*, which appeared in 1866.

Other full-length ghost stories to be placed in the first class are Mrs. Riddell's *The Haunted River*, whose pages are dank with a mist that is not wholly material, with shadows and doom ; Lanoe Falconer's *Cecilia de Noel*, a book of real genius, in which the effect of an apparition on varying individuals is shown ; Lucas Malet's *The Gateless Barrier* and *The Tall Villa* ; Mrs. Oliphant's *The Beleaguered City* ; *The White People* by Francis Hodgson Burnett.

All these are works of great beauty, and this they owe to their apprehension of the spiritual. In other phrase, to produce a flaw-less piece of work the writer must believe in the motive of the tale. This indeed I have emphasised before, and I will not enlarge upon the point now. I would merely add that if a ghost story has not the note of spirituality which may be beauty—a beauty not without awe—or may be horror, it will fail because of its insincerity and untruth. I do not know, and I do not care to know, how far Henry James believed in the possibility of *The Turn of the Screw*, but his genius succeeded in creating an atmosphere of spiritual dread because he realised that this was necessary to his art. I understand that actually *The Turn of the Screw* is a brilliant *tour de force*, but I am convinced that Henry James was less sceptic than appears.

It seems to me that it is exactly this lack of spirituality which so fatally flaws the vast majority of the tales in a series generally known as " Not at Night," which has now attained six volumes of similar if slightly varying titles. If there is a note of spiritual horror, whether it be vampire horror, as in *Four Wooden Stakes*, or Satanism, as in *The Devil's Martyr* and *The Witch-Baiter*, the story is raised to another plane far higher than the rather nauseous sensationalism of fiendish serums, foul experiments of lunatic surgeons, half-human plants, monstrous insects and the like.

Not forgetting the admirable work that has been done in the last thirty years, the nineteenth century may be acclaimed as the hey-day of the good old-fashioned ghost story, even if only in view of the fact that from 1838 to 1873 was writing one who has been justly termed " *the* Master of Horror and the Mysterious," Joseph Sheridan Le Fanu, whose place in literature has been so precisely estimated by Mr. S. M. Ellis in a fine essay in *Mainly Victorian*. Dr. M. R. James, who is, with the exception of Vernon Lee, of all writers of ghost stories to-day *facile princeps*, has also declared his admiration for Le Fanu, and has collected with a valuable preface and bibliographical notes some dozen or more of Le Fanu's stories in *Madam Crowl's Ghost*. Both Mr. Ellis and Dr. James are agreed that Le Fanu was the supreme master of the supernatural, and I am glad to pay my own tribute also by writing that certainly in my opinion he has seldom, if ever, been approached, and most assuredly never excelled. It should be remarked that Le Fanu had the habit of refashioning his tales, and would often develop a short story until it was of considerable length. Finally it might even attain the dimensions of a three-volume novel. I mention this inasmuch as *An Account of some Strange Disturbances in Aungier Street* (1853) is the first form of *Mr. Justice Harbottle* which appeared in the volume published in 1872 under the title *In a Glass Darkly*. These stories, once difficult to procure, have of late years been reissued, but I felt that, however accessible they may be, no collection of the supernatural could go forth without the seal of Le Fanu.

It should be remarked, and I hardly think that the point has been noticed before in this connexion, what gloomy yet intensive delight the mid-Victorians took in funerals, interments, and all the trappings of mortuary woe. How raven-black was the velvet pall, how solemnly nodded the hearse-plumes, how awful stood the train of mutes, how long was the deep *crape* worn by relics of the deceased, how fruity was the old port wine, how rich the slabs of cake ! Their minds loved to dwell upon sepulture and the charnel. Dickens, in *Martin Chuzzlewit* and other of his novels, has shown how prominent a part was played by the undertakers, Mr. Mould, Mr. Sowerby, Mr. Joram, and the rest. What an event was a funeral from a house ! The way to all these sadly sentimental lachrymals had been paved before by the lugubrious cortèges of the time of Anne, the funerals at night with a train of flambeaux, the mourning coaches, and all the rest of the lugubrious paraphernalia. We must not forget, too, those expressions of elegant piety such as Blair's *The Grave*, Young's *The Last Day*, Samuel Boyse's *A Deity*, and *Death* by Bishop Beilby Porteus, which for a century and a half exercised an almost universal influence in the spheres of such theology as loved to ponder upon the skull, the hour-glass, crossbones, hatchments, mournful and sorrowing cherubim.

A typically Victorian writer was Mrs. Riddell, whose *The Haunted River* I have mentioned above, and who published in one volume half a dozen tales under the attractive title *Weird Stories*, 1885. Miss Braddon and Mrs. Henry Wood both wrote some first-rate ghost stories. *The Cold Embrace* and *Eveline's Visitant* (which I have included here) by the former lady are particularly good, and, although it does not actually deal with the supernatural, I am constrained to mention as an example of her uncanny power *The Mystery at Fernwood*, where Laurence Wendale is horribly murdered apparently by himself, as through the door of the billiard-room is seen his exact image bending over and slashing at the corpse. The double suddenly mops and grins furiously. It is the dead man's twin brother, an idiot, whose brain was injured owing to an accident in earliest childhood.

A large number of stories of the supernatural may be found in the magazines : in *Tinsley's Magazine*, *Temple Bar*, *Belgravia*, *London Society*, *Blackwood's*, the *Argosy*, the *English Illustrated*, as also in the forgotten *Family Herald Supplement* and *Young Ladies' Journal*. To come to a later date, there was no richer storehouse than the *Pall Mall Magazine*. In this last, in May, June and October, 1893, was published a study by James Mew, *The Black Art*, which is particularly interesting as a young and unknown artist, Aubrey Beardsley, contributed a full-page illustration (June, 1893, p. 177), " Of a Neophyte And How The Black Art Was Revealed Unto Him By The Fiend Asomuel." In July, 1893, of the *Pall Mall Magazine* appeared *The Last of the Flying Dutchman*, by W. L. Alden, which cleverly ended with a query ; and *A Kiss of Judas*, a vampire story by X. L., the author of a tale of Satanism, *Aut Diabolus aut Nihil*, and who in the same magazine (September to December, 1898) published *With All the Powders of the Merchant*. In October, 1893, appeared *The Luck of the Devil* ; in May, 1894, *A Cry Across the Black Water*, and in August of the same year Howard Pease's *Mine Host the Cardinal*, an excellent ghost story. In January, 1895, was given *The Devil Stone*, by Beatrice Heron Maxwell ; in March, *The*

Hands of Earl Rothes, by E. M. Hewitt, and also *Huguenin's Wife*, by M. P. Shiel. In December of that year we welcomed one of Dr. M. R. James's best stories, *Lost Hearts*. It is interesting to notice that some four years later, in April, 1899, another of our leading writers of ghost fiction, Algernon Blackwood, was represented by his *The Haunted Island*. June, 1896, has *The Story of a Tusk*, by H. A. Boyden, and *The Stone Chamber of Taverndale Manor House*, this latter a good spooky yarn of the real old Christmassy kind. In March, 1897, a horrible tale of psychic invasion, *The Case of the Rev. Mr. Toomey*, was given, as also *Doctor Armstrong*, which tells how to a leading surgeon was brought for a serious operation a man in feeblest health, who had suffered terribly all his life. In this invalid Doctor Armstrong, who has never known a day's illness, recognises by some uprush from a past life the Grand Inquisitor, who at Toledo centuries before had doomed him to the rack and the screw, to a death of agony by fire. In a moment of time, as it were, he passes through those days and months of excruciating anguish once more and is convulsed in throes of fiercest pain. Revenge, completest revenge, is in his grasp. He takes the steel instruments, and, administering no anæsthetic, in his turn becomes tormentor. He wrenches the muscles, tears the flesh and twists the nerves of the helpless writhing thing before him until the unhappy wretch draws his last moaning breath. But then a voice of infinite pity, yet infinitely just, sounds in the doctor's ear, telling him that by indulging his own bad passions and wreaking vengeance instead of showing mercy so has he forfeited his claim upon the mercy of Heaven.

August and September of the *Pall Mall Magazine*, 1897, gave *A Tribute of Souls*, by Lord Frederic Hamilton and Robert Hichens, which was afterwards reprinted in the latter writer's *Byways*. October, 1900, had *A Night on the Moor*, by R. Murray Gilchrist, and one of the best vampire stories I know appropriately appeared in December of that year—*The Tomb of Sarah*, by F. G. Loring.

Even just this hasty sketch—and I have omitted a large number of stories of great merit—will serve to show the interest taken in the supernatural by many of the writers prominent before the public in those years.

Stories of the supernatural, many of a rare excellence, have been penned by R. L. Stevenson, W. W. Jacobs, Rudyard Kipling, H. G. Wells, Richard Middleton, Robert Hichens, Lord Dunsany, Walter de la Mare, Edith Wharton, Mrs. Molesworth, Fergus

Hume, Barry Pain, John Buchan, Ambrose Bierce, Oliver Onions, Arthur Machen, Mary Heaton Vorse, Elliot O'Donnell, Bram Stoker, M. H. Austin, Hugh Conway, Fred G. Smale, Fitz-James O'Brien, Robert W. Chambers, Arthur Johnson, Clark Russell, Perceval Landon, Conan Doyle, Marjorie Bowen, Howard Pease, Ingulphus (Arthur Gray), Saki, Sir T. G. Jackson, Edward H. Cooper, A. M. Burrage, Grace V. Christmas, H. R. Wakefield, Mrs. Campbell Praed, Evelyn Nesbit, the Rev. E. G. Swain, L. P. Hartley, Mrs. Belloc Lowndes, Elizabeth Bowen, Baring Gould, Katherine Tynan, Vincent O'Sullivan, Vernon Lee, Amyas Northcote, E. and H. Heron, Roger Pater, John Guinan, W. J. Wintle, A. C. Benson, May Sinclair, and many others, the omission of whose names from this list, set down well-nigh at random as I glance at my shelves, must not be taken as any criticism of or judgement upon their quality, but rather because in making a terrier of ghost stories it is well-nigh impossible to aim at anything like a complete and exhaustive survey.

Although his work is widely read, I have always felt that the ghost stories of the late Monsignor Hugh Benson never receive their just meed of appreciation. Yet it would not be easy to find a better symposium than *The Mirror of Shalott*, and there are few stories more horrible than *My Own Tale*, the house which had no soul. A fine story, too, is *The Traveller*, in *The Light Invisible*, and, in spite of the fact that Monsignor Benson himself declared that this book was written " in moods of great feverishness " and " largely insincere," frankly I would give twenty apocalyptic romances such as *The Lord of the World* and *The Dawn of All*, and fifty novels such as *Initiation* and *Loneliness*, both of which seem to me to trench far too nearly upon a calamitous pessimism, to call it nothing worse, for another *Light Invisible* ; although I am very well aware that certain points, and these not the least important, are open to criticism.

It is hardly necessary for me to speak of the most notable living exponents of the ghost story. Mr. E. F. Benson has shown himself a supremely accomplished artist in *Spook Stories* and *The Room in the Tower*. *The Empty House*, by Algernon Blackwood, is worthy of Le Fanu himself, and praise can reach no higher. *Keeping his Promise* and *Smith* are also of a rare quality, whilst there is nobody fascinated by the supernatural who does not wish for further experiences of *John Silence*. Dr. James uses his vast antiquarian and archæological erudition to create an appropriate atmosphere for his malignant ghosts, and no better setting could be devised. His care for detail is admirable, and tells immensely. In fact, I know only one living writer who can be compared with him in this point. I refer to Vernon Lee (Violet Paget), from whose *Hauntings* I am privileged to give two stories, *Amour Dure* and *Oke of Okehurst*. In the first the old Italian town among the hills, and in the other the English manor house, are drawn with marvellous felicity. No less cleverly done are Venice, Padua, and the Italian *podere* in *That Wicked Voice*. *Hauntings* is a masterpiece of literature, and even Le Fanu and M. R. James cannot be ranked above the genius of this lady. Unfortunately, Vernon Lee has given us no further ghost stories since 1890, save that she once refashioned a tale or so as was the wont of Sheridan Le Fanu.

Particularly happy is Dr. James in his descriptions of those tall, red-brick houses, whose probable date is 1770 or thereabouts, in the eastern counties : such are Wilsthorpe, Castringham (although the Hall was mainly Elizabethan) in Suffolk, Aswarby Hall, Betton Court, Brockstone Court, and the Residence at Whitminster. I, too, like the pillared portico, the hall, the library, the pictures ; and I, too, " wish to have one of these houses and enough money to keep it together and entertain my friends in it modestly."

Dr. James tells us, as we might well guess, that for him places are prolific in suggestion.

.   .   .   .

It may be asked in what spirit should the stories in this collection be taken. With the exception of three (and these I will not specify), they are all ostensibly fiction, but I am sure that of the others, too, more than half a dozen could be very closely paralleled by real experience. I can hardly expect, although I might desire, that they should have the same effect upon the readers as *The Castle of Otranto* had upon Gray, who wrote : " It makes some of us cry a little, and all in general afraid to go to bed o' nights."

The best way to appreciate a ghost story is to believe in ghosts. Yet if one cannot, at least imitate the wittily truthful Madame du Deffand, who, when asked, " Do you believe in ghosts ? " replied : " No, but I am afraid of them."

MONTAGUE SUMMERS.

Note.—Many of the stories in this book are copyright, and may not be reprinted without the permission of the authors and publishers concerned. Whilst the utmost care and great diligence have been exercised to ascertain the owners of the rights so that the necessary permission to include the stories in the present collection should be secured, the editor and publishers desire to offer their apologies in any possible case of accidental infringement.

My best thanks and all acknowledgements are particularly due to the following for generous permissions so courteously accorded : To Miss Violet Paget (Vernon Lee) and Messrs. John Lane for *Amour Dure* and *Oke of Okehurst* ; Miss Rosalie Muspratt (Jasper John) and Messrs. Henry Walker for *The Spirit of Stonehenge* and *The Seeker of Souls* ; Mr. John Guinan for *The Watcher O' The Dead*; Messrs. Routledge for *The Judge's House* ; Messrs. Burns, Oates & Washbourne for *De Profundis*, *The Astrologer's Legacy*, and *A Porta Inferi* ; Messrs. C. Arthur Pearson for *The Story of The Spaniards, Hammersmith*, *The Story of Konnor Old House*, *The Story of Yand Manor House* ; Messrs. John Lane for *Brickett Bottom* ; Messrs. William Heinemann for *Thurnley Abbey*; Messrs. George G. Harrap for *Tousell's Pale Bride*.

I am further much indebted to Mr. H. Stuart-Forbes for his invaluable help in the collection of material, as also for his spirited and discerning criticisms of Ghost Stories, suggestions which have gone far to make my task easier and (if possible) more interesting.

M. S.

SECTION I

STORIES OF
HAUNTINGS AND HORROR

J. *Sheridan de Fanu*

NARRATIVE OF THE GHOST OF A HAND

from THE HOUSE BY THE CHURCHYARD

Tinsley, 1863

I'm sure she believed every word she related, for old Sally was veracious. But all this was worth just so much as such talk commonly is—marvels, fabulæ, what our ancestors called winter's tales —which gathered details from every narrator, and dilated in the act of narration. Still it was not quite for nothing that the house was held to be haunted. Under all this smoke there smouldered just a little spark of truth—an authenticated mystery, for the solution of which some of my readers may possibly suggest a theory, though I confess I can't.

Miss Rebecca Chattesworth, in a letter dated late in the autumn of 1753, gives a minute and curious relation of occurrences in the Tiled House, which, it is plain, although at starting she protests against all such fooleries, she has heard with a peculiar sort of interest, and relates it certainly with an awful sort of particularity.

I was for printing the entire letter, which is really very singular as well as characteristic. But my publisher meets me with his *veto* ; and I believe he is right. The worthy old lady's letter *is*, perhaps, too long ; and I must rest content with a few hungry notes of its tenor.

That year, and somewhere about the 24th October, there broke out a strange dispute between Mr. Alderman Harper, of High Street, Dublin, and my Lord Castlemallard, who, in virtue of his cousinship to the young heir's mother, had undertaken for him the management of the tiny estate on which the Tiled or Tyled House—for I find it spelt both ways—stood.

This Alderman Harper had agreed for a lease of the house for his daughter, who was married to a gentleman named Prosser. He furnished it and put up hangings, and otherwise went to considerable expense. Mr. and Mrs. Prosser came there sometime in June, and after having parted with a good many servants in the interval, she made up her mind that she could not live in the house, and her father waited on Lord Castlemallard, and told him

plainly that he would not take out the lease because the house was
subjected to annoyances which he could not explain. In plain
terms, he said it was haunted, and that no servants would live
there more than a few weeks, and that after what his son-in-law's
family had suffered there, not only should he be excused from
taking a lease of it, but that the house itself ought to be pulled
down as a nuisance and the habitual haunt of something worse
than human malefactors.

Lord Castlemallard filed a bill in the Equity side of the Exche-
quer to compel Mr. Alderman Harper to perform his contract, by
taking out the lease. But the Alderman drew an answer, supported
by no less than seven long affidavits, copies of all which were
furnished to his lordship, and with the desired effect ; for rather
than compel him to place them upon the file of the court, his
lordship struck, and consented to release him.

I am sorry the cause did not proceed at least far enough to place
upon the files of the court the very authentic and unaccountable
story which Miss Rebecca relates.

The annoyances described did not begin till the end of August,
when, one evening, Mrs. Prosser, quite alone, was sitting in the
twilight at the back parlour window, which was open, looking out
into the orchard, and plainly saw a hand stealthily placed upon the
stone window-sill outside, as if by some one beneath the window,
at her right side, intending to climb up. There was nothing but the
hand, which was rather short but handsomely formed, and white
and plump, laid on the edge of the window-sill ; and it was not a
very young hand, but one aged, somewhere about forty, as she
conjectured. It was only a few weeks before that the horrible
robbery at Clondalkin had taken place, and the lady fancied that
the hand was that of one of the miscreants who was now about to
scale the windows of the Tiled House. She uttered a loud scream
and an ejaculation of terror, and at the same moment the hand was
quietly withdrawn.

Search was made in the orchard, but no indications of any
person's having been under the window, beneath which, ranged
along the wall, stood a great column of flower-pots, which it
seemed must have prevented any one's coming within reach
of it.

The same night there came a hasty tapping, every now and
then, at the window of the kitchen. The women grew frightened,
and the servant-man, taking fire-arms with him, opened the

back-door, but discovered nothing. As he shut it, however, he said, "a thump came on it," and a pressure as of somebody striving to force his way in, which frightened *him* ; and though the tapping went on upon the kitchen window panes, he made no further explorations.

About six o'clock on the Saturday evening following, the cook, "an honest, sober woman, now aged nigh sixty years," being alone in the kitchen, saw, on looking up, it is supposed, the same fat but aristocratic-looking hand, laid with its palm against the glass, near the side of the window, and this time moving slowly up and down, pressed all the while against the glass, as if feeling carefully for some inequality in its surface. She cried out, and said something like a prayer on seeing it. But it was not withdrawn for several seconds after.

After this, for a great many nights, there came at first a low, and afterwards an angry rapping, as it seemed with a set of clenched knuckles at the back-door. And the servant-man would not open it, but called to know who was there ; and there came no answer, only a sound as if the palm of the hand was placed against it, and drawn slowly from side to side with a sort of soft, groping motion.

All this time, sitting in the back parlour, which, for the time, they used as a drawing-room, Mr. and Mrs. Prosser were disturbed by rappings at the window, sometimes very low and furtive, like a clandestine signal, and at others sudden and so loud as to threaten the breaking of the pane.

This was all at the back of the house, which looked upon the orchard as you know. But on a Tuesday night, at about half-past nine, there came precisely the same rapping at the hall-door, and went on, to the great annoyance of the master and terror of his wife, at intervals, for nearly two hours.

After this, for several days and nights, they had no annoyance whatsoever, and began to think that the nuisance had expended itself. But on the night of the 13th September, Jane Easterbrook, an English maid, having gone into the pantry for the small silver bowl in which her mistress's posset was served, happening to look up at the little window of only four panes, observed through an augur-hole which was drilled through the window frame, for the admission of a bolt to secure the shutter, a white pudgy finger —first the tip, and then the two first joints introduced, and turned about this way and that, crooked against the inside, as if in search of a fastening which its owner designed to push aside.

When the maid got back into the kitchen, we are told "she fell into
' a swounde,' and was all the next day very weak."

Mr. Prosser being, I've heard, a hard-headed and conceited
sort of fellow, scouted the ghost, and sneered at the fears of his
family. He was privately of opinion that the whole affair was a
practical joke or a fraud, and waited an opportunity of catching
the rogue *flagrante delicto*. He did not long keep this theory to himself, but let it out by degrees with no stint of oaths and threats,
believing that some domestic traitor held the thread of the conspiracy.

Indeed it was time something were done ; for not only his
servants, but good Mrs. Prosser herself, had grown to look unhappy
and anxious. They kept at home from the hour of sunset, and
would not venture about the house after night-fall, except in
couples.

The knocking had ceased for about a week ; when one night,
Mrs. Prosser being in the nursery, her husband, who was in the
parlour, heard it begin very softly at the hall-door. The air was
quite still, which favoured his hearing distinctly. This was the
first time there had been any disturbance at that side of the house,
and the character of the summons was changed.

Mr. Prosser, leaving the parlour-door open, it seems, went
quietly into the hall. The sound was that of beating on the outside
of the stout door, softly and regularly, "with the flat of the hand."
He was going to open it suddenly, but changed his mind ; and
went back very quietly, and on to the head of the kitchen stair,
where was a "strong closet" over the pantry, in which he kept his
firearms, swords, and canes.

Here he called his man-servant, whom he believed to be honest,
and, with a pair of loaded pistols in his own coat-pockets, and
giving another pair to him, he went as lightly as he could, followed by the man, and with a stout walking-cane in his hand,
forward to the door.

Everything went as Mr. Prosser wished. The besieger of his
house, so far from taking fright at their approach, grew more impatient ; and the sort of patting which had aroused his attention
at first assumed the rhythm and emphasis of a series of double-
knocks.

Mr. Prosser, angry, opened the door with his right arm across,
cane in hand. Looking, he saw nothing ; but his arm was jerked
up oddly, as it might be with the hollow of a hand, and something

passed under it, with a kind of gentle squeeze. The servant neither saw nor felt anything, and did not know why his master looked back so hastily, cutting with his cane, and shutting the door with so sudden a slam.

From that time Mr. Prosser discontinued his angry talk and swearing about it, and seemed nearly as averse from the subject as the rest of his family. He grew, in fact, very uncomfortable, feeling an inward persuasion that when, in answer to the summons, he had opened the hall-door, he had actually given admission to the besieger.

He said nothing to Mrs. Prosser, but went up earlier to his bedroom, " where he read a while in his Bible, and said his prayers." I hope the particular relation of this circumstance does not indicate its singularity. He lay awake a good while, it appears ; and, as he supposed, about a quarter past twelve he heard the soft palm of a hand patting on the outside of the bedroom-door, and then brushed slowly along it.

Up bounced Mr. Prosser, very much frightened, and locked the door, crying, " Who's there ? " but receiving no answer, but the same brushing sound of a soft hand drawn over the panels, which he knew only too well.

In the morning the housemaid was terrified by the impression of a hand in the dust of the " little parlour " table, where they had been unpacking delft and other things the day before. The print of the naked foot in the sea-sand did not frighten Robinson Crusoe half so much. They were by this time all nervous, and some of them half-crazed, about the hand.

Mr. Prosser went to examine the mark, and, made light of it, but, as he swore afterwards, rather to quiet his servants than from any comfortable feeling about it in his own mind ; however, he had them all, one by one, into the room, and made each place his or her hand, palm downward, on the same table, thus taking a similar impression from every person in the house, including himself and his wife ; and his " affidavit " deposed that the formation of the hand so impressed differed altogether from those of the living inhabitants of the house, and corresponded with that of the hand seen by Mrs. Prosser and by the cook.

Whoever or whatever the owner of that hand might be, they all felt this subtle demonstration to mean that it was declared he was no longer out of doors, but had established himself in the house.

And now Mrs. Prosser began to be troubled with strange and

horrible dreams, some of which as set out in detail, in Aunt Rebecca's long letter, are really very appalling nightmares. But one night, as Mr. Prosser closed his bedchamber-door, he was struck somewhat by the utter silence of the room, there being no sound of breathing, which seemed unaccountable to him, as he knew his wife was in bed, and his ears were particularly sharp.

There was a candle burning on a small table at the foot of the bed, besides the one he held in one hand, a heavy ledger, connected with his father-in-law's business being under his arm. He drew the curtain at the side of the bed, and saw Mrs. Prosser lying, as for a few seconds he mortally feared, dead, her face being motionless, white, and covered with a cold dew ; and on the pillow, close beside her head, and just within the curtains, was, as he first thought, a toad—but really the same fattish hand, the wrist resting on the pillow, and the fingers extended towards her temple.

Mr. Prosser, with a horrified jerk, pitched the ledger right at the curtains, behind which the owner of the hand might be supposed to stand. The hand was instantaneously and smoothly snatched away, the curtains made a great wave, and Mr. Prosser got round the bed in time to see the closet-door, which was at the other side, pulled to by the same white, puffy hand, as he believed.

He drew the door open with a fling, and stared in : but the closet was empty, except for the clothes hanging from the pegs on the wall, and the dressing-table and looking-glass facing the windows. He shut it sharply, and locked it, and felt for a minute, he says, " as if he were like to lose his wits " ; then, ringing at the bell, he brought the servants, and with much ado they recovered Mrs. Prosser from a sort of " trance," in which, he says, from her looks, she seemed to have suffered " the pains of death " : and Aunt Rebecca adds, " from what she told me of her visions, with her own lips, he might have added, ' and of hell also.' "

But the occurrence which seems to have determined the crisis was the strange sickness of their eldest child, a little boy aged between two and three years. He lay awake, seemingly in paroxysms of terror, and the doctors who were called in, set down the symptoms to incipient water on the brain. Mrs. Prosser used to sit up with the nurse, by the nursery fire, much troubled in mind about the condition of her child.

His bed was placed sideways along the wall, with its head against the door of a press or cupboard, which, however, did not shut quite close. There was a little valance, about a foot deep, round the top of the child's bed, and this descended within some ten or twelve inches of the pillow on which it lay.

They observed that the little creature was quieter whenever they took it up and held it on their laps. They had just replaced him, as he seemed to have grown quite sleepy and tranquil, but he was not five minutes in his bed when he began to scream in one of his frenzies of terror ; at the same moment the nurse, for the first time, detected, and Mrs. Prosser equally plainly saw, following the direction of *her* eyes, the real cause of the child's sufferings.

Protruding through the aperture of the press, and shrouded in the shade of the valance, they plainly saw the white fat hand, palm downwards, presented towards the head of the child. The mother uttered a scream, and snatched the child from its little bed, and she and the nurse ran down to the lady's sleeping-room, where Mr. Prosser was in bed, shutting the door as they entered ; and they had hardly done so, when a gentle tap came to it from the outside.

There is a great deal more, but this will suffice. The singularity of the narrative seems to me to be this, that it describes the ghost of a hand, and no more. The person to whom that hand belonged never once appeared ; nor was it a hand separated from a body, but only a hand so manifested and introduced that its owner was always, by some crafty accident, hidden from view.

In the year 1819, at a college breakfast, I met a Mr. Prosser—a thin, grave, but rather chatty old gentleman, with very white hair drawn back into a pigtail—and he told us all, with a concise particularity, a story of his cousin, James Prosser, who, when an infant, had slept for some time in what his mother said was a haunted nursery in an old house near Chapelizod, and who, whenever he was ill, over-fatigued, or in anywise feverish, suffered all through his life as he had done from a time he could scarce remember, from a vision of a certain gentleman, fat and pale, every curl of whose wig, every button and fold of whose laced clothes, and every feature and line of whose sensual, benignant, and unwholesome face, was as minutely engraven upon his memory as the dress and lineaments of his own grandfather's portrait, which hung before him every day at breakfast, dinner, and supper.

Mr. Prosser mentioned this as an instance of a curiously monotonous, individualised, and persistent nightmare, and hinted the extreme horror and anxiety with which his cousin, of whom he

spoke in the past tense as " poor Jemmie," was at any time induced to mention it.

I hope the reader will pardon me for loitering so long in the
Tiled House, but this sort of lore has always had a charm for me ;
and people, you know, especially old people, will talk of what
most interests themselves, too often forgetting that others may
have had more than enough of it.

J. Sheridan Le Fanu

AN ACCOUNT OF SOME STRANGE DISTURBANCES IN AUNGIER STREET

from DUBLIN UNIVERSITY MAGAZINE, 1853

It is not worth telling, this story of mine—at least, not worth
writing. Told, indeed, as I have sometimes been called upon to
tell it, to a circle of intelligent and eager faces, lighted up by a
good after-dinner fire on a winter's evening, with a cold wind
rising and wailing outside, and all snug and cosy within, it has
gone off—though I say it, who should not—indifferent well. But
it is a venture to do as you would have me. Pen, ink, and paper are
cold vehicles for the marvellous, and a " reader " decidedly a
more critical animal than a " listener." If, however, you can
induce your friends to read it after nightfall, and when the fireside
talk has run for a while on thrilling tales of shapeless terror ; in
short, if you will secure me the *mollia tempora fandi*, I will go to my
work, and say my say, with better heart. Well, then, these conditions presupposed, I shall waste no more words, but tell you simply
how it all happened.

My cousin (Tom Ludlow) and I studied medicine together. I think he would have succeeded, had he stuck to the profession ; but he preferred the Church, poor fellow, and died early, a sacrifice to contagion, contracted in the noble discharge of his duties. For my present purpose, I say enough of his character when I mention that he was of a sedate but frank and cheerful nature ; very exact in his observance of truth, and not by any means like myself—of an excitable or nervous temperament.

My Uncle Ludlow—Tom's father—while we were attending lectures, purchased three or four old houses in Aungier Street, one of which was unoccupied. *He* resided in the country, and Tom proposed that we should take up our abode in the untenanted house, so long as it should continue unlet ; a move which would accomplish the double end of settling us nearer alike to our lecture-rooms and to our amusements, and of relieving us from the weekly charge of rent for our lodgings.

Our furniture was very scant—our whole equipage remarkably modest and primitive ; and, in short, our arrangements pretty nearly as simple as those of a bivouac. Our new plan was, therefore, executed almost as soon as conceived. The front drawing-room was our sitting-room. I had the bedroom over it, and Tom the back bedroom on the same floor, which nothing could have induced me to occupy.

The house, to begin with, was a very old one. It had been, I believe, newly fronted about fifty years before ; but with this exception, it had nothing modern about it. The agent who bought it and looked into the titles for my uncle, told me that it was sold, along with much other forfeited property, at Chichester House, I think, in 1702 ; and had belonged to Sir Thomas Hacket, who was Lord Mayor of Dublin in James II's time. How old it was *then*, I can't say ; but, at all events, it had seen years and changes enough to have contracted all that mysterious and saddened air, at once exciting and depressing, which belongs to most old mansions.

There had been very little done in the way of modernising details ; and, perhaps, it was better so ; for there was something queer and by-gone in the very walls and ceilings—in the shape of doors and windows—in the odd diagonal site of the chimney-pieces—in the beams and ponderous cornices—not to mention the singular solidity of all the woodwork, from the banisters to the window-frames, which hopelessly defied disguise, and would have emphatically proclaimed their antiquity through any conceivable amount of modern finery and varnish.

An effort had, indeed, been made, to the extent of papering the drawing-rooms ; but, somehow the paper looked raw and out of keeping ; and the old woman, who kept a little dirt-pie of a shop in the lane, and whose daughter—a girl of two and fifty—was our solitary handmaid, coming in at sunrise, and chastely receding again as soon as she had made all ready for tea in our state apartment ;—this woman, I say, remembered it, when old Judge Horrocks (who, having earned the reputation of a particularly " hanging judge," ended by hanging himself, as the coroner's jury found, under an impulse of " temporary insanity," with a child's skipping-rope, over the massive old banisters) resided there, entertaining good company, with fine venison and rare old port. In those halcyon days, the drawing-rooms were hung with gilded leather, and, I dare say, cut a good figure, for they were really spacious rooms.

The bedrooms were wainscoted, but the front one was not gloomy ; and in it the cosiness of antiquity quite overcame its sombre associations. But the back bedroom, with its two queerly-placed melancholy windows, staring vacantly at the foot of the bed, and with the shadowy recess to be found in most old houses in Dublin, like a large ghostly closet, which, from congeniality of temperament, had amalgamated with the bedchamber, and dissolved the partition. At night-time, this " alcove "—as our " maid " was wont to call it—had, in my eyes, a specially sinister and suggestive character. Tom's distant and solitary candle glimmered vainly into its darkness. *There* it was always over-looking him—always itself impenetrable. But this was only part of the effect. The whole room was, I can't tell how, repulsive to me. There was, I suppose, in its proportions and features, a latent discord—a certain mysterious and indescribable relation, which jarred indistinctly upon some secret sense of the fitting and the safe, and raised indefinable suspicions and apprehensions of the imagination. On the whole, as I began by saying, nothing could have induced me to pass a night alone in it.

I had never pretended to conceal from poor Tom my superstitious weakness ; and he, on the other hand, most unaffectedly ridiculed my tremors. The sceptic was, however, destined to receive a lesson, as you shall hear.

We had not been very long in occupation of our respective dormitories, when I began to complain of uneasy nights and disturbed sleep. I was, I suppose, the more impatient under this annoyance, as I was usually a sound sleeper, and by no means prone to nightmares. It was now, however, my destiny, instead of enjoying my customary repose, every night to " sup full of horrors." After a preliminary course of disagreeable and frightful dreams, my troubles took a definite form, and the same vision, without an appreciable variation in a single detail, visited me at least (on an average) every second night in the week.

Now, this dream, nightmare, or infernal illusion—which you please—of which I was the miserable sport, was on this wise :—

I saw, or thought I saw, with the most abominable distinctness, although at the time in profound darkness, every article of furniture and accidental arrangement of the chamber in which I lay. This, as you know, is incidental to ordinary nightmare. Well, while in this clairvoyant condition, which seemed but the lighting up of the theatre in which was to be exhibited the monotonous tableau of horror, which made my nights insupportable, my attention invariably became, I know not why, fixed upon the windows opposite the foot of my bed ; and, uniformly with the same effect, a sense of dreadful anticipation always took slow but sure possession of me. I became somehow conscious of a sort of horrid but undefined preparation going forward in some unknown quarter, and by some unknown agency, for my torment ; and, after an interval, which always seemed to me of the same length, a picture suddenly flew up to the window, where it remained fixed, as if by an electrical attraction, and my discipline of horror then commenced, to last perhaps for hours. The picture thus mysteriously glued to the window-panes, was the portrait of an old man, in a crimson flowered silk dressing-gown, the folds of which I could now describe, with a countenance embodying a strange mixture of intellect, sensuality, and power, but withal sinister and full of malignant omen. His nose was hooked, like the beak of a vulture ; his eyes large, grey, and prominent, and lighted up with a more than mortal cruelty and coldness. These features were surmounted by a crimson velvet cap, the hair that peeped from under which was white with age, while the eyebrows retained their original blackness. Well I remember every line, hue, and shadow of that stony countenance, and well I may ! The gaze of this hellish visage was fixed upon me, and mine returned it with the inexplicable fascination of nightmare, for what appeared to me to be hours of agony. At last—

" The cock he crew, away then flew "

the fiend who had enslaved me through the awful watches of the night ; and, harassed and nervous, I rose to the duties of the day.

I had—I can't say exactly why, but it may have been from the exquisite anguish and profound impressions of unearthly horror, with which this strange phantasmagoria was associated—an insurmountable antipathy to describing the exact nature of my nightly troubles to my friend and comrade. Generally, however, I told him that I was haunted by abominable dreams ; and, true to the imputed materialism of medicine, we put our heads together to dispel my horrors, not by exorcism, but by a tonic.

I will do this tonic justice, and frankly admit that the accursed portrait began to intermit its visits under its influence. What of that ? Was this singular apparition—as full of character as of terror—therefore the creature of my fancy, or the invention of my poor stomach ? Was it, in short, *subjective* (to borrow the technical slang of the day) and not the palpable aggression and intrusion of an external agent ? That, good friend, as we will both admit, by no means follows. The evil spirit, who enthralled my senses in the shape of that portrait, may have been just as near me, just as energetic, just as malignant, though I saw him not. What means the whole moral code of revealed religion regarding the due keeping of our own bodies, soberness, temperance, etc. ? here is an obvious connexion between the material and the invisible ; the healthy tone of the system, and its unimpaired energy, may, for aught we can tell, guard us against influences which would otherwise render life itself terrific. The mesmerist and the electro-biologist will fail upon an average with nine patients out of ten—so may the evil spirit. Special conditions of the corporeal system are indispensable to the production of certain spiritual phenomena. The operation succeeds sometimes—sometimes fails—that is all.

I found afterwards that my would-be sceptical companion had his troubles too. But of these I knew nothing yet. One night, for a wonder, I was sleeping soundly, when I was roused by a step on the lobby outside my room, followed by the loud clang of what turned out to be a large brass candlestick, flung with all his force by poor Tom Ludlow over the banisters, and rattling with a rebound down the second flight of stairs ; and almost concurrently with this, Tom burst open my door, and bounced into my room backwards, in a state of extraordinary agitation.

I had jumped out of bed and clutched him by the arm before I had any distinct idea of my own whereabouts. There we were—in our shirts—standing before the open door—staring through the great old banister opposite, at the lobby window, through which the sickly light of a clouded moon was gleaming.

" What's the matter, Tom ? What's the matter with you ? What the devil's the matter with you, Tom ? " I demanded, shaking him with nervous impatience.

He took a long breath before he answered me, and then it was not very coherently.

" It's nothing, nothing at all—did I speak ?—what did I say ?—where's the candle, Richard ? It's dark ; I—I had a candle ! "

" Yes, dark enough," I said ; " but what's the matter ?—what is it ?—why don't you speak, Tom ?—have you lost your wits ?—what is the matter ? "

" The matter ?—oh, it is all over. It must have been a dream—nothing at all but a dream—don't you think so ? It could not be anything more than a dream."

" Of *course*," said I, feeling uncommonly nervous, " it *was* a dream."

" I thought," he said, " there was a man in my room, and—and I jumped out of bed ; and—and—where's the candle ? "

" In your room, most likely," I said, " shall I go and bring it ? "

" No ; stay here—don't go ; it's no matter—don't, I tell you ; it was all a dream. Bolt the door, Dick ; I'll stay here with you—I feel nervous. So, Dick, like a good fellow, light your candle and open the window—I am in a *shocking state*."

I did as he asked me, and robing himself like Granuaile in one of my blankets, he seated himself close beside my bed.

Everybody knows how contagious is fear of all sorts, but more especially that particular kind of fear under which poor Tom was at that moment labouring. I would not have heard, nor I believe would he have recapitulated, just at that moment, for half the world, the details of the hideous vision which had so unmanned him.

" Don't mind telling me anything about your nonsensical dream, Tom," said I, affecting contempt, really in a panic ; " let us talk about something else ; but it is quite plain that this dirty old house disagrees with us both, and hang me if I stay here any longer, to be pestered with indigestion and—and—bad nights, so we may as well look out for lodgings—don't you think so ?—at once."

Tom agreed, and, after an interval, said—

" I have been thinking, Richard, that it is a long time since I saw my father, and I have made up my mind to go down to-morrow and return in a day or two, and you can take rooms for us in the meantime."

I fancied that this resolution, obviously the result of the vision which had so profoundly scared him, would probably vanish next morning with the damps and shadows of night. But I was mistaken. Off went Tom at peep of day to the country, having agreed that so soon as I had secured suitable lodgings, I was to recall him by letter from his visit to my Uncle Ludlow.

Now, anxious as I was to change my quarters, it so happened, owing to a series of petty procrastinations and accidents, that nearly a week elapsed before my bargain was made and my letter of recall on the wing to Tom ; and, in the meantime, a trifling adventure or two had occurred to your humble servant, which, absurd as they now appear, diminished by distance, did certainly at the time serve to whet my appetite for change considerably.

A night or two after the departure of my comrade, I was sitting by my bedroom fire, the door locked, and the ingredients of a tumbler of hot whisky-punch upon the crazy spider-table ; for, as the best mode of keeping the

> " *Black spirits and white,*
> *Blue spirits and grey,*"

with which I was environed, at bay, I had adopted the practice recommended by the wisdom of my ancestors, and " kept my spirits up by pouring spirits down." I had thrown aside my volume of Anatomy, and was treating myself by way of a tonic, prepara-tory to my punch and bed, to half-a-dozen pages of the *Spectator*, when I heard a step on the flight of stairs descending from the attics. It was two o'clock, and the streets were as silent as a church-yard—the sounds were, therefore, perfectly distinct. There was a slow, heavy tread, characterised by the emphasis and deliberation of age, descending by the narrow staircase from above ; and, what made the sound more singular, it was plain that the feet which produced it were perfectly bare, measuring the descent with some-thing between a pound and a flop, very ugly to hear.

I knew quite well that my attendant had gone away many hours before, and that nobody but myself had any business in the house. It was quite plain also that the person who was coming downstairs had no intention whatever of concealing his movements ; but, on the contrary, appeared disposed to make even more noise, and proceed more deliberately, than was at all necessary. When the step reached the foot of the stairs outside my room, it seemed to stop ; and I expected every moment to see my door open spontaneously, and give admission to the original of my detested portrait. I was, however, relieved in a few seconds by hearing the descent renewed, just in the same manner, upon the staircase leading down to the drawing-rooms, and thence, after another pause, down the next flight, and so on to the hall, whence I heard no more.

Now, by the time the sound had ceased, I was wound up, as they say, to a very unpleasant pitch of excitement. I listened, but there was not a stir. I screwed up my courage to a decisive experiment—opened my door, and in a stentorian voice bawled over the banisters, " Who's there ? " There was no answer, but the ringing of my own voice through the empty old house,—no renewal of the movement ; nothing, in short, to give my unpleasant sensations a definite direction. There is, I think, something most disagreeably disenchanting in the sound of one's own voice under such circumstances, exerted in solitude and in vain. It redoubled my sense of isolation, and my misgivings increased on perceiving that the door, which I certainly thought I had left open, was closed behind me ; in a vague alarm, lest my retreat should be cut off, I got again into my room as quickly as I could, where I remained in a state of imaginary blockade, and very uncomfortable indeed, till morning.

Next night brought no return of my barefooted fellow-lodger ; but the night following, being in my bed, and in the dark—somewhere, I suppose, about the same hour as before, I distinctly heard the old fellow again descending from the garrets.

This time I had had my punch, and the *morale* of the garrison was consequently excellent. I jumped out of bed, clutched the poker as I passed the expiring fire, and in a moment was upon the lobby. The sound had ceased by this time—the dark and chill were discouraging ; and, guess my horror, when I saw, or thought I saw, a black monster, whether in the shape of a man or a bear I could not say, standing, with its back to the wall, on the lobby, facing me, with a pair of great greenish eyes shining dimly out. Now, I must be frank, and confess that the cupboard which displayed our plates and cups stood just there, though at the moment I did not recollect it. At the same time I must honestly say, that making every allowance for an excited imagination, I never could satisfy myself that I was made the dupe of my own fancy in this matter ; for this apparition, after one or two shiftings of shape, as if in the act of incipient transformation, began, as it seemed on second thoughts, to advance upon me in its original form. From an instinct of terror rather than of courage, I hurled the poker, with all my force, at its head ; and to the music of a horrid crash made my way into my room, and double-locked the door. Then, in a minute more, I heard the horrid bare feet walk down the stairs, till the sound ceased in the hall, as on the former occasion.

If the apparition of the night before was an ocular delusion of my fancy sporting with the dark outlines of our cupboard, and if its horrid eyes were nothing but a pair of inverted teacups, I had, at all events, the satisfaction of having launched the poker with admirable effect, and in true " fancy " phrase, " knocked its two daylights into one," as the commingled fragments of my tea-service testified. I did my best to gather comfort and courage from these evidences ; but it would not do. And then what could I say of those horrid bare feet, and the regular tramp, tramp, tramp, which measured the distance of the entire staircase through the solitude of my haunted dwelling, and at an hour when no good influence was stirring ? Confound it !—the whole affair was abominable. I was out of spirits, and dreaded the approach of night.

It came, ushered ominously in with a thunder-storm and dull torrents of depressing rain. Earlier than usual the streets grew silent ; and by twelve o'clock nothing but the comfortless pattering of the rain was to be heard.

I made myself as snug as I could. I lighted *two* candles instead of one. I forswore bed, and held myself in readiness for a sally, candle in hand ; for, *coute qui coute*, I was resolved to *see* the being, if visible at all, who troubled the nightly stillness of my mansion. I was fidgety and nervous and, tried in vain to interest myself with my books. I walked up and down my room, whistling in turn martial and hilarious music, and listening ever and anon for the dreaded noise. I sate down and stared at the square label on the solemn and reserved-looking black bottle, until " FLANAGAN & Co.'s BEST OLD MALT WHISKY " grew into a sort of subdued accompaniment to all the fantastic and horrible speculations which chased one another through my brain.

Silence, meanwhile, grew more silent, and darkness darker. I listened in vain for the rumble of a vehicle, or the dull clamour of a distant row. There was nothing but the sound of a rising wind, which had succeeded the thunder-storm that had travelled over the Dublin mountains quite out of hearing. In the middle of this great city I began to feel myself alone with nature, and Heaven knows what beside. My courage was ebbing. Punch, however, which makes beasts of so many, made a man of me again—just in time to hear with tolerable nerve and firmness the lumpy, flabby, naked feet deliberately descending the stairs again.

I took a candle, not without a tremor. As I crossed the floor I tried to extemporise a prayer, but stopped short to listen, and never finished it. The steps continued. I confess I hesitated for some seconds at the door before I took heart of grace and opened it. When I peeped out the lobby was perfectly empty—there was no monster standing on the staircase ; and as the detested sound ceased, I was reassured enough to venture forward nearly to the banisters. Horror of horrors ! within a stair or two beneath the spot where I stood the unearthly tread smote the floor. My eye caught something in motion ; it was about the size of Goliath's foot—it was grey, heavy, and flapped with a dead weight from one step to another. As I am alive, it was the most monstrous grey rat I ever beheld or imagined.

Shakespeare says—" Some men there are cannot abide a gaping pig, and some that are mad if they behold a cat." I went well-nigh out of my wits when I beheld this *rat* ; for, laugh at me as you may, it fixed upon me, I thought, a perfectly human expression of malice ; and, as it shuffled about and looked up into my face almost from between my feet, I saw, I could swear it—I felt it then, and know it now, the infernal gaze and the accursed countenance of my old friend in the portrait, transfused into the visage of the bloated vermin before me.

I bounced into my room again with a feeling of loathing and horror I cannot describe, and locked and bolted my door as if a lion had been at the other side. D——n him or *it* ; curse the portrait and its original ! I felt in my soul that the rat—yes, the *rat*, the RAT I had just seen, was that evil being in masquerade, and rambling through the house upon some infernal night lark.

Next morning I was early trudging through the miry streets ; and, among other transactions, posted a peremptory note recalling Tom. On my return, however, I found a note from my absent " chum," announcing his intended return next day. I was doubly rejoiced at this, because I had succeeded in getting rooms ; and because the change of scene and return of my comrade were rendered specially pleasant by the last night's half ridiculous half horrible adventure.

I slept extemporaneously in my new quarters in Digges' Street that night, and next morning returned for breakfast to the haunted mansion, where I was certain Tom would call immediately on his arrival.

I was quite right—he came ; and almost his first question referred to the primary object of our change of residence.

" Thank God," he said with genuine fervour, on hearing that all was arranged. " On *your* account I am delighted. As to myself, I assure you that no earthly consideration could have induced me ever again to pass a night in this disastrous old house."

" Confound the house ! " I ejaculated, with a genuine mixture of fear and detestation, " we have not had a pleasant hour since we came to live here " ; and so I went on, and related incidentally my adventure with the plethoric old rat.

" Well, if that were *all*," said my cousin, affecting to make light of the matter, " I don't think I should have minded it very much."

" Ay, but its eye—its countenance, my dear Tom," urged I ; " if you had seen *that*, you would have felt it might be *anything* but what it seemed."

" I am inclined to think the best conjurer in such a case would be an able-bodied cat," he said, with a provoking chuckle.

" But let us hear your own adventure," I said tartly.

At this challenge he looked uneasily round him. I had poked up a very unpleasant recollection.

" You shall hear it, Dick ; I'll tell it to you," he said. " Begad, sir, I should feel quite queer, though, telling it *here*, though we are too strong a body for ghosts to meddle with just now."

Though he spoke this like a joke, I think it was serious calculation. Our Hebe was in a corner of the room, packing our cracked delf tea and dinner-services in a basket. She soon suspended operations, and with mouth and eyes wide open became an absorbed listener. Tom's experiences were told nearly in these words :—

" I saw it three times, Dick—three distinct times ; and I am perfectly certain it meant me some infernal harm. I was, I say, in danger—in *extreme* danger ; for, if nothing else had happened, my reason would most certainly have failed me, unless I had escaped so soon. Thank God. I *did* escape.

" The first night of this hateful disturbance, I was lying in the attitude of sleep, in that lumbering old bed. I hate to think of it. I was really wide awake, though I had put out my candle, and was lying as quietly as if I had been asleep ; and although accidentally restless, my thoughts were running in a cheerful and agreeable channel.

" I think it must have been two o'clock at least when I thought I heard a sound in that—that odious dark recess at the far end of the bedroom. It was as if someone was drawing a piece of cord slowly along the floor, lifting it up, and dropping it softly down again in coils. I sate up once or twice in my bed, but could see nothing, so I concluded it must be mice in the wainscot. I felt no emotion graver than curiosity, and after a few minutes ceased to observe it.

" While lying in this state, strange to say ; without at first a suspicion of anything supernatural, on a sudden I saw an old man, rather stout and square, in a sort of roan-red dressing-gown, and with a black cap on his head, moving stiffly and slowly in a diagonal direction, from the recess, across the floor of the bedroom, passing my bed at the foot, and entering the lumber-closet at the left. He had something under his arm ; his head hung a little at one side ; and merciful God ! when I saw his face."

Tom stopped for a while, and then said—

" That awful countenance, which living or dying I never can forget, disclosed what he was. Without turning to the right or left, he passed beside me, and entered the closet by the bed's head.

" While this fearful and indescribable type of death and guilt was passing, I felt that I had no more power to speak or stir than if I had been myself a corpse. For hours after it had disappeared, I was too terrified and weak to move. As soon as daylight came, I took courage, and examined the room, and especially the course which the frightful intruder had seemed to take, but there was not a vestige to indicate anybody's having passed there ; no sign of any disturbing agency visible among the lumber that strewed the floor of the closet.

" I now began to recover a little. I was fagged and exhausted, and at last, overpowered by a feverish sleep. I came down late ; and finding you out of spirits, on account of your dreams about the portrait, whose *original* I am now certain disclosed himself to me, I did not care to talk about the infernal vision. In fact, I was trying to persuade myself that the whole thing was an illusion, and I did not like to revive in their intensity the hated impressions of the past night—or, to risk the constancy of my scepticism, by recounting the tale of my sufferings.

" It required some nerve, I can tell you, to go to my haunted chamber next night, and lie down quietly in the same bed," continued Tom. " I did so with a degree of trepidation, which, I am not ashamed to say, a very little matter would have sufficed to stimulate to downright panic. This night, however, passed off quietly enough, as also the next ; and so too did two or three more. I grew more confident, and began to fancy that I believed in the theories of spectral illusions, with which I had at first vainly tried to impose upon my convictions.

" The apparition had been, indeed, altogether anomalous. It had crossed the room without any recognition of my presence : I had not disturbed *it*, and *it* had no mission to *me*. What, then, was the imaginable use of its crossing the room in a visible shape at all ? Of course it might have *been* in the closet instead of *going* there, as easily as it introduced itself into the recess without entering the chamber in a shape discernible by the senses. Besides, how the deuce *had* I seen it ? It was a dark night ; I had no candle ; there was no fire ; and yet I saw it as distinctly, in colouring and outline, as ever I beheld human form ! A cataleptic dream would explain it all ; and I was determined that a dream it should be.

" One of the most remarkable phenomena connected with the practice of mendacity is the vast number of deliberate lies we tell ourselves, whom, of all persons, we can least expect to deceive. In all this, I need hardly tell you, Dick, I was simply lying to myself, and did not believe one word of the wretched humbug. Yet I went on, as men will do, like persevering charlatans and impostors, who tire people into credulity by the mere force of reiteration ; so I hoped to win myself over at last to a comfortable scepticism about the ghost.

" He had not appeared a second time—that certainly was a comfort ; and what, after all, did I care for him, and his queer old toggery and strange looks ? Not a fig ! I was nothing the worse for having seen him, and a good story the better. So I tumbled into bed, put out my candle, and, cheered by a loud drunken quarrel in the back lane, went fast asleep.

" From this deep slumber I awoke with a start. I knew I had had a horrible dream ; but what it was I could not remember. My heart was thumping furiously ; I felt bewildered and feverish ; I sate up in the bed and looked about the room. A broad flood of moonlight came in through the curtainless window ; everything was as I had last seen it ; and though the domestic squabble in the back lane was, unhappily for me, allayed, I yet could hear a pleasant fellow singing, on his way home, the then popular comic ditty called, ' Murphy Delany.' Taking advantage of this diversion I lay down again, with my face towards the fireplace, and closing my eyes, did my best to think of nothing else but the song, which was every moment growing fainter in the distance :—

> ' 'Twas Murphy Delany, so funny and frisky,
>   Stept into a shebeen shop to get his skin full ;
> He reeled out again pretty well lined with whiskey,
>   As fresh as a shamrock, as blind as a bull.'

" The singer, whose condition I dare say resembled that of his hero, was soon too far off to regale my ears any more ; and as his music died away, I myself sank into a doze, neither sound nor refreshing. Somehow the song had got into my head, and I went meandering on through the adventures of my respectable fellow-countryman, who, on emerging from the ' shebeen shop,' fell into a river, from which he was fished up to be ' sat upon ' by a coroner's jury, who having learned from a ' horse-doctor ' that he was ' dead as a door-nail, so there was an end,' returned their verdict accordingly, just as he returned to his senses, when an angry altercation and a pitched battle between the body and the coroner winds up the lay with due spirit and pleasantry.

" Through this ballad I continued with a weary monotony to plod, down to the very last line, and then *da capo*, and so on, in my uncomfortable half-sleep, for how long, I can't conjecture. I found myself at last, however, muttering, ' *dead* as a door-nail, so there was an end ' ; and something like another voice within me, seemed to say, very faintly, but sharply, ' dead ! dead ! *dead !* and may the Lord have mercy on your soul ! " and instantaneously I was wide awake, and staring right before me from the pillow.

" Now—will you believe it, Dick ?—I saw the same accursed figure standing full front, and gazing at me with its stony and fiendish countenance, not two yards from the bedside."

Tom stopped here, and wiped the perspiration from his face. I felt very queer. The girl was as pale as Tom ; and, assembled as we were in the very scene of these adventures, we were all, I dare say, equally grateful for the clear daylight and the resuming bustle out of doors.

" For about three seconds only I saw it plainly ; then it grew indistinct ; but, for a long time, there was something like a column of dark vapour where it had been standing between me and the wall ; and I felt sure that he was still there. After a good while, this appearance went too. I took my clothes downstairs to the hall, and dressed there, with the door half open ; then went out into the street, and walked about the town till morning, when I came back, in a miserable state of nervousness and exhaustion. I was such a fool, Dick, as to be ashamed to tell you how I came to be so upset. I thought you would laugh at me ; especially as I had always talked philosophy, and treated *your* ghosts with contempt. I concluded you would give me no quarter ; and so kept my tale of horror to myself.

" Now, Dick, you will hardly believe me, when I assure you, that for many nights after this last experience, I did not go to my room at all. I used to sit up for a while in the drawing-room after you had gone up to your bed ; and then steal down softly to the hall-door, let myself out, and sit in the ' Robin Hood ' tavern until the last guest went off ; and then I got through the night like a sentry, pacing the streets till morning.

" For more than a week I never slept in bed. I sometimes had a snooze on a form in the ' Robin Hood,' and sometimes a nap in a chair during the day ; but regular sleep I had absolutely none.

" I was quite resolved that we should get into another house ; but I could not bring myself to tell you the reason, and I somehow put it off from day to day, although my life was, during every hour of this procrastination, rendered as miserable as that of a felon with the constables on his track. I was growing absolutely ill from this wretched mode of life.

" One afternoon I determined to enjoy an hour's sleep upon your bed. I hated mine ; so that I had never, except in a stealthy visit every day to unmake it, lest Martha should discover the secret of my nightly absence, entered the ill-omened chamber.

" As ill-luck would have it, you had locked your bedroom, and taken away the key. I went into my own to unsettle the bedclothes, as usual, and give the bed the appearance of having been slept in. Now, a variety of circumstances concurred to bring about the dreadful scene through which I was that night to pass. In the first place, I was literally overpowered with fatigue, and longing for sleep ; in the next place, the effect of this extreme exhaustion upon my nerves resembled that of a narcotic, and rendered me less susceptible than, perhaps I should in any other condition have been, of the exciting fears which had become habitual to me. Then again, a little bit of the window was open, a pleasant freshness pervaded the room, and, to crown all, the cheerful sun of day was making the room quite pleasant. What was to prevent my enjoying an hour's nap *here* ? The whole air was resonant with the cheerful hum of life, and the broad matter-of-fact light of day filled every corner of the room.

" I yielded—stifling my qualms—to the almost overpowering temptation ; and merely throwing off my coat, and loosening my cravat, I lay down, limiting myself to *half*-an-hour's doze in the unwonted enjoyment of a feather bed, a coverlet, and a bolster.

" It was horribly insidious ; and the demon, no doubt, marked my infatuated preparations. Dolt that I was, I fancied, with mind and body worn out for want of sleep, and an arrear of a full week's rest to my credit, that such measure as *half*-an-hour's sleep, in such a situation, was possible. My sleep was death-like, long, and dreamless.

" Without a start or fearful sensation of any kind, I waked gently, but completely. It was, as you have good reason to remember, long past midnight—I believe, about two o'clock. When sleep has been deep and long enough to satisfy nature thoroughly, one often wakens in this way, suddenly, tranquilly, and completely.

" There was a figure seated in that lumbering, old sofa-chair, near the fireplace. Its back was rather towards me, but I could not be mistaken ; it turned slowly round, and, merciful heavens ! there was the stony face, with its infernal lineaments of malignity and despair, gloating on me. There was now no doubt as to its consciousness of my presence, and the hellish malice with which it was animated, for it arose, and drew close to the bedside. There was a rope about its neck, and the other end, coiled up, it held stiffly in its hand.

" My good angel nerved me for this horrible crisis. I remained for some seconds transfixed by the gaze of this tremendous phantom. He came close to the bed, and appeared on the point of mounting upon it. The next instant I was upon the floor at the far side, and in a moment more was, I don't know how, upon the lobby.

" But the spell was not yet broken ; the valley of the shadow of death was not yet traversed. The abhorred phantom was before me there ; it was standing near the banisters, stooping a little, and with one end of the rope round its own neck, was poising a noose at the other, as if to throw over mine ; and while engaged in this baleful pantomime, it wore a smile so sensual, so unspeakably dreadful, that my senses were nearly overpowered. I saw and remember nothing more, until I found myself in your room.

" I had a wonderful escape, Dick—there is no disputing *that*—an escape for which, while I live, I shall bless the mercy of heaven. No one can conceive or imagine what it is for flesh and blood to stand in the presence of such a thing, but one who has had the terrific experience. Dick, Dick, a shadow has passed over me—a chill has crossed my blood and marrow, and I will never be the same again—never, Dick—never ! "

Our handmaid, a mature girl of two-and-fifty, as I have said, stayed her hand, as Tom's story proceeded, and by little and little drew near to us, with open mouth, and her brows contracted over her little, beady black eyes, till stealing a glance over her shoulder now and then, she established herself close behind us. During the relation, she had made various earnest comments, in an under-tone ; but these and her ejaculations, for the sake of brevity and simplicity, I have omitted in my narration.

" It's often I heard tell of it," she now said, " but I never believed it rightly till now—though, indeed, why should not I ? Does not my mother, down there in the lane, know quare stories, God bless us, beyant telling about it ? But you ought not to have slept in the back bedroom. She was loath to let me be going in and out of that room even in the day time, let alone for any Christian to spend the night in it ; for sure she says it was his own bedroom."

" *Whose* own bedroom ? " we asked, in a breath.

" Why, *his*—the ould Judge's—Judge Horrock's, to be sure, God rest his sowl " ; and she looked fearfully round.

" Amen ! " I muttered. " But did he die there ? "

" Die there ! No, not quite *there*," she said. " Shure, was not it

over the banisters he hung himself, the ould sinner, God be
merciful to us all ? and was not it in the alcove they found the
handles of the skipping-rope cut off, and the knife where he was
settling the cord, God bless us, to hang himself with ? It was his
housekeeper's daughter owned the rope, my mother often told me,
and the child never throve after, and used to be starting up out
of her sleep, and screeching in the night time, wid dhrames and
frights that cum an her ; and they said how it was the speerit of the
ould Judge that was tormentin' her ; and she used to be roaring
and yelling out to hould back the big ould fellow with the crooked
neck ; and then she'd screech ' Oh, the master ! the master ! he's
stampin' at me, and beckoning to me ! Mother, darling, don't
let me go ! ' And so the poor crathure died at last, and the
docthers said it was wather on the brain, for it was all they could
say."

"How long ago was all this ? " I asked.

"Oh, then, how would I know ? " she answered. " But it must
be a wondherful long time ago, for the housekeeper was an ould
woman, with a pipe in her mouth, and not a tooth left, and better
nor eighty years ould when my mother was first married ; and
they said she was a rale buxom, fine-dressed woman when the ould
Judge come to his end ; an', indeed, my mother's not far from
eighty years ould herself this day ; and what made it worse for the
unnatural ould villain, God rest his soul, to frighten the little girl
out of the world the way he did, was what was mostly thought and
believed by everyone. My mother says how the poor little crathure
was his own child ; for he was by all accounts an ould villain every
way, an' the hangin'est judge that ever was known in Ireland's
ground."

"From what you said about the danger of sleeping in that bedroom," said I, "I suppose there were stories about the ghost
having appeared there to others."

"Well, there *was* things said—quare things, surely," she
answered, as it seemed, with some reluctance. "And why would
not there ? Sure was it not up in that same room he slept for more
than twenty years ? and was it not in the *alcove* he got the rope
ready that done his own business at last, the way he done many
a betther man's in his lifetime ?—and was not the body lying in
the same bed after death, and put in the coffin there, too, and
carried out to his grave from it in Pether's churchyard, after the
coroner was done ? But there was quare stories—my mother has

them all—about how one Nicholas Spaight got into trouble on the head of it."

" And what did they say of this Nicholas Spaight ? " I asked.

" Oh, for that matther, it's soon told," she answered.

And she certainly did relate a very strange story, which so piqued my curiosity, that I took occasion to visit the ancient lady, her mother, from whom I learned many very curious particulars. Indeed, I am tempted to tell the tale, but my fingers are weary, and I must defer it. But if you wish to hear it another time, I shall do my best.

When we had heard the strange tale I have *not* told you, we put one or two further questions to her about the alleged spectral visitations, to which the house had, ever since the death of the wicked old Judge, been subjected.

" No one ever had luck in it," she told us. " There was always cross accidents, sudden deaths, and short times in it. The first that tuck it was a family—I forget their name—but at any rate there was two young ladies and their papa. He was about sixty, and a stout healthy gentleman as you'd wish to see at that age. Well, he slept in that unlucky back bedroom ; and, God between us an' harm ! sure enough he was found dead one morning, half out of the bed, with his head as black as a sloe, and swelled like a puddin', hanging down near the floor. It was a fit, they said. He was as dead as a mackerel, and so *he* could not say what it was ; but the ould people was all sure that it was nothing at all but the ould Judge, God bless us ! that frightened him out of his senses and his life together.

" Some time after there was a rich old maiden lady took the house. I don't know which room *she* slept in, but she lived alone ; and at any rate, one morning, the servants going down early to their work, found her sitting on the passage-stairs, shivering and talkin' to herself, quite mad ; and never a word more could any of *them* or her friends get from her ever afterwards but, ' Don't ask me to go, for I promised to wait for him.' They never made out from her who it was she meant by *him*, but of course those that knew all about the ould house were at no loss for the meaning of all that happened to her.

" Then afterwards, when the house was let out in lodgings, there was Micky Byrne that took the same room, with his wife and three little children ; and sure I heard Mrs. Byrne myself telling how the children used to be lifted up in the bed at night, she could not see by what mains ; and how they were starting and screeching every hour, just all as one as the housekeeper's little girl that died, till at last one night poor Micky had a dhrop in him, the way he used now and again ; and what do you think in the middle of the night he thought he heard a noise on the stairs, and being in liquor, nothing less id do him but out he must go himself to see what was wrong. Well, after that, all she ever heard of him was himself sayin', ' Oh, God ! ' and a tumble that shook the very house ; and there, sure enough, he was lying on the lower stairs, under the lobby, with his neck smashed double undher him, where he was flung over the banisters."

Then the handmaiden added—

" I'll go down to the lane, and send up Joe Gavvey to pack up the rest of the taythings, and bring all the things across to your new lodgings."

And so we all sallied out together, each of us breathing more freely, I have no doubt, as we crossed that ill-omened threshold for the last time.

Now, I may add thus much, in compliance with the immemorial usage of the realm of fiction, which sees the hero not only through his adventures, but fairly out of the world. You must have perceived that what the flesh, blood, and bone hero of romance proper is to the regular compounder of fiction, this old house of brick, wood, and mortar is to the humble recorder of this true tale. I, therefore, relate, as in duty bound, the catastrophe which ultimately befell it, which was simply this—that about two years subsequently to my story it was taken by a quack doctor, who called himself Baron Duhlstoerf, and filled the parlour windows with bottles of indescribable horrors preserved in brandy, and the newspapers with the usual grandiloquent and mendacious advertisements. This gentleman among his virtues did not reckon sobriety, and one night, being overcome with much wine, he set fire to his bed curtains, partially burned himself, and totally consumed the house. It was afterwards rebuilt, and for a time an undertaker established himself in the premises.

I have now told you my own and Tom's adventures, together with some valuable collateral particulars ; and having acquitted myself of my engagement, I wish you a very good night, and pleasant dreams.

E. Nesbit

MAN-SIZE IN MARBLE

from GRIM TALES

A. D. Innes, 1893

Although every word of this story is as true as despair, I do not expect people to believe it. Nowadays a " rational explanation " is required before belief is possible. Let me then, at once, offer the " rational explanation " which finds most favour among those who have heard the tale of my life's tragedy. It is held that we were "under a delusion," Laura and I, on that 31st of October ; and that this supposition places the whole matter on a satisfactory and believable basis. The reader can judge, when he, too, has heard my story, how far this is an " explanation," and in what sense it is " rational." There were three who took part in this : Laura and I and another man. The other man still lives, and can speak to the truth of the least credible part of my story.

. . . .

I never in my life knew what it was to have as much money as I required to supply the most ordinary needs—good colours, books, and cab-fares—and when we were married we knew quite well that we should only be able to live at all by " strict punctuality and attention to business." I used to paint in those days, and Laura used to write, and we felt sure we could keep the pot at least simmering. Living in town was out of the question, so we went to look for a cottage in the country, which should be at once sanitary and picturesque. So rarely do these two qualities meet in one cottage that our search was for some time quite fruitless. We tried advertisements, but most of the desirable rural residences which we did look at proved to be lacking in both essentials, and when a cottage chanced to have drains it always had stucco as well and was shaped like a tea-caddy. And if we found a vine or rose-covered porch, corruption invariably lurked within. Our minds got so befogged by the eloquence of house-agents and the rival disadvantages of the fever-traps and outrages to beauty which we had seen and scorned, that I very much doubt whether either of us, on our wedding morning, knew the difference between a house and a haystack. But when we got away from friends and house-agents, on our honeymoon, our wits grew clear again, and we knew a pretty cottage when at last we saw one. It was at Brenzett—a little village set on a hill over against the southern marshes. We had gone there, from the seaside village where we were staying, to see the church, and two fields from the church we found this cottage. It stood quite by itself, about two miles from the village. It was a long, low building, with rooms sticking out in unexpected places. There was a bit of stone-work —ivy-covered and moss-grown, just two old rooms, all that was left of a big house that had once stood there—and round this stone-work the house had grown up. Stripped of its roses and jasmine it would have been hideous. As it stood it was charming, and after a brief examination we took it. It was absurdly cheap. The rest of our honeymoon we spent in grubbing about in second-hand shops in the county town, picking up bits of old oak and Chippendale chairs for our furnishing. We wound up with a run up to town and a visit to Liberty's, and soon the low oak-beamed lattice-windowed rooms began to be home. There was a jolly old-fashioned garden, with grass paths, and no end of holly-hocks and sunflowers, and big lilies. From the window you could see the marsh-pastures, and beyond them the blue, thin line of the sea. We were as happy as the summer was glorious, and settled down into work sooner than we ourselves expected. I was never tired of sketching the view and the wonderful cloud effects from the open lattice, and Laura would sit at the table and write verses about them, in which I mostly played the part of foreground.

We got a tall old peasant woman to do for us. Her face and figure were good, though her cooking was of the homeliest; but she understood all about gardening, and told us all the old names of the coppices and cornfields, and the stories of the smugglers and highwaymen, and, better still, of the " things that walked," and of the " sights " which met one in lonely glens of a starlight night. She was a great comfort to us, because Laura hated housekeeping as much as I loved folklore, and we soon came to leave all the domestic business to Mrs. Dorman, and to use her legends in little magazine stories which brought in the jingling guinea.

We had three months of married happiness, and did not have a single quarrel. One October evening I had been down to smoke a pipe with the doctor—our only neighbour—a pleasant young Irishman. Laura had stayed at home to finish a comic sketch of a village episode for the *Monthly Marplot*. I left her laughing over her own jokes, and came in to find her a crumpled heap of pale muslin weeping on the window seat.

"Good heavens, my darling, what's the matter?" I cried, taking her in my arms. She leaned her little dark head against my shoulder and went on crying. I had never seen her cry before—we had always been so happy, you see—and I felt sure some frightful misfortune had happened.

"What is the matter? Do speak."

"It's Mrs. Dorman," she sobbed.

"What has she done?" I inquired, immensely relieved.

"She says she must go before the end of the month, and she says her niece is ill; she's gone down to see her now, but I don't believe that's the reason, because her niece is always ill. I believe someone has been setting her against us. Her manner was so queer——"

"Never mind, Pussy," I said; "whatever you do, don't cry, or I shall have to cry too, to keep you in countenance, and then you'll never respect your man again!"

She dried her eyes obediently on my handkerchief, and even smiled faintly.

"But you see," she went on, "it is really serious, because these village people are so sheepy, and if one won't do a thing you may be quite sure none of the others will. And I shall have to cook the dinners, and wash up the hateful greasy plates; and you'll have to carry cans of water about, and clean the boots and knives—and we shall never have any time for work, or earn any money, or anything. We shall have to work all day, and only be able to rest when we are waiting for the kettle to boil!"

I represented to her that even if we had to perform these duties, the day would still present some margin for other toils and recreations. But she refused to see the matter in any but the greyest light. She was very unreasonable, my Laura, but I could not have loved her any more if she had been as reasonable as Whately.

"I'll speak to Mrs. Dorman when she comes back, and see if I can't come to terms with her," I said. "Perhaps she wants a rise in her screw. It will be all right. Let's walk up to the church.

The church was a large and lonely one, and we loved to go there, especially upon bright nights. The path skirted a wood, cut through it once, and ran along the crest of the hill through two meadows, and round the churchyard wall, over which the old yews loomed in black masses of shadow. This path, which was partly paved, was called " the bier-balk," for it had long been the way by which the corpses had been carried to burial. The church-yard was richly treed, and was shaded by great elms which stood just outside and stretched their majestic arms in benediction over the happy dead. A large, low porch let one into the building by a Norman doorway and a heavy oak door studded with iron. Inside, the arches rose into darkness, and between them the reticulated windows, which stood out white in the moonlight. In the chancel, the windows were of rich glass, which showed in faint light their noble colouring, and made the black oak of the choir pews hardly more solid than the shadows. But on each side of the altar lay a grey marble figure of a knight in full plate armour lying upon a low slab, with hands held up in everlasting prayer, and these figures, oddly enough, were always to be seen if there was any glimmer of light in the church. Their names were lost, but the peasants told of them that they had been fierce and wicked men, marauders by land and sea, who had been the scourge of their time, and had been guilty of deeds so foul that the house they had lived in—the big house, by the way, that had stood on the site of our cottage—had been stricken by lightning and the vengeance of Heaven. But for all that, the gold of their heirs had bought them a place in the church. Looking at the bad hard faces re-produced in the marble, this story was easily believed.

The church looked at its best and weirdest on that night, for the shadows of the yew trees fell through the windows upon the floor of the nave and touched the pillars with tattered shade. We sat down together without speaking, and watched the solemn beauty of the old church, with some of that awe which inspired its early builders. We walked to the chancel and looked at the sleeping warriors. Then we rested some time on the stone seat in the porch, looking out over the stretch of quiet moonlit meadows, feeling in every fibre of our being the peace of the night and of our happy love ; and came away at last with a sense that even scrubbing and blackleading were but small troubles at their worst.

Mrs. Dorman had come back from the village, and I at once invited her to a *tête-à-tête*.

" Now, Mrs. Dorman," I said, when I had got her into my painting room, " what's all this about your not staying with us?"

" I should be glad to get away, sir, before the end of the month," she answered, with her usual placid dignity.

" Have you any fault to find, Mrs. Dorman ? "

" None at all, sir ; you and your lady have always been most kind, I'm sure——"

" Well, what is it ? Are your wages not high enough ? "

" No, sir, I gets quite enough."

" Then why not stay ? "

" I'd rather not "—with some hesitation—" my niece is ill."

" But your niece has been ill ever since we came."

No answer. There was a long and awkward silence. I broke it.

" Can't you stay for another month ? " I asked.

" No, sir. I'm bound to go by Thursday."

And this was Monday !

" Well, I must say, I think you might have let us know before. There's no time now to get any one else, and your mistress is not fit to do heavy housework. Can't you stay till next week ? "

" I might be able to come back next week."

I was now convinced that all she wanted was a brief holiday, which we should have been willing enough to let her have, as soon as we could get a substitute.

" But why must you go this week ? " I persisted. " Come, out with it."

Mrs. Dorman drew the little shawl, which she always wore, tightly across her bosom, as though she were cold. Then she said, with a sort of effort—

" They say, sir, as this was a big house in Catholic times, and there was a many deeds done here."

The nature of the " deeds " might be vaguely inferred from the inflection of Mrs. Dorman's voice—which was enough to make one's blood run cold. I was glad that Laura was not in the room. She was always nervous, as highly-strung natures are, and I felt that these tales about our house, told by this old peasant woman, with her impressive manner and contagious credulity, might have made our home less dear to my wife.

" Tell me all about it, Mrs. Dorman," I said ; " you needn't mind about telling me. I'm not like the young people who make fun of such things."

Which was partly true.

" Well, sir "—she sank her voice—" you may have seen in the church, beside the altar, two shapes."

" You mean the effigies of the knights in armour," I said cheerfully.

" I mean them two bodies, drawed out man-size in marble,"
she returned, and I had to admit that her description was a
thousand times more graphic than mine, to say nothing of a certain
weird force and uncanniness about the phrase " drawed out
man-size in marble."

" They do say, as on All Saints' Eve them two bodies sits up on
their slabs, and gets off of them, and then walks down the aisle,
in their marble "—(another good phrase, Mrs. Dorman)—" and
as the church clock strikes eleven they walks out of the church
door, and over the graves, and along the bier-balk, and if it's a
wet night there's the marks of their feet in the morning."

" And where do they go ? " I asked, rather fascinated.

" They comes back here to their home, sir, and if any one meets
them——"

" Well, what then ? " I asked.

But no—not another word could I get from her, save that her
niece was ill and she must go. After what I had heard I scorned to
discuss the niece, and tried to get from Mrs. Dorman more details
of the legend. I could get nothing but warnings.

" Whatever you do, sir, lock the door early on All Saints' Eve,
and make the cross-sign over the doorstep and on the windows."

" But has any one ever seen these things ? " I persisted.

" That's not for me to say. I know what I know, sir."

" Well, who was here last year ? "

" No one, sir ; the lady as owned the house only stayed here in
summer, and she always went to London a full month afore *the
night*. And I'm sorry to inconvenience you and your lady, but my
niece is ill and I must go on Thursday."

I could have shaken her for her absurd reiteration of that
obvious fiction, after she had told me her real reasons.

She was determined to go, nor could our united entreaties move
her in the least.

I did not tell Laura the legend of the shapes that " walked in
their marble," partly because a legend concerning our house
might perhaps trouble my wife, and partly, I think, from some
more occult reason. This was not quite the same to me as any other
story, and I did not want to talk about it till the day was over. I
had very soon ceased to think of the legend, however. I was painting a portrait of Laura, against the lattice window, and I could not
think of much else. I had got a splendid background of yellow
and grey sunset, and was working away with enthusiasm at her

lace. On Thursday Mrs. Dorman went. She relented, at parting, so far as to say—

"Don't you put yourself about too much, ma'am, and if there's any little thing I can do next week, I'm sure I shan't mind."

From which I inferred that she wished to come back to us after Hallowe'en. Up to the last she adhered to the fiction of the niece with touching fidelity.

Thursday passed off pretty well. Laura showed marked ability in the matter of steak and potatoes, and I confess that my knives, and the plates, which I insisted upon washing, were better done than I had dared to expect.

Friday came. It is about what happened on that Friday that this is written. I wonder if I should have believed it, if any one had told it to me. I will write the story of it as quickly and plainly as I can. Everything that happened on that day is burnt into my brain. I shall not forget anything, nor leave anything out.

I got up early, I remember, and lighted the kitchen fire, and had just achieved a smoky success, when my little wife came running down, as sunny and sweet as the clear October morning itself. We prepared breakfast together, and found it very good fun. The housework was soon done, and when brushes and brooms and pails were quiet again, the house was still indeed. It is wonderful what a difference one makes in a house. We really missed Mrs. Dorman, quite apart from considerations concerning pots and pans. We spent the day in dusting our books and putting them straight, and dined gaily on cold steak and coffee. Laura was, if possible, brighter and gayer and sweeter than usual, and I began to think that a little domestic toil was really good for her. We had never been so merry since we were married, and the walk we had that afternoon was, I think, the happiest time of all my life. When we had watched the deep scarlet clouds slowly pale into leaden grey against a pale-green sky, and saw the white mists curl up along the hedgerows in the distant marsh, we came back to the house, silently, hand in hand.

"You are sad, my darling," I said, half-jestingly, as we sat down together in our little parlour. I expected a disclaimer, for my own silence had been the silence of complete happiness. To my surprise she said—

"Yes. I think I am sad, or rather I am uneasy. I don't think I'm very well. I have shivered three or four times since we came in, and it is not cold, is it ? "

" No," I said, and hoped it was not a chill caught from the treacherous mists that roll up from the marshes in the dying light. No—she said, she did not think so. Then, after a silence, she spoke suddenly—

" Do you ever have presentiments of evil ? "

" No," I said, smiling, " and I shouldn't believe in them if I had."

" I do," she went on ; " the night my father died I knew it, though he was right away in the north of Scotland." I did not answer in words.

She sat looking at the fire for some time in silence, gently stroking my hand. At last she sprang up, came behind me, and, drawing my head back, kissed me.

" There, it's over now," she said. " What a baby I am ! Come, light the candles, and we'll have some of these new Rubinstein duets."

And we spent a happy hour or two at the piano.

At about half-past ten I began to long for the good-night pipe, but Laura looked so white that I felt it would be brutal of me to fill our sitting-room with the fumes of strong cavendish.

" I'll take my pipe outside," I said.

" Let me come, too."

" No, sweetheart, not to-night ; you're much too tired. I shan't be long. Get to bed, or I shall have an invalid to nurse to-morrow as well as the boots to clean."

I kissed her and was turning to go, when she flung her arms round my neck, and held me as if she would never let me go again. I stroked her hair.

" Come, Pussy, you're over-tired. The housework has been too much for you."

She loosened her clasp a little and drew a deep breath.

" No. We've been very happy to-day, Jack, haven't we ? Don't stay out too long."

" I won't, my dearie."

I strolled out of the front door, leaving it unlatched. What a night it was ! The jagged masses of heavy dark cloud were rolling at intervals from horizon to horizon, and thin white wreaths covered the stars. Through all the rush of the cloud river, the moon swam, breasting the waves and disappearing again in the darkness. When now and again her light reached the woodlands they seemed to be slowly and noiselessly waving in time to the

swing of the clouds above them. There was a strange grey light
over all the earth ; the fields had that shadowy bloom over them
which only comes from the marriage of dew and moonshine, or
frost and starlight.

I walked up and down, drinking in the beauty of the quiet
earth and the changing sky. The night was absolutely silent.
Nothing seemed to be abroad. There was no skurrying of rabbits,
or twitter of the half-asleep birds. And though the clouds went
sailing across the sky, the wind that drove them never came low
enough to rustle the dead leaves in the woodland paths. Across the
meadows I could see the church tower standing out black and
grey against the sky. I walked there thinking over our three months
of happiness—and of my wife, her dear eyes, her loving ways. Oh,
my little girl ! my own little girl ; what a vision came then of a
long, glad life for you and me together !

I heard a bell-beat from the church. Eleven already ! I turned
to go in, but the night held me. I could not go back into our
little warm rooms yet. I would go up to the church. I felt vaguely
that it would be good to carry my love and thankfulness to the
sanctuary whither so many loads of sorrow and gladness had been
borne by the men and women of the dead years.

I looked in at the low window as I went by. Laura was half
lying on her chair in front of the fire. I could not see her face, only
her little head showed dark against the pale blue wall. She was
quite still. Asleep, no doubt. My heart reached out to her, as I
went on. There must be a God, I thought, and a God who was
good. How otherwise could anything so sweet and dear as she
have ever been imagined ?

I walked slowly along the edge of the wood. A sound broke the
stillness of the night, it was a rustling in the wood. I stopped and
listened. The sound stopped too. I went on, and now distinctly
heard another step than mine answer mine like an echo. It was a
poacher or a wood-stealer, most likely, for these were not unknown
in our Arcadian neighbourhood. But whoever it was, he was a
fool not to step more lightly. I turned into the wood, and now the
footstep seemed to come from the path I had just left. It must be
an echo, I thought. The wood looked perfect in the moonlight.
The large dying ferns and the brushwood showed where through
thinning foliage the pale light came down. The tree trunks stood
up like Gothic columns all around me. They reminded me of the
church, and I turned into the bier-balk, and passed through the

corpse-gate between the graves to the low porch. I paused for a moment on the stone seat where Laura and I had watched the fading landscape. Then I noticed that the door of the church was open, and I blamed myself for having left it unlatched the other night. We were the only people who ever cared to come to the church except on Sundays, and I was vexed to think that through our carelessness the damp autumn airs had had a chance of getting in and injuring the old fabric. I went in. It will seem strange, perhaps, that I should have gone half-way up the aisle before I remembered—with a sudden chill, followed by as sudden a rush of self-contempt—that this was the very day and hour when, according to tradition, the " shapes drawed out man-size in marble " began to walk.

Having thus remembered the legend, and remembered it with a shiver, of which I was ashamed, I could not do otherwise than walk up towards the altar, just to look at the figures—as I said to myself ; really what I wanted was to assure myself, first, that I did not believe the legend, and, secondly, that it was not true. I was rather glad that I had come. I thought now I could tell Mrs. Dorman how vain her fancies were, and how peacefully the marble figures slept on through the ghastly hour. With my hands in my pockets I passed up the aisle. In the grey dim light the eastern end of the church looked larger than usual, and the arches above the two tombs looked larger too. The moon came out and showed me the reason. I stopped short, my heart gave a leap that nearly choked me, and then sank sickeningly.

The " bodies drawed out man-size " *were gone*, and their marble slabs lay wide and bare in the vague moonlight that slanted through the east window.

Were they really gone ? or was I mad ? Clenching my nerves, I stooped and passed my hand over the smooth slabs, and felt their flat unbroken surface. Had some one taken the things away? Was it some vile practical joke ? I would make sure, anyway. In an instant I had made a torch of a newspaper, which happened to be in my pocket, and lighting it held it high above my head. Its yellow glare illumined the dark arches and those slabs. The figures *were* gone. And I was alone in the church ; or was I alone ?

And then a horror seized me, a horror indefinable and indescribable—an overwhelming certainty of supreme and accomplished calamity. I flung down the torch and tore along the aisle and out through the porch, biting my lips as I ran to keep myself from shrieking aloud. Oh, was I mad—or what was this that possessed me ? I leaped the churchyard wall and took the straight cut across the fields, led by the light from our windows. Just as I got over the first stile, a dark figure seemed to spring out of the ground. Mad still with that certainty of misfortune, I made for the thing that stood in my path, shouting, " Get out of the way, can't you ! "

But my push met with a more vigorous resistance than I had expected. My arms were caught just above the elbow and held as in a vice, and the raw-boned Irish doctor actually shook me.

" Would ye ? " he cried, in his own unmistakable accents— " would ye, then ? "

" Let me go, you fool," I gasped. " The marble figures have gone from the church ; I tell you they've gone."

He broke into a ringing laugh. " I'll have to give ye a draught to-morrow, I see. Ye've bin smoking too much and listening to old wives' tales."

" I tell you, I've seen the bare slabs."

" Well, come back with me. I'm going up to old Palmer's—his daughter's ill ; we'll look in at the church and let me see the bare slabs."

" You go, if you like," I said, a little less frantic for his laughter ; " I'm going home to my wife."

" Rubbish, man," said he ; " d'ye think I'll permit of that ? Are ye to go saying all yer life that ye've seen solid marble endowed with vitality, and me to go all me life saying ye were a coward ? No, sir—ye shan't do ut."

The night air—a human voice—and I think also the physical contact with this six feet of solid common sense, brought me back a little to my ordinary self, and the word " coward " was a mental shower-bath.

" Come on, then," I said sullenly ; " perhaps you're right.

He still held my arm tightly. We got over the stile and back to the church. All was still as death. The place smelt very damp and earthy. We walked up the aisle. I am not ashamed to confess that I shut my eyes : I knew the figures would not be there. I heard Kelly strike a match.

" Here they are, ye see, right enough ; ye've been dreaming or drinking, asking yer pardon for the imputation."

I opened my eyes. By Kelly's expiring vesta I saw two shapes lying " in their marble " on their slabs. I drew a deep breath, and caught his hand.

" I'm awfully indebted to you," I said. " It must have been some trick of light, or I have been working rather hard, perhaps that's it. Do you know, I was quite convinced they were gone."

" I'm aware of that," he answered rather grimly ; " ye'll have to be careful of that brain of yours, my friend, I assure ye."

He was leaning over and looking at the right-hand figure, whose stony face was the most villainous and deadly in expression.

" By Jove," he said, " something has been afoot here—this hand is broken."

And so it was. I was certain that it had been perfect the last time Laura and I had been there.

" Perhaps some one has *tried* to remove them," said the young doctor.

" That won't account for my impression," I objected.

" Too much painting and tobacco will account for that, well enough."

" Come along,'' I said, " or my wife will be getting anxious. You'll come in and have a drop of whisky and drink confusion to ghosts and better sense to me."

" I ought to go up to Palmer's, but it's so late now I'd best leave it till the morning," he replied. " I was kept late at the Union, and I've had to see a lot of people since. All right, I'll come back with ye."

I think he fancied I needed him more than did Palmer's girl, so, discussing how such an illusion could have been possible, and deducing from this experience large generalities concerning ghostly apparitions, we walked up to our cottage. We saw, as we walked up the garden-path, that bright light streamed out of the front door, and presently saw that the parlour door was open too. Had she gone out ?

" Come in," I said, and Dr. Kelly followed me into the parlour. It was all ablaze with candles, not only the wax ones, but at least a dozen guttering, glaring tallow dips, stuck in vases and orna-ments in unlikely places. Light, I knew, was Laura's remedy for nervousness. Poor child ! Why had I left her ? Brute that I was.

We glanced round the room, and at first we did not see her. The window was open, and the draught set all the candles flaring one way. Her chair was empty and her handkerchief and book lay on the floor. I turned to the window. There, in the recess of the window, I saw her. Oh, my child, my love, had she gone to that window to watch for me? And what had come into the room behind her? To what had she turned with that look of frantic fear and horror? Oh, my little one, had she thought that it was I whose step she heard, and turned to meet—what?

She had fallen back across a table in the window, and her body lay half on it and half on the window-seat, and her head hung down over the table, the brown hair loosened and fallen to the carpet. Her lips were drawn back, and her eyes wide, wide open. They saw nothing now. What had they seen last?

The doctor moved towards her, but I pushed him aside and sprang to her; caught her in my arms and cried—

" It's all right, Laura! I've got you safe, wifie."

She fell into my arms in a heap. I clasped her and kissed her, and called her by all her pet names, but I think I knew all the time that she was dead. Her hands were tightly clenched. In one of them she held something fast. When I was quite sure that she was dead, and that nothing mattered at all any more, I let him open her hand to see what she held.

It was a grey marble finger.

———

Bram Stoker

THE JUDGE'S HOUSE
from DRACULA'S GUEST

Routledge & Sons, 1914

When the time for his examination drew near Malcolm Malcolmson made up his mind to go somewhere to read by himself. He feared the attractions of the seaside, and also he feared completely rural isolation, for of old he knew its charms, and so he determined to find some unpretentious little town where there would be nothing to distract him. He refrained from asking suggestions from any of his friends, for he argued that each would recommend some place of which he had knowledge, and where he had already acquaintances. As Malcolmson wished to avoid friends he had no wish to encumber himself with the attention or friends' friends, and so he determined to look out for a place for himself. He packed a portmanteau with some clothes and all the books he required, and then took ticket for the first name on the local time-table which he did not know.

When at the end of three hours' journey he alighted at Benchurch, he felt satisfied that he had so far obliterated his tracks as to be sure of having a peaceful opportunity of pursuing his studies. He went straight to the one inn which the sleepy little place contained, and put up for the night. Benchurch was a market town, and once in three weeks was crowded to excess, but for the remainder of the twenty-one days it was as attractive as a desert. Malcolmson looked around the day after his arrival to try to find quarters more isolated than even so quiet an inn as " The Good Traveller " afforded. There was only one place which took his fancy, and it certainly satisfied his wildest ideas regarding quiet ; in fact, quiet was not the proper word to apply to it—desolation was the only term conveying any suitable idea of its isolation. It was an old rambling, heavy-built house of the Jacobean style, with heavy gables and windows, unusually small, and set higher than was customary in such houses, and was surrounded with a high brick wall massively built. Indeed, on examination, it looked more like a fortified house than an ordinary dwelling. But all these things pleased Malcolmson. " Here," he thought, " is the very spot I have been looking for, and if I can only get opportunity of using it I shall be happy." His joy was increased when he realised beyond doubt that it was not at present inhabited.

From the post-office he got the name of the agent, who was rarely surprised at the application to rent a part of the old house. Mr. Carnford, the local lawyer and agent, was a genial old gentleman, and frankly confessed his delight at anyone being willing to live in the house.

" To tell you the truth," said he, " I should be only too happy, on behalf of the owners, to let anyone have the house rent free for a term of years if only to accustom the people here to see it inhabited. It has been so long empty that some kind of absurd prejudice has grown up about it, and this can be best put down by its occupation—if only," he added with a sly glance at Malcomson, " by a scholar like yourself, who wants its quiet for a time."

Malcolmson thought it needless to ask the agent about the " absurd prejudice " ; he knew he would get more information, if he should require it, on that subject from other quarters. He paid his three months' rent, got a receipt, and the name of an old woman who would probably undertake to " do " for him, and came away with the keys in his pocket. He then went to the land-lady of the inn, who was a cheerful and most kindly person, and asked her advice as to such stores and provisions as he would be likely to require. She threw up her hands in amazement when he told her where he was going to settle himself.

" Not in the Judge's House ! " she said, and grew pale as she spoke. He explained the locality of the house, saying that he did not know its name. When he had finished she answered :

" Aye, sure enough—sure enough the very place ! It is the Judge's House sure enough." He asked her to tell him about the place, why so called, and what there was against it. She told him that it was so called locally because it had been many years before —how long she could not say, as she was herself from another part of the country, but she thought it must have been a hundred years or more—the abode of a judge who was held in great terror on account of his harsh sentences and his hostility to prisoners at Assizes. As to what there was against the house itself she could not tell. She had often asked, but no one could inform her ; but there was a general feeling that there was *something*, and for her own part she would not take all the money in Drinkwater's Bank and stay in the house an hour by herself. Then she apologised to Malcolm-son for her disturbing talk.

" It is too bad of me, sir, and you—and a young gentleman, too —if you will pardon me saying it, going to live there all alone. If you were my boy—and you'll excuse me for saying it—you wouldn't sleep there a night, not if I had to go there myself and pull the big alarm bell that's on the roof ! " The good creature was so manifestly in earnest, and was so kindly in her intentions, that Malcolmson, although amused, was touched. He told her kindly how much he appreciated her interest in him, and added :

" But, my dear Mrs. Witham, indeed you need not be concerned about me ! A man who is reading for the Mathematical Tripos has too much to think of to be disturbed by any of these mysterious somethings,' and his work is of too exact and prosaic a kind to allow of his having any corner in his mind for mysteries of any kind. Harmonical Progression, Permutations and Combinations, and Elliptic Functions have sufficient mysteries for me ! " Mrs. Witham kindly undertook to see after his commissions, and he went himself to look for the old woman who had been recommended to him. When he returned to the Judge's House with her, after an interval of a couple of hours, he found Mrs. Witham herself waiting with several men and boys carrying parcels, and an upholsterer's man with a bed in a cart, for she said, though tables and chairs might be all very well, a bed that hadn't been aired for mayhap fifty years was not proper for young bones to lie on. She was evidently curious to see the inside of the house ; and though manifestly so afraid of the ' somethings ' that at the slightest sound she clutched on to Malcolmson, whom she never left for a moment, went over the whole place.

After his examination of the house, Malcolmson decided to take up his abode in the great dining-room, which was big enough to serve for all his requirements ; and Mrs. Witham, with the aid of the charwoman, Mrs. Dempster, proceeded to arrange matters. When the hampers were brought in and unpacked, Malcolmson saw that with much kind forethought she had sent from her own kitchen sufficient provisions to last for a few days. Before going she expressed all sorts of kind wishes ; and at the door turned and said :

" And perhaps, sir, as the room is big and draughty it might be well to have one of those big screens put round your bed at night— though, truth to tell, I would die myself if I were to be so shut in with all kinds of—of ' things,' that put their heads round the sides, or over the top, and look on me ! " The image which she had called up was too much for her nerves, and she fled incontinently.

Mrs. Dempster sniffed in a superior manner as the landlady disappeared, and remarked that for her own part she wasn't afraid of all the bogies in the kingdom.

" I'll tell you what it is, sir," she said ; " bogies is all kinds and sorts of things—except bogies ! Rats and mice, and beetles ; and creaky doors, and loose slates, and broken panes, and stiff drawer handles, that stay out when you pull them and then fall down in the middle of the night. Look at the wainscot of the room ! It is old—hundreds of years old ! Do you think there's no rats and beetles there ! And do you imagine, sir, that you won't see none of them ! Rats is bogies, I tell you, and bogies is rats ; and don't you get to think anything else ! "

" Mrs. Dempster," said Malcolmson gravely, making her a polite bow, " you know more than a Senior Wrangler ! And let me say, that, as a mark of esteem for your indubitable soundness of head and heart, I shall, when I go, give you possession of this house, and let you stay here by yourself for the last two months of my tenancy, for four weeks will serve my purpose."

"Thank you kindly, sir !" she answered, "but I couldn't sleep away from home a night. I am in Greenhow's Charity, and if I slept a night away from my rooms I should lose all I have got to live on. The rules is very strict ; and there's too many watching for a vacancy for me to run any risks in the matter. Only for that, sir, I'd gladly come here and attend on you altogether during your stay."

"My good woman," said Malcolmson hastily, "I have come here on purpose to obtain solitude ; and believe me that I am grateful to the late Greenhow for having so organised his admirable charity—whatever it is—that I am perforce denied the opportunity of suffering from such a form of temptation ! Saint Anthony himself could not be more rigid on the point !"

The old woman laughed harshly. "Ah, you young gentlemen," she said, "you don't fear for naught ; and belike you'll get all the solitude you want here." She set to work with her cleaning ; and by nightfall, when Malcolmson returned from his walk—he always had one of his books to study as he walked—he found the room swept and tidied, a fire burning in the old hearth, the lamp lit, and the table spread for supper with Mrs. Witham's excellent fare. "This is comfort, indeed," he said, as he rubbed his hands.

When he had finished his supper, and lifted the tray to the other end of the great oak dining-table, he got out his books again, put fresh wood on the fire, trimmed his lamp, and set himself down to a spell of real hard work. He went on without pause till about eleven o'clock, when he knocked off for a bit to fix his fire and lamp, and to make himself a cup of tea. He had always been a tea-drinker, and during his college life had sat late at work and had taken tea late. The rest was a great luxury to him, and he enjoyed it with a sense of delicious, voluptuous ease. The renewed fire leaped and sparkled, and threw quaint shadows through the great old room ; and as he sipped his hot tea he revelled in the sense of isolation from his kind. Then it was that he began to notice for the first time what a noise the rats were making.

"Surely," he thought, "they cannot have been at it all the time I was reading. Had they been, I must have noticed it !" Presently, when the noise increased, he satisfied himself that it was really new. It was evident that at first the rats had been frightened at the presence of a stranger, and the light of fire and lamp ; but that as the time went on they had grown bolder and were now disporting themselves as was their wont.

How busy they were ! and hark to the strange noises ! Up and down behind the old wainscot, over the ceiling and under the floor they raced, and gnawed, and scratched ! Malcolmson smiled to himself as he recalled to mind the saying of Mrs. Dempster, " Bogies is rats, and rats is bogies ! " The tea began to have its effect of intellectual and nervous stimulus, he saw with joy another long spell of work to be done before the night was past, and in the sense of security which it gave him, he allowed himself the luxury of a good look round the room. He took his lamp in one hand, and went all around, wondering that so quaint and beautiful an old house had been so long neglected. The carving of the oak on the panels of the wainscot was fine, and on and round the doors and windows it was beautiful and of rare merit. There were some old pictures on the walls, but they were coated so thick with dust and dirt that he could not distinguish any detail of them, though he held his lamp as high as he could over his head. Here and there as he went round he saw some crack or hole blocked for a moment by the face of a rat with its bright eyes glittering in the light, but in an instant it was gone, and a squeak and a scamper followed.

The thing that most struck him, however, was the rope of the great alarm bell on the roof, which hung down in a corner of the room on the right-hand side of the fireplace. He pulled up close to the hearth a great high-backed carved oak chair, and sat down to his last cup of tea. When this was done he made up the fire, and went back to his work, sitting at the corner of the table, having the fire to his left. For a while the rats disturbed him somewhat with their perpetual scampering, but he got accustomed to the noise as one does to the ticking of a clock or to the roar of moving water ; and he became so immersed in his work that everything in the world, except the problem which he was trying to solve, passed away from him.

He suddenly looked up, his problem was still unsolved, and there was in the air that sense of the hour before the dawn, which is so dread to doubtful life. The noise of the rats had ceased. Indeed it seemed to him that it must have ceased but lately and that it was the sudden cessation which had disturbed him. The fire had fallen low, but still it threw out a deep red glow. As he looked he started in spite of his *sang froid*.

There on the great high-backed carved oak chair by the right side of the fireplace sat an enormous rat, steadily glaring at him with baleful eyes. He made a motion to it as though to hunt it away, but it did not stir. Then he made the motion of throwing something. Still it did not stir, but showed its great white teeth angrily, and its cruel eyes shone in the lamplight with an added vindictiveness.

Malcolmson felt amazed, and seizing the poker from the hearth ran at it to kill it. Before, however, he could strike it, the rat, with a squeak that sounded like the concentration of hate, jumped upon the floor, and, running up the rope of the alarm bell, disappeared in the darkness beyond the range of the green-shaded lamp. Instantly, strange to say, the noisy scampering of the rats in the wainscot began again.

By this time Malcolmson's mind was quite off the problem ; and as a shrill cock-crow outside told him of the approach of morning, he went to bed and to sleep.

He slept so sound that he was not even waked by Mrs. Dempster coming in to make up his room. It was only when she had tidied up the place and got his breakfast ready and tapped on the screen which closed in his bed that he woke. He was a little tired still after his night's hard work, but a strong cup of tea soon freshened him up, and, taking his book, he went out for his morning walk, bringing with him a few sandwiches lest he should not care to return till dinner time. He found a quiet walk between high elms some way outside the town, and here he spent the greater part of the day studying his Laplace. On his return he looked in to see Mrs. Witham and to thank her for her kindness. When she saw him coming through the diamond-paned bay-window of her sanctum she came out to meet him and asked him in. She looked at him searchingly and shook her head as she said :

" You must not overdo it, sir. You are paler this morning than you should be. Too late hours and too hard work on the brain isn't good for any man ! But tell me, sir, how did you pass the night ? Well, I hope ? But, my heart ! sir, I was glad when Mrs. Dempster told me this morning that you were all right and sleeping sound when she went in."

" Oh, I was all right," he answered, smiling, " the ' something ' didn't worry me, as yet. Only the rats ; and they had a circus, I tell you, all over the place. There was one wicked looking old devil that sat up on my own chair by the fire, and wouldn't go till I took the poker to him, and then he ran up the rope of the alarm bell and got to somewhere up the wall or the ceiling—I couldn't see where, it was so dark."

" Mercy on us," said Mrs. Witham, " an old devil, and sitting on a chair by the fireside ! Take care, sir ! take care ! There's many a true word spoken in jest."

" How do you mean ? 'Pon my word I don't understand."

" An old devil ! The old devil, perhaps. There ! sir, you needn't laugh," for Malcolmson had broken into a hearty peal. " You young folks thinks it easy to laugh at things that makes older ones shudder. Never mind, sir ! never mind ! Please God, you'll laugh all the time. It's what I wish you myself ! " and the good lady beamed all over in sympathy with his enjoyment, her fears gone for a moment.

" Oh, forgive me ! " said Malcolmson presently. " Don't think me rude ; but the idea was too much for me—that the old devil himself was on the chair last night ! " And at the thought he laughed again. Then he went home to dinner.

This evening the scampering of the rats began earlier ; indeed it had been going on before his arrival, and only ceased whilst his presence by its freshness disturbed them. After dinner he sat by the fire for a while and had a smoke ; and then, having cleared his table, began to work as before. To-night the rats disturbed him more than they had done on the previous night. How they scampered up and down and under and over ! How they squeaked, and scratched, and gnawed ! How they, getting bolder by degrees, came to the mouths of their holes and to the chinks and cracks and crannies in the wainscoting till their eyes shone like tiny lamps as the firelight rose and fell. But to him, now doubtless accustomed to them, their eyes were not wicked ; only their playfulness touched him. Sometimes the boldest of them made sallies out on the floor or along the mouldings of the wainscot. Now and again as they disturbed him Malcolmson made a sound to frighten them, smiting the table with his hand or giving a fierce " Hsh, hsh," so that they fled straightway to their holes.

And so the early part of the night wore on ; and despite the noise Malcolmson got more and more immersed in his work.

All at once he stopped, as on the previous night, being overcome by a sudden sense of silence. There was not the faintest sound of gnaw, or scratch, or squeak. The silence was as of the grave. He remembered the odd occurrence of the previous night, and instinctively he looked at the chair standing close by the fireside. And then a very odd sensation thrilled through him.

There, on the great old high-backed carved oak chair beside the fireplace sat the same enormous rat, steadily glaring at him with baleful eyes.

Instinctively he took the nearest thing to his hand, a book of logarithms, and flung it at it. The book was badly aimed and the rat did not stir, so again the poker performance of the previous night was repeated ; and again the rat, being closely pursued, fled up the rope of the alarm bell. Strangely too, the departure of this rat was instantly followed by the renewal of the noise made by the general rat community. On this occasion, as on the previous one, Malcolmson could not see at what part of the room the rat disappeared, for the green shade of his lamp left the upper part of the room in darkness, and the fire had burned low.

On looking at his watch he found it was close on midnight ; and, not sorry for the *divertissement*, he made up his fire and made himself his nightly pot of tea. He had got through a good spell of work, and thought himself entitled to a cigarette ; and so he sat on the great carved oak chair before the fire and enjoyed it. Whilst smoking he began to think that he would like to know where the rat disappeared to, for he had certain ideas for the morrow not entirely disconnected with a rat-trap. Accordingly he lit another lamp and placed it so that it would shine well into the right-hand corner of the wall by the fireplace. Then he got all the books he had with him, and placed them handy to throw at the vermin. Finally he lifted the rope of the alarm bell and placed the end of it on the table, fixing the extreme end under the lamp. As he handled it he could not help noticing how pliable it was, especially for so strong a rope, and one not in use. " You could hang a man with it," he thought to himself. When his preparations were made he looked around, and said complacently :

" There now, my friend, I think we shall learn something of you this time ! " He began his work again, and though as before somewhat disturbed at first by the noise of the rats, soon lost himself in his propositions and problems.

Again he was called to his immediate surroundings suddenly. This time it might not have been the sudden silence only which took his attention ; there was a slight movement of the rope, and the lamp moved. Without stirring, he looked to see if his pile of books was within range, and then cast his eye along the rope. As he looked he saw the great rat drop from the rope on the oak armchair and sit there glaring at him. He raised a book in his right hand, and taking careful aim, flung it at the rat. The latter, with a quick movement, sprang aside and dodged the missile. He then took another book, and a third, and flung them one after another at the rat, but each time unsuccessfully. At last, as he stood with a book poised in his hand to throw, the rat squeaked and seemed afraid. This made Malcolmson more than ever eager to strike, and the book flew and struck the rat a resounding blow. It gave a terrified squeak, and turning on its pursuer a look of terrible malevolence, ran up the chair-back and made a great jump to the rope of the alarm bell and ran up it like lightning. The lamp rocked under the sudden strain, but it was a heavy one and did not topple over. Malcolmson kept his eyes on the rat, and saw it by the light of the second lamp leap to a moulding of the wainscot and disappear through a hole in one of the great pictures which hung on the wall, obscured and invisible through its coating of dirt and dust.

" I shall look up my friend's habitation in the morning," said the student, as he went over to collect his books. " The third picture from the fireplace ; I shall not forget." He picked up the books one by one, commenting on them as he lifted them. " *Conic Sections* he does not mind, nor *Cycloidal Oscillations*, nor the *Principia*, nor *Quaternions*, nor *Thermodynamics*. Now for the book that fetched him ! " Malcolmson took it up and looked at it. As he did so he started, and a sudden pallor overspread his face. He looked round uneasily and shivered slightly, as he murmured to himself :

" The Bible my mother gave me ! What an odd coincidence." He sat down to work again, and the rats in the wainscot renewed their gambols. They did not disturb him, however ; somehow their presence gave him a sense of companionship. But he could not attend to his work, and after striving to master the subject on which he was engaged gave it up in despair, and went to bed as the first streak of dawn stole in through the eastern window.

He slept heavily but uneasily, and dreamed much ; and when Mrs. Dempster woke him late in the morning he seemed ill at ease, and for a few minutes did not seem to realise exactly where he was. His first request rather surprised the servant.

" Mrs. Dempster, when I am out to-day I wish you would get the steps and dust or wash those pictures—specially that one the third from the fireplace—I want to see what they are."

Late in the afternoon Malcolmson worked at his books in the shaded walk, and the cheerfulness of the previous day came back to him as the day wore on, and he found that his reading was progressing well. He had worked out to a satisfactory conclusion all the problems which had as yet baffled him, and it was in a state of jubilation that he paid a visit to Mrs. Witham at " The Good Traveller." He found a stranger in the cosy sitting-room with the landlady, who was introduced to him as Dr. Thornhill. She was not quite at ease, and this, combined with the Doctor's plunging at once into a series of questions, made Malcolmson come to the conclusion that his presence was not an accident, so without preliminary he said :

" Dr. Thornhill, I shall with pleasure answer you any question you may choose to ask me if you will answer me one question first."

The Doctor seemed surprised, but he smiled and answered at once. " Done ! What is it ? "

" Did Mrs. Witham ask you to come here and see me and advise me ? "

Dr. Thornhill for a moment was taken aback, and Mrs. Witham got fiery red and turned away ; but the doctor was a frank and ready man, and he answered at once and openly :

" She did : but she didn't intend you to know it. I suppose it was my clumsy haste that made you suspect. She told me that she did not like the idea of your being in that house all by yourself, and that she thought you took too much strong tea. In fact, she wants me to advise you if possible to give up the tea and the very late hours. I was a keen student in my time, so I suppose I may take the liberty of a college man, and without offence, advise you not quite as a stranger."

Malcolmson with a bright smile held out his hand. "Shake ! as they say in America," he said. " I must thank you for your kindness and Mrs. Witham too, and your kindness deserves a return on my part. I promise to take no more strong tea—no tea at all till you let me—and I shall go to bed to-night at one o'clock at latest. Will that do ? "

" Capital," said the Doctor. "Now tell us all that you noticed in the old house," and so Malcolmson then and there told in minute detail all that had happened in the last two nights. He was interrupted every now and then by some exclamation from Mrs. Witham, till finally when he told of the episode of the Bible the landlady's pent-up emotions found vent in a shriek ; and it was not till a stiff glass of brandy and water had been administered that she grew composed again. Dr. Thornhill listened with a face of growing gravity, and when the narrative was complete and Mrs. Witham had been restored he asked :

" The rat always went up the rope of the alarm bell ? "

" Always."

" I suppose you know," said the Doctor after a pause, " what the rope is ? "

" No ! "

" It is," said the Doctor slowly, " the very rope which the hangman used for all the victims of the Judge's judicial rancour ! " Here he was interrupted by another scream from Mrs. Witham, and steps had to be taken for her recovery. Malcolmson having looked at his watch, and found that it was close to his dinner hour, had gone home before her complete recovery.

When Mrs. Witham was herself again she almost assailed the Doctor with angry questions as to what he meant by putting such horrible ideas into the poor young man's mind. " He has quite enough there already to upset him," she added. Dr. Thornhill replied :

" My dear madam, I had a distinct purpose in it ! I wanted to draw his attention to the bell rope, and to fix it there. It may be that he is in a highly overwrought state, and has been studying too much, although I am bound to say that he seems as sound and healthy a young man, mentally and bodily, as ever I saw—but then the rats—and that suggestion of the devil." The doctor shook his head and went on. " I would have offered to go and stay the first night with him but that I felt sure it would have been a cause of offence. He may get in the night some strange fright or hallucination ; and if he does I want him to pull that rope. All alone as he is it will give us warning, and we may reach him in time to be of service. I shall be sitting up pretty late to-night and shall keep my ears open. Do not be alarmed if Benchurch gets a surprise before morning."

" Oh, Doctor, what do you mean ? What do you mean ? "

" I mean this ; that possibly—nay, more probably—we shall hear the great alarm bell from the Judge's House to-night," and the Doctor made about as effective an exit as could be thought of.

When Malcolmson arrived home he found that it was a little after his usual time, and Mrs. Dempster had gone away—the rules of Greenhow's Charity were not to be neglected. He was glad to see that the place was bright and tidy with a cheerful fire and a well-trimmed lamp. The evening was colder than might have been expected in April, and a heavy wind was blowing with such rapidly-increasing strength that there was every promise of a storm during the night. For a few minutes after his entrance the noise of the rats ceased ; but so soon as they became accustomed to his presence they began again. He was glad to hear them, for he felt once more the feeling of companionship in their noise, and his mind ran back to the strange fact that they only ceased to manifest themselves when that other—the great rat with the baleful eyes—came upon the scene. The reading-lamp only was lit and its green shade kept the ceiling and the upper part of the room in darkness, so that the cheerful light from the hearth spreading over the floor and shining on the white cloth laid over the end of the table was warm and cheery. Malcolmson sat down to his dinner with a good appetite and a buoyant spirit. After his dinner and a cigarette he sat steadily down to work, determined not to let anything disturb him, for he remembered his promise to the doctor, and made up his mind to make the best of the time at his disposal.

For an hour or so he worked all right, and then his thoughts began to wander from his books. The actual circumstances around him, the calls on his physical attention, and his nervous susceptibility were not to be denied. By this time the wind had become a gale, and the gale a storm. The old house, solid though it was, seemed to shake to its foundations, and the storm roared and raged through its many chimneys and its queer old gables, producing strange, unearthly sounds in the empty rooms and corridors. Even the great alarm bell on the roof must have felt the force of the wind, for the rope rose and fell slightly, as though the bell were moved a little from time to time, and the limber rope fell on the oak floor with a hard and hollow sound.

As Malcolmson listened to it he bethought himself of the doctor's words, " It is the rope which the hangman used for the victims of the Judge's judicial rancour," and he went over to the corner of the fireplace and took it in his hand to look at it. There seemed a sort of deadly interest in it, and as he stood there he lost himself for a moment in speculation as to who these victims were, and the grim wish of the Judge to have such a ghastly relic ever under his eyes. As he stood there the swaying of the bell on the roof still lifted the rope now and again ; but presently there came a new sensation—a sort of tremor in the rope, as though something was moving along it.

Looking up instinctively Malcolmson saw the great rat coming slowly down towards him, glaring at him steadily. He dropped the rope and started back with a muttered curse, and the rat turning ran up the rope again and disappeared, and at the same instant Malcolmson became conscious that the noise of the rats, which had ceased for a while, began again.

All this set him thinking, and it occurred to him that he had not investigated the lair of the rat or looked at the pictures, as he had intended. He lit the other lamp without the shade, and, holding it up, went and stood opposite the third picture from the fireplace on the right-hand side where he had seen the rat disappear on the previous night.

At the first glance he started back so suddenly that he almost dropped the lamp, and a deadly pallor overspread his face. His knees shook, and heavy drops of sweat came on his forehead, and he trembled like an aspen. But he was young and plucky, and pulled himself together, and after the pause of a few seconds stepped forward again, raised the lamp, and examined the picture which had been dusted and washed, and now stood out clearly.

It was of a judge dressed in his robes of scarlet and ermine. His face was strong and merciless, evil, crafty, and vindictive, with a sensual mouth, hooked nose of ruddy colour, and shaped like the beak of a bird of prey. The rest of the face was of a cadaverous colour. The eyes were of peculiar brilliance and with a terribly malignant expression. As he looked at them, Malcolmson grew cold, for he saw there the very counterpart of the eyes of the great rat. The lamp almost fell from his hand, he saw the rat with its baleful eyes peering out through the hole in the corner of the picture, and noted the sudden cessation of the noise of the other rats. However, he pulled himself together, and went on with his examination of the picture.

The Judge was seated in a great high-backed carved oak chair, on the right-hand side of a great stone fireplace where, in the corner, a rope hung down from the ceiling, its end lying coiled on the floor. With a feeling of something like horror, Malcolmson recognised the scene of the room as it stood, and gazed around him in an awe-struck manner as though he expected to find some strange presence behind him. Then he looked over to the corner of the fireplace—and with a loud cry he let the lamp fall from his hand.

There, in the Judge's arm-chair, with the rope hanging behind, sat the rat with the Judge's baleful eyes, now intensified and with a fiendish leer. Save for the howling of the storm without there was silence.

The fallen lamp recalled Malcolmson to himself. Fortunately it was of metal, and so the oil was not spilt. However, the practical need of attending to it settled at once his nervous apprehensions. When he had turned it out, he wiped his brow and thought for a moment.

" This will not do," he said to himself. " If I go on like this I shall become a crazy fool. This must stop ! I promised the Doctor I would not take tea. Faith, he was pretty right ! My nerves must have been getting into a queer state. Funny I did not notice it. I never felt better in my life. However, it is all right now, and I shall not be such a fool again."

Then he mixed himself a good stiff glass of brandy and water and resolutely sat down to his work.

It was nearly an hour when he looked up from his book, disturbed by the sudden stillness. Without, the wind howled and roared louder than ever, and the rain drove in sheets against the windows, beating like hail on the glass ; but within there was no sound whatever save the echo of the wind as it roared in the great chimney, and now and then a hiss as a few raindrops found their way down the chimney in a lull of the storm. The fire had fallen low and had ceased to flame, though it threw out a red glow. Malcolmson listened attentively, and presently heard a thin, squeaking noise, very faint. It came from the corner of the room where the rope hung down, and he thought it was the creaking of the rope on the floor as the swaying of the bell raised and lowered it. Looking up, however, he saw in the dim light the great rat clinging to the rope and gnawing it. The rope was already nearly gnawed through—he could see the lighter colour where the strands were laid bare. As he looked the job was completed, and the severed end of the rope fell clattering on the oaken floor, whilst for an instant the great rat remained like a knob or tassel at the end of the rope, which now began to sway to and fro. Malcolmson felt for a moment another pang of terror as he thought that now the possibility of calling the outer world to his assistance was cut off, but an intense anger took its place, and seizing the book he was reading he hurled it at the rat. The blow was well aimed, but before the missile could reach it the rat dropped off and struck the floor with a soft thud. Malcolmson instantly rushed over towards it, but it darted away and disappeared in the darkness of the shadows of the room. Malcolmson felt that his work was over for the night, and determined then and there to vary the monotony of the proceedings by a hunt for the rat, and took off the green shade of the lamp so as to insure a wider spreading light. As he did so the gloom of the upper part of the room was relieved, and in the new flood of light, great by comparison with the previous darkness, the pictures on the wall stood out boldly. From where he stood, Malcolmson saw right opposite to him the third picture on the wall from the right of the fireplace. He rubbed his eyes in surprise, and then a great fear began to come upon him.

In the centre of the picture was a great irregular patch of brown canvas, as fresh as when it was stretched on the frame. The background was as before, with chair and chimney-corner and rope, but the figure of the Judge had disappeared.

Malcolmson, almost in a chill of horror, turned slowly round, and then he began to shake and tremble like a man in a palsy. His strength seemed to have left him, and he was incapable of action or movement, hardly even of thought. He could only see and hear.

There, on the great high-backed carved oak chair sat the Judge in his robes of scarlet and ermine, with his baleful eyes glaring vindictively, and a smile of triumph on the resolute, cruel mouth, as he lifted with his hands a *black cap*. Malcolmson felt as if the blood was running from his heart, as one does in moments of prolonged suspense. There was a singing in his ears. Without, he could hear the roar and howl of the tempest, and through it, swept on the storm, came the striking of midnight by the great chimes in the market place. He stood for a space of time that seemed to him endless, still as a statue and with wide-open, horror-struck eyes, breathless. As the clock struck, so the smile of triumph on the Judge's face intensified, and at the last stroke of midnight he placed the black cap on his head.

Slowly and deliberately the Judge rose from his chair and picked up the piece of the rope of the alarm bell which lay on the floor, drew it through his hands as if he enjoyed its touch, and then deliberately began to knot one end of it, fashioning it into a noose. This he tightened and tested with his foot, pulling hard at it till he was satisfied and then making a running noose of it, which he held in his hand. Then he began to move along the table on the opposite side to Malcolmson, keeping his eyes on him until he had passed him, when with a quick movement he stood in front of the door. Malcolmson then began to feel that he was trapped, and tried to think of what he should do. There was some fascination in the Judge's eyes, which he never took off him, and he had, perforce, to look. He saw the Judge approach—still keeping between him and the door—and raise the noose and throw it towards him as if to entangle him. With a great effort he made a quick movement to one side, and saw the rope fall beside him, and heard it strike the oaken floor. Again the Judge raised the noose and tried to ensnare him, ever keeping his baleful eyes fixed on him, and each time by a mighty effort the student just managed to evade it. So this went on for many times, the Judge seeming never discouraged nor discomposed at failure, but playing as a cat does with a mouse. At last in despair, which had reached its climax, Malcolmson cast a quick glance round him. The lamp seemed to have blazed up, and there was a fairly good light in the room. At the many rat-holes and in the chinks and crannies of the wainscot he saw the rats' eyes ; and this aspect, that was purely physical, gave him a gleam of comfort. He looked around and saw that the rope of the great alarm bell was laden with rats. Every inch of it was covered with them, and more and more were pouring through the small circular hole in the ceiling whence it emerged, so that with their weight the bell was beginning to sway.

Hark ! it had swayed till the clapper had touched the bell. The sound was but a tiny one, but the bell was only beginning to sway, and it would increase.

At the sound the Judge, who had been keeping his eyes fixed on Malcolmson, looked up, and a scowl of diabolical anger overspread his face. His eyes fairly glowed like hot coals, and he stamped his foot with a sound that seemed to make the house shake. A dreadful peal of thunder broke overhead as he raised the rope again, whilst the rats kept running up and down the rope as though working against time. This time, instead of throwing it, he drew close to his victim, and held open the noose as he approached. As he came closer there seemed something paralysing in his very presence, and Malcolmson stood rigid as a corpse. He felt the Judge's icy fingers touch his throat as he adjusted the rope. The noose tightened—tightened. Then the Judge, taking the rigid form of the student in his arms, carried him over and placed him standing in the oak chair, and stepping up beside him, put his hand up and caught the end of the swaying rope of the alarm bell. As he raised his hand the rats fled squeaking, and disappeared through the hole in the ceiling. Taking the end of the noose which was round Malcolmson's neck he tied it to the hanging bell-rope, and then descending pulled away the chair.

.   .   .   .

When the alarm bell of the Judge's House began to sound a crowd soon assembled. Lights and torches of various kinds appeared, and soon a silent crowd was hurrying to the spot. They knocked loudly at the door, but there was no reply. Then they burst in the door, and poured into the great dining-room, the doctor at the head.

There at the end of the rope of the great alarm bell hung the body of the student, and on the face of the Judge in the picture was a malignant smile.

Perceval Landon

THURNLEY ABBEY

from RAW EDGES

William Heinemann, 1908

Three years ago I was on my way out to the East, and as an extra day in London was of some importance, I took the Friday evening mail-train to Brindisi instead of the usual Thursday morning Marseilles express. Many people shrink from the long forty-eight-hour train journey through Europe, and the subsequent rush across the Mediterranean on the nineteen-knot *Isis* or *Osiris* ; but there is really very little discomfort on either the train or the mail-boat, and unless there is actually nothing for me to do, I always like to save the extra day and a half in London before I say good-bye to her for one of my longer tramps. This time—it was early, I remember, in the shipping season, probably about the beginning of September—there were few passengers, and I had a compartment in the P. & O. Indian express to myself all the way from

Calais. All Sunday I watched the blue waves dimpling the Adriatic, and the pale rosemary along the cuttings ; the plain white towns, with their flat roofs and their bold " duomos," and the grey-green gnarled olive orchards of Apulia. The journey was just like any other. We ate in the dining-car as often and as long as we decently could. We slept after luncheon ; we dawdled the after-noon away with yellow-backed novels ; sometimes we exchanged platitudes in the smoking-room, and it was there that I met Alastair Colvin.

Colvin was a man of middle height, with a resolute, well-cut jaw ; his hair was turning grey ; his moustache was sun-whitened, otherwise he was clean-shaven—obviously a gentleman, and obviously also a pre-occupied man. He had no great wit. When spoken to, he made the usual remarks in the right way, and I dare say he refrained from banalities only because he spoke less than the rest of us ; most of the time he buried himself in the Wagon-lit Company's time-table, but seemed unable to concentrate his attention on any one page of it. He found that I had been over the Siberian railway, and for a quarter of an hour he discussed it with me. Then he lost interest in it, and rose to go to his compartment. But he came back again very soon, and seemed glad to pick up the conversation again.

Of course this did not seem to me to be of any importance. Most travellers by train become a trifle infirm of purpose after thirty-six hours' rattling. But Colvin's restless way I noticed in somewhat marked contrast with the man's personal importance and dignity ; especially ill suited was it to his finely made large hand with strong, broad, regular nails and its few lines. As I looked at his hand I noticed a long, deep, and recent scar of ragged shape. However, it is absurd to pretend that I thought anything was unusual. I went off at five o'clock on Sunday afternoon to sleep away the hour or two that had still to be got through before we arrived at Brindisi.

Once there, we few passengers transhipped our hand baggage, verified our berths—there were only a score of us in all—and then, after an aimless ramble of half an hour in Brindisi, we returned to dinner at the Hôtel International, not wholly surprised that the town had been the death of Virgil. If I remember rightly, there is a gaily painted hall at the International—I do not wish to advertise anything, but there is no other place in Brindisi at which to await the coming of the mails—and after dinner I was looking with awe at a trellis overgrown with blue vines, when Colvin moved across the room to my table. He picked up *Il Secolo*, but almost immediately gave up the pretence of reading it. He turned squarely to me and said :

" Would you do me a favour ? "

One doesn't do favours to stray acquaintances on Continental expresses without knowing something more of them than I knew of Colvin. But I smiled in a noncommittal way, and asked him what he wanted. I wasn't wrong in part of my estimate of him ; he said bluntly :

" Will you let me sleep in your cabin on the *Osiris* ? " And he coloured a little as he said it.

Now, there is nothing more tiresome than having to put up with a stable-companion at sea, and I asked him rather pointedly :

" Surely there is room for all of us ? " I thought that perhaps he had been partnered off with some mangy Levantine, and wanted to escape from him at all hazards.

Colvin, still somewhat confused, said : " Yes ; I am in a cabin by myself. But you would do me the greatest favour if you would allow me to share yours."

This was all very well, but, besides the fact that I always sleep better when alone, there had been some recent thefts on board English liners, and I hesitated, frank and honest and self-conscious as Colvin was. Just then the mail-train came in with a clatter and a rush of escaping steam, and I asked him to see me again about it on the boat when we started. He answered me curtly—I suppose he saw the mistrust in my manner—" I am a member of White's." I smiled to myself as he said it, but I remembered in a moment that the man—if he were really what he claimed to be, and I make no doubt that he was—must have been sorely put to it before he urged the fact as a guarantee of his respectability to a total stranger at a Brindisi hotel.

That evening, as we cleared the red and green harbour-lights of Brindisi, Colvin explained. This is his story in his own words.

" When I was travelling in India some years ago, I made the acquaintance of a youngish man in the Woods and Forests. We camped out together for a week, and I found him a pleasant companion. John Broughton was a light-hearted soul when off duty, but a steady and capable man in any of the small emergencies that continually arise in that department. He was liked and trusted by the natives, and though a trifle over-pleased with himself when he escaped to civilisation at Simla or Calcutta, Broughton's future was well assured in Government service, when a fair-sized estate was unexpectedly left to him, and he joyfully shook the dust of the Indian plains from his feet and returned to England. For five years he drifted about London. I saw him now and then. We dined together about every eighteen months, and I could trace pretty exactly the gradual sickening of Broughton with a merely idle life. He then set out on a couple of long voyages, returned as restless as before, and at last told me that he had decided to marry and settle down at his place, Thurnley Abbey, which had long been empty. He spoke about looking after the property and standing for his constituency in the usual way. Vivien Wilde, his *fiancée*, had, I suppose, begun to take him in hand. She was a pretty girl with a deal of fair hair and rather an exclusive manner ; deeply religious in a narrow school, she was still kindly and high-spirited, and I thought that Broughton was in luck. He was quite happy and full of information about his future.

" Among other things, I asked him about Thurnley Abbey. He confessed that he hardly knew the place. The last tenant, a man called Clarke, had lived in one wing for fifteen years and seen no one. He had been a miser and a hermit. It was the rarest thing for a light to be seen at the Abbey after dark. Only the barest necessities of life were ordered, and the tenant himself received them at the side-door. His one half-caste manservant, after a month's stay in the house, had abruptly left without warning, and had returned to the Southern States. One thing Broughton complained bitterly about : Clarke had wilfully spread the rumour among the villagers that the Abbey was haunted, and had even condescended to play childish tricks with spirit-lamps and salt in order to scare trespassers away at night. He had been detected in the act of this tomfoolery, but the story spread, and no one, said Broughton, would venture near the house except in broad daylight. The hauntedness of Thurnley Abbey was now, he said with a grin, part of the gospel of the countryside, but he and his young wife were going to change all that. Would I propose myself any time I liked? I, of course, said I would, and equally, of course, intended to do nothing of the sort without a definite invitation.

" The house was put in thorough repair, though not a stick of the old furniture and tapestry were removed. Floors and ceilings

were relaid : the roof was made watertight again, and the dust
of half a century was scoured out. He showed me some photo-
graphs of the place. It was called an Abbey, though as a matter of
fact it had been only the infirmary of the long-vanished Abbey
of Closter some five miles away. The larger part of this building
remained as it had been in pre-Reformation days, but a wing had
been added in Jacobean times, and that part of the house had been
kept in something like repair by Mr. Clarke. He had in both the
ground and first floors set a heavy timber door, strongly barred
with iron, in the passage between the earlier and the Jacobean
parts of the house, and had entirely neglected the former. So there
had been a good deal of work to be done.

" Broughton, whom I saw in London two or three times about
this period, made a deal of fun over the positive refusal of the
workmen to remain after sundown. Even after the electric light
had been put into every room, nothing would induce them to
remain, though, as Broughton observed, electric light was death
on ghosts. The legend of the Abbey's ghosts had gone far and wide,
and the men would take no risks. They went home in batches of
five and six, and even during the daylight hours there was an
inordinate amount of talking between one and another, if either
happened to be out of sight of his companion. On the whole,
though nothing of any sort or kind had been conjured up even by
their heated imaginations during their five months' work upon the
Abbey, the belief in the ghosts was rather strengthened than
otherwise in Thurnley because of the men's confessed nervousness,
and local tradition declared itself in favour of the ghost of an
immured nun.

" ' Good old nun ! ' said Broughton.

" I asked him whether in general he believed in the possibility
of ghosts, and, rather to my surprise, he said that he couldn't say
he entirely disbelieved in them. A man in India had told him one
morning in camp that he believed that his mother was dead in
England, as her vision had come to his tent the night before. He
had not been alarmed, but had said nothing, and the figure
vanished again. As a matter of fact, the next possible dak-walla
brought on a telegram announcing the mother's death. ' There
the thing was,' said Broughton. But at Thurnley he was practical
enough. He roundly cursed the idiotic selfishness of Clarke, whose
silly antics had caused all the inconvenience. At the same time,
he couldn't refuse to sympathise to some extent with the ignorant

workmen. ' My own idea,' said he, ' is that if a ghost ever does come in one's way, one ought to speak to it.'

" I agreed. Little as I knew of the ghost world and its conventions, I had always remembered that a spook was in honour bound to wait to be spoken to. It didn't seem much to do, and I felt that the sound of one's own voice would at any rate reassure oneself as to one's wakefulness. But there are few ghosts outside Europe— few, that is, that a white man can see—and I had never been troubled with any. However, as I have said, I told Broughton that I agreed.

" So the wedding took place, and I went to it in a tall hat which I bought for the occasion, and the new Mrs. Broughton smiled very nicely at me afterwards. As it had to happen, I took the Orient Express that evening and was not in England again for nearly six months. Just before I came back I got a letter from Broughton. He asked if I could see him in London or come to Thurnley, as he thought I should be better able to help him than anyone else he knew. His wife sent a nice message to me at the end, so I was reassured about at least one thing. I wrote from Budapest that I would come and see him at Thurnley two days after my arrival in London, and as I sauntered out of the Pannonia into the Kerepesi Utcza to post my letters, I wondered of what earthly service I could be to Broughton. I had been out with him after tiger on foot, and I could imagine few men better able at a pinch to manage their own business. However, I had nothing to do, so after dealing with some small accumulations of business during my absence, I packed a kit-bag and departed to Euston.

" I was met by Broughton's great limousine at Thurnley Road station, and after a drive of nearly seven miles we echoed through the sleepy streets of Thurnley village, into which the main gates of the park thrust themselves, splendid with pillars and spread-eagles and tom-cats rampant atop of them. I never was a herald, but I know that the Broughtons have the right to supporters— Heaven knows why ! From the gates a quadruple avenue of beech-trees led inwards for a quarter of a mile. Beneath them a neat strip of fine turf edged the road and ran back until the poison of the dead beech-leaves killed it under the trees. There were many wheel-tracks on the road, and a comfortable little pony trap jogged past me laden with a country parson and his wife and daughter. Evidently there was some garden party going on at the Abbey.

The road dropped away to the right at the end of the avenue, and I could see the Abbey across a wide pasturage and a broad lawn thickly dotted with guests.

" The end of the building was plain. It must have been almost mercilessly austere when it was first built, but time had crumbled the edges and toned the stone down to an orange-lichened grey wherever it showed behind its curtain of magnolia, jasmine, and ivy. Farther on was the three-storied Jacobean house, tall and hand-some. There had not been the slightest attempt to adapt the one to the other, but the kindly ivy had glossed over the touching-point. There was a tall flèche in the middle of the building, sur-mounting a small bell tower. Behind the house there rose the mountainous verdure of Spanish chestnuts all the way up the hill.

" Broughton had seen me coming from afar, and walked across from his other guests to welcome me before turning me over to the butler's care. This man was sandy-haired and rather inclined to be talkative. He could, however, answer hardly any questions about the house ; he had, he said, only been there three weeks. Mindful of what Broughton had told me, I made no inquiries about ghosts, though the room into which I was shown might have justified anything. It was a very large low room with oak beams projecting from the white ceiling. Every inch of the walls, including the doors, was covered with tapestry, and a remarkably fine Italian fourpost bedstead, heavily draped, added to the darkness and dignity of the place. All the furniture was old, well made, and dark. Underfoot there was a plain green pile carpet, the only new thing about the room except the electric light fittings and the jugs and basins. Even the looking-glass on the dressing-table was an old pyramidal Venetian glass set in heavy repoussé frame of tarnished silver.

" After a few minutes' cleaning up, I went downstairs and ou upon the lawn, where I greeted my hostess. The people gathered there were of the usual country type, all anxious to be pleased and roundly curious as to the new master of the Abbey. Rather to my surprise, and quite to my pleasure, I rediscovered Glenham, whom I had known well in old days in Barotseland : he lived quite close, as, he remarked with a grin, I ought to have known. ' But,' he added, ' I don't live in a place like this.' He swept his hand to the long, low lines of the Abbey in obvious admiration, and then, to my intense interest, muttered beneath his breath,

' Thank God ! ' He saw that I had overheard him, and turning
to me said decidedly, ' Yes, "thank God"' I said, and I meant it.
I wouldn't live at the Abbey for all Broughton's money.'

" ' But surely,' I demurred, ' you know that old Clarke was
discovered in the very act of setting light to his bug-a-boos ? '

" Glenham shrugged his shoulders. ' Yes, I know about that.
But there is something wrong with the place still. All I can say is
that Broughton is a different man since he has lived here. I don't
believe that he will remain much longer. But—you're staying
here?—well, you'll hear all about it to-night. There's a big
dinner, I understand.' The conversation turned off to old remin-
iscences, and Glenham soon after had to go.

" Before I went to dress that evening I had twenty minutes'
talk with Broughton in his library. There was no doubt that the
man was altered, gravely altered. He was nervous and fidgety,
and I found him looking at me only when my eye was off him. I
naturally asked him what he wanted of me. I told him I would
do anything I could, but that I couldn't conceive what he lacked
that I could provide. He said with a lustreless smile that there was,
however, something, and that he would tell me the following
morning. It struck me that he was somehow ashamed of himself,
and perhaps ashamed of the part he was asking me to play.
However, I dismissed the subject from my mind and went up to
dress in my palatial room. As I shut the door a draught blew out
the Queen of Sheba from the wall, and I noticed that the tapestries
were not fastened to the wall at the bottom. I have always held
very practical views about spooks, and it has often seemed to me
that the slow waving in firelight of loose tapestry upon a wall
would account for ninety-nine per cent. of the stories one hears.
Certainly the dignified undulation of this lady with her attendants
and huntsmen—one of whom was untidily cutting the throat of a
fallow deer upon the very steps on which King Solomon, a grey-
faced Flemish nobleman with the order of the Golden Fleece,
awaited his fair visitor—gave colour to my hypothesis.

" Nothing much happened at dinner. The people were very
much like those of the garden party. A young woman next me
seemed anxious to know what was being read in London. As
she was far more familiar than I with the most recent magazines
and literary supplements, I found salvation in being myself
instructed in the tendencies of modern fiction. All true art, she
said, was shot through and through with melancholy. How vulgar

were the attempts at wit that marked so many modern books ! From the beginning of literature it had always been tragedy that embodied the highest attainment of every age. To call such works morbid merely begged the question. No thoughtful man—she looked sternly at me through the steel rim of her glasses—could fail to agree with me. Of course, as one would, I immediately and properly said that I slept with Pett Ridge and Jacobs under my pillow at night, and that if *Jorrocks* weren't quite so large and cornery, I would add him to the company. She hadn't read any of them, so I was saved—for a time. But I remember grimly that she said that the dearest wish of her life was to be in some awful and soul-freezing situation of horror, and I remember that she dealt hardly with the hero of Nat Paynter's vampire story, between nibbles at her brown-bread ice. She was a cheerless soul, and I couldn't help thinking that if there were many such in the neighbourhood, it was not surprising that old Glenham had been stuffed with some nonsense or other about the Abbey. Yet nothing could well have been less creepy than the glitter of silver and glass, and the subdued lights and cackle of conversation all round the dinner-table.

" After the ladies had gone I found myself talking to the rural dean. He was a thin, earnest man, who at once turned the conversation to old Clarke's buffooneries. But, he said, Mr. Broughton had introduced such a new and cheerful spirit, not only into the Abbey, but, he might say, into the whole neighbourhood, that he had great hopes that the ignorant superstitions of the past were from henceforth destined to oblivion. Thereupon his other neighbour, a portly gentleman of independent means and position, audibly remarked ' Amen,' which damped the rural dean, and we talked of partridges past, partridges present, and pheasants to come. At the other end of the table Broughton sat with a couple of his friends, red-faced hunting men. Once I noticed that they were discussing me, but I paid no attention to it at the time. I remembered it a few hours later.

" By eleven all the guests were gone, and Broughton, his wife, and I were alone together under the fine plaster ceiling of the Jacobean drawing-room. Mrs. Broughton talked about one or two of the neighbours, and then, with a smile, said that she knew I would excuse her, shook hands with me, and went off to bed. I am not very good at analysing things, but I felt that she talked a little uncomfortably and with a suspicion of effort, smiled rather conventionally, and was obviously glad to go. These things seem trifling enough to repeat, but I had throughout the faint feeling that everything was not square. Under the circumstances, this was enough to set me wondering what on earth the service could be that I was to render—wondering also whether the whole business were not some ill-advised jest in order to make me come down from London for a mere shooting-party.

"Broughton said little after she had gone. But he was evidently labouring to bring the conversation round to the so-called haunting of the Abbey. As soon as I saw this, of course I asked him directly about it. He then seemed at once to lose interest in the matter. There was no doubt about it : Broughton was somehow a changed man, and to my mind he had changed in no way for the better. Mrs. Broughton seemed no sufficient cause. He was clearly very fond of her, and she of him. I reminded him that he was going to tell me what I could do for him in the morning, pleaded my journey, lighted a candle, and went upstairs with him. At the end of the passage leading into the old house he grinned weakly and said, ' Mind, if you see a ghost, do talk to it ; you said you would.' He stood irresolutely a moment and then turned away. At the door of his dressing-room he paused once more : ' I'm here,' he called out, ' if you should want anything. Good night,' and he shut his door.

"I went along the passage to my room, undressed, switched on a lamp beside my bed, read a few pages of *The Jungle Book*, and then, more than ready for sleep, turned the light off and went fast asleep.

"Three hours later I woke up. There was not a breath of wind outside. There was not even a flicker of light from the fireplace. As I lay there, an ash tinkled slightly as it cooled, but there was hardly a gleam of the dullest red in the grate. An owl cried among the silent Spanish chestnuts on the slope outside. I idly reviewed the events of the day, hoping that I should fall off to sleep again before I reached dinner. But at the end I seemed as wakeful as ever. There was no help for it. I must read my *Jungle Book* again till I felt ready to go off, so I fumbled for the pear at the end of the cord that hung down inside the bed, and I switched on the bedside lamp. The sudden glory dazzled me for a moment. I felt under my pillow for my book with half-shut eyes. Then, growing used to the light, I happened to look down to the foot of my bed.

" I can never tell you really what happened then. Nothing I could ever confess in the most abject words could even faintly picture to you what I felt. I know that my heart stopped dead, and my throat shut automatically. In one instinctive movement I crouched back up against the head-boards of the bed, staring at the horror. The movement set my heart going again, and the sweat dripped from every pore. I am not a particularly religious man, but I had always believed that God would never allow any supernatural appearance to present itself to man in such a guise and in such circumstances that harm, either bodily or mental, could result to him. I can only tell you that at that moment both my life and my reason rocked unsteadily on their seats."

The other *Osiris* passengers had gone to bed. Only he and I remained leaning over the starboard railing, which rattled uneasily now and then under the fierce vibration of the over-engined mail-boat. Far over, there were the lights of a few fishing-smacks riding out the night, and a great rush of white combing and seething water fell out and away from us overside.

At last Colvin went on :

" Leaning over the foot of my bed, looking at me, was a figure swathed in a rotten and tattered veiling. This shroud passed over the head, but left both eyes and the right side of the face bare. It then followed the line of the arm down to where the hand grasped the bed-end. The face was not entirely that of a skull, though the eyes and the flesh of the face were totally gone. There was a thin, dry skin drawn tightly over the features, and there was some skin left on the hand. One wisp of hair crossed the forehead. It was perfectly still. I looked at it, and it looked at me, and my brains turned dry and hot in my head. I had still got the pear of the electric lamp in my hand, and I played idly with it ; only I dared not turn the light out again. I shut my eyes, only to open them in a hideous terror the same second. The thing had not moved. My heart was thumping, and the sweat cooled me as it evaporated. Another cinder tinkled in the grate, and a panel creaked in the wall.

" My reason failed me. For twenty minutes, or twenty seconds, I was able to think of nothing else but this awful figure, till there came, hurtling through the empty channels of my senses, the remembrance that Broughton and his friends had discussed me furtively at dinner. The dim possibility of its being a hoax stole gratefully into my unhappy mind, and once there, one's pluck came creeping back along a thousand tiny veins. My first sensation was one of blind unreasoning thankfulness that my brain was going to stand the trial. I am not a timid man, but the best of us needs some human handle to steady him in time of extremity, and in this faint but growing hope that after all it might be only a brutal hoax, I found the fulcrum that I needed. At last I moved.

" How I managed to do it I cannot tell you, but with one spring towards the foot of the bed I got within arm's-length and struck out one fearful blow with my fist at the thing. It crumbled under it, and my hand was cut to the bone. With a sickening revulsion after my terror, I dropped half-fainting across the end of the bed. So it was merely a foul trick after all. No doubt the trick had been played many a time before : no doubt Broughton and his friends had had some large bet among themselves as to what I should do when I discovered the gruesome thing. From my state of abject terror I found myself transported into an insensate anger. I shouted curses upon Broughton. I dived rather than climbed over the bed-end on to the sofa. I tore at the robed skeleton—how well the whole thing had been carried out, I thought—I broke the skull against the floor, and stamped upon its dry bones. I flung the head away under the bed, and rent the brittle bones of the trunk in pieces. I snapped the thin thigh-bones across my knee, and flung them in different directions. The shin-bones I set up against a stool and broke with my heel. I raged like a Berserker against the loathly thing, and stripped the ribs from the backbone and slung the breastbone against the cupboard. My fury increased as the work of destruction went on. I tore the frail rotten veil into twenty pieces, and the dust went up over everything, over the clean blotting-paper and the silver inkstand. At last my work was done. There was but a raffle of broken bones and strips of parchment and crumbling wool. Then, picking up a piece of the skull— it was the cheek and temple bone of the right side, I remember—I opened the door and went down the passage to Broughton's dressing-room. I remember still how my sweat-dripping pyjamas clung to me as I walked. At the door I kicked and entered.

" Broughton was in bed. He had already turned the light on and seemed shrunken and horrified. For a moment he could hardly pull himself together. Then I spoke. I don't know what I

said. Only I know that from a heart full and over-full with hatred
and contempt, spurred on by shame of my own recent cowardice,
I let my tongue run on. He answered nothing. I was amazed at
my own fluency. My hair still clung lankily to my wet temples, my
hand was bleeding profusely, and I must have looked a strange
sight. Broughton huddled himself up at the head of the bed just
as I had. Still he made no answer, no defence. He seemed pre-
occupied with something besides my reproaches, and once or
twice moistened his lips with his tongue. But he could say nothing
though he moved his hands now and then, just as a baby who
cannot speak moves its hands.

"At last the door into Mrs. Broughton's room opened and she
came in, white and terrified. 'What is it? What is it? Oh, in
God's name! what is it?' she cried again and again, and then
she went up to her husband and sat on the bed in her night-dress,
and the two faced me. I told her what the matter was. I spared her
husband not a word for her presence there. Yet he seemed hardly
to understand. I told the pair that I had spoiled their cowardly
joke for them. Broughton looked up.

"'I have smashed the foul thing into a hundred pieces,' I said.
Broughton licked his lips again and his mouth worked. 'By God!'
I shouted, 'it would serve you right if I thrashed you within an
inch of your life. I will take care that not a decent man or woman
of my acquaintance ever speaks to you again. And there,' I
added, throwing the broken piece of the skull upon the floor
beside his bed, 'there is a souvenir for you, of your damned work
to-night!'

"Broughton saw the bone, and in a moment it was his turn to
frighten me. He squealed like a hare caught in a trap. He screamed
and screamed till Mrs. Broughton, almost as bewildered as myself,
held on to him and coaxed him like a child to be quiet. But
Broughton—and as he moved I thought that ten minutes ago
I perhaps looked as terribly ill as he did—thrust her from him, and
scrambled out of the bed on to the floor, and still screaming put
out his hand to the bone. It had blood on it from my hand. He
paid no attention to me whatever. In truth I said nothing. This
was a new turn indeed to the horrors of the evening. He rose from
the floor with the bone in his hand and stood silent. He seemed to
be listening. 'Time, time, perhaps,' he muttered, and almost at
the same moment fell at full length on the carpet, cutting his
head against the fender. The bone flew from his hand and came

to rest near the door. I picked Broughton up, haggard and broken, with blood over his face. He whispered hoarsely and quickly, ' Listen, listen ! ' We listened.

" After ten seconds' utter quiet, I seemed to hear something. I could not be sure, but at last there was no doubt. There was a quiet sound as of one moving along the passage. Little regular steps came towards us over the hard oak flooring. Broughton moved to where his wife sat, white and speechless, on the bed, and pressed her face into his shoulder.

" Then, the last thing that I could see as he turned the light out, he fell forward with his own head pressed into the pillow of the bed. Something in their company, something in their cowardice, helped me, and I faced the open doorway of the room, which was outlined fairly clearly against the dimly lighted passage. I put out one hand and touched Mrs. Broughton's shoulder in the darkness. But at the last moment I too failed. I sank on my knees and put my face in the bed. Only we all heard. The footsteps came to the door, and there they stopped. The piece of bone was lying a yard inside the door. There was a rustle of moving stuff, and the thing was in the room. Mrs. Broughton was silent : I could hear Broughton's voice praying, muffled in the pillow : I was cursing my own cowardice. Then the steps moved out again on the oak boards of the passage, and I heard the sounds dying away. In a flash of remorse I went to the door and looked out. At the end of the corridor I thought I saw something that moved away. A moment later the passage was empty. I stood with my forehead against the jamb of the door almost physically sick.

" ' You can turn the light on,' I said, and there was an answering flare. There was no bone at my feet. Mrs. Broughton had fainted. Broughton was almost useless, and it took me ten minutes to bring her to. Broughton only said one thing worth remembering. For the most part he went on muttering prayers. But I was glad afterwards to recollect that he had said that thing. He said in a colourless voice, half as a question, half as a reproach, ' You didn't speak to her.'

" We spent the remainder of the night together. Mrs. Broughton actually fell off into a kind of sleep before dawn, but she suffered so horribly in her dreams that I shook her into consciousness again. Never was dawn so long in coming. Three or four times Broughton spoke to himself. Mrs. Broughton would then just tighten her hold on his arm, but she could say nothing. As for me, I can honestly

say that I grew worse as the hours passed and the light strengthened. The two violent reactions had battered down my steadiness of view, and I felt that the foundations of my life had been
built upon the sand. I said nothing, and after binding up my hand
with a towel, I did not move. It was better so. They helped me and
I helped them, and we all three knew that out reason had gone
very near to ruin that night. At last, when the light came in pretty
strongly, and the birds outside were chattering and singing, we
felt that we must do something. Yet we never moved. You might
have thought that we should particularly dislike being found as
we were by the servants : yet nothing of that kind mattered a
straw, and an overpowering listlessness bound us as we sat, until
Chapman, Broughton's man, actually knocked and opened the
door. None of us moved. Broughton, speaking hardly and stiffly,
said, ' Chapman you can come back in five minutes.' Chapman,
was a discreet man, but it would have made no difference to us if
he had carried his news to the ' room ' at once.

" We looked at each other and I said I must go back. I meant
to wait outside till Chapman returned. I simply dared not re-
enter my bedroom alone. Broughton roused himself and said that
he would come with me. Mrs. Broughton agreed to remain in her
own room for five minutes if the blinds were drawn up and all the
doors left open.

" So Broughton and I, leaning stiffly one against the other, went
down to my room. By the morning light that filtered past the
blinds we could see our way, and I released the blinds. There was
nothing wrong in the room from end to end, except smears of my
own blood on the end of the bed, on the sofa, and on the carpet
where I had torn the thing to pieces."

Colvin had finished his story. There was nothing to say. Seven
bells stuttered out from the fo'c'sle, and the answering cry wailed
through the darkness. I took him downstairs.

" Of course I am much better now, but it is a kindness of you
to let me sleep in your cabin."

E. and H. Heron

THE STORY OF THE
SPANIARDS, HAMMERSMITH

from "Real Ghost Stories," PEARSON'S MAGAZINE, *January
1898, afterwards reprinted in* GHOST STORIES
C. Arthur Pearson, 1916

Lieutenant Roderick Houston, of H.M.S. *Sphinx*, had practically nothing beyond his pay, and he was beginning to be very tired
of the West African station, when he received the pleasant intelligence that a relative had left him a legacy. This consisted of
a satisfactory sum in ready money and a house in Hammersmith,
which was rated at over £200 a year, and was said in addition to
be comfortably furnished. Houston, therefore, counted on its
rental to bring his income up to a fairly desirable figure. Further
information from home, however, showed him that he had been
rather premature in his expectations, whereupon, being a man
of action, he applied for two months' leave, and came home to
look after his affairs himself.

When he had been a week in London he arrived at the conclusion that he could not possibly hope single-handed to tackle the
difficulties which presented themselves. He accordingly wrote the
following letter to his friend, Flaxman Low :

"The Spaniards, Hammersmith, 23-3-1892.

"DEAR LOW,—Since we parted some three years ago, I have
heard very little of you. It was only yesterday that I met our
mutual friend, Sammy Smith ('Silkworm' of our schooldays)
who told me that your studies have developed in a new direction,
and that you are now a good deal interested in psychical subjects. If this be so, I hope to induce you to come and stay with
me here for a few days by promising to introduce you to a problem in your own line. I am just now living at 'The Spaniards,'
a house that has lately been left to me, and which in the first
instance was built by an old fellow named Van Nuysen, who
married a great-aunt of mine. It is a good house, but there is
said to be 'something wrong' with it. It lets easily, but unluckily the tenants cannot be persuaded to remain above a week
or two. They complain that the place is haunted by something
—presumably a ghost—because its vagaries bear just that brand

of inconsequence which stamps the common run of manifestations.

" It occurs to me that you may care to investigate the matter with me. If so, send me a wire when to expect you.

" Yours ever,
" RODERICK HOUSTON."

Houston waited in some anxiety for an answer. Low was the sort of man one could rely on in almost any emergency. Sammy Smith had told him a characteristic anecdote of Low's career at Oxford, where, although his intellectual triumphs may be forgotten, he will always be remembered by the story that when Sands, of Queen's, fell ill on the day before the 'Varsity sports, a telegram was sent to Low's rooms : " Sands ill. You must do the hammer for us." Low's reply was pithy : " I'll be there." Thereupon he finished the treatise upon which he was engaged, and next day his strong, lean figure was to be seen swinging the hammer amidst vociferous cheering, for that was the occasion on which he not only won the event, but beat the record.

On the fifth day Low's answer came from Vienna. As he read it, Houston recalled the high forehead, long neck—with its accompanying low collar—and thin moustache of his scholarly, athletic friend, and smiled. There was so much more in Flaxman Low than anyone gave him credit for.

" MY DEAR HOUSTON,—Very glad to hear of you again. In response to your kind invitation, I thank you for the opportunity of meeting the ghost, and still more for the pleasure of your companionship. I came here to inquire into a somewhat similar affair. I hope, however, to be able to leave to-morrow, and will be with you some time on Friday evening.

" Very sincerely yours,
" FLAXMAN LOW."

" P.S.—By the way, will it be convenient to give your servants a holiday during the term of my visit, as, if my investigations are to be of any value, not a grain of dust must be disturbed in your house, excepting by ourselves ?—F. L."

" The Spaniards " was within some fifteen minutes' walk of Hammersmith Bridge. Set in the midst of a fairly respectable neighbourhood, it presented an odd contrast to the commonplace dullness of the narrow streets crowded about it. As Flaxman Low drove up in the evening light, he reflected that the house might have come from the back of beyond—it gave an impression of something old-world and something exotic.

It was surrounded by a ten-foot wall, above which the upper storey was visible, and Low decided that this intensely English house still gave some curious suggestion of the tropics. The interior of the house carried out the same idea, with its sense of space and air, cool tints and wide, matted passages.

" So you have seen something yourself since you came ? " Low said, as they sat at dinner, for Houston had arranged that meals should be sent in for them from an hotel.

" I've heard tapping up and down the passage upstairs. It is an uncarpeted landing which runs the whole length of the house. One night, when I was quicker than usual, I saw what looked like a bladder disappear into one of the bedrooms—your room it is to be, by the way—and the door closed behind it," replied Houston discontentedly. " The usual meaningless antics of a ghost."

" What had the tenants who lived here to say about it ? " went on Low.

" Most of the people saw and heard just what I have told you, and promptly went away. The only one who stood out for a little while was old Filderg—you know the man ? Twenty years ago he made an effort to cross the Australian deserts—he stopped for eight weeks. When he left he saw the house-agent, and said he was afraid he had done a little shooting practice in the upper passage, and he hoped it wouldn't count against him in the bill, as it was done in defence of his life. He said something had jumped on to the bed and tried to strangle him. He described it as cold and glutinous, and he pursued it down the passage, firing at it. He advised the owner to have the house pulled down ; but, of course, my cousin did nothing of the kind. It's a very good house, and he did not see the sense of spoiling his property."

" That's very true," replied Flaxman Low, looking round. " Mr. Van Nuysen had been in the West Indies, and kept his liking for spacious rooms."

" Where did you hear anything about him ? " asked Houston in surprise.

" I have heard nothing beyond what you told me in your let-ter ; but I see a couple of bottles of Gulf weed and a lace-plant ornament, such as people used to bring from the West Indies in former days."

"Perhaps I should tell you the history of the old man," said Houston doubtfully ; " but we aren't proud of it ! "

Flaxman Low considered a moment.

"When was the ghost seen for the first time ? "

"When the first tenant took the house. It was let after old Van Nuysen's time."

"Then it may clear the way if you will tell me something of him."

"He owned sugar plantations in Trinidad, where he passed the greater part of his life, while his wife mostly remained in England—incompatibility of temper it was said. When he came home for good and built this house they still lived apart, my aunt declaring that nothing on earth would persuade her to return to him. In course of time he became a confirmed invalid, and he then insisted on my aunt joining him. She lived here for perhaps a year, when she was found dead in bed one morning—in your room."

"What caused her death ? "

"She had been in the habit of taking narcotics, and it was supposed that she smothered herself while under their influence."

"That doesn't sound very satisfactory," remarked Flaxman Low.

"Her husband was satisfied with it anyhow, and it was no one else's business. The family were only too glad to have the affair hushed up."

"And what became of Mr. Van Nuysen ? "

"That I can't tell you. He disappeared a short time after. Search was made for him in the usual way, but nobody knows to this day what became of him."

"Ah, that was strange, as he was such an invalid," said Low, and straightway fell into a long fit of abstraction, from which he was roused by hearing Houston curse the incurable foolishness and imbecility of ghostly behaviour. Flaxman woke up at this. He broke a walnut thoughtfully and began in a gentle voice :

"My dear fellow, we are apt to be hasty in our condemnation of the general behaviour of ghosts. It may appear incalculably foolish in our eyes, and I admit there often seems to be a total absence of any apparent object or intelligent action. But remember that what appears to us to be foolishness may be wisdom in the spirit world, since our unready senses can only catch broken glimpses of what is, I have not the slightest doubt, a coherent whole, if we could trace the connection."

" There may be something in that," replied Houston indifferently. " People naturally say that this ghost is the ghost of old Van Nuysen. But what connection can possibly exist between what I have told you of him and the manifestations—a tapping up and down the passage and the drawing about of a bladder like a child at play ? It sounds idiotic ! "

" Certainly. Yet it need not necessarily be so. There are isolated facts, we must look for the links which lie between. Suppose a saddle and a horse-shoe were to be shown to a man who had never seen a horse, I doubt whether he, however intelligent, could evolve the connecting idea ! The ways of spirits are strange to us simply because we need further data to help us to interpret them."

" It's a new point of view," returned Houston, " but upon my word, you know, Low, I think you're wasting your time ! "

Flaxman Low smiled slowly ; his grave, melancholy face brightened.

" I have," said he, " gone somewhat deeply into the subject. In other sciences one reasons by analogy. Psychology is unfortunately a science with a future but without a past, or more probably it is a lost science of the ancients. However that may be, we stand to-day on the frontier of an unknown world, and progress is the result of individual effort ; each solution of difficult phenomena forms a step towards the solution of the next problem. In this case, for example, the bladder-like object may be the key to the mystery."

Houston yawned.

" It all seems pretty senseless, but perhaps you may be able to read reason into it. If it were anything tangible, anything a man could meet with his fists, it would be easier."

" I entirely agree with you. But suppose we deal with this affair as it stands, on similar lines, I mean on prosaic, rational lines, as we should deal with a purely human mystery."

" My dear fellow," returned Houston, pushing his chair back from the table wearily, " you shall do just as you like, only get rid of the ghost ! "

For some time after Low's arrival nothing very special happened. The tappings continued, and more than once Low had been in time to see the bladder disappear into the closing door of his bedroom, though, unluckily, he never chanced to be inside the room on these occasions, and however quickly he followed the bladder, he never succeeded in seeing anything further. He made a thorough examination of the house, and left no space unaccounted for in his careful measurement. There were no cellars, and the foundation of the house consisted of a thick layer of concrete.

At length, on the sixth night, an event took place, which, as Flaxman Low remarked, came very near to putting an end to the investigations as far as he was concerned. For the preceding two nights he and Houston had kept watch in the hope of getting a glimpse of the person or thing which tapped so persistently up and down the passage. But they were disappointed, for there were no manifestations. On the third evening, therefore, Low went off to his room a little earlier than usual, and fell asleep almost immediately.

He says he was awakened by feeling a heavy weight upon his feet, something that seemed inert and motionless. He recollected that he had left the gas burning, but the room was now in darkness.

Next he was aware that the thing on the bed had slowly shifted, and was gradually travelling up towards his chest. How it came on the bed he had no idea. Had it leaped or climbed ? The sensation he experienced as it moved was of some ponderous, pulpy body, not crawling or creeping, but spreading ! It was horrible ! He tried to move his lower limbs, but could not because of the deadening weight. A feeling of drowsiness began to overpower him, and a deadly cold, such as he said he had before felt at sea when in the neighbourhood of icebergs, chilled upon the air.

With a violent struggle he managed to free his arms, but the thing grew more irresistible as it spread upwards. Then he became conscious of a pair of glassy eyes, with livid, everted lids, looking into his own. Whether they were human eyes or beast eyes, he could not tell, but they were watery, like the eyes of a dead fish, and gleamed with a pale, internal lustre.

Then he owns he grew afraid. But he was still cool enough to notice one peculiarity about this ghastly visitant—although the head was within a few inches of his own, he could detect no breathing. It dawned upon him that he was about to be suffocated, for, by the same method of extension, the thing was now coming over his face ! It felt cold and clammy, like a mass of mucilage or a monstrous snail. And every instant the weight became greater.

He is a powerful man, and he struck with his fists again and again at the head. Some substance yielded under the blows with a sickening sensation of bruised flesh.

With a lucky twist he raised himself in the bed and battered away with all the force he was capable of in his cramped position. The only effect was an occasional shudder or quake that ran through the mass as his half-arm blows rained upon it. At last, by chance, his hand knocked against the candle beside him. In a moment he recollected the matches. He seized the box, and struck a light.

As he did so, the lump slid to the floor. He sprang out of bed, and lit the candle. He felt a cold touch upon his leg, but when he looked down there was nothing to be seen. The door, which he had locked overnight, was now open, and he rushed out into the passage. All was still and silent with the throbbing vacancy of night time.

After searching round, he returned to his room. The bed still gave ample proof of the struggle that had taken place, and by his watch he saw the hour to be between two and three.

As there seemed nothing more to be done, he put on his dressing-gown, lit his pipe, and sat down to write an account of the experience he had just passed through for the Psychical Research Society—from which paper the above is an abstract.

He is a man of strong nerves, but he could not disguise from himself that he had been at handgrips with some grotesque form of death. What might be the nature of his assailant he could not determine, but his experience was supported by the attack which had been made on Filderg, and also—it was impossible to avoid the conclusion—by the manner of Mrs. Van Nuysen's death.

He thought the whole situation over carefully in connection with the tapping and the disappearing bladder, but, turn these events how he would, he could make nothing of them. They were entirely incongruous. A little later he went and made a shake-down in Houston's room.

" What was the thing ? " asked Houston, when Low had ended his story of the encounter.

Low shrugged his shoulders.

" At least it proves that Filderg did not dream," he said.

" But this is monstrous ! We are more in the dark than ever. There's nothing for it but to have the house pulled down. Let us leave to-day."

" Don't be in a hurry, my dear fellow. You would rob me of a very great pleasure ; besides, we may be on the verge of some valuable discovery. This series of manifestations is even more interesting than the Vienna mystery I was telling you of."

" Discovery or not," replied the other, " I don't like it."

The first thing next morning Low went out for a quarter of an hour. Before breakfast a man with a barrowful of sand came into the garden. Low looked up from his paper, leant out of the window, and gave some order.

When Houston came down a few minutes later he saw the yellowish heap on the lawn with some surprise.

" Hullo ! What's this ? " he asked.

" I ordered it," replied Low.

" All right. What's it for ? "

" To help us in our investigations. Our visitor is capable of being felt, and he or it left a very distinct impression on the bed. Hence I gather it can also leave an impression on sand. It would be an immense advance if we could arrive at any correct notion of what sort of feet the ghost walks on. I propose to spread a layer of this sand in the upper passage, and the result should be footmarks if the tapping comes to-night."

That evening the two men made a fire in Houston's bedroom, and sat there smoking and talking, to leave the ghost " a free run for once," as Houston phrased it. The tapping was heard at the usual hour, and presently the accustomed pause at the other end of the passage and the quiet closing of the door.

Low heaved a long sigh of satisfaction as he listened.

" That's my bedroom door," he said ; " I know the sound of it perfectly. In the morning, and with the help of daylight, we shall see what we shall see."

As soon as there was light enough for the purpose of examining the footprints, Low roused Houston.

Houston was as full of excitement as a boy, but his spirits fell by the time he had passed from end to end of the passage.

" There are marks," he said, " but they are as perplexing as everything else about this haunting brute, whatever it is. I suppose you think this is the print left by the thing which attacked you the night before last ? "

" I fancy it is," said Low, who was still bending over the floor eagerly. " What do you make of it, Houston ? "

" The brute has only one leg, to start with," replied Houston,

" and that leaves the mark of a large, clawless pad ! It's some animal—some ghoulish monster ! "

" On the contrary," said Low, " I think we have now every reason to conclude that it is a man ? "

" A man ? What man ever left footmarks like these ? "

" Look at these hollows and streaks at the sides ; they are the traces of the sticks we have heard tapping."

" You don't convince me," returned Houston doggedly.

" Let us wait another twenty-four hours, and to-morrow night, if nothing further occurs, I will give you my conclusions. Think it over. The tapping, the bladder, and the fact that Mr. Van Nuysen had lived in Trinidad. Add to these things this single pad-like print. Does nothing strike you by way of a solution ? "

Houston shook his head.

" Nothing. And I fail to connect any of these things with what happened both to you and Filderg."

" Ah ! now," said Flaxman Low, his face clouding a little, " I confess you lead me into a somewhat different region, though to me the connection is perfect."

Houston raised his eyebrows and laughed.

" If you can unravel this tangle of hints and events and diagnose the ghost, I shall be extremely astonished," he said. " What can you make of the footless impression ? "

" Something, I hope. In fact, that mark may be a clue—an outrageous one, perhaps, but still a clue."

That evening the weather broke, and by night the storm had risen to a gale, accompanied by sharp bursts of rain.

" It's a noisy night," remarked Houston ; " I don't suppose we'll hear the ghost, supposing it does turn up."

This was after dinner, as they were about to go into the smoking-room. Houston, finding the gas low in the hall, stopped to turn it higher ; at the same time asking Low to see if the jet on the upper landing was also alight.

Flaxman Low glanced up and uttered a slight exclamation, which brought Houston to his side.

Looking down at them from over the banisters was a face— a blotched, yellowish face, flanked by two swollen, protruding ears, the whole aspect being strangely leonine. It was but a glimpse, a clash of meeting glances, as it were, a glare of defiance, and the face was quickly withdrawn as the two men literally leapt up the stairs.

" There's nothing here," exclaimed Houston, after a search had been carried out through every room above.

" I didn't suppose we'd find anything," returned Low.

" This fairly knots up the thread," said Houston. " You can't pretend to unravel it now."

" Come down," said Low briefly ; " I'm ready to give you my opinion, such as it is."

Once in the smoking-room, Houston busied himself in turning on all the light he could procure, then he saw to securing the windows, and piled up an immense fire, while Flaxman Low, who, as usual, had a cigarette in his mouth, sat on the edge of the table and watched him with some amusement.

" You saw that abominable face ? " cried Houston, as he threw himself into a chair. " It was as material as yours or mine. But where did he go to ? He must be somewhere about."

" We saw him clearly. That is sufficient for our purpose."

" You are very good at enumerating points, Low. Now just listen to my list. The difficulties grow with every fresh discovery. We're at a deadlock now, I take it ? The sticks and the tapping point to an old man, the playing with a bladder to a child ; the footmark might be the pad of a tiger minus claws, yet the thing that attacked you at night was cold and pulpy. And, lastly, by way of a wind-up, we see a lion-like, human face ! If you can make all these items square with each other, I'll be happy to hear what you have got to say."

" You must first allow me to ask you a question. I understood you to say that no blood relationship existed between you and old Mr. Van Nuysen ? "

" Certainly not. He was quite an outsider," answered Houston brusquely.

" In that case you are welcome to my conclusions. All the things you have mentioned point to one explanation. This house is haunted by the ghost of Mr. Van Nuysen, and he was a leper."

Houston stood up and stared at his companion.

" What a horrible notion ! I must say I fail to see how you have arrived at such a conclusion."

" Take the chain of evidence in rather different order," said Low. " Why should a man tap with a stick ? "

" Generally because he's blind."

" In cases of blindness, one stick is used for guidance. Here we have two for support."

" A man who has lost the use of his feet."

" Exactly ; a man who has from some cause partially lost the use of his feet."

" But the bladder and the lion-like face ? " went on Houston.

" The bladder, or what seemed to us to resemble a bladder, was one of his feet, contorted by the disease and probably swathed in linen, which foot he dragged rather than used ; consequently, in passing through a door, for example, he would be in the habit of drawing it in after him. Now, as regards the single footmark we saw. In one form of leprosy, the smaller bones of the extremities frequently fall away. The pad-like impression was, as I believe, the mark of the other foot—a toeless foot which he used, because in a more advanced stage of the disease the maimed hand or foot heals and becomes callous."

" Go on," said Houston ; " it sounds as if it might be true. And the lion-like face I can account for myself. I have been in China, and have seen it before in lepers."

" Mr. Van Nuysen had been in Trinidad for many years, as we know, and while there he probably contracted the disease."

" I suppose so. After his return," added Houston, " he shut himself up almost entirely, and gave out that he was a martyr to rheumatic gout, this awful thing being the true explanation."

" It also accounts for Mrs. Van Nuysen's determination not to return to her husband."

Houston appeared much disturbed.

" We can't drop it here, Low," he said, in a constrained voice. "" There is a good deal more to be cleared up yet. Can you tell me more ? "

" From this point I find myself on less certain ground," replied Low unwillingly. " I merely offer a suggestion, remember—I don't ask you to accept it. I believe Mrs. Van Nuysen was murdered ! "

" What ? " exclaimed Houston. " By her husband ? "

" Indications tend that way."

" But, my good fellow——"

" He suffocated her and then made away with himself. It is a pity that his body was not recovered. The condition of the remains would be the only really satisfactory test of my theory. If the skeleton could even now be found, the fact that he was a leper would be finally settled."

There was a prolonged pause until Houston put another question.

" Wait a minute, Low," he said. " Ghosts are admittedly im-material. In this instance our spook has an extremely palpable body. Surely this is rather unusual ? You have made everything else more or less plain. Can you tell me why this dead leper should have tried to murder you and old Filderg ? And also how he came to have the actual physical power to do so ? "

Low removed his cigarette to look thoughtfully at the end of it. " Now I lapse into the purely theoretical," he answered. " Cases have been known where the assumption of diabolical agency is apparently justifiable."

" Diabolical agency ?—I don't follow you."

" I will try to make myself clear, though the subject is still in a stage of vagueness and immaturity. Van Nuysen committed a murder of exceptional atrocity, and afterwards killed himself. Now, bodies of suicides are known to be peculiarly susceptible to spiritual influences, even to the point of arrested corruption. Add to this our knowledge that the highest aim of an evil spirit is to gain possession of a material body. If I carried out my theory to its logical conclusion, I should say that Van Nuysen's body is hid-den somewhere on these premises—that this body is intermittently animated by some spirit, which at certain periods is forced to re-enact the gruesome tragedy of the Van Nuysens. Should any living person chance to occupy the position of the first victim, so much the worse for him ! "

For some minutes Houston made no remark on this singular expression of opinion.

" But have you ever met with anything of the sort before ? " he said at last.

" I can recall," replied Flaxman Low thoughtfully, " quite a number of cases which would seem to bear out this hypothesis. Among them a curious problem of haunting exhaustively exam-ined by Busner in the early part of 1888, at which I was myself lucky enough to assist. Indeed, I may add that the affair which I have recently been engaged upon in Vienna offers some rather similar features. There, however, we had to stop short of excava-tion, by which alone any specific results might have been at-tained."

" Then you are of opinion," said Houston, " that pulling the house to pieces might cast some further light upon this affair ? "

" I cannot see any better course," said Mr. Low.

Then Houston closed the discussion by a very definite declaration.

" This house shall come down ! "

So " The Spaniards " was pulled down.

Such is the story of " The Spaniards," Hammersmith, and it has been given the first place in this series because, although it may not be of so strange a nature as some that will follow it, yet it seems to us to embody in a high degree the peculiar methods by which Mr. Flaxman Low is wont to approach these cases.

The work of demolition, begun at the earliest possible moment, did not occupy very long, and during its early stages, under the boarding at an angle of the landing was found a skeleton. Several of the phalanges were missing, and other indications also established beyond a doubt the fact that the remains were the remains of a leper.

The skeleton is now in the museum of one of our city hospitals. It bears a scientific ticket, and is the only evidence extant of the correctness of Mr. Flaxman Low's methods and the possible truth of his extraordinary theories.

Amelia B. Edwards

THE PHANTOM COACH

from ALL THE YEAR ROUND, 1864

The circumstances I am about to relate to you have truth to recommend them. They happened to myself, and my recollection of them is as vivid as if they had taken place only yesterday. Twenty years, however, have gone by since that night. During those twenty years I have told the story to but one other person. I tell it now with a reluctance which I find it difficult to overcome. All I entreat, meanwhile, is that you will abstain from forcing your own conclusions upon me. I want nothing explained away. I desire no arguments. My mind on this subject is quite made up, and, having the testimony of my own senses to rely upon, I prefer to abide by it.

Well ! It was just twenty years ago, and within a day or two

of the end of the grouse season. I had been out all day with my
gun, and had had no sport to speak of. The wind was due east ;
the month, December ; the place, a bleak wide moor in the far
north of England. And I had lost my way. It was not a pleasant
place in which to lose one's way, with the first feathery flakes of
a coming snowstorm just fluttering down upon the heather, and
the leaden evening closing in all around. I shaded my eyes with
my hand, and stared anxiously into the gathering darkness, where
the purple moorland melted into a range of low hills, some ten or
twelve miles distant. Not the faintest smoke-wreath, not the tiniest
cultivated patch, or fence, or sheep-track, met my eyes in any
direction. There was nothing for it but to walk on, and take my
chance of finding what shelter I could, by the way. So I shouldered
my gun again, and pushed wearily forward ; for I had been on
foot since an hour after daybreak, and had eaten nothing since
breakfast.

Meanwhile, the snow began to come down with ominous steadiness, and the wind fell. After this, the cold became more intense,
and the night came rapidly up. As for me, my prospects darkened
with the darkening sky, and my heart grew heavy as I thought
how my young wife was already watching for me through the
window of our little inn parlour, and thought of all the suffering
in store for her throughout this weary night. We had been married
four months, and, having spent our autumn in the Highlands,
were now lodging in a remote little village situated just on the
verge of the great English moorlands. We were very much in love,
and, of course, very happy. This morning, when we parted, she
had implored me to return before dusk, and I had promised her
that I would. What would I not have given to have kept my word !

Even now, weary as I was, I felt that with a supper, an hour's
rest, and a guide, I might still get back to her before midnight,
if only guide and shelter could be found.

And all this time, the snow fell and the night thickened. I
stopped and shouted every now and then, but my shouts seemed
only to make the silence deeper. Then a vague sense of uneasiness
came upon me, and I began to remember stories of travellers who
had walked on and on in the falling snow until, wearied out, they
were fain to lie down and sleep their lives away. Would it be
possible, I asked myself, to keep on thus through all the long dark
night ? Would there not come a time when my limbs must fail,
and my resolution give way ? When I, too, must sleep the sleep

of death. Death ! I shuddered. How hard to die just now, when
life lay all so bright before me ! How hard for my darling, whose
whole loving heart——but that thought was not to be borne ! To
banish it, I shouted again, louder and longer, and then listened
eagerly. Was my shout answered, or did I only fancy that I heard
a far-off cry ? I halloed again, and again the echo followed. Then
a wavering speck of light came suddenly out of the dark, shifting,
disappearing, growing momentarily nearer and brighter. Running
towards it at full speed, I found myself, to my great joy, face to
face with an old man and a lantern.

"Thank God ! " was the exclamation that burst involuntarily
from my lips.

Blinking and frowning, he lifted his lantern and peered into
my face.

"What for ? " growled he, sulkily.

"Well—for you. I began to fear I should be lost in the snow."

"Eh, then, folks do get cast away hereabouts fra' time to time,
an' what's to hinder you from bein' cast away likewise, if the
Lord's so minded ? "

"If the Lord is so minded that you and I shall be lost together,
friend, we must submit," I replied ; "but I don't mean to be lost
without you. How far am I now from Dwolding ? "

"A gude twenty mile, more or less."

"And the nearest village ? "

"The nearest village is Wyke, an' that's twelve mile t'other
side."

"Where do you live, then ? "

"Out yonder," said he, with a vague jerk of the lantern.

"You're going home, I presume ? "

"Maybe I am."

"Then I'm going with you."

The old man shook his head, and rubbed his nose reflectively
with the handle of the lantern.

"It ain't o' no use," growled he. "He 'ont let you in—not he."

"We'll see about that," I replied, briskly. "Who is He ? "

"The master."

"Who is the master ? "

"That's nowt to you," was the unceremonious reply.

"Well, well ; you lead the way, and I'll engage that the master
shall give me shelter and a supper to-night."

"Eh, you can try him ! " muttered my reluctant guide ; and,

still shaking his head, he hobbled, gnome-like, away through the falling snow. A large mass loomed up presently out of the darkness, and a huge dog rushed out, barking furiously.

" Is this the house ? " I asked.

" Ay, it's the house. Down, Bey ! " And he fumbled in his pocket for the key.

I drew up close behind him, prepared to lose no chance of entrance, and saw in the little circle of light shed by the lantern that the door was heavily studded with iron nails, like the door of a prison. In another minute he had turned the key and I had pushed past him into the house.

Once inside, I looked round with curiosity, and found myself in a great raftered hall, which served, apparently, a variety of uses. One end was piled to the roof with corn, like a barn. The other was stored with flour-sacks, agricultural implements, casks, and all kinds of miscellaneous lumber ; while from the beams overhead hung rows of hams, flitches, and bunches of dried herbs for winter use. In the centre of the floor stood some huge object gauntly dressed in a dingy wrapping-cloth, and reaching half way to the rafters. Lifting a corner of this cloth, I saw, to my surprise, a telescope of very considerable size, mounted on a rude movable platform, with four small wheels. The tube was made of painted wood, bound round with bands of metal rudely fashioned ; the speculum, so far as I could estimate its size in the dim light, measured at least fifteen inches in diameter. While I was yet examining the instrument, and asking myself whether it was not the work of some self-taught optician, a bell rang sharply.

" That's for you," said my guide, with a malicious grin. " Yonder's his room."

He pointed to a low black door at the opposite side of the hall. I crossed over, rapped somewhat loudly, and went in, without waiting for an invitation. A huge, white-haired old man rose from a table covered with books and papers, and confronted me sternly.

" Who are you ? " said he. " How came you here ? What do you want ? "

" James Murray, barrister-at-law. On foot across the moor. Meat, drink, and sleep."

He bent his bushy brows into a portentous frown.

" Mine is not a house of entertainment," he said, haughtily. " Jacob, how dared you admit this stranger ? "

" I didn't admit him," grumbled the old man. " He followed

me over the muir, and shouldered his way in before me. I'm no
match for six foot two."

" And pray, sir, by what right have you forced an entrance into
my house ? "

" The same by which I should have clung to your boat, if
I were drowning. The right of self-preservation."

" Self-preservation ? "

" There's an inch of snow on the ground already," I replied,
briefly ; " and it would be deep enough to cover my body before
daybreak."

He strode to the window, pulled aside a heavy black curtain,
and looked out.

" It is true," he said. " You can stay, if you choose, till morning. Jacob, serve the supper."

With this he waved me to a seat, resumed his own, and became
at once absorbed in the studies from which I had disturbed him.

I placed my gun in a corner, drew a chair to the hearth, and
examined my quarters at leisure. Smaller and less incongruous
in its arrangements than the hall, this room contained, nevertheless, much to awaken my curiosity. The floor was carpetless. The
whitewashed walls were in parts scrawled over with strange diagrams, and in others covered with shelves crowded with philosophical instruments, the uses of many of which were unknown
to me. On one side of the fireplace, stood a bookcase filled with
dingy folios ; on the other, a small organ, fantastically decorated
with painted carvings of mediæval saints and devils. Through the
half-opened door of a cupboard at the further end of the room,
I saw a long array of geological specimens, surgical preparations,
crucibles, retorts, and jars of chemicals ; while on the mantelshelf
beside me, amid a number of small objects, stood a model of the
solar system, a small galvanic battery, and a microscope. Every
chair had its burden. Every corner was heaped high with books.
The very floor was littered over with maps, casts, papers, tracings,
and learned lumber of all conceivable kinds.

I stared about me with an amazement increased by every fresh
object upon which my eyes chanced to rest. So strange a room
I had never seen ; yet seemed it stranger still, to find such a room
in a lone farmhouse amid those wild and solitary moors ! Over
and over again, I looked from my host to his surroundings, and
from his surroundings back to my host, asking myself who and
what he could be ? His head was singularly fine ; but it was more

the head of a poet than of a philosopher. Broad in the temples, prominent over the eyes, and clothed with a rough profusion of perfectly white hair, it had all the ideality and much of the ruggedness that characterises the head of Louis von Beethoven. There were the same deep lines about the mouth, and the same stern furrows in the brow. There was the same concentration of expression. While I was yet observing him, the door opened, and Jacob brought in the supper. His master then closed his book, rose, and with more courtesy of manner than he had yet shown, invited me to the table.

A dish of ham and eggs, a loaf of brown bread, and a bottle of admirable sherry, were placed before me.

" I have but the homeliest farmhouse fare to offer you, sir," said my entertainer. " Your appetite, I trust, will make up for the deficiencies of our larder."

I had already fallen upon the viands, and now protested, with the enthusiasm of a starving sportsman, that I had never eaten anything so delicious.

He bowed stiffly, and sat down to his own supper, which consisted, primitively, of a jug of milk and a basin of porridge. We ate in silence, and, when we had done, Jacob removed the tray. I then drew my chair back to the fireside. My host, somewhat to my surprise, did the same, and turning abruptly towards me, said :

" Sir, I have lived here in strict retirement for three-and-twenty years. During that time, I have not seen as many strange faces, and I have not read a single newspaper. You are the first stranger who has crossed my threshold for more than four years. Will you favour me with a few words of information respecting that outer world from which I have parted company so long ? "

" Pray interrogate me," I replied. " I am heartily at your service."

He bent his head in acknowledgment ; leaned forward, with his elbows resting on his knees and his chin supported in the palms of his hands ; stared fixedly into the fire ; and proceeded to question me.

His inquiries related chiefly to scientific matters, with the later progress of which, as applied to the practical purposes of life, he was almost wholly unacquainted. No student of science myself, I replied as well as my slight information permitted ; but the task was far from easy, and I was much relieved when, passing from interrogation to discussion, he began pouring forth his own conclusions upon the facts which I had been attempting to place before him. He talked, and I listened spellbound. He talked till I believe he almost forgot my presence, and only thought aloud. I had never heard anything like it then ; I have never heard anything like it since. Familiar with all systems of all philosophies, subtle in analysis, bold in generalisation, he poured forth his thoughts in an uninterrupted stream, and, still leaning forward in the same moody attitude with his eyes fixed upon the fire, wandered from topic to topic, from speculation to speculation, like an inspired dreamer. From practical science to mental philosophy ; from electricity in the wire to electricity in the nerve ; from Watts to Mesmer, from Mesmer to Reichenbach, from Reichenbach to Swedenborg, Spinoza, Condillac, Descartes, Berkeley, Aristotle, Plato, and the Magi and mystics of the East, were transitions which, however bewildering in their variety and scope, seemed easy and harmonious upon his lips as sequences in music. By-and-by—I forget now by what link of conjecture or illustration—he passed on to that field which lies beyond the boundary line of even conjectural philosophy, and reaches no man knows whither. He spoke of the soul and its aspirations ; of the spirit and its powers ; of second sight ; of prophecy ; of those phenomena which, under the names of ghosts, spectres, and supernatural appearances, have been denied by the sceptics and attested by the credulous, of all ages.

" The world," he said, " grows hourly more and more sceptical of all that lies beyond its own narrow radius ; and our men of science foster the fatal tendency. They condemn as fable all that resists experiment. They reject as false all that cannot be brought to the test of the laboratory or the dissecting-room. Against what superstition have they waged so long and obstinate a war, as against the belief in apparitions ? And yet what superstition has maintained its hold upon the minds of men so long and so firmly ? Show me any fact in physics, in history, in archæology, which is supported by testimony so wide and so various. Attested by all races of men, in all ages, and in all climates, by the soberest sages of antiquity, by the rudest savage of to-day, by the Christian, the Pagan, the Pantheist, the Materialist, this phenomenon is treated as a nursery tale by the philosophers of our century. Circumstantial evidence weighs with them as a feather in the balance. The comparison of causes with effects, however valuable in physical science, is put aside as worthless and unreliable. The evidence of competent witnesses, however conclusive in a court of justice, counts for nothing. He who pauses before he pronounces, is condemned as a trifler. He who believes, is a dreamer or a fool."

He spoke with bitterness, and, having said thus, relapsed for some minutes into silence. Presently he raised his head from his hands, and added, with an altered voice and manner,

" I, sir, paused, investigated, believed, and was not ashamed to state my convictions to the world. I, too, was branded as a visionary, held up to ridicule by my contemporaries, and hooted from that field of science in which I had laboured with honour during all the best years of my life. These things happened just three-and-twenty years ago. Since then, I have lived as you see me living now, and the world has forgotten me, as I have forgotten the world. You have my history."

" It is a very sad one," I murmured, scarcely knowing what to answer.

" It is a very common one," he replied. " I have only suffered for the truth, as many a better and wiser man has suffered before me."

He rose, as if desirous of ending the conversation, and went over to the window.

" It has ceased snowing," he observed, as he dropped the curtain, and came back to the fireside.

" Ceased ! " I exclaimed, starting eagerly to my feet. " Oh, if it were only possible—but no ! it is hopeless. Even if I could find my way across the moor, I could not walk twenty miles to-night."

" Walk twenty miles to-night ! " repeated my host. " What are you thinking of ? "

" Of my wife," I replied, impatiently. " Of my young wife, who does not know that I have lost my way, and who is at this moment breaking her heart with suspense and terror."

" Where is she ? "

" At Dwolding, twenty miles away."

" At Dwolding," he echoed, thoughtfully. " Yes, the distance, it is true, is twenty miles ; but—are you so very anxious to save the next six or eight hours ? "

" So very, very anxious, that I would give ten guineas at this moment for a guide and a horse."

" Your wish can be gratified at a less costly rate," said he, smiling. " The night mail from the north, which changes horses at Dwolding, passes within five miles of this spot, and will be due

at a certain cross-road in about an hour and a quarter. If Jacob
were to go with you across the moor, and put you into the old
coach-road, you could find your way, I suppose, to where it joins
the new one ? "

" Easily—gladly."

He smiled again, rang the bell, gave the old servant his directions, and, taking a bottle of whisky and a wineglass from the cupboard in which he kept his chemicals, said :

" The snow lies deep, and it will be difficult walking to-night
on the moor. A glass of usquebaugh before you start ? "

I would have declined the spirit, but he pressed it on me, and
I drank it. It went down my throat like liquid flame, and almost
took my breath away.

" It is strong," he said ; " but it will help to keep out the cold.
And now you have no moments to spare. Good night ! "

I thanked him for his hospitality, and would have shaken hands,
but that he had turned away before I could finish my sentence.
In another minute I had traversed the hall, Jacob had locked the
outer door behind me, and we were out on the wide white moor.

Although the wind had fallen, it was still bitterly cold. Not a
star glimmered in the black vault overhead. Not a sound, save
the rapid crunching of the snow beneath our feet, disturbed the
heavy stillness of the night. Jacob, not too well pleased with his
mission, shambled on before in sullen silence, his lantern in his
hand, and his shadow at his feet. I followed, with my gun over
my shoulder, as little inclined for conversation as himself. My
thoughts were full of my late host. His voice yet rang in my ears.
His eloquence yet held my imagination captive. I remember to
this day, with surprise, how my over-excited brain retained whole
sentences and parts of sentences, troops of brilliant images, and
fragments of splendid reasoning, in the very words in which he
had uttered them. Musing thus over what I had heard, and striving to recall a lost link here and there, I strode on at the heels of
my guide, absorbed and unobservant. Presently—at the end, as
it seemed to me, of only a few minutes—he came to a sudden halt,
and said :

" Yon's your road. Keep the stone fence to your right hand,
and you can't fail of the way."

" This, then, is the old coach-road ? "

" Ay, 'tis the old coach-road."

" And how far do I go, before I reach the cross-roads ? "

" Nigh upon three mile."

I pulled out my purse, and he became more communicative.

" The road's a fair road enough," said he, " for foot passengers ; but 'twas over steep and narrow for the northern traffic. You'll mind where the parapet's broken away, close again the sign-post. It's never been mended since the accident."

" What accident ? "

" Eh, the night mail pitched right over into the valley below —a gude fifty feet an' more—just at the worst bit o' road in the whole county."

" Horrible ! Were many lives lost ? "

" All. Four were found dead, and t'other two died next morning."

" How long is it since this happened ? "

" Just nine year."

" Near the sign-post, you say ? I will bear it in mind. Good night."

" Gude night, sir, and thankee." Jacob pocketed his half-crown, made a faint pretence of touching his hat, and trudged back by the way he had come.

I watched the light of his lantern till it quite disappeared, and then turned to pursue my way alone. This was no longer matter of the slightest difficulty, for, despite the dead darkness overhead, the line of stone fence showed distinctly enough against the pale gleam of the snow. How silent it seemed now, with only my footsteps to listen to ; how silent and how solitary ! A strange disagreeable sense of loneliness stole over me. I walked faster. I hummed a fragment of a tune. I cast up enormous sums in my head, and accumulated them at compound interest. I did my best, in short, to forget the startling speculations to which I had but just been listening, and, to some extent, I succeeded.

Meanwhile the night air seemed to become colder and colder, and though I walked fast I found it impossible to keep myself warm. My feet were like ice. I lost sensation in my hands, and grasped my gun mechanically. I even breathed with difficulty, as though, instead of traversing a quiet north country highway, I were scaling the uppermost heights of some gigantic Alp. This last symptom became presently so distressing, that I was forced to stop for a few minutes, and lean against the stone fence. As I did so, I chanced to look back up the road, and there, to my infinite relief, I saw a distant point of light, like the gleam of an approaching lantern. I at first concluded that Jacob had retraced his steps and followed me ; but even as the conjecture presented itself, a second light flashed into sight—a light evidently parallel with the first, and approaching at the same rate of motion. It needed no second thought to show me that these must be the carriage-lamps of some private vehicle, though it seemed strange that any private vehicle should take a road professedly disused and dangerous.

There could be no doubt, however, of the fact, for the lamps grew larger and brighter every moment, and I even fancied I could already see the dark outline of the carriage between them. It was coming up very fast, and quite noiselessly, the snow being nearly a foot deep under the wheels.

And now the body of the vehicle became distinctly visible behind the lamps. It looked strangely lofty. A sudden suspicion flashed upon me. Was it possible that I had passed the cross-roads in the dark without observing the sign-post, and could this be the very coach which I had come to meet ?

No need to ask myself that question a second time, for here it came round the bend of the road, guard and driver, one outside passenger, and four steaming greys, all wrapped in a soft haze of light, through which the lamps blazed out, like a pair of fiery meteors.

I jumped forward, waved my hat, and shouted. The mail came down at full speed, and passed me. For a moment I feared that I had not been seen or heard, but it was only for a moment. The coachman pulled up ; the guard, muffled to the eyes in capes and comforters, and apparently sound asleep in the rumble, neither answered my hail nor made the slightest effort to dismount ; the outside passenger did not even turn his head. I opened the door for myself, and looked in. There were but three travellers inside, so I stepped in, shut the door, slipped into the vacant corner, and congratulated myself on my good fortune.

The atmosphere of the coach seemed, if possible, colder than that of the outer air, and was pervaded by a singularly damp and disagreeable smell. I looked round at my fellow-passengers. They were all three, men, and all silent. They did not seem to be asleep, but each leaned back in his corner of the vehicle, as if absorbed in his own reflections. I attempted to open a conversation.

" How intensely cold it is to-night," I said, addressing my opposite neighbour.

He lifted his head, looked at me, but made no reply.

" The winter," I added, " seems to have begun in earnest."

Although the corner in which he sat was so dim that I could distinguish none of his features very clearly, I saw that his eyes were still turned full upon me. And yet he answered never a word.

At any other time I should have felt, and perhaps expressed, some annoyance, but at the moment I felt too ill to do either. The icy coldness of the night air had struck a chill to my very marrow, and the strange smell inside the coach was affecting me with an intolerable nausea. I shivered from head to foot, and, turning to my left-hand neighbour, asked if he had any objection to an open window ?

He neither spoke nor stirred.

I repeated the question somewhat more loudly, but with the same result. Then I lost patience, and let the sash down. As I did so, the leather strap broke in my hand, and I observed that the glass was covered with a thick coat of mildew, the accumulation, apparently, of years. My attention being thus drawn to the condition of the coach, I examined it more narrowly, and saw by the uncertain light of the outer lamps that it was in the last stage of dilapidation. Every part of it was not only out of repair, but in a condition of decay. The sashes splintered at a touch. The leather fittings were crusted over with mould, and literally rotting from the woodwork. The floor was almost breaking away beneath my feet. The whole machine, in short, was foul with damp, and had evidently been dragged from some outhouse in which it had been mouldering away for years, to do another day or two of duty on the road.

I turned to the third passenger, whom I had not yet addressed, and hazarded one more remark.

" This coach," I said, " is in a deplorable condition. The regular mail, I suppose, is under repair ? "

He moved his head slowly, and looked me in the face, without speaking a word. I shall never forget that look while I live. I turned cold at heart under it. I turn cold at heart even now when I recall it. His eyes glowed with a fiery unnatural lustre. His face was livid as the face of a corpse. His bloodless lips were drawn back as if in the agony of death, and showed the gleaming teeth between.

The words that I was about to utter died upon my lips, and a strange horror—a dreadful horror—came upon me. My sight had by this time become used to the gloom of the coach, and I could see with tolerable distinctness. I turned to my opposite neighbour. He, too, was looking at me, with the same startling pallor in his face, and the same stony glitter in his eyes. I passed my hand across my brow. I turned to the passenger on the seat beside my own, and saw—oh Heaven ! how shall I describe what I saw ? I saw that he was no living man—that none of them were living men, like myself ! A pale phosphorescent light—the light of putrefaction—played upon their awful faces ; upon their hair, dank with the dews of the grave ; upon their clothes, earth-stained and dropping to pieces ; upon their hands, which were as the hands of corpses long buried. Only their eyes, their terrible eyes, were living ; and those eyes were all turned menacingly upon me !

A shriek of terror, a wild unintelligible cry for help and mercy, burst from my lips as I flung myself against the door, and strove in vain to open it.

In that single instant, brief and vivid as a landscape beheld in the flash of summer lightning, I saw the moon shining down through a rift of stormy cloud—the ghastly sign-post rearing its warning finger by the wayside—the broken parapet—the plunging horses—the black gulf below. Then, the coach reeled like a ship at sea. Then, came a mighty crash—a sense of crushing pain—and then, darkness.

It seemed as if years had gone by when I awoke one morning from a deep sleep, and found my wife watching by my bedside. I will pass over the scene that ensued, and give you, in half a dozen words, the tale she told me with tears of thanksgiving. I had fallen over a precipice, close against the junction of the old coach-road and the new, and had only been saved from certain death by lighting upon a deep snowdrift that had accumulated at the foot of the rock beneath. In this snowdrift I was discovered at daybreak, by a couple of shepherds, who carried me to the nearest shelter, and brought a surgeon to my aid. The surgeon found me in a state of raving delirium, with a broken arm and a compound fracture of the skull. The letters in my pocket-book showed my name and address ; my wife was summoned to nurse me ; and, thanks to youth and a fine constitution, I came out of danger at last. The place of my fall, I need scarcely say, was precisely that at which a frightful accident had happened to the north mail nine years before.

I never told my wife the fearful events which I have just related to you. I told the surgeon who attended me ; but he treated the whole adventure as a mere dream born of the fever in my brain.

We discussed the question over and over again, until we found that we could discuss it with temper no longer, and then we dropped it. Others may form what conclusions they please—I *know* that twenty years ago I was the fourth inside passenger in that Phantom Coach.

————

Amyas Northcote

BRICKETT BOTTOM

from IN GHOSTLY COMPANY

John Lane, 1922

The Reverend Arthur Maydew was the hard-working incumbent of a large parish in one of our manufacturing towns. He was also a student and a man of no strong physique, so that when an opportunity was presented to him to take an annual holiday by exchanging parsonages with an elderly clergyman, Mr. Roberts, the Squarson of the Parish of Overbury, and an acquaintance of his own, he was glad to avail himself of it.

Overbury is a small and very remote village in one of our most lovely and rural counties, and Mr. Roberts had long held the living of it.

Without further delay we can transport Mr. Maydew and his family, which consisted only of two daughters, to their temporary home. The two young ladies, Alice and Maggie, the heroines of this narrative, were at that time aged twenty-six and twenty-four years respectively. Both of them were attractive girls, fond of such society as they could find in their own parish and, the former especially, always pleased to extend the circle of their acquaintance. Although the elder in years, Alice in many ways yielded place to her sister, who was the more energetic and practical and upon whose shoulders the bulk of the family cares and responsibilities rested. Alice was inclined to be absent-minded and emotional and to devote more of her thoughts and time to speculations of an abstract nature than her sister.

Both of the girls, however, rejoiced at the prospect of a period of quiet and rest in a pleasant country neighbourhood, and both were

gratified at knowing that their father would find in Mr. Roberts'
library much that would entertain his mind, and in Mr. Roberts'
garden an opportunity to indulge freely in his favourite game of
croquet. They would have, no doubt, preferred some cheerful
neighbours, but Mr. Roberts was positive in his assurances that
there was no one in the neighbourhood whose acquaintance would
be of interest to them.

The first few weeks of their new life passed pleasantly for the
Maydew family. Mr. Maydew quickly gained renewed vigour in
his quiet and congenial surroundings, and in the delightful air,
while his daughters spent much of their time in long walks about
the country and in exploring its beauties.

One evening late in August the two girls were returning from
a long walk along one of their favourite paths, which led along the
side of the Downs. On their right, as they walked, the ground fell
away sharply to a narrow glen, named Brickett Bottom, about
three-quarters of a mile in length, along the bottom of which ran
a little-used country road leading to a farm, known as Blaise's
Farm, and then onward and upward to lose itself as a sheep track
on the higher Downs. On their side of the slope some scattered
trees and bushes grew, but beyond the lane and running up over
the farther slope of the glen was a thick wood, which extended
away to Carew Court, the seat of a neighbouring magnate, Lord
Carew. On their left the open Down rose above them and beyond
its crest lay Overbury.

The girls were walking hastily, as they were later than they had
intended to be and were anxious to reach home. At a certain point
at which they had now arrived the path forked, the right hand
branch leading down into Brickett Bottom and the left hand turning up over the Down to Overbury.

Just as they were about to turn into the left hand path Alice
suddenly stopped and pointing downwards exclaimed :

" How very curious, Maggie ! Look, there is a house down there
in the Bottom, which we have, or at least I have, never noticed
before, often as we have walked up the Bottom."

Maggie followed with her eyes her sister's pointing finger.

" I don't see any house," she said.

" Why, Maggie," said her sister, " can't you see it ! A quaint-
looking, old-fashioned red brick house, there just where the road
bends to the right. It seems to be standing in a nice, well-kept
garden too."

Maggie looked again, but the light was beginning to fade in the glen and she was short-sighted to boot.

" I certainly don't see anything," she said. " but then I am so blind and the light is getting bad ; yes, perhaps I do see a house," she added, straining her eyes.

" Well, it is there," replied her sister, " and to-morrow we will come and explore it."

Maggie agreed readily enough, and the sisters went home, still speculating on how they had happened not to notice the house before and resolving firmly on an expedition thither the next day. However, the expedition did not come off as planned, for that evening Maggie slipped on the stairs and fell, spraining her ankle in such a fashion as to preclude walking for some time.

Notwithstanding the accident to her sister, Alice remained possessed by the idea of making further investigations into the house she had looked down upon from the hill the evening before ; and the next day, having seen Maggie carefully settled for the afternoon, she started off for Brickett Bottom. She returned in triumph and much intrigued over her discoveries, which she eagerly narrated to her sister.

Yes. There was a nice, old-fashioned red brick house, not very large and set in a charming, old-world garden in the Bottom. It stood on a tongue of land jutting out from the woods, just at the point where the lane, after a fairly straight course from its junction with the main road half a mile away, turned sharply to the right in the direction of Blaise's Farm. More than that, Alice had seen the people of the house, whom she described as an old gentleman and a lady, presumably his wife. She had not clearly made out the gentleman, who was sitting in the porch, but the old lady, who had been in the garden busy with her flowers, had looked up and smiled pleasantly at her as she passed. She was sure, she said, that they were nice people and that it would be pleasant to make their acquaintance.

Maggie was not quite satisfied with Alice's story. She was of a more prudent and retiring nature than her sister ; she had an uneasy feeling that, if the old couple had been desirable or attractive neighbours, Mr. Roberts would have mentioned them, and knowing Alice's nature she said what she could to discourage her vague idea of endeavouring to make acquaintance with the owners of the red brick house.

On the following morning, when Alice came to her sister's room to inquire how she did, Maggie noticed that she looked pale and rather absent-minded, and, after a few commonplace remarks had passed, she asked :

"What is the matter, Alice? You don't look yourself this morning."

Her sister gave a slightly embarrassed laugh.

"Oh, I am all right," she replied, "only I did not sleep very well. I kept on dreaming about the house. It was such an odd dream too : the house seemed to be home, and yet to be different."

"What, that house in Brickett Bottom?" said Maggie. "Why, what is the matter with you, you seem to be quite crazy about the place?"

"Well, it is curious, isn't it, Maggie, that we should have only just discovered it, and that it looks to be lived in by nice people? I wish we could get to know them."

Maggie did not care to resume the argument of the night before and the subject dropped, nor did Alice again refer to the house or its inhabitants for some little time. In fact, for some days the weather was wet and Alice was forced to abandon her walks, but when the weather once more became fine she resumed them, and Maggie suspected that Brickett Bottom formed one of her sister's favourite expeditions. Maggie became anxious over her sister, who seemed to grow daily more absent-minded and silent, but she refused to be drawn into any confidential talk, and Maggie was nonplussed.

One day, however, Alice returned from her afternoon walk in an unusually excited state of mind, of which Maggie sought an explanation. It came with a rush. Alice said that, that afternoon, as she approached the house in Brickett Bottom, the old lady, who as usual was busy in her garden, had walked down to the gate as she passed and had wished her good day.

Alice had replied and, pausing, a short conversation had followed. Alice could not remember the exact tenor of it, but, after she had paid a compliment to the old lady's flowers, the latter had rather diffidently asked her to enter the garden for a closer view. Alice had hesitated, and the old lady had said : " Don't be afraid of me, my dear, I like to see young ladies about me and my husband finds their society quite necessary to him." After a pause she went on: " Of course nobody has told you about us. My husband is Colonel Paxton, late of the Indian Army, and we have been here for many, many years. It's rather lonely, for so few people ever see us. Do come in and meet the Colonel."

" I hope you didn't go in," said Maggie rather sharply.

" Why not ? " replied Alice.

" Well, I don't like Mrs. Paxton asking you in that way," answered Maggie.

" I don't see what harm there was in the invitation," said Alice. " I didn't go in because it was getting late and I was anxious to get home ; but——"

" But what ? " asked Maggie.

Alice shrugged her shoulders.

" Well," she said, " I have accepted Mrs. Paxton's invitation to pay her a little visit to-morrow." And she gazed defiantly at Maggie.

Maggie became distinctly uneasy on hearing of this resolution. She did not like the idea of her impulsive sister visiting people on such slight acquaintance, especially as they had never heard them mentioned before. She endeavoured by all means, short of appealing to Mr. Maydew, to dissuade her sister from going, at any rate until there had been time to make some inquiries as to the Paxtons. Alice, however, was obdurate.

What harm could happen to her ? she asked. Mrs. Paxton was a charming old lady. She was going early in the afternoon for a short visit. She would be back for tea and croquet with her father and, anyway, now that Maggie was laid up, long solitary walks were unendurable and she was not going to let slip the chance of following up what promised to be a pleasant acquaintance.

Maggie could do nothing more. Her ankle was better and she was able to get down to the garden and sit in a long chair near her father, but walking was still quite out of the question, and it was with some misgivings that on the following day she watched Alice depart gaily for her visit, promising to be back by half-past four at the very latest.

The afternoon passed quietly till nearly five, when Mr. Maydew, looking up from his book, noticed Maggie's uneasy expression and asked :

" Where is Alice ? "

" Out for a walk," replied Maggie ; and then after a short pause she went on : " And she has also gone to pay a call on some neighbours whom she has recently discovered."

" Neighbours," ejaculated Mr. Maydew, " what neighbours ? Mr. Roberts never spoke of any neighbours to me."

" Well, I don't know much about them," answered Maggie. " Only Alice and I were out walking the day of my accident and saw or at least she saw, for I am so blind I could not quite make it out, a house in Brickett Bottom. The next day she went to look at it closer, and yesterday she told me that she had made the acquaintance of the people living in it. She says that they are a retired Indian officer and his wife, a Colonel and Mrs. Paxton, and Alice describes Mrs. Paxton as a charming old lady, who pressed her to come and see them. So she has gone this afternoon, but she promised me she would be back long before this."

Mr. Maydew was silent for a moment and then said :

" I am not well pleased about this. Alice should not be so impulsive and scrape acquaintance with absolutely unknown people. Had there been nice neighbours in Brickett Bottom, I am certain Mr. Roberts would have told us."

The conversation dropped ; but both father and daughter were disturbed and uneasy and, tea having been finished and the clock striking half-past five, Mr. Maydew asked Maggie :

" When did you say Alice would be back ? "

" Before half-past four at the latest, father."

" Well, what can she be doing ? What can have delayed her ? You say you did not see the house," he went on.

" No," said Maggie, " I cannot say I did. It was getting dark and you know how short-sighted I am."

" But surely you must have seen it at some other time," said her father.

" That is the strangest part of the whole affair," answered Maggie. " We have often walked up the Bottom, but I never noticed the house, nor had Alice till that evening. I wonder," she went on after a short pause, " if it would not be well to ask Smith to harness the pony and drive over to bring her back. I am not happy about her—I am afraid——"

" Afraid of what ? " said her father in the irritated voice of a man who is growing frightened. " What can have gone wrong in this quiet place ? Still, I'll send Smith over for her."

So saying he rose from his chair and sought out Smith, the rather dull-witted gardener-groom attached to Mr. Roberts' service.

" Smith," he said, " I want you to harness the pony at once and go over to Colonel Paxton's in Brickett Bottom and bring Miss Maydew home."

The man stared at him.

" Go where, sir ? " he said.

Mr. Maydew repeated the order and the man, still staring stupidly, answered :

" I never heard of Colonel Paxton, sir. I don't know what house you mean."

Mr. Maydew was now growing really anxious.

" Well, harness the pony at once," he said ; and going back to Maggie he told her of what he called Smith's stupidity, and asked her if she felt that her ankle would be strong enough to permit her to go with him and Smith to the Bottom to point out the house.

Maggie agreed readily and in a few minutes the party started off. Brickett Bottom, although not more than three-quarters of a mile away over the Downs, was at least three miles by road ; and as it was nearly six o'clock before Mr. Maydew left the Vicarage, and the pony was old and slow, it was getting late before the entrance to Brickett Bottom was reached. Turning into the lane the cart proceeded slowly up the Bottom, Mr. Maydew and Maggie looking anxiously from side to side, whilst Smith drove stolidly on looking neither to the right nor left.

" Where is the house ? " said Mr. Maydew presently.

" At the bend of the road," answered Maggie, her heart sickening as she looked out through the failing light to see the trees stretching their ranks in unbroken formation along it. The cart reached the bend. " It should be here," whispered Maggie.

They pulled up. Just in front of them the road bent to the right round a tongue of land, which, unlike the rest of the right hand side of the road, was free from trees and was covered only by rough grass and stray bushes. A closer inspection disclosed evident signs of terraces having once been formed on it, but of a house there was no trace.

" Is this the place ? " said Mr. Maydew in a low voice.

Maggie nodded.

" But there is no house here," said her father. " What does it all mean ? Are you sure of yourself, Maggie ? Where is Alice ? "

Before Maggie could answer a voice was heard calling " Father ! Maggie ! " The sound of the voice was thin and high and, paradoxically, it sounded both very near and yet as if it came from some infinite distance. The cry was thrice repeated and then silence fell. Mr. Maydew and Maggie stared at each other.

" That was Alice's voice," said Mr. Maydew huskily, " she is near and in trouble, and is calling us. Which way did you think it came from, Smith ? " he added, turning to the gardener.

" I didn't hear anybody calling," said the man.

" Nonsense ! " answered Mr. Maydew.

And then he and Maggie both began to call " Alice. Alice. Where are you ? " There was no reply and Mr. Maydew sprang from the cart, at the same time bidding Smith to hand the reins to Maggie and come and search for the missing girl. Smith obeyed him and both men, scrambling up the turfy bit of ground, began to search and call through the neighbouring wood. They heard and saw nothing, however, and after an agonised search Mr. Maydew ran down to the cart and begged Maggie to drive on to Blaise's Farm for help leaving himself and Smith to continue the search. Maggie followed her father's instructions and was fortunate enough to find Mr. Rumbold, the farmer, his two sons and a couple of labourers just returning from the harvest field. She explained what had happened, and the farmer and his men promptly volunteered to form a search party, though Maggie, in spite of her anxiety, noticed a queer expression on Mr. Rumbold's face as she told him her tale.

The party, provided with lanterns, now went down the Bottom, joined Mr. Maydew and Smith and made an exhaustive but absolutely fruitless search of the woods near the bend of the road. No trace of the missing girl was to be found, and after a long and anxious time the search was abandoned, one of the young Rumbolds volunteering to ride into the nearest town and notify the police.

Maggie, though with little hope in her own heart, endeavoured to cheer her father on their homeward way with the idea that Alice might have returned to Overbury over the Downs whilst they were going by road to the Bottom, and that she had seen them and called to them in jest when they were opposite the tongue of land.

However, when they reached home there was no Alice and, though the next day the search was resumed and full inquiries were instituted by the police, all was to no purpose. No trace of Alice was ever found, the last human being that saw her having been an old woman, who had met her going down the path into the Bottom on the afternoon of her disappearance, and who described her as smiling but looking " queerlike."

This is the end of the story, but the following may throw some light upon it.

The history of Alice's mysterious disappearance became widely known through the medium of the Press and Mr. Roberts, distressed beyond measure at what had taken place, returned in all haste to Overbury to offer what comfort and help he could give to his afflicted friend and tenant. He called upon the Maydews and, having heard their tale, sat for a short time in silence. Then he said :

" Have you ever heard any local gossip concerning this Colonel and Mrs. Paxton ? "

" No," replied Mr. Maydew, " I never heard their names until the day of my poor daughter's fatal visit."

" Well," said Mr. Roberts, " I will tell you all I can about them, which is not very much, I fear." He paused and then went on : " I am now nearly seventy-five years old, and for nearly seventy years no house has stood in Brickett Bottom. But when I was a child of about five there was an old-fashioned, red brick house standing in a garden at the bend of the road, such as you have described. It was owned and lived in by a retired Indian soldier and his wife, a Colonel and Mrs. Paxton. At the time I speak of, certain events having taken place at the house and the old couple having died, it was sold by their heirs to Lord Carew, who shortly after pulled it down on the ground that it interfered with his shooting. Colonel and Mrs. Paxton were well known to my father, who was the clergyman here before me, and to the neighbourhood in general. They lived quietly and were not unpopular, but the Colonel was supposed to possess a violent and vindictive temper. Their family consisted only of themselves, their daughter and a couple of servants, the Colonel's old Army servant and his Eurasian wife. Well, I cannot tell you details of what happened, I was only a child ; my father never liked gossip and in later years, when he talked to me on the subject, he always avoided any appearance of exaggeration or sensationalism. However, it is known that Miss Paxton fell in love with and became engaged to a young man to whom her parents took a strong dislike. They used every possible means to break off the match, and many rumours were set on foot as to their conduct—undue influence, even cruelty were charged against them. I do not know the truth, all I can say

is that Miss Paxton died and a very bitter feeling against her
parents sprang up. My father, however, continued to call, but was
rarely admitted. In fact, he never saw Colonel Paxton after his
daughter's death and only saw Mrs. Paxton once or twice. He
described her as an utterly broken woman, and was not surprised at her following her daughter to the grave in about three
months' time. Colonel Paxton became, if possible, more of a recluse than ever after his wife's death and himself died not more
than a month after her under circumstances which pointed to
suicide. Again a crop of rumours sprang up, but there was no one
in particular to take action, the doctor certified Death from
Natural Causes, and Colonel Paxton, like his wife and daughter,
was buried in this churchyard. The property passed to a distant
relative, who came down to it for one night shortly afterwards ; he
never came again, having apparently conceived a violent dislike
to the place, but arranged to pension off the servants and then
sold the house to Lord Carew, who was glad to purchase this
little island in the middle of his property. He pulled it down soon
after he had bought it, and the garden was left to relapse into a
wilderness."

Mr. Roberts paused.

" Those are all the facts," he added.

" But there is something more," said Maggie.

Mr. Roberts hesitated for a while.

" You have a right to know all," he said almost to himself ; then
louder he continued : " What I am now going to tell you is really
rumour, vague and uncertain ; I cannot fathom its truth or its
meaning. About five years after the house had been pulled down
a young maidservant at Carew Court was out walking one afternoon. She was a stranger to the village and a new-comer to the
Court. On returning home to tea she told her fellow-servants that
as she walked down Brickett Bottom, which place she described
clearly, she passed a red brick house at the bend of the road and
that a kind-faced old lady had asked her to step in for a while.
She did not go in, not because she had any suspicions of there
being anything uncanny, but simply because she feared to be late
for tea.

" I do not think she ever visited the Bottom again and she had
no other similar experience, so far as I am aware.

" Two or three years later, shortly after my father's death, a
travelling tinker with his wife and daughter camped for the night

at the foot of the Bottom. The girl strolled away up the glen to gather blackberries and was never seen or heard of again. She was searched for in vain—of course, one does not know the truth —and she may have run away voluntarily from her parents, although there was no known cause for her doing so.

"That," concluded Mr. Roberts, " is all I can tell you of either facts or rumours ; all that I can now do is to pray for you and for her."

Miss Braddon

THE COLD EMBRACE
from RALPH THE BAILIFF
Ward & Lock, 1862

He was an artist—such things as happened to him happen sometimes to artists.

He was a German—such things as happened to him happen sometimes to Germans.

He was young, handsome, studious, enthusiastic, metaphysical, reckless, unbelieving, heartless.

And being young, handsome, and eloquent, he was beloved.

He was an orphan, under the guardianship of his dead father's brother, his uncle Wilhelm, in whose house he had been brought up from a little child ; and she who loved him was his cousin—his cousin Gertrude, whom he swore he loved in return.

Did he love her ? Yes, when he first swore it. It soon wore out, this passionate love ; how threadbare and wretched a sentiment it became at last in the selfish heart of the student ! But in its first golden dawn, when he was only nineteen, and had just returned from his apprenticeship to a great painter at Antwerp, and they wandered together in the most romantic outskirts of the city at rosy sunset, by holy moonlight, or bright and joyous morning, how beautiful a dream !

They keep it a secret from Wilhelm, as he has the father's ambition of a wealthy suitor for his only child—a cold and dreary vision beside the lover's dream.

So they are betrothed ; and standing side by side when the dying sun and the pale rising moon divide the heavens, he puts the betrothal ring upon her finger, the white and taper finger whose slender shape he knows so well. This ring is a peculiar one, a massive golden serpent, its tail in its mouth, the symbol of eternity ; it had been his mother's, and he would know it amongst a thousand. If he were to become blind to-morrow, he could select it from amongst a thousand by the touch alone.

He places it on her finger, and they swear to be true to each other for ever and ever—through trouble and danger—in sorrow and change—in wealth or poverty. Her father must needs be won to consent to their union by and by, for they were now betrothed, and death alone could part them.

But the young student, the scoffer at revelation, yet the enthusiastic adorer of the mystical asks :

" Can death part us ? I would return to you from the grave, Gertrude. My soul would come back to be near my love. And you—you, if you died before me—the cold earth would not hold you from me ; if you loved me, you would return, and again these fair arms would be clasped round my neck as they are now."

But she told him, with a holier light in her deep-blue eyes than had ever shone in his—she told him that the dead who die at peace with God are happy in heaven, and cannot return to the troubled earth ; and that it is only the suicide—the lost wretch on whom sorrowful angels shut the door of Paradise—whose unholy spirit haunts the footsteps of the living.

The first year of their betrothal is passed, and she is alone, for he has gone to Italy, on a commission for some rich man, to copy Raphaels, Titians, Guidos, in a gallery at Florence. He has gone to win fame, perhaps ; but it is not the less bitter—he is gone !

Of course her father misses his young nephew, who has been as a son to him ; and he thinks his daughter's sadness no more than a cousin should feel for a cousin's absence.

In the meantime, the weeks and months pass. The lover writes— often at first, then seldom—at last, not at all.

How many excuses she invents for him ! How many times she goes to the distant little post-office, to which he is to address his letters ! How many times she hopes, only to be disappointed ! How many times she despairs only to hope again !

But real despair comes at last, and will not be put off any more. The rich suitor appears on the scene, and her father is determined.

She is to marry at once. The wedding-day is fixed—the fifteenth of June.

The date seems burnt into her brain.

The date, written in fire, dances for ever before her eyes.

The date, shrieked by the Furies, sounds continually in her ears.

But there is time yet—it is the middle of May—there is time for a letter to reach him at Florence ; there is time for him to come to Brunswick, to take her away and marry her, in spite of her father—in spite of the whole world.

But the days and weeks fly by, and he does not write—he does not come. This is indeed despair which usurps her heart, and will not be put away.

It is the fourteenth of June. For the last time she goes to the little post-office ; for the last time she asks the old question, and they give her for the last time the dreary answer, " No ; no letter."

For the last time—for to-morrow is the day appointed for her bridal. Her father will hear no entreaties ; her rich suitor will not listen to her prayers. They will not be put off a day—an hour ; to-night alone is hers—this night, which she may employ as she will.

She takes another path than that which leads home ; she hurries through some by-streets of the city, out on to a lonely bridge, where he and she had stood so often in the sunset, watching the rose-coloured light glow, fade, and die upon the river.

.   .   .   .

He returns from Florence. He had received her letter. That letter, blotted with tears, entreating, despairing—he had received it, but he loved her no longer. A young Florentine, who has sat to him for a model, had bewitched his fancy—that fancy which with him stood in place of a heart—and Gertrude had been half-forgotten. If she had a richer suitor, good ; let her marry him ; better for her, better far for himself. He had no wish to fetter himself with a wife. Had he not his art always ?—his eternal bride, his unchanging mistress.

Thus he thought it wiser to delay his journey to Brunswick, so that he should arrive when the wedding was over—arrive in time to salute the bride.

And the vows—the mystical fancies—the belief in his return, even after death, to the embrace of his beloved ? O, gone out of his life ; melted away for ever, those foolish dreams of his boyhood.

So on the fifteenth of June he enters Brunswick, by that very bridge on which she stood, the stars looking down on her, the night before. He strolls across the bridge and down by the water's edge, a great rough dog at his heels, and the smoke from his short meerschaum-pipe curling in blue wreaths fantastically in the pure morning air. He has his sketch-book under his arm, and attracted now and then by some object that catches his artist's eye, stops to draw : a few weeds and pebbles on the river's brink—a crag on the opposite shore—a group of pollard willows in the distance. When he has done, he admires his drawing, shuts his sketch-book, empties the ashes from his pipe, refills from this tobacco-pouch, sings the refrain of a gay drinking-song, calls to his dog, smokes again, and walks on. Suddenly he opens his sketch-book again ; this time that which attracts him is a group of figures : but what is it ?

It is not a funeral, for there are no mourners.

It is not a funeral, but it is a corpse lying on a rude bier, covered with an old sail, carried between two bearers.

It is not a funeral, for the bearers are fishermen—fishermen in their everyday garb.

About a hundred yards from him they rest their burden on a bank—one stands at the head of the bier, the other throws himself down at the foot of it.

And thus they form a perfect group ; he walks back two or three paces, selects his point of sight, and begins to sketch a hurried outline. He has finished it before they move ; he hears their voices, though he cannot hear their words, and wonders what they can be talking of. Presently he walks on and joins them.

" You have a corpse there, my friends ? " he says.

" Yes ; a corpse washed ashore an hour ago."

" Drowned ? "

" Yes, drowned. A young girl, very handsome."

" Suicides are always handsome," says the painter ; and then he stands for a little while idly smoking and meditating, looking at the sharp outline of the corpse and the stiff folds of the rough canvas covering.

Life is such a golden holiday for him—young, ambitious, clever—that it seems as though sorrow and death could have no part in his destiny.

At last he says that, as this poor suicide is so handsome, he should like to make a sketch of her.

He gives the fishermen some money, and they offer to remove the sailcloth that covers her features.

No ; he will do it himself. He lifts the rough, coarse, wet canvas from her face. What face ?

The face that shone on the dreams of his foolish boyhood ; the face which once was the light of his uncle's home. His cousin Gertrude—his betrothed !

He sees, as in one glance, while he draws one breath, the rigid features—the marble arms—the hands crossed on the cold bosom ; and, on the third finger of the left hand, the ring which had been his mother's—the golden serpent ; the ring which, if he were to become blind, he could select from a thousand others by the touch alone.

But he is a genius and a metaphysician—grief, true grief, is not for such as he. His first thought is flight—flight anywhere out of that accursed city—anywhere far from the brink of that hideous river—anywhere away from memory, away from remorse—anywhere to forget.

.   .   .   .

He is miles on the road that leads away from Brunswick before he knows that he has walked a step.

It is only when his dog lies down panting at his feet that he feels how exhausted he is himself, and sits down upon a bank to rest. How the landscape spins round and round before his dazzled eyes, while his morning's sketch of the two fishermen and the canvas-covered bier glares redly at him out of the twilight !

At last, after sitting a long time by the roadside, idly playing with his dog, idly smoking, idly lounging, looking as any idle, light-hearted travelling student might look, yet all the while acting over that morning's scene in his burning brain a hundred times a minute ; at last he grows a little more composed, and tries presently to think of himself as he is, apart from his cousin's suicide. Apart from that, he was no worse off than he was yesterday. His genius was not gone ; the money he had earned at Florence still lined his pocket-book ; he was his own master, free to go whither he would.

And while he sits on the roadside, trying to separate himself from the scene of that morning—trying to put away the image of the corpse covered with the damp canvas sail—trying to think of what he should do next, where he should go, to be farthest away from Brunswick and remorse, the old diligence comes rumbling and jingling along. He remembers it ; it goes from Brunswick to Aix-la-Chapelle.

He whistles to his dog, shouts to the postillion to stop, and springs into the *coupé*.

During the whole evening, through the long night, though he does not once close his eyes, he never speaks a word ; but when morning dawns, and the other passengers awake and begin to talk to each other, he joins in the conversation. He tells them that he is an artist, that he is going to Cologne and to Antwerp to copy the Rubenses, and the great picture by Quentin Matsys, in the museum. He remembered afterwards that he talked and laughed boisterously, and that when he was talking and laughing loudest, a passenger, older and graver than the rest, opened the window near him, and told him to put his head out. He remembered the fresh air blowing in his face, the singing of the birds in his ears, and the flat fields and roadside reeling before his eyes. He remembered this, and then falling in a lifeless heap on the floor of the diligence.

It is a fever that keeps him for six long weeks laid on a bed at a hotel in Aix-la-Chapelle.

He gets well, and, accompanied by his dog, starts on foot for Cologne. By this time he is his former self once more. Again the blue smoke from his short meerschaum curls upwards in the morning air—again he sings some old university drinking-song—again stops here and there, meditating and sketching.

He is happy, and has forgotten his cousin—and so on to Cologne.

It is by the great cathedral he is standing, with his dog at his side. It is night, the bells have just chimed the hour, and the clocks are striking eleven ; the moonlight shines full upon the magnificent pile, over which the artist's eye wanders, absorbed in the beauty of form.

He is not thinking of his drowned cousin, for he has forgotten her and is happy.

Suddenly someone, something from behind him, puts two cold arms round his neck, and clasps its hands on his breast.

And yet there is no one behind him, for on the flags bathed in the broad moonlight there are only two shadows, his own and his dog's. He turns quickly round—there is no one—nothing to be seen in the broad square but himself and his dog ; and though he feels, he cannot see the cold arms clasped round his neck.

It is not ghostly, this embrace, for it is palpable to the touch—it cannot be real, for it is invisible.

He tries to throw off the cold caress. He clasps the hands in his own to tear them asunder, and to cast them off his neck. He can feel the long delicate fingers cold and wet beneath his touch, and on the third finger of the left hand he can feel the ring which was his mother's—the golden serpent—the ring which he has always said he would know among a thousand by the touch alone. He knows it now !

His dead cousin's cold arms are round his neck—his dead cousin's wet hands are clasped upon his breast. He asks himself if he is mad. " Up, Leo ! " he shouts. " Up, up, boy ! " and the Newfoundland leaps to his shoulders—the dog's paws are on the dead hands, and the animal utters a terrific howl, and springs away from his master.

The student stands in the moonlight, the dead arms around his neck, and the dog at a little distance moaning piteously.

Presently a watchman, alarmed by the howling of the dog, comes into the square to see what is wrong.

In a breath the cold arms are gone.

He takes the watchman home to the hotel with him and gives him money ; in his gratitude he could have given that man half his little fortune.

Will it ever come to him again, this embrace of the dead ?

He tries never to be alone ; he makes a hundred acquaintances, and shares the chamber of another student. He starts up if he is left by himself in the public room at the inn where he is staying, and runs into the street. People notice his strange actions, and begin to think that he is mad.

But, in spite of all, he is alone once more ; for one night the public room being empty for a moment, when on some idle pretence he strolls into the street, the street is empty too, and for the second time he feels the cold arms round his neck, and for the second time, when he calls his dog, the animal slinks away from him with a piteous howl.

After this he leaves Cologne, still travelling on foot—of necessity now, for his money is getting low. He joins travelling hawkers, he walks side by side with labourers, he talks to every foot-passenger he falls in with, and tries from morning till night to get company on the road.

At night he sleeps by the fire in the kitchen of the inn at which he stops ; but do what he will, he is often alone, and it is now a common thing for him to feel the cold arms around his neck.

Many months have passed since his cousin's death—autumn,

winter, early spring. His money is nearly gone, his health is utterly broken, he is the shadow of his former self, and he is getting near Paris. He will reach that city at the time of the Carnival. To this he looks forward. In Paris, in Carnival time, he need never, surely, be alone, never feel that deadly caress ; he may even recover his lost gaiety, his lost health, once more resume his profession, once more earn fame and money by his art.

How hard he tries to get over the distance that divides him from Paris, while day by day he grows weaker, and his step slower and more heavy !

But there is an end at last ; the long dreary roads are passed. This is Paris, which he enters for the first time—Paris, of which he has dreamed so much—Paris, whose million voices are to exorcise his phantom.

To him to-night Paris seems one vast chaos of lights, music, and confusion—lights which dance before his eyes and will not be still—music that rings in his ears and deafens him—confusion which makes his head whirl round and round.

But, in spite of all, he finds the opera-house, where there is a masked ball. He has enough money left to buy a ticket of admission, and to hire a domino to throw over his shabby dress. It seems only a moment after his entering the gates of Paris that he is in the very midst of all the wild gaiety of the opera-house ball.

No more darkness, no more loneliness, but a mad crowd, shouting and dancing, and a lovely Débardeuse hanging on his arm.

The boisterous gaiety he feels surely is his old light-heartedness come back. He hears the people round him talking of the outrageous conduct of some drunken student, and it is to him they point when they say this—to him, who has not moistened his lips since yesterday at noon, for even now he will not drink ; though his lips are parched, and his throat burning, he cannot drink. His voice is thick and hoarse, and his utterance indistinct ; but still this must be his old light-heartedness come back that makes him so wildly gay.

The little Débardeuse is wearied out—her arm rests on his shoulder heavier than lead—the other dancers one by one drop off.

The lights in the chandeliers one by one die out.

The decorations look pale and shadowy in that dim light which is neither night nor day.

A faint glimmer from the dying lamps, a pale streak of cold grey light from the new-born day, creeping in through half-opened shutters.

And by this light the bright-eyed Débardeuse fades sadly. He looks her in the face. How the brightness of her eyes dies out ! Again he looks her in the face. How white that face has grown ! Again—and now it is the shadow of a face alone that looks in his.

Again—and they are gone—the bright eyes, the face, the shadow of the face. He is alone ; alóne in that vast saloon.

Alone, and, in the terrible silence, he hears the echoes of his own footsteps in that dismal dance which has no music.

No music but the beating of his heart against his breast. For the cold arms are round his neck—they whirl him round, they will not be flung off, or cast away ; he can no more escape from their icy grasp than he can escape from death. He looks behind him—there is nothing but himself in the great empty *salle* ; but he can feel— cold, deathlike, but O, how palpable !—the long slender fingers, and the ring which was his mother's.

He tries to shout, but he has no power in his burning throat. The silence of the place is only broken by the echoes of his own footsteps in the dance from which he cannot extricate himself. Who says he has no partner ? The cold hands are clasped on his breast, and now he does not shun their caress. No ! One more polka, if he drops down dead.

The lights are all out, and, half an hour after, the *gendarmes* come in with a lantern to see that the house is empty ; they are followed by a great dog that they have found seated howling on the steps of the theatre. Near the principal entrance they stumble over——

The body of a student, who has died from want of food, exhaustion, and the breaking of a blood-vessel.

———

Amelia B. Edwards

HOW THE THIRD FLOOR
KNEW THE POTTERIES

from ALL THE YEAR ROUND, 1863

I am a plain man, Major, and you may not dislike to hear a plain statement of facts from me. Some of those facts lie beyond my understanding. I do not pretend to explain them. I only know that they happened as I relate them, and that I pledge myself for the truth of every word of them.

I began life roughly enough, down among the Potteries. I was an orphan ; and my earliest recollections are of a great porcelain manufactory in the country of the Potteries, where I helped about the yard, picked up what halfpence fell in my way, and slept in a harness-loft over the stable. Those were hard times ; but things bettered themselves as I grew older and stronger, especially after George Barnard had come to be foreman of the yard.

George Barnard was a Wesleyan—we were mostly dissenters in the Potteries—sober, clear-headed, somewhat sulky and silent, but a good fellow every inch of him, and my best friend at the time when I most needed a good friend. He took me out of the yard, and set me to the furnace-work. He entered me on the books at a fixed rate of wages. He helped me to pay for a little cheap schooling four nights a week ; and he led me to go with him on Sundays to the chapel down by the river-side, where I first saw Leah Payne. She was his sweetheart, and so pretty that I used to forget the preacher and everybody else, when I looked at her. When she joined in the singing, I heard no voice but hers. If she asked me for the hymn-book, I used to blush and tremble. I believe I worshipped her, in my stupid ignorant way ; and I think I worshipped Barnard almost as blindly, though after a different fashion. I felt I owed him everything. I knew that he had saved me, body and mind ; and I looked up to him as a savage might look up to a missionary.

Leah was the daughter of a plumber, who lived close by the chapel. She was twenty, and George about seven or eight-and-thirty. Some captious folks said there was too much difference in their ages ; but she was so serious-minded, and they loved each other so earnestly and quietly, that, if nothing had come between them during their courtship, I don't believe the question of disparity would ever have troubled the happiness of their married lives. Something did come, however ; and that something was a Frenchman, called Louis Laroche. He was a painter on porcelain, from the famous works at Sèvres ; and our master, it was said, had engaged him for three years certain, at such wages as none of our own people, however skilful, could hope to command. It was about the beginning or middle of September when he first came among us. He looked very young ; was small, dark, and well made ; had little white soft hands, and a silky moustache ; and spoke English nearly as well as I do. None of us liked him ; but that was only natural, seeing how he was put over the head of every Englishman in the place. Besides, though he was always smiling and civil, we couldn't help seeing that he thought himself ever so much better than the rest of us ; and that was not pleasant. Neither was it pleasant to see him strolling about the town, dressed just like a gentleman, when working hours were over ; smoking good cigars, when we were forced to be content with a pipe of common tobacco ; hiring a horse on Sunday afternoons, when we were trudging a-foot ; and taking his pleasure as if the world was made for him to enjoy, and us to work in.

" Ben, boy," said George, " there's something wrong about that Frenchman."

It was on a Saturday afternoon, and we were sitting on a pile of empty seggars against the door of my furnace-room, waiting till the men should all have cleared out of the yard. Seggars are deep earthen boxes in which the pottery is put, while being fired in the kiln.

I looked up, inquiringly.

" About the Count ? " said I, for that was the nickname by which he went in the pottery.

George nodded, and paused for a moment with his chin resting on his palms.

" He has an evil eye," said he ; " and a false smile. Something wrong about him."

I drew nearer, and listened to George as if he had been an oracle.

" Besides," added he, in his slow quiet way, with his eyes fixed straight before him as if he was thinking aloud, " there's a young look about him that isn't natural. Take him just at sight, and you'd think he was almost a boy ; but look close at him—see the little fine wrinkles under his eyes, and the hard lines about his mouth, and then tell me his age, if you can ! Why, Ben boy, he's as old as I am, pretty near ; ay, and as strong, too. You stare ; but I tell you that, slight as he looks, he could fling you over his shoulder as if you were a feather. And as for his hands, little and white as they are, there are muscles of iron inside them, take my word for it."

" But, George, how can you know ? "

" Because I have a warning against him," replied George, very gravely. " Because, whenever he is by, I feel as if my eyes saw clearer, and my ears heard keener, than at other times. Maybe it's presumption, but I sometimes feel as if I had a call to guard myself and others against him. Look at the children, Ben, how they shrink away from him ; and see there, now ! Ask Captain what he thinks of him ! Ben, that dog likes him no better than I do."

I looked, and saw Captain crouching by his kennel with his ears laid back, growling audibly, as the Frenchman came slowly down the steps leading from his own workshop at the upper end of the yard. On the last step he paused ; lighted a cigar ; glanced round, as if to see whether anyone was by ; and then walked straight over to within a couple of yards of the kennel. Captain gave a short angry snarl, and laid his muzzle close down upon his paws, ready for a spring. The Frenchman folded his arms deliberately, fixed his eyes on the dog, and stood calmly smoking. He knew exactly how far he dared go, and kept just that one foot out of harm's way. All at once he stooped, puffed a mouthful of smoke in the dog's eyes, burst into a mocking laugh, turned lightly on his heel, and walked away ; leaving Captain straining at his chain, and barking after him like a mad creature.

Days went by, and I, at work in my own department, saw no more of the Count. Sunday came—the third, I think, after I had talked with George in the yard. Going with George to chapel, as usual, in the morning, I noticed that there was something strange and anxious in his face, and that he scarcely opened his lips to me on the way. Still I said nothing. It was not my place to question him ; and I remember thinking to myself that the cloud would all clear off as soon as he found himself by Leah's side, holding the same book, and joining in the same hymn. It did not, however, for no Leah was there. I looked every moment to the door, expecting to see her sweet face coming in ; but George never lifted his eyes from his book, or seemed to notice that her place was empty. Thus the whole service went by, and my thoughts wandered continually from the words of the preacher. As soon as the last blessing was spoken, and we were fairly across the threshold, I turned to George, and asked if Leah was ill?

"No," said he, gloomily. "She's not ill."

"Then why wasn't she—— ?"

"I'll tell you why," he interrupted, impatiently. "Because you've seen her here for the last time. She's never coming to chapel again."

"Never coming to the chapel again?" I faltered, laying my hand on his sleeve in the earnestness of my surprise. "Why, George, what is the matter?"

But he shook my hand off, and stamped with his iron heel till the pavement rang again.

"Don't ask me," said he, roughly. "Let me alone. You'll know soon enough."

And with this he turned off down a by-lane leading towards the hills, and left me without another word.

I had had plenty of hard treatment in my time; but never, until that moment, an angry look or syllable from George. I did not know how to bear it. That day my dinner seemed as if it would choke me; and in the afternoon I went out and wandered restlessly about the fields till the hour for evening prayers came round. I then returned to the chapel, and sat down on a tomb outside, waiting for George. I saw the congregation go in by twos and threes; I heard the first psalm-tune echo solemnly through the evening stillness; but no George came. Then the service began, and I knew that, punctual as his habits were, it was of no use to expect him any longer. Where could he be? What could have happened? Why should Leah Payne never come to chapel again? Had she gone over to some other sect, and was that why George seemed so unhappy?

Sitting there in the little dreary churchyard with the darkness fast gathering around me, I asked myself these questions over and over again, till my brain ached; for I was not much used to thinking about anything in those times. At last, I could bear to sit quiet no longer. The sudden thought struck me that I would go to Leah, and learn what the matter was, from her own lips. I sprang to my feet, and set off at once towards her home.

It was quite dark, and a light rain was beginning to fall. I found the garden-gate open, and a quick hope flashed across me that George might be there. I drew back for a moment, hesitating whether to knock or ring, when a sound of voices in the passage, and the sudden gleaming of a bright line of light under the door, warned me that someone was coming out. Taken by surprise, and quite unprepared for the moment with anything to say, I shrank back behind the porch, and waited until those within should have passed out. The door opened, and the light streamed suddenly upon the roses and the wet gravel.

" It rains," said Leah, bending forward and shading the candle with her hand.

" And is as cold as Siberia," added another voice, which was not George's, and yet sounded strangely familiar. " Ugh ! what a climate for such a flower as my darling to bloom in ! "

" Is it so much finer in France ? " asked Leah, softly.

" As much finer as blue skies and sunshine can make it. Why, my angel, even your bright eyes will be ten times brighter, and your rosy cheeks ten times rosier, when they are transplanted to Paris. Ah ! I can give you no idea of the wonders of Paris—the broad streets planted with trees, the palaces, the shops, the gardens !—it is a city of enchantment."

" It must be, indeed ! " said Leah. " And you will really take me to see all those beautiful shops ? "

" Every Sunday, my darling—Bah ! don't look so shocked. The shops in Paris are always open on Sunday, and everybody makes holiday. You will soon get over these prejudices."

" I fear it is very wrong to take so much pleasure in the things of this world," sighed Leah.

The Frenchman laughed, and answered her with a kiss.

" Good night, my sweet little saint ! " and he ran lightly down the path, and disappeared in the darkness. Leah sighed again, lingered a moment, and then closed the door.

Stupefied and bewildered, I stood for some seconds like a stone statue, unable to move ; scarcely able to think. At length, I roused myself, as it were mechanically, and went towards the gate. At that instant a heavy hand was laid upon my shoulder, and a hoarse voice close beside my ear, said :

" Who are you ? What are you doing here ? "

It was George. I knew him at once, in spite of the darkness, and stammered his name. He took his hand quickly from my shoulder.

" How long have you been here ? " said he, fiercely. " What right have you to lurk about, like a spy in the dark ? God help me, Ben—I'm half mad. I don't mean to be harsh to you."

" I'm sure you don't," I cried, earnestly.

" It's that cursed Frenchman," he went on, in a voice that sounded like the groan of one in pain. " He's a villain. I know he's a villain ; and I've had a warning against him ever since the first moment he came among us. He'll make her miserable, and break her heart some day—my pretty Leah—and I loved her so ! But I'll be revenged—as sure as there's a sun in heaven, I'll be revenged ! "

His vehemence terrified me. I tried to persuade him to go home ; but he would not listen to me.

" No, no," he said. " Go home yourself, boy, and let me be. My blood is on fire : this rain is good for me, and I am better alone."

" If I could only do something to help you——"

" You can't," interrupted he. " Nobody can help me. I'm a ruined man, and I don't care what becomes of me. The Lord forgive me ! my heart is full of wickedness, and my thoughts are the promptings of Satan. There go—for Heaven's sake, go. I don't know what I say, or what I do ! "

I went, for I did not dare refuse any longer ; but I lingered a while at the corner of the street, and watched him pacing to and fro, to and fro in the driving rain. At length I turned reluctantly away, and went home.

I lay awake that night for hours, thinking over the events of the day, and hating the Frenchman from my very soul. I could not hate Leah. I had worshipped her too long and too faithfully for that ; but I looked upon her as a creature given over to destruction. I fell asleep towards morning, and woke again shortly after daybreak. When I reached the pottery, I found George there before me, looking very pale, but quite himself, and setting the men to their work the same as usual. I said nothing about what had happened the day before. Something in his face silenced me ; but seeing him so steady and composed, I took heart, and began to hope he had fought through the worst of his trouble. By-and-by the Frenchman came through the yard, gay and off-hand, with his cigar in his mouth, and his hands in his pockets. George turned sharply away into one of the workshops, and shut the door. I drew a deep breath of relief. My dread was to see them come to an open quarrel ; and I felt that as long as they kept clear of that, all would be well.

Thus the Monday went by, and the Tuesday ; and still George kept aloof from me. I had sense enough not to be hurt by this. I felt he had a good right to be silent, if silence helped him to bear his trial better ; and I made up my mind never to breathe another syllable on the subject, unless he began.

Wednesday came. I had overslept myself that morning, and came to work a quarter after the hour, expecting to be fined ; for George was very strict as foreman of the yard, and treated friends and enemies just the same. Instead of blaming me, however, he called me up, and said :

" Ben, whose turn is it this week to sit up ? "

" Mine, sir," I replied. (I always called him " Sir " in working hours.)

" Well, then, you may go home to-day, and the same on Thursday and Friday ; for there's a large batch of work for the ovens to-night, and there'll be the same to-morrow night and the night after."

" All right, sir," said I. " Then I'll be here by seven this evening."

" No, half-past nine will be soon enough. I've some accounts to make up, and I shall be here myself till then. Mind you are true to time, though."

" I'll be as true as the clock, sir," I replied, and was turning away when he called me back again.

" You're a good lad, Ben," said he. " Shake hands."

I seized his hand, and pressed it warmly.

" If I'm good for anything, George," I answered with all my heart, " it's you who have made me so. God bless you for it ! "

" Amen ! " said he, in a troubled voice, putting his hand to his hat.

And so we parted.

In general, I went to bed by day when I was attending to the firing by night ; but this morning I had already slept longer than usual, and wanted exercise more than rest. So I ran home ; put a bit of bread and meat in my pocket ; snatched up my big thorn stick ; and started off for a long day in the country. When I came home, it was quite dark and beginning to rain, just as it had begun to rain at about the same time that wretched Sunday evening : so I changed my wet boots, had an early supper and a nap in the chimney-corner, and went down to the works at a few minutes before half-past nine. Arriving at the factory-gate, I found it ajar, and so walked in and closed it after me. I remember thinking at the time that it was unlike George's usual caution to leave it so ; but it passed from my mind next moment. Having slipped in the bolt, I then went straight over to George's little counting-house, where the gas was shining cheerfully in the window. Here also, somewhat to my surprise, I found the door open, and the room empty. I went in. The threshold and part of the floor was wetted by the driving rain. The wages-book was open on the desk, George's pen stood in the ink, and his hat hung on its usual peg in the corner. I concluded, of course, that he had gone round to the ovens ; so, following him, I took down his hat and carried it with me, for it was now raining fast.

The baking-houses lay just opposite, on the other side of the yard. There were three of them, opening one out of the other ; and in each, the great furnace filled all the middle of the room. These furnaces are, in fact, large kilns built of brick, with an oven closed in by an iron door in the centre of each, and a chimney going up through the roof. The pottery, enclosed in seggars, stands round inside on shelves, and has to be turned from time to time while the firing is going on. To turn these seggars, test the heat, and keep the fires up, was my work at the period of which I am now telling you, Major.

Well ! I went through the baking-houses one after the other, and found all empty alike. Then a strange, vague, uneasy feeling came over me, and I began to wonder what could have become of George. It was possible that he might be in one of the work-shops ; so I ran over to the counting-house, lighted a lantern, and made a thorough survey of the yards. I tried the doors ; they were all locked as usual. I peeped into the open sheds ; they were all vacant. I called " George ! George ! " in every part of the outer premises ; but the wind and rain drove back my voice, and no other voice replied to it. Forced at last to believe that he was really gone, I took his hat back to the counting-house, put away the wages-book, extinguished the gas, and prepared for my solitary watch.

The night was mild, and the heat in the baking-rooms intense. I knew, by experience, that the ovens had been overheated, and that none of the porcelain must go in at least for the next two hours ; so I carried my stool to the door, settled myself in a sheltered corner where the air could reach me, but not the rain, and fell to wondering where George could have gone, and why he should not have waited till the time appointed. That he had left in haste was clear—not because his hat remained behind, for he might have had a cap with him—but because he had left the book open, and the gas lighted. Perhaps one of the workmen had met with some accident, and he had been summoned away so urgently that he had no time to think of anything ; perhaps he would even now come back presently to see that all was right before he went home to his lodgings. Turning these things over in my mind, I grew drowsy, my thoughts wandered, and I fell asleep.

I cannot tell how long my nap lasted. I had walked a great distance that day, and I slept heavily ; but I awoke all in a moment, with a sort of terror upon me, and, looking up, saw George Barnard sitting on a stool before the oven door, with the firelight full upon his face.

Ashamed to be found sleeping, I started to my feet. At the same instant, he rose, turned away without even looking towards me, and went out into the next room.

" Don't be angry, George ! " I cried, following him. " None of the seggars are in. I knew the fires were too strong, and——"

The words died on my lips. I had followed him from the first room to the second, from the second to the third, and in the third —I lost him !

I could not believe my eyes. I opened the end door leading into the yard, and looked out ; but he was nowhere in sight. I went round to the back of the baking-houses, looked behind the furnaces, ran over to the counting-house, called him by his name over and over again ; but all was dark, silent, lonely, as ever.

Then I remembered how I had bolted the outer gate, and how impossible it was that he should have come in without ringing. Then, too, I began again to doubt the evidence of my own senses, and to think I must have been dreaming.

I went back to my old post by the door of the first baking-house, and sat down for a moment to collect my thoughts.

" In the first place," said I to myself, " there is but one outer gate. That outer gate I bolted on the inside, and it is bolted still. In the next place, I searched the premises, and found all the sheds empty, and the workshop-doors padlocked as usual on the outside. I proved that George was nowhere about, when I came, and I know he could not have come in since, without my knowledge.

Therefore it is a dream. It is certainly a dream, and there's an end of it."

And with this I trimmed my lantern and proceeded to test the temperature of the furnaces. We used to do this, I should tell you, by the introduction of little roughly-moulded lumps of common fire-clay. If the heat is too great, they crack ; if too little, they remain damp and moist ; if just right, they become firm and smooth all over, and pass into the biscuit stage. Well ! I took my three little lumps of clay, put one in each oven, waited while I counted five hundred, and then went round again to see the results. The two first were in capital condition, the third had flown into a dozen pieces. This proved that the seggars might at once go into ovens One and Two, but that number Three had been overheated, and must be allowed to go on cooling for an hour or two longer.

I therefore stocked One and Two with nine rows of seggars, three deep on each shelf ; left the rest waiting till number Three was in a condition to be trusted ; and, fearful of falling asleep again, now that the firing was in progress, walked up and down the rooms to keep myself awake. This was hot work, however, and I could not stand it very long ; so I went back presently to my stool by the door, and fell to thinking about my dream. The more I thought of it, the more strangely real it seemed, and the more I felt convinced that I was actually on my feet, when I saw George get up and walk into the adjoining room. I was also certain that I had still continued to see him as he passed out of the second room into the third, and that at that time I was even following his very footsteps. Was it possible, I asked myself, that I could have been up and moving, and yet not quite awake ? I had heard of people walking in their sleep. Could it be that I was walking in mine, and never waked till I reached the cool air of the yard ? All this seemed likely enough, so I dismissed the matter from my mind, and passed the rest of the night in attending to the seggars, adding fresh fuel from time to time to the furnaces of the first and second ovens, and now and then taking a turn through the yards. As for number Three, it kept up its heat to such a degree that it was almost day before I dared trust the seggars to go in it.

Thus the hours went by ; and at half-past seven on Thursday morning, the men came to their work. It was now my turn to go off duty, but I wanted to see George before I left, and so waited for him in the counting-house, while a lad named Steve Storr took my place at the ovens. But the clock went on from half-past seven to a quarter to eight ; then to eight o'clock ; then to a quarter-past eight—and still George never made his appearance. At length, when the hand got round to half-past eight, I grew weary of waiting, took up my hat, ran home, went to bed, and slept profoundly until past four in the afternoon.

That evening I went down to the factory quite early ; for I had a restlessness upon me, and I wanted to see George before he left for the night. This time, I found the gate bolted, and I rang for admittance.

" How early you are, Ben ! " said Steve Storr, as he let me in.

" Mr. Barnard's not gone ? " I asked, quickly ; for I saw at the first glance that the gas was out in the counting-house.

" He's not gone," said Steve, " because he's never been."

" Never been ? "

" No : and what's stranger still, he's not been home either, since dinner yesterday."

" But he was here last night."

" Oh yes, he was here last night, making up the books. John Parker was with him till past six ; and you found him here, didn't you, at half-past nine ? "

I shook my head.

" Well, he's gone, anyhow. Good night ! "

" Good night ! "

I took the lantern from his hand, bolted him out mechanically, and made my way to the baking-houses like one in a stupor. George gone? Gone without a word of warning to his employer, or of farewell to his fellow-workmen ? I could not understand it. I could not believe it. I sat down bewildered, incredulous, stunned. Then came hot tears, doubts, terrifying suspicions. I remembered the wild words he had spoken a few nights back ; the strange calm by which they were followed ; my dream of the evening before. I had heard of men who drowned themselves for love ; and the turbid Severn ran close by—so close, that one might pitch a stone into it from some of the workshop windows.

These thoughts were too horrible. I dared not dwell upon them. I turned to work, to free myself from them, if I could ; and began by examining the ovens. The temperature of all was much higher than on the previous night, the heat having been gradually increased during the last twelve hours. It was now my business to keep the heat on the increase for twelve more ; after which it would be allowed, as gradually, to subside, until the pottery was cool enough for removal. To turn the seggars, and add fuel to the two first furnaces, was my first work. As before, I found number Three in advance of the others, and so left it for half an hour, or an hour. I then went round the yard ; tried the doors ; let the dog loose ; and brought him back with me to the baking-houses, for company. After that, I set my lantern on a shelf beside the door, took a book from my pocket, and began to read.

I remember the title of the book as well as possible. It was called *Bowlker's Art of Angling*, and contained little rude cuts of all kinds of artificial flies, hooks, and other tackle. But I could not keep my mind to it for two minutes together ; and at last I gave it up in despair, covered my face with my hands, and fell into a long absorbing painful train of thought. A considerable time had gone by thus—maybe an hour—when I was roused by a low whimpering howl from Captain, who was lying at my feet. I looked up with a start, just as I had started from sleep the night before, and with the same vague terror ; and saw, exactly in the same place and in the same attitude, with the firelight full upon him—George Barnard !

At this sight, a fear heavier than the fear of death fell upon me, and my tongue seemed paralysed in my mouth. Then, just as last night, he rose, or seemed to rise, and went slowly out into the next room. A power stronger than myself appeared to compel me, reluctantly, to follow him. I saw him pass through the second room—cross the threshold of the third room—walk straight up to the oven—and there pause. He then turned, for the first time, with the glare of the red firelight pouring out upon him from the open door of the furnace, and looked at me, face to face. In the same instant, his whole frame and countenance seemed to glow and become transparent, as if the fire were all within him and around him—and in that glow he became, as it were, absorbed into the furnace, and disappeared !

I uttered a wild cry, tried to stagger from the room, and fell insensible before I reached the door.

When I next opened my eyes, the grey dawn was in the sky ; the furnace-doors were all closed as I had left them when I last went round ; the dog was quietly sleeping not far from my side ; and the men were ringing at the gate, to be let in.

I told my tale from beginning to end, and was laughed at, as a matter of course, by all who heard it. When it was found, however,

that my statements never varied, and, above all, that George
Barnard continued absent, some few began to talk it over seriously,
and among those few, the master of the works. He forbade the
furnace to be cleared out, called in the aid of a celebrated naturalist,
and had the ashes submitted to a scientific examination. The
result was as follows :

The ashes were found to have been largely saturated with some
kind of fatty animal matter. A considerable portion of those ashes
consisted of charred bone. A semi-circular piece of iron, which
evidently had once been the heel of a workman's heavy boot, was
found, half fused, at one corner of the furnace. Near it, a tibia
bone, which still retained sufficient of its original form and texture
to render identification possible. This bone, however, was so much
charred, that it fell into powder on being handled.

After this, not many doubted that George Barnard had been
foully murdered, and that his body had been thrust into the
furnace. Suspicion fell upon Louis Laroche. He was arrested, a
coroner's inquest was held, and every circumstance connected
with the night of the murder was as thoroughly sifted and investigated as possible. All the sifting in the world, however, failed
either to clear or to condemn Louis Laroche. On the very night
of his release, he left the place by the mail-train, and was never
seen or heard of there, again. As for Leah, I know not what became of her. I went away myself before many weeks were over,
and never have set foot among the Potteries from that hour to this.

Rosa Mulholland

NOT TO BE TAKEN AT
BED-TIME

from ALL THE YEAR ROUND, 1865

This is the legend of a house called the Devil's Inn, standing in
the heather on the top of the Connemara mountains, in a shallow
valley hollowed between five peaks. Tourists sometimes come in
sight of it on September evenings ; a crazy and weather-stained

apparition, with the sun glaring at it angrily between the hills, and striking its shattered window-panes. Guides are known to shun it, however.

The house was built by a stranger, who came no one knew whence, and whom the people nicknamed Coll Dhu (Black Coll), because of his sullen bearing and solitary habits. His dwelling they called the Devil's Inn, because no tired traveller had ever been asked to rest under its roof, nor friend known to cross its threshold. No one bore him company in his retreat but a wizen-faced old man, who shunned the good-morrow of the trudging peasant when he made occasional excursions to the nearest village for provisions for himself and master, and who was as secret as a stone concerning all the antecedents of both.

For the first year of their residence in the country, there had been much speculation as to who they were, and what they did with themselves up there among the clouds and eagles. Some said that Coll Dhu was a scion of the old family from whose hands the surrounding lands had passed ; and that, embittered by poverty and pride, he had come to bury himself in solitude, and brood over his misfortunes. Others hinted of crime, and flight from an-other country ; others again whispered of those who were cursed from their birth, and could never smile, nor yet make friends with a fellow-creature till the day of their death. But when two years had passed, the wonder had somewhat died out, and Coll Dhu was little thought of, except when a herd looking for sheep crossed the track of a big dark man walking the mountains gun in hand, to whom he did not dare say " Lord save you ! " or when a house-wife rocking her cradle of a winter's night, crossed herself as a gust of storm thundered over her cabin-roof, with the exclamation, " Oh, then, it's Coll Dhu that has enough o' the fresh air about his head up there this night, the crature ! "

Coll Dhu had lived thus in his solitude for some years, when it became known that Colonel Blake, the new lord of the soil, was coming to visit the country. By climbing one of the peaks encircling his eyrie, Coll could look sheer down a mountain-side, and see in miniature beneath him, a grey old dwelling with ivied chimneys and weather-slated walls, standing amongst straggling trees and grim warlike rocks, that gave it the look of a fortress, gazing out to the Atlantic for ever with the eager eyes of all its windows, as if demanding perpetually, " What tidings from the New World ? "

He could see now masons and carpenters crawling about below, like ants in the sun, over-running the old house from base to chimney, daubing here and knocking there, tumbling down walls that looked to Coll, up among the clouds, like a handful of jackstones, and building up others that looked like the toy fences in a child's Farm. Throughout several months he must have watched the busy ants at their task of breaking and mending again, disfiguring and beautifying ; but when all was done he had not the curiosity to stride down and admire the handsome panelling of the new billiard-room, nor yet the fine view which the enlarged bay-window in the drawing-room commanded of the watery highway to Newfoundland.

Deep summer was melting into autumn, and the amber streaks of decay were beginning to creep out and trail over the ripe purple of moor and mountain, when Colonel Blake, his only daughter, and a party of friends, arrived in the country. The grey house below was alive with gaiety, but Coll Dhu no longer found an interest in observing it from his eyrie. When he watched the sun rise or set, he chose to ascend some crag that looked on no human habitation. When he sallied forth on his excursions, gun in hand, he set his face towards the most isolated wastes, dipping into the loneliest valleys, and scaling the nakedest ridges. When he came by chance within call of other excursionists, gun in hand he plunged into the shade of some hollow, and avoided an encounter. Yet it was fated, for all that, that he and Colonel Blake should meet.

Towards the evening of one bright September day, the wind changed, and in half an hour the mountains were wrapped in a thick blinding mist. Coll Dhu was far from his den, but so well had he searched these mountains, and inured himself to their climate, that neither storm, rain, nor fog, had power to disturb him. But while he stalked on his way, a faint and agonised cry from a human voice reached him through the smothering mist. He quickly tracked the sound, and gained the side of a man who was stumbling along in danger of death at every step.

" Follow me ! " said Coll Dhu to this man, and, in an hour's time, brought him safely to the lowlands, and up to the walls of the eager-eyed mansion.

" I am Colonel Blake," said the frank soldier, when, having left the fog behind him, they stood in the starlight under the lighted windows. " Pray tell me quickly to whom I owe my life."

As he spoke, he glanced up at his benefactor, a large man with a sombre sun-burned face.

" Colonel Blake," said Coll Dhu, after a strange pause, " your father suggested to my father to stake his estates at the gaming-table. They were staked, and the tempter won. Both are dead ; but you and I live, and I have sworn to injure you."

The colonel laughed good humouredly at the uneasy face above him.

" And you began to keep your oath to-night by saving my life ? " said he. " Come ! I am a soldier, and know how to meet an enemy ; but I had far rather meet a friend. I shall not be happy till you have eaten my salt. We have merrymaking to-night in honour of my daughter's birthday. Come in and join us ? "

Coll Dhu looked at the earth doggedly.

" I have told you," he said, " who and what I am, and I will not cross your threshold."

But at this moment (so runs my story) a French window opened among the flower-beds by which they were standing, and a vision appeared which stayed the words on Coll's tongue. A stately girl, clad in white satin, stood framed in the ivied window, with the warm light from within streaming around her richly-moulded figure into the night. Her face was as pale as her gown, her eyes were swimming in tears, but a firm smile sat on her lips as she held out both hands to her father. The light behind her, touched the glistening folds of her dress—the lustrous pearls round her throat —the coronet of blood-red roses which encircled the knotted braids at the back of her head. Satin, pearls, and roses—had Coll Dhu, of the Devil's Inn, never set eyes upon such things before ?

Evleen Blake was no nervous tearful miss. A few quick words —" Thank God ! you're safe ; the rest have been home an hour " —and a tight pressure of her father's fingers between her own jewelled hands, were all that betrayed the uneasiness she had suffered.

" Faith, my love, I owe my life to this brave gentleman ! " said the blithe colonel. " Press him to come in and be our guest, Evleen. He wants to retreat to his mountains, and lose himself again in the fog where I found him ; or, rather, where he found me ! Come, sir " (to Coll), " you must surrender to this fair besieger."

An introduction followed. " Coll Dhu ! " murmured Evleen Blake, for she had heard the common tales of him ; but with a frank welcome she invited her father's preserver to taste the hospitality of that father's house.

" I beg you to come in, sir," she said ; " but for you our gaiety must have been turned into mourning. A shadow will be upon our mirth if our benefactor disdains to join in it."

With a sweet grace, mingled with a certain hauteur from which she was never free, she extended her white hand to the tall looming figure outside the window ; to have it grasped and wrung in a way that made the proud girl's eyes flash their amazement, and the same little hand clench itself in displeasure, when it had hid itself like an outraged thing among the shining folds of her gown. Was this Coll Dhu mad, or rude ?

The guest no longer refused to enter, but followed the white figure into a little study where a lamp burned ; and the gloomy stranger, the bluff colonel, and the young mistress of the house, were fully discovered to each other's eyes. Evleen glanced at the newcomer's dark face, and shuddered with a feeling of indescribable dread and dislike ; then, to her father, accounted for the shudder after a popular fashion, saying lightly : " There is someone walking over my grave."

So Coll Dhu was present at Evleen Blake's birthday ball. Here he was, under a roof which ought to have been his own, a stranger, known only by a nickname, shunned and solitary. Here he was, who had lived among the eagles and foxes, lying in wait with a fell purpose, to be revenged on the son of his father's foe for poverty and disgrace, for the broken heart of a dead mother, for the loss of a self-slaughtered father, for the dreary scattering of brothers and sisters. Here he stood, a Samson shorn of his strength ; and all because a haughty girl had melting eyes, a winning mouth, and looked radiant in satin and roses.

Peerless where many were lovely, she moved among her friends, trying to be unconscious of the gloomy fire of those strange eyes which followed her unweariedly wherever she went. And when her father begged her to be gracious to the unsocial guest whom he would fain conciliate, she courteously conducted him to see the new picture-gallery adjoining the drawing-rooms ; explained under what odd circumstances the colonel had picked up this little painting or that ; using every delicate art her pride would allow to achieve her father's purpose, whilst maintaining at the same time her own personal reserve ; trying to divert the guest's oppressive attention from herself to the objects for which she claimed his notice. Coll Dhu followed his conductress and listened to her voice, but what she said mattered nothing ; nor did she wring many words of comment or reply from his lips, until they paused in a retired corner where the light was dim, before a window from which the curtain was withdrawn. The sashes were open, and nothing was visible but water ; the night Atlantic, with the full moon riding high above a bank of clouds, making silvery tracks outward towards the distance of infinite mystery dividing two worlds. Here the following little scene is said to have been enacted.

" This window of my father's own planning, is it not creditable to his taste ? " said the young hostess, as she stood, herself glittering like a dream of beauty, looking on the moonlight.

Coll Dhu made no answer ; but suddenly, it is said, asked her for a rose from a cluster of flowers that nestled in the lace on her bosom.

For the second time that night Evleen Blake's eyes flashed with no gentle light. But this man was the saviour of her father. She broke off a blossom, and with such good grace, and also with such queen-like dignity as she might assume, presented it to him. Whereupon, not only was the rose seized, but also the hand that gave it, which was hastily covered with kisses.

Then her anger burst upon him.

" Sir," she cried, " if you are a gentleman you must be mad ! If you are not mad, then you are not a gentleman ! "

" Be merciful " said Coll Dhu ; " I love you. My God, I never loved a woman before ! Ah ! " he cried, as a look of disgust crept over her face, " you hate me. You shuddered the first time your eyes met mine. I love you, and you hate me ! "

" I do," cried Evleen, vehemently, forgetting everything but her indignation. " Your presence is like something evil to me. Love me ?—your looks poison me. Pray, sir, talk no more to me in this strain."

" I will trouble you no longer," said Coll Dhu. And, stalking to the window, he placed one powerful hand upon the sash, and vaulted from it out of her sight.

Bare-headed as he was, Coll Dhu strode off to the mountains, but not towards his own home. All the remaining dark hours of that night he is believed to have walked the labyrinths of the hills, until dawn began to scatter the clouds with a high wind. Fasting, and on foot from sunrise the morning before, he was then glad enough to see a cabin right in his way. Walking in, he asked for water to drink, and a corner where he might throw himself to rest.

There was a wake in the house, and the kitchen was full of people, all wearied out with the night's watch ; old men were dozing over their pipes in the chimney-corner, and here and there a woman was fast asleep with her head on a neighbour's knee. All who were awake crossed themselves when Coll Dhu's figure darkened the door, because of his evil name ; but an old man of the house invited him in, and offering him milk, and promising him a roasted potato by-and-by, conducted him to a small room off the kitchen, one end of which was strewed with heather, and where there were only two women sitting gossiping over a fire.

" A thraveller," said the old man, nodding his head at the women, who nodded back, as if to say " he has the traveller's right." And Coll Dhu flung himself on the heather, in the furthest corner of the narrow room.

The women suspended their talk for a while ; but presently, guessing the intruder to be asleep, resumed it in voices above a whisper. There was but a patch of window with the grey dawn behind it, but Coll could see the figures by the firelight over which they bent : an old woman sitting forward with her withered hands extended to the embers, and a girl reclining against the hearth wall, with her healthy face, bright eyes, and crimson draperies, glowing by turns in the flickering blaze.

" I do' know," said the girl, " but it's the quarest marriage iver I h'ard of. Sure it's not three weeks since he tould right an' left that he hated her like poison ! "

" Whist, asthoreen ! " said the colliagh, bending forward confidentially ; " throth an' we all know that o' him. But what could he do, the crature ! When she put the burragh-bos on him ! "

" The *what* ? " asked the girl.

" Then the burragh-bos machree-o ? That's the spanchel o' death, avourneen ; an' well she has him tethered to her now, bad luck to her ! "

The old woman rocked herself and stifled the Irish cry breaking from her wrinkled lips by burying her face in her cloak.

" But what is it ? " asked the girl, eagerly. " What's the burragh-bos, anyways, an' where did she get it ? "

" Och, och ! it's not fit for comin' over to young ears, but cuggir (whisper), acushla ! It's a sthrip o' the skin o' a corpse, peeled from the crown o' the head to the heel, without crack or split, or the charrm's broke ; an' that, rowled up, an' put on a sthring roun' the neck o' the wan that's cowld by the wan that wants to be loved. An' sure enough it puts the fire in their hearts, hot an' sthrong, afore twenty-four hours is gone."

The girl had started from her lazy attitude, and gazed at her companion with eyes dilated by horror.

" Marciful Saviour ! " she cried. " Not a sowl on airth would bring the curse out o' heaven by sich a black doin' ! "

" Aisy, Biddeen alanna ! an' there's wan that does it, an' isn't the divil. Arrah, asthoreen, did ye niver hear tell o' Pexie na Pishrogie, that lives betune two hills o' Maam Turk ? "

" I h'ard o' her," said the girl, breathlessly.

" Well, sorra bit lie, but it's hersel' that does it. She'll do it for money any day. Sure they hunted her from the graveyard o' Salruck, where she had the dead raised ; an' glory be to God ! they would ha' murthered her, only they missed her thracks, an' couldn't bring it home to her afther."

" Whist, a-wauher " (my mother), said the girl ; " here's the thraveller gettin' up to set off on his road again ! Och, then, it's the short rest he tuk, the sowl ! "

It was enough for Coll, however. He had got up, and now went back to the kitchen, where the old man had caused a dish of potatoes to be roasted, and earnestly pressed his visitor to sit down and eat of them. This Coll did readily ; having recruited his strength by a meal, he betook himself to the mountains again, just as the rising sun was flashing among the waterfalls, and sending the night mists drifting down the glens. By sundown the same evening he was striding over the hills of Maam Turk, asking of herds his way to the cabin of one Pexie na Pishrogie.

In a hovel on a brown desolate heath, with scared-looking hills flying off into the distance on every side, he found Pexie : a yellow-faced hag, dressed in a dark-red blanket, with elf-locks of coarse black hair protruding from under an orange kerchief swathed round her wrinkled jaws. She was bending over a pot upon her fire, where herbs were simmering, and she looked up with an evil glance when Coll Dhu darkened her door.

" The burragh-bos is it her honour wants ? " she asked, when he had made known his errand. " Ay, ay ; but the arighad, the arighad (money) for Pexie. The burragh-bos is ill to get."

" I will pay," said Coll Dhu, laying a sovereign on the bench before her.

The witch sprang upon it, and chuckling, bestowed on her visitor a glance which made even Coll Dhu shudder.

" Her honour is a fine king," she said, " an' her is fit to get the burragh-bos. Ha ! ha ! her sall get the burragh-bos from Pexie. But the arighad is not enough. More, more ! "

She stretched out her claw-like hand, and Coll dropped another sovereign into it. Whereupon she fell into more horrible convulsions of delight.

" Hark ye ! " cried Coll. " I have paid you well, but if your infernal charm does not work, I will have you hunted for a witch ! "

" Work ! " cried Pexie, rolling up her eyes. " If Pexie's charrm not work, then her honour come back here an' carry these bits o' mountain away on her back. Ay, her will work. If the colleen hate her honour like the old diaoul hersel', still an' withal her love will love her honour like her own white sowl afore the sun sets or rises. That, (with a furtive leer,) or the colleen dhas go wild mad afore wan hour."

" Hag ! " returned Coll Dhu ; " the last part is a hellish invention of your own. I heard nothing of madness. If you want more money, speak out, but play none of your hideous tricks on me."

The witch fixed her cunning eyes on him, and took her cue at once from his passion.

" Her honour guess thrue," she simpered ; " it is only the little bit more arighad poor Pexie want."

Again the skinny hand was extended. Coll Dhu shrank from touching it, and threw his gold upon the table.

" King, king ! " chuckled Pexie. " Her honour is a grand king. Her honour is fit to get the burragh-bos. The colleen dhas sall love her like her own white sowl. Ha, ha ! "

" When shall I get it ? " asked Coll Dhu, impatiently.

" Her honour sall come back to Pexie in so many days, do-deag (twelve), so many days, fur that the burragh-bos is hard to get. The lonely graveyard is far away, an' the dead man is hard to raise——"

" Silence ! " cried Coll Dhu ; " not a word more. I will have your hideous charm, but what it is, or where you get it, I will not know."

Then, promising to come back in twelve days, he took his departure. Turning to look back when a little way across the heath, he saw Pexie gazing after him, standing on her black hill in relief against the lurid flames of the dawn, seeming to his dark imagination like a fury with all hell at her back.

At the appointed time Coll Dhu got the promised charm. He sewed it with perfumes into a cover of cloth of gold, and slung it to a fine-wrought chain. Lying in a casket which had once held the jewels of Coll's broken-hearted mother, it looked a glittering bauble enough. Meantime the people of the mountains were cursing over their cabin fires, because there had been another unholy raid upon their graveyard, and were banding themselves to hunt the criminal down.

A fortnight passed. How or where could Coll Dhu find an opportunity to put the charm round the neck of the colonel's proud daughter ? More gold was dropped into Pexie's greedy claw, and then she promised to assist him in his dilemma.

Next morning the witch dressed herself in decent garb, smoothed her elf-locks under a snowy cap, smoothed the evil wrinkles out of her face, and with a basket on her arm locked the door of the hovel, and took her way to the lowlands. Pexie seemed to have given up her disreputable calling for that of a simple mushroom-gatherer. The housekeeper at the grey house bought poor Muireade's mushrooms of her every morning. Every morning she left unfailingly a nosegay of wild flowers for Miss Evleen Blake, " God bless her ! She had never seen the darling young lady with her own two longing eyes, but sure hadn't she heard tell of her sweet purty face, miles away ! " And at last, one morning, whom should she meet but Miss Evleen herself returning alone from a ramble. Whereupon poor Muireade " made bold " to present her flowers in person.

" Ah," said Evleen, " it is you who leave me the flowers every morning ? They are very sweet."

Muireade had sought her only for a look at her beautiful face. And now that she had seen it, as bright as the sun, and as fair as the lily, she would take up her basket and go away contented. Yet she lingered a little longer.

" My lady never walk up big mountain ? " said Pexie.

" No," said Evleen, laughing ; she feared she could not walk up a mountain.

" Ah yes ; my lady ought to go, with more gran' ladies an' gentlemen, ridin' on purty little donkeys, up the big mountains. Oh, gran' things up big mountains for my lady to see ! "

Thus she set to work, and kept her listener enchained for an hour, while she related wonderful stories of those upper regions. And as Evleen looked up to the burly crowns of the hills, perhaps she thought there might be sense in this wild old woman's suggestion. It ought to be a grand world up yonder.

Be that as it may, it was not long after this when Coll Dhu got notice that a party from the grey house would explore the mountains next day; that Evleen Blake would be one of the number; and that he, Coll, must prepare to house and refresh a crowd of weary people, who in the evening should be brought, hungry and faint, to his door. The simple mushroom gatherer should be discovered laying in her humble stock among the green places between the hills, should volunteer to act as guide to the party, should lead them far out of their way through the mountains and up and down the most toilsome ascents and across dangerous places; to escape safely from which, the servants should be told to throw away the baskets of provisions which they carried.

Coll Dhu was not idle. Such a feast was set forth, as had never been spread so near the clouds before. We are told of wonderful dishes furnished by unwholesome agency, and from a place believed much hotter than is necessary for purposes of cookery. We are told also how Coll Dhu's barren chambers were suddenly hung with curtains of velvet, and with fringes of gold; how the blank white walls glowed with delicate colours and gilding; how gems of pictures sprang into sight between the panels; how the tables blazed with plate and gold, and glittered with the rarest glass; how such wines flowed, as the guests had never tasted; how servants in the richest livery, amongst whom the wizen-faced old man was a mere nonentity, appeared, and stood ready to carry in the wonderful dishes, at whose extraordinary fragrance the eagles came pecking to the windows, and the foxes drew near the walls, snuffing. Sure enough, in all good time, the weary party came within sight of the Devil's Inn, and Coll Dhu sallied forth to invite them across his lonely threshold. Colonel Blake (to whom Evleen, in her delicacy, had said no word of the solitary's strange behaviour to herself) hailed his appearance with delight, and the whole party sat down to Coll's banquet in high good humour. Also, it is said, in much amazement at the magnificence of the mountain recluse.

All went in to Coll's feast, save Evleen Blake, who remained standing on the threshold of the outer door; weary, but unwilling to rest there ; hungry, but unwilling to eat there. Her white cambric dress was gathered on her arms, crushed and sullied with the toils of the day ; her bright cheek was a little sunburned ; her small dark head with its braids a little tossed, was bared to the mountain air and the glory of the sinking sun ; her hands were loosely tangled in the strings of her hat ; and her foot sometimes tapped the threshold-stone. So she was seen.

The peasants tell that Coll Dhu and her father came praying her to enter, and that the magnificent servants brought viands to the threshold ; but no step would she move inward, no morsel would she taste.

" Poison, poison ! " she murmured, and threw the food in handfuls to the foxes, who were snuffing on the heath.

But it was different when Muireade, the kindly old woman, the simple mushroom-gatherer, with all the wicked wrinkles smoothed out of her face, came to the side of the hungry girl, and coaxingly presented a savoury mess of her own sweet mushrooms, served on a common earthen platter.

" An' darlin', my lady, poor Muireade her cook them hersel', an' no thing o' this house touch them or look at poor Muireade's mushrooms."

Then Evleen took the platter and ate a delicious meal. Scarcely was it finished when a heavy drowsiness fell upon her; and, unable to sustain herself on her feet, she presently sat down upon the door-stone. Leaning her head against the framework of the door, she was soon in a deep sleep, or trance. So she was found.

" Whimsical, obstinate little girl ! " said the colonel, putting his hand on the beautiful slumbering head. And taking her in his arms, he carried her into a chamber which had been (say the story-tellers) nothing but a bare and sorry closet in the morning but which was now fitted up with Oriental splendour. And here on a luxurious couch she was laid, with a crimson coverlet wrapping her feet. And here in the tempered light coming through jewelled glass, where yesterday had been a coarse rough-hung window, her father looked his last upon her lovely face.

The colonel returned to his host and friends, and by-and-by the whole party sallied forth to see the after-glare of a fierce sunset swathing the hills in flames. It was not until they had gone some distance that Coll Dhu remembered to go back and fetch his telescope. He was not long absent. But he was absent long enough to enter that glowing chamber with a stealthy step, to throw a light chain around the neck of the sleeping girl, and to slip among the folds of her dress the hideous glittering burragh-bos.

After he had gone away again, Pexie came stealing to the door, and, opening it a little, sat down on the mat outside, with her cloak wrapped round her. An hour passed, and Evleen Blake still slept, her breathing scarcely stirring the deadly bauble on her breast. After that, she began to murmur and moan, and Pexie pricked up her ears. Presently a sound in the room told that the victim was awake and had risen. Then Pexie put her face to the aperture of the door and looked in, gave a howl of dismay, and fled from the house, to be seen in that country no more.

The light was fading among the hills, and the ramblers were returning towards the Devil's Inn, when a group of ladies who were considerably in advance of the rest, met Evleen Blake advancing towards them on the heath, with her hair disordered as by sleep, and no covering on her head. They noticed something bright, like gold, shifting and glancing with the motion of her figure. There had been some jesting among them about Evleen's fancy for falling asleep on the door-step instead of coming in to dinner, and they advanced laughing, to rally her on the subject. But she stared at them in a strange way, as if she did not know them, and passed on. Her friends were rather offended, and commented on her fantastic humour ; only one looked after her, and got laughed at by her companions for expressing uneasiness on the wilful young lady's account.

So they kept their way, and the solitary figure went fluttering on, the white robe blushing, and the fatal burragh-bos glittering in the reflexion from the sky. A hare crossed her path, and she laughed out loudly, and clapping her hands, sprang after it. Then she stopped and asked questions of the stones, striking them with her open palm because they would not answer. (An amazed little herd sitting behind a rock, witnessed these strange proceedings.) By-and-by she began to call after the birds, in a wild shrill way startling the echoes of the hills as she went along. A party of gentlemen returning by a dangerous path, heard the unusual sound and stopped to listen.

" What is that ? " asked one.

" A young eagle," said Coll Dhu, whose face had become livid ; " they often give such cries."

" It was uncommonly like a woman's voice ! " was the reply ; and immediately another wild note rang towards them from the

rocks above : a bare saw-like ridge, shelving away to some distance
ahead, and projecting one hungry tooth over an abyss. A few more
moments and they saw Evleen Blake's light figure fluttering out
towards this dizzy point.

"My Evleen !" cried the colonel, recognising his daughter,
"she is mad to venture on such a spot !"

"Mad !" repeated Coll Dhu. And then dashed off to the rescue
with all the might and swiftness of his powerful limbs.

When he drew near her, Evleen had almost reached the verge
of the terrible rock. Very cautiously he approached her, his object
being to seize her in his strong arms before she was aware of his
presence, and carry her many yards away from the spot of danger.
But in a fatal moment Evleen turned her head and saw him. One
wild ringing cry of hate and horror, which startled the very eagles
and scattered a flight of curlews above her head, broke from her
lips. A step backward brought her within a foot of death.

One desperate though wary stride, and she was struggling in
Coll's embrace. One glance in her eyes, and he saw that he was
striving with a mad woman. Back, back, she dragged him, and he
had nothing to grasp by. The rock was slippery and his shod feet
would not cling to it. Back, back ! A hoarse panting, a dire
swinging to and fro ; and then the rock was standing naked
against the sky, no one was there, and Coll Dhu and Evleen Blake
lay shattered far below.

Charles Dickens

TO BE TAKEN WITH A GRAIN
OF SALT

from ALL THE YEAR ROUND, 1865

I have always noticed a prevalent want of courage, even among
persons of superior intelligence and culture, as to imparting their
own psychological experiences when those have been of a strange
sort. Almost all men are afraid that what they could relate in such
wise would find no parallel or response in a listener's internal life,
and might be suspected or laughed at. A truthful traveller who

should have seen some extraordinary creature in the likeness of a sea-serpent, would have no fear of mentioning it ; but the same traveller having had some singular presentiment, impulse, vagary of thought, vision (so-called), dream, or other remarkable mental impression, would hesitate considerably before he would own to it. To this reticence I attribute much of the obscurity in which such subjects are involved. We do not habitually communicate our experiences of these subjective things, as we do our experiences of objective creation. The consequence is, that the general stock of experience in this regard appears exceptional, and really is so, in respect of being miserably imperfect.

In what I am going to relate I have no intention of setting up, opposing, or supporting, any theory whatever. I know the history of the Bookseller of Berlin, I have studied the case of the wife of a late Astronomer Royal as related by Sir David Brewster, and I have followed the minutest details of a much more remarkable case of Spectral Illusion occurring within my private circle of friends. It may be necessary to state as to this last that the sufferer (a lady) was in no degree, however distant, related to me. A mistaken assumption on that head, might suggest an explanation of a part of my own case—but only a part—which would be wholly without foundation. It cannot be referred to my inheritance of any developed peculiarity, nor had I ever before any at all similar experience, nor have I ever had any at all similar experience since.

It does not signify how many years ago, or how few, a certain Murder was committed in England, which attracted great attention. We hear more than enough of Murderers as they rise in succession to their atrocious eminence, and I would bury the memory of this particular brute, if I could, as his body was buried, in Newgate Jail. I purposely abstain from giving any direct clue to the criminal's individuality.

When the murder was first discovered, no suspicion fell—or I ought rather to say, for I cannot be too precise in my facts, it was nowhere publicly hinted that any suspicion fell—on the man who was afterwards brought to trial. As no reference was at that time made to him in the newspapers, it is obviously impossible that any description of him can at that time have been given in the newspapers. It is essential that this fact be remembered.

Unfolding at breakfast my morning paper, containing the account of that first discovery, I found it to be deeply interesting, and I read it with close attention. I read it twice, if not three times.

The discovery had been made in a bedroom, and, when I laid down the paper, I was aware of a flash—rush—flow—I do not know what to call it—no word I can find is satisfactorily descriptive—in which I seemed to see that bedroom passing through my room, like a picture impossibly painted on a running river. Though almost instantaneous in its passing, it was perfectly clear ; so clear that I distinctly, and with a sense of relief, observed the absence of the dead body from the bed.

It was in no romantic place that I had this curious sensation, but in chambers in Piccadilly, very near to the corner of Saint James's-street. It was entirely new to me. I was in my easy-chair at the moment, and the sensation was accompanied with a peculiar shiver which started the chair from its position. (But it is to be noted that the chair ran easily on castors.) I went to one of the windows (there are two in the room, and the room is on the second floor) to refresh my eyes with the moving objects down in Piccadilly. It was a bright autumn morning, and the street was sparkling and cheerful. The wind was high. As I looked out, it brought down from the Park a quantity of fallen leaves, which a gust took, and whirled into a spiral pillar. As the pillar fell and the leaves dispersed, I saw two men on the opposite side of the way, going from West to East. They were one behind the other. The foremost man often looked back over his shoulder. The second man followed him, at a distance of some thirty paces, with his right hand menacingly raised. First, the singularity and steadiness of this threatening gesture in so public a thoroughfare, attracted my attention ; and next, the more remarkable circumstance that nobody heeded it. Both men threaded their way among the other passengers, with a smoothness hardly consistent even with the action of walking on a pavement, and no single creature that I could see, gave them place, touched them, or looked after them. In passing before my windows, they both stared up at me. I saw their two faces very distinctly, and I knew that I could recognise them anywhere. Not that I had consciously noticed anything very remarkable in either face, except that the man who went first had an unusually lowering appearance, and that the face of the man who followed him was of the colour of impure wax.

I am a bachelor, and my valet and his wife constitute my whole establishment. My occupation is in a certain Branch Bank, and I wish that my duties as head of a Department were as light as they are popularly supposed to be. They kept me in town that autumn,

when I stood in need of a change. I was not ill, but I was not well.
My reader is to make the most that can be reasonably made of my
feeling jaded, having a depressing sense upon me of a monotonous
life, and being " slightly dyspeptic." I am assured by my renowned
doctor that my real state of health at that time justifies no stronger
description, and I quote his own from his written answer to my
request for it.

As the circumstances of the Murder, gradually unravelling,
took stronger and stronger possession of the public mind, I kept
them away from mine, by knowing as little about them as was
possible in the midst of the universal excitement. But I knew that a
verdict of Wilful Murder had been found against the suspected
Murderer, and that he had been committed to Newgate for trial.
I also knew that his trial had been postponed over one Sessions
of the Central Criminal Court, on the ground of general prejudice
and want of time for the preparation of the defence. I may further
have known, but I believe I did not, when, or about when, the
Sessions to which his trial stood postponed would come on.

My sitting-room, bedroom, and dressing-room, are all on one
floor. With the last, there is no communication but through the
bedroom. True, there is a door in it, once communicating with the
staircase ; but a part of the fitting of my bath has been—and had
then been for some years—fixed across it. At the same period, and
as a part of the same arrangement, the door had been nailed up
and canvased over.

I was standing in my bedrom late one night, giving some directions to my servant before he went to bed. My face was towards
the only available door of communication with the dressing-room,
and it was closed. My servant's back was towards that door. While
I was speaking to him I saw it open, and a man look in, who very
earnestly and mysteriously beckoned to me. That man was the man
who had gone second of the two along Piccadilly, and whose face
was of the colour of impure wax.

The figure, having beckoned, drew back and closed the door.
With no longer pause than was made by my crossing the bedroom,
I opened the dressing-room door, and looked in. I had a lighted
candle already in my hand. I felt no inward expectation of seeing
the figure in the dressing-room, and I did not see it there.

Conscious that my servant stood amazed, I turned round to
him, and said : " Derrick, could you believe that in my cool senses
I fancied I saw a——" As I there laid my hand upon his breast,

with a sudden start he trembled violently, and said, " O Lord yes sir ! A dead man beckoning ! "

Now, I do not believe that this John Derrick, my trusty and attached servant for more than twenty years, had any impression whatever of having seen any such figure, until I touched him. The change in him was so startling when I touched him, that I fully believe he derived his impression in some occult manner from me at that instant.

I bade John Derrick bring some brandy, and I gave him a dram, and was glad to take one myself. Of what had proceeded that night's phenomenon, I told him not a single word. Reflecting on it, I was absolutely certain that I had never seen that face before, except on the one occasion in Piccadilly. Comparing its expression when beckoning at the door, with its expression when it had stared up at me as I stood at my window, I came to the conclusion that on the first occasion it had sought to fasten itself upon my memory, and that on the second occasion it had made sure of being immediately remembered.

I was not very comfortable that night, though I felt a certainty, difficult to explain, that the figure would not return. At daylight, I fell into a heavy sleep, from which I was awakened by John Derrick's coming to my bedside with a paper in his hand.

This paper, it appeared, had been the subject of an altercation at the door between its bearer and my servant. It was a summons to me to serve upon a Jury at the forthcoming Sessions of the Central Criminal Court at the Old Bailey. I had never before been summoned on such a Jury, as John Derrick well knew. He believed— I am not certain at this hour whether with reason or otherwise— that that class of Jurors were customarily chosen on a lower qualification than mine, and he had at first refused to accept the summons. The man who served it had taken the matter very coolly. He had said that my attendance or non-attendance was nothing to him ; there the summons was ; and I should deal with it at my own peril, and not at his.

For a day or two I was undecided whether to respond to this call, or take no notice of it. I was not conscious of the slightest mysterious bias, influence, or attraction, one way or other. Of that I am as strictly sure as of every other statement that I make here. Ultimately I decided, as a break in the monotony of my life, that I would go.

The appointed morning was a raw morning in the month of

November. There was a dense brown fog in Piccadilly, and it
became positively black and in the last degree oppressive East of
Temple Bar. I found the passages and staircases of the Court House
flaringly lighted with gas, and the Court itself similarly illuminated. I *think* that until I was conducted by officers into the Old
Court and saw its crowded state, I did not know that the Murderer
was to be tried that day. I *think* that until I was so helped into the
Old Court with considerable difficulty, I did not know into which
of the two Courts sitting, my summons would take me. But this
must not be received as a positive assertion, for I am not completely satisfied in my mind on either point.

I took my seat in the place appropriated to Jurors in waiting,
and I looked about the Court as well as I could through the cloud
of fog and breath that was heavy in it. I noticed the black vapour
hanging like a murky curtain outside the great windows, and I
noticed the stifled sound of wheels on the straw or tan that
was littered in the street ; also, the hum of the people gathered
there, which a shrill whistle, or a louder song or hail than the rest,
occasionally pierced. Soon afterwards the Judges, two in number,
entered and took their seats. The buzz in the Court was awfully
hushed. The direction was given to put the Murderer to the bar.
He appeared there. And in that same instant I recognised in him,
the first of the two men who had gone down Piccadilly.

If my name had been called then, I doubt if I could have answered to it audibly. But it was called about sixth or eighth in the
panel, and I was by that time able to say " Here ! " Now, observe.
As I stepped into the box, the prisoner, who had been looking on
attentively but with no sign of concern, became violently agitated,
and beckoned to his attorney. The prisoner's wish to challenge
me was so manifest, that it occasioned a pause, during which the
attorney, with his hand upon the dock, whispered with his client,
and shook his head. I afterwards had it from that gentleman, that
the prisoner's first affrighted words to him were, " *At all hazards
challenge that man !* " But, that as he would give no reason for it,
and admitted that he had not even known my name until he
heard it called and I appeared, it was not done.

Both on the ground already explained, that I wish to avoid
reviving the unwholesome memory of that Murderer, and also
because a detailed account of his long trial is by no means indispensable to my narrative, I shall confine myself closely to such
incidents in the ten days and nights during which we, the Jury,

were kept together, as directly bear on my own curious personal experience. It is in that, and not in the Murderer, that I seek to interest my reader. It is to that, and not to a page of the Newgate Calendar, that I beg attention.

I was chosen Foreman of the Jury. On the second morning of the trial, after evidence had been taken for two hours (I heard the church clocks strike), happening to cast my eyes over my brother-jurymen, I found an inexplicable difficulty in counting them. I counted them several times, yet always with the same difficulty. In short, I made them one too many.

I touched the brother-juryman whose place was next to me, and I whispered to him, " Oblige me by counting us." He looked surprised by the request, but turned his head and counted. " Why," says he, suddenly, "" we are Thirt—— ; but no, it's not possible. No. We are twelve."

According to my counting that day, we were always right in detail, but in the gross we were always one too many. There was no appearance—no figure—to account for it ; but I had now an inward foreshadowing of the figure that was surely coming.

The Jury were housed at the London Tavern. We all slept in one large room on separate tables, and we were constantly in the charge and under the eye of the officer sworn to hold us in safe-keeping. I see no reason for suppressing the real name of that officer. He was intelligent, highly polite, and obliging, and (I was glad to hear) much respected in the City. He had an agreeable presence, good eyes, enviable black whiskers, and a fine sonorous voice. His name was Mr. Harker.

When we turned into our twelve beds at night, Mr. Harker's bed was drawn across the door. On the night of the second day, not being disposed to lie down, and seeing Mr. Harker sitting on his bed, I went and sat beside him, and offered him a pinch of snuff. As Mr. Harker's hand touched mine in taking it from my box, a peculiar shiver crossed him, and he said : " Who is this ! "

Following Mr. Harker's eyes and looking along the room, I saw again the figure I expected—the second of the two men who had gone down Piccadilly. I rose, and advanced a few steps ; then stopped, and looked round at Mr. Harker. He was quite uncon-cerned, laughed, and said in a pleasant way, " I thought for a moment we had a thirteenth juryman, without a bed. But I see it is the moonlight."

Making no revelation to Mr. Harker, but inviting him to take a

walk with me to the end of the room, I watched what the figure did.
It stood for a few moments by the bedside of each of my eleven
brother-jurymen, close to the pillow. It always went to the right-
hand side of the bed, and always passed out crossing the foot of the
next bed. It seemed from the action of the head, merely to look
down pensively at each recumbent figure. It took no notice of me,
or of my bed, which was that nearest to Mr. Harker's. It seemed
to go out where the moonlight came in, through a high window,
as by an aërial flight of stairs.

Next morning at breakfast, it appeared that everybody present
had dreamed of the murdered man last night, except myself and
Mr. Harker.

I now felt as convinced that the second man who had gone down
Piccadilly was the murdered man (so to speak), as if it had been
borne into my comprehension by his immediate testimony. But
even this took place, and in a manner for which I was not at all
prepared.

On the fifth day of the trial, when the case for the prosecution
was drawing to a close, a miniature of the murdered man, missing
from his bedroom upon the discovery of the deed, and afterwards
found in a hiding-place where the Murderer had been seen digging, was put in evidence. Having been identified by the witness
under examination, it was handed up to the Bench, and thence
handed down to be inspected by the Jury. As an officer in a black
gown was making his way with it across to me, the figure of the
second man who had gone down Piccadilly, impetuously started
from the crowd, caught the miniature from the officer, and gave
it to me with its own hands, at the same time saying in a low and
hollow tone—before I saw the miniature, which was in a locket—
" *I was younger then, and my face was not then drained of blood.*" It
also came between me and the brother-juryman to whom I would
have given the miniature, and between him and the brother-
juryman to whom he would have given it, and so passed it on
through the whole of our number, and back into my possession.
Not one of them, however, detected this.

At table, and generally when we were shut up together in Mr.
Harker's custody, we had from the first naturally discussed the
day's proceedings a good deal. On that fifth day, the case for the
prosecution being closed, and we having that side of the question
in a completed shape before us, our discussion was more animated
and serious. Among our number was a vestryman—the densest

idiot I have ever seen at large—who met the plainest evidence with the most preposterous objections, and who was sided with by two flabby parochial parasites ; all the three empanelled from a district so delivered over to Fever that they ought to have been upon their own trial, for five hundred Murders. When these mischievous blockheads were at their loudest, which was towards midnight while some of us were already preparing for bed, I again saw the murdered man. He stood grimly behind them, beckoning to me. On my going towards them and striking into the conversation, he immediately retired. This was the beginning of a separate series of appearances, confined to that long room in which *we* were confined. Whenever a knot of my brother jurymen laid their heads together, I saw the head of the murdered man among theirs. Whenever their comparison of notes was going against him, he would solemnly and irresistibly beckon to me.

It will be borne in mind that down to the production of the miniature on the fifth day of the trial, I had never seen the Appearance in Court. Three changes occurred, now that we entered on the case for the defence. Two of them I will mention together, first. The figure was now in Court continually, and it never there addressed itself to me, but always to the person who was speaking at the time. For instance. The throat of the murdered man had been cut straight across. In the opening speech for the defence, it was suggested that the deceased might have cut his own throat. At that very moment, the figure with its throat in the dreadful condition referred to (this it had concealed before) stood at the speaker's elbow, motioning across and across its windpipe, now with the right hand, now with the left, vigorously suggesting to the speaker himself, the impossibility of such a wound having been self-inflicted by either hand. For another instance. A witness to character, a woman, deposed to the prisoner's being the most amiable of mankind. The figure at that instant stood on the floor before her, looking her full in the face, and pointing out the prisoner's evil countenance with an extended arm and an outstretched finger.

The third change now to be added, impressed me strongly, as the most marked and striking of all. I do not theorise upon it ; I accurately state it, and there leave it. Although the Appearance was not itself perceived by those whom it addressed, its coming close to such persons was invariably attended by some trepidation or disturbance on their part. It seemed to me as if it were prevented by laws to which I was not amenable, from fully revealing itself to others, and yet as if it could, invisibly, dumbly and darkly, overshadow their minds. When the leading counsel for the defence suggested that hypothesis of suicide and the figure stood at the learned gentleman's elbow, frightfully sawing at its severed throat, it is undeniable that the counsel faltered in his speech, lost for a few seconds the thread of his ingenious discourse, wiped his forehead with his handkerchief, and turned extremely pale. When the witness to character was confronted by the Appearance, her eyes most certainly did follow the direction of its pointed finger, and rest in great hesitation and trouble upon the prisoner's face. Two additional illustrations will suffice. On the eighth day of the trial, after the pause which was every day made early in the afternoon for a few minutes' rest and refreshment, I came back into Court with the rest of the Jury, some little time before the return of the Judges. Standing up in the box and looking about me, I thought the figure was not there, until, chancing to raise my eyes to the gallery, I saw it bending forward and leaning over a very decent woman, as if to assure itself whether the Judges had resumed their seats or not. Immediately afterwards, that woman screamed, fainted, and was carried out. So with the venerable, sagacious, and patient Judge who conducted the trial. When the case was over, and he settled himself and his papers to sum up, the murdered man entering by the Judges' door, advanced to his Lordship's desk, and looked eagerly over his shoulder at the pages of his notes which he was turning. A change came over his Lordship's face ; his hand stopped ; the peculiar shiver that I knew so well, passed over him ; he faltered, " Excuse me gentlemen, for a few moments. I am somewhat oppressed by the vitiated air ; " and did not recover until he had drunk a glass of water.

Through all the monotony of six of those interminable ten days —the same Judges and others on the bench, the same Murderer in the dock, the same lawyers at the table, the same tones of question and answer rising to the roof of the court, the same scratching of the Judge's pen, the same ushers going in and out, the same lights kindled at the same hour when there had been any natural light of day, the same foggy curtain outside the great windows when it was foggy, the same rain pattering and dripping when it was rainy, the same footmarks of turnkeys and prisoner day after day on the same sawdust, the same keys locking and unlocking the same heavy doors—through all the wearisome monotony which made me feel as if I had been Foreman of the Jury for a vast period of time, and Piccadilly had flourished coevally with Babylon, the murdered man never lost one trace of his distinctness in my eyes, nor was he at any moment less distinct than anybody else. I must not omit, as a matter of fact, that I never once saw the Appearance which I call by the name of the murdered man, look at the Murderer. Again and again I wondered, " Why does he not ? " But he never did.

Nor did he look at me, after the production of the miniature, until the last closing minutes of the trial arrived. We retired to consider, at seven minutes before ten at night. The idiotic vestry- man and his two parochial parasites gave us so much trouble, that we twice returned into Court, to beg to have certain extracts from the Judge's notes re-read. Nine of us had not the smallest doubt about those passages, neither, I believe, had any one in Court ; the dunder-headed triumvirate however, having no idea but obstruction, disputed them for that very reason. At length we prevailed, and finally the Jury returned into Court at ten minutes past twelve.

The murdered man at that time stood directly opposite the Jury- box, on the other side of the Court. As I took my place, his eyes rested on me, with great attention ; he seemed satisfied, and slowly shook a great grey veil, which he carried on his arm for the first time, over his head and whole form. As I gave in our verdict "Guilty," the veil collapsed, all was gone, and his place was empty.

The Murderer being asked by the Judge, according to usage, whether he had anything to say before sentence of Death should be passed upon him, indistinctly muttered something which was described in the leading newspapers of the following day as " a few rambling, incoherent, and half-audible words, in which he was understood to complain that he had not had a fair trial, because the Foreman of the Jury was prepossessed against him." The remarkable declaration that he really made, was this : " *My Lord, I knew I was a doomed man when the Foreman of my Jury came into the box. My Lord, I knew he would never let me off, because, before I was taken, he somehow got to my bedside in the night, woke me, and put a rope round my neck.*"

———————

Charles Dickens

THE SIGNAL-MAN

from ALL THE YEAR ROUND, 1866

"Halloa ! Below there !"

When he heard a voice thus calling to him, he was standing at the door of his box, with a flag in his hand, furled round its short pole. One would have thought, considering the nature of the ground, that he could not have doubted from what quarter the voice came ; but, instead of looking up to where I stood on the top of the steep cutting nearly over his head, he turned himself about and looked down the Line. There was something remarkable in his manner of doing so, though I could not have said, for my life, what. But, I know it was remarkable enough to attract my notice, even though his figure was foreshortened and shadowed, down in the deep trench, and mine was high above him, so steeped in the glow of an angry sunset that I had shaded my eyes with my hand before I saw him at all.

" Halloa ! Below ! "

From looking down the Line, he turned himself about again, and, raising his eyes, saw my figure high above him.

" Is there any path by which I can come down and speak to you ? "

He looked up at me without replying, and I looked down at him without pressing him too soon with a repetition of my idle question. Just then, there came a vague vibration in the earth and air, quickly changing into a violent pulsation, and an oncoming rush that caused me to start back, as though it had force to draw me down. When such vapour as rose to my height from this rapid train, had passed me and was skimming away over the landscape, I looked down again, and saw him re-furling the flag he had shown while the train went by.

I repeated my inquiry. After a pause, during which he seemed to regard me with fixed attention, he motioned with his rolled-up flag towards a point on my level, some two or three hundred yards distant. I called down to him, " All right ! " and made for that point. There, by dint of looking closely about me, I found a rough zig-zag descending path notched out : which I followed.

The cutting was extremely deep, and unusually precipitate.

It was made through a clammy stone that became oozier and wetter as I went down. For these reasons, I found the way long enough to give me time to recall a singular air of reluctance or compulsion with which he had pointed out the path.

When I came down low enough upon the zig-zag descent, to see him again, I saw that he was standing between the rails on the way by which the train had lately passed, in an attitude as if he were waiting for me to appear. He had his left hand at his chin, and that left elbow rested on his right hand crossed over his breast. His attitude was one of such expectation and watchfulness, that I stopped a moment, wondering at it.

I resumed my downward way, and, stepping out upon the level of the railroad and drawing nearer to him, saw that he was a dark sallow man, with a dark beard and rather heavy eyebrows. His post was in as solitary and dismal a place as ever I saw. On either side, a dripping-wet wall of jagged stone, excluding all view but a strip of sky ; the perspective one way, only a crooked prolongation of this great dungeon ; the shorter perspective in the other direction, terminating in a gloomy red light, and the gloomier entrance to a black tunnel, in whose massive architecture there was a barbarous, depressing, and forbidding air. So little sunlight ever found its way to this spot, that it had an earthy deadly smell ; and so much cold wind rushed through it, that it struck chill to me, as if I had left the natural world.

Before he stirred, I was near enough to him to have touched him. Not even then removing his eyes from mine, he stepped back one step, and lifted his hand.

This was a lonesome post to occupy (I said), and it had riveted my attention when I looked down from up yonder. A visitor was a rarity, I should suppose ; not an unwelcome rarity, I hoped ? In me, he merely saw a man who had been shut up within narrow limits all his life, and who, being at last set free, had a newly-awakened interest in these great works. To such purpose I spoke to him ; but I am far from sure of the terms I used, for, besides that I am not happy in opening any conversation, there was something in the man that daunted me.

He directed a most curious look towards the red light near the tunnel's mouth, and looked all about it, as if something were missing from it, and then looked at me.

That light was part of his charge ? Was it not ?

He answered in a low voice : " Don't you know it is ? "

The monstrous thought came into my mind as I perused the fixed eyes and the saturnine face, that this was a spirit, not a man. I have speculated since, whether there may have been infection in his mind.

In my turn, I stepped back. But in making the action, I detected in his eyes some latent fear of me. This put the monstrous thought to flight.

" You look at me," I said, forcing a smile, " as if you had a dread of me."

" I was doubtful," he returned, " whether I had seen you before."

" Where ? "

He pointed to the red light he had looked at.

" There ? " I said.

Intently watchful of me, he replied (but without sound), Yes.

" My good fellow, what should I do there ? However, be that as it may, I never was there, you may swear."

" I think I may," he rejoined. " Yes. I am sure I may."

His manner cleared, like my own. He replied to my remarks with readiness, and in well-chosen words. Had he much to do there ? Yes ; that was to say, he had enough responsibility to bear ; but exactness and watchfulness were what was required of him, and of actual work—manual labour he had next to none. To change that signal, to trim those lights, and to turn this iron handle now and then, was all he had to do under that head. Regarding those many long and lonely hours of which I seemed to make so much, he could only say that the routine of his life had shaped itself into that form, and he had grown used to it. He had taught himself a language down here—if only to know it by sight, and to have formed his own crude ideas of its pronunciation, could be called learning it. He had also worked at fractions and decimals, and tried a little algebra ; but he was, and had been as a boy, a poor hand at figures. Was it necessary for him when on duty, always to remain in that channel of damp air, and could he never rise into the sunshine from between those high stone walls ? Why, that depended upon times and circumstances. Under some conditions there would be less upon the Line than under others, and the same held good as to certain hours of the day and night. In bright weather, he did choose occasions for getting a little above these lower shadows ; but, being at all times liable to be called by his electric bell, and at such times listening for it with redoubled anxiety, the relief was less than I would suppose.

He took me into his box, where there was a fire, a desk for an official book in which he had to make certain entries, a telegraphic instrument with its dial face and needles, and the little bell of which he had spoken. On my trusting that he would excuse the remark that he had been well-educated, and (I hoped I might say without offence), perhaps educated above that station, he observed that instances of slight incongruity in such-wise would rarely be found wanting among large bodies of men ; that he had heard it was so in workhouses, in the police force, even in that last desperate resource, the army ; and that he knew it was so, more or less, in any great railway staff. He had been, when young (if I could believe it, sitting in that, hut ; he scarcely could), a student of natural philosophy, and had attended lectures ; but he had run wild, misused his opportunities, gone down, and never risen again. He had no complaint to offer about that. He had made his bed, and he lay upon it. It was far too late to make another.

All that I have here condensed, he said in a quiet manner, with his grave dark regards divided between me and the fire. He threw in the word " Sir " from time to time, and especially when he referred to his youth : as though to request me to understand that he claimed to be nothing but what I found him. He was several times interrupted by the little bell, and had to read off messages, and send replies. Once, he had to stand without the door, and display a flag as a train passed, and make some verbal communication to the driver. In the discharge of his duties I observed him to be remarkably exact and vigilant, breaking off his discourse at a syllable, and remaining silent until what he had to do was done.

In a word, I should have set this man down as one of the safest of men to be employed in that capacity, but for the circumstance that while he was speaking to me he twice broke off with a fallen colour, turned his face towards the little bell when it did NOT ring, opened the door of the hut (which was kept shut to exclude the unhealthy damp), and looked out towards the red light near the mouth of the tunnel. On both of those occasions, he came back to the fire with the inexplicable air upon him which I had remarked, without being able to define, when we were so far asunder.

Said I when I rose to leave him : " You almost make me think that I have met with a contented man."

(I am afraid I must acknowledge that I said it to lead him on.)

" I believe I used to be so," he rejoined, in the low voice in which he had first spoken; " but I am troubled, sir, I am troubled."

He would have recalled the words if he could. He had said them, however, and I took them up quickly.

" With what ? What is your trouble ? "

" It is very difficult to impart, sir. It is very, very difficult to speak of. If ever you make me another visit, I will try to tell you."

" But I expressly intend to make you another visit. Say, when shall it be ? "

" I go off early in the morning, and I shall be on again at ten to-morrow night, sir."

" I will come at eleven."

He thanked me, and went out at the door with me. " I'll show my white light, sir," he said, in his peculiar low voice, " till you have found the way up. When you have found it, don't call out ! And when you are at the top, don't call out ! "

His manner seemed to make the place strike colder to me, but I said no more than " Very well."

" And when you come down to-morrow night, don't call out ! Let me ask you a parting question. What made you cry ' Halloa ! Below there ! ' to-night ? "

⌐" ' Heaven knows,'' said I. " I cried something to that effect——"

" Not to that effect, sir. Those were the very words. I know them well."

" Admit those were the very words. I said them, no doubt, because I saw you below."

" For no other reason ? "

" What other reason could I possibly have ! "

" You had no feeling that they were conveyed to you in any supernatural way ? "

" No."

He wished me good night, and held up his light. I walked by the side of the down Line of rails (with a very disagreeable sensation of a train coming behind me), until I found the path. It was easier to mount than to descend, and I got back to my inn without any adventure.

Punctual to my appointment, I placed my foot on the first notch of the zig-zag next night, as the distant clocks were striking eleven. He was waiting for me at the bottom, with his white light on. " I have not called out," I said, when we came close together ; " may I speak now ? " " By all means, sir " " Good night then, and here's my hand." " Good night, sir, and here's mine." With that, we walked side by side to his box, entered it, closed the door, and sat down by the fire.

" I have made up my mind, sir," he began, bending forward as soon as we were seated, and speaking in a tone but a little above a whisper, " that you shall not have to ask me twice what troubles me. I took you for someone else yesterday evening. That troubles me."

" That mistake ? "

" No. That someone else."

" Who is it ? "

" I don't know."

" Like me ? "

" I don't know. I never saw the face. The left arm is across the face, and the right arm is waved. Violently waved. This way."

I followed his action with my eyes, and it was the action of an arm gesticulating with the utmost passion and vehemence : " For God's sake clear the way ! "

" One moonlight night," said the man, " I was sitting here, when I heard a voice cry ' Halloa ! Below there !' I started up, looked from that door, and saw this Some one else standing by the red light near the tunnel, waving as I just now showed you. The voice seemed hoarse with shouting, and it cried, ' Look out ! Look out ! ' And then again ' Halloa ! Below there ! Look out ! ' I caught up my lamp, turned it on red, and ran towards the figure, calling, ' What's wrong ? What has happened ? Where ? ' It stood just outside the blackness of the tunnel. I advanced so close upon it that I wondered at its keeping the sleeve across its eyes. I ran right up at it, and had my hand stretched out to pull the sleeve away, when it was gone."

" Into the tunnel," said I.

" No. I ran on into the tunnel, five hundred yards. I stopped and held my lamp above my head, and saw the figures of the measured distance, and saw the wet stains stealing down the walls and trickling through the arch. I ran out again, faster than I had run in (for I had a mortal abhorrence of the place upon me), and I looked all round the red light with my own red light, and I went up the iron ladder to the gallery atop of it, and I came down again, and ran back here. I telegraphed both ways, ' An alarm has been given. Is anything wrong ? ' The answer came back, both ways : ' All well.' "

Resisting the slow touch of a frozen finger tracing out my spine, I showed him how that this figure must be a deception of his sense of sight, and how that figures, originating in disease of the delicate nerves that minister to the functions of the eye, were known to have often troubled patients, some of whom had become conscious of the nature of their affliction, and had even proved it by experiments upon themselves. " As to an imaginary cry," said I, " do but listen for a moment to the wind in this unnatural valley while we speak so low, and to the wild harp it makes of the telegraph wires ! "

That was all very well, he returned, after we had sat listening for a while, and he ought to know something of the wind and the wires, he who so often passed long winter nights there, alone and watching. But he would beg to remark that he had not finished.

I asked his pardon, and he slowly added these words, touching my arm :

" Within six hours after the Appearance, the memorable accident on this Line happened, and within ten hours the dead and wounded were brought along through the tunnel over the spot where the figure had stood."

A disagreeable shudder crept over me, but I did my best against it. It was not to be denied, I rejoined, that this was a remarkable coincidence, calculated deeply to impress his mind. But it was unquestionable that remarkable coincidences did continually occur, and they must be taken into account in dealing with such a subject. Though to be sure I must admit, I added (for I thought I saw that he was going to bring the objection to bear upon me), men of common sense did not allow much for coincidences in making the ordinary calculations of life.

He again begged to remark that he had not finished.

I again begged his pardon for being betrayed into interruptions.

" This," he said, again laying his hand upon my arm, and glancing over his shoulder with hollow eyes, " was just a year ago. Six or seven months passed, and I had recovered from the surprise and shock, when one morning, as the day was breaking, I, standing at that door, looked towards the red light, and saw the spectre again." He stopped, with a fixed look at me.

" Did it cry out ? "

" No. It was silent."

" Did it wave its arm ? "

"No. It leaned against the shaft of the light, with both hands before the face. Like this."

Once more, I followed his action with my eyes. It was an action of mourning. I have seen such an attitude in stone figures on tombs.

"Did you go up to it?"

"I came in and sat down, partly to collect my thoughts, partly because it had turned me faint. When I went to the door again, daylight was above me, and the ghost was gone."

"But nothing followed? Nothing came of this?"

He touched me on the arm with his forefinger twice or thrice, giving a ghastly nod each time:

"That very day, as a train came out of the tunnel, I noticed, at a carriage window on my side, what looked like a confusion of hands and heads, and something waved. I saw it, just in time to signal the driver, Stop! He shut off, and put his brake on, but the train drifted past here a hundred and fifty yards or more. I ran after it, and, as I went along, heard terrible screams and cries. A beautiful young lady had died instantaneously in one of the compartments, and was brought in here, and laid down on this floor between us."

Involuntarily, I pushed my chair back, as I looked from the boards at which he pointed, to himself.

"True, sir. True. Precisely as it happened, so I tell it you."

I could think of nothing to say, to any purpose, and my mouth was very dry. The wind and the wires took up the story with a long lamenting wail.

He resumed. "Now, sir, mark this, and judge how my mind is troubled. The spectre came back, a week ago. Ever since, it has been there, now and again, by fits and starts."

"At the light?"

"At the Danger-light."

"What does it seem to do?"

He repeated, if possible with increased passion and vehemence, that former gesticulation of "For God's sake clear the way!"

Then, he went on. "I have no peace or rest for it. It calls to me, for many minutes together, in an agonised manner, 'Below there! Look out! Look out!' It stands waving to me. It rings my little bell——"

I caught at that. "Did it ring your bell yesterday evening when I was here, and you went to the door?"

" Twice."

" Why, see," said I, " how your imagination misleads you. My eyes were on the bell, and my ears were open to the bell, and if I am a living man, it did NOT ring at those times. No, nor at any other time, except when it was rung in the natural course of physical things by the station communicating with you."

He shook his head. " I have never made a mistake as to that, yet, sir. I have never confused the spectre's ring with the man's. The ghost's ring is a strange vibration in the bell that it derives from nothing else, and I have not asserted that the bell stirs to the eye. I don't wonder that you failed to hear it. But *I* heard it."

" And did the spectre seem to be there, when you looked out ? "

" It WAS there."

" Both times ? "

He repeated firmly : " Both times."

" Will you come to the door with me, and look for it now ? "

He bit his under-lip as though he were somewhat unwilling, but arose. I opened the door, and stood on the step, while he stood in the doorway. There, was the Danger-light. There, was the dismal mouth of the tunnel. There, were the high wet stone walls of the cutting. There, were the stars above them.

" Do you see it ? " I asked him, taking particular note of his face. His eyes were prominent and strained ; but not very much more so, perhaps, than my own had been when I had directed them earnestly towards the same spot.

" No," he answered. " It is not there."

" Agreed," said I.

We went in again, shut the door, and resumed our seats. I was thinking how best to improve this advantage, if it might be called one, when he took up the conversation in such a matter of course way, so assuming that there could be no serious question of fact between us, that I felt myself placed in the weakest of positions.

" By this time you will fully understand, sir," he said, " that what troubles me so dreadfully, is the question, What does the spectre mean ? "

I was not sure, I told him, that I did fully understand.

" What is its warning against ? " he said, ruminating, with his eyes on the fire, and only by times turning them on me. " What is the danger ? Where is the danger ? There is danger overhanging, somewhere on the Line. Some dreadful calamity will happen.

It is not to be doubted this third time, after what has gone before. But surely this is a cruel haunting of *me*. What can *I* do ? "

He pulled out his handkerchief, and wiped the drops from his heated forehead.

" If I telegraph Danger, on either side of me, or on both, I can give no reason for it," he went on, wiping the palms of his hands. " I should get into trouble, and do no good. They would think I was mad. This is the way it would work :—Message : ' Danger ! Take care ! ' Answer : ' What danger ? Where ? ' Message : ' Don't know. But for God's sake take care ! ' They would displace me. What else could they do ? "

His pain of mind was most pitiable to see. It was the mental torture of a conscientious man, oppressed beyond endurance by an unintelligible responsibility involving life.

" When it first stood under the Danger-light," he went on, putting his dark hair back from his head, and drawing his hands outward across and across his temples in an extremity of feverish distress, " why not tell me where that accident was to happen— if it must happen ? Why not tell me how it could be averted—if it could have been averted ? When on its second coming it hid its face, why not tell me instead : ' She is going to die. Let them keep her at home ' ? If it came, on those two occasions, only to show me that its warnings were true, and so to prepare me for the third, why not warn me plainly now ? And I, Lord help me ! A mere poor signalman on this solitary station ! Why not go to somebody with credit to be believed, and power to act ! "

When I saw him in this state, I saw that for the poor man's sake, as well as for the public safety, what I had to do for the time was, to compose his mind. Therefore, setting aside all question of reality or unreality between us, I represented to him that whoever thoroughly discharged his duty, must do well, and that at least it was his comfort that he understood his duty, though he did not understand these confounding Appearances. In this effort I succeeded far better than in the attempt to reason him out of his conviction. He became calm ; the occupations incidental to his post as the night advanced, began to make larger demands on his attention ; and I left him at two in the morning. I had offered to stay through the night, but he would not hear of it.

That I more than once looked back at the red light as I ascended the pathway, that I did not like the red light, and that I should have slept but poorly if my bed had been under it, I see no reason to conceal. Nor, did I like the two sequences of the accident and the dead girl. I see no reason to conceal that, either.

But, what ran most in my thoughts was the consideration how ought I to act, having become the recipient of this disclosure? I had proved the man to be intelligent, vigilant, painstaking, and exact; but how long might he remain so, in his state of mind? Though in a subordinate position, still he held a most important trust, and would I (for instance) like to stake my own life on the chances of his continuing to execute it with precision?

Unable to overcome a feeling that there would be something treacherous in my communicating what he had told me, to his superiors in the Company, without first being plain with himself and proposing a middle course to him, I ultimately resolved to offer to accompany him (otherwise keeping his secret for the present) to the wisest medical practitioner we could hear of in those parts, and to take his opinion. A change in his time of duty would come round next night, he had apprised me, and he would be off an hour or two after sunrise, and on again soon after sunset. I had appointed to return accordingly.

Next evening was a lovely evening, and I walked out early to enjoy it. The sun was not yet quite down when I traversed the field-path near the top of the deep cutting. I would extend my walk for an hour, I said to myself, half an hour on and half an hour back, and it would then be time to go to my signal-man's box.

Before pursuing my stroll, I stepped to the brink, and mechanically looked down, from the point from which I had first seen him. I cannot describe the thrill that seized upon me, when, close at the mouth of the tunnel, I saw the appearance of a man, with his left sleeve across his eyes, passionately waving his right arm.

The nameless horror that oppressed me, passed in a moment, for in a moment I saw that this appearance of a man was a man indeed, and that there was a little group of other men standing at a short distance, to whom he seemed to be rehearsing the gesture he made. The Danger-light was not yet lighted. Against its shaft, a little low hut, entirely new to me, had been made of some wooden supports and tarpaulin. It looked no bigger than a bed.

With an irresistible sense that something was wrong—with a flashing self-reproachful fear that fatal mischief had come of my leaving the man there, and causing no one to be sent to overlook or correct what he did—I descended the notched path with all the speed I could make.

"What is the matter ? " I asked the men.

"Signal-man killed this morning, sir."

"Not the man belonging to that box ? "

"Yes, sir."

"Not the man I know ? "

"You will recognise him, sir, if you knew him," said the man who spoke for the others, solemnly uncovering his own head and raising an end of the tarpaulin, "for his face is quite composed."

"O ! how did this happen, how did this happen ? " I asked, turning from one to another as the hut closed in again.

"He was cut down by an engine, sir. No man in England knew his work better. But somehow he was not clear of the outer rail. It was just at broad day. He had struck the light, and had the lamp in his hand. As the engine came out of the tunnel, his back was towards her, and she cut him down. That man drove her, and was showing how it happened. Show the gentleman, Tom."

The man, who wore a rough dark dress, stepped back to his former place at the mouth of the tunnel !

"Coming round the curve in the tunnel, sir," he said, "I saw him at the end, like as if I saw him down a perspective-glass. There was no time to check speed, and I knew him to be very careful. As he didn't seem to take heed of the whistle, I shut it off when we were running down upon him, and called to him as loud as I could call."

"What did you say ? "

"I said, Below there ! Look out ! Look out ! For God's sake clear the way ! "

I started.

"Ah ! it was a dreadful time, sir. I never left off calling to him. I put this arm before my eyes, not to see, and I waved this arm to the last ; but it was no use."

Without prolonging the narrative to dwell on any one of its curious circumstances more than on any other, I may, in closing it, point out the coincidence that the warning of the Engine-Driver included, not only the words which the unfortunate Signal-man had repeated to me as haunting him, but also the words which I myself—not he—had attached, and that only in my own mind, to the gesticulation he had imitated.

Charles Collins

THE COMPENSATION HOUSE

from ALL THE YEAR ROUND, 1866

"There's not a looking-glass in all the house, sir. It's some peculiar fancy of my master's. There isn't one in any single room in the house."

It was a dark and gloomy-looking building, and had been purchased by this Company for an enlargement of their Goods Station. The value of the house had been referred to what was popularly called "a compensation jury," and the house was called, in consequence, The Compensation House. It had become the Company's property; but its tenant still remained in possession, pending the commencement of active building operations. My attention was originally drawn to this house because it stood directly in front of a collection of huge pieces of timber which lay near this part of the Line, and on which I sometimes sat for half an hour at a time, when I was tired by my wanderings about Mugby Junction.

It was square, cold, grey-looking, built of rough-hewn stone, and roofed with thin slabs of the same material. Its windows were few in number, and very small for the size of the building. In the great blank, grey broadside, there were only four windows. The entrance-door was in the middle of the house; there was a window on either side of it, and there were two more in the single story above. The blinds were all closely drawn, and when the door was shut, the dreary building gave no sign of life or occupation.

But the door was not always shut. Sometimes it was opened from within, with a great jingling of bolts and door-chains, and then a man would come forward and stand upon the doorstep, snuffing the air as one might do who was ordinarily kept on rather a small allowance of that element. He was stout, thickset, and perhaps fifty or sixty years old—a man whose hair was cut exceedingly close, who wore a large bushy beard, and whose eye had a sociable twinkle in it which was prepossessing. He was dressed, whenever I saw him, in a greenish-brown frock-coat made of some material which was not cloth, wore a waistcoat and trousers of light colour, and had a frill to his shirt—an ornament, by the way, which did not seem to go at all well with the beard, which was continually in contact with it. It was the custom of this worthy person, after standing for a short time on the threshold inhaling the air, to come forward into the road, and, after glancing at one of the upper windows in a half mechanical way, to cross over to the logs, and, leaning over the fence which guarded the railway, to look up and down the Line (it passed before the house) with the air of a man accomplishing a self-imposed task of which nothing was expected to come. This done, he would cross the road again, and turning on the threshold to take a final sniff of air, disappeared once more within the house, bolting and chaining the door again as if there were no probability of its being reopened for at least a week. Yet half an hour had not passed before he was out in the road again, sniffing the air and looking up and down the Line as before.

It was not very long before I managed to scrape acquaintance with this restless personage. I soon found out that my friend with the shirt-frill was the confidential servant, butler, valet, factotum, what you will, of a sick gentleman, a Mr. Oswald Strange, who had recently come to inhabit the house opposite, and concerning whose history my new acquaintance, whose name I ascertained was Masey, seemed disposed to be somewhat communicative. His master, it appeared, had come down to this place, partly for the sake of reducing his establishment—not, Mr. Masey was swift to inform me, on economical principles, but because the poor gentleman, for particular reasons, wished to have few dependents about him—partly in order that he might be near his old friend, Dr. Garden, who was established in the neighbourhood, and whose society and advice were necessary to Mr. Strange's life. That life was, it appeared, held by this suffering gentleman on a precarious tenure. It was ebbing away fast with each passing hour. The servant already spoke of his master in the past tense, describing him to me as a young gentleman not more than five-and-thirty years of age, with a young face, as far as the features and build of it went, but with an expression which had nothing of youth about it. This was the great peculiarity of the man. At a distance he looked younger than he was by many years, and strangers, at the time when he had been used to get about, always took him for a man of seven or eight-and-twenty, but they changed their minds on getting nearer to him. Old Masey had a way of his own of summing up the peculiarities of his master, repeating twenty times over : " Sir, he was Strange by name, and Strange by nature, and Strange to look at into the bargain."

It was during my second or third interview with the old fellow that he uttered the words quoted at the beginning of this plain narrative.

" Not such a thing as a looking-glass in all the house," the old man said, standing beside my piece of timber, and looking across reflectively at the house opposite. " Not one."

" In the sitting-rooms, I suppose you mean ? "

" No, sir, I mean sitting-rooms and bedrooms both ; there isn't so much as a shaving-glass as big as the palm of your hand anywhere."

" But how is it ? " I asked. " Why are there no looking-glasses in any of the rooms ? "

" Ah, sir ! " replied Masey, " that's what none of us can ever tell. There is the mystery. It's just a fancy on the part of my master. He had some strange fancies, and this was one of them. A pleasant gentleman he was to live with, as any servant could desire. A liberal gentleman, and one who gave but little trouble ; always ready with a kind word, and a kind deed, too, for the matter of that. There was not a house in all the parish of St. George's (in which we lived before we came down here) where the servants had more holidays or a better table kept ; but, for all that, he had his queer ways and his fancies, as I may call them, and this was one of them. And the point he made of it, sir," the old man went on ; " the extent to which that regulation was enforced, whenever a new servant was engaged ; and the changes in the establishment it occasioned ! In hiring a new servant, the very first stipulation made, was that about the looking-glasses. It was one of my duties to explain the thing, as far as it could be explained, before any servant was taken into the house. ' You'll find it an easy place,' I used to say, ' with a liberal table, good wages, and a deal of leisure ; but there's one thing you must make up your mind to ; you must do without looking-glasses while you're here, for there isn't one in the house, and, what's more, there never will be."

" But how did you know there never would be one ? " I asked.

" Lor' bless you, sir ! If you'd seen and heard all that I'd seen and heard, you could have no doubt about it. Why, only to take one instance :—I remember a particular day when my master had occasion to go into the housekeeper's room, where the cook lived, to see about some alterations that were making, and when a pretty scene took place. The cook—she was a very ugly woman, and awful vain—had left a little bit of a looking-glass, about six inches square, upon the chimney-piece ; she had got it *surreptitious*, and kept it always locked up ; but she'd left it out, being called away suddenly, while titivating her hair. I had seen the glass, and was making for the chimney-piece as fast as I could ; but master came in front of it before I could get there, and it was all over in a moment. He gave one long piercing look into it, turned deadly pale, and seizing the glass, dashed it into a hundred pieces on the floor, and then stamped upon the fragments and ground them into powder with his feet. He shut himself up for the rest of that day in his own room, first ordering me to discharge the cook, then and there, at a moment's notice."

" What an extraordinary thing ! " I said, pondering.

" Ah, sir," continued the old man, " it was astonishing what trouble I had with those women-servants. It was difficult to get any that would take the place at all under the circumstances. ' What not so much as a mossul to do one's 'air at ? ' they would say, and they'd go off, in spite of extra wages. Then those who did consent to come, what lies they would tell, to be sure ! They would protest that they didn't want to look in the glass, that they never had been in the habit of looking in the glass, and all the while that very wench would have her looking-glass, of some kind or another, hid away among her clothes upstairs. Sooner or later, she would bring it out too, and leave it about somewhere or other (just like the cook), where it was as likely as not that master might see it. And then—for girls like that have no consciences, sir— when I had caught one of 'em at it, she'd turn round as bold as brass, ' And how am I to know whether my 'air's parted straight ? ' she'd say, just as if it hadn't been considered in her wages that that was the very thing which she never *was* to know while she lived in our house. A vain lot, sir, and the ugly ones always the vainest. There was no end to their dodges. They'd have looking-glasses in the interiors of their workbox-lids, where it was next to impossible that I could find 'em, or inside the covers of hymn-books, or cookery-books, or in their caddies. I recollect one girl, a sly one she was, and marked with the small-pox terrible, who was always reading her prayer-book at odd times. Sometimes I used to think what a religious mind she'd got, and at other times (depending on the mood I was in) I would conclude that it was the marriage-service she was studying ; but one day, when I got behind her to satisfy my doubts—lo and behold ! it was the old story : a bit of glass, without a frame, fastened into the kiver with the outside edges of the sheets of postage-stamps. Dodges ! Why they'd keep their looking-glasses in the scullery or the coal-cellar, or leave them in charge of the servants next door, or with the milk-woman round the corner ; but have 'em they would. And I don't mind confessing, sir," said the old man, bringing his long speech to an end, " that it *was* an inconveniency not to have so much as a scrap to shave before. I used to go to the barber's at first, but I soon gave that up, and took to wearing my beard as my master did ; likewise to keeping my hair "—Mr. Masey touched his head as he spoke—" so short, that it didn't require any parting, before or behind."

I sat for some time lost in amazement, and staring at my companion. My curiosity was powerfully stimulated, and the desire to learn more was very strong within me.

" Had your master any personal defect," I inquired, " which might have made it distressing to him to see his own image reflected ? "

" By no means, sir," said the old man. " He was as handsome a gentleman as you would wish to see : a little delicate-looking and care-worn, perhaps, with a very pale face ; but as free from any deformity as you or I, sir. No, sir, no ; it was nothing of that."

" Then what was it ? What is it ? " I asked, desperately. " Is there no one who is, or has been, in your master's confidence ? "

" Yes, sir," said the old fellow, with his eyes turning to that window opposite. " There is one person who knows all my master's secrets, and this secret among the rest."

" And who is that ? "

The old man turned round and looked at me fixedly. " The doctor here," he said. " Dr. Garden. My master's very old friend."

" I should like to speak with this gentleman," I said, involuntarily.

" He is with my master now," answered Masey. " He will be coming out presently, and I think I may say he will answer any question you may like to put to him." As the old man spoke, the door of the house opened, and a middle-aged gentleman, who was tall and thin, but who lost something of his height by a habit of stooping, appeared on the step. Old Masey left me in a moment. He muttered something about taking the doctor's directions, and hastened across the road. The tall gentleman spoke to him for a minute or two very seriously, probably about the patient upstairs, and it then seemed to me from their gestures that I myself was the subject of some further conversation between them. At all events, when old Masey retired into the house, the doctor came across to where I was standing, and addressed me with a very agreeable smile.

" John Masey tells me that you are interested in the case of my poor friend, sir. I am now going back to my house, and if you don't mind the trouble of walking with me, I shall be happy to enlighten you as far as I am able."

I hastened to make my apologies and express my acknowledgments, and we set off together. When we had reached the doctor's house and were seated in his study, I ventured to inquire after the health of this poor gentleman.

" I am afraid there is no amendment, nor any prospect of amendment," said the doctor. " Old Masey has told you something of his strange condition, has he not ? "

" Yes, he has told me something," I answered, " and he says you know all about it."

Dr. Garden looked very grave. " I don't know all about it. I only know what happens when he comes into the presence of a looking-glass. But as to the circumstances which have led to his being haunted in the strangest fashion that I ever heard of, I know no more of them than you do."

" Haunted ? " I repeated. " And in the strangest fashion that you ever heard of ? "

Dr. Garden smiled at my eagerness, seemed to be collecting his thoughts, and presently went on :

" I made the acquaintance of Mr. Oswald Strange in a curious way. It was on board of an Italian steamer, bound from Civita Vecchia to Marseilles. We had been travelling all night. In the morning I was shaving myself in the cabin, when suddenly this man came behind me, glanced for a moment into the small mirror before which I was standing, and then, without a word of warning, tore it from the nail, and dashed it to pieces at my feet. His face was at first livid with passion—it seemed to me rather the passion of fear than of anger—but it changed after a moment, and he seemed ashamed of what he had done. Well," continued the doctor, relapsing for a moment into a smile, " of course I was in a devil of a rage. I was operating on my under-jaw, and the start the thing gave me caused me to cut myself. Besides, altogether it seemed an outrageous and insolent thing, and I gave it to poor Strange in a style of language which I am sorry to think of now, but which, I hope, was excusable at the time. As to the offender himself, his confusion and regret, now that his passion was at an end, disarmed me. He sent for the steward, and paid most liberally for the damage done to the steamboat property, explaining to him, and to some other passengers who were present in the cabin, that what had happened had been accidental. For me, however, he had another explanation. Perhaps he felt that I must know it to have been no accident—perhaps he really wished to confide in someone. At all events, he owned to me that what he had done was done under the influence of an uncontrollable impulse—a seizure which took him, he said, at times—something like a fit. He begged my pardon, and entreated that I would endeavour to disassociate him personally from this action, of which he was heartily ashamed. Then he attempted a sickly joke, poor fellow, about his wearing a beard, and feeling a little spiteful, in consequence, when he saw other people taking the trouble to shave ; but he said nothing about any infirmity or delusion, and shortly after left me.

" In my professional capacity I could not help taking some interest in Mr. Strange. I did not altogether lose sight of him after our sea-journey to Marseilles was over. I found him a pleasant companion up to a certain point ; but I always felt that there was a reserve about him. He was uncommunicative about his past life, and especially would never allude to anything connected with his travels or his residence in Italy, which, however, I could make out had been a long one. He spoke Italian well, and seemed familiar with the country, but disliked to talk about it.

" During the time we spent together there were seasons when he was so little himself, that I, with a pretty large experience, was almost afraid to be with him. His attacks were violent and sudden in the last degree ; and there was one most extraordinary feature connected with them all :—some horrible association of ideas took possession of him whenever he found himself before a looking-glass. And after we had travelled together for a time, I dreaded the sight of a mirror hanging harmlessly against a wall, or a toilet-glass standing on a dressing-table, almost as much as he did.

" Poor Strange was not always affected in the same manner by a looking-glass. Sometimes it seemed to madden him with fury ; at other times, it appeared to turn him to stone : remaining motionless and speechless as if attacked by catalepsy. One night— the worst things always happen at night, and oftener than one would think on stormy nights—we arrived at a small town in the central district of Auvergne : a place but little known, out of the line of railways, and to which we had been drawn, partly by the antiquarian attractions which the place possessed, and partly by the beauty of the scenery. The weather had been rather against us. The day had been dull and murky, the heat stifling, and the sky had threatened mischief since the morning. At sundown, these threats were fulfilled. The thunderstorm, which had been all day coming up—as it seemed to us, against the wind—burst over the place where we were lodged, with very great violence.

" There are some practical-minded persons with strong con-stitutions, who deny roundly that their fellow-creatures are, or can be, affected, in mind or body, by atmospheric influences. I am not a disciple of that school, simply because I cannot believe that those changes of weather, which have so much effect upon animals, and even on inanimate objects, can fail to have some influence on a piece of machinery so sensitive and intricate as the human frame. I think, then, that it was in part owing to the disturbed state of the atmosphere that, on this particular evening I felt nervous and depressed. When my new friend Strange and I parted for the night, I felt as little disposed to go to rest as I ever did in my life. The thunder was still lingering among the moun-tains in the midst of which our inn was placed. Sometimes it seemed nearer, and at other times further off ; but it never left off altogether, except for a few minutes at a time. I was quite unable to shake off a succession of painful ideas which persistently besieged my mind.

" It is hardly necessary to add that I thought from time to time of my travelling-companion in the next room. His image was almost continually before me. He had been dull and depressed all the evening, and when we parted for the night there was a look in his eyes which I could not get out of my memory.

" There was a door between our rooms, and the partition divid-ing them was not very solid ; and yet I had heard no sound since I parted from him which could indicate that he was there at all, much less that he was awake and stirring. I was in a mood, sir, which made this silence terrible to me, and so many foolish fancies —as that he was lying there dead, or in a fit, or what not—took possession of me, that at last I could bear it no longer. I went to the door, and, after listening, very attentively but quite in vain, for any sound, I at last knocked pretty sharply. There was no answer. Feeling that longer suspense would be unendurable, I, without more ceremony, turned the handle and went in.

" It was a great bare room, and so imperfectly lighted by a single candle that it was almost impossible—except when the lightning flashed—to see into its great dark corners. A small rickety bedstead stood against one of the walls, shrouded by yellow cotton curtains, passed through a great iron ring in the ceiling. There was, for all other furniture, an old chest-of-drawers which served also as a washing-stand, having a small basin and ewer and a single towel arranged on the top of it. There were, moreover, two ancient chairs and a dressing-table. On this last, stood a large old-fashioned looking-glass with a carved frame.

" I must have seen all these things, because I remember them so well now, but I do not know how I could have seen them, for it seems to me that, from the moment of my entering that room, the action of my senses and of the faculties of my mind was held fast by the ghastly figure which stood motionless before the looking-glass in the middle of the empty room.

" How terrible it was ! The weak light of one candle standing on the table shone upon Strange's face, lighting it from below, and throwing (as I now remember) his shadow, vast and black, upon the wall behind him and upon the ceiling overhead. He was leaning rather forward, with his hands upon the table supporting him, and gazing into the glass which stood before him with a horrible fixity. The sweat was on his white face ; his rigid features and his pale lips showed in that feeble light were horrible, more than words can tell, to look at. He was so completely stupefied and lost, that the noise I had made in knocking and in entering the room was unobserved by him. Not even when I called him loudly by name did he move or did his face change.

" What a vision of horror that was, in the great dark empty room, in a silence that was something more than negative, that ghastly figure frozen into stone by some unexplained terror ! And the silence and the stillness ! The very thunder had ceased now. My heart stood still with fear. Then, moved by some instinctive feeling, under whose influence I acted mechanically, I crept with slow steps nearer and nearer to the table, and at last, half expecting to see some spectre even more horrible than this which I saw already, I looked over his shoulder into the looking-glass. I happened to touch his arm, though only in the lightest manner. In that one moment the spell which had held him—who knows how

long ?—enchained, seemed broken, and he lived in this world
again. He turned round upon me, as suddenly as a tiger makes
its spring, and seized me by the arm.

"I have told you that even before I entered my friend's room
I had felt, all that night, depressed and nervous. The necessity
for action at this time was, however, so obvious, and this man's
agony made all that I had felt, appear so trifling, that much of
my own discomfort seemed to leave me. I felt that I *must* be strong.

"The face before me almost unmanned me. The eyes which
looked into mine were so scared with terror, the lips—if I may
say so—looked so speechless. The wretched man gazed long into
my face, and then, still holding me by the arm, slowly, very slowly,
turned his head. I had gently tried to move him away from the
looking-glass, but he would not stir, and now he was looking into
it as fixedly as ever. I could bear this no longer, and, using such
force as was necessary, I drew him gradually away, and got him
to one of the chairs at the foot of the bed. 'Come !' I said—after
the long silence my voice, even to myself, sounded strange and
hollow—'come ! You are over-tired, and you feel the weather.
Don't you think you ought to be in bed ? Suppose you lie down.
Let me try my medical skill in mixing you a composing draught.'

"He held my hand, and looked eagerly into my eyes. 'I am
better now,' he said, speaking at last very faintly. Still he looked
at me in that wistful way. It seemed as if there were something
that he wanted to do or say, but had not sufficient resolution. At
length he got up from the chair to which I had led him, and
beckoning me to follow him, went across the room to the dressing-
table, and stood again before the glass. A violent shudder passed
through his frame as he looked into it ; but apparently forcing
himself to go through with what he had now begun, he remained
where he was, and, without looking away, moved to me with his
hand to come and stand beside him. I complied.

"'Look in there !' he said, in an almost inaudible tone. He
was supported, as before, by his hands resting on the table, and
could only bow with his head towards the glass to intimate what
he meant. 'Look in there !' he repeated.

"I did as he asked me.

"'What do you see ?' he asked next.

"'See ?' I repeated, trying to speak as cheerfully as I could,
and describing the reflexion of his own face as nearly as I could.
'I see a very, very pale face with sunken cheeks——'

" ' What ? ' he cried, with an alarm in his voice which I could not understand.

" ' With sunken cheeks,' I went on, ' and two hollow eyes with large pupils.'

" I saw the reflexion of my friend's face change, and felt his hand clutch my arm even more tightly than he had done before. I stopped abruptly and looked round at him. He did not turn his head towards me, but, gazing still into the looking-glass, seemed to labour for utterance.

" ' What,' he stammered at last. ' Do—you—see it—too ? '

" ' See what ? ' I asked, quickly.

" ' That face ! ' he cried, in accents of horror. ' That face— which is not mine—and which—I SEE INSTEAD OF MINE—always ! '

" I was struck speechless by the words. In a moment this mystery was explained—but what an explanation ! Worse, a hundred times worse, than anything I had imagined. What ! Had this man lost the power of seeing his own image as it was reflected there before him ? and, in its place, was there the image of another ? Had he changed reflexions with some other man ? The frightfulness of the thought struck me speechless for a time—then I saw how false an impression my silence was conveying.

" ' No, no, no ! ' I cried, as soon as I could speak—' a hundred times, no ! I see you, of course, and only you. It was your face I attempted to describe, and no other.'

" He seemed not to hear me. ' Why, look there ! ' he said, in a low, indistinct voice, pointing to his own image in the glass. ' Whose face do you see there ? '

" ' Why yours, of course.' And then, after a moment, I added, ' Whose do you see ? '

" He answered, like one in a trance, ' *His*—only his—always his ! ' He stood still a moment, and then, with a loud and terrific scream, repeated those words, ' ALWAYS HIS, ALWAYS HIS,' and fell down in a fit before me.

" I knew what to do now. Here was a thing which, at any rate, I could understand. I had with me my usual small stock of medicines and surgical instruments, and I did what was necessary : first to restore my unhappy patient, and next to procure for him the rest he needed so much. He was very ill—at death's door for some days —and I could not leave him, though there was urgent need that I should be back in London. When he began to mend, I sent over to England for my servant—John Masey—whom I knew I could trust. Acquainting him with the outlines of the case, I left him in charge of my patient, with orders that he should be brought over to this country as soon as he was fit to travel.

" That awful scene was always before me. I saw this devoted man day after day, with the eyes of my imagination, sometimes destroying in his rage the harmless looking-glass, which was the immediate cause of his suffering, sometimes transfixed before the horrid image that turned him to stone. I recollect coming upon him once when we were stopping at a roadside inn, and seeing him stand so by broad daylight. His back was turned towards me, and I waited and watched him for nearly half an hour as he stood there motionless and speechless, and appearing not to breathe. I am not sure but that this apparition seen so by daylight was more ghastly than that apparition seen in the middle of the night, with the thunder rumbling among the hills.

" Back in London in his own house, where he could command in some sort the objects which should surround him, poor Strange was better than he would have been elsewhere. He seldom went out except at night, but once or twice I have walked with him by daylight, and have seen him terribly agitated when we have had to pass a shop in which looking-glasses were exposed for sale.

" It is nearly a year now since my poor friend followed me down to this place, to which I have retired. For some months he has been daily getting weaker and weaker, and a disease of the lungs has become developed in him, which has brought him to his death-bed. I should add, by-the-by, that John Masey has been his constant companion ever since I brought them together, and I have had, consequently, to look after a new servant.

" And now tell me," the doctor added, bringing his tale to an end, " did you ever hear a more miserable history, or was ever man haunted in a more ghastly manner than this man ? "

I was about to reply, when we heard a sound of footsteps outside, and before I could speak old Masey entered the room, in haste and disorder.

" I was just telling this gentleman," the doctor said : not at the moment observing old Masey's changed manner : " how you deserted me to go over to your present master."

" Ah ! sir," the man answered, in a troubled voice, " I'm afraid he won't be my master long."

The doctor was on his legs in a moment. " What ! Is he worse ? "

" I think, sir, he is dying," said the old man.

" Come with me, sir ; you may be of use if you can keep quiet."
The doctor caught up his hat as he addressed me in those words,
and in a few minutes we had reached The Compensation House.
A few seconds more and we were standing in a darkened room on
the first floor, and I saw lying on a bed before me—pale, emaciated
and, as it seemed, dying—the man whose story I had just heard.

He was lying with closed eyes when we came into the room,
and I had leisure to examine his features. What a tale of misery
they told ! They were regular and symmetrical in their arrangement, and not without beauty—the beauty of exceeding refinement and delicacy. Force there was none, and perhaps it was to
the want of this that the faults—perhaps the crime—which had
made the man's life so miserable were to be attributed. Perhaps
the crime ? Yes, it was not likely that an affliction, lifelong and
terrible, such as this he had endured, would come upon him unless some misdeed had provoked the punishment. What misdeed
we were soon to know.

It sometimes—I think generally—happens that the presence of
anyone who stands and watches beside a sleeping man will wake
him, unless his slumbers are unusually heavy. It was so now. While
we looked at him, the sleeper awoke very suddenly, and fixed his
eyes upon us. He put out his hand and took the doctor's in its
feeble grasp. " Who is that ? " he asked next, pointing towards me.

" Do you wish him to go ? The gentleman knows something of
your sufferings, and is powerfully interested in your case ; but he
will leave us, if you wish it," the doctor said.

" No. Let him stay."

Seating myself out of sight, but where I could both see and hear
what passed, I waited for what should follow. Dr. Garden and John
Masey stood beside the bed. There was a moment's pause.

" I want a looking-glass," said Strange, without a word of
preface.

We all started to hear him say those words.

" I am dying," said Strange ; " will you not grant me my
request ? "

Dr. Garden whispered to old Masey ; and the latter left the
room. He was not absent long, having gone no further than the
next house. He held an oval-framed mirror in his hand when he
returned. A shudder passed through the body of the sick man as
he saw it.

" Put it down," he said, faintly—" anywhere—for the present."

No one of us spoke. I do not think, in that moment of suspense, that we *could*, any of us, have spoken if we had tried.

The sick man tried to raise himself a little. " Prop me up," he said. " I speak with difficulty—I have something to say."

They put pillows behind him, so as to raise his head and body.

" I have presently a use for it," he said, indicating the mirror. " I want to see——" He stopped, and seemed to change his mind. He was sparing of his words. " I want to tell you—all about it." Again he was silent. Then he seemed to make a great effort, and spoke once more, beginning very abruptly.

" I loved my wife fondly. I loved her—her name was Lucy. She was English ; but, after we were married, we lived long abroad—in Italy. She liked the country, and I liked what she liked. She liked to draw, too, and I got her a master. He was an Italian. I will not give his name. We always called him ' the Master.' A treacherous insidious man this was, and, under cover of his profession, took advantage of his opportunities, and taught my wife to love him—to love him.

" I am short of breath. I need not enter into details as to how I found them out ; but I *did* find them out. We were away on a sketching expedition when I made my discovery. My rage maddened me, and there was one at hand who fomented my madness. My wife had a maid, who, it seemed, had also loved this man— the Master—and had been ill-treated and deserted by him. She told me all. She had played the part of go-between—had carried letters. When she told me these things, it was night, in a solitary Italian town, among the mountains. ' He is in his room now,' she said, ' writing to her.'

" A frenzy took possession of me as I listened to those words. I am naturally vindictive—remember that—and now my longing for revenge was like a thirst. Travelling in those lonely regions, I was armed, and when the woman said, ' He is writing to your wife,' I laid hold of my pistols, as by an instinct. It has been some comfort to me since, that I took them both. Perhaps, at that moment, I may have meant fairly by him—meant that we should fight. I don't know what I meant, quite. The woman's words, ' He is in his own room now, writing to her,' rung in my ears.

The sick man stopped to take breath. It seemed an hour, though it was probably not more than two minutes, before he spoke again.

" I managed to get into his room unobserved. Indeed, he was

altogether absorbed in what he was doing. He was sitting at the only table in the room, writing at a travelling-desk, by the light of a single candle. It was a rude dressing-table, and—and before him—exactly before him—there was—there was a looking-glass.

" I stole up behind him as he sat and wrote by the light of the candle. I looked over his shoulder at the letter, and I read, ' Dearest Lucy, my love, my darling.' As I read the words, I pulled the trigger of the pistol I held in my right hand, and killed him—killed him—but, before he died, he looked up once—not at me, but at my image before him in the glass, and his face— such a face—has been there—ever since, and mine—my face— is gone ! "

He fell back exhausted, and we all pressed forward thinking that he must be dead, he lay so still.

But he had not yet passed away. He revived under the influence of stimulants. He tried to speak, and muttered indistinctly from time to time words of which we could sometimes make no sense. We understood, however, that he had been tried by an Italian tribunal, and had been found guilty ; but with such extenuating circumstances that his sentence was commuted to imprisonment, during, we thought we made out, two years. But we could not understand what he said about his wife, though we gathered that she was still alive, from something he whispered to the doctor of there being provision made for her in his will.

He lay in a doze for something more than an hour after he had told his tale, and then he woke up quite suddenly, as he had done when we had first entered the room. He looked round uneasily in all directions, until his eye fell on the looking-glass.

" I want it," he said, hastily ; but I noticed that he did not shudder now as it was brought near. When old Masey approached, holding it in his hand, and crying like a child, Dr. Garden came forward and stood between him and his master, taking the hand of poor Strange in his.

" Is this wise ? " he asked. " Is it good, do you think, to revive this misery of your life now, when it is so near its close ? The chastisement of your crime," he added, solemnly, " has been a terrible one. Let us hope in God's mercy that your punishment is over."

The dying man raised himself with a last great effort, and looked up at the doctor with such an expression on his face as none of us had seen on any face, before.

" I do hope so," he said, faintly, " but you must let me have my way in this—for if, now, when I look, I see aright—once more —I shall then hope yet more strongly—for I shall take it as a sign."

The doctor stood aside without another word, when he heard the dying man speak thus, and the old servant drew near, and, stooping over softly, held the looking-glass before his master. Presently afterwards, we, who stood around looking breathlessly at him, saw such a rapture upon his face, as left no doubt upon our minds that the face which had haunted him so long, had, in his last hour, disappeared.

Amelia B. Edwards

THE ENGINEER
from ALL THE YEAR ROUND, 1866

His name, sir, was Matthew Price ; mine is Benjamin Hardy. We were born within a few days of each other ; bred up in the same village ; taught at the same school. I cannot remember the time when we were not close friends. Even as boys, we never knew what it was to quarrel. We had not a thought, we had not a possession, that was not in common. We would have stood by each other, fearlessly, to the death. It was such a friendship as one reads about sometimes in books : fast and firm as the great Tors upon our native moorlands, true as the sun in the heavens.

The name of our village was Chadleigh. Lifted high above the pasture flats which stretched away at our feet like a measureless green lake and melted into mist on the furthest horizon, it nestled, a tiny stone-built hamlet, in a sheltered hollow about midway between the plain and the plateau. Above us, rising ridge beyond ridge, slope beyond slope, spread the mountainous moor-country, bare and bleak for the most part, with here and there a patch of cultivated field or hardy plantation, and crowned highest of all with masses of huge grey crag, abrupt, isolated, hoary, and older than the deluge. These were the Tors—Druids' Tor, King's Tor, Castle Tor, and the like ; sacred places, as I have heard, in the ancient time, where crownings, burnings, human sacrifices, and all kinds of bloody heathen rites were performed. Bones, too, had been found there, and arrow-heads, and ornaments of gold and glass. I had a vague awe of the Tors in those boyish days, and would not have gone near them after dark for the heaviest bribe.

I have said that we were born in the same village. He was the son of a small farmer, named William Price, and the eldest of a family of seven ; I was the only child of Ephraim Hardy, the Chadleigh blacksmith—a well-known man in those parts, whose memory is not forgotten to this day. Just so far as a farmer is supposed to be a bigger man than a blacksmith, Mat's father might be said to have a better standing than mine ; but William Price with his small holding and his seven boys, was, in fact, as poor as many a day-labourer ; whilst, the blacksmith, well-to-do, bustling, popular, and open-handed, was a person of some importance in the place. All this, however, had nothing to do with Mat and myself. It never occurred to either of us that his jacket was out at elbows, or that our mutual funds came altogether from my pocket. It was enough for us that we sat on the same school-bench, conned our tasks from the same primer, fought each other's battles, screened each other's faults, fished, nutted, played truant, robbed orchards and birds' nests together, and spent every half-hour, authorised or stolen, in each other's society. It was a happy time ; but it could not go on for ever. My father, being prosperous, resolved to put me forward in the world. I must know more, and do better, than himself. The forge was not good enough, the little world of Chadleigh not wide enough, for me. Thus it happened that I was still swinging the satchel when Mat was whistling at the plough, and that at last, when my future course was shaped out, we were separated, as it then seemed to us, for life. For, blacksmith's son as I was, furnace and forge, in some form or other, pleased me best, and I chose to be a working engineer. So my father by-and-by apprenticed me to a Birmingham iron-master ; and, having bidden farewell to Mat, and Chadleigh, and the grey old Tors in the shadow of which I had spent all the days of my life, I turned my face northward, and went over into " the Black Country."

I am not going to dwell on this part of my story. How I worked out the term of my apprenticeship ; how, when I had served my full time and become a skilled workman, I took Mat from the plough and brought him over to the Black Country, sharing with him lodging, wages, experience—all, in short, that I had to give ;

how he, naturally quick to learn and brimful of quiet energy, worked his way up a step at a time, and came by-and-by to be a " first hand " in his own department ; how, during all these years of change, and trial, and effort, the old boyish affection never wavered or weakened, but went on, growing with our growth and strengthening with our strength—are facts which I need do no more than outline in this place.

About this time—it will be remembered that I speak of the days when Mat and I were on the bright side of thirty—it happened that our firm contracted to supply six first-class locomotives to run on the new line, then in process of construction, between Turin and Genoa. It was the first Italian order we had taken. We had had dealings with France, Holland, Belgium, Germany ; but never with Italy. The connection, therefore, was new and valuable —all the more valuable because our Transalpine neighbours had but lately begun to lay down the iron roads, and would be safe to need more of our good English work as they went on. So the Birmingham firm set themselves to the contract with a will, lengthened our working hours, increased our wages, took on fresh hands, and determined, if energy and promptitude could do it, to place themselves at the head of the Italian labour-market, and stay there. They deserved and achieved success. The six loco-motives were not only turned out to time, but were shipped, despatched, and delivered with a promptitude that fairly amazed our Piedmontese consignee. I was not a little proud, you may be sure, when I found myself appointed to superintend the transport of the engines. Being allowed a couple of assistants, I contrived that Mat should be one of them ; and thus we enjoyed together the first great holiday of our lives.

It was a wonderful change for two Birmingham operatives fresh from the Black Country. The fairy city, with its crescent back-ground of Alps ; the port crowded with strange shipping ; the marvellous blue sky and the bluer sea ; the painted houses on the quays ; the quaint cathedral, faced with black and white marble ; the street of jewellers, like an Arabian Nights' bazaar ; the street of palaces, with its Moorish courtyards, its fountains and orange-trees ; the women veiled like brides ; the galley-slaves chained two and two ; the processions of priests and friars ; the everlasting clangour of bells ; the babble of a strange tongue ; the singular lightness and brightness of the climate—made, altogether, such a combination of wonders that we wandered about, the first day, in a kind of bewildered dream, like children at a fair. Before that week was ended, being tempted by the beauty of the place and the liberality of the pay, we had agreed to take service with the Turin and Genoa Railway Company, and to turn our backs upon Birmingham for ever.

Then began a new life—a life so active and healthy. so steeped in fresh air and sunshine, that we sometimes marvelled how we could have endured the gloom of the Black Country. We were constantly up and down the line : now at Genoa, now at Turin, taking trial trips with the locomotives, and placing our old experiences at the service of our new employers.

In the meanwhile we made Genoa our headquarters, and hired a couple of rooms over a small shop in a by-street sloping down to the quays. Such a busy little street—so steep and winding that no vehicles could pass through it, and so narrow that the sky looked like a mere strip of deep-blue ribbon overhead ! Every house in it, however, was a shop, where the goods encroached on the footway, or were piled about the door, or hung like tapestry from the balconies ; and all day long, from dawn to dusk, an incessant stream of passers-by poured up and down between the port and the upper quarter of the city.

Our landlady was the widow of a silver-worker, and lived by the sale of filigree ornaments, cheap jewellery, combs, fans, and toys in ivory and jet. She had an only daughter named Gianetta, who served in the shop, and was simply the most beautiful woman I ever beheld. Looking back across this weary chasm of years, and bringing her image before me (as I can and do) with all the vividness of life, I am unable, even now, to detect a flaw in her beauty. I do not attempt to describe her. I do not believe there is a poet living who could find the words to do it ; but I once saw a picture that was somewhat like her (not half so lovely, but still like her), and, for aught I know, that picture is still hanging where I last looked at it—upon the walls of the Louvre. It represented a woman with brown eyes and golden hair, looking over her shoulder into a circular mirror held by a bearded man in the background. In this man, as I then understood, the artist had painted his own portrait ; in her, the portrait of the woman he loved. No picture that I ever saw was half so beautiful, and yet it was not worthy to be named in the same breath with Gianetta Coneglia.

You may be certain the widow's shop did not want for customers.

All Genoa knew how fair a face was to be seen behind that dingy little counter ; and Gianetta, flirt as she was, had more lovers than she cared to remember, even by name. Gentle and simple, rich and poor, from the red-capped sailor buying his ear-rings or his amulet, to the nobleman carelessly purchasing half the filigrees in the window, she treated them all alike—encouraged them, laughed at them, led them on and turned them off at her pleasure. She had no more heart than a marble statue ; as Mat and I discovered by-and-by, to our bitter cost.

I cannot tell to this day how it came about, or what first led me to suspect how things were going with us both ; but long before the waning of that autumn a coldness had sprung up between my friend and myself. It was nothing that could have been put into words. It was nothing that either of us could have explained or justified, to save his life. We lodged together, ate together, worked together, exactly as before ; we even took our long evening's walk together, when the day's labour was ended ; and except, perhaps, that we were more silent than of old, no mere looker-on could have detected a shadow of change. Yet there it was, silent and subtle, widening the gulf between us every day.

It was not his fault. He was too true and gentle-hearted to have willingly brought about such a state of things between us. Neither do I believe—fiery as my nature is—that it was mine. It was all hers—hers from first to last—the sin, and the shame, and the sorrow.

If she had shown a fair and open preference for either of us, no real harm could have come of it. I would have put any constraint upon myself, and, Heaven knows ! have borne any suffering, to see Mat really happy. I know that he would have done the same, and more if he could, for me. But Gianetta cared not one sou for either. She never meant to choose between us. It gratified her vanity to divide us ; it amused her to play with us. It would pass my power to tell how, by a thousand imperceptible shades of coquetry—by the lingering of a glance, the substitution of a word, the flitting of a smile—she contrived to turn our heads, and torture our hearts, and lead us on to love her. She deceived us both. She buoyed us both up with hope ; she maddened us with jealousy ; she crushed us with despair. For my part, when I seemed to wake to a sudden sense of the ruin that was about our path and I saw how the truest friendship that ever bound two lives together was drifting on to wreck and ruin, I asked myself whether any

woman in the world was worth what Mat had been to me and
I to him. But this was not often. I was readier to shut my eyes
upon the truth than to face it ; and so lived on, wilfully, in a dream.

Thus the autumn passed away, and winter came—the strange,
treacherous Genoese winter, green with olive and ilex, brilliant
with sunshine, and bitter with storm. Still, rivals at heart and
friends on the surface, Mat and I lingered on in our lodging in
the Vicolo Balba. Still Gianetta held us with her fatal wiles and
her still more fatal beauty. At length there came a day when I felt
I could bear the horrible misery and suspense of it no longer. The
sun, I vowed, should not go down before I knew my sentence. She
must choose between us. She must either take me or let me go.
I was reckless. I was desperate. I was determined to know the
worst, or the best. If the worst, I would at once turn my back
upon Genoa, upon her, upon all the pursuits and purposes of my
past life, and begin the world anew. This I told her, passionately
and sternly, standing before her in the little parlour at the back
of the shop, one bleak December morning.

" If it's Mat whom you care for most," I said, " tell me so in
one word, and I will never trouble you again. He is better worth
your love. I am jealous and exacting ; he is as trusting and unselfish as a woman. Speak, Gianetta ; am I to bid you good-bye
for ever and ever, or am I to write home to my mother in England,
bidding her pray to God to bless the woman who has promised
to be my wife ? "

" You plead your friend's cause well," she replied, haughtily.
" Matteo ought to be grateful. This is more than he ever did for
you."

" Give me my answer, for pity's sake," I exclaimed, " and let
me go ! "

" You are free to go or stay, Signor Inglese," she replied. " I
am not your jailor."

" Do you bid me leave you ? "

" Beata Madre ! not I."

" Will you marry me, if I stay ? "

She laughed aloud—such a merry, mocking, musical laugh,
like a chime of silver bells !

" You ask too much," she said.

" Only what you have led me to hope these five or six months
past ! "

" That is just what Matteo says. How tiresome you both are ! "

" O, Gianetta," I said, passionately, " be serious for one moment ! I am a rough fellow, it is true—not half good enough or
clever enough for you ; but I love you with my whole heart, and
an Emperor could do no more."

" I am glad of it," she replied ; " I do not want you to love me
less."

" Then you cannot wish to make me wretched ! Will you promise me ? "

" I promise nothing," said she, with another burst of laughter ;
" except that I will not marry Matteo ! "

Except that she would not marry Matteo ! Only that. Not a
word of hope for myself. Nothing but my friend's condemnation.
I might get comfort, and selfish triumph, and some sort of base
assurance out of that, if I could. And so, to my shame, I did. I
grasped at the vain encouragement, and, fool that I was ! let her
put me off again unanswered. From that day, I gave up all effort
at self-control, and let myself drift blindly on—to destruction.

At length things became so bad between Mat and myself that
it seemed as if an open rupture must be at hand. We avoided each
other, scarcely exchanged a dozen sentences in a day, and fell
away from all our old familiar habits. At this time—I shudder to
remember it !—there were moments when I felt that I hated him.

Thus, with the trouble deepening and widening between us day
by day, another month or five weeks went by ; and February
came ; and, with February, the Carnival. They said in Genoa
that it was a particularly dull carnival ; and so it must have been ;
for, save a flag or two hung out in some of the principal streets,
and a sort of festa look about the women, there were no special
indications of the season. It was, I think, the second day when,
having been on the line all the morning, I returned to Genoa at
dusk, and, to my surprise, found Mat Price on the platform. He
came up to me, and laid his hand on my arm.

" You are in late," he said. " I have been waiting for you three-
quarters of an hour. Shall we dine together to-day ? "

Impulsive as I am, this evidence of returning goodwill at once
called up my better feelings.

" With all my heart, Mat," I replied ; " shall we go to
Gozzoli's ? "

" No, no," he said, hurriedly. " Some quieter place—some
place where we can talk. I have something to say to you."

I noticed now that he looked pale and agitated, and an uneasy sense of apprehension stole upon me. We decided on the " Pesca-tore," a little out-of-the-way trattoria, down near the Molo Vecchio. There, in a dingy salon, frequented chiefly by seamen, and redolent of tobacco, we ordered our simple dinner. Mat scarcely swallowed a morsel ; but, calling presently for a bottle of Sicilian wine, drank eagerly.

" Well, Mat," I said, as the last dish was placed on the table, " what news have you ? "

" Bad."

" I guessed that from your face."

" Bad for you—bad for me. Gianetta."

" What of Gianetta ? "

He passed his hand nervously across his lips.

" Gianetta is false—worse than false," he said, in a hoarse voice. " She values an honest man's heart just as she values a flower for her hair—wears it for a day, then throws it aside for ever. She has cruelly wronged us both."

" In what way ? Good Heavens, speak out ! "

" In the worst way that a woman can wrong those who love her. She has sold herself to the Marchese Loredano."

The blood rushed to my head and face in a burning torrent. I could scarcely see, and dared not trust myself to speak.

" I saw her going towards the cathedral," he went on, hurriedly. " It was about three hours ago. I thought she might be going to confession, so I hung back and followed her at a distance. When she got inside, however, she went straight to the back of the pulpit, where this man was waiting for her. You remember him—an old man who used to haunt the shop a month or two back. Well, see-ing how deep in conversation they were, and how they stood close under the pulpit with their backs towards the church, I fell into a passion of anger and went straight up the aisle, intending to say or do something : I scarcely knew what ; but, at all events, to draw her arm through mine, and take her home. When I came within a few feet, however, and found only a big pillar between myself and them, I paused. They could not see me, nor I them ; but I could hear their voices distinctly, and—and I listened."

" Well, and you heard——"

" The terms of a shameful bargain—beauty on the one side, gold on the other ; so many thousand francs a year ; a villa near Naples—— Pah ! it makes me sick to repeat it."

And, with a shudder, he poured out another glass of wine and drank it at a draught.

"After that," he said, presently, "I made no effort to bring her away. The whole thing was so cold-blooded, so deliberate, so shameful, that I felt I had only to wipe her out of my memory, and leave her to her fate. I stole out of the cathedral, and walked about here by the sea for ever so long, trying to get my thoughts straight. Then I remembered you, Ben ; and the recollection of how this wanton had come between us and broken up our lives drove me wild. So I went up to the station and waited for you. I felt you ought to know it all ; and—and I thought, perhaps, that we might go back to England together."

"The Marchese Loredano ! "

It was all that I could say ; all that I could think. As Mat had just said of himself, I felt " like one stunned."

"There is one other thing I may as well tell you," he added, reluctantly, " if only to show you how false a woman can be. We —we were to have been married next month."

"*We* ? Who ? What do you mean ? "

"I mean that we were to have been married—Gianetta and I."

A sudden storm of rage, of scorn, of incredulity, swept over me at this, and seemed to carry my senses away.

"*You !* " I cried. "Gianetta marry you ! I don't believe it."

"I wish I had not believed it,".he replied, looking up as if puzzled by my vehemence. " But she promised me ; and I thought, when she promised it, she meant it."

"She told me, weeks ago, that she would never be your wife ! "

His colour rose, his brow darkened ; but when his answer came, it was as calm as the last.

"Indeed ! " he said. " Then it is only one baseness more. She told me that she had refused you ; and that was why we kept our engagement secret."

"Tell the truth, Mat Price," I said, well-nigh beside myself with suspicion. " Confess that every word of this is false ! Confess that Gianetta will not listen to you, and that you are afraid I may succeed where you have failed. As perhaps I shall—as perhaps I shall, after all ! "

"Are you mad ? " he exclaimed. " What do you mean ? "

"That I believe it's just a trick to get me away to England— that I don't credit a syllable of your story. You're a liar, and I hate you ! "

He rose, and, laying one hand on the back of his chair, looked me sternly in the face.

" If you were not Benjamin Hardy," he said, deliberately, " I would thrash you within an inch of your life."

The words had no sooner passed his lips than I sprang at him. I have never been able distinctly to remember what followed. A curse—a blow—a struggle—a moment of blind fury—a cry—a confusion of tongues—a circle of strange faces. Then I see Mat lying back in the arms of a bystander ; myself trembling and be-wildered—the knife dropping from my grasp ; blood upon the floor ; blood upon my hands ; blood upon his shirt. And then I hear those dreadful words :

" O, Ben, you have murdered me ! "

He did not die—at least, not there and then. He was carried to the nearest hospital, and lay for some weeks between life and death. His case, they said, was difficult and dangerous. The knife had gone in just below the collar-bone, and pierced down into the lungs. He was not allowed to speak or turn—scarcely to breathe with freedom. He might not even lift his head to drink. I sat by him day and night all through that sorrowful time. I gave up my situation on the railway ; I quitted my lodging in the Vicolo Balba ; I tried to forget that such a woman as Gianetta Coneglia had ever drawn breath. I lived only for Mat ; and he tried to live more, I believe, for my sake than his own. Thus, in the bitter silent hours of pain and penitence, when no hand but mine ap-proached his lips or smoothed his pillow, the old friendship came back with even more than its old trust and faithfulness. He forgave me, fully and freely ; and I would thankfully have given my life for him.

At length there came one bright spring morning, when, dis-missed as convalescent, he tottered out through the hospital gates, leaning on my arm, and feeble as an infant. He was not cured ; neither, as I then learned to my horror and anguish, was it possible that he ever could be cured. He might live, with care, for some years ; but the lungs were injured beyond hope of remedy, and a strong or healthy man he could never be again. These, spoken aside to me, were the parting words of the chief physician, who advised me to take him further south without delay.

I took him to a little coast-town called Rocca, some thirty miles beyond Genoa—a sheltered lonely place along the Riviera, where the sea was even bluer than the sky, and the cliffs were green with strange tropical plants, cacti, and aloes, and Egyptian palms. Here we lodged in the house of a small tradesman ; and Mat, to use his own words, " set to work at getting well in good earnest." But, alas ! it was a work which no earnestness could forward. Day after day he went down to the beach, and sat for hours drinking the sea air and watching the sails that came and went in the offing. By-and-by he could go no further than the garden of the house in which we lived. A little later, and he spent his days on a couch beside the open window, waiting patiently for the end. Ay, for the end ! It had come to that. He was fading fast, waning with the waning summer, and conscious that the Reaper was at hand. His whole aim now was to soften the agony of my remorse, and prepare me for what must shortly come.

" I would not live longer, if I could," he said, lying on his couch one summer evening. and looking up to the stars. " If I had my choice at this moment, I would ask to go. I should like Gianetta to know that I forgave her."

" She shall know it," I said, trembling suddenly from head to foot.

He pressed my hand.

" And you'll write to father ? "

" I will."

I had drawn a little back, that he might not see the tears raining down my cheeks ; but he raised himself on his elbow, and looked round.

" Don't fret, Ben," he whispered ; laid his head back wearily upon the pillow—and so died.

And this was the end of it. This was the end of all that made life life to me. I buried him there, in hearing of the wash of a strange sea on a strange shore. I stayed by the grave till the priest and the bystanders were gone. I saw the earth filled in to the last sod, and the gravedigger stamped it down with his feet. Then, and not till then, I felt that I had lost him for ever—the friend I had loved, and hated, and slain. Then, and not till then, I knew that all rest, and joy, and hope were over for me. From that moment my heart hardened within me, and my life was filled with loathing. Day and night, land and sea, labour and rest, food and sleep, were alike hateful to me. It was the curse of Cain, and that my brother had pardoned me made it lie none the lighter. Peace on earth was for me no more, and goodwill towards men was dead in my heart for ever. Remorse softens some natures ; but it poisoned mine. I hated all mankind ; but above all mankind I hated the woman who had come between us two, and ruined both our lives.

He had bidden me seek her out, and be the messenger of his forgiveness. I had sooner have gone down to the port of Genoa and taken upon me the serge cap and shotted chain of any galley-slave at his toil in the public works ; but for all that I did my best to obey him. I went back, alone and on foot. I went back, intending to say to her, " Gianetta Coneglia, he forgave you ; but God never will." But she was gone. The little shop was let to a fresh occupant ; and the neighbours only knew that mother and daughter had left the place quite suddenly, and that Gianetta was supposed to be under the " protection " of the Marchese Loredano. How I made inquiries here and there—how I heard that they had gone to Naples—and how, being restless and reckless of my time, I worked my passage in a French steamer, and followed her —how, having found the sumptuous villa that was now hers, I learned that she had left there some ten days and gone to Paris, where the Marchese was ambassador for the Two Sicilies—how, working my passage back again to Marseilles, and thence, in part by the river and in part by the rail, I made my way to Paris— how, day after day, I paced the streets and the parks, watched at the ambassador's gates, followed his carriage, and at last, after weeks of waiting, discovered her address—how, having written to request an interview, her servants spurned me from her door and flung my letter in my face—how, looking up at her windows, I then, instead of forgiving, solemnly cursed her with the bitterest curses my tongue could devise—and how, this done, I shook the dust of Paris from my feet, and became a wanderer upon the face of the earth, are facts which I have now no space to tell.

The next six or eight years of my life were shifting and unsettled enough. A morose and restless man, I took employment here and there, as opportunity offered, turning my hand to many things, and caring little what I earned, so long as the work was hard and the change incessant. First of all I engaged myself as chief engineer in one of the French steamers plying between Marseilles and Constantinople. At Constantinople I changed to one of the Austrian Lloyd's boats, and worked for some time to and from Alexandria, Jaffa, and those parts. After that, I fell in with a party of Mr. Layard's men at Cairo, and so went up the

Nile and took a turn at the excavations of the mound of Nimroud. Then I became a working engineer on the new desert line between Alexandria and Suez ; and by-and-by I worked my passage out to Bombay, and took service as an engine fitter on one of the great Indian railways. I stayed a long time in India ; that is to say, I stayed nearly two years, which was a long time for me ; and I might not even have left so soon, but for the war that was declared just then with Russia. That tempted me. For I loved danger and hardship as other men love safety and ease ; and as for my life, I had sooner have parted from it than kept it, any day. So I came straight back to England ; betook myself to Portsmouth, where my testimonials at once procured me the sort of berth I wanted. I went out to the Crimea in the engine-room of one of her Majesty's war steamers.

I served with the fleet, of course, while the war lasted ; and when it was over, went wandering off again, rejoicing in my liberty. This time I went to Canada, and after working on a railway then in progress near the American frontier. I presently passed over into the States ; journeyed from north to south ; crossed the Rocky Mountains ; tried a month or two of life in the gold country ; and then, being seized with a sudden, aching, unaccountable longing to revisit that solitary grave so far away on the Italian coast, I turned my face once more towards Europe.

Poor little grave ! I found it rank with weeds, the cross half shattered, the inscription half effaced. It was as if no one had loved him, or remembered him. I went back to the house in which we had lodged together. The same people were still living there, and made me kindly welcome. I stayed with them for some weeks. I weeded, and planted, and trimmed the grave with my own hands, and set up a fresh cross in pure white marble. It was the first season of rest that I had known since I laid him there ; and when at last I shouldered my knapsack and set forth again to battle with the world, I promised myself that, God willing, I would creep back to Rocca, when my days drew near to ending, and be buried by his side.

From hence, being, perhaps, a little less inclined than formerly for very distant parts, and willing to keep within reach of that grave, I went no further than Mantua, where I engaged myself as an engine-driver on the line, then not long completed, between that city and Venice. Somehow, although I had been trained to the working engineering, I preferred in these days to earn my bread by driving. I liked the excitement of it, the sense of power, the rush of the air, the roar of the fire, the flitting of the landscape. Above all, I enjoyed to drive a night express. The worse the weather, the better it suited with my sullen temper. For I was as hard, and harder than ever. The years had done nothing to soften me. They had only confirmed all that was blackest and bitterest in my heart.

I continued pretty faithful to the Mantua line, and had been working on it steadily for more than seven months when that which I am now about to relate took place.

It was in the month of March. The weather had been unsettled for some days past, and the nights stormy ; and at one point along the line, near Ponte di Brenta, the waters had risen and swept away some seventy yards of embankment. Since this accident, the trains had all been obliged to stop at a certain spot between Padua and Ponte di Brenta, and the passengers, with their luggage, had thence to be transported in all kinds of vehicles, by a circuitous country road, to the nearest station on the other side of the gap, where another train and engine awaited them. This, of course, caused great confusion and annoyance, put all our time-tables wrong, and subjected the public to a large amount of inconvenience. In the mean while an army of navvies was drafted to the spot, and worked day and night to repair the damage. At this time I was driving two through trains each day ; namely, one from Mantua to Venice in the early morning, and a return train from Venice to Mantua in the afternoon—a tolerably full days' work, covering about one hundred and ninety miles of ground, and occupying between ten and eleven hours. I was therefore not best pleased when, on the third or fourth day after the accident, I was informed that, in addition to my regular allowance of work, I should that evening be required to drive a special train to Venice. This special train, consisting of an engine, a single carriage, and a break-van, was to leave the Mantua platform at eleven ; at Padua the passengers were to alight and find post-chaises waiting to convey them to Ponte di Brenta ; at Ponte di Brenta another engine, carriage, and break-van were to be in readiness, I was charged to accompany them throughout.

" Corpo di Bacco," said the clerk who gave me my orders, " you need not look so black, man. You are certain of a handsome gratuity. Do you know who goes with you ? "

" Not I."

" Not you, indeed ! Why, it's the Duca Loredano, the Nea-
politan ambassador."

" Loredano ! " I stammered. " What Loredano ? There was a
Marchese——"

" Certo. He was the Marchese Loredano some years ago ; but he
has come into his dukedom since then."

" He must be a very old man by this time."

" Yes, he is old ; but what of that ? He is as hale, and bright,
and stately as ever. You have seen him before ? "

" Yes," I said, turning away ; " I have seen him—years ago."

" You have heard of his marriage ? "

I shook my head.

The clerk chuckled, rubbed his hands, and shrugged his
shoulders.

" An extraordinary affair," he said. " Made a tremendous
esclandre at the time. He married his mistress—quite a common,
vulgar girl—a Genoese—very handsome ; but not received, of
course. Nobody visits her."

" Married her ! " I exclaimed. " Impossible."

" True, I assure you."

I put my hand to my head. I felt as if I had had a fall or a blow.

" Does she—does she go to-night ? " I faltered.

" O dear, yes—goes everywhere with him—never lets him out
of her sight. You'll see her—la bella Duchessa ! "

With this my informant laughed, and rubbed his hands again,
and went back to his office.

The day went by, I scarcely know how, except that my whole
soul was in a tumult of rage and bitterness. I returned from my
afternoon's work about 7.25, and at 10.30 I was once again at
the station. I had examined the engine ; given instructions to the
Fochista, or stoker, about the fire ; seen to the supply of oil ;
and got all in readiness, when, just as I was about to compare
my watch with the clock in the ticket-office, a hand was laid
upon my arm, and a voice in my ear said :

" Are you the engine-driver who is going on with this special
train ? "

I had never seen the speaker before. He was a small, dark man,
muffled up about the throat, with blue glasses, a large black
beard, and his hat drawn low upon his eyes.

" You are a poor man, I suppose," he said, in a quick, eager
whisper, " and, like other poor men, would not object to be

better off. Would you like to earn a couple of thousand florins ? "

" In what way ? "

" Hush ! You are to stop at Padua, are you not, and to go on again at Ponte di Brenta ? "

I nodded.

" Suppose you did nothing of the kind. Suppose, instead of turning off the steam, you jump off the engine, and let the train run on ? "

" Impossible. There are seventy yards of embankment gone, and——"

" Basta ! I know that. Save yourself, and let the train run on. It would be nothing but an accident."

I turned hot and cold ; I trembled ; my heart beat fast, and my breath failed.

" Why do you tempt me ? " I faltered.

" For Italy's sake," he whispered ; " for liberty's sake. I know you are no Italian ; but, for all that, you may be a friend. This Loredano is one of his country's bitterest enemies. Stay, here are the two thousand florins."

I thrust his hand back fiercely.

" No—no," I said. " No blood-money. If I do it, I do it neither for Italy nor for money ; but for vengeance."

" For vengeance ! " he repeated.

At this moment the signal was given for backing up to the platform. I sprang to my place upon the engine without another word. When I again looked towards the spot where he had been standing, the stranger was gone.

I saw them take their places—Duke and Duchess, secretary and priest, valet and maid. I saw the station-master bow them into the carriage, and stand, bareheaded, beside the door. I could not distinguish their faces ; the platform was too dusk, and the glare from the engine fire too strong ; but I recognised her stately figure, and the poise of her head. Had I not been told who she was, I should have known her by those traits alone. Then the guard's whistle shrilled out, and the station-master made his last bow ; I turned the steam on ; and we started.

My blood was on fire. I no longer trembled or hesitated. I felt as if every nerve was iron, and every pulse instinct with deadly purpose. She was in my power, and I would be avenged. She should die—she, for whom I had stained my soul with my friend's blood ! She should die, in the plenitude of her wealth and her beauty, and no power upon earth should save her !

The stations flew past. I put on more steam ; I bade the fireman heap in the coke, and stir the blazing mass. I would have out-stripped the wind, had it been possible. Faster and faster—hedges and trees, bridges, and stations, flashing past—villages no sooner seen than gone—telegraph wires twisting, and dipping, and twin-ing themselves in one, with the awful swiftness of our pace ! Faster and faster, till the fireman at my side looks white and scared, and refuses to add more fuel to the furnace. Faster and faster, till the wind rushes in our faces and drives the breath back upon our lips.

I would have scorned to save myself. I meant to die with the rest. Mad as I was—and I believe from my very soul that I was utterly mad for the time—I felt a passing pang of pity for the old man and his suite. I would have spared the poor fellow at my side, too, if I could ; but the pace at which we were going made escape impossible.

Vicenza was passed—a mere confused vision of lights. Pojana flew by. At Padua, but nine miles distant, our passengers were to alight. I saw the fireman's face turned upon me in remonstrance ; I saw his lips move, though I could not hear a word ; I saw his expression change suddenly from remonstrance to a deadly terror, and then—merciful Heaven ! then, for the first time, I saw that he and I were no longer alone upon the engine.

There was a third man—a third man standing on my right hand, as the fireman was standing on my left—a tall, stalwart man, with short curling hair, and a flat Scotch cap upon his head. As I fell back in the first shock of surprise, he stepped nearer ; took my place at the engine, and turned the steam off. I opened my lips to speak to him ; he turned his head slowly, and looked me in the face.

Matthew Price !

I uttered one long wild cry, flung my arms wildly up above my head, and fell as if I had been smitten with an axe.

I am prepared for the objections that may be made to my story. I expect, as a matter of course, to be told that this was an optical illusion, or that I was suffering from pressure on the brain, or even that I laboured under an attack of temporary insanity. I have heard all these arguments before, and, if I may be forgiven for saying so, I have no desire to hear them again. My own mind has been made up upon this subject for many a year. All that I can say—all that I *know* is—that Matthew Price came back from the dead, to save my soul and the lives of those whom I, in my guilty rage, would have hurried to destruction. I believe this as I believe in the mercy of Heaven and the forgiveness of repentant sinners.

Vincent O'Sullivan

WHEN I WAS DEAD

from A BOOK OF BARGAINS

Leonard Smithers, 1896

" And yet my heart
Will not confess he owes the malady
That doth my life besiege."

All's Well that Ends Well.

That was the worst of Ravenel Hall. The passages were long and gloomy, the rooms were musty and dull, even the pictures were sombre and their subjects dire. On an autumn evening, when the wind soughed and wailed through the trees in the park, and the dead leaves whistled and chattered, while the rain clamoured at the windows, small wonder that folks with gentle nerves went a-straying in their wits ! An acute nervous system is a grievous burthen on the deck of a yacht under sunlit skies : at Ravenel the chain of nerves was prone to clash and jangle a funeral march. Nerves must be pampered in a tea-drinking community ; and the ghost that your grandfather, with a skinful of port, could face and never tremble, sets you, in your sobriety, sweating and shivering ; or, becoming scared (poor ghost !) of your bulged eyes and dropping jaw, he quenches expectation by not appearing at all. So I am left to conclude that it was tea which made my acquaintance afraid to stay at Ravenel. Even Wilvern gave over ; and as he is in the Guards, and a polo player his nerves ought to be strong enough. On the night before he went I was explaining to him my theory, that if you place some drops of human blood near you, and then concentrate your thoughts, you will after a while see before you a man or a woman who will stay with you during long hours of the night, and even meet you at unexpected places during the day. I was explaining this theory, I repeat, when he interrupted me with words, senseless enough, which sent me fencing and parrying strangers,—on my guard.

" I say, Alistair, my dear chap ! " he began, " you ought to get out of this place and go up to Town and knock about a bit—you really ought, you know."

" Yes," I replied, " and get poisoned at the hotels by bad food and at the clubs by bad talk, I suppose. No, thank you : and let me say that your care for my health enervates me."

" Well, you can do as you like," says he, rapping with his feet on the floor. " I'm hanged if I stay here after to-morrow—I'll be staring mad if I do ! "

He was my last visitor. Some weeks after his departure I was sitting in the library with my drops of blood by me. I had got my theory nearly perfect by this time ; but there was one difficulty.

The figure which I had ever before me was the figure of an old woman with her hair divided in the middle, and her hair fell to her shoulders, white on one side and black on the other. She was a very complete old woman ; but, alas ! she was eyeless, and when I tried to construct the eyes she would shrivel and rot in my sight. But to-night I was thinking, thinking, as I had never thought before, and the eyes were just creeping into the head when I heard a terrible crash outside as if some heavy substance had fallen. Of a sudden the door was flung open and two maid-servants entered. They glanced at the rug under my chair, and at that they turned a sick white, cried on God, and huddled out.

" How dare you enter the library in this manner ? " I demanded sternly. No answer came back from them, so I started in pursuit. I found all the servants in the house gathered in a knot at the end of the passage.

" Mrs. Pebble," I said smartly, to the housekeeper, " I want those two women discharged to-morrow. It's an outrage ! You ought to be more careful."

But she was not attending to me. Her face was distorted with terror.

" Ah dear, ah dear ! " she went. " We had better all go to the library together," says she to the others.

" Am I master of my own house, Mrs. Pebble ? " I inquired, bringing my knuckles down with a bang on the table.

None of them seemed to see me or hear me : I might as well have been shrieking in a desert. I followed them down the passage, and forbade them with strong words to enter the library.

But they trooped past me, and stood with a clutter round the hearth-rug. Then three or four of them began dragging and lifting, as if they were lifting a helpless body, and stumbled with their imaginary burthen over to a sofa. Old Soames, the butler, stood near.

" Poor young gentleman ! " he said with a sob. " I've knowed him since he was a baby. And to think of him being dead like this —and so young, too ! "

I crossed the room. " What's all this, Soames ? " I cried, shaking him roughly by the shoulders. " I'm not dead. I'm here—here ! " As he did not stir I got a little scared. " Soames, old friend ! " I called, " don't you know me ? Don't you know the little boy you used to play with ? Say I'm not dead, Soames, please, Soames ! "

He stooped down and kissed the sofa. " I think one of the men ought to ride over to the village for the doctor, Mr. Soames," says Mrs. Pebble ; and he shuffled out to give the order.

Now, this doctor was an ignorant dog, whom I had been forced to exclude from the house because he went about proclaiming his belief in a saving God, at the same time that he proclaimed himself a man of science. He, I was resolved, should never cross my threshold, and I followed Mrs. Pebble through the house, screaming out prohibition. But I did not catch even a groan from her, not a nod of the head, nor a cast of the eye, to show that she had heard.

I met the doctor at the door of the library. " Well," I sneered, throwing my hand in his face, " have you come to teach me some new prayers ? "

He brushed by me as if he had not felt the blow, and knelt down by the sofa.

" Rupture of a vessel on the brain, I think," he says to Soames and Mrs. Pebble after a short moment. " He has been dead some hours. Poor fellow ! You had better telegraph for his sister, and I will send up the undertaker to arrange the body."

" You liar ! " I yelled. " You whining liar ! How have you the insolence to tell my servants that I am dead, when you see me here face to face ? "

He was far in the passage, with Soames and Mrs. Pebble at his heels, ere I had ended, and not one of the three turned round.

All that night I sat in the library. Strangely enough, I had no wish to sleep nor during the time that followed, had I any craving to eat. In the morning the men came, and although I ordered them out, they proceeded to minister about something I could not see. So all day I stayed in the library or wandered about the house, and at night the men came again bringing with them a coffin. Then, in my humour, thinking it shame that so fine a coffin should be empty I lay the night in it and slept a soft dreamless sleep—the softest sleep I have ever slept. And when the men came the next day I rested still, and the undertaker shaved me. A strange valet !

On the evening after that, I was coming downstairs, when I noted some luggage in the hall, and so learned that my sister had arrived. I had not seen this woman since her marriage, and I loathed her more than I loathed any creature in this ill-organised world. She was very beautiful, I think—tall, and dark, and straight as a ram-rod—and she had an unruly passion for scandal and dress. I suppose the reason I disliked her so intensely was, that she had a habit of making one aware of her presence when she was several yards off. At half-past nine o'clock my sister came down to the library in a very charming wrap, and I soon found that she was as insensible to my presence as the others. I trembled with rage to see her kneel down by the coffin—my coffin ; but when she bent over to kiss the pillow I threw away control.

A knife which had been used to cut string was lying upon a table : I seized it and drove it into her neck. She fled from the room screaming.

" Come ! come ! " she cried, her voice quivering with anguish. " The corpse is bleeding from the nose."

Then I cursed her.

On the morning of the third day there was a heavy fall of snow. About eleven o'clock I observed that the house was filled with blacks and mutes and folk of the county, who came for the obsequies. I went into the library and sat still, and waited. Soon came the men, and they closed the lid of the coffin and bore it out on their shoulders. And yet I sat, feeling rather sadly that something of mine had been taken away : I could not quite think what. For half-an-hour perhaps—dreaming, dreaming : and then I glided to the hall door. There was no trace left of the funeral ; but after a while I sighted a black thread winding slowly across the white plain.

" I'm not dead ! " I moaned, and rubbed my face in the pure snow and tossed it on my neck and hair. " Sweet God, I am not dead."

E. and H. Heron

THE STORY OF YAND MANOR HOUSE

from "Real Ghost Stories," PEARSONS'S MAGAZINE *June,*
1898; afterwards reprinted in GHOST STORIES
C. Arthur Pearson Ltd. 1916

Looking through the notes of Mr. Flaxman Low, one sometimes catches through the steel-blue hardness of facts, the pink
flush of romance, or more often the black corner of a horror un-
nameable. The following story may serve as an instance of the
latter. Mr. Low not only unravelled the mystery at Yand, but at
the same time justified his life-work to M. Thierry, the well-known
French critic and philosopher.

At the end of a long conversation, M. Thierry, arguing from his
own standpoint as a materialist, had said :

" The factor in the human economy which you call ' soul '
cannot be placed."

" I admit that," replied Low. " Yet, when a man dies, is there
not one factor unaccounted for in the change that comes upon
him ? Yes ! For though his body still exists, it rapidly falls to pieces,
which proves that that has gone which held it together."

The Frenchman laughed, and shifted his ground.

" Well, for my part, I don't believe in ghosts ! Spirit manifestations, occult phenomena—is not this the ashbin into which a
certain clique shoot everything they cannot understand, or for
which they fail to account ? "

" Then what should you say to me, Monsieur, if I told you that
I have passed a good portion of my life in investigating this particular ashbin, and have been lucky enough to sort a small part of
its contents with tolerable success ? " replied Flaxman Low.

" The subject is doubtless interesting—but I should like to have
some personal experience in the matter," said Thierry dubiously.

" I am at present investigating a most singular case," said Low.
" Have you a day or two to spare ? "

Thierry thought for a minute or more.

" I am grateful," he replied. " But, forgive me, is it a convincing ghost ? "

" Come with me to Yand and see. I have been there once

already, and came away for the purpose of procuring information
from MSS. to which I have the privilege of access, for I confess
that the phenomena at Yand lie altogether outside any former
experience of mine."

Low sank back into his chair with his hands clasped behind his
head—a favourite position of his—and the smoke of his long pipe
curled up lazily into the golden face of an Isis, which stood behind
him on a bracket. Thierry, glancing across, was struck by the
strange likeness between the faces of the Egyptian goddess and this
scientist of the nineteenth century. On both rested the calm,
mysterious abstraction of some unfathomable thought. As he
looked, he decided.

" I have three days to place at your disposal."

" I thank you heartily," replied Low. " To be associated with
so brilliant a logician as yourself in an inquiry of this nature is
more than I could have hoped for ! The material with which I
have to deal is so elusive, the whole subject is wrapped in such
obscurity and hampered by so much prejudice, that I can find
few really qualified persons who care to approach these investigations seriously. I go down to Yand this evening, and hope not
to leave without clearing up the mystery. You will accompany
me ? "

" Most certainly. Meanwhile pray tell me something of the
affair."

" Briefly the story is as follows. Some weeks ago I went to Yand
Manor House at the request of the owner, Sir George Blackburton,
to see what I could make of the events which took place there. All
they complain of is the impossibility of remaining in one room—
the dining-room."

" What then is he like, this M. le Spook ? " asked the Frenchman, laughing.

" No one has ever seen him, or for that matter heard him."

" Then how——"

" You can't see him, nor hear him, nor smell him," went on
Low, " but you can feel him and—taste him ! "

" *Mon Dieu !* But this is singular ! Is he then of so bad a
flavour ? "

" You shall taste for yourself," answered Flaxman Low smiling.
" After a certain hour no one can remain in the room, they are
simply crowded out."

" But who crowds them out ? " asked Thierry.

"That is just what I hope we may discover to-night or to-morrow."

The last train that night dropped Mr. Flaxman Low and his companion at a little station near Yand. It was late, but a trap in waiting soon carried them to the Manor House. The big bulk of the building stood up in absolute blackness before them.

"Blackburton was to have met us, but I suppose he has not yet arrived," said Low. "Hullo! the door is open," he added as he stepped into the hall.

Beyond a dividing curtain they now perceived a light. Passing behind this curtain they found themselves at the end of the long hall, the wide staircase opening up in front of them.

"But who is this?" exclaimed Thierry.

Swaying and stumbling at every step, there tottered slowly down the stairs the figure of a man. He looked as if he had been drinking, his face was livid, and his eyes sunk into his head.

"Thank Heaven you've come! I heard you outside," he said in a weak voice.

"It's Sir George Blackburton," said Low, as the man lurched forward and pitched into his arms.

They laid him down on the rugs and tried to restore consciousness.

"He has the air of being drunk, but it is not so," remarked Thierry. "Monsieur has had a bad shock of the nerves. See the pulses drumming in his throat."

In a few minutes Blackburton opened his eyes and staggered to his feet.

"Come. I could not remain there alone. Come quickly."

They went rapidly across the hall, Blackburton leading the way down a wide passage to a double-leaved door, which, after a perceptible pause, he threw open, and they all entered together.

On the great table in the centre stood an extinguished lamp, some scattered food, and a big, lighted candle. But the eyes of all three men passed at once to a dark recess beside the heavy, carved chimneypiece, where a rigid shape sat perched on the back of a huge, oak chair.

Flaxman Low snatched up the candle and crossed the room towards it.

On the top of the chair, with his feet upon the arms, sat a powerfully-built young man huddled up. His mouth was open, and his eyes twisted upwards. Nothing further could be seen from below but the ghastly pallor of cheek and throat.

" Who is this ? " cried Low. Then he laid his hand gently on the man's knee.

At the touch the figure collapsed in a heap upon the floor, the gaping, set, terrified face turned up to theirs.

" He's dead ! " said Low after a hasty examination. " I should say he's been dead some hours."

" Oh, Lord ! Poor Batty ! " groaned Sir George, who was entirely unnerved. " I'm glad you've come."

" Who is he ? " said Thierry, " and what was he doing here ? "

" He's a gamekeeper of mine. He was always anxious to try conclusions with the ghost, and last night he begged me to lock him in here with food for twenty-four hours. I refused at first, but then I thought if anything happened while he was in here alone, it would interest you. Who could imagine it would end like this ? "

" When did you find him ? " asked Low.

" I only got here from my mother's half an hour ago. I turned on the light in the hall and came in here with a candle. As I entered the room, the candle went out, and—and—I think I must be going mad."

" Tell us everything you saw," urged Low.

" You will think I am beside myself ; but as the light went out and I sank almost paralysed into an armchair, I saw two barred eyes looking at me ! "

" Barred eyes ? What do you mean ? "

" Eyes that looked at me through thin vertical bars, like the bars of a cage. What's that ? "

With a smothered yell Sir George sprang back. He had approached the dead man and declared something had brushed his face.

" You were standing on this spot under the overmantel. I will remain here. Meantime, my dear Thierry, I feel sure you will help Sir George to carry this poor fellow to some more suitable place," said Flaxman Low.

When the dead body of the young gamekeeper had been carried out, Low passed slowly round and about the room. At length he stood under the old carved overmantel, which reached to the ceiling and projected bodily forward in quaint heads of satyrs and animals. One of these on the side nearest the recess represented a griffin with a flanged mouth. Sir George had been standing directly below this at the moment when he felt the touch on his face. Now alone in the dim, wide room, Flaxman Low stood on the same spot and waited. The candle threw its dull yellow rays on the shadows which seemed to gather closer and wait also. Presently a distant door banged, and Low, leaning forward to listen, distinctly felt something on the back of his neck !

He swung round. There was nothing ! He searched carefully on all sides, then put his hand up to the griffin's head. Again came the same soft touch, this time upon his hand, as if something had floated past on the air.

This was definite. The griffin's head located it. Taking the candle to examine more closely, Low found four long black hairs depending from the jagged fangs. He was detaching them when Thierry reappeared.

" We must get Sir George away as soon as possible," he said.

" Yes, we must take him away, I fear," agreed Low. " Our investigation must be put off till to-morrow."

On the following day they returned to Yand. It was a large country-house, pretty and old-fashioned, with lattice windows and deep gables, that looked out between tall shrubs and across lawns set with beaupots, where peacocks sunned themselves on the velvet turf. The church spire peered over the trees on one side ; and an old wall covered with ivy and creeping plants, and pierced at intervals with arches, alone separated the gardens from the churchyard.

The haunted room lay at the back of the house. It was square and handsome, and furnished in the style of the last century. The oak overmantel reached to the ceiling, and a wide window, which almost filled one side of the room, gave a view of the west door of the church.

Low stood for a moment at the open window looking out at the level sunlight which flooded the lawns and parterres.

" See that door sunk in the church wall to the left ? " said Sir George's voice at his elbow. " That is the door of the family vault. Cheerful outlook, isn't it ? "

" I should like to walk across there presently," remarked Low.

" What ! Into the vault ? " asked Sir George, with a harsh laugh. " I'll take you if you like. Anything else I can show you or tell you . "

" Yes. Last night I found this hanging from the griffin's head," said Low, producing the thin wisp of black hair. " It must have touched your cheek as you stood below. Do you know to whom it can belong ? "

" It's a woman's hair ! No, the only woman who has been in this room to my knowledge for months is an old servant with grey hair, who cleans it," returned Blackburton. " I'm sure it was not here when I locked Batty in."

" It is human hair, exceedingly coarse and long uncut," said Low ; " but it is not necessarily a woman's."

" It is not mine at any rate, for I'm sandy ; and poor Batty was fair. Good-night ; I'll come round for you in the morning."

Presently, when the night closed in, Thierry and Low settled down in the haunted room to await developments. They smoked and talked deep into the night. A big lamp burned brightly on the table, and the surroundings looked homely and desirable.

Thierry made a remark to that effect, adding that perhaps the ghost might see fit to omit his usual visit.

" Experience goes to prove that ghosts have a cunning habit of choosing persons either credulous or excitable to experiment upon," he added.

To M. Thierry's surprise, Flaxman Low agreed with him.

" They certainly choose suitable persons," he said, " that is, not credulous persons, but those whose senses are sufficiently keen to detect the presence of a spirit. In my own investigations, I try to eliminate what you would call the supernatural element. I deal with these mysterious affairs as far as possible on material lines."

" Then what do you say of Batty's death ? He died of fright—simply."

" I hardly think so. The manner of his death agrees in a peculiar manner with what we know of the terrible history of this room. He died of fright and pressure combined. Did you hear the doctor's remark ? It was significant. He said : ' The indications are precisely those I have observed in persons who have been crushed and killed in a crowd ! ' "

" That is sufficiently curious, I allow. I see that it is already past two o'clock. I am thirsty ; I will have a little seltzer." Thierry rose from his chair, and, going to the side-board, drew a tumblerful from the syphon. " Pah ! What an abominable taste ! "

" What ? The seltzer ? "

" Not at all ? " returned the Frenchman irritably. " I have not touched it yet. Some horrible fly has flown into my mouth, I suppose. Pah ! Disgusting ! "

" What is it like ? " asked Flaxman Low, who was at the moment wiping his own mouth with his handkerchief.

" Like ? As if some repulsive fungus had burst in the mouth."

" Exactly. I perceive it also. I hope you are about to be convinced."

" What ? " exclaimed Thierry, turning his big figure round and staring at Low. " You don't mean——"

As he spoke the lamp suddenly went out.

" Why, then, have you put the lamp out at such a moment ? " cried Thierry,

" I have not put it out. Light the candle beside you on the table."

Low heard the Frenchman's grunt of satisfaction as he found the candle, then the scratch of a match. It sputtered and went out. Another match and another behaved in the same manner, while Thierry swore freely under his breath.

" Let me have your matches, Monsieur Flaxman ; mine are, no doubt damp," he said at last.

Low rose to feel his way across the room. The darkness was dense.

" It is the darkness of Egypt—it may be felt. Where then are you, my dear friend ? " he heard Thierry saying, but the voice seemed a long way off.

" I am coming," he answered, " but it's so hard to get along."

After Low had spoken the words, their meaning struck him. He paused and tried to realise in what part of the room he was. The silence was profound, and the growing sense of oppression seemed like a nightmare. Thierry's voice sounded again, faint and receding.

" I am suffocating, Monsieur Flaxman, where are you ? I am near the door. Ach ! "

A strangling bellow of pain and fear followed, that scarcely reached Low through the thickening atmosphere.

" Thierry, what is the matter with you ? " he shouted. " Open the door."

But there was no answer. What had become of Thierry in that hideous, clogging gloom ! Was he also dead, crushed in some ghastly fashion against the wall ? What was this ?

The air had become palpable to the touch, heavy, repulsive, with the sensation of cold humid flesh !

Low pushed out his hands with a mad longing to touch a table, a chair, anything but this clammy, swelling softness that thrust itself upon him from every side, baffling him and filling his grasp.

He knew now that he was absolutely alone—struggling against what ?

His feet were slipping in his wild efforts to feel the floor—the dank flesh was creeping upon his neck, his cheek—his breath came short and labouring as the pressure swung him gently to and fro, helpless, nauseated !

The clammy flesh crowded upon him like the bulk of some fat, horrible creature ; then came a stinging pain on the cheek. Low clutched at something—there was a crash and a rush of air——

The next sensation of which Mr. Flaxman Low was conscious was one of deathly sickness. He was lying on wet grass, the wind blowing over him, and all the clean, wholesome smells of the open air in his nostrils.

He sat up and looked about him. Dawn was breaking windily in the east, and by its light he saw that he was on the lawn of Yand Manor House. The latticed window of the haunted room above him was open. He tried to remember what had happened. He took stock of himself, in fact, and slowly felt that he still held something clutched in his right hand—something dark-coloured, slender, and twisted. It might have been a long shred of bark or the cast skin of an adder—it was impossible to see in the dim light.

After an interval the recollection of Thierry recurred to him. Scrambling to his feet, he raised himself to the window-sill and looked in. Contrary to his expectation, there was no upsetting of furniture ; everything remained in position as when the lamp went out. His own chair and the one Thierry had occupied were just as when they had arisen from them. But there was no sign of Thierry.

Low jumped in by the window. There was the tumbler full of seltzer, and the litter of matches about it. He took up Thierry's box of matches and struck a light. It flared, and he lit the candle with ease. In fact, everything about the room was perfectly normal ; all the horrible conditions prevailing but a couple of hours ago had disappeared.

But where was Thierry ? Carrying the lighted candle, he passed out of the door, and searched in the adjoining rooms. In one of them, to his relief, he found the Frenchman sleeping profoundly in an armchair.

Low touched his arm. Thierry leapt to his feet, fending off an imaginary blow with his arm. Then he turned his scared face on Low.

" What ! You, Monsieur Flaxman ! How have you escaped ? "

" I should rather ask you how you escaped," said Low, smiling at the havoc the night's experiences had worked on his friend's looks and spirits.

" I was crowded out of the room against the door. That infernal thing—what was it ?—with its damp, swelling flesh, inclosed me ! " A shudder of disgust stopped him. " I was a fly in an aspic. I could not move. I sank into the stifling pulp. The air grew thick. I called to you, but your answers became inaudible. Then I was suddenly thrust against the door by a huge hand—it felt like one, at least. I had a struggle for my life, I was all but crushed, and then, I do not know how, I found myself outside the door. I shouted to you in vain. Therefore, as I could not help you, I came here, and—I will confess it, my dear friend—I locked and bolted the door. After some time I went again into the hall and listened ; but, as I heard nothing, I resolved to wait until daylight and the return of Sir George."

" That's all right," said Low. " It was an experience worth having."

" But, no ! Not for me ! I do not envy you your researches into mysteries of this abominable description. I now comprehend perfectly that Sir George has lost his nerve if he has had to do with this horror. Besides, it is entirely impossible to explain these things."

At this moment they heard Sir George's arrival, and went out to meet him.

" I could not sleep all night for thinking of you ! " exclaimed Blackburton on seeing them ; "and I came along as soon as it was light. Something has happened."

" But certainly something has happened," cried M. Thierry shaking his head solemnly ; " something of the most bizarre, of the most horrible ! Monsieur Flaxman, you shall tell Sir George this story. You have been in that accursed room all night, and remain alive to tell the tale ! "

As Low came to the conclusion of the story Sir George suddenly exclaimed :

" You have met with some injury to your face, Mr. Low."

Low turned to the mirror. In the now strong light three parallel weals from eye to mouth could be seen.

" I remember a stinging pain like a lash on my cheek. What would you say these marks were caused by, Thierry ? " asked Low.

Thierry looked at them and shook his head.

" No one in their senses would venture to offer any explanation of the occurrences of last night," he replied.

" Something of this sort, do you think ? " asked Low again, putting down the object he held in his hand on the table.

Thierry took it up and described it aloud.

" A long and thin object of a brown and yellow colour and twisted like a sabre-bladed corkscrew," then he started slightly and glanced at Low.

" It's a human nail, I imagine," suggested Low.

" But no human being has talons of this kind—except, perhaps, a Chinaman of high rank."

" There are no Chinamen about here, nor ever have been, to my knowledge," said Blackburton shortly. " I'm very much afraid that, in spite of all you have so bravely faced, we are no nearer to any rational explanation."

" On the contrary, I fancy I begin to see my way. I believe, after all, that I may be able to convert you, Thierry," said Flaxman Low.

" Convert me ? "

" To a belief in the definite aim of my work. But you shall judge for yourself. What do you make of it so far ? I claim that you know as much of the matter as I do."

" My dear good friend, I make nothing of it," returned Thierry, shrugging his shoulders and spreading out his hands. " Here we have a tissue of unprecedented incidents that can be explained on no theory whatever."

" But this is definite," and Flaxman Low held up the blackened nail.

" And how do you propose to connect that nail with the black hairs—with the eyes that looked through the bars of a cage—the fate of Batty, with its symptoms of death by pressure and suffocation—our experience of swelling flesh, that something which filled and filled the room to the exclusion of all else ? How are you going to account for these things by any kind of connected hypothesis ? " asked Thierry, with a shade of irony.

" I mean to try," replied Low.

At lunch time Thierry inquired how the theory was getting on.

" It progresses," answered Low. " By the way, Sir George, who lived in this house for some time prior to, say, 1840 ? He was a man—it may have been a woman, but, from the nature of his studies, I am inclined to think it was a man—who was deeply read in ancient necromancy, Eastern magic, mesmerism, and subjects of a kindred nature. And was he not buried in the vault you pointed out ? "

" Do you know anything more about him ? " asked Sir George in surprise.

" He was I imagine," went on Flaxman Low reflectively, " hirsute and swarthy, probably a recluse, and suffered from a morbid and extravagant fear of death."

" How do you know all this ? "

" I only asked about it. Am I right ? "

" You have described my cousin, Sir Gilbert Blackburton, in every particular. I can show you his portrait in another room."

As they stood looking at the painting of Sir Gilbert Black-burton, with his long, melancholy, olive face and thick, black beard, Sir George went on. " My grandfather succeeded him at Yand. I have often heard my father speak of Sir Gilbert, and his strange studies and extraordinary fear of death. Oddly enough, in the end he died rather suddenly, while he was still hale and strong. He predicted his own approaching death, and had a doctor in attendance for a week or two before he died. He was placed in a coffin he had had made on some plan of his own and buried in the vault. His death occurred in 1842 or 1843. If you care to see them I can show you some of his papers, which may interest you."

Mr. Flaxman Low spent the afternoon over the papers. When evening came, he rose from his work with a sigh of content, stretched himself, and joined Thierry and Sir George in the garden.

They dined at Lady Blackburton's, and it was late before Sir George found himself alone with Mr. Flaxman Low and his friend.

" Have you formed any opinion about the thing which haunts the Manor House ? " he asked anxiously.

Thierry elaborated a cigarette, crossed his legs, and added :

" If you have in truth come to any definite conclusion, pray let us hear it, my dear Monsieur Flaxman."

" I have reached a very definite and satisfactory conclusion," replied Low. " The Manor House is haunted by Sir Gilbert Blackburton, who died, or, rather, who seemed to die, on the 15th of August, 1842."

" Nonsense ! The nail fifteen inches long at the least—how do you connect it with Sir Gilbert ? " asked Blackburton testily.

" I am convinced that it belonged to Sir Gilbert," Low answered.

" But the long black hair like a woman's ? "

" Dissolution in the case of Sir Gilbert was not complete—not consummated, so to speak—as I hope to show you later. Even in the case of dead persons the hair and nails have been known to grow. By a rough calculation as to the growth of nails in such cases, I was enabled to indicate approximately the date of Sir Gilbert's death. The hair too grew on his head."

" But the barred eyes ? I saw them myself ! " exclaimed the young man.

" The eyelashes grow also. You follow me ? "

" You have, I presume, some theory in connection with this ? " observed Thierry. " It must be a very curious one."

" Sir Gilbert in his fear of death appears to have mastered and elaborated a strange and ancient formula by which the grosser factors of the body being eliminated, the more ethereal portions continue to retain the spirit, and the body is thus preserved from absolute disintegration. In this manner true death may be indefinitely deferred. Secure from the ordinary chances and changes of existence, this spiritualised body could retain a modified life practically for ever."

" This is a most extraordinary idea, my dear fellow," remarked Thierry.

" But why should Sir Gilbert haunt the Manor House, and one special room ? "

" The tendency of spirits to return to the old haunts of bodily life is almost universal. We cannot yet explain the reason of this attraction of environment."

" But the expansion—the crowding substance which we ourselves felt ? You cannot meet that difficulty," said Thierry persistently.

" Not as fully as I could wish, perhaps. But the power of expanding and contracting to a degree far beyond our comprehension is a well-known attribute of spiritualised matter."

" Wait one little moment, my dear Monsieur Flaxman," broke in Thierry's voice after an interval ; " this is very clever and ingenious indeed. As a theory I give it my sincere admiration. But proof—proof is what we now demand."

Flaxman Low looked steadily at the two incredulous faces.

" This," he said slowly, " is the hair of Sir Gilbert Blackburton, and this nail is from the little finger of his left hand. You can prove my assertion by opening the coffin."

Sir George, who was pacing up and down the room impatiently, drew up.

" I don't like it at all, Mr. Low, I tell you frankly. I don't like it at all. I see no object in violating the coffin. I am not concerned to verify this unpleasant theory of yours. I have only one desire ; I want to get rid of this haunting presence, whatever it is."

" If I am right," replied Low, " the opening of the coffin and exposure of the remains to strong sunshine for a short time will free you for ever from this presence."

In the early morning, when the summer sun struck warmly on the lawns of Yand, the three men carried the coffin from the vault to a quiet spot among the shrubs where, secure from observation, they raised the lid.

Within the coffin lay the semblance of Gilbert Blackburton, maned to the ears with long and coarse black hair. Matted eye-lashes swept the fallen cheeks, and beside the body stretched the bony hands, each with its dependent sheaf of switch-like nails. Low bent over and raised the left hand gingerly.

The little finger was without a nail !

Two hours later they came back and looked again. The sun had in the meantime done its work ; nothing remained but a fleshless skeleton and a few half-rotten shreds of clothing.

The ghost of Yand Manor House has never since been heard of.

When Thiery bade Flaxman Low good-bye, he said :

" In time, my dear Monsieur Flaxman, you will add another to our sciences. You establish your facts too well for my peace of mind."

Vincent O'Sullivan

THE BUSINESS OF
MADAME JAHN
from A BOOK OF BARGAINS

Leonard Smithers. 1896

How we all stared, how frightened we all were, how we passed opinions, on that morning when Gustave Herbout was found swinging by the neck from the ceiling of his bedroom ! The whole *Faubourg*, even the ancient folk who had not felt a street under them for years, turned out and stood gaping at the house with amazement and loud conjecture. For why should Gustave Herbout, of all men, take to the rope ? Only last week he had inherited all the money of his aunt, Madame Jahn, together with her house and the shop with the five assistants, and life looked fair enough for him. No ; clearly it was not wise of Gustave to hang himself !

Besides, his aunt's death had happened at a time when Gustave was in sore straits for money. To be sure, he had his salary from the bank in which he worked ; but what is a mere salary to one who (like Gustave) threw off the clerkly habit when working hours were over to assume the dress and lounge of the accustomed *boulevardier* : while he would relate to obsequious friends vague but satisfactory stories of a Russian Prince who was his uncle, and of an extremely rich English lady to whose death he looked forward with hope. Alas ! with a clerk's salary one cannot make much of a figure in Paris. It took all of that, and more, to maintain the renown he had gained among his acquaintance of having to his own a certain little lady with yellow hair who danced divinely. So he was forced to depend on the presents which Madame Jahn gave him from time to time ; and for those presents he had to pay his aunt a most sedulous and irksome attention. At times, when he was almost sick from his craving for the *boulevard*, the *café*, the theatre, he would have to repair as the day grew to an end, to our *Faubourg*, and the house behind the shop, where he would sit to an old-fashioned supper with his aunt, and listen with a sort of dull impatience while she asked him when he had last been at Confession, and told him long dreary stories of his dead father and mother. Punctually at nine o'clock the deaf servant, who was the only person besides Madame Jahn that lived in the house, would let in the fat old priest, who came for his game of dominoes, and betake herself to bed. Then the dominoes would begin, and with them the old man's prattle which Gustave knew so well : about his daily work, about the uselessness of all things here on earth, and the happiness and glory of the Kingdom of Heaven ; and, of course, our *boulevardier* noticed, with the usual cheap sneer of the modern, that whilst the priest talked of the Kingdom of Heaven he yet showed the greatest anxiety if he had symptoms of a cold, or any other petty malady. However, Gustave would sit there with a hypocrite's grin and inwardly raging, till the clock chimed eleven. At that hour Madame Jahn would rise, and, if she was pleased with her nephew, would go over to her writing-desk and give him, with a rather pretty air of concealment from the priest, perhaps fifty or a hundred francs. Whereupon Gustave would bid her a manifestly affectionate goodnight ! and depart in the company of the priest. As soon as he could get rid of the priest, he would hasten to his favourite *cafés*, to discover that all the people worth seeing had long since grown tired of waiting and had departed on their own affairs. The money, indeed, was a kind of consolation ; but then there were nights when he did not get a *sou*. Ah ! they amuse themselves in Paris, but not in this way—this is not amusing.

One cannot live a proper life upon a salary and an occasional gift of fifty or a hundred francs. And it is not entertaining to tell men that your uncle, the Prince at Moscow, is in a sorry case, and even now lies a-dying, or that the rich English lady is in the grip of a vile consumption and is momently expected to succumb, if these men only shove up their shoulders, wink at one another, and continue to present their bills. Further, the little Mademoiselle with yellow hair had lately shown signs of a very pretty temper, because her usual flowers and *bon-bons* were not apparent. So, since things were come to this dismal pass, Gustave fell to attending the race-meetings at Chantilly. During the first week Gustave won largely, for that is sometimes the way with ignorant men : during that week, too, the little Mademoiselle was charming, for she had her *bouquets* and boxes of *bon-bons*. But the next week Gustave lost heavily, for that is also very often the way with ignorant men : and he was thrown into the blackest despair, when one night at a place where he used to sup, Mademoiselle took the arm of a great fellow whom he much suspected to be a German, and tossed him a scornful nod as she went off.

On the evening after this happened, he was standing between five and six o'clock, in the *Place de la Madeleine*, blowing on his fingers and trying to plan his next move, when he heard his name called by a familiar voice, and turned to face his aunt's adviser, the priest.

" Ah, Gustave, my friend, I have just been to see a colleague of mine here ! " cried the old man, pointing to the great church. " And are you going to your good aunt to-night ? " he added, with a look at Gustave's neat dress.

Gustave was in a flame that the priest should have detected him in his gay clothes, for he always made a point of appearing at Madame Jahn's clad staidly in black ; but he answered pleasantly enough :

" No, my Father, I'm afraid I can't to-night. You see I'm a little behind with my office work, and I have to stay at home and catch up."

" Well, well ! " said the priest, with half a sigh, " I suppose young men will always be the same. I myself can only be with her till nine o'clock to-night because I must see a sick parishioner. But let me give you one bit of advice, my friend," he went on, taking hold of a button on Gustave's coat : " Don't neglect your aunt ; for, mark my words, one day everything of Madame Jahn's will be yours ! " And the omnibus he was waiting for happening to swing by at that moment, he departed without another word.

Gustave strolled along the *Boulevard des Capucines* in a study. Yes ; it was certain that the house, and the shop with the five assistants, would one day be his ; for the priest knew all his aunt's affairs. But how soon would they be his ? Madame Jahn was now hardly sixty ; her mother had lived to be ninety ; when she was ninety he would be—— And meanwhile, what about the numerous bills ; what (above all !) about the little lady with yellow hair ? He paused and struck his heel on the pavement with such force, that two men passing nudged one another and smiled. Then he made certain purchases, and set about wasting his time till nine o'clock.

It is curious to consider, that although when he started out at nine o'clock, Gustave was perfectly clear as to what he meant to do, yet he was chiefly troubled by the fear that the priest had told his aunt about his fine clothes. But when he had passed through the deserted *Faubourg*, and had come to the house behind the shop,

he found his aunt only very pleased to see him, and a little surprised. So he sat with her, and listened to her gentle, homely
stories, and told lies about himself and his manner of life, till the
clock struck eleven. Then he rose, and Madame Jahn rose too
and went to her writing-desk and opened a small drawer.

" You have been very kind to a lonely old woman to-night, my
Gustave," said Madame Jahn, smiling.

" How sweet of you to say that, dearest aunt ! " replied Gustave.
He went over and passed his arm caressingly across her shoulders,
and stabbed her in the heart.

For a full five minutes after the murder he stood still ; as men
often do in a great crisis when they know that any movement
means decisive action. Then he started, laid hold of his hat, and
made for the door. But there the stinging knowledge of his crime
came to him for the first time ; and he turned back into the room.
Madame Jahn's bedroom candle was on a table : he lit it, and
passed through a door which led from the house into the shop.
Crouching below the counters covered with white sheets, lest a
streak of light on the windows might attract the observation of
some passenger, he proceeded to a side entrance to the shop, un-
barred and unlocked the door and put the key in his pocket. Then,
in the same crouching way, he returned to the room, and started
to ransack the small drawer. The notes he scattered about the
floor ; but two small bags of coin went into his coat. Then he took
the candle and dropped some wax on the face and hands and
dress of the corpse ; he spilt wax, too, over the carpet, and then he
broke the candle and ground it under his foot. He even tore with
long nervous fingers at the dead woman's bodice until her breasts
lay exposed ; and plucked out a handful of her hair and threw it
on the floor to stick to the wax. When all these things had been
accomplished he went to the house door and listened. The *Faubourg* is always very quiet about twelve o'clock, and a single footstep falls on the night with a great sound. He could not hear the
least noise ; so he darted out and ran lightly until he came to a
turning. There he fell into a sauntering walk, lit a cigarette, and,
hailing a passing *fiacre*, directed the man to drive to the *Pont
Saint-Michel*. At the bridge he alighted, and noting that he was
not eyed, he threw the key of the shop into the river. Then assuming the swagger and assurance of a half-drunken man, he marched
up the *Boulevard* and entered the *Café d'Harcourt*.

The place was filled with the usual crowd of men and women of the *Quartier Latin*. Gustave looked round, and observing a young student with a flushed face who was talking eagerly about the rights of man, he sat down by him. It was his part to act quickly : so before the student had quite finished a sentence for his ear, the murderer gave him the lie. The student, however, was not so ready for a fight as Gustave had supposed ; and when he began to argue again, Gustave seized a glass full of brandy and water and threw the stuff in his face. Then indeed there was a row, till the *gendarmes* interfered, and haled Gustave to the station. At the police-station he bitterly lamented his misdeed, which he attributed to an extra glass of absinthe, and he begged the authorities to carry word of his plight to his good aunt, Madame Jahn, in our *Faubourg*. So to the house behind the shop they went, and there they found her—sitting with her breasts hanging out, her poor head clotted with blood, and a knife in her heart.

The next morning, Gustave was set free. A man and a woman, two of the five assistants in the shop, had been charged with the murder. The woman had been severely reprimanded by Madame Jahn on the day before, and the man was known to be the girl's paramour. It was the duty of the man to close at night all the entrances into the shop, save the main entrance, which was closed by Madame Jahn and her deaf servant ; and the police had formed a theory (worked out with the amazing zeal and skill which cause the Paris police so often to overreach themselves !) that the man had failed to bolt one of the side doors, and had, by his subtilty, got possession of the key whereby he and his accomplice re-entered the place about midnight. Working on this theory, the police had woven a web round the two unfortunates with threads of steel ; and there was little doubt that both of them would stretch their necks under the guillotine, with full consent of Press and public. At least, this was Gustave's opinion ; and Gustave's opinion now went for a great deal in the *Faubourg*. Of course there were a few who murmured that it was a good thing poor Madame Jahn had not lived to see her nephew arrested for a drunken brawler ; but with full remembrance of who owned the house and shop we were most of us inclined to say, after the priest : That if the brave Gustave had been with his aunt, the shocking affair could never have occurred. And, indeed, what had we more inspiring than the inconsolable grief he showed? Why ! on the day of the funeral, when he heard the earth clatter down on the coffin-lid in *Père la Chaise*, he even swooned to the ground, and had to be carried out in the midst of the mourners. " Oh, yes," (quoth the gossips), " Gustave Herbout loved his aunt passing well ! "

On the night after the funeral, Gustave was sitting alone before the fire in Madame Jahn's room, smoking and making his plans. He thought, that when all this wretched mock grief and pretence of decorum was over, he would again visit the *cafés* which he greatly savoured, and the little Mademoiselle with yellow hair would once more smile on him delicious smiles with a gleaming regard. Thus he was thinking when the clock on the mantel-piece tinkled eleven ; and at that moment a very singular thing happened. The door was suddenly opened : a girl came in, and walked straight over to the writing-desk, pulled out the small drawer, and then sat staring at the man by the fire. She was distinctly beautiful ; although there was a certain old-fashioned-ness in her peculiar silken dress, and the manner of wearing her hair. Not once did it occur to Gustave, as he gazed in terror, that he was gazing on a mortal woman : the doors were too well bolted to allow anyone from outside to enter, and besides, there was a strange baffling familiarity in the face and mien of the in-truder. It might have been an hour as he sat there ; and then, the silence becoming too horrible, by a supreme effort of his wonderful courage he rushed out of the room and up-stairs to get his hat. There in his murdered aunt's bedroom,—there, smiling at him from the wall—was a vivid presentment of the dread vision that sat below : a portrait of Madame Jahn as a girl. He fled into the street, and walked, perhaps two miles, before he thought at all. But when he did think, he found that he was drawn against his will back to the house to see if *It* was still there : just as the police here believe a murderer is drawn to the *Morgue* to view the body of his victim. Yes ; the girl was there still, with her great reproachless eyes ; and throughout that solemn night Gustave, haggard and mute, sat glaring at her. Towards dawn he fell into an uneasy doze ; and when he awoke with a scream, he found that the girl was gone.

At noon the next day Gustave, heartened by several glasses of brandy, and cheered by the sunshine in the *Champs-Elysées*, en-deavoured to make light of the affair. He would gladly have ar-ranged not to go back to the house : but then people would talk so much, and he could not afford to lose any custom out of the shop. Moreover, the whole matter was only an hallucination—the effect of jaded nerves. He dined well, and went to see a musical comedy ; and so contrived, that he did not return to the house until after two o'clock. There was someone waiting for him, sitting at the desk with the small drawer open ; not the girl of last night, but a somewhat older woman—and the same reproachless eyes. So great was the fascination of those eyes, that, although he left the house at once with an iron resolution not to go back, he found himself drawn under them again, and he sat through the night as he had sat through the night before, sobbing and stupidly glaring. And all day long he crouched by the fire shuddering ; and all the night till eleven o'clock ; and then a figure of his aunt came to him again, but always a little older and more withered. And this went on for five days ; the figure that sat with him becoming older and older as the days ran, till on the sixth night he gazed through the hours at his aunt as she was on the night he killed her. On these nights he was used sometimes to start up and make for the street, swearing never to return ; but always he would be dragged back to the eyes. The policemen came to know him from these night walks, and people began to notice his bad looks : these could not spring from grief, folk said, and so they thought he was leading a wild life.

On the seventh night there was a delay of about five minutes after the clock had rung eleven, before the door opened. And then —then, merciful God ! The body of a woman in grave-clothes came into the room, as if borne by unseen men, and lay in the air across the writing-desk, while the small drawer flew open of its own accord. Yes ; there was the shroud and the brown scapular, the prim white cap, the hands folded on the shrunken breast. Grey from slimy horror, Gustave raised himself up, and went over to look for the eyes. When he saw them pressed down with pennies, he reeled back and vomited into the grate. And blind, and sick, and loathing, he stumbled up-stairs.

But as he passed by Madame Jahn's bedroom the corpse came out to meet him, with the eyes closed and the pennies pressing them down. Then, at last, reeking and dabbled with sweat, with his tongue lolling out, and the spittle running down his beard, Gustave breathed :

" Are you alive ? "

" No, no ! " wailed the *thing*, with a burst of awful weeping ; " I have been dead many days."

_____

Vernon Lee

AMOUR DURE

Passages from the Diary of Spiridion Trepka

from Hauntings

Heinemann, 1890 ; Second Edition, John Lane, 1906

PART I

Urbania, August 20th, 1885.—I had longed, these years and years, to be in Italy, to come face to face with the Past ; and was this Italy, was this the Past ? I could have cried, yes cried, for disappointment when I first wandered about Rome, with an invitation to dine at the German Embassy in my pocket, and three or four Berlin and Munich Vandals at my heels, telling me where the best beer and sauerkraut could be had, and what the last article by Grimm or Mommsen was about.

Is this folly ? Is it falsehood ? Am I not myself a product of modern, northern civilisation ; is not my coming to Italy due to this very modern scientific vandalism, which has given me a travelling scholarship because I have written a book like all those other atrocious books of erudition and art-criticism ? Nay, am I not here at Urbania on the express understanding that, in a certain number of months, I shall produce just another such book ? Dost thou imagine, thou miserable Spiridion, thou Pole grown into the semblance of a German pedant, doctor of philosophy, professor even, author of a prize essay on the despots of the fifteenth century, dost thou imagine that thou, with thy ministerial letters and proof-sheets in thy black professorial coat-pocket, canst ever come in spirit into the presence of the Past ?

Too true, alas ! But let me forget it, at least, every now and then ; as I forgot it this afternoon, while the white bullocks dragged my gig slowly winding along interminable valleys, crawling along interminable hill-sides, with the invisible droning torrent far below, and only the bare grey and reddish peaks all around, up to this town of Urbania, forgotten of mankind, towered and battlemented on the high Apennine ridge. Sigillo, Penna, Fossombrone, Mercatello, Montemurlo—each single village name, as the driver pointed it out, brought to my mind the recollection of some battle or some great act of treachery of former days. And as

the huge mountains shut out the setting sun, and the valleys filled
with bluish shadow and mist, only a band of threatening smoke-
red remaining behind the towers and cupolas of the city on its
mountain-top, and the sound of church bells floated across the
precipice from Urbania, I almost expected, at every turning of the
road, that a troop of horsemen, with beaked helmets and clawed
shoes, would emerge, with armour glittering and pennons waving
in the sunset. And then, not two hours ago, entering the town at
dusk, passing along the deserted streets, with only a smoky light
here and there under a shrine or in front of a fruit-stall, or a fire
reddening the blackness of a smithy ; passing beneath the battlements and turrets of the palace. . . . Ah, that was Italy, it was the
Past !

August 21st.—And this is the Present ! Four letters of introduction to deliver, and an hour's polite conversation to endure with
the Vice-Prefect, the Syndic, the Director of the Archives, and the
good man to whom my friend Max had sent me for lodgings. . . .

August 22nd–27th.—Spent the greater part of the day in the
Archives, and the greater part of my time there in being bored to
extinction by the Director thereof, who to-day spouted Æneas
Sylvius' Commentaries for three-quarters of an hour without taking breath. From this sort of martyrdom (what are the sensations of
a former racehorse being driven in a cab ? If you can conceive
them, they are those of a Pole turned Prussian professor) I take
refuge in long rambles through the town. This town is a handful
of tall black houses huddled on to the top of an Alp, long narrow
lanes trickling down its sides, like the slides we made on hillocks in
our boyhood, and in the middle the superb red brick structure,
turreted and battlemented, of Duke Ottobuono's palace, from
whose windows you look down upon a sea, a kind of whirlpool, of
melancholy grey mountains. Then there are the people, dark,
bushy-bearded men, riding about like brigands, wrapped in green-
lined cloaks upon their shaggy pack-mules ; or loitering about,
great, brawny, low-headed youngsters, like the parti-coloured
bravos in Signorelli's frescoes ; the beautiful boys, like so many
young Raphaels, with eyes like the eyes of bullocks, and the huge
women, Madonnas or St. Elizabeths, as the case may be, with
their clogs firmly poised on their toes and their brass pitchers on
their heads, as they go up and down the steep black alleys. I do
not talk much to these people ; I fear my illusions being dispelled.
At the corner of a street, opposite Francesco di Giorgio's beautiful

little portico, is a great blue and red advertisement, representing an angel descending to crown Elias Howe, on account of his sewing-machines ; and the clerks of the Vice-Prefecture, who dine at the place where I get my dinner, yell politics, Minghetti, Cairoli, Tunis, ironclads, etc., at each other, and sing snatches of *La Fille de Mme. Angot*, which I imagine they have been performing here recently.

No ; talking to the natives is evidently a dangerous experiment. Except indeed, perhaps, to my good landlord, Signor Notaro Porri, who is just as learned, and takes considerably less snuff (or rather brushes it off his coat more often) than the Director of the Archives. I forgot to jot down (and I feel I must jot down, in the vain belief that some day these scraps will help, like a withered twig of olive or a three-wicked Tuscan lamp on my table, to bring to my mind, in that hateful Babylon of Berlin, these happy Italian days)—I forgot to record that I am lodging in the house of a dealer in antiquities. My window looks up the principal street to where the little column with Mercury on the top rises in the midst of the awnings and porticoes of the market-place. Bending over the chipped ewers and tubs full of sweet basil, clove pinks, and marigolds, I can just see a corner of the palace turret, and the vague ultramarine of the hills beyond. The house, whose back goes sharp down into the ravine, is a queer up-and-down black place, whitewashed rooms, hung with the Raphaels and Francias and Peruginos, whom mine host regularly carries to the chief inn whenever a stranger is expected ; and surrounded by old carved chairs, sofas of the Empire, embossed and gilded wedding-chests, and the cupboards which contain bits of old damask and embroidered altarcloths scenting the place with the smell of old incense and mustiness ; all of which are presided over by Signor Porri's three maiden sisters—Sora Serafina, Sora Lodovica, and Sora Adalgisa—the three Fates in person, even to the distaffs and their black cats.

Sor Asdrubale, as they call my landlord, is also a notary. He regrets the Pontifical Government, having had a cousin who was a Cardinal's train-bearer, and believes that if only you lay a table for two, light four candles made of dead men's fat, and perform certain rites about which he is not very precise, you can, on Christmas Eve and similar nights, summon up San Pasquale Baylon, who will write you the winning numbers of the lottery upon the smoked back of a plate, if you have previously slapped him on both cheeks and repeated three Ave Marias. The difficulty

consists in obtaining the dead men's fat for the candles, and also
in slapping the saint before he have time to vanish.

"If it were not for that," says Sor Asdrubale, "the Government
would have had to suppress the lottery ages ago—eh ! "

Sept. 9th.—This history of Urbania is not without its romance,
although that romance (as usual) has been overlooked by our
Dryasdusts. Even before coming here I felt attracted by the
strange figure of a woman, which appeared from out of the dry
pages of Gualterio's and Padre de Sanctis' histories of this place.
This woman is Medea, daughter of Galeazzo IV Malatesta, Lord
of Carpi, wife first of Pierluigi Orsini, Duke of Stimigliano, and
subsequently of Guidalfonso II, Duke of Urbania, predecessor of
the great Duke Robert II.

This woman's history and character remind one of that of
Bianca Cappello, and at the same time of Lucrezia Borgia. Born
in 1556, she was affianced at the age of twelve to a cousin, a Malatesta of the Rimini family. This family having greatly gone down
in the world, her engagement was broken, and she was betrothed
a year later to a member of the Pico family, and married to him
by proxy at the age of fourteen. But this match not satisfying her
own or her father's ambition, the marriage by proxy was, upon
some pretext, declared null, and the suit encouraged of the Duke
of Stimigliano, a great Umbrian feudatory of the Orsini family.
But the bridegroom, Giovanfrancesco Pico, refused to submit,
pleaded his case before the Pope, and tried to carry off by force
his bride, with whom he was madly in love, as the lady was most
lovely and of most cheerful and amiable manner, says an old
anonymous chronicle. Pico waylaid her litter as she was going to
a villa of her father's, and carried her to his castle near Miran-
dola, where he respectfully pressed his suit ; insisting that he had a
right to consider her as his wife. But the lady escaped by letting
herself into the moat by a rope of sheets, and Giovanfrancesco
Pico was discovered stabbed in the chest, by the hand of Madonna
Medea da Carpi. He was a handsome youth only eighteen years old.

The Pico having been settled, and the marriage with him declared null by the Pope, Medea da Carpi was solemnly married to
the Duke of Stimigliano, and went to live upon his domains near
Rome.

Two years later, Pierluigi Orsini was stabbed by one of his
grooms at his castle of Stimigliano, near Orvieto ; and suspicion
fell upon his widow, more especially as, immediately after the

event, she caused the murderer to be cut down by two servants in her own chamber ; but not before he had declared that she had induced him to assassinate his master by a promise of her love. Things became so hot for Medea da Carpi that she fled to Urbania and threw herself at the feet of Duke Guidalfonso II, declaring that she had caused the groom to be killed merely to avenge her good fame, which he had slandered, and that she was absolutely guiltless of the death of her husband. The marvellous beauty of the widowed Duchess of Stimigliano, who was only nineteen, entirely turned the head of the Duke of Urbania. He affected implicit belief in her innocence, refused to give her up to the Orsinis, kinsmen of her late husband, and assigned to her magnificent apartments in the left wing of the palace, among which the room containing the famous fireplace ornamented with marble Cupids on a blue ground. Guidalfonso fell madly in love with his beautiful guest. Hitherto timid and domestic in character, he began publicly to neglect his wife, Maddalena Varano of Camerino, with whom, although childless, he had hitherto lived on excellent terms ; he not only treated with contempt the admonitions of his advisers and of his suzerain the Pope, but went so far as to take measures to repudiate his wife, on the score of quite imaginary ill-conduct. The Duchess Maddalena, unable to bear this treatment, fled to the convent of the barefooted sisters at Pesaro, where she pined away, while Medea da Carpi reigned in her place at Urbania, embroiling Duke Guidalfonso in quarrels both with the powerful Orsinis, who continued to accuse her of Stimigliano's murder, and with the Varanos, kinsmen of the injured Duchess Maddalena ; until at length, in the year 1576, the Duke of Urbania, having become suddenly, and not without suspicious circumstances, a widower, publicly married Medea da Carpi two days after the decease of his unhappy wife. No child was born of this marriage ; but such was the infatuation of Duke Guidalfonso, that the new Duchess induced him to settle the inheritance of the Duchy (having, with great difficulty, obtained the consent of the Pope) on the boy Bartolommeo, her son by Stimigliano, but whom the Orsinis refused to acknowledge as such, declaring him to be the child of that Giovanfrancesco Pico to whom Medea had been married by proxy, and whom, in defence, as she had said, of her honour, she had assassinated ; and this investiture of the Duchy of Urbania on to a stranger and a bastard was at the expense of the obvious rights of the Cardinal Robert, Guidalfonso's younger brother.

In May 1579 Duke Guidalfonso died suddenly and mysteriously, Medea having forbidden all access to his chamber, lest, on his deathbed, he might repent and reinstate his brother in his rights. The Duchess immediately caused her son, Bartolommeo Orsini, to be proclaimed Duke of Urbania, and herself regent ; and, with the help of two or three unscrupulous young men, particularly a certain Captain Oliverotto da Narni, who was rumoured to be her lover, seized the reins of government with extraordinary and terrible vigour, marching an army against the Varanos and Orsinis, who were defeated at Sigillo, and ruthlessly exterminating every person who dared question the lawfulness of the succession ; while, all the time, Cardinal Robert, who had flung aside his priest's garb and vows, went about in Rome, Tuscany, Venice— nay, even to the Emperor and the King of Spain, imploring help against the usurper. In a few months he had turned the tide of sympathy against the Duchess-Regent ; the Pope solemnly de- clared the investiture of Bartolommeo Orsini worthless, and pub- lished the accession of Robert II, Duke of Urbania and Count of Montemurlo ; the Grand Duke of Tuscany and the Venetians secretly promised assistance, but only if Robert were able to assert his rights by main force. Little by little, one town after the other of the Duchy went over to Robert, and Medea da Carpi found herself surrounded in the mountain citadel of Urbania like a scorpion surrounded by flames. (This simile is not mine, but be- longs to Raffaello Gualterio, historiographer to Robert II.) But, unlike the scorpion, Medea refused to commit suicide. It is per- fectly marvellous how, without money or allies, she could so long keep her enemies at bay ; and Gualterio attributes this to those fatal fascinations which had brought Pico and Stimigliano to their deaths, which had turned the once honest Guidalfonso into a vil- lain, and which were such that, of all her lovers, not one but pre- ferred dying for her, even after he had been treated with ingrati- tude and ousted by a rival ; a faculty which Messer Raffaello Gualterio clearly attributed to hellish connivance.

At last the ex-Cardinal Robert succeeded, and triumphantly entered Urbania in November 1579. His accession was marked by moderation and clemency. Not a man was put to death, save Oliverotto da Narni, who threw himself on the new Duke, tried to stab him as he alighted at the palace, and who was cut down by the Duke's men, crying, " Orsini, Orsini ! Medea, Medea ! Long live Duke Bartolommeo ! " with his dying breath, although it is said that the Duchess had treated him with ignominy. The little Bartolommeo was sent to Rome to the Orsinis ; the Duchess, respectfully confined to the left wing of the palace.

It is said that she haughtily requested to see the new Duke, but that he shook his head, and, in his priest's fashion, quoted a verse about Ulysses and the Sirens ; and it is remarkable that he persistently refused to see her, abruptly leaving his chamber one day that she had entered it by stealth. After a few months a conspiracy was discovered to murder Duke Robert, which had obviously been set on foot by Medea. But the young man, one Marcantonio Frangipani of Rome, denied, even under the severest torture, any complicity of hers ; so that Duke Robert, who wished to do nothing violent, merely transferred the Duchess from his villa at Sant' Elmo to the convent of the Clarisse in town, where she was guarded and watched in the closest manner. It seemed impossible that Medea should intrigue any further, for she certainly saw and could be seen by no one. Yet she contrived to send a letter and her portrait to one Prinzivalle degli Ordelaffi, a youth, only nineteen years old, of noble Romagnole family, and who was betrothed to one of the most beautiful girls of Urbania. He immediately broke off his engagement, and, shortly afterwards, attempted to shoot Duke Robert with a holster-pistol as he knelt at mass on the festival of Easter Day. This time Duke Robert was determined to obtain proofs against Medea. Prinzivalle degli Ordelaffi was kept some days without food, then submitted to the most violent tortures, and finally condemned. When he was going to be flayed with red-hot pincers and quartered by horses, he was told that he might obtain the grace of immediate death by confessing the complicity of the Duchess ; and the confessor and nuns of the convent, which stood in the place of execution outside Porta San Romano, pressed Medea to save the wretch, whose screams reached her, by confessing her own guilt. Medea asked permission to go to a balcony, where she could see Prinzivalle and be seen by him. She looked on coldly, then threw down her embroidered kerchief to the poor mangled creature. He asked the executioner to wipe his mouth with it, kissed it, and cried out that Medea was innocent. Then, after several hours of torments, he died. This was too much for the patience even of Duke Robert. Seeing that as long as Medea lived his life would be in perpetual danger, but unwilling to cause a scandal (somewhat of the priest-nature remaining), he had Medea strangled in the convent, and, what is remarkable, insisted that only women—two infanticides to whom he remitted their sentence—should be employed for the deed.

"This clement prince," writes Don Arcangelo Zappi in his life of him, published in 1725, "can be blamed only for one act of cruelty, the more odious as he had himself, until released from his vows by the Pope, been in holy orders. It is said that when he caused the death of the infamous Medea da Carpi, his fear lest her extraordinary charms should seduce any man was such, that he not only employed women as executioners, but refused to permit her a priest or monk, thus forcing her to die unshriven, and refusing her the benefit of any penitence that may have lurked in her adamantine heart."

Such is the story of Medea da Carpi, Duchess of Stimigliano Orsini, and then wife of Duke Guidalfonso II of Urbania. She was put to death just two hundred and ninety-seven years ago, December 1582, at the age of barely seven-and-twenty, and having, in the course of her short life, brought to a violent end five of her lovers, from Giovanfrancesco Pico to Prinzivalle degli Ordelaffi.

Sept. 20th.—A grand illumination of the town in honour of the taking of Rome fifteen years ago. Except Sor Asdrubale, my landlord, who shakes his head at the Piedmontese, as he calls them, the people here are all Italianissimi. The Popes kept them very much down since Urbania lapsed to the Holy See in 1645.

Sept. 28th.—I have for some time been hunting for portraits of the Duchess Medea. Most of them, I imagine, must have been destroyed, perhaps by Duke Robert II's fear lest even after her death this terrible beauty should play him a trick. Three or four I have, however, been able to find—one a miniature in the Archives, said to be that which she sent to poor Prinzivalle degli Ordelaffi in order to turn his head ; one a marble bust in the palace lumber-room ; one in a large composition, possibly by Baroccio, representing Cleopatra at the feet of Augustus. Augustus is the idealised portrait of Robert II, round cropped head, nose a little awry, clipped beard and scar as usual, but in Roman dress. Cleopatra seems to me, for all her Oriental dress, and although she wears a black wig, to be meant for Medea da Carpi ; she is kneeling, baring her breast for the victor to strike, but in reality to captivate him, and he turns away with an awkward gesture of loathing. None of these portraits seem very good, save the miniature, but that is an exquisite work, and with it, and the suggestions of the bust, it is easy to reconstruct the beauty of this terrible being. The type is that most admired by the late Renaissance, and, in some measure, immortalised by Jean Goujon and the French. The face is a perfect oval, the forehead somewhat over-round, with minute curls, like a fleece, of bright auburn hair ; the nose a trifle over-aquiline, and the cheek-bones a trifle too low ; the eyes grey, large, prominent, beneath exquisitely curved brows and lids just a little too tight at the corners ; the mouth also, brilliantly red and most delicately designed, is a little too tight, the lips strained a trifle over the teeth. Tight eyelids and tight lips give a strange refinement, and, at the same time, an air of mystery, a somewhat sinister seductiveness ; they seem to take, but not to give. The mouth with a kind of childish pout, looks as if it could bite or suck like a leech. The complexion is dazzlingly fair, the perfect transparent roset lily of a red-haired beauty ; the head, with hair elaborately curled and plaited close to it, and adorned with pearls, sits like that of the antique Arethusa on a long, supple, swan-like neck. A curious, at first rather conventional, artificial-looking sort of beauty, voluptuous yet cold, which, the more it is contemplated, the more it troubles and haunts the mind. Round the lady's neck is a gold chain with little gold lozenges at intervals, on which is engraved the posy or pun (the fashion of French devices is common in those days), " Amour Dure—Dure Amour." The same posy is inscribed in the hollow of the bust, and, thanks to it, I have been able to identify the latter as Medea's portrait. I often examine these tragic portraits, wondering what this face, which led so many men to their death, may have been like when it spoke or smiled, what at the moment when Medea da Carpi fascinated her victims into love unto death—" Amour Dure—Dure Amour," as runs her device—love that lasts, cruel love—yes indeed, when one thinks of the fidelity and fate of her lovers.

Oct. 13th.—I have literally not had time to write a line of my diary all these days. My whole mornings have gone in those Archives, my afternoons taking long walks in this lovely autumn weather (the highest hills are just tipped with snow). My evenings go in writing that confounded account of the Palace of Urbania which Government requires, merely to keep me at work at something useless. Of my history I have not yet been able to write a word. . . . By the way, I must note down a curious circumstance mentioned in an anonymous MS. life of Duke Robert, which I fell upon to-day. When this prince had the equestrian statue of himself by Antonio Tassi, Gianbologna's pupil, erected in the square of

the *Corte*, he secretly caused to be made, says my anonymous MS.,
a silver statuette of his familiar genius or angel—" familiaris ejus
angelus seu genius, quod a vulgo dicitur *idolino* "—which statuette
or idol, after having been consecrated by the astrologers—" ab
astrologis quibusdam ritibus sacrato "—was placed in the cavity
of the chest of the effigy by Tassi, in order, says the MS., that his
soul might rest until the general Resurrection. This passage is
curious, and to me somewhat puzzling ; how could the soul of
Duke Robert await the general Resurrection, when, as a Catholic,
he ought to have believed that it must, as soon as separated from
his body, go to Purgatory ? Or is there some semi-pagan superstition of the Renaissance (most strange, certainly, in a man who
had been a Cardinal) connecting the soul with a guardian genius,
who could be compelled, by magic rites (" ab astrologis sacrato,"
the MS. says of the little idol), to remain fixed to earth, so that the
soul should sleep in the body until the Day of Judgment ? I confess this story baffles me. I wonder whether such an idol ever
existed, or exists nowadays, in the body of Tassi's bronze effigy ?

Oct. 20th.—I have been seeing a good deal of late of the Vice-
Prefect's son : an amiable young man with a love-sick face and a
languid interest in Urbanian history and archæology, of which he
is profoundly ignorant. This young man, who has lived at Siena
and Lucca before his father was promoted here, wears extremely
long and tight trousers, which almost preclude his bending his
knees, a stick-up collar and an eyeglass, and a pair of fresh kid
gloves stuck in the breast of his coat, speaks of Urbania as Ovid
might have spoken of Pontus, and complains (as well he may) of
the barbarism of the young men, the officials who dine at my inn
and howl and sing like madmen, and the nobles who drive gigs
showing almost as much throat as a lady at a ball. This person
frequently entertains me with his *amori*, past, present, and future ;
he evidently thinks me very odd for having none to entertain him
with in return ; he points out to me the pretty (or ugly) servant-
girls and dressmakers as we walk in the street, sighs deeply or
sings in falsetto behind every tolerably young-looking woman, and
has finally taken me to the house of the lady of his heart, a great
black-moustachioed countess, with a voice like a fish-crier ; here,
he says, I shall meet all the best company in Urbania and some
beautiful women—ah, too beautiful, alas ! I find three huge
half-furnished rooms, with bare brick floors, petroleum lamps, and
horribly bad pictures on bright wash-ball-blue and gamboge walls,

and in the midst of it all, every evening, a dozen ladies and gentlemen seated in a circle, vociferating at each other the same news
a year old ; the younger ladies in bright yellows and greens, fan-
ning themselves while my teeth chatter, and having sweet things
whispered behind their fans by officers with hair brushed up like
a hedgehog. And these are the women my friend expects me to
fall in love with ! I vainly wait for tea or supper which does not
come, and rush home, determined to leave alone the Urbanian
beau monde.

It is quite true that I have no *amori*, although my friend does
not believe it. When I came to Italy first, I looked out for romance ; I sighed, like Goethe in Rome, for a window to open
and a wondrous creature to appear, " welch mich versengend
erquickt." Perhaps it is because Goethe was a German, accustomed to German *Fraus*, and I am, after all, a Pole, accustomed to
something very different from *Fraus* ; but anyhow, for all my efforts
in Rome, Florence, and Siena, I never could find a woman to go
mad about, either among the ladies, chattering bad French, or
among the lower classes, as 'cute and cold as money-lenders ; so
I steer clear of Italian womankind, its shrill voice and gaudy
toilettes. I am wedded to history, to the Past, to women like
Lucrezia Borgia, Vittoria Accoramboni, or that Medea da Carpi,
for the present ; some day I shall perhaps find a grand passion, a
woman to play the Don Quixote about, like the Pole that I am ;
a woman out of whose slipper to drink, and for whose pleasure to
die ; but not here ! Few things strike me so much as the degeneracy
of Italian women. What has become of the race of Faustinas,
Marozias, Bianca Cappellos ? Where discover nowadays (I confess she haunts me) another Medea da Carpi ? Were it only possible to meet a woman of that extreme distinction of beauty, of
that terribleness of nature, even if only potential, I do believe I
could love her, even to the Day of Judgment, like any Oliverotto
da Narni, or Frangipani or Prinzivalle.

Oct. 27th.—Fine sentiments the above are for a professor, a
learned man ! I thought the young artists of Rome childish because they played practical jokes and yelled at night in the streets,
returning from the Caffé Greco or the cellar in the Via Palom-
bella ; but am I not as childish to the full—I, melancholy wretch,
whom they called Hamlet and the Knight of the Doleful Countenance ?

Nov. 5th.—I can't free myself from the thought of this Medea da

Carpi. In my walks, my mornings in the Archives, my solitary evenings, I catch myself thinking over the woman. Am I turning novelist instead of historian ? And still it seems to me that I understand her so well ; so much better than my facts warrant. First, we must put aside all pedantic modern ideas of right and wrong. Right and wrong in a century of violence and treachery does not exist, least of all for creatures like Medea. Go preach right and wrong to a tigress, my dear sir ! Yet is there in the world anything nobler than the huge creature, steel when she springs, velvet when she treads, as she stretches her supple body, or smooths her beautiful skin, or fastens her strong claws into her victim ?

Yes ; I can understand Medea. Fancy a woman of superlative beauty, of the highest courage and calmness, a woman of many resources, of genius, brought up by a petty princelet of a father, upon Tacitus and Sallust, and the tales of the great Malatestas, of Cæsar Borgia and such-like !—a woman whose one passion is conquest and empire—fancy her, on the eve of being wedded to a man of the power of the Duke of Stimigliano, claimed, carried off by a small fry of a Pico, locked up in his hereditary brigand's castle, and having to receive the young fool's red-hot love as an honour and a necessity ! The mere thought of any violence to such a nature is an abominable outrage ; and if Pico chooses to embrace such a woman at the risk of meeting a sharp piece of steel in her arms, why, it is a fair bargain. Young hound—or, if you prefer, young hero—to think to treat a woman like this as if she were any village wench ! Medea marries her Orsini. A marriage, let it be noted, between an old soldier of fifty and a girl of sixteen. Reflect what that means : it means that this imperious woman is soon treated like a chattel, made roughly to understand that her business is to give the Duke an heir, not advice ; that she must never ask " wherefore this or that ? " that she must courtesy before the Duke's counsellors, his captains, his mistresses ; that, at the least suspicion of rebelliousness, she is subject to his foul words and blows ; at the least suspicion of infidelity, to be strangled or starved to death, or thrown down an oubliette. Suppose that she know that her husband has taken it into his head that she has looked too hard at this man or that, that one of his lieutenants or one of his women have whispered that, after all, the boy Bartolommeo might as soon be a Pico as an Orsini. Suppose she know that she must strike or be struck ? Why, she strikes, or gets some one to strike for her. At what price ? A promise of love, of love to a groom, the son of a serf! Why, the dog must be mad or drunk to believe such a thing possible; his very belief in anything so monstrous makes him worthy of death. And then he dares to blab! This is much worse than Pico. Medea is bound to defend her honour a second time; if she could stab Pico, she can certainly stab this fellow, or have him stabbed.

Hounded by her husband's kinsmen, she takes refuge at Urbania. The Duke, like every other man, falls wildly in love with Medea, and neglects his wife; let us even go so far as to say, breaks his wife's heart. Is this Medea's fault? Is it her fault that every stone that comes beneath her chariot-wheels is crushed? Certainly not. Do you suppose that a woman like Medea feels the smallest ill-will against a poor, craven Duchess Maddalena? Why, she ignores her very existence. To suppose Medea a cruel woman is as grotesque as to call her an immoral woman. Her fate is, sooner or later, to triumph over her enemies, at all events to make their victory almost a defeat; her magic faculty is to enslave all the men who come across her path; all those who see her, love her, become her slaves; and it is the destiny of all her slaves to perish. Her lovers, with the exception of Duke Guidalfonso, all come to an untimely end; and in this there is nothing unjust. The possession of a woman like Medea is a happiness too great for a mortal man; it would turn his head, make him forget even what he owed her; no man must survive long who conceives himself to have a right over her; it is a kind of sacrilege. And only death, the willingness to pay for such happiness by death, can at all make a man worthy of being her lover; he must be willing to love and suffer and die. This is the meaning of her device—" Amour Dure —Dure Amour." The love of Medea da Carpi cannot fade, but the lover can die; it is a constant and a cruel love.

Nov. 11th.—I was right, quite right in my idea. I have found— Oh, joy! I treated the Vice-Prefect's son to a dinner of five courses at the Trattoria La Stella d'Italia out of sheer jubilation —I have found in the Archives, unknown, of course, to the Director, a heap of letters—letters of Duke Robert about Medea da Carpi, letters of Medea herself! Yes, Medea's own hand-writing—a round, scholarly character, full of abbreviations, with a Greek look about it, as befits a learned princess who could read Plato as well as Petrarch. The letters are of little importance, mere drafts of business letters for her secretary to copy, during the time that she governed the poor weak Guidalfonso. But they are her letters, and I can imagine almost that there hangs about these mouldering pieces of paper a scent as of a woman's hair.

The few letters of Duke Robert show him in a new light. A cunning, cold, but craven priest. He trembles at the bare thought of Medea—" la pessima Medea "—worse than her namesake of Colchis, as he calls her. His long clemency is a result of mere fear of laying violent hands upon her. He fears her as something almost supernatural ; he would have enjoyed having had her burnt as a witch. After letter on letter, telling his crony, Cardinal Sanseverino, at Rome his various precautions during her lifetime—how he wears a jacket of mail under his coat ; how he drinks only milk from a cow which he has milked in his presence ; how he tries his dog with morsels of his food, lest it be poisoned ; how he suspects the wax-candles because of their peculiar smell ; how he fears riding out lest some one should frighten his horse and cause him to break his neck—after all this, and when Medea has been in her grave two years, he tells his correspondent of his fear of meeting the soul of Medea after his own death, and chuckles over the ingenious device (concocted by his astrologer and a certain Fra Gaudenzio, a Capuchin) by which he shall secure the absolute peace of his soul until that of the wicked Medea be finally " chained up in hell among the lakes of boiling pitch and the ice of Caina described by the immortal bard "—old pedant ! Here, then, is the explanation of that silver image—*quod vulgo dicitur idolino*—which he caused to be soldered into his effigy by Tassi. As long as the image of his soul was attached to the image of his body, he should sleep awaiting the Day of Judgment, fully convinced that Medea's soul will then be properly tarred and feathered, while his—honest man !—will fly straight to Paradise. And to think that, two weeks ago, I believed this man to be a hero ! Aha ! my good Duke Robert, you shall be shown up in my history ; and no amount of silver idolinos shall save you from being heartily laughed at !

Nov. 15th.—Strange ! That idiot of a Prefect's son, who has heard me talk a hundred times of Medea da Carpi, suddenly recollects that, when he was a child at Urbania, his nurse used to threaten him with a visit from Madonna Medea, who rode in the sky on a black he-goat. My Duchess Medea turned into a bogey for naughty little boys !

Nov. 20th.—I have been going about with a Bavarian Professor of mediæval history, showing him all over the country. Among

other places we went to Rocca Sant' Elmo, to see the former villa
of the Dukes of Urbania, the villa where Medea was confined between the accession of Duke Robert and the conspiracy of Marcantonio Frangipani, which caused her removal to the nunnery
immediately outside the town. A long ride up the desolate Apennine valleys, bleak beyond words just now with their thin fringe
of oak scrub turned russet, thin patches of grass sered by the frost,
the last few yellow leaves of the poplars by the torrents shaking
and fluttering about in the chill Tramontana ; the mountain-tops
are wrapped in thick grey cloud ; to-morrow, if the wind con-
tinues, we shall see them round masses of snow against the cold
blue sky. Sant' Elmo is a wretched hamlet high on the Apennine
ridge, where the Italian vegetation is already replaced by that of
the North. You ride for miles through leafless chestnut woods, the
scent of the soaking brown leaves filling the air, the roar of the
torrent, turbid with autumn rains, rising from the precipice below ; then suddenly the leafless chestnut woods are replaced, as
at Vallonbrosa, by a belt of black, dense fir plantations. Emerging
from these, you come to an open space, frozen blasted meadows,
the rocks of snow clad peak, the newly fallen snow, close above
you ; and in the midst, on a knoll, with a gnarled larch on either
side, the ducal villa of Sant' Elmo, a big black stone box with a
stone escutcheon, grated windows, and a double flight of steps in
front. It is now let out to the proprietor of the neighbouring woods,
who uses it for the storage of chestnuts, faggots, and charcoal from
the neighbouring ovens. We tied our horses to the iron rings and
entered : an old woman, with dishevelled hair, was alone in the
house. The villa is a mere hunting-lodge, built by Ottobuono IV,
the father of Dukes Guidalfonso and Robert, about 1530. Some of
the rooms have at one time been frescoed and panelled with oak
carvings, but all this has disappeared. Only, in one of the big
rooms, there remains a large marble fireplace, similar to those in
the palace at Urbania, beautifully carved with Cupids on a blue
ground ; a charming naked boy sustains a jar on either side, one
containing clove pinks, the other roses. The room was filled with
stacks of faggots.

We returned home late, my companion in excessively bad
humour at the fruitlessness of the expedition. We were caught in
the skirt of a snowstorm as we got into the chestnut woods. The
sight of the snow falling gently, of the earth and bushes whitened
all round, made me feel back at Posen, once more a child. I sang

and shouted, to my companion's horror. This will be a bad point against me if reported at Berlin. A historian of twenty-four who shouts and sings, and that when another historian is cursing at the snow and the bad roads ! All night I lay awake watching the embers of my wood fire, and thinking of Medea da Carpi mewed up, in winter, in that solitude of Sant' Elmo, the firs groaning, the torrent roaring, the snow falling all round ; miles and miles away from human creatures. I fancied I saw it all, and that I, somehow, was Marcantonio Frangipani come to liberate her—or was it Prinzivalle degli Ordelaffi ? I suppose it was because of the long ride, the unaccustomed pricking feeling of the snow in the air ; or perhaps the punch which my professor insisted on drinking after dinner.

Nov. 23rd.—Thank goodness, that Bavarian professor has finally departed ! Those days he spent here drove me near crazy. Talking over my work, I told him one day my views on Medea da Carpi ; whereupon he condescended to answer that those were the usual tales due to the mythopœic (old idiot !) tendency of the Renaissance ; that research would disprove the greater part of them, as it had disproved the stories current about the Borgias, etc. ; that, moreover, such a woman as I made out was psychologically and physiologically impossible. Would that one could say as much of such professors as he and his fellows !

Nov. 24th.—I cannot get over my pleasure in being rid of that imbecile ; I felt as if I could have throttled him every time he spoke of the Lady of my thoughts—for such she has become— *Metea*, as the animal called her !

Nov. 30th.—I feel quite shaken at what has just happened ; I am beginning to fear that that old pedant was right in saying that it was bad for me to live all alone in a strange country, that it would make me morbid. It is ridiculous that I should be put into such a state of excitement merely by the chance discovery of a portrait of a woman dead these three hundred years. With the case of my uncle Ladislas, and other suspicions of insanity in my family, I ought really to guard against such foolish excitement.

Yet the incident was really dramatic, uncanny. I could have sworn that I knew every picture in the palace here ; and particularly every picture of Her. Anyhow, this morning, as I was leaving the Archives, I passed through one of the many small rooms— irregular-shaped closets—which fill up the ins and outs of this curious palace, turreted like a French château. I must have passed through that closet before, for the view was so familiar out of its window ; just the particular bit of round tower in front, the cypress on the other side of the ravine, the belfry beyond, and the piece of the line of Monte Sant' Agata and the Leonessa, covered with snow, against the sky. I suppose there must be twin rooms, and that I had got into the wrong one ; or rather, perhaps some shutter had been opened or curtain withdrawn. As I was passing, my eye was caught by a very beautiful old mirror-frame let into the brown and yellow inlaid wall. I approached, and looking at the frame, looked also, mechanically, into the glass. I gave a great start, and almost shrieked, I do believe—(it's lucky the Munich professor is safe out of Urbania !). Behind my own image stood another, a figure close to my shoulder, a face close to mine ; and that figure, that face, hers ! Medea da Carpi's ! I turned sharp round, as white, I think, as the ghost I expected to see. On the wall opposite the mirror, just a pace or two behind where I had been standing, hung a portrait. And such a portrait !—Bronzino never painted a grander one. Against a background of harsh, dark blue, there stands out the figure of the Duchess (for it is Medea, the real Medea, a thousand times more real, individual, and powerful than in the other portraits), seated stiffly in a high-backed chair, sustained, as it were, almost rigid, by the stiff brocade of skirts and stomacher, stiffer for plaques of embroidered silver flowers and rows of seed pearl. The dress is, with its mixture of silver and pearl, of a strange dull red, a wicked poppy-juice colour, against which the flesh of the long, narrow hands with fringe-like fingers ; of the long slender neck, and the face with bared forehead, looks white and hard, like alabaster. The face is the same as in the other portraits : the same rounded forehead, with the short fleece-like, yellowish-red curls ; the same beautifully curved eyebrows, just barely marked ; the same eyelids, a little tight across the eyes ; the same lips, a little tight across the mouth ; but with a purity of line, a dazzling splendour of skin, and intensity of look immeasurably superior to all the other portraits.

She looks out of the frame with a cold, level glance ; yet the lips smile. One hand holds a dull-red rose ; the other, long, narrow, tapering, plays with a thick rope of silk and gold and jewels hanging from the waist ; round the throat, white as marble, partially confined in the tight dull-red bodice, hangs a gold collar, with the device on alternate enamelled medallions, " AMOUR DURE— DURE AMOUR."

On reflection, I see that I simply could never have been in that room or closet before ; I must have mistaken the door. But, although the explanation is so simple, I still, after several hours, feel terribly shaken in all my being. If I grow so excitable I shall have to go to Rome at Christmas for a holiday. I feel as if some danger pursued me here (can it be fever ?) ; and yet, and yet, I don't see how I shall ever tear myself away.

Dec. 10th.—I have made an effort, and accepted the Vice-Prefect's son's invitation to see the oil-making at a villa of theirs near the coast. The villa, or farm, is an old fortified, towered place, standing on a hillside among olive-trees and little osier-bushes, which look like a bright orange flame. The olives are squeezed in a tremendous black cellar, like a prison : you see, by the faint white daylight, and the smoky yellow flare of resin burning in pans, great white bullocks moving round a huge millstone ; vague figures working at pulleys and handles : it looks, to my fancy, like some scene of the Inquisition. The Cavaliere regaled me with his best wine and rusks. I took some long walks by the seaside ; I had left Urbania wrapped in snow-clouds ; down on the coast there was a bright sun ; the sunshine, the sea, the bustle of the little port on the Adriatic seemed to do me good. I came back to Urbania another man. Sor Asdrubale, my landlord, poking about in slippers among the gilded chests, the Empire sofas, the old cups and saucers and pictures which no one will buy, congratulated me upon the improvement in my looks. " You work too much," he says ; " youth requires amusement, theatres, promenades, *amori*—it is time enough to be serious when one is bald "—and he took off his greasy red cap. Yes, I am better ! and, as a result, I take to my work with delight again. I will cut them out still, those wise-acres at Berlin !

Dec. 14th.—I don't think I have ever felt so happy about my work. I see it all so well—that crafty, cowardly Duke Robert ; that melancholy Duchess Maddalena ; that weak, showy, would-be chivalrous Duke Guidalfonso ; and above all, the splendid figure of Medea. I feel as if I were the greatest historian of the age ; and, at the same time, as if I were a boy of twelve. It snowed yesterday for the first time in the city, for two good hours. When it had done, I actually went into the square and taught the raga-muffins to make a snow-man ; no, a snow-woman ; and I had the fancy to call her Medea. " La pessima Medea ! " cried one of the boys—" the one who used to ride through the air on a goat ? "

"No, no," I said; "she was a beautiful lady, the Duchess of Urbania, the most beautiful woman that ever lived." I made her a crown of tinsel, and taught the boys to cry "Evviva, Medea!" But one of them said, "She is a witch! She must be burnt!" At which they all rushed to fetch burning faggots and tow; in a minute the yelling demons had melted her down.

Dec. 15th.—What a goose I am, and to think I am twenty-four, and known in literature! In my long walks I have composed to a tune (I don't know what it is) which all the people are singing and whistling in the street at present, a poem in frightful Italian, beginning "Medea, mia dea," calling on her in the name of her various lovers. I go about humming between my teeth, "Why am I not Marcantonio? or Prinzivalle? or he of Narni? or the good Duke Alfonso? that I might be beloved by thee, Medea, mia dea," etc., etc. Awful rubbish! My landlord, I think, suspects that Medea must be some lady I met while I was staying by the seaside. I am sure Sora Serafina, Sora Lodovica, and Sora Adalgisa— the three Parcæ or *Norns*, as I call them—have some such notion. This afternoon, at dusk, while tidying my room, Sora Lodovica said to me, "How beautifully the Signorino has taken to singing!" I was scarcely aware that I had been vociferating, "Vieni, Medea, mia dea," while the old lady bobbed about making up my fire. I stopped; a nice reputation I shall get! I thought, and all this will somehow get to Rome, and thence to Berlin. Sora Lodovica was leaning out of the window, pulling in the iron hook of the shrine-lamp which marks Sor Asdrubale's house. As she was trimming the lamp previous to swinging it out again, she said in her odd, prudish little way, "You are wrong to stop singing, my son" (she varies between calling me Signor Professore and such terms of affection as "Nino," "Viscere mie," etc.); "you are wrong to stop singing, for there is a young lady there in the street who has actually stopped to listen to you."

I ran to the window. A woman, wrapped in a black shawl, was standing in an archway, looking up to the window.

"Eh, eh! the Signor Professore has admirers," said Sora Lodovica.

"Medea, mia dea!" I burst out as loud as I could, with a boy's pleasure in disconcerting the inquisitive passer-by. She turned suddenly round to go away, waving her hand at me; at that moment Sora Lodovica swung the shrine-lamp back into its place. A stream of light fell across the street. I felt myself grow quite cold ; the face of the woman outside was that of Medea da Carpi !

What a fool I am, to be sure !

PART II

Dec. 17th.—I fear that my craze about Medea da Carpi has become well known, thanks to my silly talk and idiotic songs. That Vice-Prefect's son—or the assistant at the Archives, or perhaps some of the company at the Contessa's, is trying to play me a trick ! But take care, my good ladies and gentlemen, I shall pay you out in your own coin ! Imagine my feelings when, this morning, I found on my desk a folded letter addressed to me in a curious handwriting which seemed strangely familiar to me, and which, after a moment, I recognised as that of the letters of Medea da Carpi at the Archives. It gave me a horrible shock. My next idea was that it must be a present from some one who knew my interest in Medea—a genuine letter of hers on which some idiot had written my address instead of putting it into an envelope. But it was addressed to me, written to me, no old letter ; merely four lines, which ran as follows :

"To SPIRIDION.—A person who knows the interest you bear her will be at the Church of San Giovanni Decollato this evening at nine. Look out, in the left aisle, for a lady wearing a black mantle, and holding a rose."

By this time I understood that I was the object of a conspiracy, the victim of a hoax. I turned the letter round and round. It was written on paper such as was made in the sixteenth century, and in an extraordinarily precise imitation of Medea da Carpi's characters. Who had written it ? I thought over all the possible people. On the whole, it must be the Vice-Prefect's son, perhaps in combination with his lady-love, the Countess. They must have torn a blank page off some old letter ; but that either of them should have had the ingenuity of inventing such a hoax, or the power of committing such a forgery, astounds me beyond measure. There is more in these people than I should have guessed. How pay them off ? By taking no notice of the letter ? Dignified, but dull. No, I will go ; perhaps some one will be there, and I will mystify them in their turn. Or, if no one is there, how I shall crow over them for their imperfectly carried out plot ! Perhaps this is some folly of the Cavalier Muzio's to bring me into the presence of some lady whom he destines to be the flame of my future *amori*. That is likely enough. And it would be too idiotic and professorial to refuse such an invitation ; the lady must be worth knowing who can forge sixteenth-century letters like this, for I am sure that languid swell Muzio never could. I will go ! By Heaven ! I'll pay them back in their own coin ! It is now five—how long these days are !

Dec. 18th.—Am I mad ? Or are there really ghosts ? That adventure of last night has shaken me to the very depth of my soul.

I went at nine, as the mysterious letter had bid me. It was bitterly cold, and the air full of fog and sleet ; not a shop open, not a window unshuttered, not a creature visible ; the narrow black streets, precipitous between their high walls and under their lofty archways, were only the blacker for the dull light of an oil-lamp here and there, with its flickering yellow reflection on the wet flags. San Giovanni Decollato is a little church, or rather oratory, which I have always hitherto seen shut up (as so many churches here are shut up except on great festivals) ; and situate behind the ducal palace, on a sharp ascent, and forming the bifurcation of two steep paved lanes. I have passed by the place a hundred times, and scarcely noticed the little church, except for the marble high relief over the door, showing the grizzly head of the Baptist in the charger, and for the iron cage close by, in which were formerly exposed the heads of criminals ; the decapitated, or, as they call him here, decollated, John the Baptist, being apparently the patron of axe and block.

A few strides took me from my lodgings to San Giovanni Decollato. I confess I was excited ; one is not twenty-four and a Pole for nothing. On getting to the kind of little platform at the bifurcation of the two precipitious streets, I found, to my surprise, that the windows of the church or oratory were not lighted, and that the door was locked ! So this was the precious joke that had been played upon me ; to send me on a bitter cold, sleety night, to a church which was shut up and had perhaps been shut up for years ! I don't know what I couldn't have done in that moment of rage ; I felt inclined to break open the church door, or to go and pull the Vice-Prefect's son out of bed (for I felt sure that the joke was his). I determined upon the latter course ; and was walking towards his door, along the black alley to the left of the church, when I was suddenly stopped by the sound as of an organ close by ; an organ, yes, quite plainly, and the voice of choristers and the drone of a litany. So that church was not shut, after all ! I retraced my steps to the top of the lane. All was dark and in complete silence. Suddenly there came again a faint gust of organ and voices. I listened ; it clearly came from the other lane, the one on the right-hand side. Was there, perhaps, another door there ? I passed beneath the archway, and descended a little way in the direction whence the sounds seemed to come. But no door, no light, only the black walls, the black wet flags, with their faint yellow reflections of flickering oil-lamps ; moreover, complete silence. I stopped a minute, and then the chant rose again ; this time it seemed to me most certainly from the lane I had just left. I went back—nothing. Thus backwards and forwards, the sounds always beckoning, as it were, one way, only to beckon me back, vainly, to the other.

At last I lost patience ; and I felt a sort of creeping terror, which only a violent action could dispel. If the mysterious sounds came neither from the street to the right, nor from the street to the left, they could come only from the church. Half-maddened, I rushed up the two or three steps, and prepared to wrench the door open with a tremendous effort. To my amazement, it opened with the greatest ease. I entered, and the sounds of the litany met me louder than before, as I paused a moment between the outer door and the heavy leathern curtain. I raised the latter and crept in. The altar was brilliantly illuminated with tapers and garlands of chandeliers ; this was evidently some evening service connected with Christmas. The nave and aisles were comparatively dark, and about half-full. I elbowed my way along the right aisle towards the altar. When my eyes had got accustomed to the unexpected light, I began to look round me, and with a beating heart. The idea that all this was a hoax, that I should meet merely some acquaintance of my friend the Cavaliere's, had somehow departed : I looked about. The people were all wrapped up, the men in big cloaks, the women in woollen veils and mantles. The body of the church was comparatively dark, and I could not make out anything very clearly, but it seemed to me, somehow, as if under the cloaks and veils, these people were dressed in a rather extraordinary fashion. The man in front of me, I remarked, showed yellow stockings beneath his cloak ; a woman, hard by, a red bodice, laced behind with gold tags. Could these be peasants from some remote part come for the Christmas festivities, or did the inhabitants of Urbania don some old-fashioned garb in honour of Christmas ?

As I was wondering, my eye suddenly caught that of a woman standing in the opposite aisle, close to the altar, and in the full blaze of its lights. She was wrapped in black, but held, in a very conspicuous way, a red rose, an unknown luxury at this time of the year in a place like Urbania. She evidently saw me, and turning even more fully into the light, she loosened her heavy black cloak, displaying a dress of deep red, with gleams of silver and gold embroideries ; she turned her face towards me ; the full blaze of the chandeliers and tapers fell upon it. It was the face of Medea da Carpi ! I dashed across the nave, pushing people roughly aside, or rather, it seemed to me, passing through impalpable bodies. But the lady turned and walked rapidly down the aisle towards the door. I followed close upon her, but somehow I could not get up with her. Once, at the curtain, she turned round again. She was within a few paces of me. Yes, it was Medea. Medea herself, no mistake, no delusion, no sham ; the oval face, the lips tightened over the mouth, the eyelids tight over the corner of the eyes, the exquisite alabaster complexion ! She raised the curtain and glided out. I followed ; the curtain alone separated me from her. I saw the wooden door swing to behind her. One step ahead of me ! I tore open the door ; she must be on the steps, within reach of my arm !

I stood outside the church. All was empty, merely the wet pavement and the yellow reflections in the pools : a sudden cold seized me ; I could not go on. I tried to re-enter the church ; it was shut. I rushed home, my hair standing on end, and trembling in all my limbs, and remained for an hour like a maniac. Is it a delusion ? Am I too going mad ? O God, God ! am I going mad ?

Dec. 19th.—A brilliant, sunny day ; all the black snow-slush has disappeared out of the town, off the bushes and trees. The snow-clad mountains sparkle against the bright blue sky. A Sunday, and Sunday weather ; all the bells are ringing for the approach of Christmas. They are preparing for a kind of fair in the square with the colonnade, putting up booths filled with coloured cotton and woollen ware, bright shawls and kerchiefs, mirrors, ribbons, brilliant pewter lamps ; the whole turn-out of the pedlar in " Winter's Tale." The pork-shops are all garlanded with green and with paper flowers, the hams and cheeses stuck full of little flags and green twigs. I strolled out to see the cattle-fair outside the gate ;

a forest of interlacing horns, an ocean of lowing and stamping :
hundreds of immense white bullocks, with horns a yard long and
red tassels, packed close together on the little piazza d'armi under
the city walls. Bah ! why do I write this trash ? What's the use of
it all ? While I am forcing myself to write about bells, and Christmas festivities, and cattle-fairs, one idea goes on like a bell within
me : Medea, Medea ! Have I really seen her, or am I mad ?

Two hours later.—That Church of San Giovanni Decollato—so
my landlord informs me—has not been made use of within the
memory of man. Could it have been all a hallucination or a dream
—perhaps a dream dreamed that night ? I have been out again
to look at that church. There it is, at the bifurcation of the two
steep lanes, with its bas-relief of the Baptist's head over the door.
The door does look as if it had not been opened for years. I can
see the cobwebs in the window-panes ; it does look as if, as Sor
Asdrubale says, only rats and spiders congregated within it. And
yet—and yet ; I have so clear a remembrance, so distinct a consciousness of it all. There was a picture of the daughter of Herodias
dancing, upon the altar ; I remember her white turban with a
scarlet tuft of feathers, and Herod's blue caftan ; I remember the
shape of the central chandelier ; it swung round slowly, and one of
the wax lights had got bent almost in two by the heat and draught.

Things, all these, which I may have seen elsewhere, stored un-
awares in my brain, and which may have come out, somehow, in
a dream ; I have heard physiologists allude to such things. I will
go again : if the church be shut, why then it must have been a
dream, a vision, the result of over-excitement. I must leave at once
for Rome and see doctors, for I am afraid of going mad. If, on the
other hand—pshaw ! there *is no other hand* in such a case. Yet if
there were—why then, I should really have seen Medea ; I might
see her again ; speak to her. The mere thought sets my blood in a
whirl, not with horror, but with . . . I know not what to call it.
The feeling terrifies me, but it is delicious. Idiot ! There is some
little coil of my brain, the twentieth of a hair's breadth out of
order—that's all !

Dec. 20th.—I have been again ; I have heard the music ; I have
been inside the church ; I have seen Her ! I can no longer doubt
my senses. Why should I ? Those pedants say that the dead are
dead, the past is past. For them, yes ; but why for me ?—why for a
man who loves, who is consumed with the love of a woman ?—
a woman who, indeed—yes, let me finish the sentence. Why should

there not be ghosts to such as can see them? Why should she not
return to the earth, if she knows that it contains a man who thinks
of, desires, only her?

A hallucination? Why, I saw her, as I see this paper that I
write upon; standing there, in the full blaze of the altar. Why, I
heard the rustle of her skirts, I smelt the scent of her hair, I raised
the curtain which was shaking from her touch. Again I missed
her. But this time, as I rushed out into the empty moonlit street,
I found upon the church steps a rose—the rose which I had seen
in her hand the moment before—I felt it, smelt it; a rose, a real,
living rose, dark red and only just plucked. I put it into water when
I returned, after having kissed it, who knows how many times? I
placed it on the top of the cupboard; I determined not to look at
it for twenty-four hours lest it should be a delusion. But I must
see it again; I must. . . . Good Heavens! this is horrible, horrible;
if I had found a skeleton it could not have been worse! The rose,
which last night seemed freshly plucked, full of colour and perfume, is brown, dry—a thing kept for centuries between the leaves
of a book—it has crumbled into dust between my fingers. Horrible, horrible! But why so, pray? Did I not know that I was in
love with a woman dead three hundred years? If I wanted fresh
roses which bloomed yesterday, the Countess Fiammetta or any
little semptress in Urbania might have given them me. What if
the rose has fallen to dust? If only I could hold Medea in my arms
as I held it in my fingers, kiss her lips as I kissed its petals, should
I not be satisfied if she too were to fall to dust the next moment, if
I were to fall to dust myself?

Dec. 22nd, Eleven at night.—I have seen her once more!—almost
spoken to her. I have been promised her love? Ah, Spiridion! you
were right when you felt that you were not made for any earthly
amori. At the usual hour I betook myself this evening to San Giovanni Decollato. A bright winter night; the high houses and bel-
fries standing out against a deep blue heaven luminous, shimmering like steel with myriads of stars; the moon has not yet risen.
There was no light in the windows; but, after a little effort, the
door opened and I entered the church, the altar, as usual, brilliantly illuminated. It struck me suddenly that all this crowd of
men and women standing all round, these priests chanting and
moving about the altar, were dead—that they did not exist for any
man save me. I touched, as if by accident, the hand of my neighbour; it was cold, like wet clay. He turned round, but did not

seem to see me : his face was ashy, and his eyes staring, fixed, like those of a blind man or a corpse. I felt as if I must rush out. But at that moment my eyes fell upon Her, standing as usual by the altar steps, wrapped in a black mantle, in the full blaze of the lights. She turned round ; the light fell straight upon her face, the face with the delicate features, the eyelids and lips a little tight, the alabaster skin faintly tinged with pale pink. Our eyes met.

I pushed my way across the nave towards where she stood by the altar steps ; she turned quickly down the aisle, and I after her. Once or twice she lingered, and I thought I should overtake her ; but again, when, not a second after the door had closed upon her, I stepped out into the street, she had vanished. On the church step lay something white. It was not a flower this time, but a letter. I rushed back to the church to read it ; but the church was fast shut, as if it had not been opened for years. I could not see by the flickering shrine-lamps—I rushed home, lit my lamp, pulled the letter from my breast. I have it before me. The handwriting is hers ; the same as in the Archives, the same as in that first letter :

" To Spiridion.—Let thy courage be equal to thy love, and thy love shall be rewarded. On the night preceding Christmas, take a hatchet and saw ; cut boldly into the body of the bronze rider who stands on the Corte, on the left side, near the waist. Saw open the body, and within it thou wilt find the silver effigy of a winged genius. Take it out, hack it into a hundred pieces, and fling them in all directions, so that the winds may sweep them away. That night she whom thou lovest will come to reward thy fidelity."

On the brownish wax is the device—

" Amour Dure—Dure Amour."

Dec. 23rd.—So it is true ! I was reserved for something wonderful in this world. I have at last found that after which my soul has been straining. Ambition, love of art, love of Italy, these things which have occupied my spirit, and have yet left me continually unsatisfied, these were none of them my real destiny. I have sought for life, thirsting for it as a man in the desert thirsts for a well ; but the life of the senses of other youths, the life of the intellect of other men, have never slaked that thirst. Shall life for me mean the love of a dead woman ? We smile at what we choose to call the super-stition of the past, forgetting that all our vaunted science of to-day

may seem just such another superstition to the men of the future ;
but why should the present be right and the past wrong ? The
men who painted the pictures and built the palaces of three hundred years ago were certainly of as delicate fibre, of as keen reason,
as ourselves, who merely print calico and build locomotives.
What makes me think this, is that I have been calculating my
nativity by help of an old book belonging to Sor Asdrubale—and
see, my horoscope tallies almost exactly with that of Medea da Carpi,
as given by a chronicler. May this explain ? No, no ; all is explained
by the fact that the first time I read of this woman's career, the
first time I saw her portrait, I loved her, though I hid my love to
myself in the garb of historical interest. Historical interest indeed !

I have got the hatchet and the saw. I bought the saw of a poor
joiner, in a village some miles off ; he did not understand at first
what I meant, and I think he thought me mad ; perhaps I am.
But if madness means the happiness of one's life, what of it ? The
hatchet I saw lying in a timber-yard, where they prepare the
great trunks of the fir-trees which grow high on the Apennines of
Sant' Elmo. There was no one in the yard, and I could not resist
the temptation ; I handled the thing, tried its edge, and stole it.
This is the first time in my life that I have been a thief ; why did I
not go into a shop and buy a hatchet ? I don't know ; I seemed
unable to resist the sight of the shining blade. What I am going to
do is, I suppose, an act of vandalism ; and certainly I have no
right to spoil the property of this city of Urbania. But I wish no
harm either to the statue or the city ; if I could plaster up the
bronze, I would do so willingly. But I must obey Her ; I must
avenge Her ; I must get at that silver image which Robert of
Montemurlo had made and consecrated in order that his
cowardly soul might sleep in peace, and not encounter that of
the being whom he dreaded most in the world. Aha ! Duke Robert,
you forced her to die unshriven, and you stuck the image of your
soul into the image of your body, thinking thereby that, while she
suffered the tortures of Hell, you would rest in peace, until your
well-scoured little soul might fly straight up to Paradise ;—you
were afraid of Her when both of you should be dead, and thought
yourself very clever to have prepared for all emergencies ! Not so,
Serene Highness. You too shall taste what it is to wander after
death, and to meet the dead whom one has injured.

What an interminable day ! But I shall see her again to-night.

Eleven o'clock.—No ; the church was fast closed ; the spell had ceased. Until to-morrow I shall not see her. But to-morrow ! Ah, Medea ! did any of thy lovers love thee as I do ?

Twenty-four hours more till the moment of happiness—the moment for which I seem to have been waiting all my life. And after that, what next ? Yes, I see it plainer every minute ; after that, nothing more. All those who loved Medea da Carpi, who loved and who served her, died : Giovanfrancesco Pico, her first husband, whom she left stabbed in the castle from which she fled ; Stimigliano, who died of poison , the groom who gave him the poison, cut down by her orders ; Oliverotto da Narni, Marcantonio Frangipani, and that poor boy of the Ordelaffi, who had never even looked upon her face, and whose only reward was that handkerchief with which the hangman wiped the sweat off his face, when he was one mass of broken limbs and torn flesh : all had to die, and I shall die also.

The love of such a woman is enough, and is fatal—" Amour Dure," as her device says. I shall die also. But why not ? Would it be possible to live in order to love another woman ? Nay, would it be possible to drag on a life like this one after the happiness of to-morrow ? Impossible ; the others died, and I must die. I always felt that I should not live long ; a gipsy in Poland told me once that I had in my hand the cut-line which signifies a violent death. I might have ended in a duel with some brother-student, or in a railway accident. No, no ; my death will not be of that sort ! Death —and is not she also dead ? What strange vistas does such a thought not open ! Then the others—Pico, the Groom, Stimigliano, Oliverotto, Frangipani, Prinzivalle degli Ordelaffi—will they all be *there* ? But she shall love me best—me by whom she has been loved after she has been three hundred years in the grave !

Dec. 24th.—I have made all my arrangements. To-night at eleven I slip out ; Sor Asdrubale and his sisters will be sound asleep. I have questioned them ; their fear of rheumatism prevents their attending midnight mass. Luckily there are no churches between this and the Corte ; whatever movement Christmas night may entail will be a good way off. The Vice-Prefect's rooms are on the other side of the palace ; the rest of the square is taken up with state-rooms, archives, and empty stables and coach-houses of the palace. Besides, I shall be quick at my work.

I have tried my saw on a stout bronze vase I bought of Sor Asdrubale ; and the bronze of the statue, hollow and worn away by rust (I have even noticed holes), cannot resist very much, especially after a blow with the sharp hatchet. I have put my papers in order, for the benefit of the Government which has sent me hither. I am sorry to have defrauded them of their " History of Urbania." To pass the endless day and calm the fever of impatience, I have just taken a long walk. This the coldest day we have had. The bright sun does not warm in the least, but seems only to increase the impression of cold, to make the snow on the mountains glitter, the blue air to sparkle like steel. The few people who are out are muffled to the nose, and carry earthenware braziers beneath their cloaks ; long icicles hang from the fountain with the figure of Mercury upon it ; one can imagine the wolves trooping down through the dry scrub and beleaguering this town. Somehow this cold makes me feel wonderfully calm—it seems to bring back to me my boyhood.

As I walked up the rough, steep, paved alleys, slippery with frost, and with their vista of snow mountains against the sky, and passed by the church steps strewn with box and laurel, with the faint smell of incense coming out, there returned to me—I know not why—the recollection, almost the sensation, of those Christmas Eves long ago at Posen and Breslau, when I walked as a child along the wide streets, peeping into the windows where they were beginning to light the tapers of the Christmas-trees, and wondering whether I too, on returning home, should be let into a wonderful room all blazing with lights and gilded nuts and glass beads. They are hanging the last strings of those blue and red metallic beads, fastening on the last gilded and silvered walnuts on the trees out there at home in the North ; they are lighting the blue and red tapers ; the wax is beginning to run on to the beautiful spruce green branches ; the children are waiting with beating hearts behind the door, to be told that the Christ-Child has been. And I, for what am I waiting ? I don't know ; all seems a dream ; everything vague and unsubstantial about me, as if time had ceased, nothing could happen, my own desires and hopes were all dead, myself absorbed into I know not what passive dreamland. Do I long for to-night ? Do I dread it ? Will to-night ever come ? Do I feel anything, does anything exist all round me ? I sit and seem to see that street at Posen, the wide street with the windows illuminated by the Christmas lights, the green fir-branches grazing the window-panes.

Christmas Eve, Midnight.—I have done it. I slipped out noiselessly. Sor Asdrubale and his sisters were fast asleep. I feared I had waked them for my hatchet fell as I was passing through the principal room where my landlord keeps his curiosities for sale ; it struck against some old armour which he has been piecing. I heard him exclaim, half in his sleep ; and blew out my light and hid in the stairs. He came out in his dressing-gown, but finding no one, went back to bed again. " Some cat, no doubt ! " he said. I closed the house door softly behind me. The sky had become stormy since the afternoon, luminous with the full moon, but strewn with grey and buff-coloured vapours ; every now and then the moon disappeared entirely. Not a creature abroad ; the tall gaunt houses staring in the moonlight.

I know not why, I took a roundabout way to the Corte, past one or two church doors, whence issued the faint flicker of midnight mass. For a moment I felt a temptation to enter one of them ; but something seemed to restrain me. I caught snatches of the Christmas hymn. I felt myself beginning to be unnerved, and hastened towards the Corte. As I passed under the portico at San Francesco I heard steps behind me ; it seemed to me that I was followed. I stopped to let the other pass. As he approached his pace flagged ; he passed close by me and murmured, " Do not go : I am Giovanfrancesco Pico." I turned round ; he was gone. A coldness numbed me ; but I hastened on.

Behind the cathedral apse, in a narrow lane, I saw a man leaning against a wall. The moonlight was full upon him ; it seemed to me that his face, with a thin pointed beard, was streaming with blood. I quickened my pace ; but as I grazed by him he whispered, " Do not obey her ; return home : I am Marcantonio Frangipani." My teeth chattered, but I hurried along the narrow lane, with the moonlight blue upon the white walls.

At last I saw the Corte before me : the square was flooded with moonlight, the windows of the palace seemed brightly illuminated, and the statue of Duke Robert, shimmering green, seemed advancing towards me on its horse. I came into the shadow. I had to pass beneath an archway. There started a figure as if out of the wall, and barred my passage with his outstretched cloaked arm. I tried to pass. He seized me by the arm, and his grasp was like a weight of ice. " You shall not pass ! " he cried, and, as the moon came out once more, I saw his face, ghastly white and bound with an embroidered kerchief ; he seemed almost a child. " You shall not pass ! " he cried ; " you shall not have her ! She is mine, and mine alone ! I am Prinzivalle degli Ordelaffi." I felt his ice-cold clutch, but with my other arm I laid about me wildly with the hatchet which I carried beneath my cloak. The hatchet struck the wall and rang upon the stone. He had vanished.

I hurried on. I did it. I cut open the bronze ; I sawed it into a wider gash. I tore out the silver image, and hacked it into innumerable pieces. As I scattered the last fragments about, the moon was suddenly veiled ; a great wind arose, howling down the square ; it seemed to me that the earth shook. I threw down the hatchet and the saw, and fled home. I felt pursued, as if by the tramp of hundreds of invisible horsemen.

Now I am calm. It is midnight ; another moment and she will be here ! Patience, my heart ! I hear it beating loud. I trust that no one will accuse poor Sor Asdrubale. I will write a letter to the authorities to declare his innocence should anything happen. . . . One ! the clock in the palace tower has just struck. . . . " I hereby certify that, should anything happen this night to me, Spiridion Trepka, no one but myself is to be held . . ." A step on the staircase ! It is she ! it is she ! At last, Medea, Medea ! Ah ! AMOUR DURE—DURE AMOUR !

NOTE.—Here ends the diary of the late Spiridion Trepka. The chief newspapers of the province of Umbria informed the public that, on Christmas morning of the year 1885, the bronze equestrian statue of Robert II had been found grievously mutilated ; and that Professor Spiridion Trepka of Posen, in the German Empire, had been discovered dead of a stab in the region of the heart, given by an unknown hand.

Vernon Lee

OKE OF OKEHURST

OR THE PHANTOM LOVER

from HAUNTINGS

Heinemann 1890 ; Second Edition, John Lane, 1906

I

That sketch up there with the boy's cap ? Yes ; that's the same woman. I wonder whether you could guess who she was. A singular being, is she not ? The most marvellous creature, quite, that I

have ever met : a wonderful elegance, exotic, far-fetched, poig-
nant ; an artificial perverse sort of grace and research in every
outline and movement and arrangement of head and neck, and
hands and fingers. Here are a lot of pencil-sketches I made while
I was preparing to paint her portrait. Yes ; there's nothing but
her in the whole sketch-book. Mere scratches, but they may give
some idea of her marvellous, fantastic kind of grace. Here she is
leaning over the staircase, and here sitting in the swing. Here she
is walking quickly out of the room. That's her head. You see she
isn't really handsome ; her forehead is too big, and her nose too
short. This gives no idea of her. It was altogether a question of
movement. Look at the strange cheeks, hollow and rather flat ;
well, when she smiled she had the most marvellous dimples here.
There was something exquisite and uncanny about it. Yes ; I
began the picture, but it was never finished. I did the husband
first. I wonder who has his likeness now ? Help me to move these
pictures away from the wall. Thanks. This is her portrait ; a huge
wreck. I don't suppose you can make much of it ; it is merely
blocked in, and seems quite mad. You see my idea was to make
her leaning against a wall—there was one hung with yellow that
seemed almost brown—so as to bring out the silhouette.

It was very singular I should have chosen that particular wall.
It does look rather insane in this condition, but I like it ; it has
something of her. I would frame it and hang it up, only people
would ask questions. Yes ; you have guessed quite right—it is
Mrs. Oke of Okehurst. I forgot you had relations in that part of
the country ; besides, I suppose the newspapers were full of it at
the time. You didn't know that it all took place under my eyes ?
I can scarcely believe now that it did : it all seems so distant, vivid
but unreal, like a thing of my own invention. It really was much
stranger than any one guessed. People could no more understand
it than they could understand her. I doubt whether any one ever
understood Alice Oke besides myself. You mustn't think me unfeeling. She was a marvellous, weird, exquisite creature, but one
couldn't feel sorry for her. I felt much sorrier for the wretched
creature of a husband. It seemed such an appropriate end for her ;
I fancy she would have liked it could she have known. Ah ! I shall
never have another chance of painting such a portrait as I wanted.
She seemed sent me from heaven or the other place. You have
never heard the story in detail ? Well, I don't usually mention it,
because people are so brutally stupid or sentimental ; but I'll tell

it you. Let me see. It's too dark to paint any more to-day, so I can tell it you now. Wait ; I must turn her face to the wall. Ah, she was a marvellous creature !

II

You remember, three years ago, my telling you I had let myself in for painting a couple of Kentish squireen ? I really could not understand what had possessed me to say yes to that man. A friend of mine had brought him one day to my studio—Mr. Oke of Oke-hurst, that was the name on his card. He was a very tall, very well-made, very good-looking young man, with a beautiful fair complexion, beautiful fair moustache, and beautifully fitting clothes ; absolutely like a hundred other young men you can see any day in the Park, and absolutely uninteresting from the crown of his head to the tip of his boots. Mr. Oke, who had been a lieutenant in the Blues before his marriage, was evidently extremely uncomfortable on finding himself in a studio. He felt misgivings about a man who could wear a velvet coat in town, but at the same time he was nervously anxious not to treat me in the very least like a trades-man. He walked round my place, looked at everything with the most scrupulous attention, stammered out a few complimentary phrases, and then, looking at his friend for assistance, tried to come to the point, but failed. The point, which the friend kindly explained, was that Mr. Oke was desirous to know whether my engagements would allow of my painting him and his wife and what my terms would be. The poor man blushed perfectly crimson during this explanation, as if he had come with the most improper proposal ; and I noticed—the only interesting thing about him—a very odd nervous frown between his eyebrows, a perfect double gash—a thing which usually means something abnormal : a mad-doctor of my acquaintance calls it the maniac-frown. When I had answered, he suddenly burst out into rather confused explana-tions : his wife—Mrs. Oke—had seen some of my—pictures—paintings—portraits—at the—the—what d'you call it ? Academy. She had—in short, they had made a very great impression upon her. Mrs. Oke had a great taste for art ; she was, in short, extremely desirous of having her portrait and his painted by me, *etcetera*.

" My wife," he suddenly added, " is a remarkable woman. I don't know whether you will think her handsome—she isn't exactly, you know. But she's awfully strange," and Mr. Oke of

Okehurst gave a little sigh and frowned that curious frown, as if so long a speech and so decided an expression of opinion had cost him a great deal.

It was a rather unfortunate moment in my career. A very influential sitter of mine—you remember the fat lady with the crimson curtain behind her ?—had come to the conclusion or been persuaded that I had painted her old and vulgar, which, in fact, she was. Her whole clique had turned against me, the newspapers had taken up the matter, and for the moment I was considered as a painter to whose brushes no woman would trust her reputation. Things were going badly. So I snapped but too gladly at Mr. Oke's offer, and settled to go down to Okehurst at the end of a fortnight. But the door had scarcely closed upon my future sitter when I began to regret my rashness ; and my disgust at the thought of wasting a whole summer upon the portrait of a totally uninteresting Kentish squire, and his doubtless equally uninteresting wife, grew greater and greater as the time for execution approached. I remember so well the frightful temper in which I got into the train for Kent, and the even more frightful temper in which I got out of it at the little station nearest to Okehurst. It was pouring floods. I felt a comfortable fury at the thought that my canvases would get nicely wetted before Mr. Oke's coachman had packed them on the top of the waggonette. It was just what served me right for coming to this confounded place to paint these confounded people. We drove off in the steady downpour. The roads were a mass of yellow mud ; the endless flat grazing-grounds under the oak-trees, after having been burnt to cinders in a long drought, were turned into a hideous brown sop ; the country seemed intolerably monotonous.

My spirits sank lower and lower. I began to meditate upon the modern Gothic country-house, with the usual amount of Morris furniture, Liberty rugs, and Mudie novels, to which I was doubtless being taken. My fancy pictured very vividly the five or six little Okes—that man certainly must have at least five children—the aunts, and sisters-in-law, and cousins ; the eternal routine of afternoon tea and lawn-tennis ; above all, it pictured Mrs. Oke, the bouncing, well-informed, model house-keeper, electioneering, charity-organising young lady, whom such an individual as Mr. Oke would regard in the light of a remarkable woman. And my spirit sank within me, and I cursed my avarice in accepting the commission, my spiritlessness in not throwing it over while yet there was time. We had meanwhile driven into a large park, or rather a long succession of grazing-grounds, dotted about with large oaks, under which the sheep were huddled together for shelter from the rain. In the distance, blurred by the sheets of rain, was a line of low hills, with a jagged fringe of bluish firs and a solitary windmill. It must be a good mile and a half since we had passed a house, and there was none to be seen in the distance— nothing but the undulation of sere grass, sopped brown beneath the huge blackish oak-trees, and whence arose, from all sides, a vague disconsolate bleating. At last the road made a sudden bend, and disclosed what was evidently the home of my sitter. It was not what I had expected. In a dip in the ground a large red-brick house, with the rounded gables and high chimney-stacks of the time of James I,—a forlorn, vast place, set in the midst of the pasture-land, with no trace of garden before it, and only a few large trees indicating the possibility of one to the back ; no lawn either, but on the other side of the sandy dip, which suggested a filled-up moat, a huge oak, short, hollow, with wreathing, blasted, black branches, upon which only a handful of leaves shook in the rain. It was not at all what I had pictured to myself the home of Mr. Oke of Okehurst.

My host received me in the hall, a large place, panelled and carved, hung round with portraits up to its curious ceiling— vaulted and ribbed like the inside of a ship's hull. He looked even more blond and pink and white, more absolutely mediocre in his tweed suit ; and also, I thought, even more good-natured and duller. He took me into his study, a room hung round with whips and fishing-tackle in place of books, while my things ere being carried upstairs. It was very damp, and a fire was smouldering. He gave the embers a nervous kick with his foot, and said, as he offered me a cigar—

" You must excuse my not introducing you at once to Mrs. Oke. My wife—in short, I believe my wife is asleep."

" Is Mrs. Oke unwell ? " I asked, a sudden hope flashing across me that I might be off the whole matter.

" Oh no ! Alice is quite well ; at least, quite as well as she usually is. My wife," he added, after a minute, and in a very decided tone, " does not enjoy very good health—a nervous constitution. Oh no ! not at all ill, nothing at all serious, you know. Only nervous, the doctors say ; mustn't be worried or excited, the doctors say ; requires lots of repose—that sort of thing."

There was a dead pause. This man depressed me, I knew not why. He had a listless, puzzled look, very much out of keeping with his evident admirable health and strength.

" I suppose you are a great sportsman ? " I asked from sheer despair, nodding in the direction of the whips and guns and fishing-rods.

" Oh no ! not now. I was once. I have given up all that," he answered, standing with his back to the fire, and staring at the polar bear beneath his feet. " I—I have no time for all that now," he added, as if an explanation were due. " A married man—you know. Would you like to come up to your rooms ? " he suddenly interrupted himself. " I have had one arranged for you to paint in. My wife said you would prefer a north light. If that one doesn't suit, you can have your choice of any other."

I followed him out of the study, through the vast entrance-hall. In less than a minute I was no longer thinking of Mr. and Mrs. Oke and the boredom of doing their likeness ; I was simply overcome by the beauty of this house, which I had pictured modern and philistine. It was, without exception, the most perfect example of an old English manor-house that I had ever seen ; the most magnificent intrinsically, and the most admirably preserved. Out of the huge hall, with its immense fireplace of delicately carved and inlaid grey and black stone, and its rows of family portraits, reaching from the wainscoting to the oaken ceiling, vaulted and ribbed like a ship's hull, opened the wide, flat-stepped staircase, the parapet surmounted at intervals by heraldic monsters, the wall covered with oak carvings of coats-of-arms, leafage, and little mythological scenes, painted a faded red and blue, and picked out with tarnished gold, which harmonised with the tarnished blue and gold of the stamped leather that reached to the oak cornice, again delicately tinted and gilded. The beautifully damascened suits of court armour looked, without being at all rusty, as if no modern hand had ever touched them ; the very rugs under foot were of sixteenth-century Persian make ; the only things of to-day were the big bunches of flowers and ferns, arranged in majolica dishes upon the landings. Everything was perfectly silent ; only from below came the chimes, silvery like an Italian palace fountain, of an old-fashioned clock.

It seemed to me that I was being led through the palace of the Sleeping Beauty.

" What a magnificent house ! " I exclaimed as I followed my

host through a long corridor, also hung with leather, wainscoted with carvings, and furnished with big wedding coffers, and chairs that looked as if they came out of some Vandyck portrait. In my mind was the strong impression that all this was natural, spontaneous—that it had about it nothing of the picturesqueness which swell studios have taught to rich and æsthetic houses. Mr. Oke misunderstood me.

" It is a nice old place," he said, " but it's too large for us. You see, my wife's health does not allow of our having many guests ; and there are no children."

I thought I noticed a vague complaint in his voice ; and he evidently was afraid there might have seemed something of the kind, for he added immediately—

" I don't care for children one jackstraw, you know, myself ; can't understand how any one can, for my part."

If ever a man went out of his way to tell a lie, I said to myself, Mr. Oke of Okehurst was doing so at the present moment.

When he had left me in one of the two enormous rooms that were allotted to me, I threw myself into an arm-chair and tried to focus the extraordinary imaginative impression which this house had given me.

I am very susceptible to such impressions ; and besides the sort of spasm of imaginative interest sometimes given to me by certain rare and eccentric personalities, I know nothing more subduing than the charm, quieter and less analytic, of any sort of complete and out-of-the-common-run sort of house. To sit in a room like the one I was sitting in, with the figures of the tapestry glimmering grey and lilac and purple in the twilight, the great bed, columned and curtained, looming in the middle, and the embers reddening beneath the overhanging mantelpiece of inlaid Italian stonework, a vague scent of rose-leaves and spices, put into the china bowls by the hands of ladies long since dead, while the clock downstairs sent up, every now and then, its faint silvery tune of forgotten days, filled the room ;—to do this is a special kind of voluptuousness, peculiar and complex and indescribable, like the half-drunkenness of opium or haschisch, and which, to be conveyed to others in any sense as I feel it, would require a genius, subtle and heady, like that of Baudelaire.

After I had dressed for dinner I resumed my place in the armchair, and resumed also my reverie, letting all these impressions of the past—which seemed faded like the figures in the arras, but

still warm like the embers in the fireplace, still sweet and subtle
like the perfume of the dead rose-leaves and broken spices in the
china bowls—permeate me and go to my head. Of Oke and Oke's
wife I did not think ; I seemed quite alone, isolated from the world,
separated from it in this exotic enjoyment.

Gradually the embers grew paler ; the figures in the tapestry
more shadowy ; the columned and curtained bed loomed out
vaguer ; the room seemed to fill with greyness ; and my eyes wandered to the mullioned bow-window, beyond whose panes, between whose heavy stone-work, stretched a greyish-brown expanse
of sere and sodden park grass, dotted with big oaks ; while far off,
behind a jagged fringe of dark Scotch firs, the wet sky was suffused
with the blood-red of the sunset. Between the falling of the raindrops from the ivy outside, there came, fainter or sharper, the
recurring bleating of the lambs separated from their mothers, a
forlorn, quavering, eerie little cry.

I started up at a sudden rap at my door.

" Haven't you heard the gong for dinner ? " asked Mr. Oke's
voice.

I had completely forgotten his existence.

III

I feel that I cannot possibly reconstruct my earliest impressions
of Mrs. Oke. My recollection of them would be entirely coloured
by my subsequent knowledge of her ; whence I conclude that I
could not at first have experienced the strange interest and admiration which that extraordinary woman very soon excited in
me. Interest and admiration, be it well understood, of a very unusual kind, as she was herself a very unusual kind of woman ; and
I, if you choose, am a rather unusual kind of man. But I can explain that better anon.

This much is certain, that I must have been immeasurably surprised at finding my hostess and future sitter so completely unlike
everything I had anticipated. Or no—now I come to think of it,
I scarcely felt surprised at all ; or if I did, that shock of surprise
could have lasted but an infinitesimal part of a minute. The fact
is, that, having once seen Alice Oke in the reality, it was quite
impossible to remember that one could have fancied her at all
different : there was something so complete, so completely unlike
every one else, in her personality, that she seemed always to have

been present in one's consciousness, although present, perhaps, as an enigma.

Let me try and give you some notion of her : not that first impression, whatever it may have been, but the absolute reality of her as I gradually learned to see it. To begin with, I must repeat and reiterate over and over again, that she was, beyond all comparison, the most graceful and exquisite woman I have ever seen, but with a grace and an exquisiteness that had nothing to do with any preconceived notion or previous experience of what goes by these names : grace and exquisiteness recognised at once as perfect, but which were seen in her for the first, and probably, I do believe, for the last time. It is conceivable, is it not, that once in a thousand years there may arise a combination of lines, a system of movements, an outline, a gesture, which is new, unprecedented, and yet hits off exactly our desires for beauty and rareness ? She was very tall ; and I suppose people would have called her thin. I don't know, for I never thought about her as a body—bones, flesh, that sort of thing ; but merely as a wonderful series of lines, and a wonderful strangeness of personality. Tall and slender, certainly, and with not one item of what makes up our notion of a well-built woman. She was as straight—I mean she had as little of what people call figure—as a bamboo ; her shoulders were a trifle high, and she had a decided stoop ; her arms and her shoulders she never once wore uncovered. But this bamboo figure of hers had a suppleness and a stateliness, a play of outline with every step she took, that I can't compare to anything else ; there was in it something of the peacock and something also of the stag ; but, above all, it was her own. I wish I could describe her. I wish, alas !—I wish, I wish, I have wished a hundred thousand times—I could paint her, as I see her now, if I shut my eyes—even if it were only a silhouette. There ! I see her so plainly, walking slowly up and down a room, the slight highness of her shoulders just completing the exquisite arrangement of lines made by the straight supple back, the long exquisite neck, the head, with the hair cropped in short pale curls, always drooping a little, except when she would suddenly throw it back, and smile, not at me, nor at any one, nor at anything that had been said, but as if she alone had suddenly seen or heard something, with the strange dimple in her thin, pale cheeks, and the strange whiteness in her full, wide-opened eyes : the moment when she had something of the stag in her movement. But where is the use of talking about her ? I don't believe, you know, that even the greatest painter can show what is the real beauty of a very beautiful woman in the ordinary sense : Titian's and Tintoretto's women must have been miles handsomer than they have made them. Something—and that the very essence—always escapes, perhaps because real beauty is as much a thing in time—a thing like music, a succession, a series— as in space. Mind you, I am speaking of a woman beautiful in the conventional sense. Imagine, then, how much more so in the case of a woman like Alice Oke ; and if the pencil and brush, imitating each line and tint, can't succeed, how is it possible to give even the vaguest notion with mere wretched words—words possessing only a wretched abstract meaning, an impotent conventional as- sociation ? To make a long story short, Mrs. Oke of Okehurst was, in my opinion, to the highest degree exquisite and strange,—an exotic creature, whose charm you can no more describe than you could bring home the perfume of some newly discovered tropical flower by comparing it with the scent of a cabbage-rose or a lily.

That first dinner was gloomy enough. Mr. Oke—Oke of Oke- hurst, as the people down there called him—was horribly shy, con- sumed with a fear of making a fool of himself before me and his wife, I then thought. But that sort of shyness did not wear off ; and I soon discovered that, although it was doubtless increased by the presence of a total stranger, it was inspired in Oke, not by me, but by his wife. He would look every now and then as if he were going to make a remark, and then evidently restrain him- self, and remain silent. It was very curious to see this big, hand- some, manly young fellow, who ought to have had any amount of success with women, suddenly stammer and grow crimson in the presence of his own wife. Nor was it the consciousness of stupidity ; for when you got him alone, Oke, although always slow and timid, had a certain amount of ideas, and very defined political and social views, and a certain childlike earnestness and desire to attain certainty and truth which was rather touching. On the other hand, Oke's singular shyness was not, so far as I could see, the result of any kind of bullying on his wife's part. You can always detect, if you have any observation, the husband or the wife who is accus- tomed to be snubbed, to be corrected, by his or her better-half : there is a self consciousness in both parties, a habit of watching and fault-finding, of being watched and found fault with. This was clearly not the case at Okehurst. Mrs. Oke evidently did not trouble herself about her husband in the very least ; he might say or do any amount of silly things without rebuke or even notice ; and he might have done so, had he chosen, ever since his wedding-day. You felt that at once. Mrs. Oke simply passed over his existence. I cannot say she paid much attention to any one's, even to mine. At first I thought it an affectation on her part—for there was something far-fetched in her whole appearance, something suggesting study, which might lead one to tax her with affectation at first ; she was dressed in a strange way, not according to any established æsthetic eccentricity, but individually, strangely, as if in the clothes of an ancestress of the seventeenth century. Well, at first I thought it a kind of pose on her part, this mixture of extreme graciousness and utter indifference which she manifested towards me. She always seemed to be thinking of something else ; and although she talked quite sufficiently, and with every sign of superior intelligence, she left the impression of having been as taciturn as her husband.

In the beginning, in the first few days of my stay at Okehurst, I imagined that Mrs. Oke was a highly superior sort of flirt ; and that her absent manner, her look, while speaking to you, into an invisible distance, her curious irrelevant smile, were so many means of attracting and baffling adoration. I mistook it for the somewhat similar manners of certain foreign women—it is beyond English ones—which mean, to those who can understand, " pay court to me." But I soon found I was mistaken. Mrs. Oke had not the faintest desire that I should pay court to her ; indeed she did not honour me with sufficient thought for that ; and I, on my part, began to be too much interested in her from another point of view to dream of such a thing. I became aware, not merely that I had before me the most marvellously rare and exquisite and baffling subject for a portrait, but also one of the most peculiar and enigmatic of characters. Now that I look back upon it, I am tempted to think that the psychological peculiarity of that woman might be summed up in an exorbitant and absorbing interest in herself—a Narcissus attitude—curiously complicated with a fantastic imagination, a sort of morbid day-dreaming, all turned inwards, and with no outer characteristic save a certain restlessness, a perverse desire to surprise and shock, to surprise and shock more particularly her husband, and thus be revenged for the intense boredom which his want of appreciation inflicted upon her.

I got to understand this much little by little, yet I did not seem to have really penetrated the something mysterious about Mrs.

Oke. There was a waywardness, a strangeness, which I felt but could not explain—a something as difficult to define as the peculiarity of her outward appearance, and perhaps very closely connected therewith. I became interested in Mrs. Oke as if I had been in love with her ; and I was not in the least in love. I neither dreaded parting from her, nor felt any pleasure in her presence. I had not the smallest wish to please or to gain her notice. But I had her on the brain. I pursued her, her physical image, her psychological explanation, with a kind of passion which filled my days, and prevented my ever feeling dull. The Okes lived a remarkably solitary life. There were but few neighbours, of whom they saw but little ; and they rarely had a guest in the house. Oke himself seemed every now and then seized with a sense of responsibility towards me. He would remark vaguely, during our walks and after-dinner chats, that I must find life at Okehurst horribly dull ; his wife's health had accustomed him to solitude, and then also his wife thought the neighbours a bore. He never questioned his wife's judgment in these matters. He merely stated the case as if resignation were quite simple and inevitable ; yet it seemed to me, sometimes, that this monotonous life of solitude, by the side of a woman who took no more heed of him than of a table or chair, was producing a vague depression and irritation in this young man, so evidently cut out for a cheerful, commonplace life. I often wondered how he could endure it at all, not having, as I had, the interest of a strange psychological riddle to solve, and of a great portrait to paint. He was, I found, extremely good—the type of the perfectly conscientious young Englishman, the sort of man who ought to have been the Christian soldier kind of thing ; devout, pure-minded, brave, incapable of any baseness, a little intellectually dense, and puzzled by all manner of moral scruples. The condition of his tenants and of his political party—he was a regular Kentish Tory—lay heavy on his mind. He spent hours every day in his study, doing the work of a land agent and a political whip, reading piles of reports and newspapers and agricultural treatises ; and emerging for lunch with piles of letters in his hand, and that odd puzzled look in his good healthy face, that deep gash between his eyebrows, which my friend the mad-doctor calls the *maniac-frown*. It was with this expression of face that I should have liked to paint him ; but I felt that he would not have liked it, that it was more fair to him to represent him in his mere wholesome pink and white and blond conventionality. I was perhaps rather unconscientious about the likeness of Mr. Oke ; I felt satisfied to paint it no matter how, I mean as regards character, for my whole mind was swallowed up in thinking how I should paint Mrs. Oke, how I could best transport on to canvas that singular and enigmatic personality. I began with her husband, and told her frankly that I must have much longer to study her. Mr. Oke couldn't understand why it should be necessary to make a hundred and one pencil-sketches of his wife before even determining in what attitude to paint her ; but I think he was rather pleased to have an opportunity of keeping me at Okehurst ; my presence evidently broke the monotony of his life. Mrs. Oke seemed perfectly indifferent to my staying, as she was perfectly indifferent to my presence. Without being rude, I never saw a woman pay so little attention to a guest ; she would talk with me sometimes by the hour, or rather let me talk to her, but she never seemed to be listening. She would lie back in a big seventeenth-century arm-chair while I played the piano, with that strange smile every now and then in her thin cheeks, that strange whiteness in her eyes ; but it seemed a matter of indifference whether my music stopped or went on. In my portrait of her husband she did not take, or pretend to take, the very faintest interest ; but that was nothing to me. I did not want Mrs. Oke to think me interesting ; I merely wished to go on studying her.

The first time that Mrs. Oke seemed to become at all aware of my presence as distinguished from that of the chairs and tables, the dogs that lay in the porch, or the clergyman or lawyer or stray neighbour who was occasionally asked to dinner, was one day—I might have been there a week—when I chanced to remark to her upon the very singular resemblance that existed between herself and the portrait of a lady that hung in the hall with the ceiling like a ship's hull. The picture in question was a full length, neither very good nor very bad, probably done by some stray Italian of the early seventeenth century. It hung in a rather dark corner, facing the portrait, evidently painted to be its companion, of a dark man, with a somewhat unpleasant expression of resolution and efficiency, in a black Vandyck dress. The two were evidently man and wife ; and in the corner of the woman's portrait were the words, " Alice Oke, daughter of Virgil Pomfret, Esq., and wife to Nicholas Oke of Okehurst," and the date 1626— " Nicholas Oke " being the name painted in the corner of the small portrait. The lady was really wonderfully like the present

Mrs. Oke, at least so far as an indifferently painted portrait of the early days of Charles I can be like a living woman of the nineteenth century. There were the same strange lines of figure and face, the same dimples in the thin cheeks, the same wide-opened eyes, the same vague eccentricity of expression, not destroyed even by the feeble painting and conventional manner of the time. One could fancy that this woman had the same walk, the same beautiful line of nape of the neck and stooping head as her descendant ; for I found that Mr. and Mrs. Oke, who were first cousins, were both descended from that Nicholas Oke and that Alice, daughter of Virgil Pomfret. But the resemblance was heightened by the fact that, as I soon saw, the present Mrs. Oke distinctly made herself up to look like her ancestress, dressing in garments that had a seventeenth-century look ; nay, that were sometimes absolutely copied from this portrait.

"You think I am like her," answered Mrs. Oke dreamily to my remark, and her eyes wandered off to that unseen something, and the faint smile dimpled her thin cheeks.

"You are like her, and you know it. I may even say you wish to be like her, Mrs. Oke," I answered, laughing.

"Perhaps I do."

And she looked in the direction of her husband. I noticed that he had an expression of distinct annoyance besides that frown of his.

"Isn't it true that Mrs. Oke tries to look like that portrait ? " I asked, with a perverse curiosity.

"Oh, fudge ! " he exclaimed, rising from his chair and walking nervously to the window. "It's all nonsense, mere nonsense. I wish you wouldn't, Alice."

"Wouldn't what ? " asked Mrs. Oke, with a sort of contemptuous indifference. "If I am like that Alice Oke, why I am ; and I am very pleased any one should think so. She and her husband are just about the only two members of our family—our most flat, stale, and unprofitable family—that ever were in the least degree interesting."

Oke grew crimson, and frowned as if in pain.

"I don't see why you should abuse our family, Alice," he said. "Thank God, our people have always been honourable and upright men and women ! "

"Excepting always Nicholas Oke and Alice his wife, daughter

of Virgil Pomfret, Esq.," she answered, laughing, as he strode out into the park.

" How childish he is ! " she exclaimed when we were alone. " He really minds, really feels disgraced by what our ancestors did two centuries and a half ago. I do believe William would have those two portraits taken down and burned if he weren't afraid of me and ashamed of the neighbours. And as it is, these two people really are the only two members of our family that ever were in the least interesting. I will tell you the story some day."

As it was, the story was told to me by Oke himself. The next day, as we were taking our morning walk, he suddenly broke a long silence, laying about him all the time at the sere grasses with the hooked stick that he carried, like the conscientious Kentish-man he was, for the purpose of cutting down his and other folk's thistles.

" I fear you must have thought me very ill-mannered towards my wife yesterday," he said shyly ; " and indeed I know I was."

Oke was one of those chivalrous beings to whom every woman, every wife—and his own most of all—appeared in the light of something holy. " But—but—I have a prejudice which my wife does not enter into, about raking up ugly things in one's own family. I suppose Alice thinks that it is so long ago that it has really got no connection with us ; she thinks of it merely as a picturesque story. I daresay many people feel like that ; in short, I am sure they do, otherwise there wouldn't be such lots of discreditable family traditions afloat. But I feel as if it were all one whether it was long ago or not ; when it's a question of one's own people, I would rather have it forgotten. I can't understand how people can talk about murders in their families, and ghosts, and so forth."

" Have you any ghosts at Okehurst, by the way ? " I asked. The place seemed as if it required some to complete it.

" I hope not," answered Oke gravely.

His gravity made me smile.

" Why, would you dislike it if there were ? " I asked.

" If there are such things as ghosts," he replied, " I don't think they should be taken lightly. God would not permit them to be, except as a warning or a punishment."

We walked on some time in silence, I wondering at the strange type of this commonplace young man, and half wishing I could put something into my portrait that should be the equivalent of this curious unimaginative earnestness. Then Oke told me the story of those two pictures—told it me about as badly and hesitatingly as was possible for mortal man.

He and his wife were, as I have said, cousins, and therefore descended from the same old Kentish stock. The Okes of Okehurst could trace back to Norman, almost to Saxon times, far longer than any of the titled or better-known families of the neighbourhood. I saw that William Oke, in his heart, thoroughly looked down upon all his neighbours. " We have never done anything particular, or been anything particular—never held any office," he said ; " but we have always been here, and apparently always done our duty. An ancestor of ours was killed in the Scotch wars, another at Agincourt—mere honest captains." Well, early in the seventeenth century, the family had dwindled to a single member. Nicholas Oke, the same who had rebuilt Okehurst in its present shape. This Nicholas appears to have been somewhat different from the usual run of the family. He had, in his youth, sought adventures in America, and seems, generally speaking, to have been less of a nonentity than his ancestors. He married, when no longer very young, Alice, daughter of Virgil Pomfret, a beautiful young heiress from a neighbouring county. " It was the first time an Oke married a Pomfret," my host informed me, " and the last time. The Pomfrets were quite different sort of people—restless, self-seeking ; one of them had been a favourite of Henry VIII." It was clear that William Oke had no feeling of having any Pomfret blood in his veins ; he spoke of these people with an evident family dislike—the dislike of an Oke, one of the old, honourable, modest stock, which had quietly done its duty, for a family of fortune-seekers and Court minions. Well, there had come to live near Okehurst, in a little house recently inherited from an uncle, a certain Christopher Lovelock, a young gallant and poet, who was in momentary disgrace at Court for some love affair. This Lovelock had struck up a great friendship with his neighbours of Okehurst —too great a friendship, apparently, with the wife, either for her husband's taste or her own. Anyhow, one evening as he was riding home alone, Lovelock had been attacked and murdered, ostensibly by highwaymen, but as was afterwards rumoured, by Nicholas Oke, accompanied by his wife dressed as a groom. No legal evidence had been got, but the tradition had remained. " They used to tell it us when we were children," said my host, in a hoarse voice, " and to frighten my cousin—I mean my wife—and me

with stories about Lovelock. It is merely a tradition, which I hope
may die out, as I sincerely pray to heaven that it may be false."
" Alice—Mrs. Oke—you see," he went on after some time,
" doesn't feel about it as I do. Perhaps I am morbid. But I do dislike having the old story raked up."

And we said no more on the subject.

IV

From that moment I began to assume a certain interest in the
eyes of Mrs. Oke ; or rather, I began to perceive that I had a
means of securing her attention. Perhaps it was wrong of me to
do so ; and I have often reproached myself very seriously later on.
But after all, how was I to guess that I was making mischief merely
by chiming in, for the sake of the portrait I had undertaken, and
of a very harmless psychological mania, with what was merely the
fad, the little romantic affectation or eccentricity, of a scatter-
brained and eccentric young woman ? How in the world should
I have dreamed that I was handling explosive substances ? A man
is surely not responsible if the people with whom he is forced to
deal, and whom he deals with as with all the rest of the world, are
quite different from all other human creatures.

So, if indeed I did at all conduce to mischief, I really cannot
blame myself. I had met in Mrs. Oke an almost unique subject for
a portrait-painter of my particular sort, and a most singular,
bizarre personality. I could not possibly do my subject justice so
long as I was kept at a distance, prevented from studying the real
character of the woman. I required to put her into play. And I ask
you whether any more innocent way of doing so could be found
than talking to a woman, and letting her talk, about an absurd
fancy she had for a couple of ancestors of hers of the time of Charles
I, and a poet whom they had murdered ?—particularly as I studiously respected the prejudices of my host, and refrained from mentioning the matter, and tried to restrain Mrs. Oke from doing so,
in the presence of William Oke himself.

I had certainly guessed correctly. To resemble the Alice Oke
of the year 1626 was the caprice, the mania, the pose, the whatever you may call it, of the Alice Oke of 1880 ; and to perceive this
resemblance was the sure way of gaining her good graces. It was
the most extraordinary craze, of all the extraordinary crazes of
childless and idle women, that I had ever met ; but it was more

than that, it was admirably characteristic. It finished off the strange figure of Mrs. Oke, as I saw it in my imagination—this *bizarre* creature of enigmatic, far-fetched exquisiteness—that she should have no interest in the present, but only an eccentric passion in the past. It seemed to give the meaning to the absent look in her eyes, to her irrelevant and far-off smile. It was like the words to a weird piece of gipsy music, this that she, who was so different, so distant from all women of her own time, should try and identify herself with a woman of the past—that she should have a kind of flirtation—— But of this anon.

I told Mrs. Oke that I had learnt from her husband the outline of the tragedy, or mystery, whichever it was, of Alice Oke, daughter of Virgil Pomfret, and the poet Christopher Lovelock. That look of vague contempt, of a desire to shock, which I had noticed before, came into her beautiful, pale, diaphanous face.

" I suppose my husband was very shocked at the whole matter," she said—" told it you with as little detail as possible, and assured you very solemnly that he hoped the whole story might be a mere dreadful calumny ? Poor Willie ! I remember already when we were children, and I used to come with my mother to spend Christmas at Okehurst, and my cousin was down here for his holidays, how I used to horrify him by insisting upon dressing up in shawls and waterproofs, and playing the story of the wicked Mrs. Oke ; and he always piously refused to do the part of Nicholas, when I wanted to have the scene on Cotes Common. I didn't know then that I was like the original Alice Oke ; I found it out only after our marriage. You really think that I am ? "

She certainly was, particularly at that moment, as she stood in a white Vandyck dress, with the green of the park-land rising up behind her, and the low sun catching her short locks and surrounding her head, her exquisitely bowed head, with a pale-yellow halo. But I confess I thought the original Alice Oke, siren and murderess though she might be, very uninteresting compared with this wayward and exquisite creature whom I had rashly promised myself to send down to posterity in all her unlikely wayward exquisiteness.

One morning while Mr. Oke was despatching his Saturday heap of Conservative manifestoes and rural decisions—he was justice of the peace in a most literal sense, penetrating into cottages and huts, defending the weak and admonishing the ill-conducted—one morning while I was making one of my many pencil-sketches (alas, they are all that remain to me now !) of my future sitter, Mrs. Oke gave me her version of the story of Alice Oke and Christopher Lovelock.

"Do you suppose there was anything between them?" I asked—"that she was ever in love with him? How do you explain the part which tradition ascribes to her in the supposed murder? One has heard of women and their lovers who have killed the husband ; but a woman who combines with her husband to kill her lover, or at least the man who is in love with her—that is surely very singular." I was absorbed in my drawing, and really thinking very little of what I was saying.

"I don't know," she answered pensively, with that distant look in her eyes. "Alice Oke was very proud, I am sure. She may have loved the poet very much, and yet been indignant with him, hated having to love him. She may have felt that she had a right to rid herself of him, and to call upon her husband to help her to do so."

"Good heavens ! what a fearful idea ! " I exclaimed, half laughing. "Don't you think, after all, that Mr. Oke may be right in saying that it is easier and more comfortable to take the whole story as a pure invention ? "

"I cannot take it as an invention," answered Mrs. Oke contemptuously, "because I happen to know that it is true."

"Indeed ! " I answered, working away at my sketch, and enjoying putting this strange creature, as I said to myself, through her paces ; "how is that ? "

"How does one know that anything is true in this world ? " she replied evasively ; "because one does, because one feels it to be true, I suppose."

And, with that far-off look in her light eyes, she relapsed into silence.

"Have you ever read any of Lovelock's poetry ? " she asked me suddenly the next day.

"Lovelock ? " I answered, for I had forgotten the name. "Lovelock, who "—— But I stopped, remembering the prejudices of my host, who was seated next to me at table.

"Lovelock who was killed by Mr. Oke's and my ancestors."

And she looked full at her husband, as if in perverse enjoyment of the evident annoyance which it caused him.

"Alice," he entreated in a low voice, his whole face crimson, "for mercy's sake, don't talk about such things before the servants."

Mrs. Oke burst into a high, light, rather hysterical laugh, the laugh of a naughty child.

" The servants ! Gracious heavens ! do you suppose they haven't heard the story ? Why, it's as well known as Okehurst itself in the neighbourhood. Don't they believe that Lovelock has been seen about the house ? Haven't they all heard his footsteps in the big corridor ? Haven't they, my dear Willie, noticed a thousand times that you never will stay a minute alone in the yellow drawing-room—that you run out of it, like a child, if I happen to leave you there for a minute ? "

True ! How was it I had not noticed that ? or rather, that I only now remembered having noticed it ? The yellow drawing-room was one of the most charming rooms in the house : a large, bright room, hung with yellow damask and panelled with carvings, that opened straight out on to the lawn, far superior to the room in which we habitually sat, which was comparatively gloomy. This time Mr. Oke struck me as really too childish. I felt an intense desire to badger him.

" The yellow drawing-room ! " I exclaimed. " Does this interesting literary character haunt the yellow drawing-room ? Do tell me about it. What happened there ? "

Mr. Oke made a painful effort to laugh.

" Nothing ever happened there, so far as I know," he said, and rose from the table.

" Really ? " I asked incredulously.

" Nothing did happen there," answered Mrs. Oke slowly, playing mechanically with a fork, and picking out the pattern of the tablecloth. " That is just the extraordinary circumstance, that, so far as any one knows, nothing ever did happen there ; and yet that room has an evil reputation. No member of our family, they say, can bear to sit there alone for more than a minute. You see, William evidently cannot."

" Have you ever seen or heard anything strange there ? " I asked of my host.

He shook his head. " Nothing," he answered curtly, and lit his cigar.

" I presume you have not," I asked, half laughing, of Mrs. Oke, " since you don't mind sitting in that room for hours alone ? How do you explain this uncanny reputation, since nothing ever happened there ? "

" Perhaps something is destined to happen there in the future,"

she answered, in her absent voice. And then she suddenly added,
" Suppose you paint my portrait in that room ? "

Mr. Oke suddenly turned round. He was very white, and looked
as if he were going to say something, but desisted.

" Why do you worry Mr. Oke like that ? " I asked, when he had
gone into his smoking-room with his usual bundle of papers. " It
is very cruel of you, Mrs. Oke. You ought to have more consideration for people who believe in such things, although you may not
be able to put yourself in their frame of mind."

" Who tells you that I don't believe in *such things*, as you call
them ? " she answered abruptly.

" Come," she said, after a minute, " I want to show you why I
believe in Christopher Lovelock. Come with me into the yellow
room."

V

What Mrs. Oke showed me in the yellow room was a large
bundle of papers, some printed and some manuscript, but all of
them brown with age, which she took out of an old Italian ebony
inlaid cabinet. It took her some time to get them, as a complicated
arrangement of double locks and false drawers had to be put in
play ; and while she was doing so, I looked round the room, in
which I had been only three or four times before. It was certainly
the most beautiful room in this beautiful house, and, as it seemed
to me now, the most strange. It was long and low, with something
that made you think of the cabin of a ship, with a great mullioned
window that let in, as it were, a perspective of the brownish green
park-land, dotted with oaks, and sloping upwards to the distant
line of bluish firs against the horizon. The walls were hung with
flowered damask, whose yellow, faded to brown, united with the
reddish colour of the carved wainscoting and the carved oaken
beams. For the rest, it reminded me more of an Italian room than
an English one. The furniture was Tuscan of the early seventeenth
century, inlaid and carved ; there were a couple of faded allegori-
cal pictures, by some Bolognese master, on the walls ; and in a
corner, among a stack of dwarf orange-trees, a little Italian harp-
sichord of exquisite curve and slenderness, with flowers and landscapes painted upon its cover. In a recess was a shelf of old books,
mainly English and Italian poets of the Elizabethan time ; and close
by it, placed upon a carved wedding-chest, a large and beautiful

melon-shaped lute. The panes of the mullioned window were open, and yet the air seemed heavy, with an indescribable heady perfume, not that of any growing flower, but like that of old stuff that should have lain for years among spices.

" It is a beautiful room ! " I exclaimed. " I should awfully like to paint you in it " ; but I had scarcely spoken the words when I felt I had done wrong. This woman's husband could not bear the room, and it seemed to me vaguely as if he were right in detesting it.

Mrs. Oke took no notice of my exclamation, but beckoned me to the table where she was standing sorting the papers.

" Look ! " she said, " these are all poems by Christopher Love-lock " ; and touching the yellow papers with delicate and reverent fingers, she commenced reading some of them out loud in a slow, half-audible voice. They were songs in the style of those of Her-rick, Waller, and Drayton, complaining for the most part of the cruelty of a lady called Dryope, in whose name was evidently con-cealed a reference to that of the mistress of Okehurst. The songs were graceful, and not without a certain faded passion ; but I was thinking not of them, but of the woman who was reading them to me.

Mrs. Oke was standing with the brownish yellow wall as a back-ground to her white brocade dress, which, in its stiff seventeenth-century make, seemed but to bring out more clearly the slight-ness, the exquisite suppleness, of her tall figure. She held the papers in one hand, and leaned the other, as if for support, on the inlaid cabinet by her side. Her voice, which was delicate, shadowy, like her person, had a curious throbbing cadence, as if she were reading the words of a melody, and restraining herself with diffi-culty from singing it ; and as she read, her long slender throat throbbed slightly, and a faint redness came into her thin face. She evidently knew the verses by heart, and her eyes were mostly fixed with that distant smile in them, with which harmonised a constant tremulous little smile in her lips.

" That is how I would wish to paint her ! " I exclaimed within myself ; and scarcely noticed, what struck me on thinking over the scene, that this strange being read these verses as one might fancy a woman would read love-verses addressed to herself.

" Those are all written for Alice Oke—Alice the daughter of Virgil Pomfret," she said slowly, folding up the papers. " I found them at the bottom of this cabinet. Can you doubt of the reality of Christopher Lovelock now ? "

The question was an illogical one, for to doubt of the existence of Christopher Lovelock was one thing, and to doubt of the mode of his death was another ; but somehow I did feel convinced.

" Look ! " she said, when she had replaced the poems, " I will show you something else." Among the flowers that stood on the upper storey of her writing-table—for I found that Mrs. Oke had a writing-table in the yellow room—stood, as on an altar, a small black carved frame, with a silk curtain drawn over it : the sort of thing behind which you would have expected to find a head of Christ or of the Virgin Mary. She drew the curtain and displayed a large-sized miniature, representing a young man, with auburn curls and a peaked auburn beard, dressed in black, but with lace about his neck, and large pear-shaped pearls in his ears : a wistful, melancholy face. Mrs. Oke took the miniature religiously off its stand, and showed me, written in faded characters upon the back, the name " Christopher Lovelock," and the date 1626.

" I found this in the secret drawer of that cabinet, together with the heap of poems," she said, taking the miniature out of my hand.

I was silent for a minute.

" Does—does Mr. Oke know that you have got it here ? " I asked ; and then wondered what in the world had impelled me to put such a question.

Mrs. Oke smiled that smile of contemptuous indifference. " I have never hidden it from any one. If my husband disliked my having it, he might have taken it away, I suppose. It belongs to him, since it was found in his house."

I did not answer, but walked mechanically towards the door. There was something heady and oppressive in this beautiful room ; something, I thought, almost repulsive in this exquisite woman. She seemed to me, suddenly, perverse and dangerous.

I scarcely know why, but I neglected Mrs. Oke that afternoon. I went to Mr. Oke's study, and sat opposite to him smoking while he was engrossed in his accounts, his reports, and electioneering papers. On the table, above the heap of paper-bound volumes and pigeon-holed documents, was, as sole ornament of his den, a little photograph of his wife, done some years before. I don't know why, but as I sat and watched him, with his florid, honest, manly beauty, working away conscientiously, with that little perplexed frown of his, I felt intensely sorry for this man.

But this feeling did not last. There was no help for it : Oke was
not as interesting as Mrs. Oke ; and it required too great an effort
to pump up sympathy for this normal, excellent, exemplary young
squire, in the presence of so wonderful a creature as his wife. So
I let myself go to the habit of allowing Mrs. Oke daily to talk over
her strange craze, or rather of drawing her out about it. I confess
that I derived a morbid and exquisite pleasure in doing so : it was
so characteristic in her, so appropriate to the house ! It completed
her personality so perfectly, and made it so much easier to conceive a way of painting her. I made up my mind little by little,
while working at William Oke's portrait (he proved a less easy
subject than I had anticipated, and, despite his conscientious
efforts, was a nervous, uncomfortable sitter, silent and brooding)
—I made up my mind that I would paint Mrs. Oke standing by
the cabinet in the yellow room, in the white Vandyck dress copied
from the portrait of her ancestress. Mr. Oke might resent it, Mrs.
Oke even might resent it ; they might refuse to take the picture, to
pay for it, to allow me to exhibit ; they might force me to run my
umbrella through the picture. No matter. That picture should be
painted, if merely for the sake of having painted it ; for I felt it
was the only think I could do, and that it would be far away my
best work. I told neither of my resolution, but prepared sketch
after sketch of Mrs. Oke, while continuing to paint her husband.

Mrs. Oke was a silent person, more silent even than her husband, for she did not feel bound, as he did, to attempt to entertain
a guest or to show any interest in him. She seemed to spend her
life—a curious, inactive, half-invalidish life, broken by sudden
fits of childish cheerfulness—in an eternal day-dream, strolling
about the house and grounds, arranging the quantities of flowers
that always filled all the rooms, beginning to read and then throwing aside novels and books of poetry, of which she always had a
large number ; and, I believe, lying for hours, doing nothing, on
a couch in that yellow drawing-room, which, with her sole exception, no member of the Oke family had ever been known to
stay in alone. Little by little I began to suspect and to verify
another eccentricity of this eccentric being, and to understand
why there were stringent orders never to disturb her in that yellow
room.

It had been a habit at Okehurst, as at one or two other English
manor-houses, to keep a certain amount of the clothes of each
generation, more particularly wedding-dresses. A certain carved

oaken press, of which Mr. Oke once displayed the contents to me, was a perfect museum of costumes, male and female, from the early years of the seventeenth to the end of the eighteenth century —a thing to take away the breath of a *bric-a-brac* collector, an antiquary, or a *genre* painter. Mr. Oke was none of these, and there-fore took but little interest in the collection, save in so far as it interested his family feeling. Still he seemed well acquainted with the contents of that press.

He was turning over the clothes for my benefit, when suddenly I noticed that he frowned. I know not what impelled me to say, " By the way, have you any dresses of that Mrs. Oke whom your wife resembles so much ? Have you got that particular white dress she was painted in, perhaps ? "

Oke of Okehurst flushed very red.

" We have it," he answered hesitatingly, " but—it isn't here at present—I can't find it. I suppose," he blurted out with an effort, " that Alice has got it. Mrs. Oke sometimes has the fancy of having some of these old things down. I suppose she takes ideas from them."

A sudden light dawned in my mind. The white dress in which I had seen Mrs. Oke in the yellow room, the day that she showed me Lovelock's verses, was not, as I had thought, a modern copy ; it was the original dress of Alice Oke, the daughter of Virgil Pomfret—the dress in which, perhaps, Christopher Lovelock had seen her in that very room.

The idea gave me a delightful picturesque shudder. I said nothing. But I pictured to myself Mrs. Oke sitting in that yellow room—that room which no Oke of Okehurst save herself ven-tured to remain in alone, in the dress of her ancestress, confronting, as it were, that vague, haunting something that seemed to fill the place—that vague presence, it seemed to me, of the murdered cavalier poet.

Mrs. Oke. as I have said, was extremely silent, as a result of being extremely indifferent. She really did not care in the least about anything except her own ideas and day-dreams, except when, every now and then, she was seized with a sudden desire to shock the prejudices or superstitions of her husband. Very soon she got into the way of never talking to me at all, save about Alice and Nicholas Oke and Christopher Lovelock ; and then, when the fit seized her, she would go on by the hour, never asking herself whether I was or was not equally interested in the strange craze that fascinated her. It so happened that I was. I loved to listen to her, going on discussing by the hour the merits of Lovelock's poems, and analysing her feelings and those of her two ancestors. It was quite wonderful to watch the exquisite, exotic creature in one of these moods, with the distant look in her grey eyes and the absent-looking smile in her thin cheeks, talking as if she had intimately known these people of the seventeenth century, discussing every minute mood of theirs, detailing every scene between them and their victim, talking of Alice, and Nicholas, and Lovelock as she might of her most intimate friends. Of Alice particularly, and of Lovelock. She seemed to know every word that Alice had spoken, every idea that had crossed her mind. It sometimes struck me as if she were telling me, speaking of herself in the third person, of her own feelings—as if I were listening to a woman's confidences, the recital of her doubts, scruples, and agonies about a living lover. For Mrs. Oke, who seemed the most self-absorbed of creatures in all other matters, and utterly incapable of understanding or sympathising with the feelings of other persons, entered completely and passionately into the feelings of this woman, this Alice, who, at some moments, seemed to be not another woman, but herself.

" But how could she do it—how could she kill the man she cared for ? " I once asked her.

" Because she loved him more than the whole world ! " she exclaimed, and rising suddenly from her chair, walked towards the window, covering her face with her hands.

I could see, from the movement of her neck, that she was sobbing. She did not turn round, but motioned me to go away.

" Don't let us talk any more about it," she said. " I am ill to-day, and silly."

I closed the door gently behind me. What mystery was there in this woman's life ? This listlessness, this strange self-engrossment and stranger mania about people long dead, this indifference and desire to annoy towards her husband—did it all mean that Alice Oke had loved or still loved some one who was not the master of Okehurst ? And his melancholy, his preoccupation, the something about him that told of a broken youth—did it mean that he knew it ?

VI

The following days Mrs. Oke was in a condition of quite unusual good spirits. Some visitors—distant relatives—were expected,
and although she had expressed the utmost annoyance at the idea
of their coming, she was now seized with a fit of housekeeping
activity, and was perpetually about arranging things and giving
orders, although all arrangements, as usual, had been made, and
all orders given, by her husband.

William Oke was quite radiant.

" If only Alice were always well like this ! " he exclaimed ; " if
only she would take, or could take, an interest in life, how different
things would be ! But," he added, as if fearful lest he should be
supposed to accuse her in any way, " how can she, usually, with
her wretched health ? Still, it does make me awfully happy to see
her like this."

I nodded. But I cannot say that I really acquiesced in his views.
It seemed to me, particularly with the recollection of yesterday's
extraordinary scene, that Mrs. Oke's high spirits were anything
but normal. There was something in her unusual activity and still
more unusual cheerfulness that was merely nervous and feverish ;
and I had, the whole day, the impression of dealing with a woman
who was ill and who would very speedily collapse.

Mrs. Oke spent her day wandering from one room to another,
and from the garden to the greenhouse, seeing whether all was in
order, when, as a matter of fact, all was always in order at Okehurst. She did not give me any sitting, and not a word was spoken
about Alice Oke or Christopher Lovelock. Indeed, to a casual
observer, it might have seemed as if all that craze about Lovelock
had completely departed, or never existed. About five o'clock, as
I was strolling among the red-brick round-gabled outhouses—
each with its armorial oak—and the old-fashioned spalliered
kitchen and fruit garden, I saw Mrs. Oke standing, her hands full
of York and Lancaster roses, upon the steps facing the stables.
A groom was currycombing a horse, and outside the coach-house
was Mr. Oke's little high-wheeled cart.

" Let us have a drive ! " suddenly exclaimed Mrs. Oke, on seeing me. " Look what a beautiful evening—and look at that dear
little cart ! It is so long since I have driven, and I feel as if I must
drive again. Come with me. And you, harness Jim at once and
come round to the door."

I was quite amazed ; and still more so when the cart drove up before the door, and Mrs. Oke called to me to accompany her. She sent away the groom, and in a minute we were rolling along, at a tremendous pace, along the yellow-sand road, with the sere pasture-lands, the big oaks, on either side.

I could scarcely believe my senses. This woman, in her mannish little coat and hat, driving a powerful young horse with the utmost skill, and chattering like a school-girl of sixteen, could not be the delicate, morbid, exotic, hot-house creature, unable to walk or to do anything, who spent her days lying about on couches in the heavy atmosphere, redolent with strange scents and associations, of the yellow drawing-room. The movement of the light carriage, the cool draught, the very grind of the wheels upon the gravel, seemed to go to her head like wine.

" It is so long since I have done this sort of thing," she kept repeating ; " so long, so long. Oh, don't you think it delightful, going at this pace, with the idea that any moment the horse may come down and we two be killed ? " and she laughed her childish laugh, and turned her face, no longer pale, but flushed with the movement and the excitement, towards me.

The cart rolled on quicker and quicker, one gate after another swinging to behind us, as we flew up and down the little hills, across the pasture lands, through the little red-brick gabled villages, where the people came out to see us pass, past the rows of willows along the streams, and the dark-green compact hop-fields, with the blue and hazy tree-tops of the horizon getting bluer and more hazy as the yellow light began to graze the ground. At last we got to an open space, a high-lying piece of common-land, such as is rare in that ruthlessly utilised country of grazing-grounds and hop-gardens. Among the low hills of the Weald, it seemed quite preternaturally high up, giving a sense that its extent of flat heather and gorse, bound by distant firs, was really on the top of the world. The sun was setting just opposite, and its lights lay flat on the ground, staining it with the red and black of the heather, or rather turning it into the surface of a purple sea, canopied over by a bank of dark-purple clouds—the jet-like sparkle of the dry ling and gorse tipping the purple like sunlit wavelets. A cold wind swept in our faces.

" What is the name of this place ? " I asked. It was the only bit of impressive scenery that I had met in the neighbourhood of Okehurst.

" It is called Cotes Common," answered Mrs. Oke, who had slackened the pace of the horse, and let the reins hang loose about his neck. " It was here that Christopher Lovelock was killed. "

There was a moment's pause ; and then she proceeded, tickling the flies from the horse's ears with the end of her whip, and looking straight into the sunset, which now rolled, a deep purple stream, across the heath to our feet—

" Lovelock was riding home one summer evening from Apple-dore, when, as he had got half-way across Cotes Common, some-where about here—for I have always heard them mention the pond in the old gravel-pits as about the place—he saw two men riding towards him, in whom he presently recognised Nicholas Oke of Okehurst accompanied by a groom. Oke of Okehurst hailed him ; and Lovelock rode up to meet him. ' I am glad to have met you, Mr. Lovelock,' said Nicholas, ' because I have some important news for you ' ; and so saying, he brought his horse close to the one that Lovelock was riding, and suddenly turning round, fired off a pistol at his head. Lovelock had time to move, and the bullet, instead of striking him, went straight into the head of his horse, which fell beneath him. Lovelock, however, had fallen in such a way as to be able to extricate himself easily from his horse ; and drawing his sword, he rushed upon Oke, and seized his horse by the bridle. Oke quickly jumped off and drew his sword ; and in a minute, Lovelock, who was much the better swordsman of the two, was having the better of him. Lovelock had completely disarmed him, and got his sword at Oke's throat, cry-ing out to him that if he would ask forgiveness he should be spared for the sake of their old friendship, when the groom suddenly rode up from behind and shot Lovelock through the back. Lovelock fell, and Oke immediately tried to finish him with his sword, while the groom drew up and held the bridle of Oke's horse. At that moment the sunlight fell upon the groom's face, and Lovelock recognised Mrs. Oke. He cried out, ' Alice, Alice ! it is you who have murdered me ! ' and died. Then Nicholas Oke sprang into his saddle and rode off with his wife, leaving Lovelock dead by the side of his fallen horse. Nicholas Oke had taken the precaution of removing Lovelock's purse and throwing it into the pond, so the murder was put down to certain highwaymen who were about in that part of the country. Alice Oke died many years afterwards, quite an old woman, in the reign of Charles II ; but Nicholas did not live very long, and shortly before his death got into a very strange condition, always brooding, and sometimes threatening to kill his wife. They say that in one of these fits, just shortly before his death, he told the whole story of the murder, and made a prophecy that when the head of his house and master of Okehurst should marry another Alice Oke, descended from himself and his wife, there should be an end of the Okes of Okehurst. You see, it seems to be coming true. We have no children, and I don't suppose we shall ever have any. I, at least, have never wished for them."

Mrs. Oke paused, and turned her face towards me with the absent smile in her thin cheeks : her eyes no longer had that distant look ; they were strangely eager and fixed. I did not know what to answer ; this woman positively frightened me. We remained for a moment in that same place, with the sunlight dying away in crimson ripples on the heather, gilding the yellow banks, the black waters of the pond, surrounded by thin rushes, and the yellow gravel-pits ; while the wind blew in our faces and bent the ragged warped bluish tops of the firs. Then Mrs. Oke touched the horse, and off we went at a furious pace. We did not exchange a single word, I think, on the way home. Mrs. Oke sat with her eyes fixed on the reins, breaking the silence now and then only by a word to the horse, urging him to an even more furious pace. The people we met along the roads must have thought that the horse was running away, unless they noticed Mrs. Oke's calm manner and the look of excited enjoyment in her face. To me it seemed that I was in the hands of a mad-woman, and I quietly prepared myself for being upset or dashed against a cart. It had turned cold, and the draught was icy in our faces when we got within sight of the red gables and high chimney-stacks of Okehurst. Mr. Oke was standing before the door. On our approach I saw a look of relieved suspense, of keen pleasure come into his face.

He lifted his wife out of the cart in his strong arms with a kind of chivalrous tenderness.

" I am so glad to have you back, darling," he exclaimed—" so glad ! I was delighted to hear you had gone out with the cart, but as you have not driven for so long, I was beginning to be frightfully anxious, dearest. Where have you been all this time ? "

Mrs. Oke had quickly extricated herself from her husband, who had remained holding her, as one might hold a delicate child who has been causing anxiety. The gentleness and affection of the poor fellow had evidently not touched her—she seemed almost to recoil from it.

" I have taken him to Cotes Common," she said, with that perverse look which I had noticed before, as she pulled off her driving-gloves. " It is such a splendid old place."

Mr. Oke flushed as if he had bitten upon a sore tooth, and the double gash painted itself scarlet between his eyebrows.

Outside, the mists were beginning to rise, veiling the park-land dotted with big black oaks, and from which, in the watery moon-light, rose on all sides the eerie little cry of the lambs separated from their mothers. It was damp and cold, and I shivered.

VII

The next day Okehurst was full of people, and Mrs. Oke, to my amazement, was doing the honours of it as if a house full of commonplace, noisy young creatures, bent upon flirting and tennis, were her usual idea of felicity.

The afternoon of the third day—they had come for an electioneering ball, and stayed three nights—the weather changed ; it turned suddenly very cold and began to pour. Every one was sent indoors, and there was a general gloom suddenly over the company. Mrs. Oke seemed to have got sick of her guests, and was listlessly lying back on a couch, paying not the slighest attention to the chattering and piano-strumming in the room, when one of the guests suddenly proposed that they should play charades. He was a distant cousin of the Okes, a sort of fashionable artistic Bohemian, swelled out to intolerable conceit by the amateur-actor vogue of a season.

" It would be lovely in this marvellous old place," he cried, " just to dress up, and parade about, and feel as if we belonged to the past. I have heard you have a marvellous collection of old costumes, more or less ever since the days of Noah, somewhere, Cousin Bill."

The whole party exclaimed in joy at this proposal. William Oke looked puzzled for a moment, and glanced at his wife, who continued to lie listless on her sofa.

" There is a press full of clothes belonging to the family," he answered dubiously, apparently overwhelmed by the desire to please his guests ; " but—but—I don't know whether it's quite respectful to dress up in the clothes of dead people."

" Oh, fiddlestick ! " cried the cousin. " What do the dead people know about it ? Besides," he added, with mock seriousness, " I assure you we shall behave in the most reverent way and feel quite solemn about it all, if only you will give us the key, old man."

Again Mr. Oke looked towards his wife, and again met only her vague, absent glance.

" Very well," he said, and led his guests upstairs.

An hour later the house was filled with the strangest crew and the strangest noises. I had entered, to a certain extent, into William Oke's feeling of unwillingness to let his ancestors' clothes and personality be taken in vain ; but when the masquerade was complete, I must say that the effect was quite magnificent. A dozen youngish men and women—those who were staying in the house and some neighbours who had come for lawn-tennis and dinner— were rigged out, under the direction of the theatrical cousin, in the contents of that oaken press : and I have never seen a more beautiful sight than the panelled corridors, the carved and escutcheoned staircase, the dim drawing-rooms with their faded tapestries, the great hall with its vaulted and ribbed ceiling, dotted about with groups or single figures that seemed to have come straight from the past. Even William Oke, who, besides myself and a few elderly people, was the only man not masqueraded, seemed delighted and fired by the sight. A certain schoolboy character suddenly came out in him ; and finding that there was no costume left for him, he rushed upstairs and presently returned in the uniform he had worn before his marriage. I thought I had really never seen so magnificent a specimen of the handsome Englishman ; he looked, despite all the modern associations of his costume, more genuinely old-world than all the rest, a knight for the Black Prince or Sidney, with his admirably regular features and beautiful fair hair and complexion. After a minute, even the elderly people had got costumes of some sort—dominoes arranged at the moment, and hoods and all manner of disguises made out of pieces of old embroidery and Oriental stuffs and furs ; and very soon this rabble of masquers had become, so to speak, completely drunk with its own amusement—with the childishness, and, if I may say so, the barbarism, the vulgarity underlying the majority even of well-bred English men and women—Mr. Oke himself doing the mountebank like a schoolboy at Christmas.

" Where is Mrs. Oke ? Where is Alice ? " some one suddenly asked.

Mrs. Oke had vanished. I could fully understand that to this eccentric being, with her fantastic, imaginative, morbid passion for the past, such a carnival as this must be positively revolting ; and, absolutely indifferent as she was to giving offence, I could imagine how she would have retired, disgusted and outraged, to dream her strange day-dreams in the yellow room.

But a moment later, as we were all noisily preparing to go in to dinner, the door opened and a strange figure entered, stranger than any of these others who were profaning the clothes of the dead : a boy, slight and tall, in a brown riding-coat, leathern belt, and big buff boots, a little grey cloak over one shoulder, a large grey hat slouched over the eyes, a dagger and pistol at the waist. It was Mrs. Oke, her eyes preternaturally bright, and her whole face lit up with a bold, perverse smile.

Every one exclaimed, and stood aside. Then there was a moment's silence, broken by faint applause. Even to a crew of noisy boys and girls playing the fool in the garments of men and women long dead and buried, there is something questionable in the sudden appearance of a young married woman, the mistress of the house, in a riding-coat and jack-boots ; and Mrs. Oke's expression did not make the jest seem any the less questionable.

"What is that costume ? " asked the theatrical cousin, who, after a second, had come to the conclusion, that Mrs. Oke was merely a woman of marvellous talent whom he must try and secure for his amateur troop next season.

" It is the dress in which an ancestress of ours, my namesake Alice Oke, used to go out riding with her husband in the days of Charles I," she answered, and took her seat at the head of the table. Involuntarily my eyes sought those of Oke of Okehurst. He, who blushed as easily as a girl of sixteen, was now as white as ashes, and I noticed that he pressed his hand almost convulsively to his mouth.

" Don't you recognise my dress, William ? " asked Mrs. Oke, fixing her eyes upon him with a cruel smile.

He did not answer, and there was a moment's silence, which the theatrical cousin had the happy thought of breaking by jumping upon his seat and emptying off his glass with the exclamation—

" To the health of the two Alice Okes, of the past and the present ! "

Mrs. Oke nodded, and with an expression I had never seen in her face before, answered in a loud and aggressive tone—

" To the health of the poet, Mr. Christopher Lovelock, if his ghost be honouring this house with its presence ! "

I felt suddenly as if I were in a madhouse. Across the table, in the midst of this room full of noisy wretches, tricked out red, blue, purple, and parti-coloured, as men and women of the sixteenth, seventeenth, and eighteenth centuries, as improvised Turks and Eskimos, and dominoes, and clowns, with faces painted and corked and floured over, I seemed to see that sanguine sunset, washing like a sea of blood over the heather, to where, by the black pond and the wind-warped firs, there lay the body of Christopher Love-lock, with his dead horse near him, the yellow gravel and lilac ling soaked crimson all around ; and above emerged, as out of the red-ness, the pale blond head covered with the grey hat, the absent eyes, and strange smile of Mrs. Oke. It seemed to me horrible, vulgar, abominable, as if I had got inside a madhouse.

VIII

From that moment I noticed a change in William Oke ; or rather, a change that had probably been coming on for some time got to the stage of being noticeable.

I don't know whether he had any words with his wife about her masquerade of that unlucky evening. On the whole I decidedly think not. Oke was with every one a diffident and reserved man, and most of all so with his wife ; besides, I can fancy that he would experience a positive impossibility of putting into words any strong feeling of disapprobation towards her, that his disgust would necessarily be silent. But be this as it may, I perceived very soon that the relations between my host and hostess had become exceedingly strained. Mrs. Oke, indeed, had never paid much at-tention to her husband, and seemed merely a trifle more indifferent to his presence than she had been before. But Oke himself, al-though he affected to address her at meals from a desire to con-ceal his feeling, and a fear of making the position disagreeable to me, very clearly could scarcely bear to speak to or even see his wife. The poor fellow's honest soul was quite brimful of pain, which he was determined not to allow to overflow, and which seemed to filter into his whole nature and poison it. This woman had shocked and pained him more than was possible to say, and yet it was evident that he could neither cease loving her nor com-mence comprehending her real nature. I sometimes felt, as we took our long walks through the monotonous country, across the oak-dotted grazing-grounds, and by the brink of the dull-green, serried hop-rows, talking at rare intervals about the value of the crops, the drainage of the estate, the village schools, the Primrose League, and the iniquities of Mr. Gladstone, while Oke of Oke-hurst carefully cut down every tall thistle that caught his eye— I sometimes felt, I say, an intense and impotent desire to enlighten this man about his wife's character. I seemed to understand it so well, and to understand it well seemed to imply such a comfort-able acquiescence ; and it seemed so unfair that just he should be condemned to puzzle for ever over this enigma, and wear out his soul trying to comprehend what now seemed so plain to me. But how would it ever be possible to get this serious, conscientious, slow-brained representative of English simplicity and honesty and thoroughness to understand the mixture of self-engrossed vanity, of shallowness, of poetic vision, of love of morbid excitement, that walked this earth under the name of Alice Oke ?

So Oke of Okehurst was condemned never to understand ; but he was condemned also to suffer from his inability to do so. The poor fellow was constantly straining after an explanation of his wife's peculiarities ; and although the effort was probably uncon-scious, it caused him a great deal of pain. The gash—the maniac-frown, as my friend calls it—between his eyebrows, seemed to have grown a permanent feature of his face.

Mrs. Oke, on her side, was making the very worst of the situa-tion. Perhaps she resented her husband's tacit reproval of that masquerade night's freak, and determined to make him swallow more of the same stuff, for she clearly thought that one of William's peculiarities, and one for which she despised him, was that he could never be goaded into an outspoken expression of disappro-bation ; that from her he would swallow any amount of bitter-ness without complaining. At any rate she now adopted a perfect policy of teasing and shocking her husband about the murder of Lovelock. She was perpetually alluding to it in her conversa-tion, discussing in his presence what had or had not been the feel-ings of the various actors in the tragedy of 1626, and insisting upon her resemblance and almost identity with the original Alice Oke. Something had suggested to her eccentric mind that it would be delightful to perform in the garden at Okehurst, under the huge ilexes and elms, a little masque which she had discovered among Christopher Lovelock's works ; and she began to scour the country and enter into vast correspondence for the purpose of effectuating this scheme. Letters arrived every other day from the theatrical cousin, whose only objection was that Okehurst was too remote a locality for an entertainment in which he foresaw great glory to himself. And every now and then there would arrive some young gentleman or lady, whom Alice Oke had sent for to see whether they would do.

I saw very plainly that the performance would never take place, and that Mrs. Oke herself had no intention that it ever should. She was one of those creatures to whom realisation of a project is nothing, and who enjoy plan-making almost the more for know-ing that all will stop short at the plan. Meanwhile, this perpetual talk about the pastoral, about Lovelock, this continual attitudin-ising as the wife of Nicholas Oke, had the further attraction to Mrs. Oke of putting her husband into a condition of frightful though suppressed irritation, which she enjoyed with the enjoy-ment of a perverse child. You must not think that I looked on in-different, although I admit that this was a perfect treat to an amateur student of character like myself. I really did feel most sorry for poor Oke, and frequently quite indignant with his wife. I was several times on the point of begging her to have more con-sideration for him, even of suggesting that this kind of behaviour, particularly before a comparative stranger like me, was very poor taste. But there was something elusive about Mrs. Oke, which made it next to impossible to speak seriously with her ; and be-sides, I was by no means sure that any interference on my part would not merely animate her perversity.

One evening a curious incident took place. We had just sat down to dinner, the Okes, the theatrical cousin, who was down for a couple of days, and three or four neighbours. It was dusk, and the yellow light of the candles mingled charmingly with the grey-ness of the evening. Mrs. Oke was not well, and had been remark-ably quiet all day, more diaphanous, strange, and far-away than ever ; and her husband seemed to have felt a sudden return of tenderness, almost of compression, for this delicate, fragile crea-ture. We had been talking of quite indifferent matters, when I saw Mr. Oke suddenly turn very white, and look fixedly for a moment at the window opposite to his seat.

" Who's that fellow looking in at the window, and making signs to you, Alice ? Damn his impudence ! " he cried, and jumping up, ran to the window, opened it, and passed out into the twilight.

We all looked at each other in surprise ; some of the party remarked upon the carelessness of servants in letting nasty-looking
fellows hang about the kitchen, others told stories of tramps and
burglars. Mrs. Oke did not speak ; but I noticed the curious, dis-
tant-looking smile in her thin cheeks.

After a minute William Oke came in, his napkin in his hand.
He shut the window behind him and silently resumed his place.

" Well, who was it ? " we all asked.

" Nobody. I—I must have made a mistake," he answered, and
turned crimson, while he busily peeled a pear.

" It was probably Lovelock," remarked Mrs. Oke, just as she
might have said, " It was probably the gardener," but with that
faint smile of pleasure still in her face. Except the theatrical cousin,
who burst into a loud laugh, none of the company had ever heard
Lovelock's name, and, doubtless imagining him to be some
natural appanage of the Oke family, groom or farmer, said nothing, so the subject dropped.

From that evening onwards things began to assume a different
aspect. That incident was the beginning of a perfect system—a
system of what ? I scarcely know how to call it. A system of grim
jokes on the part of Mrs. Oke, of superstitious fancies on the part
of her husband—a system of mysterious persecutions on the part
of some less earthly tenant of Okehurst. Well, yes, after all, why
not ? We have all heard of ghosts, had uncles, cousins, grand-
mothers, nurses, who have seen them ; we are all a bit afraid of
them at the bottom of our soul ; so why shouldn't they be? I am
too sceptical to believe in the impossibility of anything, for my
part ! Besides, when a man has lived throughout a summer in the
same house with a woman like Mrs. Oke of Okehurst, he gets to
believe in the possibility of a great many improbable things, I
assure you, as a mere result of believing in her. And when you
come to think of it, why not ? That a weird creature, visibly not
of this earth, a reincarnation of a woman who murdered her lover
two centuries and a half ago, that such a creature should have the
power of attracting about her (being altogether superior to earthly
lovers) the man who loved her in that previous existence, whose
love for her was his death—what is there astonishing in that ?
Mrs. Oke herself, I feel quite persuaded, believed or half believed
it ; indeed she very seriously admitted the possibility thereof, one
day that I made the suggestion half in jest. At all events, it rather
pleased me to think so ; it fitted in so well with the woman's

whole personality ; it explained those hours and hours spent all alone in the yellow room, where the very air, with its scent of heady flowers and old perfumed stuffs, seemed redolent of ghosts. It explained that strange smile which was not for any of us, and yet was not merely for herself—that strange, far-off look in the wide pale eyes. I liked the idea, and I liked to tease, or rather to delight her with it. How should I know that the wretched husband would take such matters seriously ?

He became day by day more silent and perplexed-looking ; and, as a result, worked harder, and probably with less effect, at his land-improving schemes and political canvassing. It seemed to me that he was perpetually listening, watching, waiting for something to happen : a word spoken suddenly, the sharp opening of a door, would make him start, turn crimson, and almost tremble ; the mention of Lovelock brought a helpless look, half a convulsion, like that of a man overcome by great heat, into his face. And his wife, so far from taking any interest in his altered looks, went on irritating him more and more. Every time that the poor fellow gave one of those starts of his, or turned crimson at the sudden sound of a footstep, Mrs. Oke would ask him, with her contemptuous indifference, whether he had seen Lovelock. I soon began to perceive that my host was getting perfectly ill. He would sit at meals never saying a word, with his eyes fixed scrutinisingly on his wife, as if vainly trying to solve some dreadful mystery ; while his wife, ethereal, exquisite, went on talking in her listless way about the masque, about Lovelock, always about Lovelock. During our walks and rides, which we continued pretty regularly, he would start whenever in the roads or lanes surrounding Okehurst, or in its grounds, we perceived a figure in the distance. I have seen him tremble at what, on nearer approach, I could scarcely restrain my laughter on discovering to be some well-known farmer or neighbour or servant. Once, as we were returning home at dusk, he suddenly caught my arm and pointed across the oak-dotted pastures in the direction of the garden, then started off almost at a run, with his dog behind him, as if in pursuit of some intruder.

" Who was it ? " I asked. And Mr. Oke merely shook his head mournfully. Sometimes in the early autumn twilights, when the white mists rose from the park-land, and the rooks formed long black lines on the palings, I almost fancied I saw him start at the very trees and bushes, the outlines of the distant oast-houses, with their conical roofs and projecting vanes, like gibing fingers in the half light.

" Your husband is ill," I once ventured to remark to Mrs. Oke, as she sat for the hundred-and-thirtieth of my preparatory sketches (I somehow could never get beyond preparatory sketches with her). She raised her beautiful, wide, pale eyes, making as she did so that exquisite curve of shoulders and neck and delicate pale head that I so vainly longed to reproduce.

" I don't see it," she answered quietly. " If he is, why doesn't he go to town and see the doctor ? It's merely one of his glum fits."

" You should not tease him about Lovelock," I added, very seriously. " He will get to believe in him."

" Why not ? If he sees him, why he sees him. He would not be the only person that has done so " ; and she smiled faintly and half perversely, as her eyes sought that usual distant indefinable something.

But Oke got worse. He was growing perfectly unstrung, like a hysterical woman. One evening that we were sitting alone in the smoking-room, he began unexpectedly a rambling discourse about his wife ; how he had first known her when they were children, and they had gone to the same dancing-school near Port-land Place ; how her mother, his aunt-in-law, had brought her for Christmas to Okehurst while he was on his holidays ; how finally, thirteen years ago, when he was twenty-three and she was eigh-teen, they had been married ; how terribly he had suffered when they had been disappointed of their baby, and she had nearly died of the illness.

" I did not mind about the child, you know," he said in an ex-cited voice ; " although there will be an end of us now, and Okehurst will go to the Curtises. I minded only about Alice." It was next to inconceivable that this poor excited creature, speaking almost with tears in his voice and in his eyes, was the quiet, well-got-up, irreproachable young ex-Guardsman who had walked into my studio a couple of months before.

Oke was silent for a moment, looking fixedly at the rug at his feet, when he suddenly burst out in a scarce audible voice—

" If you knew how I cared for Alice—how I still care for her. I could kiss the ground she walks upon. I would give anything—my life any day—if only she would look for two minutes as if she liked me a little—as if she didn't utterly despise me " ; and the poor fellow burst into a hysterical laugh, which was almost a sob. Then he suddenly began to laugh outright, exclaiming, with a sort of vulgarity of intonation which was extremely foreign to him—

" Damn it, old fellow, this *is* a queer world we live in ! " and rang for more brandy and soda, which he was beginning, I noticed, to take pretty freely now, although he had been almost a blue-ribbon man—as much so as is possible for a hospitable country gentleman—when I first arrived.

I X

It became clear to me now that, incredible as it might seem, the thing that ailed William Oke was jealousy. He was simply madly in love with his wife, and madly jealous of her. Jealous—but of whom ? He himself would probably have been quite unable to say. In the first place—to clear off any possible suspicion—certainly not of me. Besides the fact that Mrs. Oke took only just a very little more interest in me than in the butler or the upper-housemaid, I think that Oke himself was the sort of man whose imagination would recoil from realising any definite object of jealousy, even though jealousy might be killing him inch by inch. It remained a vague, permeating, continuous feeling—the feeling that he loved her, and she did not care a jackstraw about him, and that everything with which she came into contact was receiving some of that notice which was refused to him—every person, or thing, or tree, or stone : it was the recognition of that strange far-off look in Mrs. Oke's eyes, of that strange absent smile on Mrs. Oke's lips—eyes and lips that had no look and no smile for him.

Gradually his nervousness, his watchfulness, suspiciousness, tendency to start, took a definite shape. Mr. Oke was for ever alluding to steps or voices he had heard, to figures he had seen sneaking round the house. The sudden bark of one of the dogs would make him jump up. He cleaned and loaded very carefully all the guns and revolvers in his study, and even some of the old fowling-pieces and holster-pistols in the hall. The servants and tenants thought that Oke of Okehurst had been seized with a terror of tramps and burglars. Mrs. Oke smiled contemptuously at all these doings.

" My dear William," she said one day, " the persons who worry you have just as good a right to walk up and down the passages and staircase, and to hang about the house, as you or I. They were there, in all probability, long before either of us was born, and are greatly amused by your preposterous notions of privacy."

Mr. Oke laughed angrily. " I suppose you will tell me it is Lovelock—your eternal Lovelock—whose steps I hear on the gravel every night. I suppose he has as good a right to be here as you or I." And he strode out of the room.

" Lovelock—Lovelock ! Why will she always go on like that about Lovelock ? " Mr. Oke asked me that evening, suddenly staring me in the face.

I merely laughed.

" It's only because she has that play of his on the brain," I answered : " and because she thinks you superstitious, and likes to tease you."

" I don't understand," sighed Oke.

How could he ? And if I had tried to make him do so, he would merely have thought I was insulting his wife, and have perhaps kicked me out of the room. So I made no attempt to explain psychological problems to him, and he asked me no more questions until once—— But I must first mention a curious incident that happened.

The incident was simply this. Returning one afternoon from our usual walk, Mr. Oke suddenly asked the servant whether any one had come. The answer was in the negative ; but Oke did not seem satisfied. We had hardly sat down to dinner when he turned to his wife and asked, in a strange voice which I scarcely recognised as his own, who had called that afternoon.

" No one," answered Mrs. Oke ; " at least to the best of my knowledge."

William Oke looked at her fixedly.

" No one ? " he repeated, in a scrutinising tone ; " no one Alice ? "

Mrs. Oke shook her head. " No one," she replied.

There was a pause.

" Who was it, then, that was walking with you near the pond, about five o'clock ? " asked Oke slowly.

His wife lifted her eyes straight to his and answered contemptuously—

" No one was walking with me near the pond, at five o'clock or any other hour."

Mr. Oke turned purple, and made a curious hoarse noise like a man choking.

" I—I thought I saw you walking with a man this afternoon, Alice," he brought out with an effort ; adding, for the sake of appearances before me, " I thought it might have been the curate come with that report for me."

Mrs. Oke smiled.

" I can only repeat that no living creature has been near me this afternoon," she said slowly. " If you saw any one with me, it it must have been Lovelock, for there certainly was no one else."

And she gave a little sigh, like a person trying to reproduce in her mind some delightful but too evanescent impression.

I looked at my host ; from crimson his face had turned perfectly livid, and he breathed as if some one were squeezing his windpipe.

No more was said about the matter. I vaguely felt that a great danger was threatening. To Oke or to Mrs. Oke ? I could not tell which ; but I was aware of an imperious inner call to avert some dreadful evil, to exert myself, to explain, to interpose. I determined to speak to Oke the following day, for I trusted him to give me a quiet hearing, and I did not trust Mrs. Oke. That woman would slip through my fingers like a snake if I attempted to grasp her elusive character.

I asked Oke whether he would take a walk with me the next afternoon, and he accepted to do so with a curious eagerness. We started about three o'clock. It was a stormy, chilly afternoon, with great balls of white clouds rolling rapidly in the cold blue sky, and occasional lurid gleams of sunlight, broad and yellow, which made the black ridge of the storm, gathered on the horizon, look blue-black like ink.

We walked quickly across the sere and sodden grass of the park, and on to the highroad that led over the low hills, I don't know why, in the direction of Cotes Common. Both of us were silent, for both of us had something to say, and did not know how to begin. For my part, I recognised the impossibility of starting the subject : an uncalled-for interference from me would merely indispose Mr. Oke, and make him doubly dense of comprehension. So, if Oke had something to say, which he evidently had, it was better to wait for him.

Oke, however, broke the silence only by pointing out to me the condition of the hops, as we passed one of his many hop-gardens. " It will be a poor year," he said, stopping short and looking intently before him—" no hops at all. No hops this autumn."

I looked at him. It was clear that he had no notion what he was saying. The dark-green bines were covered with fruit ; and only yesterday he himself had informed me that he had not seen such a profusion of hops for many years.

I did not answer, and we walked on. A cart met us in a dip of the road, and the carter touched his hat and greeted Mr. Oke. But Oke took no heed ; he did not seem to be aware of the man's presence.

The clouds were collecting all round ; black domes, among which coursed the round grey masses of fleecy stuff.

" I think we shall be caught in a tremendous storm," I said ; " hadn't we better be turning ? " He nodded, and turned sharp round.

The sunlight lay in yellow patches under the oaks of the pasture-lands, and burnished the green hedges. The air was heavy and yet cold, and everything seemed preparing for a great storm. The rooks whirled in black clouds round the trees and the conical red caps of the oast-houses which give that country the look of being studded with turreted castles ; then they descended—a black line —upon the fields, with what seemed an unearthly loudness of caw. And all round there arose a shrill quavering bleating of lambs and calling of sheep, while the wind began to catch the top-most branches of the trees.

Suddenly Mr. Oke broke the silence.

" I don't know you very well," he began hurriedly, and with-out turning his face towards me ; " but I think you are honest, and you have seen a good deal of the world—much more than I. I want you to tell me—but truly, please—what do you think a man should do if "——and he stopped for some minutes.

" Imagine," he went on quickly, " that a man cares a great deal—a very great deal for his wife, and that he find out that she —well, that—that she is deceiving him. No—don't misunderstand me ; I mean—that she is constantly surrounded by some one else and will not admit it—some one whom she hides away. Do you understand ? Perhaps she does not know all the risk she is running, you know, but she will not draw back—she will not avow it to her husband——"

" My dear Oke," I interrupted, attempting to take the matter lightly, " these are questions that can't be solved in the abstract, or by people to whom the thing has not happened. And it cer-tainly has not happened to you or me."

Oke took no notice of my interruption. " You see," he went on,

" the man doesn't expect his wife to care much about him. It's not that ; he isn't merely jealous, you know. But he feels that she is on the brink of dishonouring herself—because I don't think a woman can really dishonour her husband ; dishonour is in our own hands, and depends only on our own acts. He ought to save her, do you see ? He must, must save her, in one way or another. But if she will not listen to him, what can he do ? Must he seek out the other one, and try and get him out of the way ? You see it's all the fault of the other—not hers, not hers. If only she would trust in her husband, she would be safe. But that other one won't let her."

" Look here, Oke," I said boldly, but feeling rather frightened ; " I know quite well what you are talking about. And I see you don't understand the matter in the very least. I do. I have watched you and watched Mrs. Oke these six weeks, and I see what is the matter. Will you listen to me ? "

And taking his arm, I tried to explain to him my view of the situation—that his wife was merely eccentric, and a little theatrical and imaginative, and that she took a pleasure in teasing him. That he, on the other hand, was letting himself get into a morbid state ; that he was ill, and ought to see a good doctor. I even offered to take him to town with me.

I poured out volumes of psychological explanations. I dissected Mrs. Oke's character twenty times over, and tried to show him that there was absolutely nothing at the bottom of his suspicions beyond an imaginative *pose* and a garden-play on the brain. I adduced twenty instances, mostly invented for the nonce, of ladies of my acquaintance who had suffered from similar fads. I pointed out to him that his wife ought to have an outlet for her imaginative and theatrical over-energy. I advised him to take her to London and plunge her into some set where every one should be more or less in a similar condition. I laughed at the notion of there being any hidden individual about the house. I explained to Oke that he was suffering from delusions, and called upon so con- scientious and religious a man to take every step to rid himself of them, adding innumerable examples of people who had cured themselves of seeing visions and of brooding over morbid fancies. I struggled and wrestled, like Jacob with the angel, and I really hoped I had made some impression. At first, indeed, I felt that not one of my words went into the man's brain—that, though silent, he was not listening. It seemed almost hopeless to present my views in such a light that he could grasp them. I felt as if I were expounding and arguing at a rock. But when I got on to the tack of his duty towards his wife and himself, and appealed to his moral and religious notions, I felt that I was making an impression.

"I daresay you are right," he said, taking my hand as we came in sight of the red gables of Okehurst, and speaking in a weak, tired, humble voice. "I don't understand you quite, but I am sure what you say is true. I daresay it is all that I'm seedy. I feel sometimes as if I were mad, and just fit to be locked up. But don't think I don't struggle against it. I do, I do continually, only sometimes it seems too strong for me. I pray God night and morning to give me the strength to overcome my suspicions, or to remove these dreadful thoughts from me. God knows, I know what a wretched creature I am, and how unfit to take care of that poor girl."

And Oke again pressed my hand. As we entered the garden, he turned to me once more.

"I am very, very grateful to you," he said, "and, indeed, I will do my best to try and be stronger. If only," he added, with a sigh, "if only Alice would give me a moment's breathing-time, and not go on day after day mocking me with her Lovelock."

X

I had begun Mrs. Oke's portrait, and she was giving me a sitting. She was unusually quiet that morning ; but, it seemed to me, with the quietness of a woman who is expecting something, and she gave me the impression of being extremely happy. She had been reading, at my suggestion, the "Vita Nuova," which she did not know before, and the conversation came to roll upon that, and upon the question whether love so abstract and so enduring was a possibility. Such a discussion, which might have savoured of flirtation in the case of almost any other young and beautiful woman, became in the case of Mrs. Oke something quite different ; it seemed distant, intangible, not of this earth, like her smile and the look in her eyes.

"Such love as that," she said, looking into the far distance of the oak-dotted park-land, "is very rare, but it can exist. It becomes a person's whole existence, his whole soul ; and it can survive the death, not merely of the beloved, but of the lover. It is unextinguishable, and goes on in the spiritual world until it meet a reincarnation of the beloved ; and when this happens, it jets out and draws to it all that may remain of that lover's soul, and takes shape and surrounds the beloved one once more."

Mrs. Oke was speaking slowly, almost to herself, and I had never, I think, seen her look so strange and so beautiful, the stiff white dress bringing out but the more the exotic exquisiteness and incorporealness of her person.

I did not know what to answer, so I said half in jest——

" I fear you have been reading too much Buddhist literature, Mrs. Oke. There is something dreadfully esoteric in all you say."

She smiled contemptuously.

" I know people can't understand such matters," she replied, and was silent for some time. But, through her quietness and silence, I felt, as it were, the throb of a strange excitement in this woman, almost as if I had been holding her pulse.

Still, I was in hopes that things might be beginning to go better in consequence of my interference. Mrs. Oke had scarcely once alluded to Lovelock in the last two or three days ; and Oke had been much more cheerful and natural since our conversation. He no longer seemed so worried ; and once or twice I had caught in him a look of great gentleness and loving-kindness, almost of pity, as towards some young and very frail thing, as he sat opposite his wife.

But the end had come. After that sitting Mrs. Oke had complained of fatigue and retired to her room, and Oke had driven off on some business to the nearest town. I felt all alone in the big house, and after having worked a little at a sketch I was making in the park, I amused myself rambling about the house.

It was a warm, enervating, autumn afternoon ; the kind of weather that brings the perfume out of everything, the damp ground and fallen leaves, the flowers in the jars, the old woodwork and stuffs ; that seems to bring on to the surface of one's consciousness all manner of vague recollections and expectations, a something half pleasurable, half painful, that makes it impossible to do or to think. I was the prey of this particular, not at all unpleasurable, restlessness. I wandered up and down the corridors, stopping to look at the pictures, which I knew already in every detail, to follow the pattern of the carvings and old stuffs, to stare at the autumn flowers, arranged in magnificent masses of colour in the big china bowls and jars. I took up one book after another and threw it aside ; then I sat down to the piano and began to play irrelevant fragments. I felt quite alone, although I had heard the grind of the wheels on the gravel, which meant that my host had returned. I was lazily turning over a book of verses—I remember it perfectly well, it was Morris's " Love is Enough "—in a corner of the drawing-room, when the door suddenly opened and William Oke showed himself. He did not enter, but beckoned to me to come out to him. There was something in his face that made me start up and follow him at once. He was extremely quiet, even stiff, not a muscle of his face moving, but very pale.

" I have something to show you," he said, leading me through the vaulted hall, hung round with ancestral pictures, into the gravelled space that looked like a filled-up moat, where stood the big blasted oak, with its twisted, pointing branches. I followed him on to the lawn, or rather the piece of park-land that ran up to the house. We walked quickly, he in front, without exchanging a word. Suddenly he stopped, just where there jutted out the bow-window of the yellow drawing-room, and I felt Oke's hand tight upon my arm.

" I have brought you here to see something," he whispered hoarsely ; and he led me to the window.

I looked in. The room, compared with the outdoor, was rather dark ; but against the yellow wall I saw Mrs. Oke sitting alone on a couch in her white dress, her head slightly thrown back, a large red rose in her hand.

" Do you believe now ? " whispered Oke's voice hot at my ear. " Do you believe now ? Was it all my fancy ? But I will have him this time. I have locked the door inside, and, by God ! he shan't escape."

The words were not out of Oke's mouth. I felt myself struggling with him silently outside that window. But he broke loose, pulled open the window, and leapt into the room, and I after him. As I crossed the threshold, something flashed in my eyes ; there was a loud report, a sharp cry, and the thud of a body on the ground.

Oke was standing in the middle of the room, with a faint smoke about him ; and at his feet, sunk down from the sofa, with her blond head resting on its seat, lay Mrs. Oke, a pool of red forming in her white dress. Her mouth was convulsed, as if in that automatic shriek, but her wide-open white eyes seemed to smile vaguely and distantly.

I know nothing of time. It all seemed to be one second, but a second that lasted hours. Oke stared, then turned round and laughed.

" The damned rascal has given me the slip again ! " he cried ; and quickly unlocking the door, rushed out of the house with dreadful cries.

That is the end of the story. Oke tried to shoot himself that evening, but merely fractured his jaw, and died a few days later, raving. There were all sorts of legal inquiries, through which I went as through a dream ; and whence it resulted that Mr. Oke had killed his wife in a fit of momentary madness. That was the end of Alice Oke. By the way, her maid brought me a locket which was found round her neck, all stained with blood. It contained some very dark auburn hair, not at all the colour of William Oke's. I am quite sure it was Lovelock's.

Miss Braddon

EVELINE'S VISITANT
from RALPH THE BAILIFF

Ward & Lock, 1862

It was at a masked ball at the Palais Royal that my fatal quarrel with my first cousin André de Brissac began. The quarrel was about a woman. The women who followed the footsteps of Philip of Orleans were the causes of many such disputes ; and there was scarcely one fair head in all that glittering throng which, to a man versed in social histories and mysteries, might not have seemed bedabbled with blood.

I shall not record the name of her for love of whom André de Brissac and I crossed one of the bridges, in the dim August dawn on our way to the waste ground beyond the church of Saint-Germain des Prés.

There were many beautiful vipers in those days, and she was one of them. I can feel the chill breath of that August morning blowing in my face, as I sit in my dismal chamber at my château of Puy Verdun to-night, alone in the stillness, writing the strange story of my life. I can see the white mist rising from the river, the grim outline of the Châtelet, and the square towers of Notre Dame black against the pale-grey sky. Even more vividly can I recall André's fair young face, as he stood opposite to me with his two friends—scoundrels both, and alike eager for that unnatural fray. We were a strange group to be seen in a summer sunrise, all of us fresh from the heat and clamour of the Regent's saloons—André in a quaint hunting-dress copied from a family portrait at Puy Verdun, I costumed as one of Law's Mississippi Indians; the other men in like garish frippery, adorned with broideries and jewels that looked wan in the pale light of dawn.

Our quarrel had been a fierce one—a quarrel which could have but one result, and that the direst. I had struck him; and the welt raised by my open hand was crimson upon his fair womanish face as he stood opposite to me. The eastern sun shone on the face presently, and dyed the cruel mark with a deeper red; but the sting of my own wrongs was fresh, and I had not yet learned to despise myself for that brutal outrage.

To André de Brissac such an insult was most terrible. He was the favourite of Fortune, the favourite of women; and I was nothing,—a rough soldier who had done my country good service, but in the boudoir of a Parabère a mannerless boor.

We fought, and I wounded him mortally. Life had been very sweet for him; and I think that a frenzy of despair took possession of him when he felt the life-blood ebbing away. He beckoned me to him as he lay on the ground. I went, and knelt at his side.

" Forgive me, André ! " I murmured.

He took no more heed of my words than if that piteous entreaty had been the idle ripple of the river near at hand.

" Listen to me, Hector de Brissac," he said. " I am not one who believes that a man has done with earth because his eyes glaze and his jaw stiffens. They will bury me in the old vault at Puy Verdun; and you will be master of the château. Ah, I know how lightly they take things in these days, and how Dubois will laugh when he hears that Ça has been killed in a duel. They will bury me, and sing masses for my soul; but you and I have not finished our affair yet, my cousin. I will be with you when you least look to see me,—I, with this ugly scar upon the face that women have praised and loved. I will come to you when your life seems brightest. I will come between you and all that you hold fairest and dearest. My ghostly hand shall drop a poison in your cup of joy. My shadowy form shall shut the sunlight from your life. Men with such iron will as mine can do what they please, Hector de Brissac. It is my will to haunt you when I am dead."

All this in short broken sentences he whispered into my ear. I had need to bend my ear close to his dying lips ; but the iron will of André de Brissac was strong enough to do battle with Death, and I believe he said all he wished to say before his head fell back upon the velvet cloak they had spread beneath him, never to be lifted again.

As he lay there, you would have fancied him a fragile stripling, too fair and frail for the struggle called life ; but there are those who remember the brief manhood of André de Brissac, and who can bear witness to the terrible force of that proud nature.

I stood looking down at the young face with that foul mark upon it, and God knows I was sorry for what I had done.

Of those blasphemous threats which he had whispered in my ear I took no heed. I was a soldier, and a believer. There was nothing absolutely dreadful to me in the thought that I had killed this man. I had killed many men on the battlefield ; and this one had done me cruel wrong.

My friends would have had me cross the frontier to escape the consequences of my act ; but I was ready to face those consequences, and I remained in France. I kept aloof from the court, and received a hint that I had best confine myself to my own province. Many masses were chanted in the little chapel of Puy Verdun, for the soul of my dead cousin, and his coffin filled a niche in the vault of our ancestors.

His death had made me a rich man ; and the thought that it was so made my newly-acquired wealth very hateful to me. I lived a lonely existence in the old château, where I rarely held converse with any but the servants of the household, all of whom had served my cousin, and none of whom liked me.

It was a hard and bitter life. It galled me, when I rode through the village, to see the peasant-children shrink away from me. I have seen old women cross themselves stealthily as I passed them by. Strange reports had gone forth about me ; and there were those who whispered that I had given my soul to the Evil One as the price of my cousin's heritage. From my boyhood I had been dark of visage and stern of manner ; and hence, perhaps, no woman's love had ever been mine. I remembered my mother's face in all its changes of expression ; but I can remember no look of affection that ever shone on me. That other woman, beneath whose feet I laid my heart, was pleased to accept my homage, but she never loved me ; and the end was treachery.

I had grown hateful to myself, and had well-nigh begun to hate my fellow-creatures, when a feverish desire seized upon me, and I pined to be back in the press and throng of the busy world once again. I went back to Paris, where I kept myself aloof from the court, and where an angel took compassion upon me.

She was the daughter of an old comrade, a man whose merits had been neglected, whose achievements had been ignored, and who sulked in his shabby lodging like a rat in a hole, while all Paris went mad with the Scotch Financier, and gentlemen and lacqueys were trampling one another to death in the Rue Quin-campoix. The only child of this little cross-grained old captain of dragoons was an incarnate sunbeam, whose mortal name was Eveline Duchalet.

She loved me. The richest blessings of our lives are often those which cost us least. I wasted the best years of my youth in the worship of a wicked woman, who jilted and cheated me at last. I gave this meek angel but a few courteous words—a little fraternal tenderness—and lo, she loved me. The life which had been so dark and desolate grew bright beneath her influence ; and I went back to Puy Verdun with a fair young bride for my companion.

Ah, how sweet a change there was in my life and in my home ! The village children no longer shrank appalled as the dark horse-man rode by, the village crones no longer crossed themselves ; for a woman rode by his side—a woman whose charities had won the love of all those ignorant creatures, and whose companionship had transformed the gloomy lord of the château into a loving husband and a gentle master. The old retainers forgot the untimely fate of my cousin, and served me with cordial willingness, for love of their young mistress.

There are no words which can tell the pure and perfect happi-ness of that time. I felt like a traveller who had traversed the frozen seas of an arctic region, remote from human love or human companionship, to find himself on a sudden in the bosom of a verdant valley, in the sweet atmosphere of home. The change seemed too bright to be real ; and I strove in vain to put away from my mind the vague suspicion that my new life was but some fantastic dream.

So brief were those halcyon hours, that, looking back on them now, it is scarcely strange if I am still half inclined to fancy the first days of my married life could have been no more than a dream.

Neither in my days of gloom nor in my days of happiness had I been troubled by the recollection of André's blasphemous oath. The words which with his last breath he had whispered in my ear were vain and meaningless to me. He had vented his rage in those idle threats, as he might have vented it in idle execrations. That he will haunt the footsteps of his enemy after death is the one revenge which a dying man can promise himself ; and if men had power thus to avenge themselves, the earth would be peopled with phantoms.

I had lived for three years at Puy Verdun ; sitting alone in the solemn midnight by the hearth where he had sat, pacing the corridors that had echoed his footfall ; and in all that time my fancy had never so played me false as to shape the shadow of the dead. Is it strange, then, if I had forgotten André's horrible promise ?

There was no portrait of my cousin at Puy Verdun. It was the age of boudoir art, and a miniature set in the lid of a gold bon-bonnière, or hidden artfully in a massive bracelet, was more fashionable than a clumsy life-size image, fit only to hang on the gloomy walls of a provincial château rarely visited by its owner. My cousin's fair face had adorned more than one bonbonnière, and had been concealed in more than one bracelet ; but it was not among the faces that looked down from the panelled walls of Puy Verdun.

In the library I found a picture which awoke painful associa-tions. It was the portrait of a De Brissac, who had flourished in the time of Francis the First ; and it was from this picture that my cousin André had copied the quaint hunting-dress he wore at the Regent's ball. The library was a room in which I spent a good deal of my life ; and I ordered a curtain to be hung before this picture.

We had been married three months, when Eveline one day asked, " Who is the lord of the château nearest to this ? "

I looked with her in astonishment.

" My dearest," I answered, " do you not know that there is no other château within forty miles of Puy Verdun ? "

" Indeed ! " she said ; " that is strange."

I asked her why the fact seemed strange to her ; and after much entreaty I obtained from her the reason of her surprise.

In her walks about the park and woods during the last month, she had met a man who, by his dress and bearing, was obviously of noble rank. She had imagined that he occupied some château near at hand, and that his estate adjoined ours. I was at a loss to imagine who this stranger could be ; for my estate of Puy Verdun lay in the heart of a desolate region, and unless when some traveller's coach went lumbering and jingling through the village, one had little more chance of encountering a gentleman than of meeting a demigod.

" Have you seen this man often, Eveline ? " I asked.

She answered, in a tone which had a touch of sadness, " I see him every day."

" Where, dearest ? "

" Sometimes in the park, sometimes in the wood. You know the little cascade, Hector, where there is some old neglected rock-work that forms a kind of cavern. I have taken a fancy to that spot, and have spent many mornings there reading. Of late I have seen the stranger there every morning."

" He has never dared to address you ? "

" Never. I have looked up from my book, and have seen him standing at a little distance, watching me silently. I have continued reading ; and when I have raised my eyes again I have found him gone. He must approach and depart with a stealthy tread, for I never hear his footfall. Sometimes I have almost wished that he would speak to me. It is so terrible to see him standing silently there."

" He is some insolent peasant who seeks to frighten you."

My wife shook her head.

" He is no peasant," she answered. " It is not by his dress alone I judge, for that is strange to me. He has an air of nobility which it is impossible to mistake."

" Is he young or old ? "

" He is young and handsome."

I was much disturbed by the idea of this stranger's intrusion on my wife's solitude ; and I went straight to the village to inquire if any stranger had been seen there. I could hear of no one. I questioned the servants closely, but without result. Then I determined to accompany my wife in her walks, and to judge for myself of the rank of the stranger.

For a week I devoted all my mornings to rustic rambles with Eveline in the park and woods ; and in all that week we saw no one but an occasional peasant in *sabots*, or one of our own household returning from a neighbouring farm.

I was a man of studious habits, and those summer rambles disturbed the even current of my life. My wife perceived this, and entreated me to trouble myself no further.

" I will spend my mornings in the pleasaunce, Hector," she said ; " the stranger cannot intrude upon me there."

" I begin to think the stranger is only a phantasm of your own romantic brain," I replied, smiling at the earnest face lifted to mine. " A châtelaine who is always reading romances may well meet handsome cavaliers in the woodlands. I daresay I have Mdlle. Scuderi to thank for this noble stranger, and that he is only the great Cyrus in modern costume."

" Ah, that is the point which mystifies me, Hector," she said. " The stranger's costume is not modern. He looks as an old picture might look if it could descend from its frame."

Her words pained me, for they reminded me of that hidden picture in the library, and the quaint hunting costume of orange and purple, which André de Brissac wore at the Regent's ball.

After this my wife confined her walks to the pleasaunce ; and for many weeks I heard no more of the nameless stranger. I dismissed all thought of him from my mind, for a graver and heavier care had come upon me. My wife's health began to droop. The change in her was so gradual as to be almost imperceptible to those who watched her day by day. It was only when she put on a rich gala dress which she had not worn for months that I saw how wasted the form must be on which the embroidered bodice hung so loosely, and how wan and dim were the eyes which had once been brilliant as the jewels she wore in her hair.

I sent a messenger to Paris to summon one of the court physicians ; but I knew that many days must needs elapse before he could arrive at Puy Verdun.

In the interval I watched my wife with unutterable fear.

It was not her health only that had declined. The change was more painful to behold than any physical alteration. The bright and sunny spirit had vanished, and in the place of my joyous young bride I beheld a woman weighed down by rooted melancholy. In vain I sought to fathom the cause of my darling's sadness. She assured me that she had no reason for sorrow or discontent, and that if she seemed sad without a motive, I must forgive her sadness, and consider it as a misfortune rather than a fault.

I told her that the court physician would speedily find some cure for her despondency, which must needs arise from physical causes, since she had no real ground for sorrow. But although she said nothing, I could see she had no hope or belief in the healing powers of medicine.

One day, when I wished to beguile her from that pensive silence in which she was wont to sit an hour at a time, I told her, laughing, that she appeared to have forgotten her mysterious cavalier of the wood, and it seemed also as if he had forgotten her.

To my wonderment, her pale face became of a sudden crimson ; and from crimson changed to pale again in a breath.

" You have never seen him since you deserted your woodland grotto ? " I said.

She turned to me with a heart-rending look.

" Hector," she cried, " I see him every day ; and it is that which is killing me."

She burst into a passion of tears when she had said this. I took her in my arms as if she had been a frightened child, and tried to comfort her.

" My darling, this is madness," I said. " You know that no stranger can come to you in the pleasaunce. The moat is ten feet wide and always full of water, and the gates are kept locked day and night by old Massou. The châtelaine of a mediæval fortress need fear no intruder in her antique garden."

My wife shook her head sadly.

" I see him every day," she said.

On this I believed that my wife was mad. I shrank from questioning her more closely concerning her mysterious visitant. It would be ill, I thought, to give a form and substance to the shadow that tormented her by too close inquiry about its look and manner, its coming and going.

I took care to assure myself that no stranger to the household could by any possibility penetrate to the pleasaunce. Having done this, I was fain to await the coming of the physician.

He came at last. I revealed to him the conviction which was my misery. I told him that I believed my wife to be mad. He saw her—

spent an hour alone with her, and then came to me. To my unspeakable relief he assured me of her sanity.

" It is just possible that she may be affected by one delusion,"
he said ; " but she is so reasonable upon all other points, that I can
scarcely bring myself to believe her the subject of a monomania.
I am rather inclined to think that she really sees the person of
whom she speaks. She described him to me with a perfect minuteness. The descriptions of scenes or individuals given by patients
afflicted with monomania are always more or less disjointed ; but
your wife spoke to me as clearly and calmly as I am now speaking
to you. Are you sure there is no one who can approach her in that
garden where she walks ? "

" I am quite sure."

" Is there any kinsman of your steward, or hanger-on of your
household,—a young man with a fair womanish face, very pale
and rendered remarkable by a crimson scar, which looks like the
mark of a blow ? "

" My God ! " I cried, as the light broke in upon me all at once.
" And the dress—the strange old-fashioned dress ? "

" The man wears a hunting costume of purple and orange,"
answered the doctor.

I knew then that André de Brissac had kept his word, and that
in the hour when my life was brightest his shadow had come
between me and happiness.

I showed my wife the picture in the library, for I would fain
assure myself that there was some error in my fancy about my
cousin. She shook like a leaf when she beheld it, and clung to me
convulsively.

" This is witchcraft, Hector," she said. " The dress in that
picture is the dress of the man I see in the pleasaunce ; but the
face is not his."

Then she described to me the face of the stranger ; and it was
my cousin's face line for line—André de Brissac, whom she had
never seen in the flesh. Most vividly of all did she describe the
cruel mark upon his face, the trace of a fierce blow from an open
hand.

After this I carried my wife away from Puy Verdun. We
wandered far—through the southern provinces, and into the very
heart of Switzerland. I thought to distance the ghastly phantom,

and I fondly hoped that change of scene would bring peace to my wife.

It was not so. Go where we would, the ghost of André de Brissac followed us. To my eyes that fatal shadow never revealed itself. *That* would have been too poor a vengeance. It was my wife's innocent heart which André made the instrument of his revenge. The unholy presence destroyed her life. My constant companionship could not shield her from the horrible intruder. In vain did I watch her ; in vain did I strive to comfort her.

" He will not let me be at peace," she said ; " he comes between us, Hector. He is standing between us now. I can see his face with the red mark upon it plainer that I see yours."

One fair moonlight night, when we were together in a mountain village in the Tyrol, my wife cast herself at my feet, and told me she was the worst and vilest of women. " I have confessed all to my director," she said ; " from the first I have not hidden my sin from Heaven. But I feel that death is near me ; and before I die I would fain reveal my sin to you."

" What sin, my sweet one ? "

" When first the stranger came to me in the forest, his presence bewildered and distressed me, and I shrank from him as from something strange and terrible. He came again and again ; by and by I found myself thinking of him, and watching for his coming. His image haunted me perpetually ; I strove in vain to shut his face out of my mind. Then followed an interval in which I did not see him ; and, to my shame and anguish, I found that life seemed dreary and desolate without him. After that came the time in which he haunted the pleasaunce ; and—O, Hector, kill me if you will, for I deserve no mercy at your hands !—I grew in those days to count the hours that must elapse before his coming, to take no pleasure save in the sight of that pale face with the red brand upon it. He plucked all old familiar joys out of my heart, and left in it but one weird unholy pleasure—the delight of his presence. For a year I have lived but to see him. And now curse me, Hector ; for this is my sin. Whether it comes of the baseness of my own heart, or is the work of witchcraft, I know not ; but I know that I have striven against this wickedness in vain."

I took my wife to my breast, and forgave her. In sooth, what had I to forgive ? Was the fatality that overshadowed us any work of hers ? On the next night she died, with her hand in mine ; and at the very last she told me, sobbing and affrighted, that *he* was by her side.

————

E. Nesbit

JOHN CHARRINGTON'S WEDDING

from GRIM TALES

A. D. Innes, 1893

No one ever thought that May Forster would marry John Charrington ; but he thought differently, and things which John Charrington intended had a queer way of coming to pass. He asked her to marry him before he went up to Oxford. She laughed and refused him. He asked her again next time he came home. Again she laughed, tossed her dainty blonde head, and again refused. A third time he asked her ; she said it was becoming a confirmed bad habit, and laughed at him more than ever.

John was not the only man who wanted to marry her : she was the belle of our village *coterie*, and we were all in love with her more or less ; it was a sort of fashion, like heliotrope ties or Inverness capes. Therefore we were as much annoyed as surprised when John Charrington walked into our little local Club—we held it in a loft over the saddler's, I remember—and invited us all to his wedding.

" Your wedding ? "

" You don't mean it ? "

" Who's the happy fair ? When's it to be ? "

John Charrington filled his pipe and lighted it before he replied. Then he said :—

" I'm sorry to deprive you fellows of your only joke—but Miss Forster and I are to be married in September."

" You don't mean it ? "

" He's got the mitten again, and it's turned his head."

" No," I said, rising, " I see it's true. Lend me a pistol someone —or a first-class fare to the other end of Nowhere. Charrington has bewitched the only pretty girl in our twenty-mile radius. Was it mesmerism, or a love-potion, Jack ? "

" Neither, sir, but a gift you'll never have—perseverance—-and the best luck a man ever had in this world."

There was something in his voice that silenced me, and all chaff of the other fellows failed to draw him further.

The queer thing about it was that when we congratulated Miss Forster, she blushed and smiled and dimpled, for all the world as though she were in love with him, and had been in love with him all the time. Upon my word, I think she had. Women are strange creatures.

We were all asked to the wedding. In Brixham everyone who was anybody knew everybody else who was any one. My sisters were, I truly believe, more interested in the *trousseau* than the bride herself, and I was to be best man. The coming marriage was much canvassed at afternoon tea-tables, and at our little Club over the saddler's, and the question was always asked : " Does she care for him ? "

I used to ask that question myself in the early days of their engagement, but after a certain evening in August I never asked it again. I was coming home from the Club through the church-yard. Our church is on a thyme-grown hill, and the turf about it is so thick and soft that one's footsteps are noiseless.

I made no sound as I vaulted the low lichened wall, and threaded my way between the tombstones. It was at the same instant that I heard John Charrington's voice, and saw Her. May was sitting on a low flat gravestone, her face turned towards the full splendour of the western sun. Its expression ended, at once and for ever, any question of love for him ; it was trans-figured to a beauty I should not have believed possible, even to that beautiful little face.

John lay at her feet, and it was his voice that broke the stillness of the golden August evening.

" My dear, my dear, I believe I should come back from the dead if you wanted me ! "

I coughed at once to indicate my presence, and passed on into the shadow fully enlightened.

The wedding was to be early in September. Two days before I had to run up to town on business. The train was late, of course, for we are on the South-Eastern, and as I stood grumbling with my watch in my hand, whom should I see but John Charrington

and May Forster. They were walking up and down the unfre-
quented end of the platform, arm in arm, looking into each other's
eyes, careless of the sympathetic interest of the porters.

Of course I knew better than to hesitate a moment before
burying myself in the booking-office, and it was not till the train
drew up at the platform, that I obtrusively passed the pair with
my Gladstone, and took the corner in a first-class smoking-
carriage. I did this with as good an air of not seeing them as I
could assume. I pride myself on my discretion, but if John were
travelling alone I wanted his company. I had it.

"Hullo, old man," came his cheery voice as he swung his bag
into my carriage ; " here's luck ; I was expecting a dull journey ! "

" Where are you off to ? " I asked, discretion still bidding me
turn my eyes away, though I saw, without looking, that hers were
red-rimmed.

" To old Branbridge's," he answered, shutting the door and
leaning out for a last word with his sweetheart.

" Oh, I wish you wouldn't go, John," she was saying in a low,
earnest voice. " I feel certain something will happen."

" Do you think I should let anything happen to keep me, and
the day after to-morrow our wedding-day ? "

" Don't go," she answered, with a pleading intensity which
would have sent my Gladstone on to the platform and me after
it. But she wasn't speaking to me. John Charrington was made
differently ; he rarely changed his opinions, never his resolutions.

He only stroked the little ungloved hands that lay on the
carriage door.

" I must, May. The old boy's been awfully good to me, and
now he's dying I must go and see him, but I shall come home in
time for——" the rest of the parting was lost in a whisper and in
the rattling lurch of the starting train.

" You're sure to come ? " she spoke as the train moved.

" Nothing shall keep me," he answered ; and we steamed out.
After he had seen the last of the little figure on the platform he
leaned back in his corner and kept silence for a minute.

When he spoke it was to explain to me that his godfather,
whose heir he was, lay dying at Peasmarsh Place, some fifty miles
away, and had sent for John, and John had felt bound to go.

" I shall be surely back to-morrow," he said, " or, if not, the
day after, in heaps of time. Thank Heaven, one hasn't to get up
in the middle of the night to get married nowadays ! "

" And suppose Mr. Branbridge dies ? "

" Alive or dead I mean to be married on Thursday ! " John answered, lighting a cigar and unfolding *The Times*.

At Peasmarsh station we said " good-bye," and he got out, and I saw him ride off ; I went on to London, where I stayed the night.

When I got home the next afternoon, a very wet one, by the way, my sister greeted me with :

" Where's Mr. Charrington ? "

" Goodness knows," I answered testily. Every man, since Cain, has resented that kind of question.

" I thought you might have heard from him," she went on, " as you're to give him away to-morrow."

" Isn't he back ? " I asked, for I had confidently expected to find him at home.

" No, Geoffrey,"—my sister Fanny always had a way of jumping to conclusions, especially such conclusions as were least favourable to her fellow-creatures—" he has not returned, and, what is more, you may depend upon it he won't. You mark my words, there'll be no wedding to-morrow."

My sister Fanny has a power of annoying me which no other human being possesses.

" You mark my words," I retorted with asperity, " you had better give up making such a thundering idiot of yourself. There'll be more wedding to-morrow than ever you'll take the first part in." A prophecy which, by the way, came true.

But though I could snarl confidently to my sister, I did not feel so comfortable when late that night, I, standing on the doorstep of John's house, heard that he had not returned. I went home gloomily through the rain. Next morning brought a brilliant blue sky, gold sun, and all such softness of air and beauty of cloud as go to make up a perfect day. I woke with a vague feeling of having gone to bed anxious, and of being rather averse to facing that anxiety in the light of full wakefulness.

But with my shaving-water came a note from John which relieved my mind and sent me up to the Forster's with a light heart.

May was in the garden. I saw her blue gown through the holly-hocks as the lodge gates swung to behind me. So I did not go up to the house, but turned aside down the turfed path.

" He's written to you too," she said, without preliminary greeting, when I reached her side.

" Yes, I'm to meet him at the station at three, and come straight on to the church."

Her face looked pale, but there was a brightness in her eyes, and a tender quiver about the mouth that spoke of renewed happiness.

" Mr. Branbridge begged him so to stay another night that he had not the heart to refuse," she went on. " He is so kind, but I wish he hadn't stayed."

I was at the station at half-past two. I felt rather annoyed with John. It seemed a sort of slight to the beautiful girl who loved him, that he should come as it were out of breath, and with the dust of travel upon him, to take her hand, which some of us would have given the best years of our lives to take.

But when the three o'clock train glided in, and glided out again having brought no passengers to our little station, I was more than annoyed. There was no other train for thirty-five minutes ; I calculated that, with much hurry, we might just get to the church in time for the ceremony ; but, oh, what a fool to miss that first train ! What other man could have done it ?

That thirty-five minutes seemed a year, as I wandered round the station reading the advertisements and the time-tables, and the company's bye-laws, and getting more and more angry with John Charrington. This confidence in his own power of getting everything he wanted the minute he wanted it was leading him too far. I hate waiting. Everyone does, but I believe I hate it more than any one else. The three thirty-five was late, of course.

I ground my pipe between my teeth and stamped with impatience as I watched the signals. Click. The signal went down. Five minutes later I flung myself into the carriage that I had brought for John.

" Drive to the church ! " I said, as someone shut the door. " Mr. Charrington hasn't come by this train."

Anxiety now replaced anger. What had become of the man ? Could he have been taken suddenly ill ? I had never known him have a day's illness in his life. And even so he might have telegraphed. Some awful accident must have happened to him. The thought that he had played her false never—no, not for a moment —entered my head. Yes, something terrible had happened to him, and on me lay the task of telling his bride. I almost wished the carriage would upset and break my head so that someone else might tell her, not I, who—but that's nothing to do with this story.

It was five minutes to four as we drew up at the churchyard

gate. A double row of eager onlookers lined the path from lychgate to porch. I sprang from the carriage and passed up between them. Our gardener had a good front place near the door. I stopped.

"Are they waiting still, Byles ? " I asked, simply to gain time, for of course I knew they were by the waiting crowd's attentive attitude.

"Waiting, sir ? No, no, sir ; why, it must be over by now."

"Over ! Then Mr. Charrington's come ? "

"To the minute, sir ; must have missed you somehow, and, I say, sir," lowering his voice, " I never see Mr. John the least bit so afore, but my opinion is he's been drinking pretty free. His clothes was all dusty and his face like a sheet. I tell you I didn't like the looks of him at all, and the folks inside are saying all sorts of things. You'll see, something's gone very wrong with Mr. John, and he's tried liquor. He looked like a ghost, and in he went with his eyes straight before him, with never a look or a word for none of us : him that was always such a gentleman ! "

I had never heard Byles make so long a speech. The crowd in the churchyard were talking in whispers and getting ready rice and slippers to throw at the bride and bridegroom. The ringers were ready with their hands on the ropes to ring out the merry peal as the bride and bridegroom should come out.

A murmur from the church announced them ; out they came. Byles was right. John Charrington did not look himself. There was dust on his coat, his hair was disarranged. He seemed to have been in some row, for there was a black mark above his eyebrow. He was deathly pale. But his palior was not greater than that of the bride, who might have been carved in ivory—dress, veil, orange blossoms, face and all.

As they passed out the ringers stooped—there were six of them —and then, on the ears expecting the gay wedding peal, came the slow tolling of the passing bell.

A thrill of horror at so foolish a jest from the ringers passed through us all. But the ringers themselves dropped the ropes and fled like rabbits out into the sunlight. The bride shuddered, and grey shadows came about her mouth, but the bridegroom led her on down the path where the people stood with the handfuls of rice ; but the handfuls were never thrown, and the wedding-bells never rang. In vain the ringers were urged to remedy their mistake : they protested with many whispered expletives that they would see themselves further first.

In a hush like the hush in the chamber of death the bridal pair passed into their carriage and its door slammed behind them.

Then the tongues were loosed. A babel of anger, wonder, conjecture from the guests and the spectators.

" If I'd seen his condition, sir," said old Forster to me as we drove off, " I would have stretched him on the floor of the church, sir, by Heaven I would, before I'd have let him marry my daughter ! "

Then he put his head out of the window.

" Drive like hell," he cried to the coachman ; " don't spare the horses."

He was obeyed. We passed the bride's carriage. I forbore to look at it, and old Forster turned his head away and swore. We reached home before it.

We stood in the hall doorway, in the blazing afternoon sun, and in about half a minute we heard wheels crunching the gravel. When the carriage stopped in front of the steps old Forster and I ran down.

" Great Heaven, the carriage is empty ! And yet——"

I had the door open in a minute, and this is what I saw—

No sign of John Charrington ; and of May, his wife, only a huddled heap of white satin lying half on the floor of the carriage and half on the seat.

" I drove straight here, sir," said the coachman, as the bride's father lifted her out ; " and I'll swear no one got out of the carriage."

We carried her into the house in her bridal dress and drew back her veil. I saw her face. Shall I ever forget it ? White, white and drawn with agony and horror, bearing such a look of terror as I have never seen since except in dreams. And her hair, her radiant blonde hair, I tell you it was white like snow.

As we stood, her father and I, half mad with the horror and mystery of it, a boy came up the avenue—a telegraph boy. They brought the orange envelope to me. I tore it open.

" *Mr. Charrington was thrown from the dogcart on his way to the station at half-past one. Killed on the spot!* "

And he was married to May Forster in our parish church at *half-past three*, in presence of half the parish.

" *I shall be married, dead or alive!* "

What had passed in that carriage on the homeward drive ? No one knows—no one will ever know. Oh, May ! oh, my dear !

Before a week was over they laid her beside her husband in our little churchyard on the thyme-covered hill—the churchyard where they had kept their love-trysts.

Thus was accomplished John Charrington's wedding.

———————

Roger Pater

DE PROFUNDIS

from MYSTIC VOICES

Burns, Oates & Washbourne, 1923

It was some little time before the subject of the old priest's experiences cropped up again, and I did not like to refer to it deliberately for fear of trying his patience, and so making him avoid the matter entirely. One day, however, he mentioned it himself, and that gave me my opportunity.

" I want to ask you something about these events," I told him. " Have you yourself any theory to account for them at all ? "

" *Distinguo*," said he, after a short pause ; " without committing myself to a theory to fit every case, they do seem to me to fall into several classes.

" In one category I should place those ' voices ' which warn me of events that have happened quite recently, or are actually happening at the moment, but a long distance away ; such as the ones that told me of the deaths of my father and brother. Cases of this kind may, perhaps, be due to thought transference, or telepathy ; as you yourself suggested, if you recollect, when I first told you of those instances.

" A second type are the ' voices ' which order me to go to some place or do some special thing, which I should probably have avoided if left to myself ; and on these I have my own opinion, but, if you do not mind, I would rather keep it to myself.

" A third class are those experienced in certain places or in connection with certain articles ; such as the story I told you of the Persecution Chalice, or of my hearing the last Mass of Father

Philip Rivers the martyr. Such as these would fall into line with
the cases we often hear of haunted houses. You know the modern
theory of the subject, of course ? "

" I'm not at all sure that I do," I answered, " but, in any case,
I should like you to explain it to me, and how it bears upon your
own experiences."

" Oh, well," he replied, " the idea is just this ; that a place or a
thing, such as a weapon or article of furniture—almost anything,
in fact, which has played a part in events that aroused very intense
emotional activity on the part of those who enacted them—
becomes itself saturated, as it were, with the emotions involved.
So much so, in fact, that it can influence people of exceptional
sympathetic powers, and enable them to perceive the original
events, more or less perfectly, as if they were re-enacted before
them. Thus, in some cases, the person will see the occurrence as if
taking place before his eyes. In my case, I hear the words or
sounds, just as if I were present on the original occasion, possibly
some centuries before."

" That is a new idea to me," I said, " but it doesn't seem impossible. Hitherto the only theory of haunting which ever seemed
at all plausible to me was the old-fashioned one that the spirit of
a guilty person was sometimes compelled, as part of its purgatory,
to frequent the scene of its crime, and there re-enact the events
which it now detested. Much in the same way as we hear of a
murderer being irresistibly drawn to revisit the spot where he slew
his victim, in spite of the evident danger he runs of arousing
suspicion thereby."

" I see no reason why both theories should not be true," he
answered ; " some cases would demand one explanation, some
another. In fact, if my experiences go to prove anything, they show
that the theory you call ' old-fashioned ' is at least as likely to be
true as the one I outlined for you just now."

" I scent another story," I cried, " for none of those you have
told me, as yet, suggested a soul in purgatory as the chief agent
in the ' direct speech.' "

" If it comes to that," said he, with a smile, " I suppose I could
give you half a dozen instances where such an explanation seems
the most obvious and natural one. But, before we leave the
question of explanations, is there anything else you would like to
ask me about the subject ? "

" Well, yes," said I, with some hesitation, " but if you think me impertinent or too inquisitive, please do not hesitate to say so. I would far sooner drop the subject altogether, than run any risk of hurting your feelings."

" My dear boy," said the old priest, with more emotion than I had seen him exhibit hitherto, " please, please do not talk to me like that. God knows I am a poor enough specimen of what a priest should be, but heaven forbid that I should allow my feelings to block the way whereby you, or I, or any man, may come to understand the manner of his dealings with his creatures. I may fail, indeed I must fail to some degree, in making clear the truth in these matters ; just as everyone who tries to express himself always fails to convey things to others as perfectly as he himself perceives them. But that is quite another thing from hiding the light that God reveals to me, in order to save my feelings from possible laceration."

" I am sorry, sir," said I, " I spoke foolishly ; but I need not assure you that no such suggestion was intended by me, for a moment."

" I know, I know," he answered quickly, " but the point is one on which I feel strongly, more strongly than most men, perhaps ; and you will humour an old man in it, will you not ? But go on and ask the question which you had in mind."

" Well, sir," I said rather slowly, for his gentle outburst had distracted me from what I meant to say, " the point I wished to put to you was this. With regard to these experiences of yours, does their occurrence, their frequency, or intensity, coincide with any special state, or set of circumstances, in yourself ? I mean such things as physical health, spiritual fervour, intellectual activity or their opposites."

" Really, I don't know that I ever analysed them in that way," he answered. " But, speaking generally, I should say that in the great majority of cases I have been in perfect health at the time, and certainly up to my normal standard of intellectual activity. As regards the spiritual atmosphere on such occasions, I have often remarked that events of this kind always seem to take place when my state of soul is absolutely calm and natural, and, consequently, when my sense perception and judgement are least likely to be deceived."

" Thank you, sir," I said, " that seems to me an important point, since for anyone who knows you personally it disposes of the idea that the whole thing may be self-deception. But you spoke just now of an instance, or possibly of half a dozen instances, where the ' voice ' you heard seemed to be that of a soul in purgatory. Would you mind telling me of such a case ? "

" I will do so with pleasure," said he, " and the story I will tell you has this further interest, that it is free from an objection you made once before ; I mean, that so many of these events seem purposeless. In this case, as you will see in the sequel, what I heard was very much to the point.

" You may remember my telling you of an Austrian priest, a great friend of mine, to whose home I was travelling when I was obliged to undertake an extraordinary ' sick call ' ; and how I next met my friend years later in Rome ? " I nodded my acquiescence, and he continued, " Well, it was then that the event took place of which I propose to tell you. By that time my friend had become the head of one of the ecclesiastical colleges in Rome, and, at the personal request of the Austrian Emperor, he had been made a titular archbishop. As he was now a *personaggio distincto*, I felt a little doubtful about intruding on him, but he was so genuinely pleased when I did call that my fears all vanished, and we soon became as intimate as ever.

" One afternoon I had arranged to call for him soon after lunch, so that we might take a long walk together ; but on my arrival he met me with apologies.

" ' I am sorry to upset our plan,' he said, ' but this morning I received a note from my sister, begging me to go and see her at once. She is a nun in one of the strictly enclosed convents here in Rome, and was solemnly professed only a few weeks ago, just before you came out from England. You have never met her, she is the youngest of the family, and a good many years my junior.'

" Of course I said that the postponement of our excursion did not matter in the least, and proposed that I should walk with him to the convent. ' I will wait in the church, during your interview,' I said, ' and afterwards we can take a stroll on the *Pincio*, if you are not kept too long.' He fell in with the proposal at once, and we set out for the convent, which was quite at the other side of the city, fully half an hour's walk from the college.

" On our arrival the out-sister conducted us both to the parlour, when I explained that I would wait in the church, while the archbishop spoke with his sister. The nun then said that she was the sacristan, and would take me to the church through the sacristy, as that was the shortest way. Accordingly, we left the archbishop, and, crossing the passage, passed through a doorway inscribed 'Sagrestia.'

'"But what a large, handsome sacristy,' I exclaimed in Italian, for I had not expected anything on such a big scale. 'Si, Signore,' answered the nun, evidently pleased at my surprise ; and she explained how, some years before, the nuns had converted the upper portion of one transept into a new choir for themselves, and the lower half had then become the sacristy. 'See,' she added, 'the old pavement is still here,' and she pointed to a number of incised slabs in the floor which marked the site of old interments. Then she opened another door and I passed into the church, asking her to let me know when the archbishop was ready.

"The building was a typical Roman church of the seventeenth century ; a nave with small side chapels off it, but no aisles, a low dome at the crossing of nave and transepts, and a shallow apsidal sanctuary. A short inspection of the interior revealed nothing of special interest, so I soon settled down in a quiet corner of the transept opposite the sacristy door and said a few prayers. After some minutes I rose from my knees and sat down on a bench at the side, chancing as I did so to glance at the windows of the nuns' choir, high up in the opposite transept.

"The windows were filled with glass, frosted in some way to prevent one seeing through, but the strong light behind cast the shadow of a kneeling nun across the window as she prayed with her face towards the Blessed Sacrament, which was reserved on the High Altar of the church below. Vaguely I wondered who she was and for what she was praying, and then the figure rose and moved to one side. The silhouette was in profile now, so evidently she was kneeling before some shrine or picture which stood in the choretto itself, at the side of the window.

"I think I have mentioned that, in some cases, when the 'direct speech' comes to me it is heralded by a kind of premonition in myself. Gradually I become less and less perceptive of the things around me, a feeling of bodily fatigue and a sense of muscular lassitude grows upon me, while my mind becomes unusually alert. Then, out of this—physical insulation, may I call it ? —a kind of sympathetic union seems to arise between myself and the unknown person, and, finally, the 'direct speech' is heard. It was so in this case, as I gazed up at the figure of the nun who knelt and prayed before the shrine. Then, as from sheer fatigue I closed my eyes, abruptly in my ears came the voice of someone speaking, speaking rapidly, in Italian, with piteous tense accents, as if in extreme pain and distress.

" ' No, no, no—do not ask *me* to pray for you. It is all wrong, I say ; terribly wrong. A saint ! My God, it is I who need your prayers. Oh, why do not they pray for me, that I may rest in peace ? O my God, I am punished indeed. Punished for my folly, my pretences, my hypocrisy. Oh, do not pray to me, pray *for* me. Pray, pray for me, the wretchedest of sinners. Oh, pray for me, that God may grant me rest.'

" This went on for some minutes, the distress of the speaker becoming more intense, as if her protests went unheeded by those to whom she spoke. Then, all at once, came silence, and, opening my eyes, I looked up at the tribune. For a moment the shadow of the nun's figure fell across the window, and then she moved away, her prayers completed, and I heard no more.

" With a sense of great relief I came back to myself again, and for some minutes sat pondering over what I had heard. What could it all mean ? Something was wrong inside the convent, I felt certain, but before I had got my thoughts clear, the Sister Sacristan returned and told me that the archbishop had left the parlour, and was waiting for me in the vestibule.

" I got up at once, and joining my companion, we left the convent together. My mind was still full of the words I had heard, and of speculation about their meaning, and we must have walked a considerable distance without either of us speaking. All at once it struck me that I was neglecting my friend, and I glanced towards him, with some trifle of small talk on my lips. To my surprise his face was set and stern, with tense lips and frowning eyes, and, as I thought, an expression half puzzled and half angry. At this the trifle I had meant to say fled from my mind, and instead of it I blurted out abruptly :

" ' Something *is* wrong, then, in the convent, as I fancied ? ' With a look of surprise the archbishop turned his gaze full upon me, and I felt that I had given myself away.

" ' Explain yourself, friend Philip,' he said at length.

" ' Oh, well ! ' I answered, as lightly as I was able, ' it is easy to see that something has upset you, and in any case your sister would not have sent you such an urgent message, unless she had some reason for it.'

" ' That is not good enough, my friend,' he answered gently. ' You spoke as if my expression of annoyance had confirmed a suspicion of your own. There is something behind those words of yours, Philip ; something which it may be important for me to know. See now, I will be quite frank with you. I left the convent, disturbed and mystified by something which had just been said to me, and your first words show that you too have been affected in the same way. My dear Philip, you must tell me the cause of your anxiety, and then, in my turn, I will tell you what is troubling me.'

" ' Well, if you must know,' I said, ' while you were in the convent, I went into the church, and, after a few prayers, I sat down and fell into a reverie ' ; and then I told him all I have just told you, and how the words I heard had left me worried and anxious. The archbishop listened to my story in silence, and I was half afraid he would laugh at me, but at its close he seemed more serious than ever.

" ' It is a strange experience,' he said, when I had finished, ' I don't know that I envy you your curious faculty. But now I must tell you what is troubling me. When you left me to go to the church I waited in the parlour ; a plain bare room with a double grille across the centre, and two or three chairs on either side of it. I sat down, and after a little while my sister came in, accompanied by one of the elder nuns—you know their rule forbids them to see a visitor alone. We talked for some time in Italian, for my sister mentioned that the other did not understand German well, but nothing was mentioned which explained why she had sent for me, and I hesitated to ask her in the presence of her companion. It struck me, however, that she seemed ill at ease, and, luckily, an opportunity arose which gave me a few words with her alone.

" ' I had inquired after the Reverend Mother, and the elder nun asked if I would like to see her. I said " Yes," and she rose and went out, saying she would go and call her to the parlour. Immediately we were alone my sister said to me, " Sigismund, for God's sake go to the Holy Father and get permission to make a visitation of the convent." Astonished at her vehemence I answered, " My dear sister, whatever is the matter ? " " I cannot tell you," she replied, " for I am sworn to secrecy ; but if you make a visitation I think you may find out for yourself."

" ' Just at that moment the other nun returned with the Reverend Mother, so I could not ask her any more questions. You will imagine I felt in no mood for further conversation, so I simply told the Superioress that I did not wish to leave without seeing her, and after a few minutes' conversation I gave them my blessing and left. Now my sister is a strong-minded woman, and I am convinced she would not have spoken as she did without good reason ; and your curious experience makes me still more determined to look into the matter carefully.'

" He stopped speaking, and we walked on in silence for some little time, and then I asked him, ' How do you propose to proceed in the affair ? '

" ' Well,' he answered, ' I shall begin by going to the Vicariate, where I have a friend who is one of the secretaries to the Cardinal Vicar, and who has charge of the archives. If there is anything out of the common in the past history of the convent, he will be able to tell me. Then I shall ask for an audience with the Cardinal Vicar himself, and tell him the whole story. I have very little doubt that he will empower me to enter the enclosure and inspect the convent as his deputy, or else will appoint some discreet person to do so. If he is not prepared to take any action at all, I shall go to the Holy Father himself, and ask his permission to make a visitation in person. In the interval I will ask you to keep the whole affair a secret. I shall probably know more in a day or two, and then I will tell you how I have got on.' By this time we had reached the college again, and I said good-bye at the door, as the archbishop was evidently disinclined for further conversation.

" During the next few days I was busy renewing my acquaintance with various favourite spots in the Eternal City, and in that congenial occupation the incident at the convent was forgotten for the time. In fact, it must have been almost a week later that, on returning to my lodgings one evening, about the hour of the *Ave Maria*, I found one of the archbishop's cards on my table, with the words ' Please come and see me at once,' written on it in English. Accordingly I put on my hat again, walked round to the college, and asked the porter to let the archbishop know that I had come.

" ' But his Excellency is expecting you, my Father,' replied the man ; ' he told me to say, when you came, that he would be in his private study, and begged you would come up to him.' I knew the way, so I thanked the porter and went upstairs, where I found the archbishop walking up and down his room as if waiting impatiently.

" ' Good,' he exclaimed, as I entered, ' I was getting afraid you might not come at all to-night ; and I want your help, Philip.'

" Of course I said I was entirely at his disposal, and asked how his inquiries had prospered.

" ' Sit down, and I will tell you all about it,' he answered, and when we were both seated he continued.

" ' I went to see my friend at the Vicariate that very evening, after you had left me, and told him exactly what had happened, including your own experience.' I suppose I changed countenance at this, for he added quickly, ' Don't be annoyed with me, Philip, he is a man of great piety and remarkable discretion, and he will not repeat the story without your express permission.

" ' Well, at the time he had nothing to tell me about the con-vent, but he promised to make a search in the archives, and see if there was anything there which seemed likely to help us ; and then, on the Friday following, he sent for me. This time he had quite a dossier of papers, and we went through them together. Some of them dated from years back, and most were merely formal documents relating to the election and approval of superiors, dispensations, appointments of confessors, and other ordinary routine business. I was beginning to despair of finding anything that would help us, when we turned up a document, dated nearly twenty years ago, and headed, " *In the matter of the late Donna Anastasia Fulloni, formerly Superioress, etc., and a Petition for the admission of a Cause of Beatification—Report.*"

" ' It proved to be a copy of a long formal report prepared for the Congregation of Rites, to whom the nuns had sent in a petition asking for the usual commission of inquiry into the heroic sanctity of their Superioress, then lately dead, which is the first preliminary step in a cause of canonisation.

" ' The whole thing was really pitiful reading, for the evidence of the chaplain to the convent and of the medical man who attended the nun on her deathbed all went to show that the poor woman, far from being a saint, was a weak-minded creature, whose vanity had led her to practise a whole series of deceptions in order to create the impression that she was favoured with visions, ecstasies, and other divine privileges. On her deathbed she had confessed the truth, and commissioned her confessor to let the real facts be known, should this become necessary. Unfortunately, he took no action in the matter, and in the interval quite a little cultus began to grow up at her grave in the south transept of the church, at-tached to the convent. Then, finally, the nuns drew up and sent in the petition of which I told you. Of course, after this report, the

Sacred Congregation dismissed the petition, and prohibited any further cultus. The whole incident was considered closed, and in fact it had been quite forgotten, until my visit led to the disinterring of the report I have mentioned.

" ' There was nothing else of any importance among the papers, but my friend promised to see the Cardinal Vicar and let me know what he decided ; then, early on the Monday, I got a note ordering me to call at the Vicariate at noon to see the Cardinal himself.

" ' When I got there I found my friend with his Eminence, who told me that he had heard the whole story, and wished me to make a visitation of the convent as his deputy. Of course I said that I would gladly undertake the task, and then he asked me to name some discreet priest whom I should like to have with me. I suggested your name, which he accepted at once, saying that he had met you himself ; and then, as the third member of the commission he appointed his secretary the archivist, adding that he knew him to be a friend of my own. To-day I received the document of authorisation for the three of us to enter the enclosure, and hold a formal visitation of the convent as agents of the Cardinal Vicar ; and the nuns have notice to expect us to-morrow about ten o'clock.'

" I was not displeased to have an opportunity of solving the mystery, if there were one, so I promised to join the archbishop and his friend at the college in good time next morning, and soon afterwards went back to my lodgings.

" Next day I reached the college about nine o'clock, and found the archbishop with his friend from the Vicariate, to whom he introduced me. The archivist was an Italian priest, about sixty years old, with white hair, and a wonderful smile that reminded me of the portraits of St. Philip Neri. We talked for some little time, and got on together so well that, when the carriage was announced, I felt as if I had known him for years.

" On arriving at the convent the archbishop produced his mandate, and the three of us were admitted into the enclosure and conducted to the chapter-room which opened off the main cloister. Here we found the whole community waiting for us, some eighteen choir-nuns and nine or ten lay-sisters. On being asked if all were present the Superioress answered that one sick nun was absent in the infirmary, and on further inquiry this one proved to be the sister of the archbishop. The archivist then explained that we had been sent by the Cardinal Vicar to hold a visitation as his deputies ; and that the three of us together would interview each of the nuns in turn.

" The community then retired, returning one by one to be interrogated by the archbishop. Most of them declared that everything about the convent was quite satisfactory, though some points of detail were mentioned ; but we heard nothing to confirm our suspicion of an illicit cultus. When all had been seen, we had a few minutes' private talk, and agreed to go through the convent first on our tour of inspection, and finally to visit the infirmary and interview the archbishop's sister, whose sickness seemed curiously inopportune.

" The Reverend Mother and four of the nuns then conducted us round the cloister and ground-floor rooms, and afterwards to the choir chapel upstairs. This chapel, you will remember, was really the upper portion of one transept of the church, but the nuns had re-decorated the walls in typical Roman style, with great panels of red silk damask, framed in gilded mouldings. All this time, I ought to say, I had felt in perfect health, and no suspicion of what was to happen had crossed my mind. But the moment we entered the chapel the physical oppression which I had felt in the convent church on my previous visit returned with overwhelming force.

" Laying my hand on the archbishop's arm, I told him in a whisper what was the matter, and he hurried me forward to a chair which stood close to the large window that opened into the church. I sank into the chair, for I was almost fainting, but after a minute or so I felt stronger and opened my eyes. Opposite to me there was a *prie-dieu*, placed so that anyone kneeling on it would face *not* towards the altar in the church beneath, but towards the side wall of the chapel.

" ' It was there the nun I saw was kneeling, Sigismund,' I whispered, ' ask the Reverend Mother to take down that red silk panel.'

" The archbishop beckoned the Superioress forward, and made the request I had suggested.

" ' But it is not meant to be removed,' the nun expostulated volubly, but with evident nervousness. ' How is one to take it down without damaging it ? '

" The archbishop turned to the group standing at the entrance of the chapel. ' Which is the sacristan ? ' he asked, and one of the nuns came forward.

" ' Remove this,' he ordered, pointing to the wall beyond the *prie-dieu*. The nun hesitated a moment, but a stern look from the archbishop decided her, and going up to the wall she kneeled down, as if to get at something near the floor. There was a click, as if a lock were turned, and the tall silk panel swung outwards like a door. As it did so a wild shriek of laughter rang through the chapel. It was the Superioress, whose self-control had suddenly failed her, and she burst into violent hysterics.

" The other nuns ran forward quickly, but the archbishop's voice rang out in a tone of command. ' Let the Sub-prioress and sacristan stay here, and the rest of you take your Prioress to her room. I will send for anyone I want, when I am ready.'

" We waited before the open panel, while the shrieks of hysterical laughter grew fainter, and finally died away in the distance, and then the archbishop turned to me.

" ' Do you feel equal to moving now, Philip ? ' he asked.

" ' Certainly,' I said, ' the faintness has passed away ' ; and in fact I felt my normal self once more.

" ' Good,' he replied, ' then we will continue our inspection ' ; and turning to the two nuns who were still with us, he bade them go before us through the door revealed in the wall.

" You will have guessed the rest of the story already. Beyond the secret door was a small room fitted up as a chapel. In the centre was a kind of shrine, decorated with a red velvet pall or covering, elaborately embroidered in gold, and surrounded by candles. It contained the remains of the late Superioress, Anastasia Fulloni, which the nuns had exhumed from their grave in the transept beneath, after it had become a sacristy.

" By dint of searching inquiries we found that the foolish women had refused to accept the decision of the Congregation of Rites in the matter of her beatification, and had developed a private cultus of their own ; converting what had been a tribune, with a gallery opening into the transept, into the secret chapel which we had discovered so dramatically." The old man paused, as if his story were ended, but I could not let him leave it so incomplete.

" Surely," I asked, " the authorities took a very grave view of the affair, did they not ? "

" Yes, indeed," replied he, " for such a thing is a most serious scandal. The archbishop reported the whole matter to the Cardinal Vicar, and a few days later was summoned to the Vatican, where he repeated it to the Holy Father in person. Within a week the convent was suppressed, each nun being sent to a different house of the Order, except the archbishop's sister, who was allowed to choose for herself the convent she preferred. A year or two later the church and conventual buildings were handed over to one of the new religious congregations of men, which had not previously possessed a house in Rome. The new-comers destroyed the nun's choir and opened the transept into the church once more, turning the tribune, which had formed the secret chapel, into an organ loft.

" The body of Anastasia Fulloni was reburied in its former grave, where you may still read the original inscription on the slab unchanged, and I doubt if there are now fifty people living who remember the poor creature's name. But, for my part, every time I have been in Rome since then, I have made a point of visiting the church and saying Mass there for the repose of her soul." [1]

[1] As one of Father Pater's friends has expressed some doubt whether he would have approved the publication of this story, seeing that he was an ardent supporter of contemplative life, especially in the case of women, it will be of interest to add the following extract from my diary of the date on which he told it to me :

" . . . Squire told me true but very curious story of convent in Rome, where private cultus of a deceased nun was developed in defiance of the authorities. I asked if occurrences of such a kind—i.e., indicating a misconception of religious ideals and contempt for authority—were at all common among enclosed religious. Squire said : ' No ; quite the contrary. In fact, the chief interest of the story is that, so far as I know, it is a unique example of such folly among nuns, who, as a class, are people of strong common sense, about the last folk in the world to originate a bizarre and improper novelty, such as a false cultus. If the event had not happened within my own personal experience. I should not have believed it possible, and even as it is, I cannot understand how it can have developed so as to involve the whole community. If we knew the inner history of the convent, I am convinced we should find some quite exceptional influence at work, to throw the good sense of the nuns off its balance so terribly. As a student of psychology—and the psychology of religion in particular—I think the story ought to be put on record, since it manifests such an abnormal development. It may be that, in the light of new psychological laws as yet unknown to us, an explanation of the whole may be forthcoming. But I want you to understand clearly that the incident is quite without a parallel, and is no more typical of the normal type of convent than the actions of a maniac are typical of a sane man. But just as the study of lunacy has cast a flood of light upon normal psychology, so a story like this may help to elucidate the laws of religious psychology, and for that reason I am anxious that it should not be forgotten.' "—R.P.

Wilkie Collins

THE DREAM WOMAN

from THE QUEEN OF HEARTS

Hurst & Blackett, 1859

This story originally appeared as " The Ostler " in the " The Holly-Tree Inn," the Christmas Number of HOUSEHOLD WORDS, 1855

I

I had not been settled much more than six weeks in my country practice, when I was sent for to a neighbouring town, to consult with the resident medical man there, on a case of very dangerous illness.

My horse had come down with me, at the end of a long ride the night before, and had hurt himself, luckily, much more than he had hurt his master. Being deprived of the animal's services, I started for my destination by the coach (there were no railways at that time) ; and I hoped to get back again, towards the afternoon, in the same way.

After the consultation was over I went to the principal inn of the town to wait for the coach. When it came up, it was full inside and out. There was no resource left me, but to get home as cheaply as I could, by hiring a gig. The price asked for this accommodation struck me as being so extortionate, that I determined to look out for an inn of inferior pretensions, and to try if I could not make a better bargain with a less prosperous establishment.

I soon found a likely-looking house, dingy and quiet, with an old-fashioned sign, that had evidently not been repainted for many years past. The landlord, in this case, was not above making a small profit ; and as soon as we came to terms, he rang the yard-bell to order the gig.

" Has Robert not come back from that errand ? " asked the landlord appealing to the waiter, who answered the bell.

" No, sir, he hasn't."

" Well, then, you must wake up Isaac."

" Wake up Isacac ? " I repeated ; " that sounds rather odd. Do your ostlers go to bed in the day-time ? "

" This one does," said the landlord, smiling to himself in rather a strange way.

" And dreams, too," added the waiter.

" Never you mind about that," retorted his master ; " you go and rouse Isaac up. The gentleman's waiting for his gig."

The landlord's manner and the waiter's manner expressed a great deal more than they either of them said. I began to suspect that I might be on the trace of something professionally interesting to me, as a medical man ; and I thought I should like to look at the ostler, before the waiter awakened him.

" Stop a minute," I interposed ; " I have rather a fancy for seeing this man before you wake him up. I am a doctor ; and if this queer sleeping and dreaming of his comes from anything wrong in his brain, I may be able to tell you what to do with him."

" I rather think you will find his complaint past all doctoring, sir," said the landlord. " But if you would like to see him, you're welcome, I'm sure."

He led the way across a yard and down a passage to the stables ; opened one of the doors ; and waiting outside himself, told me to look in.

I found myself in a two-stall stable. In one of the stalls, a horse was munching his corn. In the other, an old man was lying asleep on the litter.

I stooped, and looked at him attentively. It was a withered, woe-begone face. The eyebrows were painfully contracted ; the mouth was fast set, and drawn down at the corners. The hollow wrinkled cheeks, and the scanty grizzled hair, told their own tale of past sorrow or suffering. He was drawing his breath convulsively when I first looked at him ; and in a moment more he began to talk in his sleep.

" Wake up ! " I heard him say, in a quick whisper, through his clenched teeth. " Wake up, there ! Murder."

He moved one lean arm slowly till it rested over his throat, shuddered a little, and turned on the straw. Then the arm left his throat, the hand stretched itself out, and clutched at the side towards which he had turned, as if he fancied himself to be grasping at the edge of something. I saw his lips move, and bent lower over him. He was still talking in his sleep.

" Light grey eyes," he murmured, " and a droop in the left eyelid—flaxen hair, with a gold-yellow streak in it—all right, mother—fair white arms, with a down on them—little lady's hand, with a reddish look under the finger-nails. The knife,—always the cursed knife—first on one side, then on the other. Aha ! you she-devil, where's the knife ? "

At the last word his voice rose, and he grew restless on a sudden.

I saw him shudder on the straw ; his withered face became distorted, and he threw up both his hands with a quick hysterical gasp. They struck against the bottom of the manger under which he lay, and the blow awakened him. I had just time to slip through the door, and close it, before his eyes were fairly open, and his senses his own again.

" Do you know anything about that man's past life ? " I said to the landlord.

" Yes, sir, I know pretty well all about it," was the answer, " and an uncommon queer story it is. Most people don't believe it. It's true, though, for all that. Why, just look at him," continued the landlord, opening the stable door again. " Poor devil ! he's so worn out with his restless nights, that he's dropped back into his sleep already."

" Don't wake him," I said, " I'm in no hurry for the gig. Wait till the other man comes back from his errand. And, in the meantime, suppose I have some lunch, and a bottle of sherry ; and suppose you come and help me to get through it."

The heart of mine host, as I had anticipated, warmed to me over his own wine. He soon became communicative on the subject of the man asleep in the stable ; and by little and little, I drew the whole story out of him. Extravagant and incredible as the events must appear to everybody, they are related here just as I heard them, and just as they happened.

II

Some years ago there lived in the suburbs of a large seaport town, on the west coast of England, a man in humble circumstances, by name Isaac Scatchard. His means of subsistence were derived from any employment he could get as an ostler, and occasionally, when times went well with him, from temporary engagements in service as stable-helper in private houses. Though a faithful, steady, and honest man, he got on badly in his calling. His ill-luck was proverbial among his neighbours. He was always missing good opportunities by no fault of his own ; and always living longest in service with amiable people who were not punctual payers of wages. " Unlucky Isaac " was his nickname in his own neighbourhood—and no one could say that he did not richly deserve it.

With far more than one man's fair share of adversity to endure,

Isaac had but one consolation to support him—and that was of the dreariest and most negative kind. He had no wife and children to increase his anxieties and add to the bitterness of his various failures in life. It might have been from mere insensibility, or it might have been from generous unwillingness to involve another in his own unlucky destiny—but the fact undoubtedly was, that he had arrived at the middle term of life without marrying ; and, what is much more remarkable, without once exposing himself, from eighteen to eight-and-thirty, to the genial imputation of ever having had a sweetheart.

When he was out of service, he lived alone with his widowed mother. Mrs. Scatchard was a woman above the average in her lowly station, as to capacity and manners. She had seen better days, as the phrase is ; but she never referred to them in the presence of curious visitors ; and, though perfectly polite to every-one who approached her, never cultivated any intimacies among her neighbours. She contrived to provide, hardly enough, for her simple wants, by doing rough work for the tailors ; and always managed to keep a decent home for her son to return to, when-ever his ill-luck drove him out helpless into the world.

One bleak Autumn, when Isaac was getting fast towards forty, and when he was, as usual, out of place through no fault of his own, he set forth from his mother's cottage on a long walk inland to a gentleman's seat, where he had heard that a stable-helper was required.

It wanted then but two days of his birthday ; and Mrs. Scat-chard, with her usual fondness, made him promise, before he started, that he would be back in time to keep that anniversary with her, in as festive a way as their poor means would allow. It was easy for him to comply with this request, even supposing he slept a night each way on the road.

He was to start from home on Monday morning ; and whether he got the new place or not, he was to be back for his birthday dinner on Wednesday at two o'clock.

Arriving at his destination too late on the Monday night to make application for the stable-helper's place, he slept at the village inn, and, in good time on the Tuesday morning, presented himself at the gentleman's house, to fill the vacant situation. Here again, his ill-luck pursued him as inexorably as ever. The excellent written testimonials to his character which he was able to produce, availed him nothing ; his long walk had been taken in vain—only the day before, the stable-helper's place had been given to another man.

Isaac accepted this new disappointment resignedly, and as a matter of course. Naturally slow in capacity, he had the bluntness of sensibility and phlegmatic patience of disposition which frequently distinguish men with sluggishly-working mental powers. He thanked the gentleman's steward with his usual quiet civility, for granting him an interview, and took his departure with no appearance of unusual depression in his face or manner.

Before starting on his homeward walk, he made some inquiries at the inn, and ascertained that he might save a few miles, on his return, by following a new road. Furnished with full instructions, several times repeated, as to the various turnings he was to take, he set forth on his homeward journey, and walked on all day with only one stoppage for bread and cheese. Just as it was getting towards dark, the rain came on and the wind began to rise ; and he found himself, to make matters worse, in a part of the country with which he was entirely unacquainted, though he knew himself to be some fifteen miles from home. The first house he found to inquire at, was a lonely road-side inn, standing on the outskirts of a thick wood. Solitary as the place looked, it was welcome to a lost man who was also hungry, thirsty, footsore, and wet. The landlord was civil and respectable-looking ; and the price he asked for a bed was reasonable enough. Isaac, therefore, decided on stopping comfortably at the inn for that night.

He was constitutionally a temperate man. His supper simply consisted of two rashers of bacon, a slice of home-made bread, and a pint of ale. He did not go to bed immediately after this moderate meal, but sat up with the landlord, talking about his bad prospects and his long run of ill-luck, and diverging from these topics to the subjects of horse flesh and racing. Nothing was said either by himself, his host, or the few labourers who strayed into the tap-room, which could, in the slightest degree, excite the very small and very dull imaginative faculty which Isaac Scatchard possessed.

At a little after eleven the house was closed. Isaac went round with the landlord, and held the candle while the doors and lower-windows were being secured. He noticed with surprise the strength of the bolts, bars, and iron-sheathed shutters.

" You see, we are rather lonely here," said the landlord. " We never have had any attempts made to break in yet, but it's always as well to be on the safe side. When nobody is sleeping here I am the only man in the house. My wife and daughter are timid, and the servant-girl takes after her missuses. Another glass of ale, before you turn in ?——No !—Well, how such a sober man as you comes to be out of place, is more than I can make out, for one.— Here's where you're to sleep. You're the only lodger to-night, and I think you'll say my missus has done her best to make you comfortable. You're quite sure you won't have another glass of ale ?—very well. Good night."

It was half-past eleven by the clock in the passage as they went upstairs to the bedroom, the window of which looked on to the wood at the back of the house.

Isaac locked the door, set his candle on the chest of drawers, and wearily got ready for bed. The bleak autumn wind was still blowing, and the solemn surging moan of it in the wood was dreary and awful to hear through the night-silence. Isaac felt strangely wakeful. He resolved, as he lay down in bed, to keep the candle a-light until he began to grow sleepy ; for there was something unendurably depressing in the bare idea of lying awake in the darkness, listening to the dismal, ceaseless moan of the wind in the wood.

Sleep stole on him before he was aware of it. His eyes closed, and he fell off insensibly to rest, without having so much as thought of extinguishing the candle.

The first sensation of which he was conscious, after sinking into slumber, was a strange shivering that ran through him suddenly from head to foot, and a dreadful sinking pain at the heart, such as he had never felt before. The shivering only disturbed his slumbers—the pain woke him instantly. In one moment he passed from a state of sleep to a state of wakefulness—his eyes wide open— his mental perceptions cleared on a sudden as if by a miracle.

The candle had burnt down nearly to the last morsel of tallow, but the top of the unsnuffed wick had just fallen off, and the light in the little room was, for the moment, fair and full.

Between the foot of his bed and the closed door, there stood a woman with a knife in her hand, looking at him.

He was stricken speechless with terror, but he did not lose the preternatural clearness of his faculties ; and he never took his eyes off the woman. She said not a word as they stared each other in the face ; but she began to move slowly towards the left-hand side of the bed.

His eyes followed her. She was a fair fine woman, with yellowish flaxen hair, and light grey eyes, with a droop in the left eyelid. He noticed these things and fixed them on his mind, before she was round at the side of the bed. Speechless, with no expression in her face, with no noise following her footfall, she came closer and closer—stopped—and slowly raised the knife. He laid his right arm over his throat to save it ; but, as he saw the knife coming down, threw his hand across the bed to the right side, and jerked his body over that way, just as the knife descended on the mattress within an inch of his shoulder.

His eyes fixed on her arm and hand, as she slowly drew her knife out of the bed. A white, well-shaped arm, with a pretty down lying lightly over the fair skin. A delicate, lady's hand, with the crowning beauty of a pink flush under and round the finger-nails.

She drew the knife out, and passed back again slowly to the foot of the bed ; stopped there for a moment looking at him ; then came on—still speechless, still with no expression on the beautiful face, still with no sound following the stealthy footfalls—came on to the right side of the bed where he now lay.

As she approached, she raised the knife again, and he drew himself away to the left side. She struck, as before, right into the mattress, with a deliberate, perpendicularly downward action of the arm. This time his eyes wandered from her to the knife. It was like the large clasp-knives which he had often seen labouring men use to cut their bread and bacon with. Her delicate little fingers did not conceal more than two-thirds of the handle ; he noticed that it was made of buckhorn, clean and shining as the blade was, and looking like new.

For the second time she drew the knife out, concealed it in the wide sleeve of her gown, then stopped by the bedside, watching him. For an instant he saw her standing in that position—then the wick of the spent candle fell over into the socket. The flame diminished to a little blue point, and the room grew dark.

A moment, or less if possible, passed so—and then the wick flamed up, smokily, for the last time. His eyes were still looking eagerly over the right-hand side of the bed when the final flash of light came, but they discerned nothing. The fair woman with the knife was gone.

The conviction that he was alone again, weakened the hold of the terror that had struck him dumb up to this time. The preternatural sharpness which the very intensity of his panic had mysteriously imparted to his faculties, left them suddenly. His brain grew confused—his heart beat wildly—his ears opened for the first time since the appearance of the woman, to a sense of the woeful, ceaseless moaning of the wind among the trees. With the dreadful conviction of the reality of what he had seen still strong within him, he leapt out of bed, and screaming—" Murder !—Wake up there, wake up ! "—dashed headlong through the darkness to the door.

It was fast locked, exactly as he had left it on going to bed.

His cries, on starting up, had alarmed the house. He heard the terrified, confused exclamations of women ; he saw the master of the house approaching along the passage, with his burning rush-candle in one hand and his gun in the other.

" What is it ? " asked the landlord, breathlessly.

Isaac could only answer in a whisper. " A woman, with a knife in her hand," he gasped out. " In my room—a fair, yellow-haired woman ; she jobbed at me with the knife, twice over."

The landlord's pale cheek grew paler. He looked at Isaac eagerly by the flickering light of his candle ; and his face began to get red again—his voice altered, too, as well as his complexion.

" She seems to have missed you twice," he said.

" I dodged the knife as it came down," Isaac went on, in the same scared whisper. " It struck the bed each time."

The landlord took his candle into the bedroom immediately. In less than a minute he came out again into the passage in a violent passion.

" The devil fly away with you and your woman with the knife ! There isn't a mark in the bed-clothes anywhere. What do you mean by coming into a man's place and frightening his family out of their wits by a dream ? "

" I'll leave your house," said Isaac, faintly. " Better out on the road, in rain and dark, on my way home, than back again in that room, after what I've seen in it. Lend me a light to get my clothes by, and tell me what I'm to pay."

" Pay ! " cried the landlord, leading the way with his light sulkily into the bedroom. " You'll find your score on the slate when you go down stairs. I wouldn't have taken you in for all the money you've got about you, if I'd known your dreaming, screeching ways beforehand. Look at the bed. Where's the cut of a knife in it ? Look at the window—is the lock bursted ? Look at the door (which I heard you fasten yourself)—is it broke in ? A murdering woman with a knife in my house ! You ought to be ashamed of yourself ! "

Isaac answered not a word. He huddled on his clothes : and then they went downstairs together.

" Nigh on twenty minutes past two ! " said the landlord, as they passed the clock. " A nice time in the morning to frighten honest people out of their wits ! "

Isaac paid his bill, and the landlord let him out at the front door, asking, with a grin of contempt, as he undid the strong fastenings, whether " the murdering woman got in that way ? "

They parted without a word on either side. The rain had ceased ; but the night was dark, and the wind bleaker than ever. Little did the darkness, or the cold, or the uncertainty about the way home matter to Isaac. If he had been turned out into a wilderness in a thunderstorm, it would have been a relief, after what he had suffered in the bedroom of the inn.

What was the fair woman with the knife ? The creature of a dream, or that other creature from the unknown world, called among men by the name of ghost ? He could make nothing of the mystery—had made nothing of it, even when it was mid-day on Wednesday, and when he stood, at last, after many times missing his road, once more on the door-step of home.

III

His mother came out eagerly to receive him. His face told her in a moment that something was wrong.

" I've lost the place ; but that's my luck. I dreamed an ill dream last night, mother—or, maybe, I saw a ghost. Take it either way, it scared me out of my senses, and I'm not my own man again yet."

" Isaac ! your face frightens me. Come in to the fire. Come in, and tell mother all about it."

He was as anxious to tell as she was to hear ; for it had been his hope, all the way home, that his mother, with her quicker capacity and superior knowledge, might be able to throw some light on the mystery which he could not clear up for himself. His memory of the dream was still mechanically vivid, though his thoughts were entirely confused by it.

His mother's face grew paler and paler as he went on. She never interrupted him by so much as a single word ; but when he had done, she moved her chair close to his, put her arm round his neck, and said to him :

" Isaac, you dreamed your ill dream on this Wednesday morning.

What time was it when you saw the fair woman with the knife in her hand ? "

Isaac reflected on what the landlord had said when they had passed by the clock on his leaving the inn—allowed as nearly as he could for the time that must have elapsed between the unlocking of his bedroom door and the paying of his bill just before going away, and answered :

" Somewhere about two o'clock in the morning."

His mother suddenly quitted her hold of his neck, and struck her hands together with a gesture of despair.

" This Wednesday is your birthday, Isaac ; and two o'clock in the morning is the time when you were born ! "

Isaac's capacities were not quick enough to catch the infection of his mother's superstitious dread. He was amazed, and a little startled also, when she suddenly rose from her chair, opened her old writing-desk, took pen, ink, and paper, and then said to him :

" Your memory is but a poor one, Isaac, and now I'm an old woman, mine's not much better. I want all about this dream of yours to be as well known to both of us, years hence, as it is now. Tell me over again all you told me a minute ago, when you spoke of what the woman with the knife looked like."

Isaac obeyed, and marvelled much as he saw his mother carefully set down on paper the very words that he was saying.

" Light grey eyes," she wrote as they came to the descriptive part, " with a droop in the left eyelid. Flaxen hair, with a gold-yellow streak in it. White arms, with a down upon them. Little lady's hand, with a reddish look about the finger-nails. Clasp-knife with a buckhorn handle, that seemed as good as new." To these particulars, Mrs. Scatchard added the year, month, day of the week, and time in the morning, when the woman of the dream appeared to her son. She then locked up the paper carefully in her writing-desk.

Neither on that day, nor on any day after, could her son induce her to return to the matter of the dream. She obstinately kept her thoughts about it to herself, and even refused to refer again to the paper in her writing-desk. Ere long, Isaac grew weary of attempting to make her break her resolute silence ; and time, which sooner or later wears out all things, gradually wore out the impression produced on him by the dream. He began by thinking of it carelessly, and he ended by not thinking of it at all.

This result was the more easily brought about by the advent of some important changes for the better in his prospects, which commenced not long after his terrible night's experience at the inn. He reaped at last the reward of his long and patient suffering under adversity, by getting an excellent place, keeping it for seven years, and leaving it, on the death of his master, not only with an excellent character, but also with a comfortable annuity bequeathed to him as a reward for saving his mistress's life in a carriage accident. Thus it happened that Isaac Scatchard returned to his old mother, seven years after the time of the dream at the inn, with an annual sum of money at his disposal, sufficient to keep them both in ease and independence for the rest of their lives.

The mother, whose health had been bad of late years, profited so much by the care bestowed on her and by freedom from money anxieties, that when Isaac's birthday came round, she was able to sit up comfortably at table and dine with him.

On that day, as the evening drew on, Mrs. Scatchard discovered that a bottle of tonic medicine—which she was accustomed to take, and in which she had fancied that a dose or more was still left—happened to be empty. Isaac immediately volunteered to go to the chemist's, and get it filled again. It was as rainy and bleak an autumn night as on the memorable past occasion when he lost his way and slept at the road-side inn.

On going into the chemist's shop, he was passed hurriedly by a poorly-dressed woman coming out of it. The glimpse he had of her face struck him, and he looked back after her as she descended the door-steps.

" You're noticing that woman ? " said the chemist's apprentice behind the counter. " It's my opinion there's something wronꝽ with her. She's been asking for laudanum to put to a bad tooth. Master's out for half an hour ; and I told her I wasn't allowed to sell poison to strangers in his absence. She laughed in a queer way, and said she would come back in half an hour. If she expects master to serve her, I think she'll be disappointed. It's a case of suicide, sir, if ever there was one yet."

These words added immeasurably to the sudden interest in the woman which Isaac had felt at the first sight of her face. After he had got the medicine bottle filled, he looked about anxiously for her, as soon as he was out in the street. She was walking slowly up and down on the opposite side of the road. With his heart, very much to his own surprise, beating fast, Isaac crossed over and spoke to her.

He asked if she was in any distress. She pointed to her torn shawl, her scanty dress, her crushed, dirty bonnet—then moved under a lamp so as to let the light fall on her stern, pale, but still most beautiful face.

" I look like a comfortable, happy woman—don't I ? " she said, with a bitter laugh.

She spoke with a purity of intonation which Isaac had never heard before from other than ladies' lips. Her slightest actions seemed to have the easy, negligent grace of a thoroughbred woman. Her skin, for all its poverty-stricken paleness, was as delicate as if her life had been passed in the enjoyment of every social comfort that wealth can purchase. Even her small, finely-shaped hands, gloveless as they were, had not lost their whiteness.

Little by little, in answer to his questions, the sad story of the woman came out. There is no need to relate it here ; it is told over and over again in Police reports and paragraphs descriptive of Attempted Suicides.

" My name is Rebecca Murdoch," said the woman, as she ended. " I have ninepence left, and I thought of spending it at the chemist's over the way in securing a passage to the other world. Whatever it is, it can't be worse to me than this—so why should I stop here ? "

Besides the natural compassion and sadness moved in his heart by what he heard, Isaac felt within him some mysterious influence at work all the time the woman was speaking, which utterly confused his ideas and almost deprived him of his powers of speech. All that he could say in answer to her last reckless words was, that he would prevent her from attempting her own life, if he followed her about all night to do it. His rough, trembling earnestness seemed to impress her.

" I won't occasion you that trouble," she answered, when he repeated his threat. " You have given me a fancy for living by speaking kindly to me. No need for the mockery of protestations and promises. You may believe me without them. Come to Fuller's Meadow to-morrow at twelve, and you will find me alive, to answer for myself. No !—no money. My ninepence will do to get me as good a night's lodging as I want."

She nodded and left him. He made no attempt to follow—he felt no suspicion that she was deceiving him.

" It's strange, but I can't help believing her," he said to himself, and walked away bewildered towards home.

On entering the house, his mind was still so completely absorbed by its new subject of interest, that he took no notice of what his mother was doing when he came in with the bottle of medicine. She had opened her old writing-desk in his absence, and was now reading a paper attentively that lay inside it. On every birthday of Isaac's since she had written down the particulars of his dream from his own lips, she had been accustomed to read that same paper, and ponder over it in private.

The next day he went to Fuller's Meadow.

He had done only right in believing her so implicitly—she was there, punctual to a minute, to answer for herself. The last-left faint defences in Isaac's heart, against the fascination which a word or look from her began inscrutably to exercise over him, sank down and vanished before her for ever on that memorable morning.

When a man, previously insensible to the influence of women, forms an attachment in middle life, the instances are rare indeed, let the warning circumstances be what they may, in which he is found capable of freeing himself from the tyranny of the new ruling passion. The charm of being spoken to familiarly, fondly, and gratefully by a woman whose language and manners still retained enough of their early refinement to hint at the high social station that she had lost, would have been a dangerous luxury to a man of Isaac's rank at the age of twenty. But it was far more than that—it was certain ruin to him—now that his heart was opening unworthily to a new influence at that middle time of life when strong feelings of all kinds, once implanted, strike root most stubbornly in a man's moral nature. A few more stolen interviews after that first morning in Fuller's Meadow completed his infatuation. In less than a month from the time when he first met her, Isaac Scatchard had consented to give Rebecca Murdoch a new interest in existence, and a chance of recovering the character she had lost, by promising to make her his wife.

She had taken possession not of his passions only, but of his faculties as well. All the mind he had he put into her keeping. She directed him on every point, even instructing him how to break the news of his approaching marriage in the safest manner to his mother.

" If you tell her how you met me and who I am at first," said the cunning woman, " she will move heaven and earth to prevent our marriage. Say I am the sister of one of your fellow-servants—ask her to see me before you go into any more particulars—and leave it to me to do the rest. I mean to make her love me next best to you, Isaac, before she knows anything of who I really am."

The motive of the deceit was sufficient to sanctify it to Isaac. The stratagem proposed relieved him of his one great anxiety, and quieted his uneasy conscience on the subject of his mother. Still, there was something wanting to perfect his happiness, something that he could not realise, something mysteriously untraceable, and yet something that perpetually made itself felt—not when he was absent from Rebecca Murdoch, but strange to say, when he was actually in her presence ! She was kindness itself with him ; she never made him feel his inferior capacities and inferior manners—she showed the sweetest anxiety to please him in the smallest trifles ; but, in spite of all these attractions, he never could feel quite at his ease with her. At their first meeting, there had mingled with his admiration, when he looked in her face, a faint involuntary feeling of doubt whether that face was entirely strange to him. No after-familiarity had the slightest effect on this inexplicable, wearisome uncertainty.

Concealing the truth, as he had been directed, he announced his marriage engagement precipitately and confusedly to his mother, on the day when he contracted it. Poor Mrs. Scatchard showed her perfect confidence in her son by flinging her arms round his neck, and giving him joy of having found at last, in the sister of one of his fellow-servants, a woman to comfort and care for him after his mother was gone. She was all eagerness to see the woman of her son's choice ; and the next day was fixed for the introduction.

It was a bright sunny morning, and the little cottage parlour was full of light, as Mrs. Scatchard, happy and expectant, dressed for the occasion in her Sunday gown, sat waiting for her son and her future daughter-in-law.

Punctual to the appointed time, Isaac hurriedly and nervously led his promised wife into the room. His mother rose to receive her—advanced a few steps, smiling—looked Rebecca full in the eyes—and suddenly stopped. Her face, which had been flushed the moment before, turned white in an instant—her eyes lost their expression of softness and kindness, and assumed a blank look of terror—her outstretched hands fell to her sides, and she staggered back a few steps with a low cry to her son.

" Isaac ! " she whispered, clutching him fast by the arm, when he asked alarmedly if she was taken ill, " Isaac ! does that woman's face remind you of nothing ? "

Before he could answer, before he could look round to where Rebecca stood, astonished and angered by her reception, at the lower end of the room, his mother pointed impatiently to her writing-desk and gave him the key.

" Open it," she said, in a quick, breathless whisper.

" What does this mean ? Why am I treated as if I had no business here ? Does your mother want to insult me ? " asked Rebecca, angrily.

" Open it, and give me the paper in the left-hand drawer. Quick ! quick ! for heaven's sake ! " said Mrs. Scatchard, shrinking further back in terror.

Isaac gave her the paper. She looked it over eagerly for a moment—then followed Rebecca, who was now turning away haughtily to leave the room, and caught her by the shoulder—abruptly raised the long, loose sleeve of her gown—and glanced at her hand and arm. Something like fear began to steal over the angry expression of Rebecca's face, as she shook herself free from the old woman's grasp. " Mad ! " she said to herself, " and Isaac never told me." With those few words she left the room.

Isaac was hastening after her, when his mother turned and stopped his further progress. It wrung his heart to see the misery and terror in her face as she looked at him.

" Light grey eyes," she said, in low, mournful, awestruck tones, pointing towards the open door. " A droop in the left eyelid ; flaxen hair, with a gold-yellow streak in it ; white arms with a down on them ; little, lady's hand, with a reddish look under the finger-nails. *The Dream Woman !*—Isaac, the Dream-Woman ! "

That faint cleaving doubt which he had never been able to shake off in Rebecca Murdoch's presence, was fatally set at rest for ever. He *had* seen her face, then, before—seven years before, on his birthday, in the bedroom of the lonely inn.

" Be warned ! Oh, my son, be warned ! Isaac ! Isaac ! let her go, and do you stop with me ! "

Something darkened the parlour window as those words were said. A sudden chill ran through him, and he glanced sidelong at the shadow. Rebecca Murdoch had come back. She was peering in curiously at them over the low window-blind.

" I have promised to marry, mother," he said, " and marry
I must."

The tears came into his eyes as he spoke, and dimmed his sight ;
but he could just discern the fatal face outside, moving away
again from the window.

His mother's head sank lower.

" Are you faint ? " he whispered.

" Broken-hearted, Isaac."

He stooped down and kissed her. The shadow, as he did so,
returned to the window ; and the fatal face peered in curiously
once more.

IV

Three weeks after that day Isaac and Rebecca were man and
wife. All that was hopelessly dogged and stubborn in the man's
moral nature, seemed to have closed round his fatal passion, and
to have fixed it unassailably in his heart.

After that first interview in the cottage parlour, no consideration could induce Mrs. Scatchard to see her son's wife again, or
even to talk of her when Isaac tried hard to plead her cause after
their marriage.

This course of conduct was not in any degree occasioned by a
discovery of the degradation in which Rebecca had lived. There
was no question of that between mother and son. There was no
question of anything but the fearfully exact resemblance between
the living, breathing woman, and the spectre-woman of Isaac's
dream.

Rebecca, on her side, neither felt nor expressed the slightest
sorrow at the estrangement between herself and her mother-in-
law. Isaac, for the sake of peace, had never contradicted her first
idea that age and long illness had affected Mrs. Scatchard's mind.
He even allowed his wife to upbraid him for not having confessed
this to her at the time of their marriage engagement, rather than
risk anything by hinting at the truth. The sacrifice of his integrity
before his one all-mastering delusion, seemed but a small thing,
and cost his conscience but little, after the sacrifices he had already
made.

The time of waking from his delusion—the cruel and the rueful
time—was not far off. After some quiet months of married life,
as the summer was ending, and the year was getting on towards

the month of his birthday, Isaac found his wife altering towards him. She grew sullen and contemptuous : she formed acquaintances of the most dangerous kind, in defiance of his objections, his entreaties, and his commands ; and, worst of all, she learnt, ere long, after every fresh difference with her husband, to seek the deadly self-oblivion of drink. Little by little, after the first miserable discovery that his wife was keeping company with drunkards, the shocking certainty forced itself on Isaac that she had grown to be a drunkard herself.

He had been in a sadly desponding state for some time before the occurrence of these domestic calamities. His mother's health, as he could but too plainly discern every time he went to see her at the cottage, was failing fast ; and he upbraided himself in secret as the cause of the bodily and mental suffering she endured. When, to his remorse on his mother's account was added the shame and misery occasioned by the discovery of his wife's degradation, he sank under the double trial, his face began to alter fast, and he looked, what he was, a spirit-broken man.

His mother, still struggling bravely against the illness that was hurrying her to the grave, was the first to notice the sad alteration in him, and the first to hear of his last, worst trouble with his wife. She could only weep bitterly, on the day when he made his humiliating confession ; but on the next occasion when he went to see her, she had taken a resolution, in reference to his domestic afflictions, which astonished, and even alarmed him. He found her dressed to go out, and on asking the reason, received this answer :

" I am not long for this world, Isaac," she said ; " and I shall not feel easy on my death-bed, unless I have done my best to the last to make my son happy. I mean to put my own fears and my own feelings out of the question, and to go with you to your wife, and try what I can do to reclaim her. Give me your arm, Isaac ; and let me do the last thing I can in this world to help my son, before it is too late."

He could not disobey her ; and they walked together slowly towards his miserable home.

It was only one o'clock in the afternoon when they reached the cottage where he lived. It was their dinner hour, and Rebecca was in the kitchen. He was thus able to take his mother quietly into the parlour and then prepare his wife for the interview. She had fortunately drank but little at that early hour, and she was less sullen and capricious than usual.

He returned to his mother, with his mind tolerably at ease. His wife soon followed him into the parlour, and the meeting between her and Mrs. Scathard passed off better than he had ventured to anticipate ; though he observed with secret apprehension that his mother, resolutely as she controlled herself in other respects, could not look his wife in the face when she spoke to her. It was a relief to him, therefore, when Rebecca began to lay the cloth.

She laid the cloth, brought in the bread-tray, and cut a slice from the loaf for her husband, then returned to the kitchen. At that moment, Isaac, still anxiously watching his mother, was startled by seeing the same ghastly change pass over her face which had altered it so awfully on the morning when Rebecca and she first met. Before he could say a word, she whispered with a look of horror,—

" Take me back !—home, home, again Isaac ! Come with me and never go back again ! "

He was afraid to ask for an explanation ; he could only sign to her to be silent, and help her quickly to the door. As they passed the bread-tray on the table, she stopped and pointed to it.

" Did you see what your wife cut your bread with ? " she asked in a low whisper.

" No, mother ; I was not noticing. What was it ? "

" Look ? "

He did look. A new clasp-knife, with a buckhorn handle, lay with the loaf in the bread-tray. He stretched out his hand, shudderingly, to possess himself of it ; but at the same time, there was a noise in the kitchen, and his mother caught at his arm.

" The knife of the dream ! Isaac, I'm faint with fear—take me away, before she comes back ! "

He was hardly able to support her. The visible, tangible reality of the knife struck him with a panic, and utterly destroyed any faint doubts he might have entertained up to this time, in relation to the mysterious dream-warning of nearly eight years before. By a last desperate effort, he summoned self-possession enough to help his mother out of the house—so quietly, that the " Dream-Woman " (he thought of her by that name now) did not hear their departure.

" Don't go back, Isaac, don't go back ! " implored Mrs. Scatchard, as he turned to go away, after seeing her safely seated again in her own room.

" I must get the knife," he answered under his breath. His mother tried to stop him again ; but he hurried out without another word.

On his return, he found that his wife had discovered their secret departure from the house. She had been drinking, and was in a fury of passion. The dinner in the kitchen was flung under the grate ; the cloth was off the parlour table. Where was the knife ?

Unwisely, he asked for it. She was only too glad of the opportunity of irritating him, which the request afforded her. " He wanted the knife, did he ? Could he give her a reason why ?—No ? Then he should not have it—not if he went down on his knees to ask for it." Further recriminations elicited the fact that she had bought it a bargain, and that she considered it her own especial property. Isaac saw the uselessness of attempting to get the knife by fair means, and determined to search for it, later in the day, in secret. The search was unsuccessful. Night came on, and he left the house to walk about the streets. He was afraid now to sleep in the same room with her.

Three weeks passed. Still sullenly enraged with him, she would not give up the knife ; and still that fear of sleeping in the same room with her possessed him. He walked about at night, or dozed in the parlour, or sat watching by his mother's bed-side. Before the expiration of the first week in the new month his mother died. It wanted then but ten days of her son's birthday. She had longed to live till that anniversary. Isaac was present at her death ; and her last words in this world were addressed to him :

" Don't go back, my son—don't go back ! "

He was obliged to go back, if it were only to watch his wife. Exasperated to the last degree by his distrust of her, she had revengefully sought to add a sting to his grief, during the last days of his mother's illness, by declaring that she would assert her right to attend the funeral. In spite of all that he could do or say, she held with wicked pertinacity to her word ; and on the day appointed for the burial, forced herself—inflamed and shameless with drink—into her husband's presence, and declared that she would walk in the funeral procession to his mother's grave.

This last worst outrage, accompanied by all that was most insulting in word and look, maddened him for the moment. He struck her.

The instant the blow was dealt, he repented it. She crouched down, silent, in a corner of the room, and eyed him steadily ; it was a look that cooled his hot blood, and made him tremble. But there was no time now to think of a means of making atonement. Nothing remained, but to risk the worst till the funeral was over. There was but one way of making sure of her. He locked her into her bedroom.

When he came back, some hours after, he found her sitting, very much altered in look and bearing, by the bed-side, with a bundle on her lap. She rose and faced him quietly, and spoke with a strange stillness in her voice, a strange repose in her eyes, a strange composure in her manner.

" No man has ever struck me twice," she said ; " and my husband shall have no second opportunity. Set the door open and let me go. From this day forth we see each other no more."

Before he could answer she passed him, and left the room. He saw her walk away up the street.

Would she return ?

All that night he watched and waited ; but no footstep came near the house. The next night, overcome by fatigue, he lay down in bed in his clothes, with the door locked, the key on the table, and the candle burning. His slumber was not disturbed. The third night, the fourth, the fifth, the sixth passed, and nothing happened. He lay down on the seventh, still in his clothes, still with the door locked, the key on the table, and the candle burning ; but easier in his mind.

Easier in his mind, and in perfect health of body, when he fell off to sleep. But his rest was disturbed. He woke twice, without any sensation of uneasiness. But the third time it was that never-to-be-forgotten shivering of the night at the lonely inn, that dreadful sinking pain at the heart, which once more aroused him in an instant.

His eyes opened towards the left-hand side of the bed, and there stood—

The Dream-Woman again ? No ! His wife ; the living reality, with the dream-spectre's face—in the dream-spectre's attitude : the fair arm up ; the knife clasped in the delicate white hand.

He sprang upon her, almost at the instant of seeing her, and yet not quickly enough to prevent her from hiding the knife. Without a word from him, without a cry from her, he pinioned her in a chair. With one hand he felt up her sleeve ; and there, where the Dream-Woman had hidden the knife, his wife had hidden it—the knife with the buckhorn handle, that looked like new.

In the despair of that fearful moment his brain was steady, his heart was calm. He looked at her fixedly, with the knife in his hand, and said these last words :

" You told me we should see each other no more, and you have come back. It is my turn now to go, and to go for ever. *I* say that we shall see each other no more ; and *my* word shall not be broken."

He left her, and set forth into the night. There was a bleak wind abroad, and the smell of recent rain was in the air. The distant church clocks chimed the quarter as he walked rapidly beyond the last houses in the suburb. He asked the first policeman he met, what hour that was, of which the quarter past had just struck.

The man referred sleepily to his watch, and answered, " Two o'clock." Two in the morning. What day of the month was this day that had just begun ? He reckoned it up from the date of his mother's funeral. The fatal parallel was complete—it was his birthday !

Had he escaped the mortal peril which his dream foretold ? or had he only received a second warning ?

As this ominous doubt forced itself on his mind, he stopped, reflected, and turned back again towards the city. He was still resolute to hold to his word, and never to let her see him more ; but there was a thought now in his mind of having her watched and followed. The knife was in his possession ; the world was before him ; but a new distrust of her—a vague, unspeakable, superstitious dread—had overcome him.

" I must know where she goes, now she thinks I have left her," he said to himself, as he stole back wearily to the precincts of his house.

It was still dark. He had left the candle burning in the bed-chamber ; but when he looked up to the window of the room now, there was no light in it. He crept cautiously to the house door. On going away, he remembered to have closed it ; on trying it now, he found it open.

He waited outside, never losing sight of the house till daylight. Then he ventured indoors—listened, and heard nothing—looked into kitchen, scullery, parlour ; and found nothing : went up at last into the bedroom—it was empty. A picklock lay on the floor, betraying how she had gained entrance in the night, and that was the only trace of her.

Whither had she gone ? No mortal tongue could tell him. The

darkness had covered her flight ; and when the day broke, no man
could say where the light found her.

Before leaving the house and the town for ever, he gave instructions to a friend and neighbour to sell his furniture for anything
that it would fetch, and to apply the proceeds towards employing
the police to trace her. The directions were honestly followed, and
the money was all spent ; but the enquiries led to nothing. The
picklock on the bedroom floor remained the last useless trace of the
Dream-Woman.

.   .   .   .

At this part of the narrative the landlord paused ; and, turning
towards the window of the room in which we were sitting, looked
in the direction of the stable-yard.

" So far," he said, " I tell you what was told to me. The little
that remains to be added, lies within my own experience. Between
two and three months after the events I have just been relating,
Isaac Scatchard came to me, withered and old-looking before his
time, just as you saw him to-day. He had his testimonials to
character with him, and he asked me for employment here.
Knowing that my wife and he were distantly related, I gave him a
trial, in consideration of that relationship, and liked him in spite
of his queer habits. He is as sober, honest, and willing a man as
there is in England. As for his restlessness at night, and his sleeping
away his leisure time in the day, who can wonder at it after hearing
his story ? Besides, he never objects to being roused up, when he's
wanted, so there's not much inconvenience to complain of, after
all."

" I suppose he is afraid of a return of that dreadful dream, and
of waking out of it in the dark ? "

" No," returned the landlord. " The dream comes back to him
so often, that he has got to bear with it by this time resignedly
enough. It's his wife keeps him waking at night, as he has often
told me."

" What ! Has she never been heard of yet ? "

" Never. Isaac himself has the one perpetual thought, that she
is alive and looking for him. I believe he wouldn't let himself drop
off to sleep towards two in the morning, for a king's ransom. Two
in the morning, he says, is the time she will find him, one of these
days. Two in the morning is the time, all the year round, when he
likes to be most certain that he has got the clasp-knife safe about
him. He does not mind being alone, as long as he is awake, except

on the night before his birthday, when he firmly believes himself to be in peril of his life. The birthday has only come round once since he has been here, and then he sat up along with the night-porter. ' She's looking for me,' is all he says, when anybody speaks to him about the one anxiety of his life ; ' she's looking for me.' He may be right. She *may* be looking for him. Who can tell ? "

" Who can tell ? " said I.

DIABOLISM, WITCHCRAFT, AND EVIL LORE

Richard Barham

SINGULAR PASSAGE
IN THE LIFE OF THE LATE
HENRY HARRIS, DOCTOR
IN DIVINITY

from THE INGOLDSBY LEGENDS (*First Series*)

Richard Bentley, 1840

In order that the extraordinary circumstance which I am about
to relate may meet with the credit it deserves, I think it necessary
to premise, that my reverend friend, among whose papers I find
it recorded, was in his lifetime ever esteemed as a man of good
plain understanding, strict veracity, and unimpeached morals,—
by no means of a nervous temperament, or one likely to attach
undue weight to any occurrence out of the common course of
events, merely because his reflections might not, at the moment,
afford him a ready solution of its difficulties.

On the truth of his narrative, as far as he was personally concerned, no one who knew him would hesitate to place the most
implicit reliance. His history is briefly this :—He had married
early in life, and was a widower at the age of thirty-nine, with an
only daughter, who had then arrived at puberty, and was just
married to a near connection of our own family. The sudden death
of her husband, occasioned by a fall from his horse, only three days
after her confinement, was abruptly communicated to Mrs. S——
by a thoughtless girl, who saw her master brought lifeless into the
house, and, with all that inexplicable anxiety to be the first to
tell bad news, so common among the lower orders, rushed at once
into the sick-room with her intelligence. The shock was too severe :
and though the young widow survived the fatal event several
months, yet she gradually sank under the blow, and expired,
leaving a boy, not a twelvemonth old, to the care of his maternal
grandfather.

My poor friend was sadly shaken by this melancholy catastrophe ; time, however, and a strong religious feeling, succeeded
at length in moderating the poignancy of his grief—a consum-
mation much advanced by his infant charge, who now succeeded,
as it were by inheritance, to the place in his affections left vacant

by his daughter's decease. Frederick S—— grew up to be a fine lad ; his person and features were decidedly handsome ; still there was, as I remember, an unpleasant expression in his countenance, and an air of reserve, attributed, by the few persons who called occasionally at the vicarage, to the retired life led by his grandfather, and the little opportunity he had, in consequence, of mixing in the society of his equals in age and intellect. Brought up entirely at home, his progress in the common branches of education was, without any great display of precocity, rather in advance of the generality of boys of his own standing ; partly owing, perhaps, to the turn which even his amusements took from the first. His sole associate was the son of the village apothecary, a boy about two years older than himself, whose father being really clever in his profession, and a good operative chemist, had constructed for himself a small laboratory, in which, as he was fond of children, the two boys spent a great portion of their leisure time, witnessing many of those little experiments so attractive to youth, and in time aspiring to imitate what they admired.

In such society, it is not surprising that Frederick S—— should imbibe a strong taste for the sciences which formed his principal amusement ; or that, when, in process of time, it became necessary to choose his walk in life, a profession so intimately connected with his favourite pursuit as that of medicine should be eagerly selected. No opposition was offered by my friend, who, knowing that the greater part of his own income would expire with his life, and that the remainder would prove an insufficient resource to his grandchild, was only anxious that he should follow such a path as would secure him that moderate and respectable competency which is, perhaps, more conducive to real happiness than a more elevated or wealthy station. Frederick was, accordingly, at the proper age, matriculated at Oxford, with the view of studying the higher branches of medicine, a few months after his friend, John W——, had proceeded to Leyden, for the purpose of making himself acquainted with the practice of surgery in the hospitals and lecture-rooms attached to that university. The boyish intimacy of their younger days did not, as is frequently the case, yield to separation ; on the contrary, a close correspondence was kept up between them. Dr. Harris was even prevailed upon to allow Frederick to take a trip to Holland to see his friend : and John returned the visit to Frederick at Oxford.

Satisfactory as, for some time, were the accounts of the general course of Frederick S——'s studies, by degrees rumours of a less pleasant nature reached the ears of some of his friends ; to the vicarage, however, I have reason to believe they never penetrated. The good old Doctor was too well beloved in his parish for any one voluntarily to give him pain ; and, after all, nothing beyond whispers and surmises had reached X——, when the worthy vicar was surprised on a sudden by a request from his grandchild, that he might be permitted to take his name off the books of the university, and proceed to finish his education in conjunction with his friend W—— at Leyden. Such a proposal, made, too, at a time when the period for his graduating could not be far distant, both surprised and grieved the Doctor ; he combated the design with more perseverance than he had ever been known to exert in opposition to any declared wish of his darling boy before, but, as usual, gave way, when, more strongly pressed, from sheer inability to persist in a refusal which seemed to give so much pain to Frederick, especially when the latter, with more energy than was quite becoming their relative situations, expressed his positive determination of not returning to Oxford, whatever might be the result of his grandfather's decision. My friend, his mind, perhaps, a little weakened by a short but severe nervous attack from which he had scarcely recovered, at length yielded a reluctant consent, and Frederick quitted England.

It was not till some months had elapsed after his departure, that I had reason to suspect that the eager desire of availing himself of opportunities for study abroad, not afforded him at home, was not the sole, or even the principal, reason which had drawn Frederick so abruptly from his *Alma Mater*. A chance visit to the university, and a conversation with a senior fellow belonging to his late college convinced me of this ; still I found it impossible to extract from the latter the precise nature of his offence. That he had given way to most culpable indulgences I had before heard hinted ; and when I recollected how he had been at once launched, from a state of what might be well called seclusion, into a world where so many enticements were lying in wait to allure—with liberty, example, everything to tempt him from the straight road—regret, I frankly own, was more the predominant feeling in my mind than either surprise or condemnation. But here was evidently something more than mere ordinary excess—some act of profligacy, perhaps of a deeper stain, which had induced his superiors, who, at first, had been loud in his praises, to desire him to withdraw himself quietly, but for ever ; and such an intimation, I found, had, in fact, been conveyed to him from an authority which it was impossible to resist. Seeing that my informant was determined not to be explicit, I did not press for a disclosure, which, if made, would, in all probability, only have given me pain, and that the rather as my old friend the Doctor had recently obtained a valuable living from Lord M——, only a few miles distant from the market town in which I resided, where he now was, amusing himself in putting his grounds into order, ornamenting his house, and getting everything ready against his grandson's expected visit in the following autumn. October came, and with it came Frederick ; he rode over more than once to see me, sometimes accompanied by the Doctor, between whom and myself the recent loss of my poor daughter Louisa had drawn the cords of sympathy still closer.

More than two years had flown on in this way, in which Frederick S—— had as many times made temporary visits to his native country. The time was fast approaching when he was expecting to return and finally take up his residence in England, when the sudden illness of my wife's father obliged us to take a journey into Lancashire ; my old friend, who had himself a curate, kindly offered to fix his quarters at my parsonage, and superintend the concerns of my parish till my return. Alas ! when I saw him next he was on the bed of death !

My absence was necessarily prolonged much beyond what I had anticipated. A letter, with a foreign post-mark, had, as I afterwards found, been brought over from his own house to my venerable substitute in the interval, and barely giving himself time to transfer the charge he had undertaken to a neighbouring clergyman, he had hurried off at once to Leyden. His arrival there was however too late. Frederick *was dead* !—killed in a duel, occasioned, it was said, by no ordinary provocation on his part, although the flight of his antagonist had added to the mystery which enveloped its origin. The long journey, its melancholy termination, and the complete overthrow of all my poor friend's earthly hopes, were too much for him. He appeared too—as I was informed by the proprietor of the house in which I found him, when his summons at length had brought me to his bedside—to have received some sudden and unaccountable shock, which even the death of his grandson was inadequate to explain. There was, indeed, a wildness in his fast-glazing eye, which mingled strangely with the glance of satisfaction thrown upon me as he pressed my hand ; he endeavoured to raise himself, and would have spoken, but fell back in the effort, and closed his eyes for ever. I buried him there, by the side of the object of his more than parental affection—in a foreign land.

It is from papers that I discovered in his travelling case that I submit the following extracts, without, however, presuming to advance an opinion on the strange circumstances which they detail, or even as to the connection which some may fancy they discover between different parts of them.

The first was evidently written at my own house, and bears date August the 15th, 18—, about three weeks after my own departure for Preston.

It begins thus :—

" Tuesday, August 15.—Poor girl !—I forget who it is that says, ' The real ills of life are light in comparison with fancied evils ' ; and certainly the scene I have just witnessed goes some way towards establishing the truth of the hypothesis. Among the afflictions which flesh is heir to, a diseased imagination is far from being the lightest, even when considered separately, and without taking into the account those bodily pains and sufferings which—so close is the connection between mind and matter—are but too frequently attendant upon any disorder of the fancy. Seldom has my interest been more powerfully excited than by poor Mary Graham. Her age, her appearance, her pale, melancholy features, the very contour of her countenance, all conspire to remind me, but too forcibly, of one who, waking or sleeping, is never long absent from my thoughts ;—but enough of this.

" A fine morning had succeeded one of the most tempestuous nights I ever remember, and I was just sitting down to a substantial breakfast, which the care of my friend Ingoldsby's housekeeper, kind-hearted Mrs. Wilson, had prepared for me, when I was interrupted by a summons to the sickbed of a young parishioner whom I had frequently seen in my walks, and had remarked for the regularity of her attendance at Divine worship. Mary Graham is the elder of two daughters, residing with their mother, the widow of an attorney, who, dying suddenly in the prime of life, left his family but slenderly provided for. A strict though not parsimonious economy has, however, enabled them to live with an appearance of respectability and comfort ; and from the personal attractions which both the girls possess, their mother is evidently not without hopes of seeing one, at least, of them advantageously settled in life.

As far as poor Mary is concerned, I fear she is doomed to inevitable disappointment, as I am much mistaken if consumption has not laid its wasting finger upon her ; while this last occurrence, of what I cannot but believe to be a formidable epileptic attack, threatens to shake out, with even added velocity, the little sand that may yet remain within the hour-glass of time. Her very delusion, too, is of such a nature as, by adding to bodily illness the agitation of superstitious terror, can scarcely fail to accelerate the catastrophe, which I think I see fast approaching.

" Before I was introduced into the sickroom, her sister, who had been watching my arrival from the window, took me into their little parlour, and, after the usual civilities, began to prepare me for the visit I was about to pay. Her countenance was marked at once with trouble and alarm, and in a low tone of voice, which some internal emotion, rather than the fear of disturbing the invalid in a distant room, had subdued almost to a whisper, informed me that my presence was become necessary, not more as a clergyman than a magistrate ; that the disorder with which her sister had, during the night, been so suddenly and unaccountably seized, was one of no common kind, but attended with circumstances which, coupled with the declarations of the sufferer, took it out of all ordinary calculations, and, to use her own expression, that, ' malice was at the bottom of it.'

" Naturally supposing that these insinuations were intended to intimate the partaking of some deleterious substance on the part of the invalid, I inquired what reason she had for imagining, in the first place, that anything of a poisonous nature had been administered at all ; and, secondly, what possible incitement any human being could have for the perpetration of so foul a deed towards so innocent and unoffending an individual ? Her answer considerably relieved the apprehensions I had begun to entertain lest the poor girl should, from some unknown cause, have herself been attempting to rush uncalled into the presence of her Creator ; at the same time, it surprised me not a little by its apparent want of rationality and common-sense. She had no reason to believe, she said, that her sister had taken poison, or that any attempt upon her life had been made, or was, perhaps, contemplated, but that ' still malice was at work—the malice of villains or fiends, or of both combined ; that no causes purely natural would suffice to account for the state in which her sister had been now twice placed, or for the dreadful sufferings she had undergone while in that state ' ; and that she was determined the whole affair should undergo a thorough investigation. Seeing that the poor girl was now herself labouring under a great degree of excitement, I did not think it necessary to enter at that moment into a discussion upon the absurdity of her opinion, but applied myself to the tranquillising of her mind by assurances of a proper inquiry, and then drew her attention to the symptoms of the indisposition, and the way in which it had first made its appearance.

"The violence of the storm last night had, I found, induced the whole family to sit up far beyond their usual hour, till, wearied out at length, and, as their mother observed, 'tired of burning fire and candle to no purpose,' they repaired to their several chambers.

"The sisters occupied the same room ; Elizabeth was already at her humble toilet, and had commenced the arrangement of her hair for the night, when her attention was at once drawn from her employment by a half-smothered shriek and exclamation from her sister, who, in her delicate state of health, had found walking up two flights of stairs, perhaps a little more quickly than usual, an exertion, to recover from which she had seated herself in a large arm-chair.

"Turning hastily at the sound, she perceived Mary deadly pale, grasping, as it were convulsively, each arm of the chair which supported her, and bending forward in the attitude of listening ; her lips were trembling and bloodless, cold drops of perspiration stood upon her forehead, and in an instant after, exclaiming in a piercing tone, " Hark ! they are calling me again ! it is—*it is the same voice* ;—Oh no, no !—O my God ! save me, Betsy—hold me— save me ! " she fell forward upon the floor. Elizabeth flew to her assistance, raised her, and by her cries brought both her mother, who had not yet got into bed, and their only servant-girl, to her aid. The latter was despatched at once for medical help ; but, from the appearance of the sufferer, it was much to be feared that she would soon be beyond the reach of art. Her agonised parent and sister succeeded in bearing her between them and placing her on a bed ; a faint and intermittent pulsion was for a while perceptible ; but in a few moments a general shudder shook the whole body ; the pulse ceased, the eyes became fixed and glassy, the jaw dropped, a cold clamminess usurped the place of the genial warmth of life. Before Mr. I—— arrived everything announced that dissolution had taken place, and that the freed spirit had quitted its mortal tenement.

" The appearance of the surgeon confirmed their worst apprehensions ; a vein was opened, but the blood refused to flow, and
Mr. I—— pronounced that the vital spark was indeed extinguished.

" The poor mother, whose attachment to her children was
perhaps the most powerful, as they were the sole relatives or
connections she had in the world, was overwhelmed with a grief
amounting almost to frenzy ; it was with difficulty that she was
removed to her own room by the united strength of her daughter
and medical adviser. Nearly an hour had elapsed during the
endeavour at calming her transports ; they had succeeded, however, to a certain extent, and Mr. I—— had taken his leave, when
Elizabeth, re-entering the bedchamber in which her sister lay, in
order to pay the last sad duties to her corpse, was horrorstruck at
seeing a crimson stream of blood running down the side of the
counterpane to the floor. Her exclamation brought the girl again
to her side, when it was perceived, to their astonishment, that the
sanguine stream proceeded from the arm of the body, which was
now manifesting signs of returning life. The half-frantic mother
flew to the room, and it was with difficulty that they could prevent
her, in her agitation, from so acting as to extinguish for ever the
hope which had begun to rise in their bosoms. A long-drawn sigh,
amounting almost to a groan, followed by several convulsive gasp-
ings, was the prelude in the restoration of the animal functions in
poor Mary : a shriek, almost preternaturally loud, considering her
state of exhaustion, succeeded ; but she did recover, and, with the
help of restoratives, was well enough towards morning to express a
strong desire that I should be sent for—a desire the more readily
complied with, inasmuch as the strange expressions and declarations she had made since her restoration to consciousness, had
filled her sister with the most horrible suspicions. The nature of
these suspicions was such as would at any other time, perhaps, have
raised a smile upon my lips ; but the distress, and even agony of the
poor girl, as she half hinted and half expressed them, were such as
entirely to preclude every sensation at all approaching to mirth.
Without endeavouring, therefore, to combat ideas, evidently too
strongly impressed upon her mind at the moment to admit of
present refutation, I merely used a few encouraging words, and
requested her to precede me to the sick-chamber.

" The invalid was lying on the outside of the bed, partly
dressed, and wearing a white dimity wrapping-gown, the colour of

which corresponded but too well with the deadly paleness of her complexion. Her cheek was wan and shrunken, giving an extraordinary prominence to her eye, which gleamed with a lustrous brilliancy not unfrequently characteristic of the aberration of intellect. I took her hand ; it was chill and clammy, the pulse feeble and intermittent, and the general debility of her frame was such that I would fain have persuaded her to defer any conversation which, in her present state, she might not be equal to support. Her positive assurance that, until she had disburdened herself of what she called her ' dreadful secret,' she could know no rest either of mind or body, at length induced me to comply with her wish, opposition to which, in her then frame of mind, might perhaps be attended with even worse effects than its indulgence. I bowed acquiescence, and in a low and faltering voice, with frequent interruptions, occasioned by her weakness, she gave me the following singular account of the sensations which, she averred, had been experienced by her during her trance :—

" ' This, sir,' she began, ' is not the first time that the cruelty of others has, for what purpose I am unable to conjecture, put me to a degree of torture which I can compare to no suffering, either of body or mind, which I have ever before experienced. On a former occasion I was willing to believe it the mere effect of a hideous dream, or what is vulgarly termed the nightmare ; but this repetition, and the circumstances under which I was last *summoned*, at a time, too, when I had not even composed myself to rest, fatally convince me of the reality of what I have seen and suffered.

" ' This is no time for concealment of any kind. It is now more than a twelvemonth since I was in the habit of occasionally encountering in my walks a young man of prepossessing appearance and gentlemanly deportment. He was always alone, and generally reading ; but I could not be long in doubt that these rencounters, which became every week more frequent, were not the effect of accident, or that his attention, when we did meet, was less directed to his book than to my sister and myself. He even seemed to wish to address us, and I have no doubt would have taken some other opportunity of doing so, had not one been afforded him by a strange dog attacking us one Sunday morning on our way to church, which he beat off, and made use of this little service to promote an acquaintance. His name, he said, was Francis Somers, and added that he was on a visit to a relation of the same name, resident a few miles from X——. He gave us to understand that he was himself studying surgery with the view to a medical appointment in one of the colonies. You are not to suppose, sir, that he had entered thus into his concerns at the first interview ; it was not till our acquaintance had ripened, and he had visited our house more than once with my mother's sanction, that these particulars were elicited. He never disguised, from the first, that an attachment to myself was his object originally in introducing himself to our notice. As his prospects were compara- tively flattering, my mother did not raise any impediment to his attentions, and I own I received them with pleasure.

" ' Days and weeks elapsed ; and although the distance at which his relation resided prevented the possibility of an uninterrupted intercourse, yet neither was it so great as to preclude his frequent visits. The interval of a day, or at most of two, was all that inter- vened, and these temporary absences certainly did not decrease the pleasure of the meetings with which they terminated. At length a pensive expression began to exhibit itself upon his countenance, and I could not but remark that at every visit he became more abstracted and reserved. The eye of affection is not slow to detect any symptom of uneasiness in a quarter dear to it. I spoke to him, questioned him on the subject ; his answer was evasive, and I said no more. My mother, too, however, had marked the same appear- ance of melancholy, and pressed him more strongly. He at length admitted that his spirits were depressed, and that their depression was caused by the necessity of an early, though but a temporary, separation. His uncle, and only friend, he said, had long insisted on his spending some months on the Continent, with the view of completing his professional education, and that the time was now fast approaching when it would be necessary for him to commence his journey. A look made the inquiry which my tongue refused to utter. "Yes, dearest Mary," was his reply, "I have communicated our attachment to him, partially at least ; and though I dare not say that the intimation was received as I could have wished, yet I have, perhaps, on the whole, no fair reason to be dissatisfied with his reply.

" ' " The completion of my studies, and my settlement in the world, must, my uncle told me, be the first consideration ; when these material points were achieved, he should not interfere with any arrangement that might be found essential to my happiness : at the same time he has positively refused to sanction any engage- ment at present, which may, he says, have a tendency to divert my attention from those pursuits, on the due prosecution of which my future situation in life must depend. A compromise between love and duty was eventually wrung from me, though reluctantly. I have pledged myself to proceed immediately to my destination abroad, with a full understanding that on my return, a twelve-month hence, no obstacle shall be thrown in the way of what are, I trust, our mutual wishes."

" ' I will not attempt to describe the feelings with which I received this communication, nor will it be necessary to say any-thing of what passed at the few interviews which took place before Francis quitted X——. The evening immediately previous to that of his departure he passed in this house, and, before we separated, renewed his protestations of an unchangeable affection, requiring a similar assurance from me in return. I did not hesitate to make it. "Be satisfied, my dear Francis," said I, "that no diminution in the regard I have avowed can ever take place, and though absent in body, my heart and soul will still be with you."—" Swear this," he cried, with a suddenness and energy which surprised, and rather startled me : " promise that you will be with me *in spirit*, at least, when I am far away." I gave him my hand, but that was not sufficient. " One of these dark shining ringlets, my dear Mary," said he, " as a pledge that you will not forget your vow ! " I suffered him to take the scissors from my work-box and to sever a lock of my hair, which he placed in his bosom.—The next day he was pursuing his journey, and the waves were already bearing him from England.

" ' I had letters from him repeatedly during the first three months of his absence ; they spoke of his health, his prospects, and of his love, but by degrees the intervals between each arrival be-came longer, and I fancied I perceived some falling off from that warmth of expression which had at first characterised his com-munications.

" ' One night I had retired to rest rather later than usual, having sat by the bedside, comparing his last brief note with some of his earlier letters, and was endeavouring to convince myself that my ap-prehensions of his fickleness were unfounded, when an undefinable sensation of restlessness and anxiety seized upon me. I cannot com-pare it to anything I had ever experienced before ; my pulse fluttered, my heart beat with a quickness and violence which alarmed me, and a strange tremor shook my whole frame. I retired hastily to bed, in hopes of getting rid of so unpleasant a sensation, but in vain ; a vague apprehension of I know not what occupied my mind, and vainly did I endeavour to shake it off. I can compare my feelings to nothing but those which we sometimes experience when about to undertake a long and unpleasant journey, leaving those we love behind us. More than once did I raise myself in my bed and listen, fancying that I heard myself called, and on each of those occasions the fluttering of my heart increased. Twice I was on the point of calling to my sister, who then slept in an adjoining room, but she had gone to bed indisposed, and an unwillingness to disturb either her or my mother checked me ; the large clock in the room below at this moment began to strike the hour of twelve. I distinctly heard its vibrations, but ere its sounds had ceased, a burning heat, as if a hot iron had been applied to my temple, was succeeded by a dizziness—a swoon—a total loss of consciousness as to where or in what situation I was.

" ' A pain, violent, sharp, and piercing, as though my whole frame were lacerated by some keen-edged weapon, roused me from this stupor—but where was I ? Everything was strange around me —a shadowy dimness rendered every object indistinct and uncertain ; methought, however, that I was seated in a large, antique, high-backed chair, several of which were near, their tall black carved frames and seats interwoven with a lattice-work of cane. The apartment in which I sat was one of moderate dimensions, and, from its sloping roof, seemed to be the upper story of the edifice, a fact confirmed by the moon shining without, in full effulgence, on a huge round tower, which its light rendered plainly visible through the open casement, and the summit of which appeared but little superior in elevation to the room I occupied. Rather to the right, and in the distance, the spire of some cathedral or lofty church was visible, while sundry gable-ends, and tops of houses, told me I was in the midst of a populous but unknown city.

" ' The apartment itself had something strange in its appearance, and, in the character of its furniture and appurtenances, bore little or no resemblance to any I had ever seen before. The fireplace was large and wide, with a pair of what are sometimes called andirons, betokening that wood was the principal, if not the only fuel consumed within its recess ; a fierce fire was now blazing in it, the light from which rendered visible the remotest parts of the chamber. Over a lofty old-fashioned mantelpiece, carved heavily in imitation of fruit and flowers, hung the half-length portrait of a gentleman in a dark-coloured foreign habit, with a peaked beard and moustaches, one hand resting upon a table, the other supporting a sort of *bâton*, or short military staff, the summit of which was surmounted by a silver falcon. Several antique chairs, similar in appearance to those already mentioned, surrounded a massive oaken table, the length of which much exceeded its width. At the lower end of this piece of furniture stood the chair I occupied ; on the upper, was placed a small chafing-dish filled with burning coals, and darting forth occasionally long flashes of various-coloured fire, the brilliance of which made itself visible, even above the strong illumination emitted from the chimney. Two huge, black japanned cabinets, with clawed feet, reflecting from their polished surfaces the effulgence of the flame, were placed one on each side the casement-window to which I have alluded, and with a few shelves loaded with books, many of which were also strewed in disorder on the floor, completed the list of the furniture in the apartment. Some strange-looking instruments, of unknown form and purpose, lay on the table near the chafing-dish, on the other side of which a miniature portrait of myself hung, reflected by a small oval mirror in a dark-coloured frame, while a large open volume, traced with strange characters of the colour of blood, lay in front ; a goblet, containing a few drops of liquid of the same ensanguined hue, was by its side.

" ' But of the objects which I have endeavoured to describe, none arrested my attention so forcibly as two others. These were the figures of two young men, in the prime of life, only separated from me by the table. They were dressed alike, each in a long flowing gown, made of some sad-coloured stuff, and confined at the waist by a crimson girdle ; one of them, the shorter of the two, was occupied in feeding the embers of the chafing-dish with a resinous powder, which produced and maintained a brilliant but flickering blaze, to the action of which his companion was exposing a long lock of dark chestnut hair, that shrank and shrivelled as it approached the flame. But, O God !—that hair ! and the form of him who held it ! that face ! those features !—not for one instant could I entertain a doubt—it was He ! Francis !—the lock he grasped was mine, the very pledge of affection I had given him, and still, as it partially encountered the fire, a burning heat seemed to scorch the temple from which it had been taken, conveying a torturing sensation that affected my very brain.

" ' How shall I proceed ?—but no, it is impossible—not even to you, sir, can I—dare I—recount the proceedings of that unhallowed night of horror and of shame. Were my life extended to a term commensurate with that of the Patriarchs of old, never could its detestable, its damning pollutions be effaced from my remembrance ; and, oh ! above all, never could I forget the diabolical glee which sparkled in the eyes of my fiendish tormentors, as they witnessed the worse than useless struggles of their miserable victim. Oh ! why was it not permitted me to take refuge in unconsciousness—nay, in death itself, from the abominations of which I was compelled to be, not only a witness, but a partaker ? But it is enough, sir ; I will not further shock your nature by dwelling longer on a scene, the full horrors of which, words, if I even dared employ any, would be inadequate to express ; suffice it to say, that after being subjected to it, how long I knew not, but certainly for more than an hour, a noise from below seemed to alarm my persecutors ; a pause ensued—the lights were extinguished, and, as the sound of a footstep ascending a staircase became more distinct, my forehead felt again the excruciating sensation of heat, while the embers, kindling into a momentary flame, betrayed another portion of the ringlet consuming in the blaze. Fresh agonies succeeded, not less severe, and of a similar description to those which had seized upon me at first : oblivion again followed, and on being at length restored to consciousness, I found myself as you see me now, faint and exhausted, weakened in every limb, and every fibre quivering with agitation. My groans soon brought my sister to my aid ; it was long before I could summon resolution to confide, even to her, the dreadful secret, and when I had done so, her strongest efforts were not wanting to persuade me that I had been labouring under a severe attack of nightmare. I ceased to argue, but I was not convinced ; the whole scene was then too present, too awfully real, to permit me to doubt the character of the transaction ; and if, when a few days had elapsed, the hopelessness of imparting to others the conviction I entertained myself, produced in me an apparent acquiescence, with their opinion, I have never been the less satisfied that no cause reducible to the known laws of nature occasioned my sufferings on that hellish evening. Whether that firm belief might have eventually yielded to time, whether I might at length have been brought to consider all that had passed, and the circumstances which I could never cease to remember, as a mere phantasm, the offspring of a heated imagination, acting upon an enfeebled body, I know not—last night, however, would in any case have dispelled the flattering illusion—last night—last night was the whole horrible scene acted over again. The place—the actors—the whole infernal apparatus were the same ; the same insults, the same torments, the same brutalities—all were renewed, save that the period of my agony was not so prolonged. I became sensible to an incision in my arm, though the hand that made it was not visible ; at the same moment my persecutors paused ; they were manifestly disconcerted, and the companion of him, whose name shall never more pass my lips, muttered something to his abettor in evident agitation ; the formula of an oath of horrible import was dictated to me in terms fearfully distinct. I refused it unhesitatingly ; again and again was it proposed, with menaces I tremble to think on— but I refused ; the same sound was heard—interruption was evidently apprehended—the same ceremony was hastily repeated and I again found myself released, lying on my own bed, with my mother and my sister weeping over me. O God ! O God ! when and how is this to end ?—When will my spirit be left in peace ?— Where, or with whom, shall I find refuge ? '

" It is impossible to convey any adequate idea of the emotions with which this unhappy girl's narrative affected me. It must not be supposed that her story was delivered in the same continuous and uninterrupted strain in which I have transcribed its substance. On the contrary, it was not without frequent intervals, of longer or shorter duration, that her account was brought to a conclusion ; indeed, many passages of her strange dream were not without the greatest difficulty and reluctance communicated at all. My task was no easy one ; never, in the course of a long life spent in the active duties of my Christian calling—never had I been summoned to such a conference before.

" To the half-avowed, and palliated confession of committed guilt I had often listened, and pointed out the only road to secure its forgiveness. I had succeeded in cheering the spirit of despondency, and sometimes even in calming the ravings of despair ; but here I had a different enemy to combat, an ineradicable prejudice to encounter, evidently backed by no common share of superstition and confirmed by the mental weakness attendant upon severe bodily pain. To argue the sufferer out of an opinion so rooted was a hopeless attempt. I did, however, essay it ; I spoke to her of the strong and mysterious connection maintained between our waking images and those which haunt us in our dreams, and more especially during that morbid oppression commonly called nightmare.

I was even enabled to adduce myself as a strong and living instance of the excess to which fancy sometimes carries her freaks on those occasions ; while, by an odd coincidence, the impression made upon my own mind, which I adduced as an example, bore no slight resemblance to her own. I stated to her, that on my recovery from the fit of epilepsy, which had attacked me about two years since, just before my grandson Frederick left Oxford, it was with the greatest difficulty I could persuade myself that I had not visited him, during the interval, in his rooms at Brazenose, and even conversed with himself and his friend W——, seated in his arm-chair, and gazing through the window full upon the statue of Cain, as it stands in the centre of the quadrangle. I told her of the pain I underwent both at the commencement and termination of my attack ; of the extreme lassitude that succeeded ; but my efforts were all in vain : she listened to me, indeed, with an interest almost breathless, especially when I informed her of my having actually experienced the very burning sensation in the brain alluded to, no doubt a strong attendant symptom of this peculiar affection, and a proof of the identity of the complaint : but I could plainly perceive that I failed entirely in shaking the rooted opinion which possessed her, that her spirit had, by some nefarious and unhallowed means, been actually subtracted for a time from its earthly tenement."

The next extract which I shall give from my old friend's memoranda is dated August 24th, more than a week subsequent to his first visit at Mrs. Graham's. He appears, from his papers, to have visited the poor young woman more than once during the interval, and to have afforded her those spiritual consolations which no one was more capable of communicating. His patient, for so in a religious sense she may well be termed, had been sinking under the agitation she had experienced ; and the constant dread she was under of similar sufferings, operated so strongly on a frame already enervated, that life at length seemed to hang only by a thread. His papers go on to say—

" I have just seen poor Mary Graham,—I fear for the last time. Nature is evidently quite worn out ; she is aware that she is dying, and looks forward to the termination of her existence here, not only with resignation but with joy. It is clear that her dream, or what she persists in calling her ' subtraction,' has much to do with this. For the last three days her behaviour has been altered, she has avoided conversing on the subject of her delusion, and seems to wish that I should consider her as a convert to my view of her case. This may, perhaps, be partly owing to the flippancies of her medical attendant upon the subject, for Mr. I—— has, somehow or other, got an inkling that she has been much agitated by a dream, and thinks to laugh off the impression—in my opinion injudiciously ; but though a skilful, and a kind-hearted, he is a young man, and of a disposition, perhaps, rather too mercurial for the chamber of a nervous invalid. Her manner has since been much more reserved to both of us : in my case, probably because she suspects me of betraying her secret."

"August 26th.—Mary Graham is yet alive, but sinking fast ; her cordiality towards me has returned since her sister confessed yesterday, that she had herself told Mr. I—— that his patient's mind ' had been affected by a terrible vision.' I am evidently restored to her confidence. She asked me this morning, with much earnestness, ' What I believed to be the state of departed spirits during the interval between dissolution and the final day of account ? And whether I thought they would be safe, in another world, from the influence of wicked persons employing an agency more than human ? ' Poor child ! One cannot mistake the prevailing bias of her mind. Poor child ! "

"August 27th.—It is nearly over ; she is sinking rapidly, but quietly and without pain. I have just administered to her the sacred elements, of which her mother partook. Elizabeth declined doing the same : she cannot, she says, yet bring herself to forgive the villain who has destroyed her sister. It is singular that she, a young woman of good plain sense in ordinary matters, should so easily adopt, and so pertinaciously retain, a superstition so puerile and ridiculous. This must be matter of a future conversation between us ; at present, with the form of the dying girl before her eyes, it were vain to argue with her. The mother, I find, has written to young Somers, stating the dangerous situation of his affianced wife ; indignant as she justly is, at his long silence, it is fortunate that she has no knowledge of the suspicions entertained by her daughter. I have seen her letter ; it is addressed to Mr. Francis Somers, in the Hogewoert, at Leyden—a fellow-student, then, of Frederick's. I must remember to inquire if he is acquainted with this young man."

Mary Graham, it appears, died the same night. Before her departure she repeated to my friend the singular story she had before told him, without any material variation from the detail she had formerly given. To the last she persisted in believing that her unworthy lover had practised upon her by forbidden arts. She once more described the apartment with great minuteness, and even the person of Francis' alleged companion, who was, she said, about the middle height, hard-featured, with a rather remarkable scar upon his left cheek, extending in a transverse direction from below the eye to the nose. Several pages of my reverend friend's manuscript are filled with reflections upon this extraordinary confession, which, joined with its melancholy termination, seems to have produced no common effect upon him. He alludes to more than one subsequent discussion with the surviving sister, and piques himself on having made some progress in convincing her of the folly of her theory respecting the origin and nature of the illness itself.

His memoranda on this, and other subjects, are continued till about the middle of September, when a break ensues, occasioned, no doubt, by the unwelcome news of his grandson's dangerous state, which induces him to set out forthwith for Holland. His arrival at Leyden was, as I have already said, too late. Frederick S—— had expired after thirty hours intense suffering, from a wound received in a duel with a brother student. The cause of quarrel was variously related ; but, according to his landlord's version, it had originated in some silly dispute about a dream of his antagonist's, who had been the challenger. Such, at least, was the account given to him, as he said, by Frederick's friend and fellow-lodger, W——, who had acted as second on the occasion, thus acquitting himself of an obligation of the same kind due to the deceased, whose services he had put in requisition about a year before on a similar occasion, when he had himself been severely wounded in the face.

From the same authority I learned that my poor friend was much affected on finding that his arrival had been deferred too long. Every attention was shown him by the proprietor of the house, a respectable tradesman, and a chamber was prepared for his accommodation ; the books and few effects of his deceased grandson were delivered over to him, duly inventoried, and, late as it was in the evening when he reached Leyden, he insisted on being conducted immediately to the apartments which Frederick had occupied, there to indulge the first ebullitions of his sorrows, before he retired to his own. Madame Müller accordingly led the way to an upper room, which being situated at the top of the house, had been, from its privacy and distance from the street, selected by Frederick as his study. The Doctor entered, and taking the lamp from his conductress, motioned to be left alone. His implied wish was of course complied with ; and nearly two hours had elapsed before his kind-hearted hostess reascended, in the hope of prevailing upon him to return with her, and partake of that refreshment which he had in the first instance peremptorily declined. Her application for admission was unnoticed :—she repeated it more than once, without success ; then becoming somewhat alarmed at the continued silence, opened the door and perceived her new inmate stretched on the floor in a fainting fit. Restoratives were instantly administered, and prompt medical aid succeeded at length in restoring him to consciousness. But his mind had received a shock, from which, during the few weeks he survived, it never entirely recovered. His thoughts wandered perpetually : and though from the very slight acquaintance which his hosts had with the English language, the greater part of what fell from him remained unknown, yet enough was understood to induce them to believe that something more than the mere death of his grandson had contributed thus to paralyse his faculties.

When his situation was first discovered, a small miniature was found tightly grasped in his right hand. It had been the property of Frederick, and had more than once been seen by the Mullers in his possession. To this the patient made continued reference, and would not suffer it one moment from his sight : it was in his hand when he expired. At my request it was produced to me. The portrait was that of a young woman, in an English morning dress, whose pleasing and regular features, with their mild and somewhat pensive expression, were not, I thought, altogether unknown to me. Her age was apparently about twenty. A profusion of dark chestnut hair was arranged in the Madonna style, above a brow of unsullied whiteness, a single ringlet depending on the left side. A glossy lock of the same colour, and evidently belonging to the original, appeared beneath a small crystal, inlaid in the back of the picture, which was plainly set in gold, and bore in a cipher the letters M. G. with the date 18—. From the inspection of this portrait, I could at the time collect nothing, nor from that of the Doctor himself, which, also, I found the next morning in Frederick's desk, accompanied by two separate portions of hair. One of them was a lock, short and deeply tinged with grey, and had been taken, I have little doubt, from the head of my old friend himself ; the other corresponded in colour and appearance with that at the back of the miniature. It was not till a few days had elapsed, and I had seen the worthy Doctor's remains quietly consigned to the narrow house, that while arranging his papers previous to my intended return upon the morrow, I encountered the narrative I have already transcribed. The name of the unfortunate young woman connected with it forcibly arrested my attention. I recollected it immediately as one belonging to a parishioner of my own, and at once recognised the original of the female portrait as its owner.

I rose not from the perusal of his very singular statement till I had gone through the whole of it. It was late—and the rays of the single lamp by which I was reading did but very faintly illumine the remoter parts of the room in which I sat. The brilliancy of an unclouded November moon, then some twelve nights old, and shining full into the apartment, did much towards remedying the defect. My thoughts filled with the melancholy details I had read, I rose and walked to the window. The beautiful planet rose high in the firmament, and gave to the snowy roofs of the houses, and pendent icicles, all the sparkling radiance of clustering gems. The stillness of the scene harmonised well with the state of my feelings. I threw open the casement and looked abroad. Far below me, the waters of the principal canal shone like a broad mirror in the moonlight. To the left rose the Burght, a huge round tower of remarkable appearance, pierced with embrasures at its summit ; while a little to the right and in the distance, the spire and pinnacles of the Cathedral of Leyden rose in all their majesty, presenting a *coup d'œil* of surpassing though simple beauty. To a spectator of calm, unoccupied mind, the scene would have been delightful. On me it acted with an electric effect. I turned hastily to survey the apartment in which I had been sitting. It was the one designated as the study of the late Frederick S——. The sides of the room were covered with dark wainscot ; the spacious fireplace opposite to me, with its polished andirons, was surmounted by a large old-fashioned mantelpiece, heavily carved in the Dutch style with fruits and flowers ; above it frowned a portrait, in a Vandyke dress, with a peaked beard and moustaches ; one hand of the figure rested on a table, while the other bore a marshal's

staff, surmounted with a silver falcon ; and—either my imagination, already heated by the scene, deceived me—or a smile as of
malicious triumph curled the lip and glared in the cold leaden eye
that seemed fixed upon my own. The heavy, antique, cane-backed
chairs—the large oaken table—the book-shelves, the scattered
volumes—all, all were there ; while, to complete the picture, to
my right and left, as half-breathless I leaned my back against the
casement, rose, on each side, a tall, dark, ebony cabinet, in whose
polished sides the single lamp upon the table shone reflected as in
a mirror.

What am I to think ?—Can it be that the story I have been
reading was written by my poor friend here, and under the
influence of delirium ?—Impossible ! Besides, they all assure me,
that from the fatal night of his arrival he never left his bed—never
put pen to paper. His very directions to have me summoned from
England were verbally given, during one of those few and brief
intervals in which reason seemed partially to resume her sway.
Can it then be possible that——? W——? where is he who alone
may be able to throw light on this horrible mystery ? No one
knows. He absconded, it seems, immediately after the duel. No
trace of him exists, nor, after repeated and anxious inquiries, can
I find that any student has ever been known in the University of
Leyden by the name of Francis Somers.

> There are more things in heaven and earth
> Than are dreamt of in your philosophy ! !

Jasper John

THE SPIRIT OF STONEHENGE

from SINISTER STORIES

Henry Walker, 1930

"So you have moved from your old home ; I was rather surprised
to hear," I said to Ronald Dalton.

He nodded his head.

"We were very sorry to go, but nothing would have made us
stay after what had happened. I know I did not tell you, but then

we have not spoken of it more than is necessary, even to old friends."

We were sitting in the twilight of a June evening. Outside the rain dripped from the trees, from the roof, from the windows ; for there had been a dreadful thunderstorm.

" I would like to tell you what happened, if you care to listen," Ronald said abruptly.

I had been rather hoping he would, for he was a matter-of-fact man, and my curiosity had been stirred by the papers' accounts of the strange way one of their guests had committed suicide. So he started in his earnest way, which lent conviction to the story.

" My brother made great friends with Gavin Thomson in London. The first time I saw him was when he came to stay with us for a week. His great hobby was to dabble about in excavations, and, as his father had left him enough to live comfortably, he was able to indulge his taste.

" He was a good-looking boy, about twenty-nine, dark and manly. Though only young, he had made quite a name for himself already, even with the professors. There were tales of his living among the Bedouins, an unheard-of thing for a white man to do. But it was difficult to make him talk of his exploits.

" I took to him, as my brother had done ; he had such a magnetic personality. He told us he had been reading up all the old books on Stonehenge which he could get hold of. The Druid theory fascinated him, and he was anxious to study some facts first-hand.

" He asked us if we had ever heard of elementals ; then laughed, and said we were not to be afraid that *he* was possessed by them. We asked him what the things were, for beneath his light manner I saw that he was really serious about them. He told us that they were a sort of ugly evil spirits, which had never had a form. Their one object was to find a human body in which to reside. They were supposed to have a certain power over human beings in places where great evil had prevailed.

" Quite abruptly he stopped, and began talking about the moon's rays on the dolmen at Stonehenge, and a peculiar theory he held, of which we understood nothing. I think he meant to puzzle us and make us forget.

" Now and then he descended to our level when he explained that the Druids were fond of conducting their ceremonies at certain times of the moon. ' That is why I have to do so much of

my work at night,' he said. We had given him a latchkey so that
he could come in when he liked. He told us that he was on the
verge of a great discovery which would make history.

" After a fortnight's stay he left us to do some work in Brittany,
but not before he had covered many sheets with writing. In three
months he was back again. He looked gaunt and ill, and his eyes
were sunken and bright with fever. We begged him to rest that
night, but he would not hear of it, and when he spoke of Stonehenge his eyes gleamed in a strange manner.

" When he had gone out into the night I went up to his room to
see if there was everything that he could want. There were books
everywhere ; one lay on the table, the place was marked with
something. I opened it at the place and a knife lay snugly between
the pages. It was curved, and of pure gold. I knew enough to
know that it was a copy of a sacrificial knife ; the edge was so
sharp that I cut my finger rather badly.

" Curiosity aroused, I looked at the page, and this is what I
read :

" ' ELEMENTALS OF STONEHENGE. Though the day of the Druids
is now long passed and the cries of their victims no longer haunt
the night and the altar stone has ceased to drip blood, yet it is
dangerous to go there when the sacrificial moon is full. For the
Druids, by the blood they shed, their vile sacrifices and fellowship
with the devil, attracted forces of evil to the place. So it is said
that shapeless invisible horrors haunt the vicinity and at certain
times crave a resting place in a human body. If once they enter
in, it is only with difficulty that they are evicted.'

" The book was many centuries old. I looked at the other books ;
they were all on the same subject. Gavin seemed to be quite crazy
about it. I told my brother, and he said that he thought poor
Gavin was overstrung.

" ' Perhaps he is possessed by an elemental,' he said, and we
both laughed.

" Next night we resolved to follow him. When he went out as
usual, the dog, to our surprise, jumped into the car. Gavin threw
him out with a force that surprised us, and bade us call him back.
We endeavoured to do so, but the animal seemed demented ; he
ran after the car like a mad thing, and both were soon lost in the
distance.

" After half an hour we followed on the same road. It was a lovely night, warm, with the sky full of scudding clouds which every now and then hid the face of the moon and dimmed its light. Some little way off we left the car and started to walk across the grass. Tall and gaunt the dolmen stood out where the moonlight touched them. Somehow to me they looked unaccountably sinister, as if they longed to fall and crush one.

" We were still some way off when we saw a figure steal out from one of the great stones. In the dim light it looked like a misty wraith. I heard my brother draw in his breath sharply.

" It stopped before the altar stone, which was deeply in the shadow. Something flashed in the light—a knife ; then it seemed from the stone itself came the most ear-splitting howl of agony.

" The moon went behind a cloud ; we fled, stumbling over the wet grass, and in our haste missed the car. At last we found it, and, tumbling in, drove off at a great pace. When we got back again Gavin was already in bed and had to come down to open the door. He was too tired to notice anything wrong, and we just said that we had been for a drive.

" Next day, after rather a sleepless night, we were heartily ashamed of our weakness, and firmly resolved to follow Gavin again that night. All day he seemed very absorbed and dreamy, and talked only about the discovery that he was going to make.

" An hour after he had left we were on his track. This time there was no moon, but we had an electric torch. I soon caught sight of Gavin ; he was kneeling by the altar stone. It was reassuring to see his tweed-clad figure. We came up right behind, but he did not turn his head. Then I put my hand on his shoulder, but he did not move. He was unconscious. I raised his head and the light fell on glazed eyes, for he was dead. We laid him on the altar stone seeking for a spark of life, but all in vain. There was blood on his shirt and the hilt of a little knife stuck out. There he lay on the sacrificial stone with hair dishevelled, white upturned face and glassy eyes, while above towered the great stones, seeming to rejoice that once again homage had been paid by a sacrifice of blood. Queer shadows danced in the light of the lamp which my brother held in shaking hands.

" We stood with bowed heads in the presence of those great monuments ; tombstones that would have done honour to a king. Then we gathered courage and took the body to the car. And

Stonehenge let us go, content that once again its stones were wet with blood.

" It was an unconsidered thing we did, in that, and it might have led us into trouble ; but we found a letter written by Gavin and his will which he had made, so we were freed from all blame or share in the matter.

" He said that the first few nights of his excavations at Stonehenge he had been unassailed and in a perfectly normal state of mind. Then a strange change came over him, so that at times he almost seemed to have lived there years before and to know all manner of secrets.

" Then it was that the desire to do the most dreadful things came over him. He questioned if he were mad or if it was the spirit of Stonehenge demanding a victim. The idea of elementals occurred to him, for he had been reading much about them of late.

" At last he tore himself away and went to Brittany to bury himself in work. But Stonehenge called him back, and he seemed to lose all power over himself. At last, after many sleepless nights, he came back, as he had known that he must.

" Then, one night he had seen a dog lying on the altar stone, and an irresistible desire to kill overpowered him. After the blood was shed he felt a strange joy and deep contentment, but something told him that he was being watched, so he took the body and ran to the car. He had discovered a short cut across the grass which cut off many miles, so that was how he got home before us.

" Next morning he awoke with the blood lust strong within him ; he felt that if anything would come upon him at the Stones he must kill. All day he fought it. At times he would be filled with disgust at his thoughts, then fall to devising a plot to lure us to our fate.

" When we had mentioned our coming, a cold fear had seized him, but his words died in his throat when he tried to warn us. Then all the good that was in him seemed to make one last stand. He knew there was one way out—to offer a sacrifice of blood, and the victim to be himself.

" So that night he had offered his life as a propitiation for evil in the hope that he would regain the soul that once was his. He ended by begging us to forgive and forget.

" The letter accomplished a purpose. ' Suicide while of

unsound mind,' was brought in. Suspicion was lifted from us, but afterwards Bob and I went away from the horrible place."

No one spoke. We sat in dead silence when he had finished. Then the gong rang, and we arose and knocked the ashes from our pipes.

Jasper John

THE SEEKER OF SOULS

from SINISTER STORIES

Henry Walker, 1930

It was in a deathly silence that we awaited the coming of the hour that would release the evil thing. I heard someone cough, and it echoed through the house. The clock ticked away the minutes with a grim satisfaction, and my neighbour breathed in a noisy fashion. But for once I was grateful for both sounds ; they were something ordinary and commonplace, belonging to everyday life. The moonlight streamed in at the window, making little pools of silver here and there on the walls and floor.

A clattering whirl of machinery, and the clock in the tower commenced to strike the hour. Every stroke of the chimes rever-berated through the house. Dead silence for a moment after the last note had quivered away. Then a door banged and there was the sound of shuffling footsteps out in the passage ; a strange cry, half animal, half human, but of something enraged. For three nights it had aroused even the deepest sleepers from their slumbers.

The thing, whatever it was, started coming down the passage, banging at the doors as it did so. What was it—man or beast ? We only knew that it was horribly evil and paralysed the bravest of us with fear. Inside was darkness save where the moonlight pierced it, and outside, beyond the door, the unknown, the feared. Not for life itself would I have dared to open the barrier which stood between us.

I looked at John. He had sat up in bed. A shaft of moonlight struck him, and I saw his eyes were fixed and staring ; he shook like an aspen.

"My God, man, what is it?" His voice was strained and seemed torn from him in the horror of the moment.

But I had no explanation to offer, nor much taste for conversation, so remained silent.

After a time the thing outside grew tired of wandering and returned to its room. A wave of relief swept over us; we felt that since the hour had struck we had been very near to something from hell, something fiendish and very powerful.

Next morning, as usual, we gathered round the breakfast table, and the host looked round at the black-rimmed eyes. I remember everything: the silver vase on the table, filled with red roses, the shining tea-cups and the tense atmosphere.

Three nights of terror were telling on us all. Philip, as host, found our silence jarred on his nerves. Suddenly and irritably he broke out:

"Anyhow, that thing does no harm knocking on the doors, and I must beg you all to keep it from the servants. The other wing will be inhabitable in a few days, and then we will move over there. In the meantime, if anyone is afraid, he is welcome to go. I don't want to keep anyone against his will."

We were all sorry for him, and somehow it seemed like rats leaving a sinking ship to desert now, though afterwards we wished we had possessed the courage. If anyone had spoken we others would have joined with him, but no one wished to be the first.

It was bad luck for Philip. The place had taken his fancy; a fine, rambling old castle with good fishing and shooting, it was just what he wanted. The view was superb, for it stood high in the hills.

When he had taken it Philip had heard whisperings of ghosts and strange doings; but what Englishman could believe those things? Owing to pressing circumstances of the impoverished family who owned it, the purchase money had been paid in advance.

When the castle was up for sale only one wing was ready for occupation, and none of the servants' quarters. However, we were none of us averse to roughing it with daily helps when it was a question of first-class fishing. So, when Philip had offered the invitation, it had been eagerly accepted.

At last breakfast drew to a close, and Philip made a sign to me to follow him. He took me into the shrubbery and, sitting down on a stump, took out his pipe.

" No one is likely to bother us here," he said. " Now, Peter, I want you, as my greatest friend, to help me to get to the bottom of this. We are going to explore the haunted room in daylight while the others are busy with their letters."

" I am your man," I answered, with a laugh.

" Well, let's get to work then. I have the key of the side door."

He got up and started fumbling about until he found a door hidden away amongst the ivy. The hinges were rusty and gave a heavy groan as we pushed it open. I followed Philip up a steep staircase until we came on to the passage, just by the haunted room. He took a big key from his pocket, and the lock turned without a sound.

" Better to keep it shut," he said. Then, without the slightest misgiving, we stepped inside.

It was a beautiful room, with costly things, but what struck me was that everything was twisting ; the legs of the furniture were carved like snakes. Then my eyes wandered to the tapestry. The same design there : serpents wrought in gold, with gleaming red and green eyes, worked on a black ground, with here and there the face of a grinning devil.

It was a beautiful, dreadful room ; that was the puzzling part. There was a strong smell of damp fungus and bad, rotting things, though the sun streamed in at the window and there was no sign of mildew. It was uncanny and fascinating, the way everything twisted and writhed. There was not a breath of wind, but the bed hangings moved in a sinuous fashion, like the coils of a snake.

The actual furniture consisted of a four-poster bed, a writing-table, a few chairs and a huge cupboard. The windows were stained glass with a border of leaded panes.

It came to me suddenly, as I stood gazing, that, terror of terrors, MY SOUL WAS BEING STOLEN AWAY ; the spirit of the room was tearing it from me. I knew that I must fight as I had never fought before. The devils were trying to get it from me. The knowledge of what it meant gave me strength ; in my imagination I saw the whole army of Dante's inferno arrayed against me.

In silent horror I struggled to get out of that room. I had seen the war through ; but that was fighting against flesh and blood ; this against spirits. Then the awful thing that happened was that one half of me wanted to stay frantically. I fought against it. I suppose that the evil in my nature joined with the evil in that room to betray me to the devils.

My feet seemed as if they had leaden weights attached, my tongue was powerless, and I felt like a helpless child in the grip of a giant. But I hoped that strength would be given me to resist, and I dared not yield to despair.

How long the agony endured I do not know, for it seemed as if the power of that room would draw me to itself as a straw in a whirlpool ; but in the end I won through. It was a wonderful moment when I was out in the passage again.

Then I saw through the open door that Philip was still in the room, and experiencing the same horror. His face was white and so set that it was more like a death mask than that of a human being. I tried to call, to help him, but all power was taken from me ; I was helpless. So I stood there in mortal fear, gazing and gazing. Then he was out in the passage and the door of the unholy room banged to.

The tension released, we sank down in utter exhaustion. I heard Philip's heavy breathing coupled with my own for a few minutes ; then he made a sound between a sob and a groan, and I found the tears coursing down my face.

Fortunately no one came that way. It was fully lunch-time before we had recovered ourselves. There was a thick white streak in Philip's hair which had not been there before. We told them at lunch that we had been down the river together, and had to go through a good amount of chaff about returning empty-handed.

That afternoon a party had been planned, and we had to go. I expect that it was best for us, though we found it very difficult to listen to the idle chatter round us. I had a talk with Philip about moving before that night, but the only accommodation was cottages, and we lacked the courage to give the word to pack. It would only be a few days more until the other wing was ready.

After all, banging on the doors was nothing to what we had been through. As usual, the thing came that night, knocking at the doors ; after it had gone I fell into a deep sleep.

Next morning, when I awoke, there was a great noise ; everyone seemed to be talking outside in the passage, and someone was crying hysterically. Above all I heard Philip's calm, deep voice restoring order. A few moments afterwards he came to my room, and I saw that beneath his outward calm he was very worried.

He told me that the milkman, making his early rounds, had been attracted by somebody lying under a yew tree. It was a young boy with his throat cut. There was a blood-stained razor in his clenched hand ; it looked like a clear case of suicide.

I hastily donned some clothes, while Philip sent the women away with a few stern words about behaving in a foolish manner. All of us men went with Philip to see the body. It was that of a boy of about eighteen. He must have been a handsome lad, for his features were curiously classical and locked, under the hand of death, as if they were chiselled in marble. A long strand of hair fell across his face, and on his throat was a horrible mass of gashes and cuts, evidently wrought by an inexperienced hand.

Only—such a boy ! What could have impelled him to this deed ? Had he, too, been enmeshed in the evil of the place ? Here came to me the desolation, human and spiritual, which I know no words to describe. The wind moved the branches of the tree and a shower of drops fell, as if even Nature wept at such a tragedy.

It is only a confused memory now of what was done and said. I felt that I could have joined the women in their hysterical sobs, but there was Philip to be thought of. They told me afterward that I kept my head and gave out orders like a robot, with an unmoved face.

The police, such as they were, took most of the responsibility. The old man in charge did not appear unduly surprised ; indeed, he took it quite as a matter of course. He walked up to the house with Philip and I, and sat down in the study for a talk. Mechanically, Philip handed him a cigar, and, amid the heavy fumes of smoke, I remember hearing his voice in a rich Irish brogue.

" Well, sir," he said, warming to his task, " you don't know this place. There is something here which attracts them to come and die here. There have been some from the house too. 'Tis an evil place, and cursed so that none can live here, though 'tis a fine place. But I suppose that you did not know, sir. Anyhow, if I were you, sir, I would leave and go away." He finished with rather an air of triumph at having proved his point to a couple of prosaic Englishmen.

As for Philip, he had sat staring out of the window all this time. Now he roused himself and gave the sergeant a handsome tip for his trouble, and begged him to say as little as possible.

When he had gone we stood at the window and watched the men preparing to take the corpse away. At last the little dark-clad procession passed out of view. Philip turned to me and said : " Ever heard of an exorcist ? I have sent for one to see if he can

expel the evil spirit from this place. The car left early this morning ; he should be here this evening."

Our new guest arrived in time for the evening meal. He was
short and jovial and kept us all amused by his chatter, but he
never made any mention of spirits or ghosts. He seemed to know
most of the details when Philip tried to tell him. He warned us
that the thing would make more noise that night, but he promised that no harm should come to us.

All was quiet as usual until the hour struck. Then the thing
came out and raged up and down. When it came to the door of
the exorcist it rattled at the handle and screamed with rage. At
last it wearied of its wanderings and returned to the room. The
exorcist told us that he had passed the night in prayer.

Next morning, after breakfast, the ceremony of expelling the
evil spirit took place. We all waited outside in the passage while
the exorcist went alone into the room, having enjoined us not to
come in, whatever happened.

In a loud, clear voice he began the prayers, holding a book and
a lighted candle in his hands. First thing the candle went out ;
then his face began to distort itself in various grimaces. When the
prayer was finished candle and book fell to the ground. He appeared to be fighting for breath, and cried out that he was being
throttled.

We tried to move, but were transfixed. There were strange
moanings, cries and groans ; then he was thrown with violence
into the passage and the door banged to.

The spell being broken, we bent anxiously over the victim, but
he had gone into a dead faint and there were red marks on his
throat. We carried him to his room and laid him on the bed. When
he recovered consciousness it was very evident that he had been
face to face with something very dreadful even for a man used to
evil and sinister things.

We were debating to send for a doctor, but he overheard, and
forbade us. He said these things were among the incomprehensible and beyond the sphere of man. He spoke to Philip alone,
and told him that the place was evil and it was better to go, for
there was a terrible power hidden in that room. When Philip
came out he told us all to pack, as he had decided to leave next
day.

We were all so occupied that it was only when we heard the
powerful engines of a car coming up the drive that we remembered

Guy Dennis was expected. He was very popular, with his good nature and cheery ways. He asked if we were not glad to see him, and why we all looked like a pack of ghosts. Then Philip started to explain in a mild way what had happened. Guy burst into fits of laughter. So Philip lost his temper and told him the bare truth, and we all bore witness to it. Guy saw that we were really serious about it.

" Dreadfully sorry," he said, " to be such an unbelieving sinner." And he laughed again.

There was something very cheering to have him there laughing at our fears, with his six-foot-four of common sense.

" I suggest a drink all round now, and request that I may sleep in your haunted room," he said.

The first part of the request was granted, but Philip was very firm in his " No " to the other.

I must confess that, under Guy's influence, I almost thought that the whole thing was only overwrought imagination, but a sense of fear and depression soon returned. That evening passed fairly quickly. We all got into bed with a feeling of relief that it was to be our last night in that place !

I fell almost immediately into a heavy sleep, and I dreamt that I was in a prison cell and that all around me were people being tortured. They brought in a huge man, bound, and commenced to put out his eyes. His screams were dreadful to hear. Then I woke to find myself in bed, but the cry still rang in my ears. I leapt out of bed, for it was coming from the passage. I stumbled out with a candle, and found the others there before me.

It was with a great shock that I saw Guy Dennis rolling about in the passage, alternately laughing and crying ; for he was raving mad. I heard a voice say he had tried to sleep in that room just so as to be able to laugh at us in the morning, and this was what had happened !

We all stood there watching Guy laughing and showing his teeth. Then suddenly his mood changed and he rushed at us in a rage. There was a grim fight ; candles fell to the ground and were trodden out, but in the end we overpowered him and bound him with sheets. Most of us were bleeding, for Guy had used teeth and nails against us.

The struggle had exhausted him. He went off into a faint, while the foam dried on his lips. We threw water on him and rubbed his temples. He opened his eyes with a groan and started moving his lips, but he was inaudible at first ; then he started talking as if in a dream.

" I sorry—wanted to sleep there . . . light, such a queer light. No, it was a pillar of whitish matter, near, very near. There was something green in the middle . . . damp and wet. It came out. . . . I can see it ! It is all eyes . . . no, all hands ... no, all face, all claws ! It has hundreds of eyes. I must look at it ! They are dreadful eyes ; they scorch . . . no, they freeze me, but I must look. Now it has only half a face ; but the eyes ! . . . It laughs at me and gibbers. It is thrusting me out. I want to go back. The door is shut and the master calls me. Master, I cannot get back ; it is not my fault." He tried to rise and fell back, quieter.

For a short time he slept, but about two o'clock he woke again and started moaning and praying.

" Take me away, take me away, for Heaven's sake take me away ! Have pity, have pity ! " He tossed to and fro in his agony and fear. " It is calling me ; I must go back ! " he moaned.

We were a weird group round the figure on the bed, all dressed in oddments of clothes.

The exorcist said that we must get him away at once, out of the house ; that the power of evil was very prevalent that night.

Six of us carried Guy between us. He had gone into a trance again, so it was not difficult. Down the dark passage and the great oak staircase we went, men up against the great unknown, and very fearful.

Philip had locked and barred the door with care that night. We were obliged to put our burden down to struggle with the fastenings ; as our hands were trembling, it took some time. At last the great door swung open on its hinges.

We stepped out into the warm darkness, and the procession continued down the drive, our way lit by a storm lantern. Long, dark shadows stole across the path, and every dark bush seemed to contain some lurking terror. Then, with a soft whirl of wings, an owl flew across our path.

When we reached the gates they were as welcome for us flying from evil in the dark night, as those of Paradise. The gamekeeper's cottage was quite near, Philip said ; so we walked on in silence.

The little cabin was all in darkness, but it did not take very long to rouse the good man and his wife. The Irish are very quick to understand and they did not ask an undue number of questions until we were ready to tell them. Nor were they incredulous at our story.

The good woman made a bed for Guy and we laid him on it. Poor Guy he never recovered from that night ; we were obliged to leave him in an asylum in Dublin. From time to time he would break out in violent fits when the memory of what he had seen broke upon him. I often go and see him.

The next day Philip and I went back to shut up the house. It looked very pleasant in the sunlight, that haunt of evil. We did as little as possible ; it was too full of awful memories to linger. At the lodge gates we looked back for the last time. The sun was blazing down and the gardens were bright with colour ; then the gate shut behind us on the dreadful secret evil which reigned there.

Roger Pater

THE ASTROLOGER'S LEGACY
from MYSTIC VOICES

Burns, Oates and Washbourne, 1923

May 26th, St. Philip's feast, is the squire's birthday, and every year he celebrates the day by giving a little dinner party to a few very intimate friends. But, as he says, rather sadly, " I have out-lived most of my generation " ; and, for some years past, the whole number, including the host and a guest or two who may be staying at the Hall, has seldom reached as many as ten.

On the first birthday for which I was present there were only half a dozen of us in all at the dinner. These were, first, Father Bertrand, an English Dominican Friar, and one of the squire's oldest friends, who usually spent some weeks with him every summer. Second, Sir John Gervase, a local baronet and anti-quarian, who, besides being an F.S.A., and one of the greatest living authorities on stained glass, was also one of the few Catholic gentry in the neighbourhood of Stanton Rivers. The third was Herr Aufrecht, a German professor, who had come to England to study some manuscripts in the British Museum, and had brought a letter of introduction from a common friend in Munich. Fourth, there was the rector of the next parish, who had been a Fellow of one of the colleges at Cambridge for most of his life, but had accepted the living, which was in the gift of his college, a few years previously, and had since become very intimate with the old squire, who, with myself, completed the number.

The mansion of Stanton Rivers is built round a little quadrangle, of which the servants' quarters and kitchen occupy the north side, the dining-room being at the north end of the west wing. When we are alone, however, the squire has all meals served in the morning-room ; a small, cheerful apartment on the east side of the house, with dull, ivory-coloured walls, hung with exquisite old French pastels, and furnished entirely with Chippendale furniture, designed expressly for the squire's grandfather by the famous cabinet maker ; the original contract and bills for which are preserved in the family archives.

The birthday dinner, however, as befits an "institution," is always served in the dining-room proper, which is approached through the beautiful long apartment, stretching the whole length of the west wing, which the squire has made into the library. The dining-room is large and finely proportioned, and has its original Jacobean decoration, the walls being panelled in dark oak, with a carved cornice and plaster ceiling delicately moulded with a strapwork design, in which the cockle shells of the Rivers escutcheon are repeated again and again in combination with the leopards' heads of Stanton. The broad, deep fireplace has polished steel " dogs " instead of a grate, and above it is a carved overmantel reaching to the ceiling, and emblazoned with all the quarterings the united families can boast, with their two mottoes, which combine so happily, *Sans Dieu rien* and *Garde ta Foy*.

I think the squire would prefer not to use the dining-room even for his birthday dinner, but he hasn't the heart to sadden Avison, the butler, by suggesting this. Indeed, the occasion is Avison's annual opportunity, and he glories in decking out the table with the finest things the house possesses in the way of family plate, glass, and china : while Mrs. Parkin. the cook, and Saunders, the gardener, in their respective capacities, second his efforts with the utmost zeal.

The evening was an exquisite one, and we sat in the library talking and watching the changing effects of the fading lights as they played on the garden before the windows, until Avison threw open the folding doors and announced that dinner was served.

Hitherto I had only seen the room in *déshabillé*, and it was quite a surprise to see how beautiful it now looked. The dark panelling, reflecting the warm sunset glow which came in through the broad mullioned windows, formed a perfect background to the dinner-table, with its shaded candles, delicate flowers, and gleams of light from glass and plate : and I felt that Avison's effort was really an artistic triumph. The same thought, I fancy, struck the rest of the guests, for no sooner had Father Bertrand said grace than Sir John burst out in admiration :

" My dear squire, what exquisite things you do possess ! Some day I shall come and commit a burglary on you. Your glass and silver are a positive temptation."

The host smiled, but I noticed that his eyes were fixed on the centre of the table, and that the eyelids were slightly drawn down, an expression I had learned to recognise as a sign of annoyance, carefully controlled. Following his gaze, I glanced at the table-centre, but before I could decide what it was, the German professor, who was sitting next me, broke out in a genial roar :

" Mein Gott, Herr Pater, but what is this ? " and he pointed to the exquisite piece of plate in the centre of the table.

"We call it the Cellini fountain, Herr Aufrecht," answered the squire, " though it is certainly not a fountain, but a rose-water dish, and I can give you very little evidence that it is really Cellini's work."

" Effidence," exclaimed the German—" it has its own effidence. What more want you ? None but Benvenuto could broduce such a one. But how did you come to possess it ? "

There was no doubt about the eyelids now, and I feared the other guests would notice their host's annoyance, but the squire controlled his voice perfectly as he answered :

" Oh, it has been in the family for more than three centuries ; Sir Hubert Rivers, the ancestor whose portrait hangs at the foot of the stairs, is believed to have brought it back from Italy."

I thought I could guess the cause of his annoyance now, for the ancestor in question had possessed a most unenviable reputation, and, by a strange trick of heredity, the squire's features were practically a reproduction of Sir Hubert's—a fact which was a source of no little secret chagrin to the saintly old priest. Fortunately, at this point, the rector turned the conversation down another channel ; Herr Aufrecht did not pursue the subject further, and the squire's eyelids soon regained their normal elevation.

As the meal advanced the German came out as quite a brilliant talker, and the conversational ball was kept up so busily between Father Bertrand, the rector, and himself that the other three of us had little to do but listen and be entertained. A good deal of the talk was above my head, however, and during these periods my attention came back to the great rose-water dish which shone and glittered in the centre of the table.

In the first place I had never seen it before, which struck me as a little odd, for Avison had discovered my enthusiasm for old silver, and so had taken me to the pantry and displayed all the plate for my benefit. However, I concluded that so valuable a piece was probably put away in the strong-room, which would account for its not appearing with the rest.

What puzzled me more was the unusual character of the design, for every curve and line of the beautiful piece seemed purposely arranged to concentrate the attention on a large globe of rock crystal, which formed the centre and summit of the whole. The actual basin, filled with rose-water, extended beneath this ball, which was supported by four exquisite silver figures, and the constant play of reflected lights between the water and the crystal was so fascinating that I wondered the idea had never been repeated ; yet, so far as my knowledge went, the design was unique.

Seated as I was, at the foot of the table, I faced the squire, and after a while I noticed that he, too, had dropped out of the conversation, and had his gaze fixed on the crystal globe. All at once his eyes dilated and his lips parted quickly, as if in surprise, while his gaze became concentrated with an intensity that startled me. This lasted for fully a minute, and then Avison happened to take away his plate. The distraction evidently broke the spell, whatever it was, for he began to talk again, and, as it seemed to me, kept his eyes carefully away from the crystal during the rest of the meal.

After we had drunk the squire's health, we retired to the library, where Avison brought us coffee, and about ten o'clock Sir John's carriage was announced. He had promised to give the rector a lift home, so the two of them soon departed together, and only the professor and Father Bertrand were left with the squire and myself. I felt a little afraid lest Herr Aufrecht should return to the subject of the Cellini fountain, but to my surprise, as soon as the other two were gone, the squire himself brought up the subject, which I thought he wished to avoid.

" You seemed interested in the rose-water fountain, Herr Aufrecht," he remarked, " would you like to examine it now that the others are gone ? "

The German beamed with delight, and accepted the proposal volubly, while the squire rang the bell for Avison, and ordered him to bring the Cellini fountain to the library for Herr Aufrecht to see. The butler looked almost as pleased as the professor, and in a minute the splendid piece of plate was placed on a small table, arranged in the full light of a big shaded lamp.

The professor's flow of talk stopped abruptly as the conversationalist gave place to the connoisseur. Seating himself beside the little table, he produced a pocket lens, and proceeded to examine every part of the fountain with minute care, turning it slowly round as he did so. For fully five minutes he sat in silence, absorbed in his examination, and I noticed that his attention returned continually to the great crystal globe, supported by the four lovely figures, which formed the summit of the whole. Then he leaned back in his chair and delivered his opinion.

" It is undoubtedly by Cellini," he said, " and yet the *schema* is not like him. I think the patron for whom he laboured did compel him thus to fashion it. That great crystal ball at top—no, it is not what Benvenuto would do of himself. Think you not so ? " and he turned to the squire with a look of interrogation.

" I will tell you all I know about it in a minute, professor," answered the old priest, " but first please explain to me why you think Cellini was not left free in the design."

" Ach so," replied the German, " it is the crystal globe. He is too obvious, too assertive ; how is it you say in English, he ' hit you in the eye.' You haf read the *Memoirs* of Benvenuto ? " The squire nodded. " Ach, then you must see it, yourself. Do you not remember the great morse he make, the cope-clasp for Clemens *septimus* ? The Pope show to him his great diamond, and demand a model for a clasp with it set therein. The other artists, all of them, did make the diamond the centre of the whole design. But Cellini ? No. He put him at the feet of God the Father, so that the lustre of the great gem would set off all the work, but should not dominate the whole, for *ars est celare artem*. Now here," and he laid his hand upon the crystal globe, " here it is otherwise. These statuette, they are perfection, in efery way they are worth far more than is the crystal. Yet, the great ball, he crush them, he kill them. You see him first, last, all the time. No, he is there for a purpose, but the purpose is not that of the design, not an artistic purpose, no. I am sure of it, he is there for use."

As he finished speaking, he turned quickly towards the squire, and looked up at him with an air of conviction. I followed his example, and saw the old priest smiling quietly with an expression of admiration and agreement.

"You are perfectly right, professor," he said quietly, "the crystal was put there with a purpose, at least so I firmly believe ; and I expect you can tell us also what the purpose was."

"No, no, Herr Pater," answered the other. "If you know the reason, why make I guesses at it ? Better you should tell us all about it, is it not so ? "

"Very well," replied the squire, and he seated himself beside the little table. Father Bertrand and myself did the same, and when we were all settled, he turned to the professor and began :

"I mentioned at dinner that this piece of plate was brought from Italy by Sir Hubert Rivers, and, first of all, I must tell you something about him. He was born about the year 1500, and lived to be over ninety years old, so his life practically coincides with the sixteenth century. His father died soon after Hubert came of age, and he thus became a person of some importance while still quite young. He was knighted by Henry VIII a year or two later, and soon afterwards was sent to Rome in the train of the English Ambassador.

"There his brilliant parts attracted attention, and he soon abandoned his diplomatic position to become a member of the Papal *entourage*, though without any official position. When the breach between Henry and the Pope took place, he attached himself to the suite of the Imperial Ambassador, thus avoiding any trouble with his own sovereign, who could not afford to quarrel still further with the Emperor, as well as any awkward questions as to his religious opinions.

"Of his life in Rome I can tell you practically nothing, but if tradition be true, he was a typical son of the Renaissance. He played with art, literature, and politics ; and he more than played with astrology and the black arts, being, in fact, a member of the famous, or infamous, Academy. You may remember how that institution, which was founded in the fifteenth century by the notorious Pomponio Leto, used to hold its meetings in one of the catacombs. Under Paul II the members were arrested and tried for heresy, but nothing could be actually proved against them, and afterwards they were supposed by their contemporaries to have reformed. We know now that in reality things went from bad to worse. The study of paganism led them on to the worship of Satan, and eventually suspicion was again aroused, and a further investigation ordered.

" Sir Hubert got wind of this in time, however, so he availed himself of his position in the household of the Imperial Ambassador, and quietly retired to Naples. There he lived till he was over eighty, and no one in England ever expected him to return. But he did so, bringing with him a great store of books and manuscripts, some pictures, and this piece of plate ; and he died and was buried here in the last decade of the sixteenth century.

" His nephew, who came in for the estates on his death, was a devout Catholic, and had been educated at St. Omers. He made short work with Sir Hubert's manuscripts, most of which he burned, as being heretical or worse, but he spared one volume, which contains an inventory of the things brought from Naples. Among the items mentioned is this fountain. In fact, it has a whole page to itself, with a little sketch and a note of its attribution to Cellini, besides some other words, which I have never been able to make out. But I think it is clear that the crystal was used for evil purposes, and that is why I dislike seeing it on the table. If Avison had asked me, I should have forbidden him to produce it."

" Then I am ver' glad he did not ask you, mein Herr," observed the German, bluntly, " for I should not then have seen him. But this inventory you speak of, is it permitted that I study it ? "

" Certainly, Herr Aufrecht," replied the squire, and walking to one of the bookcases, he unlocked the glass doors and took out a small volume, bound in faded red leather with gilt ornaments.

" This is the book," he said ; " I will find you the page with the sketch," and a minute later he handed the volume to the professor. I glanced across and saw a little drawing, unquestionably depicting the piece of plate before us, with some lines of writing beneath ; the whole in faded ink, almost the colour of rust.

The professor's lens came out again and, with its aid, he read out the description beneath the picture.

" ' Item. *Vasculum argenteum, crystallo ornatum in quattuor statuas imposito. Opus Benevenuti, aurificis clarissimi. Quo crystallo Romæ in ritibus nostris pontifex noster Pomponius olim uti solebat.'* "[1]

" Well, that sounds conclusive enough," said Father Bertrand, who had been listening intently. " *Opus Benevenuti, aurificis clarissimi,* could only mean Cellini ; and the last sentence certainly sounds very suspicious, though it doesn't give one much to go upon as to the use made of the crystal."

" But there is more yet," broke in Herr Aufrecht, " it is in another script and much fainter." He peered into the page with eyes screwed up, and then exclaimed in surprise, " Why it is Greek ! "

" Indeed," said the squire, with interest, " that accounts for my failure to read it. I'm afraid I forgot all the Greek I ever knew as soon as I left school."

Meanwhile the professor had produced his pocket-book, and was jotting down the words as he deciphered them, while Father Bertrand and myself took the opportunity to examine the work on the little plaques which adorned the base of the fountain.

" I haf him all now," announced Herr Aufrecht, triumphantly, after a few minutes. " Listen and I will translate him to you," and after a little hesitation he read out the following :

" In the globe all truth is recorded, of the present, the past and the future.
To him that shall gaze it is shown ; whosoever shall seek he shall find.
O Lucifer, star of the morn, give ear to the voice of thy servant,
Enter and dwell in my heart, who adore thee as master and lord."

Fabius Britannicus.

" *Fabius Britannicus,*" exclaimed the squire, as the professor ceased reading, " why, those are the words on the base of the pagan altar in the background of Sir Hubert's portrait ! "

" I doubt not he was named *Fabius Britannicus* in the Academia," answered the German ; " all the members thereof did receive classical names in place of their own."

" It must be that," said the squire ; " so he really was a worshipper of Satan. No wonder tradition paints him in such dark colours. But, why—of course," he burst out, " I see it all now, that explains everything."

---

[1] " Item. A vessel of silver, adorned with a crystal supported on four statuettes. The work of Benvenuto, most famous of goldsmiths. This crystal our Pontiff Pomponius was wont to use in our rites at Rome in days gone by."

We all looked up, surprised at his vehemence, but he kept silent, until Father Bertrand said gently :

" I think, Philip, you can tell us something more about all this ; will you not do so ? "

The old man hesitated for a little while and then answered : " Very well, if you wish it, you shall hear the story ; but I must ask you to excuse me giving you the name. Although the principal actor in it has been dead many years now, I would rather keep his identity secret.

" When I was still quite a young man, and before I decided to take orders, I made friends in London with a man who was a spiritualist. He was on terms of intimacy with Home, the medium, and he himself possessed considerable gifts in the same direction. He often pressed me to attend some of their séances, which I always refused to do, but our relations remained quite friendly, and at length he came down here on a visit to Stanton Rivers.

" The man was a journalist by profession, a critic and writer on matters artistic, so one evening, although we were quite alone at dinner, I told the butler, Avison's predecessor, to put out the Cellini fountain for him to see. I did not warn him what to expect, as I wanted to get his unbiased opinion, but the moment he set eyes on it, he burst out in admiration, and, like our friend the professor to-night, he pronounced it to be unquestionably by Benvenuto himself.

" I said it was always believed to be his work, but purposely told him nothing about Sir Hubert, or my suspicions as to the original use of the crystal, and he did not question me about its history. As the meal advanced, however, he became curiously silent and self-absorbed. Sometimes I had to repeat what I was saying two or three times before he grasped the point ; and I began to feel uncomfortable and anxious, so that it was a real relief when the butler put the decanters on the table and left us to ourselves.

" My friend was sitting on my right, at the side of the table, so that we could talk to each other more easily, and I noticed that he kept his gaze fixed on the fountain in front of him. After all it was a very natural thing for him to do, and at first I did not connect his silence and distraction with the piece of plate.

" All at once he leaned forward until his eyes were not two feet away from the great crystal globe, into which he gazed with the deepest attention, as if fascinated. It is difficult to convey to you how intense and concentrated his manner became. It was as if he looked right into the heart of the globe—not *at* it, if you understand, but at something inside it, something beneath the surface, and that something of a compelling, absorbing nature which engrossed every fibre of his being in one act of profound attention.

" For a minute or two he sat like this in perfect silence, and I noticed the sweat beginning to stand out on his forehead, while his breath came audibly between his lips, under the strain. Then, all at once, I felt I must do something, and without stopping to deliberate I said in a loud tone, ' I command you to tell me what it is you see.'

" As I spoke, a kind of shiver ran through his frame, but his eyes never moved from the crystal ball. Then his lips moved, and after some seconds came a faint whisper, uttered as if with extreme difficulty, and what he said was something like this :

" ' There is a low, flat arch, with a kind of slab beneath it, and a picture at the back. There is a cloth on the slab, and on the cloth a tall gold cup, and lying in front of it is a thin white disc. By the side is a monster, like a huge toad,' and he shuddered, ' but it is much too big to be a toad. It glistens, and its eyes have a cruel light in them. Oh, it is horrible ! ' Then all at once the voice leaped to a shrill note, and he spoke very rapidly, as if the scene were changing quicker than he could describe it.

" ' The man in front—the one with a cross on the back of his cloak—is holding a dagger in his hand. He raises it and strikes at the white disc. He has pierced it with the dagger. It bleeds ! The white cloth beneath it is all red with blood. But the monster— some of the blood has fallen upon it as it spurted out, and the toad is writhing as if in agony. Ah ! it leaps down from the slab, it is gone. All present rise up in confusion ; there is a tumult. They rush away down the dark passages. Only one remains, the man with the cross on his back. He is lying insensible upon the ground. On the slab still stands the gold cup and white disc with the blood-stained cloth, and the picture behind——' and the voice sank to an inaudible whisper, as if the speaker were exhausted.

" Almost without thinking, I put a question to him before the sight should fade entirely. ' The picture, what is it like ? ' But instead of answering he merely whispered ' *Irene, da calda,*' and fell back as if exhausted in his chair."

There was silence for a few moments.

" And your friend, the spiritualist," began Father Bertrand, " could he tell you nothing more of what he saw ? "

" I did not ask him," answered the old priest, " for, when he came to himself, he seemed quite ignorant of what he had told me during his trance. But, some years afterwards, I got some further light on the incident, and that in quite an unexpected way. Just wait a minute, and I will show you what I believe to be the picture he saw at the back of the niche ! " And the old man walked to one of the bookcases and selected a large folio volume.

" The picture I am going to show you is an exact copy of one of the frescoes in the catacombs of SS. Peter and Marcellinus, where I came upon it, quite unexpectedly, during my period in Rome as a student ; it has been reproduced since by Lanciani in one of his books. Ah, here it is," and he laid the album on the table.

There, before us, was a copy of an undeniable catacomb fresco depicting an "agape" or love-feast ; a group of figures symbolical both of the Last Supper and the communion of the elect, Above it were the contemporary inscriptions, " IRENE DA CALDA " and " AGAPE MISCE MI," while round about were scrawled, in characters evidently much more recent, a number of names : " POMPONIUS, FABIANUS, RUFFUS, LETUS, VOLSCUS, FABIUS " and others, all of them members of the notorious Academy. There they had written them in charcoal, and there they still remain to-day, as evidence how the innermost recesses of a Christian catacomb were profaned, and the cult of Satan practised there, by the neo-pagans of the fifteenth and sixteenth centuries.

We sat looking at the picture in silence for a minute or so, and then Herr Aufrecht turned to the Dominican.

" Fra Bertrand," he said, " you are Master in *Theologia*, what is your opinion of all this ? "

The friar hesitated for a moment before he answered.

" Well, Herr Aufrecht," he said at length, " the Church has never ceased to teach the possibility of diabolical possession, and for my part I see no reason why a thing," and he pointed to the crystal, " should not become ' possessed ' in much the same way as a person can. But if you ask my opinion on the practical side of the question, I should say that, since Father Philip here cannot legally part with his heirloom, he certainly acts wisely in keeping it under lock and key."

Amelia B. Edwards

MY BROTHER'S GHOST STORY

from ALL THE YEAR ROUND, 1860

Mine is my brother's Ghost Story. It happened to my brother about thirty years ago, while he was wandering, sketch-book in hand, among the High Alps, picking up subjects for an illustrated work on Switzerland. Having entered the Oberland by the Brunig Pass, and filled his portfolio with what he used to call " bits " from the neighbourhood of Meyringen, he went over the Great Scheideck to Grindlewald, where he arrived one dusky September evening, about three-quarters of an hour after sunset. There had been a fair that day, and the place was crowded. In the best inn there was not an inch of space to spare—there were only two inns at Grindlewald, thirty years ago—so my brother went to one at the end of the covered bridge next the church, and there, with some difficulty, obtained the promise of a pile of rugs and a mattress, in a room which was already occupied by three other travellers.

The Adler was a primitive hostelry, half farm, half inn, with great rambling galleries outside, and a huge general room, like a barn. At the upper end of this room stood long stoves, like metal counters, laden with steaming-pans, and glowing underneath like furnaces. At the lower end, smoking, supping, and chatting, were congregated some thirty or forty guests, chiefly mountaineers, char drivers, and guides. Among these my brother took his seat, and was served, like the rest, with a bowl of soup, a platter of beef, a flagon of country wine, and a loaf made of Indian corn. Presently, a huge St. Bernard dog came and laid his nose upon my brother's arm. In the meantime he fell into conversation with two Italian youths, bronzed and dark-eyed, near whom he happened to be seated. They were Florentines. Their names, they told him, were Stefano and Battisto. They had been travelling for some months on commission, selling cameos, mosaics, sulphur casts, and the like pretty Italian trifles, and were now on their way to Interlaken and Geneva. Weary of the cold North, they longed, like children, for the moment which should take them back to their own blue hills and grey-green olives ; to their workshop on the Ponte Vecchio, and their home down by the Arno.

It was quite a relief to my brother, on going up to bed, to find that these youths were to be two of his fellow-lodgers. The third was already there, and sound asleep, with his face to the wall. They scarcely looked at this third. They were all tired, and all anxious to rise at daybreak, having agreed to walk together over the Wengern Alp as far as Lauterbrunnen. So, my brother and the two youths exchanged a brief good night, and, before many minutes, were all as far away in the land of dreams as their unknown companion.

My brother slept profoundly—so profoundly that, being roused in the morning by a clamour of merry voices, he sat up dreamily in his rugs, and wondered where he was.

" Good day, signor," cried Battisto. " Here is a fellow-traveller going the same way as ourselves."

" Christien Baumann, native of Kandersteg, musical-box maker by trade, stands five feet eleven in his shoes, and is at monsieur's service to command," said the sleeper of the night before.

He was as fine a young fellow as one would wish to see. Light, and strong, and well proportioned, with curling brown hair, and bright, honest eyes that seemed to dance at every word he uttered.

" Good morning," said my brother. " You were asleep last night when we came up."

" Asleep ! I should think so, after being all day in the fair, and walking from Meyringen the evening before. What a capital fair it was ! "

" Capital, indeed," said Battisto. " We sold cameos and mosaics yesterday, for nearly fifty francs."

" Oh, you sell cameos and mosaics, you two ! Show me your cameos, and I will show you my musical boxes. I have such pretty ones, with coloured views of Geneva and Chillon on the lids, playing two, four, six, and even eight tunes. Bah ! I will give you a concert ! "

And with this he unstrapped his pack, displayed his little boxes on the table, and wound them up, one after the other, to the delight of the Italians.

" I helped to make them myself, every one," said he, proudly. " Is it not pretty music ? I sometimes set one of them when I go to bed at night, and fall asleep listening to it. I am sure, then, to have pleasant dreams ! But let us see your cameos. Perhaps I may buy one for Marie, if they are not too dear. Marie is my sweetheart, and we are to be married next week."

" Next week ! " exclaimed Stefano. " That is very soon. Battisto has a sweetheart also, up at Impruneta ; but they will have to wait a long time before they can buy the ring."

Battisto blushed like a girl.

" Hush, brother ! " said he. " Show the cameos to Christien, and give your tongue a holiday ! "

But Christien was not so to be put off.

" What is her name ? " ṣaid he. " Tush ! Battisto, you must tell me her name ! Is she pretty ? Is she dark, or fair ? Do you often see her when you are at home ? Is she very fond of you ? Is she as fond of you as Marie is of me ? "

" Nay, how should I know that ? " asked the soberer Battisto. " She loves me, and I love her—that is all."

" And her name ? "

" Margherita."

" A charming name ! And she is herself as pretty as her name, I'll engage. Did you say she was fair ? "

" I said nothing about it one way or the other," said Battisto, unlocking a green box clamped with iron, and taking out tray after tray of his pretty wares. " There ! Those pictures all inlaid in little bits are Roman mosaics—these flowers on a black ground are Florentine. The ground is of hard dark stone, and the flowers are made of thin slices of jasper, onyx, cornelian, and so forth. Those forget-me-nots, for instance, are bits of turquoise, and that poppy is cut from a piece of coral."

" I like the Roman ones best," said Christien. " What place is that with all the arches ? "

" This is the Coliseum, and the one next to it is St. Peter's. But we Florentines care little for the Roman work. It is not half so fine or so valuable as ours. The Romans make their mosaics of composition."

" Composition or no, I like the little landscapes best," said Christien. " There is a lovely one, with a pointed building, and a tree, and mountains at the back. How I should like that one for Marie ! "

" You may have it for eight francs," replied Battisto ; " we sold two of them yesterday for ten each. It represents the tomb of Caius Cestius, near Rome."

" A tomb ! " echoed Christien, considerably dismayed. " Diable ! That would be a dismal present to one's bride."

" She would never guess that it was a tomb, if you did not tell her," suggested Stefano.

Christien shook his head.

" That would be next door to deceiving her," said he.

" Nay," interposed my brother, " the owner of that tomb has been dead these eighteen or nineteen hundred years. One almost forgets that he was ever buried in it."

" Eighteen or nineteen hundred years? Then he was a heathen? "

" Undoubtedly, if by that you mean that he lived before Christ." Christien's face lighted up immediately.

" Oh, that settles the question," said he, pulling out his little canvas purse, and paying his money down at once. " A heathen's tomb is as good as no tomb at all. I'll have it made into a brooch for her, at Interlaken. Tell me, Battisto, what shall you take home to Italy for your Margherita? "

Battisto laughed, and chinked his eight francs. " That depends on trade," said he ; " if we make good profits between this and Christmas, I may take her a Swiss muslin from Berne ; but we have already been away seven months, and we have hardly made a hundred francs over and above our expenses."

And with this, the talk turned upon general matters, the Florentines locked away their treasures, Christien restrapped his pack, and my brother and all went down together, and breakfasted in the open air outside the inn.

It was a magnificent morning : cloudless and sunny, with a cool breeze that rustled in the vine upon the porch, and flecked the table with shifting shadows of green leaves. All around and about them stood the great mountains, with their blue-white glaciers bristling down to the verge of the pastures, and the pine-woods creeping darkly up their sides. To the left, the Wetterhorn ; to the right, the Eigher ; straight before them, dazzling and imperishable, like an obelisk of frosted silver, the Schreckhorn, or Peak of Terror. Breakfast over, they bade farewell to their hostess, and, mountain-staff in hand, took the path to the Wengern Alp. Half in light, half in shadow, lay the quiet valley, dotted over with farms, and traversed by a torrent that rushed, milk-white, from its prison in the glacier. The three lads walked briskly in advance, their voices chiming together every now and then in chorus of laughter. Somehow my brother felt sad. He lingered behind, and, plucking a little red flower from the bank, watched it hurry away with the torrent, like a life on the stream of time. Why was his heart so heavy, and why were their hearts so light?

As the day went on, my brother's melancholy, and the mirth of the young men, seemed to increase. Full of youth and hope, they talked of the joyous future, and built up pleasant castles in the air. Battisto, grown more communicative, admitted that to marry Margherita, and become a master mosaicist, would fulfil the dearest dream of his life. Stefano, not being in love, preferred to travel. Christien, who seemed to be the most prosperous, declared that it was his darling ambition to rent a farm in his native Kander Valley, and lead the patriarchal life of his fathers. As for the musical-box trade, he said, one should live in Geneva to make it answer ; and, for his part, he loved the pine-forests and the snow-peaks, better than all the towns in Europe. Marie, too, had been born among the mountains, and it would break her heart, if she thought she were to live in Geneva all her life, and never see the Kander Thal again. Chatting thus, the morning wore on to noon, and the party rested awhile in the shade of a clump of gigantic firs festooned with trailing banners of grey-green moss.

Here they ate their lunch, to the silvery music of one of Christien's little boxes, and by-and-by heard the sullen echo of an avalanche far away on the shoulder of the Jungfrau.

Then they went on again in the burning afternoon, to heights where the Alp-rose fails from the sterile steep, and the brown lichen grows more and more scantily among the stones. Here, only the bleached and barren skeletons of a forest of dead pines varied the desolate monotony ; and high on the summit of the pass, stood a little solitary inn, between them and the sky.

At this inn they rested again, and drank to the health of Christien and his bride, in a jug of country wine. He was in uncontrollable spirits, and shook hands with them all, over and over again.

" By nightfall to-morrow," said he, " I shall hold her once more in my arms ! It is now nearly two years since I came home to see her, at the end of my apprenticeship. Now I am foreman, with a salary of thirty francs a week, and well able to marry."

" Thirty francs a week ! " echoed Battisto. " Corpo di Bacco ! that is a little fortune."

Christien's face beamed.

" Yes," said he, " we shall be very happy ; and, by-and-by— who knows ?—we may end our days in the Kander Thal, and bring up our children to succeed us. Ah ! If Marie knew that I should be there to-morrow night, how delighted she would be ! "

" How so, Christien ? " said my brother. " Does she not expect you ? "

" Not a bit of it. She has no idea that I can be there till the day after to-morrow—nor could I, if I took the road all round by Unterseen and Frütigen. I mean to sleep to-night at Lauterbrunnen, and to-morrow morning shall strike across the Tschlingel glacier to Kandersteg. If I rise a little before daybreak, I shall be at home by sunset."

At this moment the path took a sudden turn, and began to descend in sight of an immense perspective of very distant valleys. Christien flung his cap into the air, and uttered a great shout.

" Look ! " said he, stretching out his arms as if to embrace all the dear familiar scene : " O ! Look ! There are the hills and woods of Interlaken, and here, below the precipices on which we stand, lies Lauterbrunnen ! God be praised, who has made our native land so beautiful ! "

The Italians smiled at each other, thinking their own Arno valley far more fair ; but my brother's heart warmed to the boy, and echoed his thanksgiving in that spirit which accepts all beauty as a birthright and an inheritance. And now their course lay across an immense plateau, all rich with corn-fields and meadows, and studded with substantial homesteads built of old brown wood, with huge sheltering eaves, and strings of Indian corn hanging like golden ingots along the carven balconies. Blue whortleberries grew beside the footway, and now and then they came upon a wild gentian, or a star-shaped immortelle. Then the path became a mere zigzag on the face of the precipice, and in less than half an hour they reached the lowest level of the valley. The glowing afternoon had not yet faded from the uppermost pines, when they were all dining together in the parlour of a little inn looking to the Jungfrau. In the evening my brother wrote letters, while the three lads strolled about the village. At nine o'clock they bade each other good night, and went to their several rooms.

Weary as he was, my brother found it impossible to sleep. The same unaccountable melancholy still possessed him, and when at last he dropped into an uneasy slumber, it was but to start over and over again from frightful dreams, faint with a nameless terror. Towards morning, he fell into a profound sleep, and never woke until the day was fast advancing towards noon. He then found, to his regret, that Christien had long since gone. He had risen before daybreak, breakfasted by candlelight, and started off in the grey dawn—" as merry," said the host, " as a fiddler at a fair."

Stefano and Battisto were still waiting to see my brother, being charged by Christien with a friendly farewell message to him, and an invitation to the wedding. They, too, were asked, and meant to go ; so, my brother agreed to meet them at Interlaken on the following Tuesday, whence they might walk to Kandersteg by easy stages, reaching their destination on the Thursday morning, in time to go to church with the bridal party. My brother then bought some of the little Florentine cameos, wished the two boys every good fortune, and watched them down the road till he could see them no longer.

Left now to himself, he wandered out with his sketch-book, and spent the day in the upper valley ; at sunset, he dined alone in his chamber, by the light of a single lamp. This meal despatched, he drew nearer to the fire, took out a pocket edition of Goethe's Essays on Art, and promised himself some hours of pleasant reading. (Ah, how well I know that very book, in its faded cover, and how often I have heard him describe that lonely evening !) The night had by this time set in cold and wet. The damp logs spluttered on the hearth, and a wailing wind swept down the valley, bearing the rain in sudden gusts against the panes. My brother soon found that to read was impossible. His attention wandered incessantly. He read the same sentence over and over again, unconscious of its meaning, and fell into long trains of thought leading far into the dim past.

Thus the hours went by, and at eleven o'clock he heard the doors closing below, and the household retiring to rest. He determined to yield no longer to this dreaming apathy. He threw on fresh logs, trimmed the lamp, and took several turns about the room. Then he opened the casement, and suffered the rain to beat against his face, and the wind to ruffle his hair, as it ruffled the acacia leaves in the garden below. Some minutes passed thus, and when, at length, he closed the window and came back into the room, his face and hair and all the front of his shirt were thoroughly saturated. To unstrap his knapsack and take out a dry shirt was, of course, his first impulse—to drop the garment, listen eagerly, and start to his feet, breathless and bewildered, was the next.

For, borne fitfully upon the outer breeze, now sweeping past the window, now dying in the distance, he heard a well-remembered strain of melody, subtle and silvery as the " sweet airs " of Prospero's isle, and proceeding unmistakably from the musical-box which had, the day before, accompanied the lunch under the fir-trees of the Wengern Alp !

Had Christien come back, and was it thus that he announced his return ? If so, where was he ? Under the window ? Outside in the corridor ? Sheltering in the porch, and waiting for admittance ? My brother threw open the casement again, and called him by his name.

" Christien ! Is that you ? "

All without was intensely silent. He could hear the last gust of wind and rain moaning farther and farther away upon its wild course down the valley, and the pine-trees shivering, like living things.

" Christien ! " he said again, and his own voice seemed to echo strangely on his ear. " Speak ! Is it you ? "

Still no one answered. He leaned out into the dark night ; but could see nothing—not even the outline of the porch below. He began to think that his imagination had deceived him, when suddenly the strain burst forth again ;—this time, apparently in his own chamber.

As he turned, expecting to find Christien at his elbow, the sounds broke off abruptly, and a sensation of intensest cold seized him in every limb—not the mere chill of nervous terror, not the mere physical result of exposure to wind and rain, but a deadly freezing of every vein, a paralysis of every nerve, an appalling consciousness that in a few moments more the lungs must cease to play, and the heart to beat ! Powerless to speak or stir, he closed his eyes, and believed that he was dying.

This strange faintness lasted but a few seconds. Gradually the vital warmth returned, and, with it, strength to close the window, and stagger to a chair. As he did so, he found the breast of his shirt all stiff and frozen, and the rain clinging in solid icicles upon his hair.

He looked at his watch. It had stopped at twenty minutes before twelve. He took his thermometer from the chimney-piece, and found the mercury at sixty-eight. Heavenly powers ! How were these things possible in a temperature of sixty-eight degrees, and with a large fire blazing on the hearth ?

He poured out half a tumbler of cognac, and drank it at a draught. Going to bed was out of the question. He felt that he dared not sleep—that he scarcely dared to think. All he could do, was, to change his linen, pile on more logs, wrap himself in his blankets, and sit all night in an easy-chair before the fire.

My brother had not long sat thus, however, before the warmth, and probably the nervous reaction, drew him off to sleep. In the morning he found himself lying on the bed, without being able to remember in the least how or when he reached it.

It was again a glorious day. The rain and wind were gone, and the Silverhorn at the end of the valley lifted its head into an unclouded sky. Looking out upon the sunshine, he almost doubted the events of the night, and, but for the evidence of his watch, which still pointed to twenty minutes before twelve, would have been disposed to treat the whole matter as a dream. As it was, he attributed more than half his terrors to the prompting of an over-active and over-wearied brain. For all this, he still felt depressed and uneasy, and so very unwilling to pass another night at Lauterbrunnen, that he made up his mind to proceed that morning to Interlaken. While he was yet loitering over his breakfast, and considering whether he should walk the seven miles of road, or hire a vehicle, a char came rapidly up to the inn door, and a young man jumped out.

" Why, Battisto ! " exclaimed my brother, in astonishment, as he came into the room ; " what brings *you* here to-day ? Where is Stefano ? "

" I have left him at Interlaken, signor," replied the Italian.

Something there was in his voice, something in his face, both strange and startling.

" What is the matter ? " asked my brother, breathlessly. " He is not ill ? No accident has happened ? "

Battisto shook his head, glanced furtively up and down the passage, and closed the door.

" Stefano is well, signor ; but—but a circumstance has occurred—a circumstance so strange !——Signor, do you believe in spirits ? "

" In spirits, Battisto ? "

" Ay, signor ; for if ever the spirit of any man, dead or living, appealed to human ears, the spirit of Christien came to me last night, at twenty minutes before twelve o'clock."

" At twenty minutes before twelve o'clock ! " repeated my brother.

" I was in bed, signor, and Stefano was sleeping in the same room. I had gone up quite warm, and had fallen asleep, full of pleasant thoughts. By-and-by, although I had plenty of bed-clothes, and a rug over me as well, I woke, frozen with cold and scarcely able to breathe. I tried to call to Stefano ; but I had no power to utter the slightest sound. I thought my last moment was come. All at once, I heard a sound under the window—a sound which I knew to be Christien's musical-box ; and it played as it played when we lunched under the fir-trees, except that it was more wild and strange and melancholy and most solemn to hear —awful to hear ! Then, signor, it grew fainter and fainter—and then it seemed to float past upon the wind, and die away. When it ceased, my frozen blood grew warm again, and I cried out to Stefano. When I told him what had happened, he declared I had been only dreaming. I made him strike a light, that I might look at my watch. It pointed to twenty minutes before twelve, and had stopped there ; and—stranger still—Stefano's watch had done the very same. Now tell me, signor, do you believe that there is any meaning in this, or do you think, as Stefano persists in thinking, that it was all a dream ? "

"What is your own conclusion, Battisto ? "

"My conclusion, signor, is that some harm has happened to poor Christien on the glacier, and that his spirit came to me last night."

"Battisto, he shall have help if living, or rescue for his poor corpse if dead ; for I, too, believe that all is not well."

And with this, my brother told him briefly what had occurred to himself in the night ; despatched messengers for the three best guides in Lauterbrunnen ; and prepared ropes, ice-hatchets, alpen-stocks, and all such matters necessary for a glacier expedition. Hasten as he would, however, it was nearly mid-day before the party started.

Arriving in about half an hour at a place called Stechelberg, they left the char, in which they had travelled so far, at a châlet, and ascended a steep path in full view of the Breithorn glacier, which rose up to the left, like a battlemented wall of solid ice. The way now lay for some time among pastures and pine-forests. Then they came to a little colony of châlets, called Steinberg, where they filled their water-bottles, got their ropes in readiness, and prepared for the Tschlingel glacier. A few minutes more, and they were on the ice.

At this point, the guides called a halt, and consulted together. One was for striking across the lower glacier towards the left, and reaching the upper glacier by the rocks which bound it on the south. The other two preferred the north, or right side ; and this my brother finally took. The sun was now pouring down with almost tropical intensity, and the surface of the ice, which was broken into long treacherous fissures, smooth as glass and blue as the summer sky, was both difficult and dangerous. Silently and cautiously, they went, tied together at intervals of about three yards each : with two guides in front, and the third bringing up the rear. Turning presently to the right, they found themselves at the foot of a steep rock, some forty feet in height, up which they must climb to reach the upper glacier. The only way in which Battisto or my brother could hope to do this, was by the help of a rope steadied from below and above. Two of the guides accordingly clambered up the face of the crag by notches in the surface, and one remained below. The rope was then let down, and my brother prepared to go first. As he planted his foot in the first notch, a smothered cry from Battisto arrested him.

" Santa Maria ! Signor ! Look yonder ! "

My brother looked, and there (he ever afterwards declared), as surely as there is a heaven above us all, he saw Christien Baumann standing in the full sunlight, not a hundred yards distant ! Almost in the same moment that my brother recognised him, he was gone. He neither faded, nor sank down, nor moved away ; but was simply gone, as if he had never been. Pale as death, Battisto fell upon his knees, and covered his face with his hands. My brother, awe-stricken and speechless, leaned against the rock, and felt that the object of his journey was but too fatally accomplished. As for the guides, they could not conceive what had happened.

" Did you see nothing ? " asked my brother and Battisto, both together.

But the men had seen nothing, and the one who had remained below, said, " What should I see but the ice and the sun ? "

To this my brother made no other reply than by announcing his intention to have a certain crevasse, from which he had not once removed his eyes since he saw the figure standing on the brink, thoroughly explored before he went a step farther ; whereupon the two men came down from the top of the crag, resumed the ropes, and followed my brother, incredulously. At the narrow end of the fissure, he paused, and drove his alpenstock firmly into the ice. It was an unusually long crevasse—at first a mere crack, but widening gradually as it went, and reaching down to unknown depths of dark deep blue, fringed with long pendent icicles, like diamond stalactites. Before they had followed the course of this crevasse for more than ten minutes, the youngest of the guides uttered a hasty exclamation.

" I see something ! " cried he. " Something dark, wedged in the teeth of the crevasse, a great way down ! "

They all saw it : a mere indistinguishable mass, almost closed over by the ice-walls at their feet. My brother offered a hundred francs to the man who would go down and bring it up. They all hesitated.

" We don't know what it is," said one.

" Perhaps it is only a dead chamois," suggested another.

Their apathy enraged him.

" It is no chamois," he said, angrily. " It is the body of Christien Baumann, native of Kandersteg. And, by Heaven, if you are all too cowardly to make the attempt, I will go down myself ! "

The youngest guide threw off his hat and coat, tied a rope about his waist, and took a hatchet in his hand.

" I will go, monsieur," said he ; and without another word, suffered himself to be lowered in. My brother turned away. A sickening anxiety came upon him, and presently he heard the dull echo of the hatchet far down in the ice. Then there was a call for another rope, and then—the men all drew aside in silence, and my brother saw the youngest guide standing once more beside the chasm, flushed and trembling, with the body of Christien lying at his feet.

Poor Christien ! They made a rough bier with their ropes and alpenstocks, and carried him, with great difficulty, back to Steinberg. There, they got additional help as far as Stechelberg, where they laid him in the char, and so brought him on to Lauterbrunnen. The next day, my brother made it his sad business to precede the body to Kandersteg, and prepare his friends for its arrival. To this day, though all these things happened thirty years ago, he cannot bear to recall Marie's despair, or all the mourning that he innocently brought upon that peaceful valley. Poor Marie has been dead this many a year ; and when my brother last passed through the Kander Thal on his way to the Ghemmi, he saw her grave, beside the grave of Christien Baumann, in the village burial-ground.

This is my brother's Ghost Story.

J. Sheridan Le Fanu

SIR DOMINICK'S BARGAIN

A Legend of Dunoran

from All The Year Round, 1872

In the early autumn of the year 1838, business called me to
the south of Ireland. The weather was delightful, the scenery and
people were new to me, and sending my luggage on by the mail-
coach route in charge of a servant, I hired a serviceable nag at a
posting-house, and, full of the curiosity of an explorer, I commenced a leisurely journey of five-and-twenty miles on horseback,
by sequestered cross-roads, to my place of destination. By bog and
hill, by plain and ruined castle, and many a winding stream, my
picturesque road led me.

I had started late, and having made little more than half my
journey, I was thinking of making a short halt at the next convenient place, and letting my horse have a rest and a feed, and
making some provision also for the comforts of his rider.

It was about four o'clock when the road, ascending a gradual
steep, found a passage through a rocky gorge between the abrupt
termination of a range of mountain to my left and a rocky hill,
that rose dark and sudden at my right. Below me lay a little
thatched village, under a long line of gigantic beech-trees, through
the boughs of which the lowly chimneys sent up their thin turf-
smoke. To my left, stretched away for miles, ascending the mountain range I have mentioned, a wild park, through whose sward
and ferns the rock broke, time-worn and lichen-stained. This
park was studded with straggling wood, which thickened to
something like a forest, behind and beyond the little village I was
approaching, clothing the irregular ascent of the hillsides with
beautiful, and in some places discoloured foliage.

As you descend, the road winds slightly, with the grey park-wall,
built of loose stone, and mantled here and there with ivy, at its
left, and crosses a shallow ford ; and as I approached the village,
through breaks in the woodlands, I caught glimpses of the long
front of an old ruined house, placed among the trees, about half-
way up the picturesque mountain-side.

The solitude and melancholy of this ruin piqued my curiosity, and when I had reached the rude thatched public-house, with the sign of St. Columbkill, with robes, mitre, and crozier displayed over its lintel, having seen to my horse and made a good meal myself on a rasher and eggs, I began to think again of the wooded park and the ruinous house, and resolved on a ramble of half an hour among its sylvan solitudes.

The name of the place, I found, was Dunoran ; and beside the gate a stile admitted to the grounds, through which, with a pensive enjoyment, I began to saunter towards the dilapidated mansion.

A long grass-grown road, with many turns and windings, led up to the old house, under the shadow of the wood.

The road, as it approached the house skirted the edge of a precipitous glen, clothed with hazel, dwarf-oak, and thorn, and the silent house stood with its wide-open hall-door facing this dark ravine, the further edge of which was crowned with towering forest ; and great trees stood about the house and its deserted court-yard and stables.

I walked in and looked about me, through passages overgrown with nettles and weeds ; from room to room with ceilings rotted, and here and there a great beam dark and worn, with tendrils of ivy trailing over it. The tall walls with rotten plaster were stained and mouldy, and in some rooms the remains of decayed wainscoting crazily swung to and fro. The almost sashless windows were darkened also with ivy, and about the tall chimneys the jackdaws were wheeling, while from the huge trees that overhung the glen in sombre masses at the other side, the rooks kept up a ceaseless cawing.

As I walked through these melancholy passages—peeping only into some of the rooms, for the flooring was quite gone in the middle, and bowed down toward the centre, and the house was very nearly un-roofed, a state of things which made the exploration a little critical—I began to wonder why so grand a house, in the midst of scenery so picturesque, had been permitted to go to decay ; I dreamed of the hospitalities of which it had long ago been the rallying place, and I thought what a scene of Redgauntlet revelries it might disclose at midnight.

The great staircase was of oak, which had stood the weather wonderfully, and I sat down upon its steps, musing vaguely on the transitoriness of all things under the sun.

Except for the hoarse and distant clamour of the rooks, hardly audible where I sat, no sound broke the profound stillness of the spot. Such a sense of solitude I have seldom experienced before. The air was stirless, there was not even the rustle of a withered leaf along the passage. It was oppressive. The tall trees that stood close about the building darkened it, and added something of awe to the melancholy of the scene.

In this mood I heard, with an unpleasant surprise, close to me, a voice that was drawling, and, I fancied, sneering, repeat the words : " Food for worms, dead and rotten ; God over all."

There was a small window in the wall, here very thick, which had been built up, and in the dark recess of this, deep in the shadow, I now saw a sharp-featured man, sitting with his feet dangling. His keen eyes were fixed on me, and he was smiling cynically, and before I had well recovered my surprise, he repeated the distich :

> *If death was a thing that money could buy,*
> *The rich they would live, and the poor they would die.*

" It was a grand house in its day, sir," he continued, " Dunoran House, and the Sarsfields. Sir Dominick Sarsfield was the last of the old stock. He lost his life not six foot away from where you are sitting."

As he thus spoke he let himself down, with a little jump, on to the ground.

He was a dark-faced, sharp-featured, little hunchback, and had a walking-stick in his hand, with the end of which he pointed to a rusty stain in the plaster of the wall.

" Do you mind that mark, sir ? " he asked.

" Yes," I said, standing up, and looking at it, with a curious anticipation of something worth hearing.

" That's about seven or eight feet from the ground, sir, and you'll not guess what it is."

" I dare say not," said I, " unless it is a stain from the weather."

" 'Tis nothing so lucky, sir," he answered, with the same cynical smile and a wag of his head, still pointing at the mark with his stick. " That's a splash of brains and blood. It's there this hundhred years ; and it will never leave it while the wall stands."

" He was murdered, then ? "

" Worse than that, sir," he answered.

" He killed himself, perhaps ? "

" Worse than that, itself, this cross between us and harm ! I'm oulder than I look, sir ; you wouldn't guess my years."

He became silent, and looked at me, evidently inviting a guess.

" Well, I should guess you to be about five-and-fifty."

He laughed, and took a pinch of snuff, and said :

" I'm that, your honour, and something to the back of it. I was seventy last Candlemas. You would not a' thought that, to look at me."

" Upon my word I should not ; I can hardly believe it even now. Still, you don't remember Sir Dominick Sarsfield's death ? " I said, glancing up at the ominous stain on the wall.

" No, sir, that was a long while before I was born. But my grandfather was butler here long ago, and many a time I heard tell how Sir Dominick came by his death. There was no masther in the great house ever sinst that happened. But there was two sarvants in care of it, and my aunt was one o' them ; and she kep' me here wid her till I was nine year old, and she was lavin' the place to go to Dublin ; and from that time it was let to go down. The wind sthript the roof, and the rain rotted the timber, and little by little, in sixty years' time, it kem to what you see. But I have a likin' for it still, for the sake of ould times ; and I never come this way but I take a look in. I don't think it's many more times I'll be turnin' to see the ould place, for I'll be undher the sod myself before long."

" You'll outlive younger people," I said.

And, quitting that trite subject, I ran on :

" I don't wonder that you like this old place ; it is a beautiful spot, such noble trees."

" I wish ye seen the glin when the nuts is ripe ; they're the sweetest nuts in all Ireland, I think," he rejoined, with a practical sense of the picturesque. " You'd fill your pockets while you'd be lookin' about you."

" These are very fine old woods," I remarked. " I have not seen any in Ireland I thought so beautiful."

" Eiah ! your honour, the woods about here is nothing to what they wor. All the mountains along here was wood when my father was a gossoon, and Murroa Wood was the grandest of them all. All oak mostly, and all cut down as bare as the road. Not one left here that's fit to compare with them. Which way did your honour come hither—from Limerick ? "

" No. Killaloe."

" Well, then, you passed the ground where Murroa Wood was in former times. You kem undher Lisnavourra, the steep knob of a hill about a mile above the village here. 'Twas near that Murroa Wood was, and 'twas there Sir Dominick Sarsfield first met the devil, the Lord between us and harm, and a bad meeting it was for him and his."

I had become interested in the adventure which had occurred in the very scenery which had so greatly attracted me, and my new acquaintance, the little hunchback, was easily entreated to tell me the story, and spoke thus, so soon as we had each resumed his seat :

It was a fine estate when Sir Dominick came into it ; and grand doings there was entirely, feasting and fiddling, free quarters for all the pipers in the counthry round, and a welcome for every one that liked to come. There was wine, by the hogshead, for the quality ; and potteen enough to set a town a-fire, and beer and cidher enough to float a navy, for the boys and girls, and the likes o' me. It was kep' up the best part of a month, till the weather broke, and the rain spoilt the sod for the moneen jigs, and the fair of Allybally Killudeen comin' on they wor obliged to give over their divarsion, and attind to the pigs.

But Sir Dominick was only beginnin' when they wor lavin' off. There was no way of gettin' rid of his money and estates he did not try—what with drinkin', dicin', racin', cards, and all soarts, it was not many years before the estates wor in debt, and Sir Dominick a distressed man. He showed a bold front to the world as long as he could ; and then he sould off his dogs, and most of his horses, and gev out he was going to thravel in France, and the like ; and so off with him for awhile ; and no one in these parts heard tale or tidings of him for two or three years. Till at last quite unexpected, one night there comes a rapping at the big kitchen window. It was past ten o'clock, and old Connor Hanlon, the butler, my grand-father, was sittin' by the fire alone, warming his shins over it. There was keen east wind blowing along the mountains that night, and whistling cowld enough through the tops of the trees, and soundin' lonesome through the long chimneys.

(And the story-teller glanced up at the nearest stack visible from his seat.)

So he wasn't quite sure of the knockin' at the window, and up he gets, and sees his master's face.

My grandfather was glad to see him safe, for it was a long time since there was any news of him ; but he was sorry, too, for it was a changed place and only himself and old Juggy Broadrick in charge of the house, and a man in the stables, and it was a poor thing to see him comin' back to his own like that.

He shook Con by the hand, and says he :

" I came here to say a word to you. I left my horse with Dick in the stable ; I may want him again before morning, or I may never want him."

And with that he turns into the big kitchen, and draws a stool, and sits down to take an air of the fire.

" Sit down, Connor, opposite me, and listen to what I tell you, and don't be afeard to say what you think."

He spoke all the time lookin' into the fire, with his hands stretched over it, and a tired man he looked.

" An why should I be afeard, Masther Dominick ? " says my grandfather. " Yourself was a good masther to me, and so was your father, rest his sould, before you, and I'll say the truth, and dar' the devil, and more than that, for any Sarsfield of Dunoran, much less yourself, and a good right I'd have."

" It's all over with me, Con," says Sir Dominick.

" Heaven forbid ! " says my grandfather.

" 'Tis past praying for," says Sir Dominick. " The last guinea's gone ; the ould place will follow it. It must be sold, and I'm come here, I don't know why, like a ghost to have a last look round me, and go off in the dark again."

And with that he tould him to be sure, in case he should hear of his death, to give the oak box, in the closet off his room, to his cousin, Pat Sarsfield, in Dublin, and the sword and pistols his grandfather carried in Aughrim, and two or three thrifling things of the kind.

And says he, " Con, they say if the divil gives you money over-night, you'll find nothing but a bagful of pebbles, and chips, and nutshells, in the morning. If I thought he played fair, I'm in the humour to make a bargain with him to-night."

" Lord forbid ! " says my grandfather, standing up, with a start and crossing himself.

" They say the country's full of men, listin' sogers for the King o' France. If I light on one o' them, I'll not refuse his offer. How contrary things goes ! How long is it since me and Captain Waller fought the jewel at New Castle ? "

" Six years, Masther Dominick, and ye broke his thigh with the bullet the first shot."

" I did, Con," says he, " and I wish, instead, he had shot me through the heart. Have you any whisky ? "

My grandfather took it out of the buffet, and the masther pours out some into a bowl, and drank it off.

" I'll go out and have a look at my horse," says he, standing up. There was sort of a stare in his eyes, as he pulled his riding-cloak about him, as if there was something bad in his thoughts.

" Sure, I won't be a minute running out myself to the stable, and looking after the horse for you myself," says my grandfather.

" I'm not goin' to the stable," says Sir Dominick ; " I may as well tell you, for I see you found it out already—I'm goin' across the deer-park ; if I come back you'll see me in an hour's time. But, anyhow, you'd better not follow me, for if you do I'll shoot you, and that 'id be a bad ending to our friendship."

And with that he walks down this passage here, and turns the key in the side door at that end of it, and out wid him on the sod into the moonlight and the cowld wind ; and my grandfather seen him walkin' hard towards the park-wall, and then he comes in and closes the door with a heavy heart.

Sir Dominick stopped to think when he got to the middle of the deer-park, for he had not made up his mind, when he left the house and the whisky did not clear his head, only it gev him courage.

He did not feel the cowld wind now, nor fear death, nor think much of anything, but the shame and fall of the old family.

And he made up his mind, if no better thought came to him between that and there, so soon as he came to Murroa Wood, he'd hang himself from one of the oak branches with his cravat.

It was a bright moonlight night, there was just a bit of a cloud driving across the moon now and then, but, only for that, as light a'most as day.

Down he goes, right for the wood of Murroa. It seemed to him every step he took was as long as three, and it was no time till he was among the big oak-trees with their roots spreading from one to another, and their branches stretching overhead like the timbers of a naked roof, and the moon shining down through them, and casting their shadows thick and twist abroad on the ground as black as my shoe.

He was sobering a bit by this time, and he slacked his pace, and he thought 'twould be better to list in the French king's army, and thry what that might do for him, for he knew a man might take his own life any time, but it would puzzle him to take it back again when he liked.

Just as he made up his mind not to make away with himself, what should he hear but a step clinkin' along the dry ground under the trees, and soon he sees a grand gentleman right before him comin' up to meet him.

He was a handsome young man like himself, and he wore a cocked-hat with gold-lace round it, such as officers wears on their coats, and he had on a dress the same as French officers wore in them times.

He stopped opposite Sir Dominick, and he cum to a standstill also.

The two gentlemen took off their hats to one another, and says the stranger :

" I am recruiting, sir," says he, " for my sovereign, and you'll find my money won't turn into pebbles, chips, and nutshells, by to-morrow."

At the same time he pulls out a big purse full of gold.

The minute he set eyes on that gentleman, Sir Dominick had his own opinion of him ; and at those words he felt the very hair standing up on his head.

" Don't be afraid," says he, " the money won't burn you. If it proves honest gold, and if it prospers with you, I'm willing to make a bargain. This is the last day of February," says he ; " I'll serve you seven years, and at the end of that time you shall serve me, and I'll come for you when the seven years is over, when the clock turns the minute between February and March ; and the first of March ye'll come away with me, or never. You'll not find me a bad master, any more than a bad servant. I love my own ; and I command all the pleasures and the glory of the world. The bargain dates from this day, and the lease is out at midnight on the last day I told you ; and in the year "—he told him the year, it was easy reckoned, but I forget it—" and if you'd rather wait," he says, " for eight months and twenty eight days, before you sign the writin', you may, if you meet me here. But I can't do a great deal for you in the mean time ; and if you don't sign then, all you get from me, up to that time, will vanish away, and you'll be just as you are to-night, and ready to hang yourself on the first tree you meet."

Well, the end of it was, Sir Dominick chose to wait, and he came back to the house with a big bag full of money, as round as your hat a'most.

My grandfather was glad enough, you may be sure, to see the master safe and sound again so soon. Into the kitchen he bangs again, and swings the bag o' money on the table ; and he stands up straight, and heaves up his shoulders like a man that has just got shut of a load ; and he looks at the bag, and my grandfather looks at him, and from him to it, and back again. Sir Dominick looked as white as a sheet, and says he :

" I don't know, Con, what's in it ; it's the heaviest load I ever carried."

He seemed shy of openin' the bag ; and he made my grandfather heap up a roaring fire of turf and wood, and then, at last, he opens it, and, sure enough, 'twas stuffed full o' golden guineas, bright and new, as if they were only that minute out o' the Mint.

Sir Dominick made my grandfather sit at his elbow while he counted every guinea in the bag.

When he was done countin', and it wasn't far from daylight when that time came, Sir Dominick made my grandfather swear not to tell a word about it. And a close secret it was for many a day after.

When the eight months and twenty-eight days were pretty near spent and ended, Sir Dominick returned to the house here with a troubled mind, in doubt what was best to be done, and no one alive but my grandfather knew anything about the matter, and he not half what had happened.

As the day drew near, towards the end of October, Sir Dominick grew only more and more troubled in mind,

One time he made up his mind to have no more to say to such things, nor to speak again with the like of them he met with in the wood of Murroa. Then, again, his heart failed him when he thought of his debts, and he not knowing where to turn. Then, only a week before the day, everything began to go wrong with him. One man wrote from London to say that Sir Dominick paid three thousand pounds to the wrong man, and must pay it over again ; another demanded a debt he never heard of before ; and another, in Dublin, denied the payment of a thundherin' big bill, and Sir Dominick could nowhere find the receipt, and so on, wid fifty other things as bad.

Well, by the time the night of the 28th of October came round, he was a'most ready to lose his senses with all the demands that

was risin' up again him on all sides, and nothing to meet them
but the help of the one dhreadful friend he had to depind on at
night in the oak-wood down there below.

So there was nothing for it but to go through with the business
that was begun already, and about the same hour as he went last,
he takes off the little crucifix he wore round his neck, for he was a
Catholic, and his gospel, and his bit o' the thrue cross that he had
in a locket, for since he took the money from the Evil One he was
growin' frightful in himself, and got all he could to guard him
from the power of the devil. But to-night, for his life, he daren't
take them with him. So he gives them into my grandfather's hands
without a word, only he looked as white as a sheet o' paper ; and
he takes his hat and sword, and telling my grandfather to watch for
him, away he goes, to try what would come of it.

It was a fine still night, and the moon—not so bright, though,
now as the first time—was shinin' over heath and rock, and down
on the lonesome oak-wood below him.

His heart beat thick as he drew near it. There was not a sound,
not even the distant bark of a dog from the village behind him.
There was not a lonesomer spot in the country round, and if it
wasn't for his debts and losses that was drivin' him on half mad, in
spite of his fears for his soul and his hopes of paradise, and all his
good angel was whisperin' in his ear, he would a' turned back, and
sent for his clargy, and made his confession and his penance, and
changed his ways, and led a good life, for he was frightened
enough to have done a great dale.

Softer and slower he stept as he got, once more, in undher the
big branches of the oak-threes ; and when he got in a bit, near
where he met with the bad spirit before, he stopped and looked
round him, and felt himself, every bit, turning as cowld as a dead
man, and you may be sure he did not feel much betther when he
seen the same man steppin' from behind the big tree that was
touchin' his elbow a'most.

" You found the money good," says he, " but it was not enough.
No matter, you shall have enough and to spare. I'll see after your
luck, and I'll give you a hint whenever it can serve you ; and any
time you want to see me you have only to come down here, and
call my face to mind, and wish me present. You shan't owe a
shilling by the end of the year, and you shall never miss the
right card, the best throw, and the winning horse. Are you
willing ? "

The young gentleman's voice almost stuck in his throat, and his hair was rising on his head, but he did get out a word or two to signify that he consented ; and with that the Evil One handed him a needle, and bid him give him three drops of blood from his arm ; and he took them in the cup of an acorn, and gave him a pen, and bid him write some words that he repeated, and that Sir Dominick did not understand, on two thin slips of parchment. He took one himself and the other he sunk in Sir Dominick's arm at the place where he drew the blood, and he chosed the flesh over it. And that's as true as you're sittin' there !

Well, Sir Dominick went home. He was a frightened man, and well he might be. But in a little time he began to grow aisier in his mind. Anyhow, he got out of debt very quick, and money came tumbling in to make him richer, and everything he took in hand prospered, and he never made a wager, or played a game, but he won ; and for all that, there was not a poor man on the estate that was not happier than Sir Dominick.

So he took again to his old ways ; for, when the money came back, all came back, and there were hounds and horses, and wine galore, and no end of company, and grand doin's, and divarsion, up here at the great house. And some said Sir Dominick was thinkin' of gettin' married ; and more said he wasn't. But, anyhow, there was somethin' troublin' him more than common, and so one night, unknownst to all, away he goes to the lonesome oak-wood. It was something, maybe, my grandfather thought was troublin' him about a beautiful young lady he was jealous of, and mad in love with her. But that was only guess.

Well, when Sir Dominick got into the wood this time, he grew more in dread than ever ; and he was on the point of turnin' and lavin' the place, when who should he see, close beside him, but my gentleman, seated on a big stone undher one of the trees. In place of looking the fine young gentleman in goold lace and grand clothes he appeared before, he was now in rags, he looked twice the size he had been, and his face smutted with soot, and he had a murtherin' big steel hammer, as heavy as a half-hundhred, with a handle a yard long, across his knees. It was so dark under the tree, he did not see him quite clear for some time.

He stood up, and he looked awful tall entirely. And what passed between them in that discourse my grandfather never heered. But Sir Dominick was as black as night afterwards, and hadn't a laugh for anything nor a word a'most for any one, and he only grew worse and worse. and darker and darker. And now this thing, whatever it was, used to come to him of its own accord, whether he wanted it or no ; sometimes in one shape, and sometimes in another, in lonesome places, and sometimes at his side by night when he'd be ridin' home alone, until at last he lost heart altogether and sent for the priest.

The priest was with him a long time, and when he heered the whole story, he rode off all the way for the bishop, and the bishop came here to the great house next day, and he gev Sir Dominick a good advice. He toult him he must give over dicin', and swearin', and drinkin', and all bad company, and live a vartuous steady life until the seven years bargain was out, and if the divil didn't come for him the minute afther the stroke of twelve the first morning of the month of March, he was safe out of the bargain. There was not more than eight or ten months to run now before the seven years wor out, and he lived all the time according to the bishop's advice, as strict as if he was " in retreat."

Well, you may guess he felt quare enough when the mornin' of the 28th of February came.

The priest came up by appointment, and Sir Dominick and his raverence wor together in the room you see there, and kep' up their prayers together till the clock struck twelve, and a good hour after, and not a sign of a disturbance, nor nothing came near them, and the priest slep' that night in the house in the room next Sir Dominick's, and all went over as comfortable as could be, and they shook hands and kissed like two comrades after winning a battle.

So, now, Sir Dominick thought he might as well have a pleasant evening, after all his fastin' and praying ; and he sent round to half a dozen of the neighbouring gentlemen to come and dine with him, and his raverence stayed and dined also, and a roarin' bowl o' punch they had, and no end o' wine, and the swearin' and dice, and cards and guineas changing hands, and songs and stories, that wouldn't do any one good to hear, and the priest slipped away, when he seen the turn things was takin', and it was not far from the stroke of twelve when Sir Dominick, sitting at the head of his table, swears, " this is the best first of March I ever sat down with my friends."

" It ain't the first o' March," says Mr. Hiffernan of Ballyvoreen. He was a scholard, and always kep' an almanack.

" What is it, then ? " says Sir Dominick, startin' up, and

dhroppin' the ladle into the bowl, and starin' at him as if he had two heads.

" 'Tis the twenty-ninth of February, leap year," says he. And just as they were talkin', the clock strikes twelve ; and my grandfather, who was half asleep in a chair by the fire in the hall, openin' his eyes, sees a short square fellow with a cloak on, and long black hair bushin' out from under his hat, standin' just there where you see the bit o' light shinin' again' the wall.

(My hunchbacked friend pointed with his stick to a little patch of red sunset light that relieved the deepening shadow of the passage.)

" Tell your master," says he, in an awful voice, like the growl of a baist, " that I'm here by appointment, and expect him downstairs this minute."

Up goes my grandfather, by these very steps you are sittin' on.

" Tell him I can't come down yet," says Sir Dominick, and he turns to the company in the room, and says he with a cold sweat shinin' on his face, " for God's sake, gentlemen, will any of you jump from the window and bring the priest here ? " One looked at another and no one knew what to make of it, and in the meantime, up comes my grandfather again, and says he, tremblin', " He says, sir, unless you go down to him, he'll come up to you."

" I don't understand this, gentlemen, I'll see what it means," says Sir Dominick, trying to put a face on it, and walkin' out o' the room like a man through the press-room, with the hangman waitin' for him outside. Down the stairs he comes, and two or three of the gentlemen peeping over the banisters, to see. My grandfather was walking six or eight steps behind him, and he seen the stranger take a stride out to meet Sir Dominick, and catch him up in his arms, and whirl his head against the wall, and wi' that the hall-doore flies open, and out goes the candles, and the turf and wood-ashes flyin' with the wind out o' the hall-fire, ran in a drift o' sparks along the floore by his feet.

Down runs the gintlemen. Bang goes the hall-doore. Some comes runnin' up, and more runnin' down, with lights. It was all over with Sir Dominick. They lifted up the corpse, and put its shoulders again' the wall ; but there was not a gasp left in him. He was cowld and stiffenin' already.

Pat Donovan was comin' up to the great house late that night and after he passed the little brook, that the carriage track up to the house crosses, and about fifty steps to this side of it, his dog, that was by his side, makes a sudden wheel, and springs over the wall, and sets up a yowlin' inside you'd hear a mile away ; and that minute two men passed him by in silence, goin' down from the house, one of them short and square, and the other like Sir Dominick in shape, but there was little light under the trees where he was, and they looked only like shadows ; and as they passed him by he could not hear the sound of their feet and he drew back to the wall frightened ; and when he got up to the great house, he found all in confusion, and the master's body, with the head smashed to pieces, lying just on *that spot*.

The narrator stood up and indicated with the point of his stick the exact site of the body, and, as I looked, the shadow deepened, the red stain of sunlight vanished from the wall, and the sun had gone down behind the distant hill of New Castle, leaving the haunted scene in the deep grey of darkening twilight.

So I and the story-teller parted, not without good wishes on both sides, and a little " tip " which seemed not unwelcome, from me.

It was dusk and the moon up by the time I reached the village, remounted my nag, and looked my last on the scene of the terrible legend of Dunoran.

Vincent O'Sullivan

THE BARGAIN OF RUPERT ORANGE

from A BOOK OF BARGAINS

Leonard Smithers, 1896

I

The marvel is, that the memory of Rupert Orange, whose name was a signal for chatter amongst people both in Europe and America not many years ago, has now almost died out. Even in New York where he was born, and where the facts of his secret and mysterious life were most discussed, he is quite forgotten. At times, indeed, some old lady will whisper to you at dinner, that a certain young man reminds her of Rupert Orange, only he is not so handsome ; but she is one of those who keep the mere incidents of their past much more brightly polished than the important things of their present. The men who worshipped him, who copied his clothes, his walk, his mode of pronouncing words, and his manner of saying things, stare vaguely when he is mentioned. And the other day at a well-known club I was having some general talk with a man whose black hair is shot with white, when he exclaimed somewhat suddenly : " How little one hears about Rupert Orange now ! " and then added : " I wonder what became of him ? " As to the first part of this speech I kept my mouth resolutely shut ; for how could I deny his saying, since I had lately seen a weed-covered grave with the early moss growing into the letters on the headstone ? As to the second part, it is now my business to set forth the answer to that : and I think when the fire begins to blaze it will lighten certain recollections which have become dark. Of course, there are numberless people who never heard the story of Rupert Orange ; but there are also crowds of men and women who followed his brilliant life with intense interest, while his shameful death will be in many a one's remembrance.

The knowledge of this case I got over a year ago ; and I would have written then, had my hands been free. But there has recently died at Vienna the Countess de Volnay, whose notorious connection with Orange was at one time the subject of every man's bruit. Her I met two years since in Paris, where she was living like a work-woman. I learned that she had sold her house, and her goods she had given to the poor. She was still a remarkable woman, though her great beauty had faded, and despite a restless, terrified manner, which gave one the monstrous idea that she always felt the devil looking over her shoulder. Her hair was white as paper, and yet she was far from the age when women cease to grin in ball-rooms. A great fear seemed to have sprung to her face and been paralyzed there : a fear which could be detected in her shaking voice. It was from her that I learned certain primary facts of this narration ; and she cried to me not to publish them till I heard of her death—as a man on the gallows sometimes asks the hangman not to adjust the noose too tight round his neck. I am altogether sure that what Orange himself told her, he never told any one else. I wish I had her running tongue instead of my slow pen, and then I would not be writing slovenly and clumsily, doubtless, for the relation ; vainly, I am afraid, for the moral.

Now Rupert Orange lived with his aunt in New York till he was twenty-four years old, and when she died, leaving her entire estate to him, a furious contest arose over the will. Principal in the contest was Mrs. Annice, the wife of a discarded nephew ; and she prosecuted the cause with the pertinacity and virulence which we often find in women of thirty. So good a pursuivant did she prove, that she and her husband leaped suddenly from indigence to great wealth : for the Court declared that the old lady had died lunatic ; that she had been unduly influenced ; and, that consequently her testament was void. But this decision, which raised them up, brought Rupert to the ground. There is no worse fall than the fall of a man from opulence to poverty ; and Rupert, after his luxurious rearing, had to undergo this fall. Yet he had the vigour and confidence of the young. His little verses and sonnets had been praised when he was an amateur ; now he undertook to make his pen a breadwinner—with the direst results. At first, nothing would do him but the great magazines ; and from these, week after week, he received back his really clever articles, accompanied by cold refusals. Then for months he hung about the offices of every outcast paper, waiting for the editor. When at length the editor did come, he generally told Rupert that he had promised all his outlying work to some bar-room acquaintance. So push by push he was brought to his knees ; and finally he dared not walk out till nightfall, for fear some of those who knew him in prosperity might witness his destitution.

One night early in December, about six o'clock, he left the mean flat-house on the west side of the city in which he occupied one room, and started (as they say in New York) " up town." The snow had frozen in lumps, and the gas lamps gleamed warmly on it for the man who had not seen a fire in months. When he reached Fifty-ninth Street, he turned east and skirted Central Park till he came to the Fifth Avenue. And here a sudden fancy seized him to walk this street, which shame and pride had kept him off since his downfall. He had not proceeded far, when he was stopped by an old man.

" Can you tell me, sir," says the old man, politely, " if this street runs on further than Central Park ? "

" Oh, yes," answered Rupert, scraping at his throat ; for he had not spoken to a soul for five days, and the phlegm had gathered. " It goes up a considerable distance from here."

" You'll forgive me asking you," went on the ancient. " I am only passing through the city, and I want to find out all I can."

" You're quite welcome," said Orange, " That," he added, pointing, " is St. Luke's Hospital."

They spoke a few more sentences, then as the stranger turned " down town," Rupert fell in with his walk. He did this partly because he was craving for fellowship ; partly, too, from that feeling which certain men have—men who have never done anything for themselves in this world, and never will do anything—that distant relations, and even total strangers, are apt at any moment to fling fortunes into their hands. As they proceeded along the avenue, Orange turned to survey his companion. A shrewd wind was blowing, and it tossed the old gentleman's long beard over his shoulder, and ruffled the white hair under his soft hat. His clothes were plain, even shabby ; and he had an odd trick of planting his feet on the ground without bending his knees, as though his legs were broomsticks. Orange thought, bitterly enough ! how short a time had passed since the days when he would have taken poison as an alternative to walking down the Fifth Avenue with such an associate. Now, they were equal : or indeed the old man was the better off of the two : for if he wore impossible broad-toed boots, Orange had to stamp his feet to keep the cold from striking through his worn-out shoes. What cared he for the criticism of the smart, well-fed " Society " now, when numbers of that far greater society, of which he was one, were starving in garrets ! As he thought these things a late afternoon reception began to pour out its crowds, and a young man and a girl, who had known Rupert in the days of his prosperity, came forth and glared with contempt at the two mean passengers. Not a muscle in Rupert's face quivered : he even afforded those two the tribute of a sneer.

When the pair of walkers reached Thirty-fourth Street they switched into Broadway. A silence had fallen between them, and it was in silence they paraded the thoroughfare. Here all was garish light and glare : carriages darted to and fro, restaurants were thronged, theatres ablaze, women smiling : everything told of a great city starting a night of pleasure. Besides the love of pleasure which was his main characteristic, Orange was distinctly gregarious ; and the sight of all this joy, which he had once revelled in himself, struck like a knife into his hungry, lonely heart. At that moment he thought he would give his very soul to get some money.

" All these people seem happy," says the old man, suddenly.

" Yes," replied Orange. " *They* are happy enough ! "

The old man caught the reply, and noticed the sour twang in

it. He looked up quickly and saw that Rupert's eyes watered.

"Why, man," he exclaimed, "I believe you're crying ! or perhaps you're cold ! Come in here, come right in to the Hoffman House ! " he went on, tugging at Rupert's coat.

Rupert hesitated. The sensitiveness of one who had never taken a favour which he could not repay, held him back. But the desire for warmth and sympathy prevailed, so he entered. The usual crowd of loafers was about the bar, and those who composed it looked scoffingly at Orange's shiny overcoat and time-eaten trousers. Believe me, the man in rags is not half so pitiable as the poor creature who tries to maintain the appearance of a gentleman : the man who inks seams by night which grow all white by day ; who keeps his fingers close pressed to his palm lest the rents in his glove be seen ; who walks with his arm across his breast for fear his coat should fly open and proclaim its lack of buttons. Even the waiters looked disparagingly at Orange ; and a waiter's jibes, or any flunkey's, are, perhaps, the sorest of all. But the old man, without noticing, sat down at a table and ordered a bottle of champagne. When the wine was brought, the two sat together some time in a muse. Then, of a sudden, the greybeard broke out.

"Wealth ! " he cried, staring into Rupert's eyes, "wealth is the only thing worth striving for in this world ! Your tub-philosophers may laugh at it, but they only laugh to keep away from themselves a cankering envy and desire which would be more bitter than their present lack. Let any man whom you call a genius arrive at this hotel to-night, and let a millionaire arrive at the same moment, and I'll bet you the millionaire gets the attention every time ! A millionaire travels round the earth, and he gets respect everywhere he goes—why ? Because he buys it. That's the way to get respect in the nineteenth century—buy it ! Do the fine works of art which are sold each year go to the pauper student who worships them ? No, sir, they go to the man who has the money, and who shells out the biggest price. I repeat, my young friend, that what's there " (and he slapped his pocket) " is what counts in the struggle of life."

"I agree with you," answered Orange, "that money counts for a great deal."

"A great deal ! " repeated the other, scornfully, being now, perhaps, somewhat warmed with wine. "A great deal ! what have you to offer instead ? Religion ? Ministers are the parasites of rich men. Art ? Go into the studio of any friend of yours to-morrow, and see whom he'll speak to first—you, or the man with a cheque in his hand. Why, if a poor man had the brains of Shakespeare, or our Emerson, and was mud-splashed by the carriage wheels of a wealthy woman, the only answer to his protests would be a policeman's ' move on ! ' "

" I know it ! I know it ! " cried Orange, in anguish. " I know it fifty times better than you do ! I tell you I would sell my whole life now, for one year's perfect enjoyment of riches."

" Not one year," said the greybeard, leaning over the table and speaking so intensely that Rupert could hardly follow him. His old face had become ghastly and looked livid in contrast to the white hair. " Not one year, my boy, but five years ! Think, only think, of the gloriousness of it all ! This evening a despised pauper, to-morrow a rich man ! Take courage, make up your mind to yield your life at the end of five years, and in return I will promise you, pledge you, that to-morrow morning you shall be in as sound a financial position as any man in New York."

Now it is strange that this outrageous proposal, made in the bar-room of an hotel situate in one of the most prosaic cities in the world, did not strike Rupert Orange as at all preposterous. Probably on account of his mystical, dreaming mind, he never took thought to doubt the speaker's sincereness, but at once fell to balancing the advantages and drawbacks of the scheme.

Five years ! Before his young eyes they stretched out like fifty years. It did not occur to him (it rarely occurs to any young man) to hark back to the five preceding years and note how few and swift were the strides which brought him over them to this very day he was living. Five years ! They lay before him all silver with sunshine, as he looked out from his present want and darkness. This was his point of view ; and let us never forget this point of view when we are passing judgment on him. No doubt, if the matter had been placed before a man of wealth, he would have denied it even momentary consideration : but the smell of cooking is only disgusting to one who has dined ; it is the vagrant who sniffs eagerly the air of the kitchen through the iron grating on the street. For Rupert, at this moment, money meant all the world. He was a man who hated to face the bitter things of life : and money included release from insolent creditors, from snubs and flouts, from a small, cold, dark room, and, chief of all ! release from that horror which he saw drawing nearer and nearer : the gaol.

" There is one more word to be said," observed the old man, smoothly. " Leaving aside the contingency of your starving to death—which, by the way, I think very likely—there is a chance of your being run over by a cart when you leave this hotel. There is an even chance of your contracting some disease during the winter. How would you like to die in a pauper hospital, where the nurses sing as they close a dead man's eyes ? Now, what I propose is, that you shall be free from any physical pain for five years."

"If I should accept," said Orange, swirling the wine round in his glass till it creamed and foamed, " I'd desire some slight ills to take the very sweetness out of life." Probably he meant, for fear that when his time came he should hate to die.

He thought again. He was like to a man who arrives suddenly at a mountain village on the feast of the Blessed Sacrament, and loitering in the street with his eyes enchanted by the tawdry decorations and festoons of the houses, forgets to look beyond at the awful mountain standing against the sky, with menacing thunder clouds about its breast. Before Orange's mind a gay and tempting pageant defiled. He thought of the travels he would be able to make, of luxurious palaces, of exquisite banquets, of priceless wines, of laughing, rapturous women. He thought, too, for he was far from being a merely sensuous man, of the first editions he could buy, of the rare gems, of dainty bindings. Sweetest of all were the thoughts, that he would be at his ease to do the best work that it was in him to do, and that he would be powerful enough to wreak his vengeance on his enemies very slowly, inch by inch. With that, like the crack of a rifle shot, came the thought of Mrs. Annice.

He sprang to his feet. " Listen ! " he cried, in such a voice that the idlers at the bar turned round for a moment ; but observing that no row was in progress to divert them, they fell once more to their drinking. " Listen ! " cried Rupert Orange again, gripping the side of the table with one hand and pointing a shaking finger at the old man. " There is one woman alive in this city to-night who has brought me to the degradation which you witness now. She flung me to the ground, she covered me with dust, she crushed me beneath her merciless heel ! Give her to me that I may lower her pride ! let me see her as abject and despised as the poorest trull that walks the streets, and I swear by God Most High to make the bargain ! "

The old man grasped Rupert's cold hand, and pressed it

between his own feverishly hot palms. "It is an unusual taste," he murmured, glancing into Rupert's eyes, and smiling faintly.

II

Orange started " up town " with a song in his heart. Curiously enough, he had not the slightest doubt about the genuineness of the contract, nor had he the least sorrow for what he had done. It mattered little about snubs and side looks to-night : to-morrow men and women would joyfully begin pawing him and fawning. So happy was he, his blood danced through his veins so merrily, that he ran for three or four *blocks* ; and once he laughed a loud laugh, which caused a policeman to menace him with a club. But this only brought him more merriment ; to-morrow, if he liked, he could laugh from Central Park to Madison Square without molestation.

When he reached the mean flat-house on the west side, there was, as usual, no light in the entrance, and he saw a postman groping among the bells.

" Say, young feller ! " began the postman, " do you know if any one by the name of Orange is kickin' around this blamed house ? "

" I am he," said Rupert Orange, and held out his hand for the letter.

" *Yes*, you are ! " answered the postman, derisively. " Now then, come off the roof and shew us the bell."

Rupert indicated the place, and, as soon as the postman had dropped the letter, he whipped out his key, and to the postman's surprise unlocked the box and put the letter in his pocket.

" Well ! you see my business is to deliver letters, not to give them away," said the postman, making an official distinction. " When you said you was the man, how was I to know you wasn't givin' me a steer ? "

" Oh, that's all right ! " replied Rupert. " Good night, my friend."

He went upstairs to his freezing little room, and sat down to think. He would not open the letter yet : his mind was too crowded to admit any new emotion. So for two hours he remain dreaming brilliant and fantastic dreams. Then he tore open the envelope. He was so poor that the gas had been turned off from his room, but by the light of a match he read a communication from Messrs. Daroll and Kettel, the lawyers, setting forth that a distant relative of his had recently died in a town in one of the Southern States, and had left him a fortune of nearly a million dollars. But Rupert knew that this million dollars was only nominal, that money would remain with him as long as he could call life his own.

The charwoman who came into his room next morning, found him asleep in the chair, with the letter open on his knee, and a smile lighting his face. But he was only a pauper, in arrears for his rent, so she struck him smartly between the shoulders with her broom.

" I believe I've been asleep," said Rupert, starting and rubbing his eyes. The woman looked at him sourly, thinking that he would have to take his next sleep in one of the parks. She began to sweep the dust in his direction till he coughed violently.

"You have been very good to me since I've been here, Mrs. Spill," Rupert continued ; and, I think, without irony : he had not much idea of irony. He took from his pocket the last five-dollar bill he had in the world and gave it to her. " Please take that for your trouble."

The woman stared at him, as she would have stared had he cut his throat before her eyes. But Orange clapped on his hat and rushed out. He had not even the five cents necessary to travel down town in a *horse-car*, so he walked the distance to the office of Messrs. Daroll and Kettel, in Pine Street. He approached a fat clerk (who, decked as he was with doubtful jewellery, looked as if he were honouring the office by being in it at all), and asked if Mr. Kettel was within. Now it is something worthy of note, that I have often called on men occupied with difficult texts ; or painting pictures ; or writing novels ; and each one had been able to let go his work at once : while, on the other hand, it is your part to await the pleasure of a clerk, till he has finished his enthralling occupation. True to his breed, the fat man kept Rupert standing before him for about three minutes, till he had elaborately finished a copy of a bill of details ; and then looking up, and seeing only a shabby fellow, he asked sharply :—

" Eh ? What do you say ? "

Rupert repeated his question.

" Yes, I guess he's in, but this is his busy day. You just sit right down there, young man, and he'll see you when he gets good and ready."

The hard knocks which Rupert had received in his contest

with the world had taken out of him the self-assertion that goes with wealth : so he sat for half an hour, knowing well, meanwhile, that his clothes were a cause for laughter to the underbred and badly trained clerks. At length he somewhat timidly went over to the desk again.

" Perhaps if you would be kind enough to take my name into Mr. Kettel——"

" Oh, look here, you make me tired ! " exclaimed the fat clerk, irritably. " Didn't I tell you that he was busy ? Now, I don't want to see you monkeying round this desk any more ! If you don't want to wait, why the walking's pretty good !—— This young man says he wants to see you," he added, as Mr. Kettel came out of his private room.

" Well, sir, what do you want to-day ? " asked Mr. Kettel, with that most offensive tone and air which some misguided men imagine will impress the spectator as a manner for the man of great affairs. " You had better call round some other time ; we're not able to attend——" he was going on, when he happened to look narrowly into Rupert's face, and his manner changed in a second. " Why, my dear boy, how are you ! it's so long since I've seen you, that I didn't know you at first. And, how you've changed ! " he went on, and could not help a glance at Rupert's shabby dress ; for he was quite ignoble. Then this remark seeming of questionable taste even to him, he cried heartily : " But come into my private room, and we can have a good long chat ! " And in he went, with Rupert at his heels, leaving the fat clerk at gaze.

In a week Rupert was once more dawdling about clubs, and attending those social functions which go to make up what is called " a Season."   Above all, he was listening to an appalling variety of apologetic lies. To the average man who said : " We didn't know when on earth you were coming back from Europe, my dear fellow ; how did you like it over there ? " he could answer with a grave face ; but the women were different. One particular afternoon he was at a reception, when he heard a lady near him remark in clear accents to her friend : " You can't think how we missed that dear Mr. Orange while he was away in Africa ! " and this struck Rupert as so grotesque that he apparently laughed. Amid this social intercourse, however, he avoided sedulously a meeting with Mrs. Annice ; he had decided not to see her for a while. Indeed, it was not till an evening late in February, after dinner, that he took a cab to her house near Washington Square.

He found her at home, and had not waited a minute before she came into the room. She was a tall woman, and wonderfully handsome by gaslight ; but she had that tiresome habit, which many women have, of talking intensely—in *italics*, as it were : a habit found generally in women ill brought up—women without control of their feelings, or command of the expression of them.

" My dear, dear Rupert, how glad I am to see you," she exclaimed, throwing a white fluffy cloak off her bare shoulders, and holding out both hands as she glided towards him. " It is so long, that I really thought we were never going to see you again. But I am *so* glad. And how very fortunate that legacy was for you—just when I suppose you were working fearfully hard. I was quite delighted when I heard of it, and my husband too. He would have been so pleased to have seen you, but he is dining out to-night."

There was a tone of too much hypocrisy about all this, and Rupert made full allowance for it. He chatted in his easy way about his good fortune, and recited some details.

" I suppose there is not the slightest possibility of a flaw in the will ? " says Mrs. Annice, regarding him keenly. The lines round her mouth had become hard, but she kept on smiling : she had some traits like Macbeth's wife.

Orange laughed his bright, merry laugh which so few could resist. " Oh no, I think it's all right this time ! " he said, and looked at her steadfastly with his fine eyes.

Mrs. Annice suddenly flushed, and then shuddered. Her heart began to throb, her head to whirl. What was the matter with her ? What was this cursed sensation which was mastering her? She, with her self-poise, her deliberateness, her calculation, was, in the flash of an eye, brought to feel towards this man, whom but a moment ago she had hated more than any one in the world, as she had never felt towards man before. It was not love, this wretched thraldom, it was not even admiration ; it was a wild desire to abnegate herself, annihilate herself, in this man's personality ; to become his bond-woman, the slave of his controlling will. She drove the nails into her palms, and crushed her lips between her teeth, as she rose to her feet and made one desperate try for victory.

" I was just going to the opera when you came in, Rupert," she said ; " won't you come in my box ? "—and her voice had so changed, there was such a note of tenderness and desire in it, that it seemed as if she had exposed her soul. But even in her disorganised state she was conscious that there would be a certain distinction in appearing at the opera with the re-edified Rupert Orange.

Rupert murmured something about the opera being such a bore, and at that moment the footman announced the carriage.

" Won't you come ? " asked Mrs. Annice, standing with her white hand resting on the back of a chair.

" I think not," answered Rupert, with a smile.

She dismissed the carriage. As soon as the servant had gone she tried to make some trivial remark, and, half turning, looked at Orange, who rose. For an instant those two stood gazing into each other's eyes with God knows what hell in their hearts, and then, with a little cry, that was half a sob, she flung her arms about his neck, and pressed her kisses on his lips.

III

Yesterday afternoon I took from amongst my books a novel of Rupert Orange, and as I turned over the leaves, I fell to pondering how difficult it is to obtain any of his works to-day, while but a few years ago all the world was reading them ; and to lose myself in amaze at our former rapturous and enthusiastic admiration of his literary art, his wit, his pathos. For in truth his art is a very tawdry art to my present liking ; his wit is rather stale, his pathos a little vulgar. And the charm has likewise gone out of his poetry : even his *Chaunt of the Storm-Witch*, which we were used to think so melodious and sonorous, now fails to please. To explain the precise effect which his poetry has upon me now, I am forced to resort to a somewhat unhappy figure ; I am forced to say that his poetry has an effect on me like *sifted ashes* ! I cannot in the least explain this figure ; and if it fails to convey any idea to the reader, I am afraid the failure must be set down to my clumsy writing. And yet what praise we all bestowed on these works of Rupert Orange ! How eagerly we watched for them to appear ; how we prized them ; with what zeal we studied the newspapers for details of his interesting and successful life !

A particular account of that brilliant and successful life it would ill become me to chronicle, even if I were so minded : it was with no purpose of relating his social and literary triumphs, his continual victories during five years in the two fields he had chosen to conquer, that I started to write. But in dwelling on his life, we must not forget to take account of these triumphs. They were very rare, very proud, very precious triumphs, both in Europe and in the United States ; triumphs that few men ever enjoy ; triumphs which were potent enough to deaden the pallid thought of the curious limits of his life, except on three sombre occasions.

It was on the first night of a new opera at Covent Garden. Orange was in a box with a notable company, and was on the point of leaning over to whisper something amusing to the beautiful Countess of Heston, when of a sudden he shot white, and the smile left his face as if he had received a blow. On the stage a chorus had commenced in a very low tone of passionate entreaty ; by degrees it swelled louder and louder, till it burst forth into a tremendous agonised prayer for pity and pardon. As Orange listened, such a dreary sense of the littleness of life, such an awful fear of death, sang through his brain, that he grew sick, and shivered in a cold sweat.

" Why, I'm afraid Mr. Orange is ill ! " exclaimed the Countess.

" No, no ! " muttered Orange, groping for his hat. " Only a little faint ; want some air !—I tell you I want some air ! " he broke out in a voice that was like a frightened cry, as he fumbled with the door of the box.

A certain man with a kind heart followed him into the *foyer*.

" Can I do anything for you, old chap ? "

" Yes ; in the name of God leave me alone ! " replied Orange ; and he said it in such a tone, and with a face so frightfully contorted, that those standing about fell back feeling queer, and the questioner returned to the box very gravely, and thought on his soul for the rest of the evening.

But Orange rushed out, and he hailed a hansom, and he drove till the cabman refused to drive any more ; and then he walked ; and it was not till he found himself on Putney Heath in his evening dress, at half-past twelve the next day, that the devil left him.

About two years after this occurrence he was wandering one Sunday evening in Chelsea, and hearing a church bell ring for the usual service, he decided to enter. As he sat waiting a little girl of four or five, with her mother, came in and sat by him : and Rupert talked to the child in his quaint, winning way, and so won her, that when the service began she continued to cling to his hand. After a while the sermon commenced, and the preacher, taking for his text the words : " *And he died*," from the fifth chapter of Genesis, tried to set forth the suddenness and unwelcomeness of death, even to the long-lived patriarchs, and its increased suddenness and unwelcomeness to most of us. The sermon I suppose, was dull and commonplace enough, but if the speaker had verily seen into the mind of one of his listeners, the effect could not have been more disastrous. Orange waited till the torture became unbearable, till he could actually feel the horrid, stifling weight of earth pressing him down in his coffin, and keeping him there for ages and ages : then with a heavy groan he started up, and rushed forth with such vehemence, that he knocked down and trampled on the little girl, in his haste to get out of sight of the white faces of people scared at his face, and the child's sad cry was borne to him out in the dark street.

The third occasion on which this sense of despair and loss oppressed him, was at a time when he was near a rugged coast. One stormy day he rode to a certain promontory, and came suddenly in sight of the great sea. As he stood watching a lonely gull, that strained, and swooped, and dipped in the surge, while the rain drizzled, and the wind whined through the long grass, the futility of his life stung him, and he hid his face in his horse's mane and wept.

But sorest of all was the thought that he might really have won a certain fame, an easy fortune, without taking on his back the fardel which, as the months went by, became so heavy. He knew that he had done some work which would have surely gained him distinction, had he but waited. Why did you not have patience ? his outraged spirit and maimed life seemed to moan ; a little more patience !

I must not let you think, however, that he was unhappy. In every detail the promise of the old man was punctiliously carried out. The very maladies which Orange had desired, were twisted to his advantage. Thus, when he was laid up with a sprained ankle at an hotel at Aix-les-Bains, he formed his notorious connection with Gabrielle de Volnay. It was when he was kept for a day in the house by a cold that he wrote his little comedy, *Her Ladyship's Dinner*—a comedy which, at one time, we were all so forward to praise. And on the night upon which his cab was overturned in the Sixth Avenue, New York, and he was badly cut about the head, did he not recognise in the drunken prostitute who cursed him, the erstwhile brilliant Mrs. Annice ? Did he not forget his pain in the exquisite knowledge that her curses were of no avail, and flout her jeeringly, brutally ? Nay ! when an epidemic disease broke out in a certain part of the Riviera, and the foreign population presently fled, he used his immunity from death to hold his ground and tend the sick, and so gave cause to the newspapers to proclaim the courage and devotion of Mr. Orange. And all these fortunate incidents were suddenly brought to completeness by one singular event.

It was on a winter morning, about three o'clock, that he found himself in the district of Kilburn, and noticed a crimson stain on the sky. More from indolence than from anything else he went towards the fire ; but when he came in sight of it, he was startled by a somewhat strange thing. For there at a window high up in the blazing house, stood a woman with a baby in her arms, who had clearly been left to a hideous fate on account of the fierceness of the flames. With an abrupt gesture Orange flung off his cloak.

" Where can I find the chief ? " he asked a man standing near, " because I'm going up ? "

The fellow turned, and seeing Rupert in his evening suit, laughed derisively.

" I say Bill ! " he sings out to his mate, " this 'ere bloke says as how he's goin' up ! " and the other's scoffing reply struck Rupert's ears as he pushed through the crowd.

By a letter which he carried with him, or some such authority, Orange gained his request ; and the next thing that the people saw was a ladder rigged, and the figure of a man ascending through clouds of smoke. Higher and higher he went, while the flames licked and sizzled around him and seared his flesh : higher and higher till he had almost reached the window, and a wild cheer burst from the crowd for such a deed of heroism. But at that moment a long tongue of flame leaped into the sky, the building tottered and then crashed down, and Orange was safely caught by some strong arms, while the woman and child met death within the ruins. Of course this affair was noised abroad the next day ; for some weeks Orange, with his hand in a sling, was a picturesque figure in several London drawing-rooms.

Now, which one of us shall say that Orange, with the tested knowledge of his exemption from death, and strong in that knowledge, deliberately did this heroic act to improve his fame, to exalt his honour ? I have stated before that we must be cautious in passing judgment on him, and I must again insist on this caution. As for myself, I should be sorry to think that there is no beautiful, merciful Spirit to note an unselfish impulse, which took no thought of glory or advertisement, and count it to the man for honesty.

But the time ran, and the years sped, until was come the last month of that fifth year, which meant the end of years for Orange. When in the days of his happiness and strength, he had dwelt on this time at all, he had planned to seek out, on the last day of the year, some mountain crag in Switzerland, and there meet death, coming in the train of the rising sun, with calm and steady eyes. Alas ! now to his anguish he felt a desire, which was stronger than his will, tearing at his heart to visit once more the scene of his hardships, to look again on the place where his bargain was concluded. I make certain, from a letter of his which I have seen, that in taking passage for New York, Rupert had no idea of turning aside his doom. The *Cambria*, on which he sailed, was due to arrive at New York a full week before the end of the year ; but she encountered baffling winds and seas, and it was not till the evening of the thirty-first of December that she sighted the light on Fire Island.

As the steamer went at speed towards Sandy Hook, Orange stood alone on the deck, watching the smoke from her funnel rolling seaward : of a sudden he saw rise out of the cloud, the presentment, grim and menacing, of God the Father.

IV

As the *Cambria* moved up towards the city, on the morning of New Year's Day, a certain frenzy which was half insane, and a fierce loathing of familiar sights—Castle Garden, the spire of Trinity Church—took hold of Orange. He passionately cursed himself for not staying in Europe ; he cursed the hour he was born ; he cursed, above all ! the hour in which he had made that fatal bargain. As soon as the vessel was made fast to the dock, he hastened ashore ; and leaving his servant to look after his luggage, he sprang into a *hack*, and directed the driver to go " up town."

" Where to, boss ? " inquired the man, looking at him curiously.

" The Hoffman House," replied Orange, before he thought. Then he cursed himself again, but he did not change the order.

I have said that the driver looked at Orange curiously ; and in truth he was a strange sight. All the dignity of his demeanour was gone : his eyes were bloodshot, and his complexion a dirty yellow : he was unshorn, his tie was loose, and his collar open. His terror grew as he passed along the well-known streets : he screamed out hateful, obscene things, rolling about in the vehicle, while foam came from his mouth ; and as he arrived at the hotel, in his distraction he drove his hand through the window glass, which cut him into the bone.

" An accident," he panted hoarsely to the porter who opened the door : " a slight accident ! God damn you ! " he yelled, " can't you see it was an accident ? " and he went up the hall to the office, leaving behind him a trail of blood. The clerk at the desk, seeing his disorder, was on the point of refusing him a room ; but when Orange wrote his name in the visitor's book, he smirked, and ordered the best set of apartments in the house to be made ready. To these apartments Orange retired, and sat all day in a sort of dull horror. For a sudden death he had in a measure prepared himself : he had made his bargain, he had bought his freedom from the cares which are the burthen of all men, and he knew that he must pay the debt : but for some uncertain, treacherous calamity he had not prepared. He was not fool enough to dream that the one to whom the debt was owed would relent : but before his creditor's method of exacting payment he was at a stand. He thought and thought, rubbing his face in his hands, till his head was near bursting : in a sudden spasm he fell off the chair to the floor ; and that night he was lying stricken by typhoid fever.

And for weeks he lay with a fiery forehead and blazing eyes, finding the lightest covering too heavy and ice too hot. Even when the known disease seemed to have been subdued, certain strange complications arose which puzzled the physicians : amongst these a painful vomiting which racked the man's frame and left an exhaustion akin to death, and a curious loathly decay of the flesh. This last was so venomous an evil, that one of the nurses having touched the sick man in her ministrations, and neglected to immediately purify herself, within a few hours incontinently deceased. After a while, to assist these enemies of Orange, there came pneumonia. It would seem as though he were experiencing all the maladies from which he had been free during the past five years ; for besides his corporal ills he had become lunatic, and he was raving. Those who tended him, used as they were to outrageous scenes, shuddered and held each other's hands when they heard him shriek his curses, and realised his abject fear of death. At times, too, they would hear him weeping softly, and whispering the broken little prayers he had learned in childhood : praying God to save him in this dark hour from the wiles of the devil.

At length, one evening towards the end of March, the mental clearness of Orange somewhat revived, and he felt himself compelled to get up and put on his clothes. The nurse, thinking that the patient was resting quietly, and fearing the shine of the lamp might distress him, had turned it low and gone away for a little : so it was without interruption, although reeling from giddiness, and scorched with fever, that Rupert groped about till he found some garments, and his evening suit. Clad in these, and throwing a cloak over his shoulders, he went downstairs. Those whom he met, that recognised him, looked at him wonderingly and with a vague dread ; but he appeared to have his understanding as well as they, and so he passed through the hall without being stopped ; and going into the bar, he called for brandy. The bar-tender, to whom he was known, exclaimed in astonishment ; but he got no reply from Orange, who, pouring himself out a large quantity of the fiery liquor found it colder than the coldest iced water in his burning frame. When he had taken the brandy, he went into the street. It was a bleak seasonable night, and a bitter frost-rain was falling : but Orange went through it, as if the bitter weather was a not unwelcome coolness, although he shuddered in an ague-fit. As he stood on the corner of Twenty-third Street, his cloak thrown open, the sleet sowing down on his shirt, and the slush which covered his ankles soaking through his thin shoes, a member of his club came by and spoke to him.

" Why, good God ! Orange, you don't mean to say you're out on a night like this ! You must be much better—eh ? " he broke off, for Orange had given him a grey look, with eyes in which there was no speculation ; and the man hurried away scared and rather aghast. " These poet chaps are always queer fishes," he muttered uneasily, as he turned into the Fifth Avenue Hotel.

Of the events of terror and horror which happened on that awful night, when a human soul was paying the price of an astonishing violation of the order of the universe, no man shall ever tell. Blurred, hideous, and enormous visions of *dives*, of hells where the worst scum of the town consorted, of a man who spat on him, of a woman who struck him across the face with her umbrella, calling him the foulest of names—visions such as these, and more hateful than these, presented themselves to Orange, when he found himself, at three o'clock in the morning, standing under a lamp-post in that strange district of New York called " The Village."

The rain had given way to a steady fall of snow : and as he stood there, a squalid harlot, an outcast amongst outcasts, approached, and solicited him in the usual manner.

" Come along—do ! " she said, shivering : " We can get a drink at my place."

Receiving no answer, she peered into his face, and gave a cry of loathing and fear.

" Oh, look here ! " she said, roughly, coughing down her disgust : " You've been drinking too much, and you've got a load. Come ahead with me and you can have a good sleep."

At that word Orange turned, and gazed at her with a vacant, dreary, silly smile. He raised his hand, and when she shrank away— " Are you afraid of me ? " he said, not coarsely, but quietly, even gently, like a man talking in his sleep. Then they went on together, till they came to a dilapidated house close by the river. They entered, and turned into a dirty room lit by a flaring jet of gas.

" Now, dear ; let's have some money," says the woman, " and I'll get you a nice drink."

Still no answer from Orange : only that same vacant smile, which was beginning to be horrible.

" Give me some money : do you hear ! " cried the woman, stridently. Then she seized him, and went through his pockets in an accustomed style, and found three cents.

" What the hell do you mean by coming here with only this ! " bellowed the woman, holding out the mean coins to Orange. She struck him ; but she was very frightened, and went to the stairs.

" Say ! Tom—Tommy," she called ; " you'd better come down and put this loafer out ! "

A great hulking man came down the stairs, and gazed for an instant at Rupert—standing under the gas-jet, with the woman plucking the studs from his shirt. For an instant the man stood, feeling sick and in a sweat ; and then, by a great effort, he approached Orange, and seized him by the collar.

" Here, out you go ! " he said. " We don't want none of your sort around here ! " The man dragged Orange to the street door, and gave the wretch such a powerful shove, that he fell on the pavement, and rolled into the gutter.

And later in the morning, one who passed by the way found him there : dead before the squalid harlot's door.

J. Sheridan Le Fanu

CARMILLA

from IN A GLASS DARKLY

Richard Bentley, 1872

PROLOGUE

Upon a paper attached to the Narrative which follows, Doctor Hesselius has written a rather elaborate note, which he accompanies with a reference to his Essay on the strange subject which the MS. illuminates.

This mysterious subject he treats, in that Essay, with his usual learning and acumen, and with remarkable directness and condensation. It will form but one volume of the series of that extraordinary man's collected papers.

As I publish the case, in this volume, simply to interest the " laity," I shall forestall the intelligent lady, who relates it, in nothing ; and, after due consideration, I have determined, therefore, to abstain from presenting any *précis* of the learned Doctor's reasoning, or extract from his statement on a subject which he describes as " involving, not improbably, some of the profoundest arcana of our dual existence, and its intermediates."

I was anxious, on discovering this paper, to re-open the correspondence commenced by Doctor Hesselius, so many years before, with a person so clever and careful as his informant seems to have been. Much to my regret, however, I found that she had died in the interval.

She, probably, could have added little to the Narrative which she communicates in the following pages, with, so far as I can pronounce, such a conscientious particularity.

CHAPTER I

AN EARLY FRIGHT

In Styria, we, though by no means magnificent people, inhabit a castle, or schloss. A small income, in that part of the world, goes a great way. Eight or nine hundred a year does wonders. Scantily enough ours would have answered among wealthy people at home. My father is English, and I bear an English name, although I never saw England. But here, in this lonely and primitive place, where everything is so marvellously cheap, I really don't see how ever so much more money would at all materially add to our comforts, or even luxuries.

My father was in the Austrian service, and retired upon a pension and his patrimony, and purchased this feudal residence, and the small estate on which it stands, a bargain.

Nothing can be more picturesque or solitary. It stands on a slight eminence in a forest. The road, very old and narrow, passes in front of its drawbridge, never raised in my time, and its moat, stocked with perch, and sailed over by many swans, and floating on its surface white fleets of water-lilies.

Over all this the schloss shows its many-windowed front ; its towers, and its Gothic chapel.

The forest opens in an irregular and very picturesque glade before its gate, and at the right a steep Gothic bridge carries the road over a stream that winds in deep shadow through the wood.

I have said that this is a very lonely place. Judge whether I say truth. Looking from the hall door towards the road, the forest in which our castle stands extends fifteen miles to the right, and twelve to the left. The nearest inhabited village is about seven of your English miles to the left. The nearest inhabited schloss of any historic associations, is that of old General Spielsdorf, nearly twenty miles away to the right.

I have said " the nearest *inhabited* village," because there is, only three miles westward, that is to say in the direction of General Spielsdorf's schloss, a ruined village, with its quaint little church, now roofless, in the aisle of which are the mouldering tombs of the proud family of Karnstein, now extinct, who once owned the equally-desolate château which, in the thick of the forest, overlooks the silent ruins of the town.

Respecting the cause of the desertion of this striking and melancholy spot, there is a legend which I shall relate to you another time.

I must tell you now, how very small is the party who constitute the inhabitants of our castle. I don't include servants, or those dependants who occupy rooms in the buildings attached to the schloss. Listen, and wonder ! My father, who is the kindest man on earth, but growing old ; and I, at the date of my story, only nineteen. Eight years have passed since then. I and my father constituted the family at the schloss. My mother, a Styrian lady, died in my infancy, but I had a good-natured governess, who had been with me from, I might almost say, my infancy. I could not remember the time when her fat, benignant face was not a familiar picture in my memory. This was Madame Perrodon, a native of Berne, whose care and good nature in part supplied to me the loss of my mother, whom I do not even remember, so early I lost her. She made a third at our little dinner party. There was a fourth, Mademoiselle De Lafontaine, a lady such as you term, I believe, a " finishing governess." She spoke French and German, Madame Perrodon French and broken English, to which my father and I added English, which, partly to prevent its becoming a lost language among us, and partly from patriotic motives, we spoke every day. The consequence was a Babel, at which strangers used to laugh, and which I shall make no attempt to reproduce in this narrative. And there were two or three young lady friends besides, pretty nearly of my own age, who were occasional visitors, for longer or shorter terms ; and these visits I sometimes returned.

These were our regular social resources ; but of course there were chance visits from " neighbours " of only five or six leagues' distance. My life was, notwithstanding, rather a solitary one, I can assure you.

My gouvernantes had just so much control over me as you might conjecture such sage persons would have in the case of a rather spoiled girl, whose only parent allowed her pretty nearly her own way in everything.

The first occurrence in my existence, which produced a terrible impression upon my mind, which, in fact, never has been effaced, was one of the very earliest incidents of my life which I can recollect. Some people will think it so trifling that it should not be recorded here. You will see, however, by-and-by, why I mention it. The nursery, as it was called, though I had it all to myself, was a large room in the upper story of the castle, with a steep oak roof. I can't have been more than six years old, when one night I awoke, and looking round the room from my bed, failed to see the nursery-maid. Neither was my nurse there ; and I thought myself alone. I was not frightened, for I was one of those happy children who are studiously kept in ignorance of ghost stories, of fairy tales, and of all such lore as makes us cover up our heads when the door creaks suddenly, or the flicker of an expiring candle makes the shadow of a bed-post dance upon the wall, nearer to our faces. I was vexed and insulted at finding myself, as I conceived, neglected, and I began to whimper, preparatory to a hearty bout of roaring ; when to my surprise, I saw a solemn, but very pretty face looking at me from the side of the bed. It was that of a young lady who was kneeling, with her hands under the coverlet. I looked at her with a kind of pleased wonder, and ceased whimpering. She caressed me with her hands, and lay down beside me on the bed, and drew me towards her, smiling ; I felt immediately delightfully soothed, and fell asleep again. I was wakened by a sensation as if two needles ran into my breast very deep at the same moment, and I cried loudly. The lady started back, with her eyes fixed on me, and then slipped down upon the floor, and, as I thought, hid herself under the bed.

I was now for the first time frightened, and I yelled with all my might and main. Nurse, nursery-maid, housekeeper, all came running in, and hearing my story, they made light of it, soothing me all they could meanwhile. But, child as I was, I could perceive that their faces were pale with an unwonted look of anxiety, and I saw them look under the bed, and about the room, and peep under tables and pluck open cupboards ; and the housekeeper whispered to the nurse : " Lay your hand along that hollow in the bed ; some one *did* lie there, so sure as you did not ; the place is still warm."

I remember the nursery-maid petting me, and all three examining my chest, where I told them I felt the puncture, and pronouncing that there was no sign visible that any such thing had happened to me.

The housekeeper and the two other servants who were in charge of the nursery, remained sitting up all night ; and from that time a servant always sat up in the nursery until I was about fourteen.

I was very nervous for a long time after this. A doctor was called in, he was pallid and elderly. How well I remember his long saturnine face, slightly pitted with small-pox, and his chestnut wig. For a good while, every second day, he came and gave me medicine, which of course I hated.

The morning after I saw this apparition I was in a state of terror, and could not bear to be left alone, daylight though it was, for a moment.

I remember my father coming up and standing at the bedside, and talking cheerfully, and asking the nurse a number of questions, and laughing very heartily at one of the answers ; and patting me on the shoulder, and kissing me, and telling me not to be frightened, that it was nothing but a dream and could not hurt me.

But I was not comforted, for I knew the visit of the strange woman was *not* a dream ; and I was *awfully* frightened.

I was a little consoled by the nursery-maid's assuring me that it was she who had come and looked at me, and lain down beside me in the bed, and that I must have been half-dreaming not to have known her face. But this, though supported by the nurse, did not quite satisfy me.

I remember, in the course of that day, a venerable old man, in a black cassock, coming into the room with the nurse and house-keeper, and talking a little to them, and very kindly to me ; his face was very sweet and gentle, and he told me they were going to pray, and joined my hands together, and desired me to say, softly, while they were praying, " Lord, hear all good prayers for us, for Jesus' sake." I think these were the very words, for I often repeated them to myself, and my nurse used for years to make me say them in my prayers.

I remember so well the thoughtful sweet face of that white-haired old man, in his black cassock, as he stood in that rude, lofty, brown room, with the clumsy furniture of a fashion three hundred years old, about him, and the scanty light entering its shadowy atmosphere through the small lattice. He kneeled, and the three women with him, and he prayed aloud with an earnest quavering voice for, what appeared to me, a long time. I forget all my life preceding that event, and for some time after it is all obscure also ; but the scenes I have just described stand out vivid as the isolated pictures of the phantasmagoria surrounded by darkness.

CHAPTER II

A GUEST

I am now going to tell you something so strange that it will require all your faith in my veracity to believe my story. It is not only true, nevertheless, but truth of which I have been an eye-witness.

It was a sweet summer evening, and my father asked me, as he sometimes did, to take a little ramble with him along that beautiful forest vista which I have mentioned as lying in front of the schloss.

"General Spielsdorf cannot come to us so soon as I had hoped," said my father, as we pursued our walk.

He was to have paid us a visit of some weeks, and we had expected his arrival next day. He was to have brought with him a young lady, his niece and ward, Mademoiselle Rheinfeldt, whom I had never seen, but whom I had heard described as a very charming girl, and in whose society I had promised myself many happy days. I was more disappointed than a young lady living in a town, or a bustling neighbourhood can possibly imagine. This visit, and the new acquaintance it promised, had furnished my day dream for many weeks.

"And how soon does he come ? " I asked.

"Not till autumn. Not for two months, I dare say," he answered. "And I am very glad now, dear, that you never knew Mademoiselle Rheinfeldt."

"And why ? " I asked, both mortified and curious.

"Because the poor young lady is dead," he replied. " I quite forgot I had not told you, but you were not in the room when I received the General's letter this evening."

I was very much shocked. General Spielsdorf had mentioned in his first letter, six or seven weeks before, that she was not so well as he would wish her, but there was nothing to suggest the remotest suspicion of danger.

"Here is the General's letter," he said, handing it to me. " I am afraid he is in great affliction ; the letter appears to me to have been written very nearly in distraction."

We sat down on a rude bench, under a group of magnificent lime trees. The sun was setting with all its melancholy splendour behind the sylvan horizon, and the stream that flows beside our home, and passes under the steep old bridge I have mentioned, wound through many a group of noble trees, almost at our feet, reflecting in its current the fading crimson of the sky. General Spielsdorf's letter was so extraordinary, so vehement, and in some places so self-contradictory, that I read it twice over—the second time aloud to my father—and was still unable to account for it, except by supposing that grief had unsettled his mind.

It said, " I have lost my darling daughter, for as such I loved her. During the last days of dear Bertha's illness I was not able to write to you. Before then I had no idea of her danger. I have lost

her, and now learn *all*, too late. She died in the peace of innocence, and in the glorious hope of a blessed futurity. The fiend
who betrayed our infatuated hospitality has done it all. I thought
I was receiving into my house innocence, gaiety, a charming
companion for my lost Bertha. Heavens ! what a fool have I been !
I thank God my child died without a suspicion of the cause of her
sufferings. She is gone without so much as conjecturing the
nature of her illness, and the accursed passion of the agent of all
this misery. I devote my remaining days to tracking and extinguishing a monster. I am told I may hope to accomplish my
righteous and merciful purpose. At present there is scarcely a
gleam of light to guide me. I curse my conceited incredulity, my
despicable affectation of superiority, my blindness, my obstinacy
—all—too late. I cannot write or talk collectedly now. I am distracted. So soon as I shall have a little recovered, I mean to devote
myself for a time to enquiry, which may possibly lead me as far as
Vienna. Some time in the autumn, two months hence, or earlier if
I live, I will see you—that is, if you permit me ; I will then tell
you all that I scarce dare put upon paper now. Farewell. Pray
for me, dear friend."

In these terms ended this strange letter. Though I had never
seen Bertha Rheinfeldt, my eyes filled with tears at the sudden
intelligence ; I was startled, as well as profoundly disappointed.

The sun had now set, and it was twilight by the time I had
returned the General's letter to my father.

It was a soft clear evening, and we loitered, speculating upon
the possible meanings of the violent and incoherent sentences
which I had just been reading. We had nearly a mile to walk
before reaching the road that passes the schloss in front, and by
that time the moon was shining brilliantly. At the drawbridge we
met Madame Perrodon and Mademoiselle De Lafontaine, who
had come out, without their bonnets, to enjoy the exquisite
moonlight.

We heard their voices gabbling in animated dialogue as we
approached. We joined them at the drawbridge, and turned about
to admire with them the beautiful scene.

The glade through which we had just walked lay before us. At
our left the narrow road wound away under clumps of lordly
trees, and was lost to sight amid the thickening forest. At the right
the same road crosses the steep and picturesque bridge, near which
stands a ruined tower, which once guarded that pass ; and beyond

the bridge an abrupt eminence rises, covered with trees, and showing in the shadow some grey ivy-clustered rocks.

Over the sward and low grounds, a thin film of mist was stealing like smoke, marking the distances with a transparent veil ; and here and there we could see the river faintly flashing in the moonlight.

No softer, sweeter scene could be imagined. The news I had just heard made it melancholy ; but nothing could disturb its character of profound serenity, and the enchanted glory and vagueness of the prospect.

My father, who enjoyed the picturesque, and I, stood looking in silence over the expanse beneath us. The two good governesses, standing a little way behind us, discoursed upon the scene, and were eloquent upon the moon.

Madame Perrodon was fat, middle-aged, and romantic, and talked and sighed poetically. Mademoiselle De Lafontaine—in right of her father, who was a German, assumed to be psychological, metaphysical, and something of a mystic—now declared that when the moon shone with a light so intense it was well known that it indicated a special spiritual activity. The effect of the full moon in such a state of brilliancy was manifold. It acted on dreams, it acted on lunacy, it acted on nervous people ; it had marvellous physical influences connected with life. Mademoiselle related that her cousin, who was mate of a merchant ship, having taken a nap on deck on such a night, lying on his back, with his face full in the light of the moon, had awakened, after a dream of an old woman clawing him by the cheek, with his features horribly drawn to one side ; and his countenance had never quite recovered its equilibrium.

" The moon, this night," she said, " is full of odylic and magnetic influence—and see, when you look behind you at the front of the schloss, how all its windows flash and twinkle with that silvery splendour, as if unseen hands had lighted up the rooms to receive fairy guests."

There are indolent states of the spirits in which, indisposed to talk ourselves, the talk of others is pleasant to our listless ears ; and I gazed on, pleased with the tinkle of the ladies' conversation.

" I have got into one of my moping moods to-night," said my father, after a silence, and quoting Shakespeare, whom, by way of keeping up our English, he used to read aloud, he said :—

> " ' *In truth I know not why I am so sad :*
> *It wearies me ; you say it wearies you ;*
> *But how I got it—came by it.*'

" I forget the rest. But I feel as if some great misfortune were hanging over us. I suppose the poor General's afflicted letter has had something to do with it."

At this moment the unwonted sound of carriage wheels and many hoofs upon the road, arrested our attention.

They seemed to be approaching from the high ground overlooking the bridge, and very soon the equipage emerged from that point. Two horsemen first crossed the bridge, then came a carriage drawn by four horses, and two men rode behind.

It seemed to be the travelling carriage of a person of rank ; and we were all immediately absorbed in watching that very unusual spectacle. It became, in a few moments, greatly more interesting, for just as the carriage had passed the summit of the steep bridge, one of the leaders, taking fright, communicated his panic to the rest, and, after a plunge or two, the whole team broke into a wild gallop together, and dashing between the horsemen who rode in front, came thundering along the road towards us with the speed of a hurricane.

The excitement of the scene was made more painful by the clear, long-drawn screams of a female voice from the carriage window.

We all advanced in curiosity and horror ; my father in silence, the rest with various ejaculations of terror.

Our suspense did not last long. Just before you reach the castle drawbridge, on the route they were coming, there stands by the roadside a magnificent lime tree, on the other stands an ancient stone cross, at sight of which the horses, now going at a pace that was perfectly frightful, swerved so as to bring the wheel over the projecting roots of the tree.

I knew what was coming. I covered my eyes, unable to see it out, and turned my head away ; at the same moment I heard a cry from my lady-friends, who had gone on a little.

Curiosity opened my eyes, and I saw a scene of utter confusion. Two of the horses were on the ground, the carriage lay upon its side, with two wheels in the air ; the men were busy removing the traces, and a lady, with a commanding air and figure had got out, and stood with clasped hands, raising the handkerchief that was in them every now and then to her eyes. Through the carriage door was now lifted a young lady, who appeared to be lifeless. My dear old father was already beside the elder lady, with his hat in his hand, evidently tendering his aid and the resources of his schloss. The lady did not appear to hear him, or to have eyes for anything but the slender girl who was being placed against the slope of the bank.

I approached ; the young lady was apparently stunned, but she was certainly not dead. My father, who piqued himself on being something of a physician, had just had his fingers to her wrist and assured the lady, who declared herself her mother, that her pulse, though faint and irregular, was undoubtedly still distinguishable. The lady clasped her hands and looked upward, as if in a momentary transport of gratitude ; but immediately she broke out again in that theatrical way which is, I believe, natural to some people.

She was what is called a fine-looking woman for her time of life, and must have been handsome ; she was tall, but not thin, and dressed in black velvet, and looked rather pale, but with a proud and commanding countenance, though now agitated strangely.

" Was ever being so born to calamity ? " I heard her say, with clasped hands, as I came up. " Here am I, on a journey of life and death, in prosecuting which to lose an hour is possibly to lose all. My child will not have recovered sufficiently to resume her route for who can say how long. I must leave her ; I cannot, dare not, delay. How far on, sir, can you tell, is the nearest village ? I must leave her there ; and shall not see my darling, or even hear of her till my return, three months hence."

I plucked my father by the coat, and whispered earnestly in his ear, " Oh ! papa, pray ask her to let her stay with us—it would be so delightful. Do, pray."

" If Madame will entrust her child to the care of my daughter and of her good gouvernante, Madame Perrodon, and permit her to remain as our guest, under my charge, until her return, it will confer a distinction and an obligation upon us, and we shall treat her with all the care and devotion which so sacred a trust deserves."

" I cannot do that, sir, it would be to task your kindness and chivalry too cruelly," said the lady, distractedly.

" It would, on the contrary, be to confer on us a very great kindness at the moment when we most need it. My daughter has just been disappointed by a cruel misfortune, in a visit from which she had long anticipated a great deal of happiness. If you confide this young lady to our care it will be her best consolation. The nearest village on your route is distant, and affords no such inn as you could think of placing your daughter at ; you cannot allow her to continue her journey for any considerable distance without danger. If, as you say, you cannot suspend your journey, you must part with her to-night, and nowhere could you do so with more honest assurances of care and tenderness than here."

There was something in this lady's air and appearance so distinguished, and even imposing, and in her manner so engaging, as to impress one, quite apart from the dignity of her equipage, with a conviction that she was a person of consequence.

By this time the carriage was replaced in its upright position, and the horses, quite tractable, in the traces again.

The lady threw on her daughter a glance which I fancied was not quite so affectionate as one might have anticipated from the beginning of the scene ; then she beckoned slightly to my father and withdrew two or three steps with him out of hearing ; and talked to him with a fixed and stern countenance, not at all like that with which she had hitherto spoken.

I was filled with wonder that my father did not seem to perceive the change, and also unspeakably curious to learn what it could be that she was speaking, almost in his ear, with so much earnestness and rapidity.

Two or three minutes at most, I think, she remained thus employed, then she turned, and a few steps brought her to where her daughter lay, supported by Madame Perrodon. She kneeled beside her for a moment and whispered, as Madame supposed, a little benediction in her ear ; then hastily kissing her, she stepped into her carriage, the door was closed, the footmen in stately liveries jumped up behind, the outriders spurred on, the postilions cracked their whips, the horses plunged and broke suddenly into a furious canter that threatened soon again to become a gallop, and the carriage whirled away, followed at the same rapid pace by the two horsemen in the rear.

CHAPTER III

WE COMPARE NOTES

We followed the *cortège* with our eyes until it was swiftly lost to sight in the misty wood ; and the very sound of the hoofs and wheels died away in the silent night air.

Nothing remained to assure us that the adventure had not been an illusion for a moment but the young lady, who just at that moment opened her eyes. I could not see, for her face was turned from me, but she raised her head, evidently looking about her, and I heard a very sweet voice ask complainingly, " Where is mamma ? "

Our good Madame Perrodon answered tenderly, and added some comfortable assurances.

I then heard her ask :

" Where am I ? What is this place ? " and after that she said, " I don't see the carriage ; and Matska, where is she ? "

Madame answered all her questions in so far as she understood them ; and gradually the young lady remembered how the misadventure came about, and was glad to hear that no one in, or in attendance on, the carriage was hurt ; and on learning that her mamma had left her here, till her return in about three months, she wept.

I was going to add my consolations to those of Madame Perrodon when Mademoiselle De Lafontaine placed her hand upon my arm, saying :

" Don't approach, one at a time is as much as she can at present converse with ; a very little excitement would possibly overpower her now."

As soon as she is comfortably in bed, I thought, I will run up to her room and see her.

My father in the meantime had sent a servant on horseback for the physician, who lived about two leagues away ; and a bedroom was being prepared for the young lady's reception.

The stranger now rose, and leaning on Madame's arm, walked slowly over the drawbridge and into the castle gate.

In the hall the servants waited to receive her, and she was conducted forthwith to her room.

The room we usually sat in as our drawing-room is long, having four windows, that looked over the moat and drawbridge, upon the forest scene I have just described.

It is furnished in old carved oak, with large carved cabinets, and the chairs are cushioned with crimson Utrecht velvet. The walls are covered with tapestry, and surrounded with great gold frames, the figures being as large as life, in ancient and very curious costume, and the subjects represented are hunting, hawking, and generally festive. It is not too stately to be extremely comfortable ; and here we had our tea, for with his usual patriotic leanings he insisted that the national beverage should make its appearance regularly with our coffee and chocolate.

We sat here this night, and with candles lighted, were talking over the adventure of the evening.

Madame Perrodon and Mademoiselle De Lafontaine were both of our party. The younger stranger had hardly lain down in her bed when she sank into a deep sleep ; and those ladies had left her in the care of a servant.

" How do you like our guest ? " I asked, as soon as Madame entered. " Tell me all about her ? "

" I like her extremely," answered Madame, " she is, I almost think, the prettiest creature I ever saw ; about your age, and so gentle and nice."

" She is absolutely beautiful," threw in Mademoiselle, who had peeped for a moment into the stranger's room.

" And such a sweet voice ! " added Madame Perrodon.

" Did you remark a woman in the carriage, after it was set up again, who did not get out," inquired Mademoiselle, " but only looked from the window ? "

No, we had not seen her.

Then she described a hideous black woman, with a sort of coloured turban on her head, who was gazing all the time from the carriage window, nodding and grinning derisively towards the ladies, with gleaming eyes and large white eye-balls, and her teeth set as if in fury.

" Did you remark what an ill-looking pack of men the servants were ? " asked Madame.

" Yes," said my father, who had just come in, " ugly, hang-dog looking fellows, as ever I beheld in my life. I hope they mayn't rob the poor lady in the forest. They are clever rogues, however ; they got everything to rights in a minute."

" I dare say they are worn out with too long travelling," said Madame. " Besides looking wicked, their faces were so strangely lean, and dark, and sullen. I am very curious, I own ; but I dare say the young lady will tell us all about it to-morrow, if she is sufficiently recovered."

" I don't think she will," said my father, with a mysterious smile, and a little nod of his head, as if he knew more about it than he cared to tell us.

This made me all the more inquisitive as to what had passed between him and the lady in the black velvet, in the brief but earnest interview that had immediately preceded her departure.

We were scarcely alone, when I entreated him to tell me. He did not need much pressing.

" There is no particular reason why I should not tell you. She expressed a reluctance to trouble us with the care of her daughter, saying she was in delicate health, and nervous, but not subject to any kind of seizure—she volunteered that—nor to any illusion ; being, in fact, perfectly sane."

" How very odd to say all that ! " I interpolated. " It was so unnecessary."

" At all events it *was* said," he laughed, " and as you wish to know all that passed, which was indeed very little, I tell you. She then said, ' I am making a long journey of *vital* importance '— she emphasized the word— 'rapid and secret ; I shall return for my child in three months ; in the meantime, she will be silent as to who we are, whence we come, and whither we are travelling.' That is all she said. She spoke very pure French. When she said the word ' secret,' she paused for a few seconds, looking sternly, her eyes fixed on mine. I fancy she makes a great point of that. You saw how quickly she was gone. I hope I have not done a very foolish thing, in taking charge of the young lady."

For my part, I was delighted. I was longing to see and talk to her ; and only waiting till the doctor should give me leave. You who live in towns, can have no idea how great an event the introduction of a new friend is, in such a solitude as surrounded us.

The doctor did not arrive till nearly one o'clock ; but I could no more have gone to my bed and slept, than I could have overtaken, on foot, the carriage in which the princess in black velvet had driven away.

When the physician came down to the drawing-room, it was to report very favourably upon his patient. She was now sitting up, her pulse quite regular, apparently perfectly well. She had sustained no injury, and the little shock to her nerves had passed away quite harmlessly. There could be no harm certainly in my seeing her, if we both wished it ; and, with this permission, I sent, forthwith, to know whether she would allow me to visit her for a few minutes in her room.

The servant returned immediately to say that she desired nothing more.

You may be sure I was not long in availing myself of this permission.

Our visitor lay in one of the handsomest rooms in the schloss. It was, perhaps a little stately. There was a sombre piece of tapestry opposite the foot of the bed, representing Cleopatra with the asp to her bosom ; and other solemn classic scenes were displayed, a little faded, upon the other walls. But there was gold carving, and rich and varied colour enough in the other decorations of the room, to more than redeem the gloom of the old tapestry.

There were candles at the bed side. She was sitting up ; her slender pretty figure enveloped in the soft silk dressing-gown, embroidered with flowers, and lined with thick quilted silk, which her mother had thrown over her feet as she lay upon the ground.

What was it that, as I reached the bed side and had just begun my little greeting, struck me dumb in a moment, and made me recoil a step or two from before her ? I will tell you.

I saw the very face which had visited me in my childhood at night, which remained so fixed in my memory, and on which I had for so many years so often ruminated with horror, when no one suspected of what I was thinking.

It was pretty, even beautiful ; and when I first beheld it, wore the same melancholy expression.

But this almost instantly lighted into a strange fixed smile of recognition.

There was a silence of fully a minute, and then at length *she* spoke ; *I* could not.

" How wonderful ! " she exclaimed. " Twelve years ago, I saw your face in a dream, and it has haunted me ever since."

" Wonderful indeed ! " I repeated, overcoming with an effort the horror that had for a time suspended my utterances. " Twelve years ago, in vision or reality, *I* certainly saw you. I could not forget your face. It has remained before my eyes ever since."

Her smile had softened. Whatever I had fancied strange in it, was gone, and it and her dimpling cheeks were now delightfully pretty and intelligent.

I felt reassured, and continued more in the vein which hospitality indicated, to bid her welcome, and to tell her how much pleasure her accidental arrival had given us all, and especially what a happiness it was to me.

I took her hand as I spoke. I was a little shy, as lonely people are, but the situation made me eloquent, and even bold. She pressed my hand, she laid hers upon it, and her eyes glowed, as, looking hastily into mine, she smiled again, and blushed.

She answered my welcome very prettily. I sat down beside her, still wondering ; and she said :

" I must tell you my vision about you ; it is so very strange that you and I should have had, each of the other so vivid a dream, that each should have seen, I you and you me, looking as we do now, when of course we both were mere children. I was a child about six years old, and I awoke from a confused and troubled dream, and found myself in a room, unlike my nursery, wainscoted clumsily in some dark wood, and with cupboards and bedsteads, and chairs, and benches placed about it. The beds were, I thought, all empty, and the room itself without any one but myself in it ; and I, after looking about me for some time, and admiring especially an iron candlestick, with two branches, which I should certainly know again, crept under one of the beds to reach the window ; but as I got from under the bed, I heard someone crying ; and looking up, while I was still upon my knees, I saw *you* —most assuredly you—as I see you now ; a beautiful young lady, with golden hair and large blue eyes, and lips—your lips—you, as you are here. Your looks won me ; I climbed on the bed and put my arms about you, and I think we both fell asleep. I was aroused by a scream ; you were sitting up screaming. I was frightened, and slipped down upon the ground, and, it seemed to me, lost consciousness for a moment ; and when I came to myself, I was again in my nursery at home. Your face I have never forgotten since. I could not be misled by mere resemblance. You *are* the lady whom I then saw."

It was now my turn to relate my corresponding vision, which I did, to the undisguised wonder of my new acquaintance.

" I don't know which should be most afraid of the other," she said, again smiling. " If you were less pretty I think I should be very much afraid of you, but being as you are, and you and I both so young, I feel only that I have made your acquaintance twelve years ago, and have already a right to your intimacy ; at all events, it does seem as if we were destined, from our earliest childhood, to be friends. I wonder whether you feel as strangely drawn towards me as I do to you ; I have never had a friend— shall I find one now ? " She sighed, and her fine dark eyes gazed passionately on me.

Now the truth is, I felt rather unaccountably towards the beautiful stranger. I did feel, as she said, " drawn towards her," but there was also something of repulsion. In this ambiguous feeling, however, the sense of attraction immensely prevailed. She interested and won me ; she was so beautiful and so indescribably engaging.

I perceived now something of languor and exhaustion stealing over her, and hastened to bid her good-night.

" The doctor thinks," I added, " that you ought to have a maid to sit up with you to-night ; one of ours is waiting, and you will find her a very useful and quiet creature."

" How kind of you, but I could not sleep, I never could with an attendant in the room. I shan't require any assistance—and, shall I confess my weakness, I am haunted with a terror of robbers. Our house was robbed once, and two servants murdered, so I always lock my door. It has become a habit—and you look so kind I know you will forgive me. I see there is a key in the lock."

She held me close in her pretty arms for a moment and whispered in my ear, " Good-night, darling, it is very hard to part with you, but good-night ; to-morrow, but not early, I shall see you again."

She sank back on the pillow with a sigh, and her fine eyes followed me with a fond and melancholy gaze, and she murmured again, " Good-night, dear friend."

Young people like, and even love, on impulse. I was flattered by the evident, though as yet undeserved, fondness she showed me. I liked the confidence with which she at once received me. She was determined that we should be very dear friends.

Next day came and we met again. I was delighted with my companion ; that is to say, in many respects.

Her looks lost nothing in daylight—she was certainly the most beautiful creature I had ever seen, and the unpleasant remembrance of the face presented in my early dream, had lost the effect of the first unexpected recognition.

She confessed that she had experienced a similar shock on seeing me, and precisely the same faint antipathy that had mingled with my admiration of her. We now laughed together over our momentary horrors.

CHAPTER IV

HER HABITS—A SAUNTER

I told you that I was charmed with her in most particulars.

There were some that did not please me so well.

She was above the middle height of women. I shall begin by describing her. She was slender, and wonderfully graceful. Except that her movements were languid—*very* languid—indeed, there was nothing in her appearance to indicate an invalid. Her complexion was rich and brilliant ; her features were small and beautifully formed ; her eyes large, dark, and lustrous ; her hair was quite wonderful, I never saw hair so magnificently thick and long when it was down about her shoulders ; I have often placed my hands under it, and laughed with wonder at its weight. It was exquisitely fine and soft, and in colour a rich very dark brown, with something of gold. I loved to let it down, tumbling with its own weight, as, in her room, she lay back in her chair talking in her sweet low voice, I used to fold and braid it, and spread it out and play with it. Heavens ! If I had but known all !

I said there were particulars which did not please me. I have told you that her confidence won me the first night I saw her ; but I found that she exercised with respect to herself, her mother, her history, everything in fact connected with her life, plans, and people, an ever-wakeful reserve. I dare say I was unreasonable, perhaps I was wrong ; I dare say I ought to have respected the solemn injunction laid upon my father by the stately lady in black velvet. But curiosity is a restless and unscrupulous passion, and no one girl can endure, with patience, that her's should be baffled by another. What harm could it do anyone to tell me what I so ardently desired to know ? Had she no trust in my good sense or honour ? Why would she not believe me when I assured her, so solemnly, that I would not divulge one syllable of what she told me to any mortal breathing.

There was a coldness, it seemed to me, beyond her years, in her smiling melancholy persistent refusal to afford me the least ray of light.

I cannot say we quarrelled upon this point, for she would not quarrel upon any. It was, of course, very unfair of me to press her, very ill-bred, but I really could not help it ; and I might just as well have let it alone.

What she did tell me amounted, in my unconscionable estimation—to nothing.

It was all summed up in three very vague disclosures.

First.—Her name was Carmilla.

Second.—Her family was very ancient and noble.

Third.—Her home lay in the direction of the west.

She would not tell me the name of her family, nor their armorial bearings, nor the name of their estate, nor even that of the country they lived in.

You are not to suppose that I worried her incessantly on these subjects. I watched opportunity, and rather insinuated than urged my enquiries. Once or twice, indeed, I did attack her more directly. But no matter what my tactics, utter failure was invariably the result. Reproaches and caresses were all lost upon her. But I must add this, that her evasion was conducted with so pretty a melancholy and deprecation, with so many, and even passionate declarations of her liking for me, and trust in my honour, and with so many promises, that I should at last know all, that I could not find it in my heart long to be offended with her.

She used to place her pretty arms about my neck, draw me to her, and laying her cheek to mine, murmur with her lips near my ear, " Dearest, your little heart is wounded ; think me not cruel because I obey the irresistible law of my strength and weakness ; if your dear heart is wounded, my wild heart bleeds with yours. In the rapture of my enormous humiliation I live in your warm life, and you shall die—die, sweetly die—into mine. I cannot help it ; as I draw near to you, you, in your turn, will draw near to others, and learn the rapture of that cruelty, which yet is love ; so, for a while, seek to know no more of me and mine, but trust me with all your loving spirit."

And when she had spoken such a rhapsody, she would press me more closely in her trembling embrace, and her lips in soft kisses gently glow upon my cheek.

Her agitations and her language were unintelligible to me.

From these foolish embraces, which were not of very frequent occurrence, I must allow, I used to wish to extricate myself ; but my energies seemed to fail me. Her murmured words sounded like a lullaby in my ear, and soothed my resistance into a trance, from which I only seemed to recover myself when she withdrew her arms.

In these mysterious moods I did not like her. I experienced a strange tumultuous excitement that was pleasurable, ever and anon, mingled with a vague sense of fear and disgust. I had no distinct thoughts about her while such scenes lasted, but I was conscious of a love growing into adoration, and also of abhorrence. This I know is paradox, but I can make no other attempt to explain the feeling.

I now write, after an interval of more than ten years, with a trembling hand, with a confused and horrible recollection of certain occurrences and situations, in the ordeal through which I was unconsciously passing ; though with a vivid and very sharp remembrance of the main current of my story. But, I suspect, in all lives there are certain emotional scenes, those in which our passions have been most wildly and terribly roused, that are of all others the most vaguely and dimly remembered.

Sometimes after an hour of apathy, my strange and beautiful companion would take my hand and hold it with a fond pressure, renewed again and again ; blushing softly, gazing in my face with languid and burning eyes, and breathing so fast that her dress rose and fell with the tumultuous respiration. It was like the ardour of a lover ; it embarrassed me ; it was hateful and yet overpowering ; and with gloating eyes she drew me to her, and her hot lips travelled along my cheek in kisses ; and she would whisper, almost in sobs, " You are mine, you *shall* be mine, and you and I are one for ever." Then she has thrown herself back in her chair, with her small hands over her eyes, leaving me trembling.

" Are we related," I used to ask ; " what can you mean by all this ? I remind you perhaps of some one whom you love ; but you must not, I hate it ; I don't know you—I don't know myself when you look so and talk so."

She used to sigh at my vehemence, then turn away and drop my hand.

Respecting these very extraordinary manifestations I strove in vain to form any satisfactory theory—I could not refer them to affectation or trick. It was unmistakably the momentary breaking out of suppressed instinct and emotion. Was she, notwithstanding her mother's volunteered denial, subject to brief visitations of insanity ; or was there here a disguise and a romance ? I had read in old story books of such things. What if a boyish lover had found

his way into the house, and sought to prosecute his suit in masquerade, with the assistance of a clever old adventuress. But here
were many things against this hypothesis, highly interesting as it
was to my vanity.

I could boast of no little attentions such as masculine gallantry
delights to offer. Between these passionate moments there were
long intervals of common-place, of gaiety, of brooding melancholy,
during which, except that I detected her eyes so full of melancholy
fire, following me, at times I might have been as nothing to her.
Except in these brief periods of mysterious excitement her ways
were girlish ; and there was always a languor about her, quite
incompatible with a masculine system in a state of health.

In some respects her habits were odd. Perhaps not so singular
in the opinion of a town lady like you, as they appeared to us
rustic people. She used to come down very late, generally not till
one o'clock, she would then take a cup of chocolate, but eat
nothing ; we then went out for a walk, which was a mere saunter,
and she seemed, almost immediately, exhausted, and either
returned to the schloss or sat on one of the benches that were
placed, here and there, among the trees. This was a bodily languor
in which her mind did not sympathise. She was always an animated talker, and very intelligent.

She sometimes alluded for a moment to her own home, or
mentioned an adventure or situation, or an early recollection,
which indicated a people of strange manners, and described
customs of which we knew nothing. I gathered from these
chance hints that her native country was much more remote than
I had at first fancied.

As we sat thus one afternoon under the trees a funeral passed
us by. It was that of a pretty young girl, whom I had often seen,
the daughter of one of the rangers of the forest. The poor man was
walking behind the coffin of his darling ; she was his only child,
and he looked quite heartbroken. Peasants walking two-and-two
came behind, they were singing a funeral hymn.

I rose to mark my respect as they passed, and joined in the hymn
they were very sweetly singing.

My companion shook me a little roughly, and I turned surprised.

She said brusquely, " Don't you perceive how discordant that
is ? "

" I think it is very sweet, on the contrary," I answered, vexed
at the interruption, and very uncomfortable, lest the people who

composed the little procession should observe and resent what was passing.

I resumed, therefore, instantly, and was again interrupted. " You pierce my ears," said Carmilla, almost angrily, and stopping her ears with her tiny fingers. " Besides, how can you tell that your religion and mine are the same ; your forms wound me, and I hate funerals. What a fuss ! Why, *you* must die—*everyone* must die ; and all are happier when they do. Come home."

" My father has gone on with the clergyman to the churchyard. I thought you knew she was to be buried to-day."

" *She ?* I don't trouble my head about peasants. I don't know who she is," answered Carmilla, with a flash from her fine eyes.

" She is the poor girl who fancied she saw a ghost a fortnight ago, and has been dying ever since, till yesterday, when she expired."

" Tell me nothing about ghosts. I shan't sleep to-night if you do."

" I hope there is no plague or fever coming ; all this looks very like it," I continued. " The swineherd's young wife died only a week ago, and she thought something seized her by the throat as she lay in her bed, and nearly strangled her. Papa says such horrible fancies do accompany some forms of fever. She was quite well the day before. She sank afterwards, and died before a week."

" Well, *her* funeral is over, I hope, and *her* hymn sung ; and our ears shan't be tortured with that discord and jargon. It has made me nervous. Sit down here, beside me ; sit close ; hold my hand ; press it hard—hard—harder."

We had moved a little back, and had come to another seat.

She sat down. Her face underwent a change that alarmed and even terrified me for a moment. It darkened, and became horribly livid ; her teeth and hands were clenched, and she frowned and compressed her lips, while she stared down upon the ground at her feet, and trembled all over with a continued shudder as irrepressible as ague. All her energies seemed strained to suppress a fit, with which she was then breathlessly tugging ; and at length a low convulsive cry of suffering broke from her, and gradually the hysteria subsided. " There ! That comes of strangling people with hymns ! " she said at last. " Hold me, hold me still. It is passing away."

And so gradually it did ; and perhaps to dissipate the sombre impression which the spectacle had left upon me, she became unusually animated and chatty ; and so we got home.

This was the first time I had seen her exhibit any definable symptoms of that delicacy of health which her mother had spoken of. It was the first time, also, I had seen her exhibit anything like temper.

Both passed away like a summer cloud ; and never but once afterwards did I witness on her part a momentary sign of anger. I will tell you how it happened.

She and I were looking out of one of the long drawing-room windows, when there entered the court-yard, over the draw-bridge, a figure of a wanderer whom I knew very well. He used to visit the schloss generally twice a year.

It was the figure of a hunchback, with the sharp lean features that generally accompany deformity. He wore a pointed black beard, and he was smiling from ear to ear, showing his white fangs. He was dressed in buff, black, and scarlet, and crossed with more straps and belts than I could count, from which hung all manner of things. Behind, he carried a magic-langern, and two boxes, which I well knew, in one of which was a salamander, and in the other a mandrake. These monsters used to make my father laugh. They were compounded of parts of monkeys, parrots, squirrels, fish, and hedgehogs, dried and stitched together with great neatness and startling effect. He had a fiddle, a box of conjuring apparatus, a pair of foils and masks attached to his belt, several other mysterious cases dangling about him, and a black staff with copper ferrules in his hand. His companion was a rough spare dog, that followed at his heels, but stopped short, suspiciously at the drawbridge, and in a little while began to howl dismally.

In the meantime, the mountebank, standing in the midst of the court-yard, raised his grotesque hat, and made us a very cere-monious bow, paying his compliments very volubly in execrable French, and German not much better. Then, disengaging his fiddle, he began to scrape a lively air, to which he sang with a merry discord, dancing with ludicrous airs and activity, that made me laugh, in spite of the dog's howling.

Then he advanced to the window with many smiles and salutations, and his hat in his left hand, his fiddle under his arm, and with a fluency that never took breath, he gabbled a long advertisement of all his accomplishments, and the resources of the various arts which he placed at our service, and the curiosities and entertainments which it was in his power, at our bidding to display.

"Will your ladyships be pleased to buy an amulet against the oupire, which is going like the wolf, I hear, through these woods," he said, dropping his hat on the pavement. "They are dying of it right and left, and here is a charm that never fails ; only pinned to the pillow, and you may laugh in his face."

These charms consisted of oblong slips of vellum, with cabalistic ciphers and diagrams upon them.

Carmilla instantly purchased one, and so did I.

He was looking up, and we were smiling down upon him, amused ; at least, I can answer for myself. His piercing black eye, as he looked up in our faces, seemed to detect something that fixed for a moment his curiosity.

In an instant he unrolled a leather case, full of all manner of odd little steel instruments.

"See here, my lady," he said, displaying it, and addressing me, "I profess, among other things less useful, the art of dentistry. Plague take the dog !" he interpolated. "Silence, beast ! He howls so that your ladyships can scarcely hear a word. Your noble friend, the young lady at your right, has the sharpest tooth—long, thin, pointed, like an awl, like a needle ; ha, ha ! With my sharp and long sight, as I look up, I have seen it distinctly ; now if it happens to hurt the young lady, and I think it must, here am I, here are my file, my punch, my nippers ; I will make it round and blunt, if her ladyship pleases ; no longer the tooth of a fish, but of a beautiful young lady as she is. Hey ? Is the young lady displeased ? Have I been too bold ? Have I offended her ?"

The young lady, indeed, looked very angry as she drew back from the window.

"How dares that mountebank insult us so ? Where is your father ? I shall demand redress from him. My father would have had the wretch tied up to the pump, and flogged with a cart-whip, and burnt to the bones with the castle brand !"

She retired from the window a step or two, and sat down, and hardly lost sight of the offender, when her wrath subsided as suddenly as it had risen, and she gradually recovered her usual tone, and seemed to forget the little hunchback and his follies.

My father was out of spirits that evening. On coming in he told us that there had been another case very similar to the two fatal ones which had lately occurred. The sister of a young peasant on his estate, only a mile away, was very ill, had been, as she described it, attacked very nearly in the same way, and was now slowly but steadily sinking.

" All this," said my father, " is strictly referable to natural causes. These poor people infect one another with their superstitions, and so repeat in imagination the images of terror that have infested their neighbours."

" But that very circumstance frightens one horribly," said Carmilla.

" How so ? " inquired my father.

" I am so afraid of fancying I see such things ; I think it would be as bad as reality."

" We are in God's hands ; nothing can happen without His permission, and all will end well for those who love Him. He is our faithful creator ; He had made us all, and will take care of us."

" Creator ! *Nature !* " said the young lady in answer to my gentle father. " And this disease that invades the country is natural. Nature. All things proceed from Nature—don't they ? All things in the heaven, in the earth, and under the earth, act and live as Nature ordains ? I think so."

" The doctor said he would come here to-day," said my father, after a silence. " I want to know what he thinks about it, and what he thinks we had better do."

" Doctors never did me any good," said Carmilla.

" Then you have been ill ? " I asked.

" More ill than ever you were," she answered.

" Long ago ? "

" Yes, a long time. I suffered from this very illness ; but I forget all but my pain and weakness, and they were not so bad as are suffered in other diseases."

" You were very young then ? "

" I dare say ; let us talk no more of it. You would not wound a friend ? " She looked languidly in my eyes, and passed her arm round my waist lovingly, and led me out of the room. My father was busy over some papers near the window.

" Why does your papa like to frighten us ? " said the pretty girl, with a sigh and a little shudder.

" He doesn't, dear Carmilla, it is the very furthest thing from his mind."

" Are you afraid, dearest ? "

" I should be very much if I fancied there was any real danger of my being attacked as those poor people were."

" You are afraid to die ? "

" Yes, every one is."

" But to die as lovers may—to die together, so that they may live together. Girls are caterpillars while they live in the world, to be finally butterflies when the summer comes ; but in the meantime there are grubs and larvæ, don't you see—each with their peculiar propensities, necessities and structure. So says Monsieur Buffon, in his big book, in the next room."

Later in the day the doctor came, and was closeted with papa for some time. He was a skilful man, of sixty and upwards, he wore powder, and shaved his pale face as smooth as a pumpkin. He and papa emerged from the room together, and I heard papa laugh, and say as they came out :

" Well, I do wonder at a wise man like you. What do you say to hippogriffs and dragons ? "

The doctor was smiling, and made answer, shaking his head—

" Nevertheless, life and death are mysterious states, and we know little of the resources of either."

And so they walked on, and I heard no more. I did not then know what the doctor had been broaching, but I think I guess it now.

CHAPTER V

A WONDERFUL LIKENESS

This evening there arrived from Gratz the grave, dark-faced son of the picture-cleaner, with a horse and cart laden with two large packing-cases, having many pictures in each. It was a journey of ten leagues, and whenever a messenger arrived at the schloss from our little capital of Gratz, we used to crowd about him in the hall, to hear the news.

This arrival created in our secluded quarters quite a sensation. The cases remained in the hall, and the messenger was taken charge of by the servants till he had eaten his supper. Then with assistants, and armed with hammer, ripping chisel, and turnscrew he met us in the hall, where we had assembled to witness the unpacking of the cases.

Carmilla sat looking listlessly on, while one after the other the old pictures, nearly all portraits, which had undergone the process of renovation, were brought to light. My mother was of an old Hungarian family, and most of these pictures, which were about to be restored to their places, had come to us through her.

My father had a list in his hand, from which he read, as the artist rummaged out the corresponding numbers. I don't know that the pictures were very good, but they were, undoubtedly very old, and some of them very curious also. They had, for the most part, the merit of being now seen by me, I may say, for the first time ; for the smoke and dust of time had all but obliterated them.

" There is a picture that I have not seen yet," said my father. " In one corner, at the top of it, is the name, as well as I could read, ' Marcia Karnstein,' and the date ' 1698 ' ; and I am curious to see how it has turned out."

I remembered it ; it was a small picture, about a foot and a half high, and nearly square, without a frame ; but it was so blackened by age that I could not make it out.

The artist now produced it, with evident pride. It was quite beautiful ; it was startling ; it seemed to live. It was the effigy of Carmilla !

" Carmilla, dear, here is an absolute miracle. Here you are, living, smiling, ready to speak, in this picture. Isn't it beautiful, papa ? And see, even the little mole on her throat."

My father laughed, and said " Certainly it is a wonderful likeness," but he looked away, and to my surprise seemed but little struck by it, and went on talking to the picture-cleaner, who was also something of an artist, and discoursed with intelligence about the portraits or other works, which his art had just brought into light and colour, while *I* was more and more lost in wonder the more I looked at the picture.

" Will you let me hang this picture in my room, papa ? " I asked.

" Certainly, dear," said he, smiling, " I'm very glad you think it so like. It must be prettier even than I thought it, if it is."

The young lady did not acknowledge this pretty speech, did not seem to hear it. She was leaning back in her seat, her fine eyes under their long lashes gazing on me in contemplation, and she smiled in a kind of rapture.

" And now you can read quite plainly the name that is written in the corner. It is not Marcia ; it looks as if it was done in gold. The name is Mircalla, Countess Karnstein, and this is a little coronet over it, and underneath A.D. 1698. I am descended from the Karnsteins ; that is, mamma was."

" Ah ! " said the lady, languidly, " so am I, I think, a very long descent, very ancient. Are there any Karnsteins living now ? "

" None who bear the name, I believe. The family were ruined, I believe, in some civil wars, long ago but the ruins of the castle are only about three miles away."

" How interesting ! " she said, languidly. " But see what beautiful moonlight ! " She glanced through the hall door, which stood a little open. " Suppose you take a little ramble round the court and look down at the road and river."

" It is so like the night you came to us," I said.

She sighed, smiling.

She rose, and each with her arm about the other's waist, we walked out upon the pavement.

In silence, slowly we walked down to the drawbridge, where the beautiful landscape opened before us.

" And so you were thinking of the night I came here ? " she almost whispered. " Are you glad I came ? "

" Delighted, dear Carmilla," I answered.

" And you ask for the picture you think like me, to hang in your room," she murmured with a sigh, as she drew her arm closer about my waist, and let her pretty head sink upon my shoulder.

" How romantic you are, Carmilla," I said. " Whenever you tell me your story, it will be made up chiefly of some one great romance."

She kissed me silently.

" I am sure, Carmilla, you have been in love ; that there is, at this moment, an affair of the heart going on."

" I have been in love with no one, and never shall," she whispered, " unless it should be with you."

How beautiful she looked in the moonlight !

Shy and strange was the look with which she quickly hid her face in my neck and hair, with tumultuous sighs, that seemed almost to sob, and pressed in mine a hand that trembled.

Her soft cheek was glowing against mine. " Darling, darling," she murmured, " I live in you ; and you would die for me, I love you so."

I started from her.

She was gazing on me with eyes from which all fire, all meaning had flown, and a face colourless and apathetic.

" Is there a chill in the air, dear ? " she said drowsily. " I almost shiver ; have I been dreaming ? Let us come in. Come, come ; come in."

" You look ill, Carmilla ; a little faint. You certainly must take some wine," I said.

" Yes, I will. I'm better now. I shall be quite well in a few minutes. Yes, do give me a little wine," answered Carmilla, as we approached the door. " Let us look again for a moment ; it is the last time, perhaps, I shall see the moonlight with you."

" How do you feel now, dear Carmilla ? Are you really better ? " I asked.

I was beginning to take alarm, lest she should have been stricken with the strange epidemic that they said had invaded the country about us.

" Papa, would be grieved beyond measure," I added, " if he thought you were ever so little ill, without immediately letting us know. We have a very skilful doctor near this, the physician who was with papa to-day."

" I'm sure he is. I know how kind you all are ; but, dear child, I am quite well again. There is nothing ever wrong with me, but a little weakness. People say I am languid ; I am incapable of exertion ; I can scarcely walk as far as a child of three years old ; and every now and then the little strength I have falters, and I become as you have just seen me. But after all I am very easily set up again ; in a moment I am perfectly myself. See how I have recovered."

So, indeed, she had ; and she and I talked a great deal, and very animated she was ; and the remainder of that evening passed without any recurrence of what I called her infatuations. I mean her crazy talk and looks, which embarrassed, and even frightened me.

But there occurred that night an event which gave my thoughts quite a new turn, and seemed to startle even Carmilla's languid nature into momentary energy.

CHAPTER VI

A VERY STRANGE AGONY

When we got into the drawing-room, and had sat down to our coffee and chocolate, although Carmilla did not take any, she seemed quite herself again, and Madame, and Mademoiselle

De Lafontaine, joined us, and made a little card party, in the course of which papa came in for what he called his " dish of tea."

When the game was over he sat down beside Carmilla on the sofa, and asked her, a little anxiously, whether she had heard from her mother since her arrival.

She answered " No."

He then asked her whether she knew where a letter would reach her at present.

" I cannot tell," she answered, ambiguously, " but I have been thinking of leaving you ; you have been already too hospitable and too kind to me. I have given you an infinity of trouble, and I should wish to take a carriage to-morrow, and post in pursuit of her ; I know where I shall ultimately find her, although I dare not yet tell you."

" But you must not dream of any such thing," exclaimed my father, to my great relief. " We can't afford to lose you so, and I won't consent to your leaving us, except under the care of your mother, who was so good as to consent to your remaining with us till she should herself return. I should be quite happy if I knew that you heard from her ; but this evening the accounts of the progress of the mysterious disease that has invaded our neighbour-hood, grow even more alarming ; and my beautiful guest, I do feel the responsibility, unaided by advice from your mother, very much. But I shall do my best ; and one thing is certain, that you must not think of leaving us without her distinct direction to that effect. We should suffer too much in parting from you to consent to it easily."

" Thank you, sir, a thousand times for your hospitality," she answered, smiling bashfully. " You have all been too kind to me ; I have seldom been so happy in all my life before, as in your beautiful château, under your care, and in the society of your dear daughter."

So he gallantly, in his old-fashioned way, kissed her hand, smiling, and pleased at her little speech.

I accompanied Carmilla as usual to her room, and sat and chatted with her while she was preparing for bed.

" Do you think," I said, at length, " that you will ever confide fully in me ? "

She turned round smiling, but made no answer, only continued to smile on me.

" You won't answer that ? " I said. " You can't answer pleasantly ; I ought not to have asked you."

" You were quite right to ask me that, or anything. You do not know how dear you are to me, or you could not think any confidence too great to look for. But I am under vows, no nun half so awfully, and I dare not tell my story yet, even to you. The time is very near when you shall know everything. You will think me cruel, very selfish, but love is always selfish ; the more ardent the more selfish. How jealous I am you cannot know. You must come with me, loving me, to death ; or else hate me, and still come with me, and *hating* me through death and after. There is no such word as indifference in my apathetic nature."

" Now, Carmilla, you are going to talk your wild nonsense again," I said hastily.

" Not I, silly little fool as I am, and full of whims and fancies ; for your sake I'll talk like a sage. Were you ever at a ball ? "

" No ; how you do run on. What is it like ? How charming it must be."

" I almost forget, it is years ago."

I laughed.

" You are not so old. Your first ball can hardly be forgotten yet."

" I remember everything about it—with an effort. I see it all, as divers see what is going on above them, through a medium, dense, rippling, but transparent. There occurred that night what has confused the picture, and made its colours faint. I was all but assassinated in my bed, wounded *here*," she touched her breast, " and never was the same since."

" Were you near dying ? "

" Yes, very—a cruel love—strange love, that would have taken my life. Love will have its sacrifices. No sacrifice without blood. Let us go to sleep now ; I feel so lazy. How can I get up just now and lock my door ? "

She was lying with her tiny hands buried in her rich wavy hair, under her cheek, her little head upon the pillow, and her glittering eyes followed me wherever I moved, with a kind of shy smile that I could not decipher.

I bid her good-night, and crept from the room with an uncomfortable sensation.

I often wondered whether our pretty guest ever said her prayers. *I* certainly had never seen her upon her knees. In the morning she never came down until long after our family prayers were over, and at night she never left the drawing-room to attend our brief evening prayers in the hall.

If it had not been that it had casually come out in one of our careless talks that she had been baptised, I should have doubted her being a Christian. Religion was a subject on which I had never heard her speak a word. If I had known the world better, this particular neglect or antipathy would not have so much surprised me.

The precautions of nervous people are infectious, and persons of a like temperament are pretty sure, after a time, to imitate them. I had adopted Carmilla's habit of locking her bed-room door, having taken into my head all her whimsical alarms about midnight invaders, and prowling assassins. I had also adopted her precaution of making a brief search through her room, to satisfy herself that no lurking assassin or robber was " ensconced."

These wise measures taken, I got into my bed and fell asleep. A light was burning in my room. This was an old habit, of very early date, and which nothing could have tempted me to dispense with.

Thus fortified I might take my rest in peace. But dreams come through stone walls, light up dark rooms, or darken light ones, and their persons make their exits and their entrances as they please, and laugh at locksmiths.

I had a dream that night that was the beginning of a very strange agony.

I cannot call it a nightmare, for I was quite conscious of being asleep. But I was equally conscious of being in my room, and lying in bed, precisely as I actually was. I saw, or fancied I saw, the room and its furniture just as I had seen it last, except that it was very dark, and I saw something moving round the foot of the bed, which at first I could not accurately distinguish. But I soon saw that it was a sooty-black animal that resembled a monstrous cat. It appeared to me about four or five feet long, for it measured fully the length of the hearth-rug as it passed over it ; and it continued to-ing and fro-ing with the lithe sinister restlessness of a beast in a cage. I could not cry out, although as you may suppose, I was terrified. Its pace was growing faster, and the room rapidly darker and darker, and at length so dark that I could no longer see anything of it but its eyes. I felt it spring lightly on the bed. The two broad eyes approached my face, and suddenly I felt a stinging pain as if two large needles darted, an inch or two apart, deep into my breast. I waked with a scream. The room was lighted by the candle that burnt there all through the night, and I saw a female figure standing at the foot of the bed, a little at the right side. It was in a dark loose dress, and its hair was down and covered its shoulders. A block of stone could not have been more still. There was not the slightest stir of respiration. As I stared at it, the figure appeared to have changed its place, and was now nearer the door ; then, close to it, the door opened, and it passed out.

I was now relieved, and able to breathe and move. My first thought was that Carmilla had been playing me a trick, and that I had forgotten to secure my door. I hastened to it, and found it locked as usual on the inside. I was afraid to open it—I was horrified. I sprang into my bed and covered my head up in the bed-clothes, and lay there more dead than alive till morning.

CHAPTER VII

DESCENDING

It would be vain my attempting to tell you the horror with which, even now, I recall the occurrence of that night. It was no such transitory terror as a dream leaves behind it. It seemed to deepen by time, and communicated itself to the room and the very furniture that had encompassed the apparition.

I could not bear next day to be alone for a moment. I should have told papa, but for two opposite reasons. At one time I thought he would laugh at my story, and I could not bear its being treated as a jest ; and at another, I thought he might fancy that I had been attacked by the mysterious complaint which had invaded our neighbourhood. I had myself no misgivings of the kind, and as he had been rather an invalid for some time, I was afraid of alarming him.

I was comfortable enough with my good-natured companions, Madame Perrodon, and the vivacious Mademoiselle Lafontaine. They both perceived that I was out of spirits and nervous, and at length I told them what lay so heavy at my heart.

Mademoiselle laughed, but I fancied that Madame Perrodon looked anxious.

" By-the-by," said Mademoiselle, laughing, " the long lime tree walk, behind Carmilla's bedroom window, is haunted ! "

"Nonsense!" exclaimed Madame, who probably thought the theme rather inopportune, "and who tells that story, my dear?"

"Martin says that he came up twice, when the old yard-gate was being repaired before sunrise, and twice saw the same female figure walking down the lime tree avenue."

"So he well might, as long as there are cows to milk in the river fields," said Madame.

"I dare say; but Martin chooses to be frightened, and never did I see a fool *more* frightened."

"You must not say a word about it to Carmilla, because she can see down that walk from her room window," I interposed, "and she is, if possible, a greater coward than I."

Carmilla came down rather later than usual that day.

"I was so frightened last night," she said, so soon as we were together, "and I am sure I should have seen something dreadful if it had not been for that charm I bought from the poor little hunchback whom I called such hard names. I had a dream of something black coming round my bed, and I awoke in a perfect horror, and I really thought, for some seconds, I saw a dark figure near the chimney piece, but I felt under my pillow for my charm, and the moment my fingers touched it, the figure disappeared, and I felt quite certain, only that I had it by me, that something frightful would have made its appearance, and perhaps, throttled me, as it did those poor people we heard of."

"Well, listen to me," I began, and recounted my adventure, at the recital of which she appeared horrified.

"And had you the charm near you?" she asked, earnestly.

"No, I had dropped it into a china vase in the drawing-room, but I shall certainly take it with me to-night, as you have so much faith in it."

At this distance of time I cannot tell you, or even understand, how I overcame my horror so effectually as to lie alone in my room that night. I remember distinctly that I pinned the charm to my pillow. I fell asleep almost immediately, and slept even more soundly than usual all night.

Next night I passed as well. My sleep was delightfully deep and dreamless. But I wakened with a sense of lassitude and melancholy which, however, did not exceed a degree that was almost luxurious.

"Well, I told you so," said Carmilla, when I described my quiet sleep, "I had such delightful sleep myself last night; I pinned the charm to the breast of my nightdress. It was too far away the night before. I am quite sure it was all fancy, except the dreams. I used to think that evil spirits made dreams, but our doctor told me it is no such thing. Only a fever passing by, or some other malady, as they often do, he said, knocks at the door, and not being able to get in, passes on, with that alarm."

" And what do you think the charm is ? " said I.

" It has been fumigated or immersed in some drug, and is an antidote against the malaria," she answered.

" Then it acts only on the body ? "

" Certainly ; you don't suppose that evil spirits are frightened by bits of ribbon, or the perfumes of a druggist's shop ? No, these complaints, wandering in the air, begin by trying the nerves, and so infect the brain ; but before they can seize upon you, the antidote repels them. That I am sure is what the charm has done for us. It is nothing magical, it is simply natural."

I should have been happier if I could quite have agreed with Carmilla, but I did my best, and the impression was a little losing its force.

For some nights I slept profoundly ; but still every morning I felt the same lassitude, and a languor weighed upon me all day. I felt myself a changed girl. A strange melancholy was stealing over me, a melancholy that I would not have interrupted. Dim thoughts of death began to open, and an idea that I was slowly sinking took gentle, and, somehow, not unwelcome possession of me. If it was sad, the tone of mind which this induced was also sweet. Whatever it might be, my soul acquiesced in it.

I would not admit that I was ill, I would not consent to tell my papa, or to have the doctor sent for.

Carmilla became more devoted to me than ever, and her strange paroxysms of languid adoration more frequent. She used to gloat on me with increasing ardour the more my strength and spirits waned. This always shocked me like a momentary glare of insanity.

Without knowing it, I was now in a pretty advanced stage of the strangest illness under which mortal ever suffered. There was an unaccountable fascination in its earlier symptoms that more than reconciled me to the incapacitating effect of that stage of the malady. This fascination increased for a time, until it reached a certain point, when gradually a sense of the horrible mingled itself with it, deepening, as you shall hear, until it discoloured and perverted the whole state of my life.

The first change I experienced was rather agreeable. It was very near the turning point from which began the descent of Avernus.

Certain vague and strange sensations visited me in my sleep. The prevailing one was of that pleasant, peculiar cold thrill which we feel in bathing, when we move against the current of a river. This was soon accompanied by dreams that seemed interminable, and were so vague that I could never recollect their scenery and persons, or any one connected portion of their action. But they left an awful impression, and a sense of exhaustion, as if I had passed through a long period of great mental exertion and danger. After all these dreams there remained on waking a remembrance of having been in a place very nearly dark, and of having spoken to people whom I could not see ; and especially of one clear voice, of a female's, very deep, that spoke as if at a distance, slowly, and producing always the same sensation of indescribable solemnity and fear. Sometimes there came a sensation as if a hand was drawn softly along my cheek and neck. Sometimes it was as if warm lips kissed me, and longer and more lovingly as they reached my throat, but there the caress fixed itself. My heart beat faster, my breathing rose and fell rapidly and full drawn ; a sobbing, that rose into a sense of strangulation, supervened, and turned into a dreadful convulsion, in which my senses left me, and I became unconscious.

It was now three weeks since the commencement of this unaccountable state. My sufferings had, during the last week, told upon my appearance. I had grown pale, my eyes were dilated and darkened underneath, and the languor which I had long felt began to display itself in my countenance.

My father asked me often whether I was ill ; but, with an obstinacy which now seems to me unaccountable, I persisted in assuring him that I was quite well.

In a sense this was true. I had no pain, I could complain of no bodily derangement. My complaint seemed to be one of the imagination, or the nerves, and, horrible as my sufferings were, I kept them, with a morbid reserve, very nearly to myself.

It could not be that terrible complaint which the peasants call the oupire, for I had now been suffering for three weeks, and they were seldom ill for much more than three days, when death put an end to their miseries.

Carmilla complained of dreams and feverish sensations, but by no means of so alarming a kind as mine. I say that mine were extremely alarming. Had I been capable of comprehending my condition, I would have invoked aid and advice on my knees. The narcotic of an unsuspected influence was acting upon me, and my perceptions were benumbed.

I am going to tell you now of a dream that led immediately to an odd discovery.

One night, instead of the voice I was accustomed to hear in the dark, I heard one, sweet and tender, and at the same time terrible, which said, " Your mother warns you to beware of the assassin." At the same time a light unexpectedly sprang up, and I saw Carmilla, standing, near the foot of my bed, in her white night-dress, bathed, from her chin to her feet, in one great stain of blood.

I wakened with a shriek, possessed with the one idea that Carmilla was being murdered. I remember springing from my bed, and my next recollection is that of standing on the lobby, crying for help.

Madame and Mademoiselle came scurrying out of their rooms in alarm ; a lamp burned always on the lobby, and seeing me, they soon learned the cause of my terror.

I insisted on our knocking at Carmilla's door. Our knocking was unanswered. It soon became a pounding and an uproar. We shrieked her name but all was vain.

We all grew frightened, for the door was locked. We hurried back, in panic, to my room. There we rang the bell long and furiously. If my father's room had been at that side of the house, we would have called him up at once to our aid. But, alas ! he was quite out of hearing, and to reach him involved an excursion for which we none of us had courage.

Servants, however, soon came running up the stairs ; I had got on my dressing-gown and slippers meanwhile, and my companions were already similarly furnished. Recognising the voices of the servants on the lobby, we sallied out together ; and having renewed, as fruitlessly, our summons at Carmilla's door, I ordered the men to force the lock. They did so, and we stood, holding our lights aloft, in the doorway, and so stared into the room.

We called her by name ; but there was still no reply. We looked round the room. Everything was undisturbed. It was exactly in the state in which I left it on bidding her good night. But Carmilla was gone.

CHAPTER VIII

SEARCH

At sight of the room, perfectly undisturbed except for our violent entrance, we began to cool a little, and soon recovered our senses sufficiently to dismiss the men. It had struck Mademoiselle that possibly Carmilla had been wakened by the uproar at her door, and in her first panic had jumped from her bed, and hid herself in a press, or behind a curtain, from which she could not, of course, emerge until the major-domo and his myrmidons had withdrawn. We now recommenced our search, and began to call her by name again.

It was all to no purpose. Our perplexity and agitation increased. We examined the windows, but they were secured. I implored of Carmilla, if she had concealed herself, to play this cruel trick no longer—to come out, and to end our anxieties. It was 'all useless. I was by this time convinced that she was not in the room, nor in the dressing-room, the door of which was still locked on this side. She could not have passed it. I was utterly puzzled. Had Carmilla discovered one of those secret passages which the old housekeeper said were known to exist in the schloss, although the tradition of their exact situation had been lost. A little time would, no doubt, explain all—utterly perplexed as, for the present, we were.

It was past four o'clock, and I preferred passing the remaining hours of darkness in Madame's room. Daylight brought no solution of the difficulty.

The whole household, with my father at its head, was in a state of agitation next morning. Every part of the château was searched. The grounds were explored. Not a trace of the missing lady could be discovered. The stream was about to be dragged ; my father was in distraction ; what a tale to have to tell the poor girl's mother on her return. I, too, was almost beside myself, though my grief was quite of a different kind.

The morning was passed in alarm and excitement. It was now one o'clock, and still no tidings. I ran up to Carmilla's room, and found her standing at her dressing-table. I was astounded. I could not believe my eyes. She beckoned me to her with her pretty finger, in silence. Her face expressed extreme fear.

I ran to her in an ecstasy of joy ; I kissed and embraced her again and again. I ran to the bell and rang it vehemently, to bring others to the spot, who might at once relieve my father's anxiety.

" Dear Carmilla, what has become of you all this time ? We have been in agonies of anxiety about you," I exclaimed. " Where have you been ? How did you come back ? "

" Last night has been a night of wonders," she said.

" For mercy's sake, explain all you can."

" It was past two last night," she said, " when I went to sleep as usual in my bed, with my doors locked, that of the dressing-room and that opening upon the gallery. My sleep was uninterrupted, and, so far as I know, dreamless ; but I awoke just now on the sofa in the dressing-room there, and I found the door between the rooms open, and the other door forced. How could all this have happened without my being awakened ? It must have been accompanied with a great deal of noise, and I am particularly easily wakened ; and how could I have been carried out of my bed without my sleep having been interrupted, I whom the slightest stir startles ? "

By this time, Madame, Mademoiselle, my father, and a number of the servants were in the room. Carmilla was, of course, overwhelmed with enquiries, congratulations, and welcomes. She had but one story to tell, and seemed the least able of all the party to suggest any way of accounting for what had happened.

My father took a turn up and down the room, thinking. I saw Carmilla's eye follow him for a moment with a sly, dark glance.

When my father had sent the servants away, Mademoiselle having gone in search of a little bottle of valerian and sal-volatile, and there being no one now in the room with Carmilla except my father, Madame, and myself, he came to her thoughtfully, took her hand very kindly, led her to the sofa, and sat down beside her.

" Will you forgive me, my dear, if I risk a conjecture, and ask a question ? "

" Who can have a better right ? " she said. " Ask what you please, and I will tell you everything. But my story is simply one of bewilderment and darkness. I know absolutely nothing. Put any question you please. But you know, of course, the limitations mamma has placed me under."

" Perfectly, my dear child. I need not approach the topics on which she desires our silence. Now, the marvel of last night consists in your having been removed from your bed and your room without being wakened, and this removal having occurred apparently while the windows were still secured, and the two doors locked upon the inside. I will tell you my theory, and first ask you a question."

Carmilla was leaning on her hand dejectedly ; Madame and I were listening breathlessly.

" Now, my question is this. Have you ever been suspected of walking in your sleep ? "

" Never since I was very young indeed."

" But you did walk in your sleep when you were young ? "

" Yes ; I know I did. I have been told so often by my old nurse."

My father smiled and nodded.

" Well, what has happened is this. You got up in your sleep, unlocked the door, not leaving the key, as usual, in the lock, but taking it out and locking it on the outside ; you again took the key out, and carried it away with you to some one of the five-and-twenty rooms on this floor, or perhaps upstairs or downstairs. There are so many rooms and closets, so much heavy furniture, and such accumulations of lumber, that it would require a week to search this old house thoroughly. Do you see, now, what I mean ? "

" I do, but not all," she answered.

" And how, papa, do you account for her finding herself on the sofa in the dressing-room, which we had searched so carefully ? "

" She came there after you had searched it, still in her sleep, and at last awoke spontaneously, and was as much surprised to find herself where she was as any one else. I wish all mysteries were as easily and innocently explained as yours, Carmilla," he said, laughing. " And so we may congratulate ourselves on the certainty that the most natural explanation of the occurrence is one that involves no drugging, no tampering with locks, no burglars, or poisoners, or witches—nothing that need alarm Carmilla, or any one else, for our safety."

Carmilla was looking charmingly. Nothing could be more beautiful than her tints. Her beauty was, I think enhanced by that graceful languor that was peculiar to her. I think my father was silently contrasting her looks with mine, for he said :—

" I wish my poor Laura was looking more like herself " ; and he sighed.

So our alarms were happily ended, and Carmilla restored to her friends.

CHAPTER IX

THE DOCTOR

As Carmilla would not hear of an attendant sleeping in her room, my father arranged that a servant should sleep outside her door so that she could not attempt to make another such excursion without being arrested at her own door.

That night passed quietly ; and next morning early, the doctor, whom my father had sent for without telling me a word about it, arrived to see me.

Madame accompanied me to the library ; and there the grave little doctor, with white hair and spectacles, whom I mentioned before, was waiting to receive me.

I told him my story, and as I proceeded he grew graver and graver.

We were standing, he and I, in the recess of one of the windows, facing one another. When my statement was over, he leaned with his shoulders against the wall, and with his eyes fixed on me earnestly with an interest in which was a dash of horror.

After a minute's reflection, he asked Madame if he could see my father.

He was sent for accordingly, and as he entered, smiling, he said :

" I dare say, doctor, you are going to tell me that I am an old fool for having brought you here ; I hope I am."

But his smile faded into shadow as the doctor, with a very grave face, beckoned him to him.

He and the doctor talked for some time in the same recess where I had just conferred with the physician. It seemed an earnest and argumentative conversation. The room is very large, and I and Madame stood together, burning with curiosity, at the further end. Not a word could we hear, however, for they spoke in a very low tone, and the deep recess of the window quite concealed the doctor from view, and very nearly my father, whose foot, arm, and shoulder only could we see ; and the voices were, I suppose, all the less audible for the sort of closet which the thick wall and window formed.

After a time my father's face looked into the room ; it was pale, thoughtful, and, I fancied, agitated.

" Laura, dear, come here for a moment. Madame, we shan't trouble you, the doctor says, at present."

Accordingly I approached, for the first time a little alarmed ;

for, although I felt very weak, I did not feel ill ; and strength, one always fancies, is a thing that may be picked up when we please.

My father held out his hand to me as I drew near, but he was looking at the doctor, and he said :

" It certainly *is* very odd ; I don't understand it quite. Laura, come here, dear ; now attend to Doctor Spielsberg, and recollect yourself."

" You mentioned a sensation like that of two needles piercing the skin, somewhere about your neck, on the night when you experienced your first horrible dream. Is there still any soreness ? "

" None at all," I answered.

" Can you indicate with your finger about the point at which you think this occurred ? "

" Very little below my throat—*here*," I answered.

I wore a morning dress, which covered the place I pointed to.

" Now you can satisfy yourself," said the doctor. " You won't mind your papa's lowering your dress a very little. It is necessary, to detect a symptom of the complaint under which you have been suffering."

I acquiesced. It was only an inch or two below the edge of my collar.

" God bless me !—so it is," exclaimed my father, growing pale.

" You see it now with your own eyes," said the doctor, with a gloomy triumph.

" What is it ? " I exclaimed, beginning to be frightened.

" Nothing, my dear young lady, but a small blue spot, about the size of the tip of your little finger ; and now," he continued, turning to papa, " the question is what is best to be done ? "

" Is there any danger ? " I urged, in great trepidation.

" I trust not, my dear," answered the doctor. " I don't see why you should not recover. I don't see why you should not begin *immediately* to get better. That is the point at which the sense of strangulation begins ? "

" Yes," I answered.

" And—recollect as well as you can—the same point was a kind of centre of that thrill which you described just now, like the current of a cold stream running against you ? "

" It may have been ; I think it was."

" Ay, you see ? " he added, turning to my father. " Shall I say a word to Madame ? "

" Certainly," said my father.

He called Madame to him, and said :

" I find my young friend here far from well. It won't be of any great consequence, I hope ; but it will be necessary that some steps be taken, which I will explain by-and-by ; but in the mean-time, Madame, you will be so good as not to let Miss Laura be alone for one moment. That is the only direction I need give for the present. It is indispensable."

" We may rely upon your kindness, Madame, I know," added my father.

Madame satisfied him eagerly.

" And you, dear Laura, I know you will observe the doctor's direction."

" I shall have to ask your opinion upon another patient, whose symptoms slightly resemble those of my daughter, that have just been detailed to you—very much milder in degree, but I believe quite of the same sort. She is a young lady—our guest ; but as you say you will be passing this way again this evening, you can't do better than take your supper here, and you can then see her. She does not come down till the afternoon."

" I thank you," said the doctor. " I shall be with you, then, at about seven this evening."

And then they repeated their directions to me and to Madame, and with this parting charge my father left us, and walked out with the doctor ; and I saw them pacing together up and down between the road and the moat, on the grassy platform in front of the castle, evidently absorbed in earnest conversation.

The doctor did not return. I saw him mount his horse there, take his leave, and ride away eastward through the forest. Nearly at the same time I saw the man arrive from Dranfeld with the letters, and dismount and hand the bag to my father.

In the meantime, Madame and I were both busy, lost in con-jecture as to the reasons of the singular and earnest direction which the doctor and my father had concurred in imposing. Madame, as she afterwards told me, was afraid the doctor apprehended a sudden seizure, and that, without prompt assistance, I might either lose my life in a fit, or at least be seriously hurt.

This interpretation did not strike me ; and I fancied perhaps luckily for my nerves, that the arrangement was prescribed simply to secure a companion, who would prevent my taking too much exercise, or eating unripe fruit, or doing any of the fifty foolish things to which young people are supposed to be prone.

About half-an-hour after, my father came in—he had a letter in his hand—and said :

" This letter had been delayed ; it is from General Spielsdorf. He might have been here yesterday, he may not come till to-morrow, or he may be here to-day."

He put the open letter into my hand ; but he did not look pleased, as he used when a guest, especially one so much loved as the General, was coming. On the contrary, he looked as if he wished him at the bottom of the Red Sea. There was plainly something on his mind which he did not choose to divulge.

" Papa, darling, will you tell me this ? " said I, suddenly laying my hand on his arm, and looking, I am sure, imploringly in his face.

" Perhaps," he answered, smoothing my hair caressingly over my eyes.

" Does the doctor think me very ill ? "

" No, dear ; he thinks, if right steps are taken, you will be quite well again, at least on the high road to a complete recovery, in a day or two," he answered, a little drily. " I wish our good friend, the General, had chosen any other time ; that is, I wish you had been perfectly well to receive him."

" But do tell me, papa," I insisted, " *what* does he think is the matter with me ? "

" Nothing ; you must not plague me with questions," he answered, with more irritation than I ever remember him to have displayed before ; and seeing that I looked wounded, I suppose, he kissed me, and added, " You shall know all about it in a day or two ; that is, all that *I* know. In the meantime, you are not to trouble your head about it."

He turned and left the room, but came back before I had done wondering and puzzling over the oddity of all this ; it was merely to say that he was going to Karnstein and had ordered the carriage to be ready at twelve, and that I and Madame should accompany him ; he was going to see the priest who lived near those picturesque grounds, upon business, and as Carmilla had never seen them, she could follow, when she came down, with Mademoiselle, who would bring materials for what you call a pic-nic, which might be laid for us in the ruined castle.

At twelve o'clock, accordingly, I was ready, and not long after, my father, Madame and I set out upon our projected drive. Passing the drawbridge we turn to the right, and follow the road over the steep Gothic bridge westward, to reach the deserted village and ruined castle of Karnstein.

No sylvan drive can be fancied prettier. The ground breaks into gentle hills and hollows, all clothed with beautiful wood, totally destitute of the comparative formality which artificial planting and early culture and pruning impart.

The irregularities of the ground often lead the road out of its course, and cause it to wind beautifully round the sides of broken hollows and the steeper sides of the hills, among varieties of ground almost inexhaustible.

Turning one of these points, we suddenly encountered our old friend, the General, riding towards us, attended by a mounted servant. His portmanteaus were following in a hired waggon, such as we term a cart.

The General dismounted as we pulled up, and, after the usual greetings, was easily persuaded to accept the vacant seat in the carriage, and send his horse on with his servant to the schloss.

CHAPTER X

BEREAVED

It was about ten months since we had last seen him ; but that time had sufficed to make an alteration of years in his appearance. He had grown thinner ; something of gloom and anxiety had taken the place of that cordial serenity which used to characterise his features. His dark blue eyes, always penetrating, now gleamed with a sterner light from under his shaggy grey eyebrows. It was not such a change as grief alone usually induces, and angrier passions seemed to have had their share in bringing it about.

We had not long resumed our drive, when the General began to talk, with his usual soldierly directness, of the bereavement, as he termed it, which he had sustained in the death of his beloved niece and ward ; and he then broke out in a tone of intense bitterness and fury, inveighing against the " hellish arts " to which she had fallen a victim, and expressing with more exasperation than piety, his wonder that Heaven should tolerate so monstrous an indulgence of the lusts and malignity of hell.

My father, who saw at once that something very extraordinary had befallen, asked him, if not too painful to him, to detail the circumstances which he thought justified the strong terms in which he expressed himself.

" I should tell you all with pleasure," said the General, " but you would not believe me."

" Why should I not ? " he asked.

" Because," he answered testily, " you believe in nothing but what consists with your own prejudices and illusions. I remember when I was like you, but I have learned better."

" Try me," said my father ; " I am not such a dogmatist as you suppose. Besides which, I very well know that you generally require proof for what you believe, and am, therefore, very strongly predisposed to respect your conclusions."

" You are right in supposing that I have not been led lightly into a belief in the marvellous—for what I have experienced *is* marvellous—and I have been forced by extraordinary evidence to credit that which ran counter, diametrically, to all my theories. I have been made the dupe of a preternatural conspiracy."

Notwithstanding his professions of confidence in the General's penetration, I saw my father, at this point, glance at the General, with, as I thought a marked suspicion of his sanity.

The General did not see it, luckily. He was looking gloomily and curiously into the glades and vistas of the woods that were opening before us.

" You are going to the Ruins of Karnstein ? " he said. " Yes, it is a lucky coincidence ; do you know I was going to ask you to bring me there to inspect them. I have a special object in exploring. There is a ruined chapel, isn't there, with a great many tombs of that extinct family ? "

" So there are—highly interesting," said my father. " I hope you are thinking of claiming the title and estates ? "

My father said this gaily, but the General did not recollect the laugh, or even the smile, which courtesy exacts for a friend's joke ; on the contrary, he looked grave and even fierce, ruminating on a matter that stirred his anger and horror.

" Something very different," he said, gruffly. " I mean to unearth some of those fine people. I hope, by God's blessing, to accomplish a pious sacrilege here, which will relieve our earth of certain monsters, and enable honest people to sleep in their beds without being assailed by murderers. I have strange things to tell you, my dear friend, such as I myself would have scouted as incredible a few months since."

My father looked at him again, but this time not with a glance of suspicion—with an eye, rather, of keen intelligence and alarm.

" The house of Karnstein," he said, " has been long extinct : a hundred years at least. My dear wife was maternally descended from the Karnsteins. But the name and title have long ceased to exist. The castle is a ruin ; the very village is deserted ; it is fifty years since the smoke of a chimney was seen there ; not a roof left."

" Quite true. I have heard a great deal about that since I last saw you ; a great deal that will astonish you. But I had better relate everything in the order in which it occurred," said the General. "You saw my dear ward—my child, I may call her. No creature could have been more beautiful and only three months ago none more blooming."

" Yes, poor thing ! when I saw her last she certainly was quite lovely," said my father. " I was grieved and shocked more than I can tell you, my dear friend ; I knew what a blow it was to you."

He took the General's hand, and they exchanged a kind pressure. Tears gathered in the old soldier's eyes. He did not seek to conceal them. He said :

" We have been very old friends ; I knew you would feel for me, childless as I am. She had become an object of very dear interest to me, and repaid my care by an affection that cheered my home and made my life happy. That is all gone. The years that remain to me on earth may not be very long ; but by God's mercy I hope to accomplish a service to mankind before I die, and to subserve the vengeance of Heaven upon the fiends who have murdered my poor child in the spring of her hopes and beauty ! "

" You said, just now, that you intended relating everything as it occurred," said my father. " Pray do ; I assure you that it is not mere curiosity that prompts me."

By this time we had reached the point at which the Drunstall road, by which the General had come, diverges from the road which we were travelling to Karnstein.

" How far is it to the ruins ? " enquired the General, looking anxiously forward.

" About half a league," answered my father. " Pray let us hear the story you were so good as to promise."

CHAPTER XI

THE STORY

"With all my heart," said the General, with an effort ; and after a short pause in which to arrange his subject, he commenced one of the strangest narratives I ever heard.

" My dear child was looking forward with great pleasure to the visit you had been so good as to arrange for her to your charming daughter." Here he made me a gallant but melancholy bow. " In the meantime we had an invitation to my old friend the Count Carlsfeld, whose schloss is about six leagues to the other side of Karnstein. It was to attend the series of fêtes which, you remember, were given by him in honour of his illustrious visitor, the Grand Duke Charles."

" Yes ; and very splendid, I believe, they were," said my father.

" Princely ! But then his hospitalities are quite regal. He has Aladdin's lamp. The night from which my sorrow dates was devoted to a magnificent masquerade.The grounds were thrown open, the trees hung with coloured lamps. There was such a display of fireworks as Paris itself had never witnessed. And such music—music, you know, is my weakness—such ravishing music ! The finest instrumental band, perhaps, in the world, and the finest singers who could be collected from all the great operas in Europe. As you wandered through these fantastically illuminated grounds, the moon-lighted château throwing a rosy light from its long rows of windows, you would suddenly hear these ravishing voices stealing from the silence of some grove, or rising from boats upon the lake. I felt myself, as I looked and listened, carried back into the romance and poetry of my early youth.

" When the fireworks were ended, and the ball beginning, we returned to the noble suite of rooms that was thrown open to the dancers. A masked ball, you know, is a beautiful sight ; but so brilliant a spectacle of the kind I never saw before.

" It was a very aristocratic assembly. I was myself almost the only ' nobody ' present.

" My dear child was looking quite beautiful. She wore no mask. Her excitement and delight added an unspeakable charm to her features, always lovely. I remarked a young lady, dressed magnificently, but wearing a mask, who appeared to me to be observing my ward with extraordinary interest. I had seen her, earlier in the evening, in the great hall, and again, for a few minutes, walking near us, on the terrace under the castle windows, similarly employed. A lady, also masked, richly and gravely dressed, and with a stately air, like a person of rank, accompanied her as a chaperon. Had the young lady not worn a mask, I could, of course, have been much more certain upon the question whether she was really watching my poor darling. I am now well assured that she was.

" We were now in one of the *salons*. My poor dear child had been dancing, and was resting a little in one of the chairs near the door ; I was standing near. The two ladies I have mentioned had approached, and the younger took the chair next my ward ; while her companion stood beside me, and for a little time addressed herself, in a low tone, to her charge.

" Availing herself of the privilege of her mask she turned to me, and in the tone of an old friend, and calling me by my name, opened a conversation with me, which piqued my curiosity a good deal. She referred to many scenes where she had met me—at Court, and at distinguished houses. She alluded to little incidents which I had long ceased to think of, but which, I found, had only lain in abeyance in my memory, for they instantly started into life at her touch.

" I became more and more curious to ascertain who she was, every moment. She parried my attempts to discover very adroitly and pleasantly. The knowledge she showed of many passages in my life seemed to me all but unaccountable ; and she appeared to take a not unnatural pleasure in foiling my curiosity, and in seeing me flounder, in my eager perplexity, from one conjecture to another.

" In the meantime the young lady, whom her mother called by the odd name of Millarca, when she once or twice addressed her, had, with the same ease and grace, got into conversation with my ward.

" She introduced herself by saying that her mother was a very old acquaintance of mine. She spoke of the agreeable audacity which a mask rendered practicable ; she talked like a friend ; she admired her dress, and insinuated very prettily her admiration of her beauty. She amused her with laughing criticisms upon the people who crowded the ballroom, and laughed at my poor child's fun. She was very witty and lively when she pleased, and after a time they had grown very good friends, and the young stranger lowered her mask, displaying a remarkably beautiful face. I had never seen it before, neither had my dear child. But though it was new to us, the features were so engaging, as well as lovely, that it was impossible not to feel the attraction powerfully. My poor girl did so. I never saw anyone more taken with another at first sight, unless indeed, it was the stranger herself, who seemed quite to have lost her heart to her.

" In the meantime, availing myself of the licence of a masquerade, I put not a few questions to the elder lady.

" ' You have puzzled me utterly,' I said, laughing. ' Is that not enough ? won't you, now, consent to stand on equal terms, and do me the kindness to remove your mask ? '

" ' Can any request be more unreasonable ? ' she replied. ' Ask a lady to yield an advantage ! Beside, how do you know you should recognise me ? Years make changes.'

" ' As you see,' I said, with a bow, and, I suppose, a rather melancholy little laugh.

" ' As philosophers tell us,' she said ; ' and how do you know that a sight of my face would help you ? '

" ' I should take chance for that,' I answered. ' It is vain trying to make yourself out an old woman ; your figure betrays you.'

" ' Years, nevertheless, have passed since I saw you, rather since you saw me, for that is what I am considering. Millarca, there, is my daughter ; I cannot then be young, even in the opinion of people whom time has taught to be indulgent, and I may not like to be compared with what you remember me. You have no mask to remove. You can offer me nothing in exchange.'

" ' My petition is to your pity, to remove it.'

" ' And mine to yours, to let it stay where it is,' she replied.

" ' Well, then, at least you will tell me whether you are French or German ; you speak both languages so perfectly.'

" ' I don't think I shall tell you that, General ; you intend a surprise, and are meditating the particular point of attack.'

" ' At all events, you won't deny this,' I said, ' that being honoured by your permission to converse, I ought to know how to address you. Shall I say Madame la Comtesse ! '

" She laughed, and she would, no doubt, have met me with another evasion—if, indeed, I can treat any occurrence in an interview every circumstance of which was pre-arranged, as I now believe, with the profoundest cunning, as liable to be modified by accident.

" ' As to that,' she began ; but she was interrupted, almost as she opened her lips, by a gentleman, dressed in black, who looked particularly elegant and distinguished, with this drawback, that his face was the most deadly pale I ever saw, except in death. He was in no masquerade—in the plain evening dress of a gentleman ; and he said, without a smile, but with a courtly and unusually low bow :—

" ' Will Madame la Comtesse permit me to say á very few words which may interest her ? '

" The lady turned quickly to him, and touched her lip in token of silence ; she then said to me, ' Keep my place for me, General ; I shall return when I have said a few words.'

" And with this injunction, playfully given, she walked a little aside with the gentleman in black, and talked for some minutes, apparently very earnestly. They then walked away slowly together in the crowd, and I lost them for some minutes.

" I spent the interval in cudgelling my brains for conjecture as to the identity of the lady who seemed to remember me so kindly, and I was thinking of turning about and joining in the conversation between my pretty ward and the Countess's daughter, and trying whether, by the time she returned, I might not have a surprise in store for her, by having her name, title, château, and estates at my fingers' ends. But at this moment she returned, accompanied by the pale man in black, who said :

" ' I shall return and inform Madame la Comtesse when her carriage is at the door.'

" He withdrew with a bow."

CHAPTER XII

A PETITION

" ' Then we are to lose Madame la Comtesse, but I hope only for a few hours,' I said, with a low bow.

" ' It may be that only, or it may be a few weeks. It was very unlucky his speaking to me just now as he did. Do you now know me ? ' "

" I assured her I did not.

" ' You shall know me,' she said, ' but not at present. We are older and better friends than, perhaps, you suspect. I cannot yet declare myself. I shall in three weeks pass your beautiful schloss about which I have been making enquiries. I shall then look in upon you for an hour or two, and renew a friendship which I never think of without a thousand pleasant recollections. This moment a piece of news has reached me like a thunderbolt. I must set out now, and travel by a devious route, nearly a hundred miles, with all the dispatch I can possibly make. My perplexities multiply. I am only deterred by the compulsory reserve I practise as to my name from making a very singular request of you. My poor child has not quite recovered her strength. Her horse fell with her, at a hunt which she had ridden out to witness, her nerves have not yet recovered the shock, and our physician says that she must on no account exert herself for some time to come. We came here, in consequence, by very easy stages—hardly six leagues a day. I must now travel day and night, on a mission of life and death—a mission the critical and momentous nature of which I shall be able to explain to you when we meet, as I hope we shall, in a few weeks, without the necessity of any concealment.'

" She went on to make her petition, and it was in the tone of a person from whom such a request amounted to conferring, rather than seeking a favour. This was only in manner, and, as it seemed, quite unconsciously. Than the terms in which it was expressed, nothing could be more deprecatory. It was simply that I would consent to take charge of her daughter during her absence.

" This was, all things considered, a strange, not to say, an audacious request. She in some sort disarmed me, by stating and admitting everything that could be urged against it, and throwing herself entirely upon my chivalry. At the same moment, by a fatality that seems to have predetermined all that happened, my poor child came to my side, and, in an undertone, besought me to invite her new friend, Millarca, to pay us a visit. She had just been sounding her, and thought, if her mamma would allow her, she would like it extremely.

" At another time I should have told her to wait a little, until, at least, we knew who they were. But I had not a moment to think in. The two ladies assailed me together, and I must confess the refined and beautiful face of the young lady, about which there was something extremely engaging, as well as the elegance and fire of high birth, determined me ; and quite overpowered, I submitted, and undertook, too easily, the care of the young lady, whom her mother called Millarca.

" The Countess beckoned to her daughter, who listened with grave attention while she told her, in general terms, how suddenly and peremptorily she had been summoned, and also of the arrangement she had made for her under my care, adding that I was one of her earliest and most valued friends.

" I made, of course, such speeches as the case seemed to call for, and found myself, on reflection, in a position which I did not half like.

" The gentleman in black returned, and very ceremoniously conducted the lady from the room.

" The demeanour of this gentleman was such as to impress me with the conviction that the Countess was a lady of very much more importance than her modest title alone might have led me to assume.

" Her last charge to me was that no attempt was to be made to learn more about her than I might have already guessed, until her return. Our distinguished host, whose guest she was, knew her reasons.

" ' But here,' she said, ' neither I nor my daughter could safely remain for more than a day. I removed my mask imprudently for a moment, about an hour ago, and, too late, I fancied you saw me. So I resolved to seek an opportunity of talking a little to you. Had I found that you *had* seen me, I should have thrown myself on your high sense of honour to keep my secret for some weeks. As it is, I am satisfied that you did not see me ; but if you now *suspect*, or, on reflection, *should* suspect, who I am, I commit myself, in like manner, entirely to your honour. My daughter will observe the same secrecy, and I well know that you will, from time to time, remind her, lest she should thoughtlessly disclose it.'

" She whispered a few words to her daughter, kissed her hurriedly twice, and went away, accompanied by the pale gentleman in black, and disappeared in the crowd.

" ' In the next room,' said Millarca, ' there is a window that looks upon the hall door. I should like to see the last of mamma, and to kiss my hand to her.'

" We assented, of course, and accompanied her to the window. We looked out, and saw a handsome old-fashioned carriage, with a troop of couriers and footmen. We saw the slim figure of the pale gentleman in black, as he held a thick velvet cloak, and placed it about her shoulders and threw the hood over her head. She nodded to him, and just touched his hand with hers. He bowed low repeatedly as the door closed, and the carriage began to move.

" ' She is gone,' said Millarca, with a sigh.

" ' She is gone,' I repeated to myself, for the first time—in the hurried moments that had elapsed since my consent—reflecting upon the folly of my act.

"' She did not look up,' said the young lady, plaintively.

"' The Countess had taken off her mask, perhaps, and did not care to show her face,' I said ; ' and she could not know that you were in the window.'

" She sighed and looked in my face. She was so beautiful that I relented. I was sorry I had for a moment repented of my hospitality, and I determined to make her amends for the unavowed churlishness of my reception.

" The young lady, replacing her mask, joined my ward in persuading me to return to the grounds, where the concert was soon to be renewed. We did so, and walked up and down the terrace that lies under the castle windows. Millarca became very intimate with us, and amused us with lively descriptions and stories of most of the great people whom we saw upon the terrace. I liked her more and more every minute. Her gossip, without being ill-natured, was extremely diverting to me, who had been so long out of the great world. I thought what life she would give to our sometimes lonely evenings at home.

" This ball was not over until the morning sun had almost reached the horizon. It pleased the Grand Duke to dance till then, so loyal people could not go away, or think of bed.

" We had just got through a crowded saloon, when my ward asked me what had become of Millarca. I thought she had been by my side, and she fancied she was by mine. The fact was, we had lost her.

" All my efforts to find her were vain. I feared that she had mistaken, in the confusion of a momentary separation from us, other people for her new friends, and had, possibly, pursued and lost them in the extensive grounds which were thrown open to us.

" Now, in its full force, I recognised a new folly in my having undertaken the charge of a young lady without so much as knowing her name ; and fettered as I was by promises, of the reasons for imposing which I knew nothing, I could not even point my enquiries by saying that the missing young lady was the daughter of the Countess who had taken her departure a few hours before.

" Morning broke. It was clear daylight before I gave up my search. It was not till near two o'clock next day that we heard anything of my missing charge.

" At about that time a servant knocked at my niece's door, to say that he had been earnestly requested by a young lady, who appeared to be in great distress, to make out where she could find the General Baron Spielsdorf and the young lady, his daughter, in whose charge she had been left by her mother.

" There could be no doubt, notwithstanding the slight in-accuracy, that our young friend had turned up ; and so she had. Would to Heaven we had lost her !

" She told my poor child a story to account for her having failed to recover us for so long. Very late, she said, she had got into the housekeeper's bedroom in despair of finding us, and had then fallen into a deep sleep which, long as it was, had hardly sufficed to recruit her strength after the fatigues of the ball.

" That day Millarca came home with us. I was only too happy, after all, to have secured so charming a companion for my dear girl."

CHAPTER XIII

THE WOOD-MAN

"There soon, however, appeared some drawbacks. In the first place, Millarca complained of extreme languor—the weakness that remained after her late illness—and she never emerged from her room till the afternoon was pretty far advanced. In the next place, it was accidentally discovered, although she always locked her door on the inside, and never disturbed the key from its place, till she admitted the maid to assist at her toilet, that she was undoubtedly sometimes absent from her room in the very early morning, and at various times later in the day, before she wished it to be understood that she was stirring. She was repeatedly seen from the windows of the schloss, in the first faint grey of the morning, walking through the trees, in an easterly direction, and looking like a person in a trance. This convinced me that she walked in her sleep. But this hypothesis did not solve the puzzle. How did she pass out from her room, leaving the door locked on the inside. How did she escape from the house without unbarring door or window ?

" In the midst of my perplexities, an anxiety of a far more urgent kind presented itself.

" My dear child began to lose her looks and health, and that in a manner so mysterious, and even horrible, that I became thoroughly frightened.

"She was at first visited by appalling dreams ; then, as she fancied, by a spectre, something resembling Millarca, sometimes in the shape of a beast, indistinctly seen, walking round the foot of the bed, from side to side. Lastly came sensations. One, not unpleasant, but very peculiar, she said, resembled the flow of an icy stream against her breast. At a later time, she felt something like a pair of large needles pierce her, a little below the throat, with a very sharp pain. A few nights after, followed a gradual and convulsive sense of strangulation ; then came unconsciousness."

I could hear distinctly every word the kind old General was saying, because by this time we were driving upon the short grass that spreads on either side of the road as you approach the roofless village which had not shown the smoke of a chimney for more than half a century.

You may guess how strangely I felt as I heard my own symptoms so exactly described in those which had been experienced by the poor girl who, but for the catastrophe which followed, would have been at that moment a visitor at my father's château. You may suppose, also, how I felt as I heard him detail habits and mysterious peculiarities which were, in fact, those of our beautiful guest, Carmilla !

A vista opened in the forest ; we were on a sudden under the chimneys and gables of the ruined village, and the towers and battlements of the dismantled castle, round which gigantic trees are grouped, overhung us from a slight eminence.

In a frightened dream I got down from the carriage, and in silence, for we had each abundant matter for thinking ; we soon mounted the ascent, and were among the spacious chambers, winding stairs, and dark corridors of the castle.

" And this was once the palatial residence of the Karnsteins ! " said the old General at length, as from a great window he looked out across the village, and saw the wide, undulating expanse of forest. " It was a bad family, and here its blood-stained annals were written," he continued. " It is hard that they should, after death, continue to plague the human race with their atrocious lusts. That is the chapel of the Karnsteins, down there."

He pointed down to the grey walls of the Gothic building, partly visible through the foliage, a little way down the steep. " And I hear the axe of a woodman," he added, " busy among the trees that surround it ; he possibly may give us the information of which I am in search, and point out the grave of Mircalla, Countess of Karnstein. These rustics preserve the local traditions of great families, whose stories die out among the rich and titled so soon as the families themselves become extinct."

" We have a portrait, at home, of Mircalla, the Countess Karnstein ; should you like to see it ? " asked my father.

" Time enough, dear friend," replied the General. "I believe that I have seen the original ; and one motive which has led me to you earlier than I at first intended, was to explore the chapel which we are now approaching."

" What ! see the Countess Mircalla," exclaimed my father ; " why, she has been dead more than a century ! "

" Not so dead as you fancy, I am told," answered the General.

" I confess, General, you puzzle me utterly," replied my father, looking at him, I fancied, for a moment with a return of the suspicion I detected before. But although there was anger and detestation, at times, in the old General's manner, there was nothing flighty.

" There remains to me," he said, as we passed under the heavy arch of the Gothic church—for its dimensions would have justified its being so styled—" but one object which can interest me during the few years that remain to me on earth, and that is to wreak on her the vengeance which, I thank God, may still be accomplished by a mortal arm."

" What vengeance can you mean ? " asked my father, in increasing amazement.

" I mean, to decapitate the monster," he answered, with a fierce flush, and a stamp that echoed mournfully through the hollow ruin, and his clenched hand was at the same moment raised, as if it grasped the handle of an axe, while he shook it ferociously in the air.

" What ! " exclaimed my father, more than ever bewildered.

" To strike her head off."

" Cut her head off ! "

" Aye, with a hatchet, with a spade, or with anything that can cleave through her murderous throat. You shall hear," he answered, trembling with rage. And hurrying forward he said :

" That beam will answer for a seat ; your dear child is fatigued ; let her be seated, and I will, in a few sentences, close my dreadful story."

The squared block of wood, which lay on the grass-grown pavement of the chapel, formed a bench on which I was very glad to seat myself, and in the meantime the General called to the woodman, who had been removing some boughs which leaned upon the old walls ; and, axe in hand, the hardy old fellow stood before us.

He could not tell us anything of these monuments ; but there was an old man, he said, a ranger of this forest, at present sojourning in the house of the priest, about two miles away, who could point out every monument of the old Karnstein family and, for a trifle, he undertook to bring him back with him, if we would lend him one of our horses, in little more than half-an-hour.

" Have you been long employed about this forest ? " asked my father of the old man.

" I have been a woodman here," he answered in his *patois*, " under the forester, all my days ; so has my father before me, and so on, as many generations as I can count up. I could show you the very house in the village here, in which my ancestors lived."

" How came the village to be deserted ? " asked the General.

" It was troubled by *revenants*, sir ; several were tracked to their graves, there detected by the usual tests, and extinguished in the usual way, by decapitation, by the stake, and by burning ; but not until many of the villagers were killed.

" But after all these proceedings according to law," he continued—" so many graves opened, and so many vampires deprived of their horrible animation—the village was not relieved. But a Moravian nobleman, who happened to be travelling this way, heard how matters were, and being skilled—as many people are in his country—in such affairs, he offered to deliver the village from its tormentor. He did so thus : There being a bright moon that night, he ascended, shortly after sunset, the tower of the chapel here, from whence he could distinctly see the churchyard beneath him ; you can see it from that window. From this point he watched until he saw the vampire come out of his grave, and place near it the linen clothes in which he had been folded, and glide away towards the village to plague its inhabitants.

" The stranger, having seen all this, came down from the steeple, took the linen wrappings of the vampire, and carried them up to the top of the tower, which he again mounted. When the vampire returned from his prowlings and missed his clothes, he cried furiously to the Moravian, whom he saw at the summit of the tower, and who, in reply beckoned him to ascend and take them. Whereupon the vampire, accepting his invitation, began to climb the steeple, and so soon as he had reached the battlements, the Moravian, with a stroke of his sword, clove his skull in twain, hurling him down to the churchyard, whither, descending by the winding stairs, the stranger followed and cut his head off, and next day delivered it and the body to the villagers, who duly impaled and burnt them.

" This Moravian nobleman had authority from the then head of the family to remove the tomb of Mircalla, Countess Karnstein, which he did effectually, so that in a little while its site was quite forgotten."

" Can you point out where it stood ? " asked the General, eagerly.

The forester shook his head and smiled.

" Not a soul living could tell you that now," he said ; " besides they say her body was removed ; but no one is sure of that either."

Having thus spoken, as time pressed, he dropped his axe and departed, leaving us to hear the remainder of the General's strange story.

CHAPTER XIV

THE MEETING

" My beloved child," he resumed, " was now growing rapidly worse. The physician who attended her had failed to produce the slightest impression upon her disease, for such I then supposed it to be. He saw my alarm, and suggested a consultation. I called in an abler physician, from Gratz. Several days elapsed before he arrived. He was a good and pious, as well as a learned man. Having seen my poor ward together, they withdrew to my library to confer and discuss. I, from the adjoining room, where I awaited their summons, heard these two gentlemen's voices raised in something sharper than a strictly philosophical discussion. I knocked at the door and entered, I found the old physician from Gratz maintaining his theory. His rival was combating it with undisguised ridicule, accompanied with bursts of laughter. This unseemly manifestation subsided and the altercation ended on my entrance.

" ' Sir,' said my first physician, ' my learned brother seems to think that you want a conjuror, and not a doctor.'

" ' Pardon me,' said the old physician from Gratz, looking displeased, ' I shall state my own view of the case in my own way another time. I grieve, Monsieur le Général, that by my skill and science I can be of no use. Before I go I shall do myself the honour to suggest something to you.'

" He seemed thoughtful, and sat down at a table, and began to write. Profoundly disappointed, I made my bow, and as I turned to go, the other doctor pointed over his shoulder to his companion who was writing, and then, with a shrug, significantly touched his forehead.

" This consultation, then, left me precisely where I was. I walked out into the grounds, all but distracted. The doctor from Gratz, in ten or fifteen minutes, overtook me. He apologised for having followed me, but said that he could not conscientiously take his leave without a few words more. He told me that he could not be mistaken ; no natural disease exhibited the same symptoms ; and that death was already very near. There remained, however, a day, or possibly two, of life. If the fatal seizure were at once arrested, with great care and skill her strength might possibly return. But all hung now upon the confines of the irrevocable. One more assault might extinguish the last spark of vitality which is, every moment, ready to die.

" ' And what is the nature of the seizure you speak of ? ' I entreated.

" ' I have stated all fully in this note, which I place in your hands, upon the distinct condition that you send for the nearest clergyman, and open my letter in his presence, and on no account read it till he is with you ; you would despise it else, and it is a matter of life and death. Should the priest fail you, then, indeed, you may read it.'

" He asked me, before taking his leave finally, whether I would wish to see a man curiously learned upon the very subject, which, after I had read his letter, would probably interest me above all others, and he urged me earnestly to invite him to visit him there ; and so took his leave.

" The ecclesiastic was absent, and I read the letter by myself. At another time, or in another case, it might have excited my ridicule. But into what quackeries will not people rush for a last chance, where all accustomed means have failed, and the life of a beloved object is at stake ?

" Nothing, you will say, could be more absurd than the learned man's letter. It was monstrous enough to have consigned him to a madhouse. He said that the patient was suffering from the visits of a vampire ! The punctures which she described as having occurred near the throat, were, he insisted, the insertion of those two long, thin, and sharp teeth which, it is well known, are peculiar to vampires ; and there could be no doubt, he added, as to the well-defined presence of the small livid mark which all concurred in describing as that induced by the demon's lips, and every symptom described by the sufferer was in exact conformity with those recorded in every case of a similar visitation.

" Being myself wholly sceptical as to the existence of any such portent as the vampire, the supernatural theory of the good doctor furnished, in my opinion, but another instance of learning and intelligence oddly associated with some hallucination. I was so miserable, however, that, rather than try nothing, I acted upon the instructions of the letter.

" I concealed myself in the dark dressing-room, that opened upon the poor patient's room, in which a candle was burning, and watched there till she was fast asleep. I stood at the door, peeping through the small crevice, my sword laid on the table beside me, as my directions prescribed, until, a little after one, I saw a large black object, very ill-defined, crawl, as it seemed to me, over the foot of the bed, and swiftly spread itself up to the poor girl's throat, where it swelled, in a moment, into a great, palpitating mass.

" For a few moments I had stood petrified. I now sprang forward, with my sword in my hand. The black creature suddenly contracted toward the foot of the bed, glided over it, and, standing on the floor about a yard below the foot of the bed, with a glare of skulking ferocity and horror fixed on me, I saw Millarca. Speculating I know not what, I struck at her instantly with my sword ; but I saw her standing near the door, unscathed. Horrified, I pursued, and struck again. She was gone ! and my sword flew to shivers against the door.

" I can't describe to you all that passed on that horrible night. The whole house was up and stirring. The spectre Millarca was gone. But her victim was sinking fast, and before the morning dawned, she died."

The old General was agitated. We did not speak to him. My father walked to some little distance, and began reading the inscriptions on the tombstones ; and thus occupied, he strolled into the door of a side chapel to prosecute his researches. The General leaned against the wall, dried his eyes, and sighed heavily. I was relieved on hearing the voices of Carmilla and Madame, who were at that moment approaching. The voices died away.

In this solitude, having just listened to so strange a story, connected, as it was, with the great and titled dead, whose monuments were mouldering among the dust and ivy round us, and every incident of which bore so awfully upon my own mysterious case—in this haunted spot, darkened by the towering foliage that rose on every side, dense and high above its noiseless walls—a horror began to steal over me, and my heart sank as I thought that my friends were, after all, not about to enter and disturb this triste and ominous scene.

The old General's eyes were fixed on the ground, as he leaned with his hand upon the basement of a shattered monument.

Under a narrow, arched doorway, surmounted by one of those demoniacal grotesques in which the cynical and ghastly fancy of old Gothic carving delights, I saw very gladly the beautiful face and figure of Carmilla enter the shadowy chapel.

I was just about to rise and speak, and nodded smiling, in answer to her peculiarly engaging smile ; when, with a cry, the old man by my side caught up the woodman's hatchet, and started forward. On seeing him a brutalised change came over her features. It was an instantaneous and horrible transformation, as she made a crouching step backwards. Before I could utter a scream, he struck at her with all his force, but she dived under his blow, and unscathed, caught him in her tiny grasp by the wrist. He struggled for a moment to release his arm, but his hand opened, the axe fell to the ground, and the girl was gone.

He staggered against the wall. His grey hair stood upon his head, and a moisture shone over his face, as if he were at the point of death.

The frightful scene had passed in a moment. The first thing I recollect after, is Madame standing before me, and impatiently repeating again and again, the question, " Where is Mademoiselle Carmilla ? "

I answered at length, " I don't know—I can't tell—she went there," and I pointed to the door through which Madame had just entered ; " only a minute or two since."

" But I have been standing there, in the passage, ever since Mademoiselle Carmilla entered ; and she did not return."

She then began to call " Carmilla " through every door and passage and from the windows, but no answer came.

" She called herself Carmilla ? " asked the General, still agitated.

" Carmilla, yes," I answered.

" Aye," he said ; that is Millarca. That is the same person who long ago was called Mircalla, Countess Karnstein. Depart from this accursed ground, my poor child, as quickly as you can. Drive to the clergyman's house, and stay there till we come. Begone ! May you never behold Carmilla more ; you will not find her here."

CHAPTER XV

ORDEAL AND EXECUTION

As he spoke one of the strangest-looking men I ever beheld, entered the chapel at the door through which Carmilla had made her entrance and her exit. He was tall, narrow-chested, stooping, with high shoulders, and dressed in black. His face was brown and dried in with deep furrows ; he wore an oddly-shaped hat with a broad leaf. His hair, long and grizzled, hung on his shoulders. He wore a pair of gold spectacles, and walked slowly, with an odd shambling gait, and his face sometimes turned up to the sky, and sometimes bowed down toward the ground, seemed to wear a perpetual smile ; his long thin arms were swinging, and his lank hands, in old black gloves ever so much too wide for them, waving and gesticulating in utter abstraction.

" The very man ! " exclaimed the General, advancing with manifest delight. " My dear Baron, how happy I am to see you, I had no hope of meeting you so soon." He signed to my father, who had by this time returned, and leading the fantastic old gentleman, whom he called the Baron, to meet him. He introduced him formally, and they at once entered into earnest conversation. The stranger took a roll of paper from his pocket, and spread it on the worn surface of a tomb that stood by. He had a pencil case in his fingers, with which he traced imaginary lines from point to point on the paper, which from their often glancing from it, together, at certain points of the building, I concluded to be a plan of the chapel. He accompanied, what I may term his lecture, with occasional readings from a dirty little book, whose yellow leaves were closely written over.

They sauntered together down the side aisle, opposite to the spot where I was standing, conversing as they went ; then they began measuring distances by paces, and finally they all stood together, facing a piece of the side-wall, which they began to examine with great minuteness ; pulling off the ivy that clung over it, and rapping the plaster with the ends of their sticks, scraping here, and knocking there. At length they ascertained the existence of a broad marble tablet, with letters carved in relief upon it.

With the assistance of the woodman, who soon returned, a monumental inscription, and carved escutcheon, were disclosed. They proved to be those of the long lost monument of Mircalla, Countess Karnstein.

The old General, though not I fear given to the praying mood, raised his hands and eyes to heaven, in mute thanksgiving for some moments.

" To-morrow," I heard him say ; " the commissioner will be here, and the Inquisition will be held according to law."

Then turning to the old man with the gold spectacles, whom I have described, he shook him warmly by both hands and said :

" Baron, how can I thank you ? How can we all thank you ? You will have delivered this region from a plague that has scourged its inhabitants for more than a century. The horrible enemy, thank God, is at last tracked."

My father led the stranger aside, and the General followed. I knew that he had led them out of hearing, that he might relate my case, and I saw them glance often quickly at me, as the discussion proceeded.

My father came to me, kissed me again and again, and leading me from the chapel, said :

" It is time to return, but before we go home, we must add to our party the good priest, who lives but a little way from this ; and persuade him to accompany us to the schloss."

In this quest we were successful : and I was glad, being unspeakably fatigued when we reached home. But my satisfaction was changed to dismay, on discovering that there were no tidings of Carmilla. Of the scene that had occurred in the ruined chapel, no explanation was offered to me, and it was clear that it was a secret which my father for the present determined to keep from me.

The sinister absence of Carmilla made the remembrance of the scene more horrible to me. The arrangements for that night were singular. Two servants and Madame were to sit up in my room that night ; and the ecclesiastic with my father kept watch in the adjoining dressing-room.

The priest had performed certain solemn rites that night, the purport of which I did not understand any more than I comprehended the reason of this extraordinary precaution taken for my safety during sleep.

I saw all clearly a few days later.

The disappearance of Carmilla was followed by the discontinuance of my nightly sufferings.

You have heard, no doubt, of the appalling superstition that prevails in Upper and Lower Styria, in Moravia, Silesia, in Turkish Servia, in Poland, even in Russia ; the superstition, so we must call it, of the vampire.

If human testimony, taken with every care and solemnity, judicially, before commissions innumerable, each consisting of many members, all chosen for integrity and intelligence, and constituting reports more voluminous perhaps than exist upon any one other class of cases, is worth anything, it is difficult to deny, or even to doubt the existence of such a phenomenon as the vampire.

For my part I have heard no theory by which to explain what I myself have witnessed and experienced, other than that supplied by the ancient and well-attested belief of the country.

The next day the formal proceedings took place in the Chapel of Karnstein. The grave of the Countess Mircalla was opened ; and the General and my father recognized each his perfidious and beautiful guest, in the face now disclosed to view. The features, though a hundred and fifty years had passed since her funeral, were tinted with the warmth of life. Her eyes were open ; no cadaverous smell exhaled from the coffin. The two medical men, one officially present, the other on the part of the promoter of the enquiry, attested the marvellous fact, that there was a faint but appreciable respiration, and a corresponding action of the heart. The limbs were perfectly flexible, the flesh elastic ; and the leaden coffin floated with blood, in which to a depth of seven inches, the body lay immersed. Here then, were all the admitted signs and proofs of vampirism. The body, therefore, in accordance with the ancient practice, was raised, and a sharp stake driven through the heart of the vampire, who uttered a piercing shriek at the moment, in all respects such as might escape from a living person in the last agony. Then the head was struck off, and a torrent of blood flowed from the severed neck. The body and head were next placed on a pile of wood, and reduced to ashes, which were thrown upon the river and borne away, and that territory has never since been plagued by the visits of a vampire.

My father has a copy of the report of the Imperial Commission, with the signatures of all who were present at these proceedings, attached in verification of the statement. It is from this official paper that I have summarised my account of this last shocking scene.

CHAPTER XVI

CONCLUSION

I write all this you suppose with composure. But far from it ; I cannot think of it without agitation. Nothing but your earnest desire so repeatedly expressed, could have induced me to sit down to a task that has unstrung my nerves for months to come, and re-induced a shadow of the unspeakable horror which years after my deliverance continued to make my days and nights dreadful, and solitude insupportably terrific.

Let me add a word or two about that quaint Baron Vordenburg, to whose curious lore we were indebted for the discovery of the Countess Mircalla's grave.

He had taken up his abode in Gratz, where, living upon a mere pittance, which was all that remained to him of the once princely estates of his family, in Upper Styria, he devoted himself to the minute and laborious investigation of the marvellously authenticated tradition of vampirism. He had at his fingers' ends all the great and little works upon the subject. *Magia Posthuma, Phlegon de Mirabilibus, Augustinus de curâ pro Mortuis, Philosophicæ et Christianæ Cogitationes de Vampiris*, by John Christofer Herenberg ; and a thousand others, among which I remember only a few of those which he lent to my father. He had a voluminous digest of all the judicial cases, from which he had extracted a system of principles that appear to govern—some always, and others occasionally only—the condition of the vampire. I may mention, in passing, that the deadly pallor attributed to that sort of *revenants*, is a mere melodramatic fiction. They present, in the grave, and when they show themselves in human society, the appearance of healthy life. When disclosed to light in their coffins, they exhibit all the

symptoms that are enumerated as those which proved the vampire-
life of the long-dead Countess Karnstein.

How they escape from their graves and return to them for certain
hours every day, without displacing the clay or leaving any trace
of disturbance in the state of the coffin or the cerements, has always been admitted to be utterly inexplicable. The amphibious
existence of the vampire is sustained by daily renewed slumber in
the grave. Its horrible lust for living blood supplies the vigour of
its waking existence. The vampire is prone to be fascinated with
an engrossing vehemence, resembling the passion of love, by particular persons. In pursuit of these it will exercise inexhaustible
patience and stratagem, for access to a particular object may be
obstructed in a hundred ways. It will never desist until it has
satiated its passion, and drained the very life of its coveted victim.
But it will, in these cases, husband and protract its murderous
enjoyment with the refinement of an epicure, and heighten it by
the gradual approaches of an artful courtship. In these cases it
seems to yearn for something like sympathy and consent. In
ordinary ones it goes direct to its object, overpowers with violence,
and strangles and exhausts often at a single feast.

The vampire is, apparently, subject, in certain situations, to
special conditions. In the particular instance of which I have
given you a relation, Mircalla seemed to be limited to a name
which, if not her real one, should at least reproduce, without the
omission or addition of a single letter, those, as we say, anagram-
matically, which compose it. *Carmilla* did this ; so did *Millarca*.

My father related to the Baron Vordenburg, who remained
with us for two or three weeks after the expulsion of Carmilla,
the story about the Moravian nobleman and the vampire at Karnstein churchyard, and then he asked the Baron how he had discovered the exact position of the long-concealed tomb of the
Countess Millarca. The Baron's grotesque features puckered up
into a mysterious smile ; he looked down, still smiling on his worn
spectacle-case and fumbled with it. Then looking up, he said :

" I have many journals, and other papers, written by that remarkable man ; the most curious among them is one treating of
the visit of which you speak, to Karnstein. The tradition, of
course, discolours and distorts a little. He might have been termed
a Moravian nobleman, for he had changed his abode to that territory, and was, beside, a noble. But he was, in truth, a native of
Upper Styria. It is enough to say that in very early youth he had

been a passionate and favoured lover of the beautiful Mircalla, Countess Karnstein. Her early death plunged him into inconsolable grief. It is the nature of vampires to increase and multiply, but according to an ascertained and ghostly law.

" Assume, at starting, a territory perfectly free from that pest. How does it begin, and how does it multiply itself? I will tell you. A person, more or less wicked, puts an end to himself. A suicide, under certain circumstances, becomes a vampire. That spectre visits living people in their slumbers ; *they* die, and almost invariably, in the grave, develop into vampires. This happened in the case of the beautiful Mircalla, who was haunted by one of those demons. My ancestor, Vordenburg, whose title I still bear, soon discovered this, and in the course of the studies to which he devoted himself, learned a great deal more.

" Among other things, he concluded that suspicion of vampirism would probably fall, sooner or later, upon the dead Countess, who in life had been his idol. He conceived a horror, be she what she might, of her remains being profaned by the outrage of a posthumous execution. He has left a curious paper to prove that the vampire, on its expulsion from its amphibious existence, is projected into a far more horrible life ; and he resolved to save his once beloved Mircalla from this.

" He adopted the stratagem of a journey here, a pretended removal of her remains, and a real obliteration of her monument. When age had stolen upon him, and from the vale of years he looked back on the scenes he was leaving, he considered, in a different spirit, what he had done, and a horror took possession of him. He made the tracings and notes which have guided me to the very spot, and drew up a confession of the deception that he had practised. If he had intended any further action in this matter, death prevented him ; and the hand of a remote descendant has too late for many, directed the pursuit to the lair of the beast."

We talked a little more, and among other things he said was this:

" One sign of the vampire is the power of the hand. The slender hand of Mircalla closed like a vice of steel on the General's wrist when he raised the hatchet to strike. But its power is not confined to its grasp ; it leaves a numbness in the limb it seizes, which is slowly, if ever, recovered from."

The following Spring my father took me a tour through Italy. We remained away for more than a year. It was long before the terror of recent events subsided ; and to this hour the image of

Carmilla returns to memory with ambiguous alternations—
sometimes the playful, languid, beautiful girl ; sometimes the
writhing fiend I saw in the ruined church ; and often from a reverie I have started, fancying I heard the light step of Carmilla
at the drawing-room door.

Frederick Marryat

THE WHITE WOLF OF THE HARTZ MOUNTAINS

from THE PHANTOM SHIP
Henry Colburn, 1839
" *The Phantom Ship* " *appeared serially in the* NEW-MONTHLY MAGAZINE
during 1837

I

Before noon Philip and Krantz had embarked, and made sail
in the peroqua.

They had no difficulty in steering their course ; the islands by
day, and the clear stars by night, were their compass. It is true
that they did not follow the more direct track, but they followed
the more secure, working up the smooth waters, and gaining to the
northward more than to the west. Many times they were chased by
the Malay proas, which infested the islands, but the swiftness of
their little peroqua was their security ; indeed, the chase was, generally speaking, abandoned as soon as the smallness of the vessel
was made out by the pirates, who expected that little or no booty
was to be gained.

One morning, as they were sailing between the isles, with less
wind than usual, Philip observed—

" Krantz, you said that there were events in your own life, or
connected with it, which would corroborate the mysterious tale
I confided to you. Will you now tell me to what you referred ? "

" Certainly," replied Krantz ; " I have often thought of doing
so, but one circumstance or another has hitherto prevented me ;
this is, however, a fitting opportunity. Prepare therefore to listen
to a strange story, quite as strange, perhaps, as your own.

" I take it for granted that you have heard people speak of the
Hartz Mountains," observed Krantz.

" I have never heard people speak of them, that I can recollect," replied Philip ; " but I have read of them in some book, and of the strange things which have occurred there."

" It is indeed a wild region," rejoined Krantz, " and many strange tales are told of it ; but strange as they are, I have good reason for believing them to be true

" My father was not born, or originally a resident, in the Hartz Mountains ; he was a serf of an Hungarian nobleman, of great possessions, in Transylvania ; but although a serf, he was not by any means a poor or illiterate man. In fact, he was rich, and his intelligence and respectability were such, that he had been raised by his lord to the stewardship ; but whoever may happen to be born a serf, a serf must he remain, even though he become a wealthy man : such was the condition of my father. My father had been married for about five years ; and by his marriage had three children—my eldest brother Cæsar, myself (Hermann), and a sister named Marcella. You know, Philip, that Latin is still the language spoken in that country ; and that will account for our high-sounding names. My mother was a very beautiful woman, unfortunately more beautiful than virtuous : she was seen and admired by the lord of the soil ; my father was sent away upon some mission ; and during his absence, my mother, flattered by the attentions, and won by the assiduities, of this nobleman, yielded to his wishes. It so happpened that my father returned very unexpectedly, and discovered the intrigue. The evidence of my mother's shame was positive : he surprised her in the company of her seducer ! Carried away by the impetuosity of his feelings, he watched the opportunity of a meeting taking place between them, and murdered both his wife and her seducer. Conscious that, as a serf, not even the provocation which he had received would be allowed as a justification of his conduct, he hastily collected together what money he could lay his hands upon, and, as we were then in the depth of winter, he put his horses to the sleigh, and taking his children with him, he set off in the middle of the night, and was far away before the tragical circumstance had transpired. Aware that he would be pursued, and that he had no chance of escape if he remained in any portion of his native country (in which the authorities could lay hold of him), he continued his flight without intermission until he had buried himself in the intricacies and seclusions of the Hartz Mountains. Of course, all that I have now told you I learned afterwards. My oldest recollections are knit to a rude, yet comfortable cottage, in which I lived with my father, brother, and sister. It was on the confines of one of those vast forests which cover the northern part of Germany ; around it were a few acres of ground, which, during the summer months, my father cultivated, and which, though they yielded a doubtful harvest, were sufficient for our support. In the winter we remained much indoors, for, as my father followed the chase, we were left alone, and the wolves during that season incessantly prowled about. My father had purchased the cottage, and land about it, of one of the rude foresters, who gain their livelihood partly by hunting, and partly by burning charcoal, for the purpose of smelting the ore from the neighbouring mines ; it was distant about two miles from any other habitation. I can call to mind the whole landscape now ; the tall pines which rose up on the mountain above us, and the wide expanse of the forest beneath, on the topmost boughs and heads of whose trees we looked down from our cottage, as the mountain below us rapidly descended into the distant valley. In summer time the prospect was beautiful : but during the severe winter a more desolate scene could not well be imagined.

" I said that, in the winter, my father occupied himself with the chase ; every day he left us, and often would he lock the door, that we might not leave the cottage. He had no one to assist him, or to take care of us—indeed, it was not easy to find a female servant who would live in such a solitude ; but, could he have found one, my father would not have received her, for he had imbibed a horror of the sex, as the difference of his conduct towards us, his two boys, and my poor little sister Marcella evidently proved. You may suppose we were sadly neglected ; indeed, we suffered much, for my father, fearful that we might come to some harm, would not allow us fuel when he left the cottage ; and we were obliged, therefore, to creep under the heaps of bears' skins, and there to keep ourselves as warm as we could until he returned in the evening, when a blazing fire was our delight. That my father chose this restless sort of life may appear strange, but the fact was, that he could not remain quiet ; whether from the remorse for having committed murder, or from the misery consequent on his change of situation, or from both combined, he was never happy unless he was in a state of activity. Children, however, when left so much to themselves, acquire a thoughtfulness not common to their age. So it was with us ; and during the short cold days of winter, we would sit silent, longing for the happy hours when the snow would melt and the leaves burst out, and the birds begin their songs, and when we should again be set at liberty.

" Such was our peculiar and savage sort of life until my brother Cæsar was nine, myself seven, and my sister five years old, when the circumstances occurred on which is based the extraordinary narrative which I am about to relate.

" One evening my father returned home rather later than usual ; he had been unsuccessful, and as the weather was very severe, and many feet of snow were upon the ground, he was not only very cold, but in a very bad humour. He had brought in wood, and we were all three gladly assisting each other in blowing on the embers to create a blaze, when he caught poor little Marcella by the arm and threw her aside ; the child fell, struck her mouth, and bled very much. My brother ran to raise her up. Accustomed to ill-usage, and afraid of my father, she did not dare to cry, but looked up in his face very piteously. My father drew his stool nearer to the hearth, muttered something in abuse of women, and busied himself with the fire, which both my brother and I had deserted when our sister was so unkindly treated. A cheerful blaze was soon the result of his exertions ; but we did not, as usual, crowd round it. Marcella, still bleeding, retired to a corner, and my brother and I took our seats beside her, while my father hung over the fire gloomily and alone. Such had been our position for about half an hour, when the howl of a wolf, close under the window of the cottage fell on our ears. My father started up, and seized his gun ; the howl was repeated ; he examined the priming, and then hastily left the cottage, shutting the door after him. We all waited (anxiously listening), for we thought that if he succeeded in shooting the wolf, he would return in a better humour ; and, although he was harsh to all of us, and particularly so to our little sister, still we loved our father, and loved to see him cheerful and happy, for what else had we to look up to ? And I may here observe, that perhaps there never were three children who were fonder of each other ; we did not, like other children, fight and dispute together ; and if, by chance, any disagreement did arise, between my elder brother and me, little Marcella would run to us, and kissing us both, seal, through her entreaties, the peace between us. Marcella was a lovely, amiable child ; I can recall her beautiful features even now. Alas ! poor little Marcella."

" She is dead, then ? " observed Philip.

" Dead ! yes, dead ! but how did she die ?—But I must not anticipate, Philip ; let me tell my story.

" We waited for some time, but the report of the gun did not reach us, and my elder brother then said, ' Our father has followed the wolf, and will not be back for some time. Marcella, let us wash the blood from your mouth, and then we will leave this corner and go to the fire to warm ourselves.'

" We did so, and remained there until near midnight, every minute wondering, as it grew later, why our father did not return. We had no idea that he was in any danger, but we thought that he must have chased the wolf for a very long time. ' I will look out and see if father is coming,' said my brother Cæsar, going to the door. ' Take care,' said Marcella, ' the wolves must be about now, and we cannot kill them, brother.' My brother opened the door very cautiously, and but a few inches ; he peeped out. ' I see nothing,' said he, after a time, and once more he joined us at the fire. ' We have had no supper,' said I, for my father usually cooked the meat as soon as he came home ; and during his absence we had nothing but the fragments of the preceding day.

" ' And if our father comes home, after his hunt, Cæsar,' said Marcella, ' he will be pleased to have some supper ; let us cook it for him and for ourselves.' Cæsar climbed upon the stool, and reached down some meat—I forget now whether it was venison or bear's meat, but we cut off the usual quantity, and proceeded to dress it, as we used to do under our father's superintendence. We were all busy putting it into the platters before the fire, to await his coming, when we heard the sound of a horn. We listened —there was a noise outside, and a minute afterwards my father entered, ushered in a young female and a large dark man in a hunter's dress.

" Perhaps I had better now relate what was only known to me many years afterwards. When my father had left the cottage, he perceived a large white wolf about thirty yards from him ; as soon as the animal saw my father, it retreated slowly, growling and snarling. My father followed ; the animal did not run, but always kept at some distance ; and my father did not like to fire until he was pretty certain that his ball would take effect ; thus they went on for some time, the wolf now leaving my father far behind, and then stopping and snarling defiance at him, and then, again, on his approach, setting off at speed.

" Anxious to shoot the animal (for the white wolf is very rare), my father continued the pursuit for several hours, during which he continually ascended the mountain.

" You must know, Philip, that there are peculiar spots on those mountains which are supposed, and, as my story will prove, truly supposed, to be inhabited by the evil influences : they are well known to the huntsmen, who invariably avoid them. Now, one of these spots, an open space in the pine forest above us, had been pointed out to my father as dangerous on that account. But whether he disbelieved these wild stories, or whether, in his eager pursuit of the chase, he disregarded them, I know not ; certain, however, it is, that he was decoyed by the white wolf to this open space, when the animal appeared to slacken her speed. My father approached, came close up to her, raised his gun to his shoulder and was about to fire, when the wolf suddenly disappeared. He thought that the snow on the ground must have dazzled his sight, and he let down his gun to look for the beast—but she was gone ; how she could have escaped over the clearance, without his seeing her, was beyond his comprehension. Mortified at the ill-success of his chase, he was about to retrace his steps, when he heard the distant sound of a horn. Astonishment at such a sound—at such an hour—in such a wilderness, made him forget for the moment his disappointment, and he remained riveted to the spot. In a minute the horn was blown a second time, and at no great distance ; my father stood still, and listened ; a third time it was blown. I forget the term used to express it, but it was the signal which, my father well knew, implied that the party was lost in the woods. In a few minutes more my father beheld a man on horseback, with a female seated on the crupper, enter the cleared space, and ride up to him. At first, my father called to mind the strange stories which he had heard of the supernatural beings who were said to frequent these mountains ; but the nearer approach of the parties satisfied him that they were mortals like himself. As soon as they came up to him, the man who guided the horse accosted him. ' Friend hunter, you are out late, the better fortune for us ; we have ridden far, and are in fear of our lives, which are eagerly sought after. These mountains have enabled us to elude our pursuers ; but if we find not shelter and refreshment, that will avail us little, as we must perish from hunger and the inclemency of the night. My daughter, who rides behind me, is now more dead than alive—say, can you assist us in our difficulty ? '

" ' My cottage is some few miles distant,' replied my father,

' but I have little to offer you besides a shelter from the weather ; to the little I have you are welcome. May I ask whence you come ? '

" ' Yes, friend, it is no secret now ; we have escaped from Transylvania, where my daughter's honour and my life were equally in jeopardy ! '

" This information was quite enough to raise an interest in my father's heart. He remembered his own escape : he remembered the loss of his wife's honour, and the tragedy by which it was wound up. He immediately, and warmly, offered all the assistance which he could afford them.

" ' There is no time to be lost, then, good sir,' observed the horseman ; ' my daughter is chilled with the frost, and cannot hold out much longer against the severity of the weather.'

" ' Follow me,' replied my father, leading the way towards his home.

" ' I was lured away in pursuit of a large white wolf,' observed my father ; ' it came to the very window of my hut, or I should not have been out at this time of night.'

" ' The creature passed by us just as we came out of the wood,' said the female, in a silvery tone.

" ' I was nearly discharging my piece at it,' observed the hunter ; ' but since it did us such good service, I am glad that I allowed it to escape.'

" In about an hour and a half, during which my father walked at a rapid pace, the party arrived at the cottage, and, as I said before, came in.

" ' We are in good time, apparently,' observed the dark hunter, catching the smell of the roasted meat, as he walked to the fire and surveyed my brother and sister and myself. ' You have young cooks here, Meinheer.' ' I am glad that we shall not have to wait,' replied my father. ' Come, mistress, seat yourself by the fire ; you require warmth after your cold ride.' ' And where can I put up my horse, Meinheer ? ' observed the huntsman. ' I will take care of him,' replied my father, going out of the cottage door.

" The female must, however, be particularly described. She was young, and apparently twenty years of age. She was dressed in a travelling dress, deeply bordered with white fur, and wore a cap of white ermine on her head. Her features were very beautiful, at least I thought so, and so my father has since declared. Her hair was flaxen, glossy, and shining, and bright as a mirror ; and her mouth, although somewhat large when it was open, showed the most brilliant teeth I have ever beheld. But there was something about her eyes, bright as they were, which made us children afraid ; they were so restless, so furtive ; I could not at that time tell why, but I felt as if there was cruelty in her eye ; and when she beckoned us to come to her, we approached her with fear and trembling. Still she was beautiful, very beautiful. She spoke kindly to my brother and myself, patted our heads and caressed us ; but Marcella would not come near her ; on the contrary, she slunk away, and hid herself in the bed, and would not wait for the supper, which half an hour before she had been so anxious for.

" My father, having put the horse into a close shed, soon returned, and supper was placed on the table. When it was over, my father requested the young lady would take possession of the bed, and he would remain at the fire, and sit up with her father. After some hesitation on her part, this arrangement was agreed to, and I and my brother crept into the other bed with Marcella, for we had as yet always slept together.

" But we could not sleep ; there was something so unusual, not only in seeing strange people, but in having those people sleep at the cottage, that we were bewildered. As for poor little Marcella, she was quiet, but I perceived that she trembled during the whole night, and sometimes I thought that she was checking a sob. My father had brought out some spirits, which he rarely used, and he and the strange hunter remained drinking and talking before the fire. Our ears were ready to catch the slightest whisper—so much was our curiosity excited.

" ' You said you came from Transylvania ? ' observed my father.

" ' Even so, Meinheer,' replied the hunter. ' I was a serf to the noble house of —— ; my master would insist upon my surrendering up my fair girl to his wishes ; it ended in my giving him a few inches of my hunting-knife.'

" ' We are countrymen and brothers in misfortune,' replied my father, taking the huntsman's hand and pressing it warmly.

" ' Indeed ! Are you then from that country ? '

" ' Yes ; and I too have fled for my life. But mine is a melancholy tale.'

" ' Your name ? ' inquired the hunter.

" ' Krantz.'

" ' What ! Krantz of —— ? I have heard your tale ; you need not renew your grief by repeating it now. Welcome, most welcome,

Meinheer, and, I may say, my worthy kinsman. I am your second cousin, Wilfred of Barnsdorf,' cried the hunter, rising up and embracing my father.

" They filled their horn-mugs to the brim, and drank to one another after the German fashion. The conversation was then carried on in a low tone ; all that we could collect from it was that our new relative and his daughter were to take up their abode in our cottage, at least for the present. In about an hour they both fell back in their chairs and appeared to sleep.

" ' Marcella, dear, did you hear ? ' said my brother, in a low tone.

" ' Yes,' replied Marcella, in a whisper, ' I heard all. Oh ! brother, I cannot bear to look upon that woman—I feel so frightened.'

" My brother made no reply, and shortly afterwards we were all three fast asleep.

" When we awoke the next morning, we found that the hunter's daughter had risen before us. I thought she looked more beautiful than ever. She came up to little Marcella and caressed her ; the child burst into tears, and sobbed as if her heart would break.

" But not to detain you with too long a story, the huntsman and his daughter were accommodated in the cottage. My father and he went out hunting daily, leaving Christina with us. She performed all the household duties ; was very kind to us children ; and gradually the dislike even of little Marcella wore away. But a great change took place in my father ; he appeared to have conquered his aversion to the sex, and was most attentive to Christina. Often, after her father and we were in bed, would he sit up with her, conversing in a low tone by the fire. I ought to have mentioned that my father and the huntsman Wilfred slept in another portion of the cottage, and that the bed which he formerly occupied, and which was in the same room as ours, had been given up to the use of Christina. These visitors had been about three weeks at the cottage, when, one night, after we children had been sent to bed, a consultation was held. My father had asked Christina in marriage, and had obtained both her own consent and that of Wilfred ; after this, a conversation took place, which was, as nearly as I can recollect, as follows :—

" ' You may take my child, Meinheer Krantz, and my blessing with her, and I shall then leave you and seek some other habitation—it matters little where.'

" ' Why not remain here, Wilfred ? '

" ' No, no, I am called elsewhere ; let that suffice, and ask no more questions. You have my child.'

" ' I thank you for her, and will duly value her ; but there is one difficulty.'

" ' I know what you would say ; there is no priest here in this wild country ; true ; neither is there any law to bind. Still must some ceremony pass between you, to satisfy a father. Will you consent to marry her after my fashion ? if so, I will marry you directly.'

" ' I will,' replied my father.

" ' Then take her by the hand. Now, Meinheer, swear.'

" ' I swear,' repeated my father.

" ' By all the spirits of the Hartz Mountains——'

" ' Nay, why not by Heaven ? ' interrupted my father.

" ' Because it is not my humour,' rejoined Wilfred. ' If I prefer that oath, less binding, perhaps, than another, surely you will not thwart me.'

" ' Well, be it so, then ; have your humour. Will you make me swear by that in which I do not believe ? '

" ' Yet many do so, who in outward appearance are Christians,' rejoined Wilfred ; ' say, will you be married, or shall I take my daughter away with me ? '

" ' Proceed,' " replied my father impatiently.

" ' I swear by all the spirits of the Hartz Mountains, by all their power for good or for evil, that I take Christina for my wedded wife ; that I will ever protect her, cherish her, and love her ; that my hand shall never be raised against her to harm her.'

" My father repeated the words after Wilfred.

" ' And if I fail in this my vow, may all the vengeance of the spirits fall upon me and upon my children ; may they perish by the vulture, by the wolf, or other beasts of the forest ; may their flesh be torn from their limbs, and their bones blanch in the wilderness : all this I swear.'

" My father hesitated, as he repeated the last words ; little Marcella could not restrain herself, and as my father repeated the last sentence, she burst into tears. This sudden interruption appeared to discompose the party, particularly my father ; he spoke harshly to the child, who controlled her sobs, burying her face under the bedclothes.

" Such was the second marriage of my father. The next morning, the hunter Wilfred mounted his horse and rode away.

" My father resumed his bed, which was in the same room as ours ; and things went on much as before the marriage, except that our new mother-in-law did not show any kindness towards us ; indeed, during my father's absence, she would often beat us, particularly little Marcella, and her eyes would flash fire, as she looked eagerly upon the fair and lovely child.

" One night my sister awoke me and my brother.

" ' What is the matter ? ' said Cæsar.

" ' She has gone out,' whispered Marcella.

" ' Gone out ! '

" ' Yes, gone out at the door, in her night-clothes,' replied the child ; ' I saw her get out of bed, look at my father to see if he slept, and then she went out at the door.'

" What could induce her to leave her bed, and all undressed to go out, in such bitter wintry weather, with the snow deep on the ground, was to us incomprehensible ; we lay awake, and in about an hour we heard the growl of a wolf close under the window.

" ' There is a wolf,' said Cæsar. ' She will be torn to pieces.'

" ' Oh, no ! ' cried Marcella.

" In a few minutes afterwards our mother-in-law appeared ; she was in her night-dress, as Marcella had stated. She let down the latch of the door, so as to make no noise, went to a pail of water, and washed her face and hands, and then slipped into the bed where my father lay.

" We all three trembled—we hardly knew why ; but we resolved to watch the next night. We did so ; and not only on the ensuing night, but on many others, and always at about the same hour, would our mother-in-law rise from her bed and leave the cottage ; and after she was gone we invariably heard the growl of a wolf under our window, and always saw her on her return wash herself before she retired to bed. We observed also that she seldom sat down to meals, and that when she did she appeared to eat with dislike ; but when the meat was taken down to be prepared for dinner, she would often furtively put a raw piece into her mouth.

" My brother Cæsar was a courageous boy ; he did not like to speak to my father until he knew more. He resolved that he would follow her out, and ascertain what she did. Marcella and I endeavoured to dissuade him from the project ; but he would not be controlled ; and the very next night he lay down in his clothes, and as soon as our mother-in-law had left the cottage he jumped up, took down my father's gun, and followed her.

" You may imagine in what a state of suspense Marcella and I remained during his absence. After a few minutes we heard the report of a gun. It did not awaken my father ; and we lay trembling with anxiety. In a minute afterwards we saw our mother-in-law enter the cottage—her dress was bloody. I put my hand to Marcella's mouth to prevent her crying out, although I was myself in great alarm. Our mother-in-law approached my father's bed, looked to see if he was asleep, and then went to the chimney and blew up the embers into a blaze.

" ' Who is there ? ' said my father, waking up.

" ' Lie still, dearest,' replied my mother-in-law ; ' it is only me ; I have lighted the fire to warm some water ; I am not quite well.'

" My father turned round, and was soon asleep ; but we watched our mother-in-law. She changed her linen, and threw the garments she had worn into the fire ; and we then perceived that her right leg was bleeding profusely, as if from a gun-shot wound. She bandaged it up, and then dressing herself, remained before the fire until the break of day.

" Poor little Marcella, her heart beat quick as she pressed me to her side—so indeed did mine. Where was our brother Cæsar ? How did my mother-in-law receive the wound unless from his gun ? At last my father rose, and then for the first time I spoke, saying, ' Father, where is my brother Cæsar ? '

" ' Your brother ? ' exclaimed he ; ' why, where can he be ? '

" ' Merciful Heaven ! I thought as I lay very restless last night,' observed our mother-in-law, ' that I heard somebody open the latch of the door ; and, dear me, husband, what has become of your gun ? '

" My father cast his eyes up above the chimney, and perceived that his gun was missing. For a moment he looked perplexed ; then, seizing a broad axe, he went out of the cottage without saying another word.

" He did not remain away from us long ; in a few minutes he returned, bearing in his arms the mangled body of my poor brother ; he laid it down, and covered up his face.

" My mother-in-law rose up, and looked at the body, while Marcella and I threw ourselves by its side, wailing and sobbing bitterly.

" ' Go to bed again, children," said she sharply. ' Husband,' continued she, ' your boy must have taken the gun down to shoot a wolf, and the animal has been too powerful for him. Poor boy ! he has paid dearly for his rashness.'

" My father made no reply. I wished to speak—to tell all—but Marcella, who perceived my intention, held my by the arm, and looked at me so imploringly, that I desisted.

" My father, therefore, was left in his error ; but Marcella and I, although we could not comprehend it, were conscious that our mother-in-law was in some way connected with my brother's death.

" That day my father went out and dug a grave ; and when he laid the body in the earth he piled up stones over it, so that the wolves should not be able to dig it up. The shock of this catastrophe was to my poor father very severe ; for several days he never went to the chase, although at times he would utter bitter anathemas and vengeance against the wolves.

" But during this time of mourning on his part, my mother-in-law's nocturnal wanderings continued with the same regularity as before.

" At last my father took down his gun to repair to the forest ; but he soon returned, and appeared much annoyed.

" ' Would you believe it, Christina, that the wolves—perdition to the whole race !—have actually contrived to dig up the body of my poor boy, and now there is nothing left of him but his bones.'

" ' Indeed ! ' replied my mother-in-law. Marcella looked at me, and I saw in her intelligent eye all she would have uttered.

" ' A wolf growls under our window every night, father,' said I.

" ' Ay, indeed ! Why did you not tell me, boy ? Wake me the next time you hear it.'

" I saw my mother-in-law turn away ; her eyes flashed fire, and she gnashed her teeth.

" My father went out again, and covered up with a larger pile of stones the little remains of my poor brother which the wolves had spared. Such was the first act of the tragedy.

" The spring now came on ; the snow disappeared, and we were permitted to leave the cottage ; but never would I quit for one moment my dear little sister, to whom, since the death of my brother, I was more ardently attached than ever ; indeed, I was afraid to leave her alone with my mother-in-law, who appeared to have a particular pleasure in ill-treating the child. My father was now employed upon his little farm, and I was able to render him some assistance.

" Marcella used to sit by us while we were at work, leaving my mother-in-law alone in the cottage. I ought to observe that, as the spring advanced, so did my mother-in-law decrease her nocturnal rambles, and that we never heard the growl of the wolf under the window after I had spoken of it to my father.

" One day, when my father and I were in the field, Marcella being with us, my mother-in-law came out, saying that she was going into the forest to collect some herbs my father wanted, and that Marcella must go to the cottage and watch the dinner. Marcella went ; and my mother-in-law soon disappeared in the forest, taking a direction quite contrary to that in which the cottage stood, and leaving my father and me, as it were, between her and Marcella.

" About an hour afterwards we were startled by shrieks from the cottage—evidently the shrieks of little Marcella. ' Marcella has burnt herself, father,' said I, throwing down my spade. My father threw down his, and we both hastened to the cottage. Before we could gain the door, out darted a large white wolf, which fled with the utmost celerity. My father had no weapon ; he rushed into the cottage, and there saw poor little Marcella expiring. Her body was dreadfully mangled and the blood pouring from it had formed a large pool on the cottage floor. My father's first intention had been to seize his gun and pursue ; but he was checked by this horrid spectacle ; he knelt down by his dying child, and burst into tears. Marcella could just look kindly on us for a few seconds, and then her eyes were closed in death.

" My father and I were still hanging over my poor sister's body when my mother-in-law came in. At the dreadful sight she expressed much concern ; but she did not appear to recoil from the sight of blood, as most women do.

" ' Poor child ! ' said she, ' it must have been that great white wolf which passed me just now, and frightened me so. She's quite dead, Krantz.'

" ' I know it !—I know it ! ' cried my father, in agony.

" I thought my father would never recover from the effects of this second tragedy ; he mourned bitterly over the body of his sweet child, and for several days would not consign it to its grave, although frequently requested by my mother-in-law to do so. At last he yielded, and dug a grave for her close by that of my poor brother, and took every precaution that the wolves should not violate her remains.

" I was now really miserable as I lay alone in the bed which I had formerly shared with my brother and sister. I could not help thinking that my mother-in-law was implicated in both their deaths, although I could not account for the manner ; but I no longer felt afraid of her ; my little heart was full of hatred and revenge.

" The night after my sister had been buried, as I lay awake, I perceived my mother-in-law get up and go out of the cottage. I waited some time, then dressed myself, and looked out through the door, which I half opened. The moon shone bright, and I could see the spot where my brother and my sister had been buried ; and what was my horror when I perceived my mother-in-law busily removing the stones from Marcella's grave !

" She was in her white night-dress, and the moon shone full upon her. She was digging with her hands, and throwing away the stones behind her with all the ferocity of a wild beast. It was some time before I could collect my senses and decide what I should do. At last I perceived that she had arrived at the body, and raised it up to the side of the grave. I could bear it no longer : I ran to my father and awoke him.

" ' Father, father ! ' cried I, ' dress yourself, and get your gun.'

" ' What ! ' cried my father, ' the wolves are there, are they ? '

" He jumped out of bed, threw on his clothes, and in his anxiety did not appear to perceive the absence of his wife. As soon as he was ready I opened the door, he went out, and I followed him.

" Imagine his horror, when (unprepared as he was for such a sight) he beheld, as he advanced towards the grave, not a wolf, but his wife, in her night-dress, on her hands and knees, crouching by the body of my sister, and tearing off large pieces of the flesh, and devouring them with all the avidity of a wolf. She was too busy to be aware of our approach. My father dropped his gun ; his hair stood on end, so did mine ; he breathed heavily, and then his breath for a time stopped. I picked up the gun and put it into his hand. Suddenly he appeared as if concentrated rage had restored him to double vigour ; he levelled his piece, fired, and with a loud shriek down fell the wretch whom he had fostered in his bosom.

" ' God of heaven ! ' cried my father, sinking down upon the earth in a swoon, as soon as he had discharged his gun.

" I remained some time by his side before he recovered. ' Where am I ? ' said he, ' what has happened ? Oh !—yes, yes ! I recollect now. Heaven forgive me ! '

" He rose and we walked up to the grave ; what again was our astonishment and horror to find that, instead of the dead body of my mother-in-law, as we expected, there was lying over the remains of my poor sister a large white she-wolf.

" ' The white wolf,' exclaimed my father, ' the white wolf which decoyed me into the forest—I see it all now—I have dealt with the spirits of the Hartz Mountains.'

" For some time my father remained in silence and deep thought. He then carefully lifted up the body of my sister, replaced it in the grave, and covered it over as before, having struck the head of the dead animal with the heel of his boot, and raving like a madman. He walked back to the cottage, shut the door, and threw himself on the bed ; I did the same, for I was in a stupor of amazement.

" Early in the morning we were both roused by a loud knocking at the door, and in rushed the hunter Wilfred.

" ' My daughter—man—my daughter !—where is my daughter ? ' cried he in a rage.

" ' Where the wretch, the fiend should be, I trust,' replied my father, starting up, and displaying equal choler : ' where she should be—in hell ! Leave this cottage, or you may fare worse.'

" ' Ha—ha ! ' replied the hunter, ' would you harm a potent spirit of the Hartz Mountains ? Poor mortal, who must needs wed a werewolf."

" ' Out, demon ! I defy thee and thy power.'

" ' Yet shall you feel it ; remember your oath—your solemn oath—never to raise your hand against her to harm her.'

" ' I made no compact with evil spirits.'

" ' You did, and if you failed in your vow, you were to meet the vengeance of the spirits. Your children were to perish by the vulture, the wolf——'

" ' Out, out, demon ! '

" ' And their bones blanch in the wilderness. Ha—ha ! '

" My father, frantic with rage, seized his axe and raised it over Wilfred's head to strike.

" ' All this I swear,' continued the huntsman mockingly.

" The axe descended ; but it passed through the form of the hunter, and my father lost his balance, and fell heavily on the floor.

" ' Mortal ! ' said the hunter, striding over my father's body, ' we have power over those only who have committed murder. You have been guilty of a double murder : you shall pay the penalty attached to your marriage vow. Two of your children are gone, the third is yet to follow—and follow them he will, for your oath is registered. Go—it were kindness to kill thee—your punishment is, that you live ! '

" With these words the spirit disappeared. My father rose from the floor, embraced me tenderly, and knelt down in prayer.

" The next morning he quitted the cottage for ever. He took me with him, and bent his steps to Holland, where we safely arrived. He had some little money with him ; but he had not been many days in Amsterdam before he was seized with a brain fever, and died raving mad. I was put into the asylum, and afterwards was sent to sea before the mast. You now know all my history. The question is, whether I am to pay the penalty of my father's oath ? I am myself perfectly convinced that, in some way or another, I shall."

II

On the twenty-second day the high land of the south of Sumatra was in view : as there were no vessels in sight, they resolved to keep their course through the Straits, and run for Pulo Penang, which they expected, as their vessel lay so close to the wind, to reach in seven or eight days. By constant exposure Philip and Krantz were now so bronzed, that with their long beards and Mussulman dresses, they might easily have passed off for natives. They had steered during the whole of the days exposed to a burning sun ; they had lain down and slept in the dew of the night ; but their health had not suffered. But for several days, since he had confided the history of his family to Philip, Krantz had become silent and melancholy ; his usual flow of spirits had vanished, and Philip had often questioned him as to the cause. As they entered the Straits, Philip talked of what they should do upon their arrival at Goa ; when Krantz gravely replied, " For some days, Philip, I have had a presentiment that I shall never see that city."

" You are out of health, Krantz," replied Philip.

" No, I am in sound health, body and mind. I have endeavoured to shake off the presentiment, but in vain ; there is a warning voice that continually tells me that I shall not be long with you. Philip, will you oblige me by making me content on one point ? I have gold about my person which may be useful to you ; oblige me by taking it, and securing it on your own."

" What nonsense, Krantz."

" It is no nonsense, Philip. Have you not had your warnings ? Why should I not have mine ? You know that I have little fear in my composition, and that I care not about death ; but I feel the presentiment which I speak of more strongly every hour. . . ."

" These are the imaginings of a disturbed brain, Krantz ; why you, young, in full health and vigour, should not pass your days in peace, and live to a good old age, there is no cause for believing. You will be better to-morrow."

" Perhaps so," replied Krantz ; " but you still must yield to my whim, and take the gold. If I am wrong, and we do arrive safe, you know, Philip, you can let me have it back," observed Krantz, with a faint smile—" but you forget, our water is nearly out, and we must look out for a rill on the coast to obtain a fresh supply."

" I was thinking of that when you commenced this unwelcome topic. We had better look out for the water before dark, and as soon as we have replenished our jars, we will make sail again."

At the time that this conversation took place, they were on the eastern side of the Strait, about forty miles to the northward. The interior of the coast was rocky and mountainous, but it slowly descended to low land of alternate forest and jungles, which continued to the beach ; the country appeared to be uninhabited. Keeping close in to the shore, they discovered, after two hours' run, a fresh stream which burst in a cascade from the mountains, and swept its devious course through the jungle, until it poured its tribute into the waters of the Strait.

They ran close into the mouth of the stream, lowered the sails, and pulled the peroqua against the current, until they had advanced far enough to assure them that the water was quite fresh. The jars were soon filled, and they were again thinking of pushing off, when enticed by the beauty of the spot, the coolness of the fresh water, and wearied with their long confinement on board of the peroqua, they proposed to bathe—a luxury hardly to be appreciated by those who have not been in a similar situation. They threw off their Mussulman dresses, and plunged into the stream, where they remained for some time. Krantz was the first to get out ; he complained of feeling chilled, and he walked on to the banks where their clothes had been laid. Philip also approached nearer to the beach, intending to follow him.

" And now, Philip," said Krantz, " this will be a good opportunity for me to give you the money. I will open my sash and pour it out, and you can put it into your own before you put it on."

Philip was standing in the water, which was about level with his waist.

" Well, Krantz," said he, " I suppose if it must be so, it must ; but it appears to me an idea so ridiculous—however, you shall have your own way."

Philip quitted the run, and sat down by Krantz, who was already busy in shaking the doubloons out of the folds of his sash ; at last he said—

" I believe, Philip, you have got them all, now ?—I feel satisfied."

" What danger there can be to you, which I am not equally exposed to, I cannot conceive," replied Philip ; " however——"

Hardly had he said these words, when there was a tremendous roar—a rush like a mighty wind through the air—a blow which threw him on his back—a loud cry—and a contention. Philip recovered himself, and perceived the naked form of Krantz carried off with the speed of an arrow by an enormous tiger through the jungle. He watched with distended eyeballs ; in a few seconds the animal and Krantz had disappeared.

" God of heaven ! would that Thou hadst spared me this," cried Philip, throwing himself down in agony on his face. " O Krantz ! my friend—my brother—too sure was your presentiment. Merciful God ! have pity—but Thy will be done." And Philip burst into a flood of tears.

For more than an hour did he remain fixed upon the spot, careless and indifferent to the danger by which he was surrounded. At last, somewhat recovered, he rose, dressed himself, and then again sat down—his eyes fixed upon the clothes of Krantz, and the gold which still lay on the sand.

" He would give me that gold. He foretold his doom. Yes ! yes ! it was his destiny, and it has been fulfilled. *His bones will bleach in the wilderness*, and the spirit-hunter and his wolfish daughter are avenged."

————

Roger Pater

A PORTA INFERI

from MYSTIC VOICES

Burns, Oates & Washbourne, 1923

Professor Aufrecht returned to London next day and I went with him as far as the junction, where I had some shopping to do, so I saw nothing of the squire and the old Dominican Father until the evening. After dinner we were talking in the library when Avison came in and removed the coffee cups.

" I'm always a little afraid of Avison," remarked Father Bertrand confidently, as the butler disappeared with his tray, " he makes me feel as if I must be on my best behaviour, like a schoolboy when the Headmaster is present."

" I know what you mean," answered the squire, " I used to feel much the same with old Wilson, Avison's predecessor. But then, you see, Wilson once caught me in the pantry, eating the dessert, when I was supposed to be safely in bed in the nursery ; and even after I became a priest and his master I felt that he half suspected I should be up to the same trick again, if he wasn't on his guard ! Now with Avison it is different ; you see, he has only been here about thirty years, whereas Wilson was butler before I was born."

" Is it really thirty years since Wilson died ? " asked Father Bertrand—" but yes, I suppose it must be. He was a splendid old man. I always used to think of him as a retainer, ' servant ' was much too undignified a term for him. On my first visit here I remember feeling that he was taking stock of me, and that, if I didn't pass muster, he would not allow you to ask me down again. Was it all my imagination, Philip, or did he exercise a veto on your visiting list ? "

" Oh no," laughed the squire, " Wilson would never have taken such a liberty, but I must admit he contrived to let me know what he thought of my friends. Don't be afraid, Bertrand, you passed with honours on the very first occasion. ' Quite a gentleman, sir, the young Dominican Father,' was his verdict. Dear old Wilson, I can hear him say it now."

" Doesn't Thackeray say somewhere that to win the approval of a butler is the highest test of good breeding ? " I asked.

" I don't remember that," answered the squire, " though I think he says that to look like a butler is the safest thing for a political leader, as it always suggests respectability. All the same, I came to trust Wilson's judgement, and it often stood me in good stead as a young man. But it is strange we should have got upon the subject to-night, for the only time I ever came near a quarrel with him was about his opinion of my friend the spiritualist, whose story I told you yesterday. The old butler took a strong dislike to him during his first visit here, and after he left we had quite a little scene. Wilson literally begged me not to make an intimate of him, and I remember getting annoyed with the old man and telling him sharply to mind his own business. He took the rebuke like a lamb and begged my pardon for venturing to speak in such a way to me. ' But you can't tell, Mr. Philip,' he added, ' what it means to me to see a man like that among your friends,' "

" I meant to ask you what became of the spiritualist," said Father Bertrand, " but it slipped my memory. Was the incident you told us the only thing of the kind, or did you come across any other examples of his faculty ? "

" Well," answered the squire, with a little hesitation, " perhaps you'll laugh at me, but old Wilson's opinion impressed me more than I cared to admit to him, and not long afterwards some facts came to my knowledge which went a long way to confirm it. In consequence I let our intimacy cool, and soon afterwards the man left England altogether, and I only met him once again, quite by accident, many years later." He paused for a moment, and then continued. " If you like I will tell you what happened on that occasion. The whole affair was over in a few hours, but while it lasted it was so startling that I have often thanked God since that I followed Wilson's advice and did not allow our former intimacy to develop.

" The incident I told you last night must have occurred about the year 1858, and the man passed out of my life within a year or so after that. Still, I never saw the Cellini fountain without it bringing him back to my mind, and I often wondered idly what had happened to him. I never heard a word about him, however, and in time I came to think he must be dead.

" More than twenty years later I was supplying at a mission on the outskirts of a large manufacturing town in the North. The place was not more than two or three miles from the heart of the city, but it was practically in the country, and the only exceptional feature about my work was the fact that I had to visit a large lunatic asylum which stood within the parish. The building had originally been the mansion of a county family, but they had died out, and when the property came into the market it was bought by the Corporation, and the mansion itself had been added to and adapted to serve its new purpose. There were a few Catholics among the inmates, and I found that one of the doctors was a Catholic too, so we soon became very good friends. One afternoon, as I was leaving the asylum, he asked me to go and have tea in his rooms. These were in a wing of the original building, where I had never been before, and his windows looked out on an old formal garden.

" 'Why,' I exclaimed, 'I thought I had seen all the grounds, but this part is quite new to me.'

" ' Yes, it would be,' he replied. ' You see, we have to keep the more serious cases separate from the others, and this part of the grounds is in their enclosure. If you like we will go round the old garden after tea ; there probably won't be more than one or two patients in it, and it will be all right if I go with you.'

" To tell the truth I was always a little uneasy when I went among the patients, even the harmless ones, but my glimpse of the garden made me long to see it all ; so I accepted the offer, and when tea was over we walked down on to the terrace beneath. The place had been laid out with great skill in the eighteenth century, and the paved walks with their old stone parapets and vases made an exquisite setting to the beds of bright flowers, relieved here and there by yew trees, clipped into fantastic shapes. There was not a soul about, and I quite forgot my uneasiness until we passed through an opening in a tall hedge at the bottom of the slope and came out on to a lawn beyond. At one end of this was a little pool, and my heart gave a great thump as I looked at it, for kneeling by the side, so that his profile was turned towards us, was a man whose face was perfectly familiar. It was my former friend the spiritualist, and, except that his shoulders were bent and his hair absolutely white, his appearance had scarcely changed in all the years, so that I recognised him in an instant. But it was not the surprise of meeting him thus unexpectedly which made me catch my breath and held me speechless. What sent the blood back to my heart, and then made it surge to the brain in a great wave of pity, was his occupation ; for carefully, with earnest gaze and rapt attention, he knelt there building castles in the mud ! The doctor must have noticed that I was upset, for he took my arm, as if to lead me back again, when I stopped him.

" ' No, no, Doctor,' I whispered, ' I'm not frightened ; it isn't that. But the man kneeling there, I used to know him well, I am certain of it.'

" ' Indeed,' he whispered back, ' he is the most curious case we have here—quite a mystery, in fact. I must get you to tell me what you know about him.'

" ' Yes, certainly,' I answered, ' but I want to speak to him. He may turn and recognise me at any moment, and I do not want him to think I have come to spy upon him.'

" ' You are right,' he replied, ' and if you can only gain his confidence it may be of great importance, for he is a case of lost identity, and your old friendship may perhaps revive his memory, and reconnect him with the vanished past.' With this he led me up to where the man was kneeling, but he never turned nor seemed to notice our presence, until the doctor addressed him in a loud voice.

" ' Come now, Lushington,' he said, ' I've brought an old friend to see you. Look up and see if you don't recognise him.' Very slowly, as if with an effort, the kneeling figure raised its head and turned towards us ; but slow as the movement was, it barely gave me time to recover from my surprise, for the doctor had addressed him by a name that was utterly unlike the one he had formerly borne, and yet here he was answering to it, as if it were his own !

" ' I wonder if you can recognise me after all these years ? ' I asked him, when he had gazed at me in silence for some moments without the smallest sign of recognition.

" ' Recognise yer ? No, I'm shot if I do,' he said at length ; and I got another surprise, for the words were spoken in a hard, vulgar voice, totally different from the quiet, refined speech of my former friend.

" ' Think again, Lushington,' said the doctor, ' for this gentleman is quite right, he used to know you well many years ago.' With a scowl the man turned upon him angrily :

" ' What the blazes do you know about it, you little body-snatcher ? ' he snarled. ' I'll trouble you to mind your own business. As if you knew anything about me and what I was " many years ago." I wouldn't have spoken to you then, and wouldn't now, but that you've got me locked in this infernal prison of yours.'

" ' It must be fully twenty years since last you saw me,' I said gently, for I wanted to calm him down if possible, ' and I was a layman then, so my dress has changed as well as my appearance ; but I hoped you might recollect my face.'

" ' I don't, anyhow,' said he, though with less confidence I thought, as if some faint glimmer of memory were returning ; ' but you says you're sure you know me, eh ? Dick Lushington ? '

" ' Quite sure of it,' I answered. ' But I must admit one thing. When I knew you, twenty years ago, you were not called Dick Lushington, but . . .' and I spoke the man's real name, which I had known him by. The effect was instantaneous and almost terrifying. No sooner had the words passed my lips than he leaped to his feet, shaking with passion. His face became livid with rage, he foamed at the mouth, and I thought he was going to have a fit.

" ' Liar, liar, liar ! ' he shrieked in my face. ' How dare you say it ? It isn't true—by Hell, I swear it isn't ! He's dead, the blackguard that you say I am—I won't soil my lips by repeating his filthy name—and now you'll be saying I killed him. You devil, why don't you say it ? It's a lie, of course, but so's what you said before—lies, lies, lies everywhere ! ' and the madman dropped to his knees again and drove his fingers deep into the mud. I noticed now that there was a warder standing behind us, and saw the doctor make a sign to him.

" ' Come away, Father,' he whispered to me, ' we must give him time to calm down. The warder will look after him, and he will recover more quickly if we go away ' ; and taking my arm again he led me back towards the mansion. When we had passed through the hedge and were well out of earshot, the doctor began to speak again.

" ' I'm afraid the experiment was not a great success, Father,' he said. ' I've never seen Lushington lose his self-control so suddenly, and the worst of it is that his heart is in a terrible state, so an outbreak like this is liable to prove fatal.'

" ' It certainly was a terrible thing to witness,' I answered ; ' but I'm not so sure we weren't successful in one respect. You are an expert in these matters and I know nothing about them, but surely the fact is clear now that he still knows his real name although he wishes others to be kept in ignorance of it.'

" ' Certainly,' answered the doctor ; ' but how does that help us, Father ? '

" ' First let me tell you what I can about his past life, in the days when I knew him,' I answered, ' and then you can say if my idea of his case is a possible one.'

" We had reached the house now, and when we were in the doctor's sitting-room again I told him all I knew. Put shortly it was this. When I first met Lushington—I will use that name, if you don't mind, as there is no reason for disclosing his identity—he was a young man, well educated, with a comfortable private income of his own, and moving in good society in London, which was only natural, for he came of an excellent family. He was then beginning to dabble in spiritualism, and had been introduced to Home, the famous medium. For my part I tried to dissuade him from this, and always refused to attend any of their séances though he often urged me to, but he ignored my advice and became more and more absorbed in his pursuit, as he found that he himself possessed special gifts as a medium ; in fact, Home often urged him to devote his whole life to ' the Cause,' as he liked to call it. I also told the doctor the story you heard last night—I mean what happened here, when I brought out the Cellini fountain for him to see—and how, later on, his reputation had become an undesirable one and he had left the country, since when I had heard and seen nothing of him until that afternoon ; and then I asked to be told the circumstances which led to his incarceration in the asylum. The doctor hesitated for a little before he answered.

" ' Well, Father,' said he, ' you know we are not allowed to let such facts be known outside the staff, but I think you may be considered as one of ourselves. Not that there's much to tell in any case, for, as I told you, Lushington is our enigma. He was brought here about five years ago by the solicitor of a well-known public man, the head of the family to which he belongs ; but even the family lawyer could tell us very little. His residence abroad, which you mentioned just now, must have terminated quite ten years ago, for he had been living in Belfast for five years or so before he came here. For a long time before that he had had no personal dealings with his relatives, but they kept in touch with him through the family solicitors, who used to send him a cheque for his half-year's income every six months, which cheques he always acknowledged.

" ' The arrangement suited both sides, for Lushington wished to avoid his family, and I gathered that they returned the feeling, though I did not learn why ; but what you say about his career as a medium no doubt supplies the explanation. However, shortly before he came here, instead of the customary formal note acknowledging their cheque, the solicitors received a long letter, full of foul language and abuse, with a deliberate accusation of dishonesty on their part, and a threat of legal proceedings for breach of trust and misappropriation of his money. The charge was manifestly absurd, but as the chief trustee was the public man I have mentioned, he could not run the risk of leaving such a charge unanswered, so one of the firm was sent over to Ireland to see Lushington and investigate the affair.

" ' He arrived in Belfast to find that his man had been arrested the day before on a criminal charge, but on examination he was found to be hopelessly insane. The solicitor obtained full powers to act on behalf of the family, and he was brought here soon afterwards. But now comes the strange part of the affair. As you know, one element in his case is that of lost identity. The man insists that he is Dick Lushington, and either refuses to admit that he ever bore his real name, or else, as to-day, maintains that the man who bore it is dead. What makes this feature of his case so odd is that, years ago, a man called Dick Lushington really lived in Belfast. He was a notorious bad lot, cunning and unscrupulous, an habitual criminal, in fact, who served numerous terms in gaol, and, when out of it, was leader of the worst gang of ruffians in the city. Finally he committed murder, and, failing to escape, took his own life to avoid being arrested and hanged. But the oddest part of it all is this, that the real Dick Lushington killed himself *nearly thirty years ago*, long before our patient ever went to Belfast—in fact, while he was still quite young and respectable ; yet one of the senior police officials there, who saw the man before he came here, declares that his voice and manner, his tricks of speech and choice of oaths, are identical with those of the notorious criminal Lushington, whose name this poor wretch has adopted, but whom he never can have seen ! '

" ' Extraordinary,' I said, ' it sounds like a case of possession ' ; but as I was speaking a knock came at the door and a warder entered.

" ' Beg pardon, sir,' he said, addressing the doctor, ' but I came to report about Lushington. After you and the other gentleman left the garden he calmed down, and I got him to come in quietly to his room. When he got there, he threw himself on the bed like one exhausted and began to cry, at the same time talking to himself in his other voice—you know what I mean, sir—like a gentleman. After a bit he called me up and said :

" ' " Tell him I want to see him."

" ' " Tell who ? " says I.

" ' " Why, Philip, of course," says he—" the gentleman who was in the garden just now."

" ' Well, sir, I didn't want to bother you with his nonsense, so I said I thought the gentleman was gone ; but no, he wouldn't have it.

" ' " Go and see," says he, and, try as I would, I couldn't put him off it. At last I said I'd go and see, so here I am, sir.'

" ' And a good thing too,' exclaimed the doctor impatiently. ' I only hope we shall not be too late, and find the quiet mood has passed. Come, Father, this is important. If Lushington is still in this state, you may be able to do something with him.'

" ' By all means, let us go at once,' I said, rising, and we hurried off to the poor creature's cell, which the doctor and myself entered, leaving the warder outside, with instructions to come in at once if either of us called. The man was lying on his bed, apparently in a state of extreme exhaustion, but as we entered he turned his head to see who we were, and a great sigh escaped his lips.

" ' Oh, Philip, come to me,' he murmured faintly, and I hastened to the bedside and took both his hands in mine.

" ' After all these years, to see you once again,' he said, almost in a whisper. ' Oh, Philip, if I had but taken your advice ! ' I pressed his fingers in my own, hardly daring to speak, and he lay silent, with eyes closed, for quite a minute. Then, all at once, his eyes opened, and he turned to me with a quick glance of terror.

" ' Take me away with you, Philip,' he cried, ' quickly, before the other one comes back ! ' and he flung his arms round me like a frightened child. Gently I laid him back upon the bed, supporting the poor feeble body in my arms, and tried to reassure him.

" ' You're all safe now, old fellow,' I whispered gently. ' He won't come back while I am here, no chance of it.'

" ' Oh, do you think so ? ' he answered eagerly. ' Then—why—then you must never leave me. My God ! how I hate him, devil that he is ; and oh, to think I let him in so willingly ! '

" ' We'll keep him out together, you and I, never fear of that,' I assured him bravely, though, even as I spoke, I was wondering what in the world it all meant ; and then I added foolishly, ' Tell me, who is he ? '

" ' Who is he ? ' he almost shrieked, his terror returning more intensely than before. ' Who is he ? Why, Dick Lushington, of course—the devil-man, who gets inside and uses me. He uses me, I tell you like a slave. My hands, my limbs, my brain, my will, he's got it all, all of me, at his mercy. The filthy, hateful devil that he is, and did it by pretending to be my friend.'

" ' Hush, hush, be calm,' I said, ' you will exhaust yourself. Be calm, he won't come back while I am here. You see, I am a priest now, did you know it ? I promise you, you will be safe with me.'

" ' Thank God for that,' he said more calmly, ' but oh, Philip, don't forsake me. I shan't last long now, I shan't keep you long. You were my friend once, be my saviour now. Promise me you'll be with me at the end. Don't leave me here to die, alone with him.'

" ' I promise you faithfully that I will do everything in my power to help you,' I answered solemnly ; ' but now you must rest yourself, and try to sleep,' and I laid his head back on the pillow, taking his hand in mine again, while he closed his eyes.

" ' I will do anything—anything you tell me,' he whispered, ' only forsake me not, or I am lost.' Then he lay still, and in less than five minutes, to my amazement, the grip on my hand relaxed, his fingers fell back, and he was sleeping like a child. The doctor crept to the door and beckoned the warder in.

" ' Stay here by the bedside,' he ordered, ' and if he wakes up, say to him at once, " Father Philip is still here and will come if you require him." If he says he does, pull the bell which communicates with my room.' Then he touched my arm and led me away on tip-toe along the gallery.

" ' Well,' I said, at length, when we had reached the doctor's room, ' I don't know what you think, but to my mind it seems a clear case of possession. I have heard of other similar cases among spiritualists.'

" ' It certainly does look like it,' he admitted ; ' but I am more concerned as to the immediate treatment than I am to explain the origin of his malady. Do you realise, my dear Father, what you have taken upon yourself ? '

" ' You mean by promising to do all I can for him ? " I asked.

" ' I mean by intervening in the case at all,' he answered

grimly. ' The man's life is in your hands now, and if you fail him, if you are not at hand whenever he calls for you, I think the consequences will probably be fatal ! '

" ' I shall certainly not shirk the consequences of my promise,' I answered ; ' but did you notice what he said to me ? " I shan't last long now, promise me you'll be with me at the end." I may be wrong, but if he is convinced that he is dying, is it not more than probable that he will do so ? '

" ' Well, yes,' admitted the doctor, ' there is something in that. In fact, if he gets another paroxysm, like you saw in the garden, I do not think he will survive it. But short of that, I shouldn't be surprised if he were to linger on for some time, or even for several weeks.'

" ' If he does, I shall have to make some arrangement about the parish work,' I answered, ' but my own belief is that he won't last many hours. I have learned to trust the instincts of a dying man.' We talked for some time longer on the point, each of us maintaining his own view, without convincing the other.

" ' Well, I only hope you may be right,' said the doctor, at length ; ' for many reasons it will be better so. Still, speaking merely from a professional point of view, I see no reason why——' but his words were cut short by the clash of a bell, ringing violently in the adjoining bedroom. The doctor leaped to his feet, and ran to the door between the two rooms.

" ' No. 17 ! ' he exclaimed, ' it is Lushington's cell. Come, Father '—and once more we hurried down the corridor. As we entered the room I could scarce believe my eyes. The man we had left, not half an hour before, in a state of utter collapse was on the floor kneeling over the prostrate figure of the warder, who was trying to tear away the fingers of the maniac, which were tightly fastened on his throat. The doctor flung himself upon the kneeling man. The weight of the charge knocked him backwards, enabling the warder to rise. The madman's arms shot out, but luckily I caught one of his wrists, and the warder, a big, powerful man, soon captured the other.

" ' The handcuffs, in my pocket—quick, Doctor,' he cried, ' get 'em out while we turn him over ! '—and in a few seconds we had the poor wretch secured, with his wrists handcuffed behind his back. He went on struggling until the warder had got his ankles fettered with a strap, but the three of us were too much for him, and in a minute or so he was lying, safely pinioned, on the bed. All this while he had never spoken, though his breath came in great gasps that shook his whole frame ; now, at length, he seemed calmer, and I thought it time to speak.

" ' You're all right now, old fellow,' I said gently, ' don't be afraid ; it is I, Philip—I am here as I promised.' The man turned his eyes upon me, and the look of hatred in them was appalling.

" ' All right, am I ? ' he shrieked savagely. ' If it wasn't for these —— handcuffs, I'd soon show yer I'm all right. A nice, mean, low sort of priest's trick to play on me. Thought you'd get hold of yer old pal, and pilot him into heaven while number one was out, did yer ? Bah ! '—and he spat at me—' you dirty swine ! '

" ' Ask the warder to wait outside, Doctor,' I said, for a sudden inspiration came to me ; and the man withdrew at his command.

" ' What yer going to do now, curse ye—sing a hymn ? ' sneered the madman on the bed, as I took my breviary from my pocket. Without answering I turned to the prayers for the dying, and, kneeling down, began to recite them aloud and slowly, while the thing that animated my poor friend's body gave a shriek of malicious hatred.

" The scene that followed was literally indescribable, but I stuck to my task, and, as calmly as I could manage, went through the litanies and all the prayers for a departing soul ; while the thing on the bed jerked itself from side to side, so far as the fastenings would allow, and the harsh, strident voice of Dick Lushington, the long-dead murderer, howled oaths, sang filthy songs, hurled curses at my head, and poured forth blasphemies unspeakable. As I reached the end of the prayers the question arose in my mind, ' What shall I do now ? ' when, all at once, a strange phenomenon occurred. It seemed as if some mighty force took hold of me, overpowering my limbs, my will, and all my faculties, so that I no more controlled my soul or body, but simply yielded myself up to serve. I was conscious that I had risen to my feet and was standing beside the bed. Then, in a tone of stern command, I heard my own voice speak the words, ' In the name of the Father and of the Son and of the Holy Ghost, I command thee, thou evil spirit, to go out of him ! '

" The body on the bed gave one tremendous heave, as if to break the bands with which it was fettered, and then fell back with a cry of baffled rage and frenzy, such as I never heard before and never wish to hear again. Then, gradually, before my astonished gaze, the face that was all distorted with anger grew calm, the purple flesh and swollen veins became deadly pale, and the eyes which looked up at me were no longer those of a madman, but the eyes of my long-lost friend. Then the lips moved feebly, and I caught a faint whisper.

" ' God bless you, Philip, you have saved me ! Jesus, be merciful to me a sinner.'

" The voice died away, one great sigh shook the frame of the dying man, and I quickly gave him the last absolution. There was silence for a minute or so, and then the doctor stepped forward.

" ' You may come away now, Father,' he said softly. ' You have kept your promise. He is dead.' "

Richard Barham

JERRY JARVIS'S WIG

A LEGEND OF THE WEALD OF KENT

from THE INGOLDSBY LEGENDS (*Third Series*)

Richard Bentley, 1847

" *The wig's the thing ! the wig ! the wig.*"—Old Song.

" Joe," said old Jarvis, looking out of his window—it was on his ground-floor back—" Joe, you seem to be very hot, Joe, and you have got no wig ! "

" Yes, sir," quoth Joseph, pausing and resting upon his spade, " it's as hot a day as ever I *see* ; but the celery must be got in, or there'll be no autumn crop, and——"

" Well, but Joe, the sun's so hot, and it shines so on your bald head, it makes one wink to look at it. You'll have a *coup de soleil*, Joe."

" A *what*, sir ? "

" No matter ; it's very hot working ; and if you'll step indoors I'll give you——"

" Thank ye, your honour, a drop of beer will be very acceptable."

Joe's countenance brightened amazingly.

" Joe, I'll give you—my old wig ! "

The countenance of Joseph fell, his grey eye had glistened as a blest vision of double X flitted athwart his fancy ; his glance faded again into the old, filmy, gooseberry-coloured hue, as he growled in a minor key, " A wig, sir ! "

" Yes, Joe, a wig. The man who does not study the comfort of his dependants is an unfeeling scoundrel. You shall have my old worn-out wig."

" I hope, sir, you'll give me a drop o' beer to drink your honour's health in ; it *is* very hot, and——"

" Come in, Joe, and Mrs. Witherspoon shall give it you."

" Heaven bless your honour ! " said honest Joe, striking his spade perpendicularly into the earth, and walking with more than usual alacrity towards the close-cut, quickset hedge which separated Mr. Jarvis's garden from the high road.

From the quickset hedge aforesaid he now raised, with all due delicacy, a well-worn and somewhat dilapidated jacket, of a stuff by drapers most pseudonymously termed " everlasting." Alack ! alack ! what is there to which *tempus edax rerum* will accord that epithet ? In its high and palmy days it had been all of a piece ; but as its master's eye now fell upon it, the expression of his countenance seemed to say with Octavian,

Those days are gone, Floranthe !

It was now, from frequent patching, a coat not unlike that of the patriarch, one of many colours.

Joseph Washford inserted his wrists into the corresponding orifices of the tattered garment, and with a steadiness of circum-gyration, to be acquired only by long and sufficient practice, swung it horizontally over his ears and settled himself into it.

" Confound your old jacket ! " cried a voice from the other side the hedge ; " keep it down, you rascal ! Don't you see my horse is frightened at it ? "

" Sensible beast ! " apostrophised Joseph, " I've been frightened at it myself every day for the last two years."

The gardener cast a rueful glance at its sleeve, and pursued his way to the door of the back kitchen.

" Joe," said Mrs. Witherspoon, a fat, comely dame, of about five-and-forty—" Joe, your master is but too good to you ; he is always kind and considerate. Joe, he has desired me to give you his old wig."

" And the beer, Ma'am Witherspoon ? " said Washford, taking
the proffered caxon, and looking at it with an expression somewhat
short of rapture ; " and the beer, ma'am ! "

" The beer, you guzzling wretch !—what beer ? Master said
nothing about no beer. You ungrateful fellow, has not he given
you a wig ? "

" Why, yes, Madam Witherspoon ! but then, you see, his honour
said it was very hot, and I'm very dry, and——"

" Go to the pump, sot ! " said Mrs. Witherspoon, as she slammed
the back-door in the face of the petitioner.

Mrs. Witherspoon was " of the Lady Huntingdon persuasion,"
and Honorary Assistant Secretary to the Appledore branch of
the " Ladies' Grand Junction Water-working Temperance
Society."

Joe remained for a few moments lost in mental abstraction ;
he looked at the door, he looked at the wig ; his first thought was
to throw it into the pigsty,—his corruption rose, but he resisted
the impulse ; he got the better of Satan ; the half-formed impreca-
tion died before it reached his lips. He looked disdainfully at the
wig ; it had once been a comely jasey enough, of the colour of
over-baked ginger-bread, one of the description commonly known
during the latter half of the last century by the name of a " brown
George." The species, it is to be feared, is now extinct, but a
few, a very few of the same description might, till very lately,
be occasionally seen,—*rari nantes in gurgite vasto*—the glorious
relics of a bygone day, crowning the *cerebellum* of some venerated
and venerable provost, or judge of assize ; but Mr. Jarvis's
wig had one peculiarity ; unlike most of its fellows, it had a
tail !—" cribbed and confined," indeed, by a shabby piece of
faded shalloon.

Washford looked at it again ; he shook his bald head ; the wig
had certainly seen its best days ; still it had about it somewhat
of an air of faded gentility ; it was " like ancient Rome, majestic
in decay,"—and as the small ale was not to be forthcoming, why—
after all, an old wig was better than nothing !

Mr. Jeremiah Jarvis, of Appledore, in the Weald of Kent, was
a gentleman by act of parliament ; one of that class of gentlemen
who, disdaining the *bourgeoise*-sounding name of " attorney-at-law,"
are, by a legal fiction, denominated solicitors. I say by a legal fiction,
surely the general tenor of the intimation received by such as enjoy
the advantage of their correspondence, has little in common with

the idea usually attached to the term " solicitation." " If you don't pay my bill, and costs, I'll send you to jail," is a very energetic *entreaty*. There are, it is true, etymologists who derive their style and title from the Latin infinitive " *solicitare*," to " make anxious," —in all probability they are right.

If this be the true etymology of his title, as it was the main end of his calling, then was Jeremiah Jarvis a worthy exemplar of the *genus* to which he belonged. Few persons in his time had created greater solicitude among his Majesty's lieges within the " Weald." He was rich, of course. The best house in the country-town is always the lawyer's, and it generally boasts a green door, stone steps, and a brass knocker. In neither of these appendages to opulence was Jeremiah deficient ; but then he was so very *rich* ; his reputed wealth, indeed, passed all the common modes of accounting for its increase. True, he was so universal a favourite that every man whose will he made was sure to leave him a legacy ; that he was a sort of general assignee to all the bankruptcies within twenty miles of Appledore ; was clerk to half the " trusts " ; and treasurer to most of the " rates," " funds," and " subscriptions," in that part of the country ; that he was land-agent to Lord Mountrhino, and steward to the rich Miss Tabbytale of Smerri- diddle Hall ; that he had been guardian (?) to three young pro- fligates who all ran through their property, which, somehow or another, came at last into his hands, " at an equitable valuation." Still his possessions were so considerable, as not to be altogether accounted for, in vulgar esteem, even by these and other honour- able modes of accumulation ; nor were there wanting those who conscientiously entertained a belief that a certain dark-coloured gentleman, of indifferent character, known principally by his predilection for appearing in perpetual mourning, had been through life his great friend and counsellor, and had mainly assisted in the acquirement of his revenues. That " old Jerry Jarvis had sold himself to the devil " was, indeed, a dogma which it was heresy to doubt in Appledore ;—on this head, at least, there were few schismatics in the parish.

When the worthy " Solicitor " next looked out of his ground- floor back, he smiled with much complacency at beholding Joe Washford again hard at work—in his wig—the little tail aforesaid oscillating like a pendulum in the breeze. If it be asked what could induce a gentleman, whose leading principle seems to have been self-appropriation, to make so magnificent a present, the answer is, that Mr. Jarvis might perhaps have thought an occasional act of benevolence necessary or politic ; he is not the only person, who, having stolen a quantity of leather, has given away a pair of shoes, *pour l'amour de Dieu*,—perhaps he had other motives.

Joe, meanwhile, worked away at the celery-bed ; but truth obliges us to say, neither with the same degree of vigour or perseverance as had marked the earlier efforts of the morning. His pauses were more frequent ; he rested longer on the handle of his spade ; while ever and anon his eye would wander from the trench beneath him to an object not unworthy the contemplation of a natural philosopher. This was an apple-tree.

Fairer fruit never tempted Eve, or any of her daughters ; the bending branches groaned beneath their luxuriant freight, and dropping to earth, seemed to ask the protecting aid of man either to support or to relieve them. The fine, rich glow of their sunstreaked clusters derived additional loveliness from the level beams of the descending day-star. An anchorite's mouth had watered at the pippins.

On the precise graft of the espalier of Eden, " Sanchoniathon, Manetho, and Berosus" are undecided ; the best-informed Talmudists, however, have, if we are to believe Dr. Pinner's German Version, pronounced it a Ribstone pippin, and a Ribstone pippin-tree it was that now attracted the optics and discomposed the inner man of the thirsty, patient, but perspiring gardener. The heat was still oppressive ; no beer had moistened his lip, though its very name, uttered as it was in the ungracious tones of a Witherspoon, had left behind a longing as intense as fruitless. His thirst seemed supernatural, when at this moment his left ear experienced a " slight and tickling sensation," such as we are assured is occasionally produced by an infinitesimal dose in homœopathy ; a still, small *voice*—it was as though a daddy long-legs were whispering in his *tympanum*—a small *voice* seemed to say, " Joe !—take an apple, Joe ! "

Honest Joseph started at the suggestion ; the rich crimson of his jolly nose deepened to a purple tint in the beams of the setting sun ; his very forehead was incarnadine. He raised his hand to scratch his ear,—the little tortuous tail had worked its way into it, —he pulled it out by the bit of shalloon, and allayed the itching, then cast his eye wistfully towards the mansion where his master was sitting by the open window. Joe pursed up his parched lips into an arid whistle, and with a desperate energy struck his spade once more into the celery-bed.

Alack ! alack ! what a piece of work is man !—how short his triumphs !—how frail his resolutions !

From this fine and very original moral reflection we turn reluctantly to record the sequel. The celery-bed, alluded to as the main scene of Mr. Washford's operations, was drawn in a rectilinear direction, nearly across the whole breadth of the parallelogram that comprised the " kitchen-garden." Its northern extremity abutted to the hedge before-mentioned, its southern one—woe is me that it should have been so !—was in fearful vicinity to the Ribstone pippin-tree. One branch, low bowed to earth, seemed ready to discharge its precious burden into the very trench. As Joseph stooped to insert the last plant with his dibble, an apple of more than ordinary beauty bobbed against his knuckles.—" He's taking snuff, Joe," whispered the same small *voice* ;—the tail had twisted itself into its old position. " He is sneezing !—now, Joe !— now ! " and, ere the agitated horticulturist could recover from his surprise and alarm, the fruit was severed, and—in his hand !

" He ! he ! he ! " shrilly laughed, or seemed to laugh, that accursed little pigtail—Washford started at once to the perpendicular ;—with an enfrenzied grasp he tore the jasey from his head, and, with that in one hand, and his ill-acquired spoil in the other, he rushed distractedly from the garden !

* * * * * * * *

All that night was the humble couch of the once-happy gardener haunted with the most fearful visions. He was stealing apples,— he was robbing hen-roosts,—he was altering the chalks upon the milk-score,—he had purloined three *chemises* from a hedge, and he awoke in the very act of cutting the throat of one of Squire Hodge's sheep ! A clammy dew stood upon his temples,—the cold perspiration burst from every pore,—he sprang in terror from the bed.

" Why, Joe, what ails thee, man ? " cried the usually incurious Mrs. Washford ; " what be the matter with thee ? Thee hast done nothing but grunt and growl all t' night long, and now thee dost stare as if thee saw summut. What bees it, Joe ? "

A long-drawn sigh was her husband's only answer ; his eye fell upon the bed. " How the devil came *that* here ? " quoth Joseph, with a sudden recoil : " who put that thing on my pillow ? "

" Why, I did, Joseph. Th' ould nightcap is in the wash, and thee didst toss and tumble so, and kick the clothes off, I thought thee mightest catch cold, so I clapt t' wig atop o' thee head."

And there it lay,—the little sinister-looking tail impudently perked up, like an infernal gnomon on a Satanic dial-plate—Larceny and Ovicide shone in every hair of it !

The dawn was overcast, the morning lower'd,
And heavily in clouds brought on the day,

when Joseph Washford once more repaired to the scene of his daily labours ; a sort of unpleasant consciousness flushed his countenance, and gave him an uneasy feeling as he opened the garden gate ; for Joe, generally speaking, was honest as the skin between his brows ; his hand faltered as it pressed the latch. " Pooh, pooh ! 'twas but an apple, after all ! " said Joseph. He pushed open the wicket, and found himself beneath the tempting tree.

But vain now were all its fascinations ; like fairy gold seen by the morning light, its charms had faded into very nothingness. Worlds, to say nothing of apples, which in shape resemble them, would not have bought him to stretch forth an unhallowed hand again ; he went steadily to his work.

The day continued cloudy ; huge drops of rain fell at intervals, stamping his bald pate with spots as big as halfpence ; but Joseph worked on. As the day advanced, showers fell thick and frequent ; the fresh-turned earth was itself fragrant as a *bouquet.*—Joseph worked on ; and when at last *Jupiter Pluvius* descended in all his majesty, soaking the ground into the consistency of dingy pudding, he put on his party-coloured jacket, and strode towards his humble home, rejoicing in his renewed integrity. " 'Twas but an apple, after all ! Had it been an apple-pie, indeed ! "—

" An apple-pie ! " the thought was a dangerous one—too dangerous to dwell on. But Joseph's better Genius was this time lord of the ascendant ;—he dismissed it, and passed on.

On arriving at his cottage, an air of bustle and confusion prevailed within, much at variance with the peaceful serenity usually observable in its economy. Mrs. Washford was in high dudgeon ! her heels clattered on the red-tiled floor, and she whisked about the house like a parched pea upon a drum-head ; her voice, generally small and low—" an excellent thing in woman,"—was pitched at least an octave above its ordinary level ; she was talking fast and furious. Something had evidently gone wrong. The mystery was soon explained. The "*cussed old twoad* of a cat" had got into the dairy, and licked off the cream from the only pan their single cow had filled that morning ! And there she now lay, purring as in scorn. Tib, heretofore the meekest of mousers, the honestest, the least " *scaddle* " of the feline race,—a cat that one would have sworn might have been trusted with untold fish,— yes,—there was no denying it,—proofs were too strong against her,—yet there she lay, hardened in her iniquity, coolly licking her whiskers, and reposing quietly upon—what ?—Jerry Jarvis's old wig ! !

The patience of a Stoic must have yielded ; it had been too much for the temperament of the Man of Uz. Joseph Washford lifted his hand—that hand which had never yet been raised on Tibby, save to fondle and caress—it now descended on her devoted head in one tremendous " dowse." Never was cat so astonished,—so enraged—all the tiger portion of her nature rose in her soul. Instead of galloping off, hissing and sputtering, with arched back, and tail erected, as any ordinary Grimalkin would unquestionably have done under similar circumstances, she paused a moment,— drew back on her haunches,—all her energies seemed concentrated for one prodigious spring ; a demoniac fire gleamed in her green and yellow eyeballs, as, bounding upwards, she fixed her talons firmly in each of her assailant's cheeks !—many and many a day after were sadly visible the marks of those envenomed claws —then dashing over his shoulder with an unearthly mew, she leaped through the open casement, and was seen no more.

" The Devil's in the cat ! " was the apostrophe of Mrs. Margaret Washford. Her husband said nothing, but thrust the old wig into his pocket, and went to bathe his scratches at the pump.

Day after day, night after night, 'twas all the same—Joe Washford's life became a burden to him ; his natural upright and honest mind struggled hard against the frailty of human nature. He was ever restless and uneasy ; his frank, open, manly look, that blenched not from the gaze of the spectator, was no more : a sly and sinister expression had usurped the place of it.

Mr. Jeremiah Jarvis had little of what the world calls " Taste," still less of Science. Ackerman would have called him a " Snob," and Buckland a " Nincompoop." Of the Horticultural Society, its *fêtes*, its fruits, and its fiddlings, he knew nothing. Little recked he of flowers—save cauliflowers—in these, indeed, he was a *connoisseur* ! to their cultivation and cookery the respective talents of Joe and Madame Witherspoon had long been dedicated ; but as for a *bouquet* !—Hardham's 37 was " the only one fit for a gentleman's nose." And yet, after all, Jerry Jarvis had a good-looking tulip-bed. A female friend of his had married a Dutch merchant ; Jerry drew the settlements ; the lady paid him by a cheque on " Child's," the gentleman by a present of a " box of roots." Jerry put the latter in his garden—he had rather they had been schalots.

Not so his neighbour, Jenkinson ; he *was* a man of " Taste " and of " Science " ; he was an F.R.C.E.B.S., which, as he told the Vicar, implied, " Fellow of the Royal Cathartico-Emetico-Botanical Society," and his autograph in Sir John Frostyface's album stood next to that of the Emperor of all the Russias. Neighbour Jenkinson fell in love with the pips and petals of " neighbour Jarvis's tulips." There were one or two among them of such brilliant, such surpassing beauty,—the " cups " so well formed,—the colours so defined. To be sure, Mr. Jenkinson had enough in his own garden ; but then " Enough," says the philosopher, " always means a little more than a man has got."—Alas ! alas ! Jerry Jarvis was never known to *bestow*,—his neighbour dared not offer to *purchase* from so wealthy a man ; and, worse than all, Joe, the gardener, was incorruptible—ay, but the wig ?

Joseph Washford was working away again in the blaze of the midday sun ; his head looked like a copper saucepan fresh from the brazier's.

" Why, where's your wig, Joseph ? " said the voice of his master from the well-known window : " what have you done with your wig ? " The question was embarrassing—its tail had tickled his ear till it had made it sore ; Joseph had put the wig in his pocket.

Mr. Jeremiah Jarvis was indignant ; he liked not that his benefits should be ill appreciated by the recipient. " Hark ye, Joseph Washford," said he, " either wear my wig, or let me have it again ! "

There was no mistaking the meaning of his tones ; they were resonant of indignation and disgust, of mingled grief and anger, the amalgamation of sentiment naturally produced by

> *Friendship unreturn'd,*
> *And unrequited love.*

Washford's heart smote him : he felt all that was implied in his master's appeal. " It's here, your Honour," said he ; " I had only taken it off because we have had a smartish shower ; but the sky is brightening now." The wig was replaced, and the little tortuous pigtail wriggled itself into its accustomed position.

At this moment neighbour Jenkinson peeped over the hedge.

" Joe Washford ! " said neighbour Jenkinson.

" Sir to you," was the reply.

" How beautiful your tulips look after the rain ! "

" Ah ! sir, master sets no great store by them flowers," returned the gardener.

" Indeed ! Then perhaps he would have no objection to part with a few ? "

" Why, no !—I don't think master would like to *give* them—or anything else,—away, sir " ; and Washford scratched his ear.

" Joe ! ! " said Mr. Jenkinson—" Joe ! "

The Sublime, observes Longinus, is often embodied in a mono-syllable—" Joe ! ! ! "—Mr. Jenkinson said no more ; but a half-crown shone from between his upraised fingers, and its " poor, poor dumb mouth " spoke for him.

How Joseph Washford's left ear *did* itch ! He looked to the ground-floor back—Mr. Jarvis had left the window.

Mr. Jenkinson's ground-plot boasted, at daybreak next morning, a splendid *Semper Augustus,* " which was not so before," and Joseph Washford was led home, much about the same time, in a most extraordinary state of " civilation," from " The Three Jolly Potboys."

From that hour he was the Fiend's ! !

.   .   .   .

" *Facilis descensus Averni !* " says Virgil. " It is only the first step that is attended with any difficulty," says—somebody else—when speaking of the decollated martyr, St. Dennis's walk with his head under his arm. " The First Step ! "—Joseph Washford had taken that step !—he had taken two—three—four steps ; and now, from a hesitating, creeping, cat-like mode of progression, he had got into a firmer tread—an amble—a positive trot ! He took the family linen " to the wash " :—one of Madame Witherspoon's best Holland *chemises* was never seen after.

" Lost !—impossible ! How *could* it be lost ?—where *could* it be gone to ?—who *could* have got it ? It was her best—her *very* best !—

she should know it among a hundred—among a thousand !—it was marked with a great W in the corner !—Lost ?—impossible— She would *see* !—Alas ! she never *did* see—the *chemise—abiit, erupit, evasit* !—it was

Like the lost Pleiad, seen on earth no more,

—but Joseph Washford's Sunday shirt *was* seen, finer and fairer than ever—the pride and *dulce decus* of the Meeting.

The Meeting ?—ay, the Meeting. Joe Washford never missed the Appledore Independent Meeting House, whether the service were in the morning or afternoon,—whether the Rev. Mr. Slyandry exhorted or made way for the Rev. Mr. Tearbrain. Let who would officiate, there was Joe. As I have said before, he never missed ;—but other people missed—one missed an umbrella,— one a pair of clogs. Farmer Johnson missed his tobacco-box,— Farmer Jackson his greatcoat,—Miss Jackson missed her hymn-book,—a diamond edition, bound in maroon-coloured velvet with gilt corners and clasps. Everything, in short, was missed— but Joe Washford ; there *he* sat, grave, sedate, and motionless— all save that restless, troublesome, fidgety little Pigtail attached to his wig, which nothing *could* keep quiet, or prevent from tickling and interfering with Miss Thompson's curls, as she sat back to back with Joe, in the adjoining pew. After the third Sunday, Nancy Thompson eloped with the tall recruiting sergeant of the Connaught Rangers.

The summer passed away,—autumn came and went,—and Christmas, jolly Christmas, that period of which we are accustomed to utter the mournful truism, it " comes but *once* a year," was at hand. It was a fine bracing morning ; the sun was just beginning to throw a brighter tint upon the Quaker-coloured ravine of Orlestone-hill, when a medical gentleman, returning to the quiet little village of Ham Street, that lies at its foot, from a farm-house at Kingsnorth rode briskly down the declivity.

After several hours of patient attention, Mr. Moneypenny had succeeded in introducing to the notice of seven little expectant brothers and sisters a " remarkably fine child," and was now hurrying home in the sweet hope of a comfortable " snooze " for a couple of hours before the announcement of tea and muffins should arouse him to fresh exertion. The road at this particular spot had, even then, been cut deep below the surface of the soil, for the purpose of diminishing the abruptness of the descent, and, as either side of the superincumbent banks was clothed with a thick mantle of tangled copsewood, the passage, even by day, was sufficiently obscure, the level beams of the rising or setting sun, as they happened to enfilade the gorge, alone illuminating its recesses. A long stream of rosy light was just beginning to make its way through the vista, and Mr. Moneypenny's nose had scarcely caught and reflected its kindred ray, when the sturdiest and most active cob that ever rejoiced in the appellation of a " Suffolk Punch," brought herself up in mid career upon her haunches, and that with a suddenness which had almost induced her rider to describe that beautiful mathematical figure, the *parabola*, between her ears. Peggy—her name was Peggy—stood stock-still, snorting like a stranded grampus, and alike insensible to the gentle hints afforded her by hand and heel.

" Tch !—tch !—get along, Peggy ! " half-exclaimed, half-whistled the equestrian. If ever steed said in its heart, " I'll be shot if I do ! " it was Peggy at that moment. She planted her forelegs deep in the sandy soil, raised her stump of a tail to an elevation approaching the horizontal, protruded her nose like a pointer at a covey, and with expanded nostril continued to snuffle most egregiously.

Mr. Geoffrey Gambado, the illustrious " Master of the Horse to the Doge of Venice," tells us, in his far-famed treatise on the Art Equestrian, that the most embarrassing position in which a rider can be placed is, when *he* wishes to go one way, and his horse is determined to go another. There is, to be sure, a *tertium quid*, which, though it "splits the difference," scarcely obviates the inconvenience ; this is when the parties compromise the matter by not going any way at all—to this compromise Peggy and her (*soi-disant*) master were now reduced ; they had fairly joined issue. " Budge ! " quoth the doctor—" Budge not ! " quoth the fiend,—for nothing short of a fiend could, of a surety, inspire Peggy at such a time with such unwanted obstinacy—Moneypenny whipped and spurred—Peggy plunged, and reared, and kicked, and for several minutes to a superficial observer the termination of the contest might have appeared uncertain ; but your profound thinker sees at a glance that, however the scales may appear to vibrate, when the question between the sexes is one of perseverance, it is quite a lost case for the masculine gender. Peggy beat the doctor " all to sticks," and when he was fairly tired of goading and thumping, maintained her position as firmly as ever.

It is of no great use, and not particularly agreeable, to sit still, on a cold frosty morning in January, upon the outside of a brute that will neither go forwards nor backwards—so Mr. Moneypenny got off, and muttering curses *both* " loud " *and* " deep " between his chattering teeth, " progressed " as near as the utmost extremity of the extended bridle would allow him, to peep among the weeds and brushwood that flanked the road, in order to discover, if possible, what it was that so exclusively attracted the instinctive attention of his Bucephalus.

His curiosity was not long at fault ; the sunbeam glanced partially upon some object ruddier even than itself—it was a scarlet waistcoat, the wearer of which, overcome perchance by Christmas compotation, seemed to have selected for his " thrice-driven bed of down " the thickest clump of the tallest and most imposing nettles, thereon to doze away the narcotic effects of superabundant juniper.

This, at least, was Mr. Moneypenny's belief, or he would scarcely have uttered, at the highest pitch of his *contralto*, " What are you doing there, you drunken rascal ? frightening my horse ! "—We have already hinted, if not absolutely asserted, that Peggy was a mare ; but this was no time for verbal criticism.—" Get up, I say— get up, and go home, you scoundrel ! "—But the " scoundrel " and " drunken rascal " answered not ; he moved not, nor could the prolonged shouting of the appellant, aided by significant explosions from a double-thonged whip, succeed in eliciting a reply. No motion indicated that the recumbent figure, whose outline alone was visible, was a living and a breathing man.

The clear, shrill tones of a ploughboy's whistle sounded at this moment from the bottom of the hill, where the broad and green expanse of Romney Marsh stretches away from its foot for many a mile, and now gleamed through the mists of morning, dotted and enamelled with its thousand flocks. In a few minutes his tiny figure was seen " slouching " up the ascent, casting a most disproportionate and ogre-like shadow before him.

" Come here, Jack " quoth the doctor,—" come here, boy ; lay hold of this bridle, and mind that my horse does not run away."

Peggy threw up her head, and snorted disdain of the insinuation, —she had not the slightest intention of doing any such thing.

Mr. Moneypenny meanwhile, disencumbered of his restive nag, proceeded, by manual application, to arouse the sleeper.

Alas ! the Seven of Ephesus might sooner have been awakened from their century of somnolency. His was that " dreamless sleep that knows no waking " ; his cares in this world were over. Vainly did Moneypenny practise his own constant precept, " To be well shaken ! "—there lay before him the lifeless body of a MURDERED MAN !

The corpse lay stretched upon its back, partially concealed, as we have before said, by the nettles which had sprung up among the stumps of the half-grubbed underwood ; the throat was fearfully lacerated, and the dark, deep, arterial dye of the coagulated blood showed that the carotid had been severed. There was little to denote the existence of any struggle ; but as the day brightened, the sandy soil of the road exhibited an impression as of a body that had fallen on its plastic surface, and had been dragged to its present position, while fresh horse-shoe prints seemed to intimate that either the assassin or his victim had been mounted. The pockets of the deceased were turned out, and empty ; a hat and heavy-loaded whip lay at no great distance from the body.

" But what have we here ? " quoth Dr. Moneypenny ; " what is that the poor fellow holds so tightly in his hand ? "

That hand had manifestly clutched some article with all the spasmodic energy of a dying grasp—IT WAS AN OLD WIG !

Those who are fortunate enough to have seen a Cinque Port court-house may possibly divine what that useful and most necessary edifice was some eighty years ago. Many of them seem to have undergone little alteration, and are in general of a composite order of architecture, a fanciful arrangement of brick and timber, with what Johnson would have styled " interstices, reticulated, and decussated " between " intersections " of lath and plaster. Its less euphonious designation in the " Weald " is a " noggin." One half the basement story is usually of the more solid material, the other, open to the street,—from which it is separated only by a row of dingy columns, supporting a portion of the superstructure, —is paved with tiles, and sometimes does duty as a market-place, while, in its centre, flanking the board staircase that leads to the sesssions-house above, stands an ominous-looking machine, of heavy perforated wood, clasped within whose stern embrace " the rude forefathers of the hamlet sleep " off occasionally the drowsiness produced by convivial excess, in a most undignified position, an inconvenience much increased at times by some mischievous urchin, who, after abstracting the shoes of the helpless *detenu*, amuses himself by tickling the soles of his feet.

It was in such a place, or rather in the Court-room above, that in the year 1761 a hale, robust man, somewhat past the middle age, with a very bald pate, save where a continued tuft of coarse, wiry hair, stretching from above each ear, swelled out into a greyish-looking bush upon the occiput, held up his hand before a grave and enlightened assemblage of Dymchurch jurymen. He stood arraigned for that offence most heinous in the sight of God and man, the deliberate and cold-blooded butchery of an unoffending, unprepared, fellow-creature,—*homicidium quod nullo vidente, nullo auscultante, clam perpetratur*.

The victim was one Humphry Bourne, a reputable grazier of Ivychurch, worthy and well-to-do, though, perhance, a thought too apt to indulge on a market-day, when " a score of ewes " had brought in a reasonable profit. Some such cause had detained him longer than usual at an Ashford cattle-show ; he had left the town late, and alone ; early in the following morning his horse was found standing at his own stable-door, the saddle turned round beneath its belly, and much about the time that the corpse of its unfortunate master was discovered some four miles off, by our friend the pharmacopolist.

That poor Bourne had been robbed and murdered there could be no question.

Who, then, was the perpetrator of the atrocious deed ?—The unwilling hand almost refuses to trace the name of—Joseph Washford.

Yet so it was. Mr. Jeremiah Jarvis was himself the coroner for that division of the county of Kent known by the name of " The Lath of Scraye." He had not sat two minutes on the body before he recognised his *quondam* property, and started at beholding in the grasp of the victim, as torn in the death-struggle from the murderer's head, his own OLD WIG !—his own perky little pigtail, tied up with a piece of shabby shalloon, now wriggling and quivering, as in salutation of its ancient master. The silver buckles of the murdered man were found in Joe Washford's shoes,—broad pieces were found in Joe Washford's pockets,—Joe Washford had himself been found, when the hue-and-cry was up, hid in a corn-rig at no great distance from the scene of slaughter, his pruning-knife red with the evidence of his crime—" the grey hairs yet stuck to the heft ! "

For their humane administration of the laws, the lieges of this portion of the realm have long been celebrated. Here it was that merciful verdict was recorded in the case of the old lady accused of larceny, " We find her Not Guilty, and hope she will never do so any more ! " Here it was that the more experienced culprit, when called upon to plead with the customary, though somewhat superfluous, inquiry, as to " how he would be tried ? " substituted for the usual reply " By God and my country," that of " By your worship and a Dymchurch Jury."—Here it was—but enough !— not even a Dymchurch jury could resist such evidence, even though the gallows (*i.e.* the expense of erecting one) stared them, as well as the criminal, in the face. The very pigtail alone !—ever at his ear !—a clearer case of *suadente Diabolo* never was made out. Had there been a doubt, its very conduct in the Court-house would have settled the question. The Rev. Joel Ingoldsby, umquhile chaplain to the Romney Bench, has left upon record that when exhibited in evidence, together with the blood-stained knife, its twistings, its caperings, its gleeful evolutions quite " flabbergasted " the jury, and threw all beholders into a consternation. It was remarked too, by many in the Court, that the Forensic Wig of the Recorder himself, was, on that trying occasion, palpably agitated, and that its three depending, learned-looking tails lost curl at once, and slunk beneath the obscurity of the powdered collar, just as the boldest dog recoils from a rabid animal of its own species, however small and insignificant.

Why prolong the painful scene ?—Joe Washford was tried— Joe Washford was convicted—Joe Washford was hanged !

The fearful black gibbet, on which his body clanked in its chains to the midnight winds, frowns no more upon Orlestone Hill ; it has sunk beneath the encroaching hand of civilisation ; but there it might be seen late in the last century, an awful warning to all bald-pated gentlemen how they wear, or accept, the old wig of a Special Attorney,

Timeo Danaos et dona ferentes !

Such gifts, as we have seen, may lead to a " Morbid Delusion, the climax of which is Murder ! "

The fate of the Wig itself is somewhat doubtful ; nobody seems to have recollected, with any degree of precision, what became of it. Mr. Ingoldsby " had heard " that, when thrown into the fire by the Court-keeper, after whizzing, and fizzling, and performing all sorts of supernatural antics and contortions, it at length whirled up the chimney with a bang that was taken for the explosion of one of the Feversham powder-mills, twenty miles off ; while others insinuate that in the " Great Storm " which took place on the night when Mr. Jeremiah Jarvis went to his " long home,"— wherever that may happen to be,—and the whole of " The Marsh " appeared as one broad sheet of flame, something that looked very like a Fiery Wig—perhaps a miniature Comet—it had unquestionably a tail—was seen careering in the blaze,—and seeming to " ride on the whirlwind and direct the storm."

John Guinan

THE WATCHER O' THE DEAD

from THE CORNHILL MAGAZINE, 1929

It is now the fall of the night. The last of the neighbours are hitting the road for home. The time they went out through that door together, for the sake of the company on the way, as they said, did they give e'er a thought at all to myself, left alone here in this desolate house ? To be sure, they asked me more than once why I refuse to leave the place, and the day is in it, by the same token. But I have no call to answer them, though what I am about to set down here in black and white will settle the question, at least for myself.

A few hours ago, and the corpse of Tim McGowan was taken from under this roof and buried deep in the clay. They laid the spade and the shovel like a rude cross on the fresh sod of his grave, and they went down on their knees and said a few hasty prayers for the good of his soul. One or two, and their faces hidden in their hats, took good care not to rise from the wet ground till they got sight of others already on their two feet. Letting on that their thoughts were on higher things, they kept in mind the old belief that the first one to leave the churchyard warm in life would not be the last to come back cold in death.

The little groups moving out began to talk of the man who was gone. Their talk ran in whispers, for fear they might trouble his long sleep. They all knew, though none had the rights of it, that he was after earning his rest dearly. An old man, whose face was hard, even for his years, took a white clay pipe from the pocket of his body coat.

" God rest your soul, Tim McGowan," he cried. It was the custom to pray for the dead before taking a " draw " from a wake pipe. " God rest you in the grave," he added, " for it's little peace or ease you had and you in the world that we know ! "

The bulk of those who heard his words caught, a little gladly, a mocking undertone which stole through the kindly feeling that had at first shaken his voice. A young man, with eager eyes and a desire to know and talk of things that should be left hidden, took courage and spoke out bluntly :

" For him to be haunting the graveyard like a ghost, and he a living man ! That was a strange vagary, for sure."

" It was the death of the good woman a year ago," the old man went on, speaking more openly, in his turn. " It was her loss turned his poor head."

" There's no denying there was a queer strain in him already," the young man said to that. " Sure they say all of that family were a bit touched ! "

They did not scruple to speak like this before myself, and I of the one blood with the man who was dead, if any of them could know or suspect that. They were after doing their duty towards his mortal remains : if there was a kink in his nature or a mystery about his life why, they might fairly ask, should it not fill the gossip of an idle hour ? But it was myself only, the stranger amongst them, who knew the true reason of Tim McGowan's nightly vigils in Gort na Marbh, why he, a living man, as was said, chose to become the Watcher o' the Dead in the lonesome grave-yard. It was ere yesterday morning he told me his secret. Tim was lying there in the settle-bed from which his stark body was carried feet foremost this day. I was trying to get ready a little food by the fire on the hearth, for Tim had not been able to rise, let alone to do a hand's turn for himself. Our wants were simple, and it was not for the first time that I had turned my poor endeavours to homely use.

" There are times," I made bold to remark, " there are times I feel this house to be haunted " ; for every night during the short spell since I came to see my kinsman, I was sure I heard the fall of footsteps on the floor after the pair of us had gone to our beds. The rattling of the door, if it was not a troubled dream, had also startled me in my sleep. I had begun to ask myself was it one of these houses where the door must be left on the latch and the hearth swept clean for Those who come back. Always at a certain hour Tim was in a hurry to rake the fire and get shut of me out of the kitchen. A pang now shot through my breast. With the poor man hardly able to raise hand or foot, it was not kind to draw down such a thing. But he looked glad that I had given him the chance to speak out.

" As you make mention of it," he said eagerly, " I want to let you know the house is haunted, surely ! But it is not by any spirit of good or evil from beyond the grave. That is a strange thing, you will be saying."

" It is a strange thing," I agreed. I had no doubt what he was going to disclose. He had already given me the story of a house built, and not without warning, on a " fairy pass," through which the Sluagh Sidhe in their hosting and revels swept gaily every night. This was the house for sure : The Gentle Folk had never passed the gates of death and know nothing of the grave.

" But," he went on, " there is one other thing as strange again. It is that same you will now be hearing, if you pay heed to me."

" You mean that this is the house "—I began, intending to say that it was the house of the story, but I checked myself—" that it is a case of a fallen angel, hanging between heaven and hell, who never had to pay the penalty of death ? "

" If you let me," he made answer, " I will tell you the truth. The place is haunted by a mortal man ! "

" One still in the world, one who goes about in his clothes, one to be seen by daylight ? " I asked, without drawing breath.

" In troth," he declared, " it is haunted by the man who tells it, and no other, if I am still in the flesh itself ! "

I lifted him slightly in the bed, not knowing what to say or think. Was this his way of speaking about some common habit, or was his reason leaving him ?

" Whisper ! " he said, and his face was flushed. " You came here to gather old stories out of the past, over and above seeing your last living relative in the world, leaving out Michael, my son, who should be here by this. I might do worse than give you the true version of my own trouble."

This made a double reason why I should hear him out. There is no man but carries in his breast the makings of a story, which, though never told, comes more home to him, than any the mind of another man can find and fashion in words.

" What harm if my story should turn out a poor thing in the telling ? " he sighed. " It will ease my mind, if it does only that. And who knows : but we will talk of that when the time comes."

He turned aside from the food I was coaxing him to take, and started :

" It is now a year since herself was laid to rest. Laid to rest ! " He laughed, a little bitterly. " That is what they call it. A week after that again, call it what you like, the graveyard was closed by orders. There are people still to the fore who have their rights under the law ; but it is hardly likely that many, if any of them, will try to make good their claim to be buried in Gort na Marbh."

Gurthnamorrav, the Field of the Dead, that is what those around and about call the lonely patch to this day. Though this generation of them are " dull of " the ancient tongue, such names, of native savour, help to keep them one in soul with the proud children of Banbha who are in eternity. Vivid imagery, symbols drawn, in a manner of speaking, from the brown earth, words of strength and beauty that stud like gems of light and grace the common speech hold not merely an abiding charm in themselves. Such heritages of the mind of the Gael evoke through active fancy the fuller life of the race of kings no less surely than those relics of skill and handicraft found by chance in tilth or red bog, the shrine of bell or battle book, the bronze spear head, the torque of gold.

" But, surely," I objected, " those who are able would like to have their bones laid beside their own when their day of nature is past ! Surely they would chose such a ground as the place of their resurrection, as the holy men of old used to say ! "

" Time and time again," he made answer, " people have left it to their deaths not to be buried in Gort na Marbh. Man and wife have been parted, mother and child. What call have I to tell you the reason ? You know it rightly. You know it is the lot of the last body brought to its long home to be from that time forth the Watcher o' the Dead ? "

" I have heard tell of that queer—of that belief," I replied. " That the poor soul cannot go to its rest, if it took years itself, till another comes to fill its place ; that it must wander about in the dead of the night amongst the graves where the mortal body is crumbling to dust ; and, as one might say in a plain way, keep an eye over the place ! "

" And who would care to be buried in ground that was shut up for ever ? " he asked. " Even at the best of times people try their best endeavours to be first through the gate with the corpse of their own friend and when two funerals happen to fall on the one day."

And then he went on to tell me, and his voice failing at that, of all he was after going through thinking of his woman, his share of the world, making the weary, dreary, rounds of the graveyard during the best part of the changing year. And, bitter agony ! he felt that she could not share in the Communion of Saints, that all his good works for her sake would not hasten her release. But the thing that made it the hardest for him to bear was this : It was through his veneration for the old customs, through his great respect even for the dead, that this awful tribulation had come to the pair of them.

" Let you not be laughing at what I'm going to tell you now," he warned me : " for I won't deny there have been times when I made merry over the like myself. It was a seldom thing two funerals to be the one day ; nor would it have come to happen at the time it did if the other people had the proper spirit, like myself, or the right regard for the things good Christians hold highly. Listen ! They knew the order to close the graveyard, the other people knew it was on the road, for the man who was dead and going to be buried on the same day as herself was himself on the Board of Guardians. That was why they waked him for one night only, and they people of means, and rushed with him in unseemly haste to Gort na Marbh. But we got wind of it, and would have been the first, for all that, only we followed the old road, the long road, and in a decent and becoming way walked in through the open gate while they took a short cut and got in over the stile. We did more than that, and so did they. While the savages, for they were little less, while they were trampling above the relics of the dead, we went round about the ground in the track of the sun till we came in the proper course to the side of the open grave."

This set me thinking of the ancient ritual by which the corpse is brought round to pay its respects, as a body might say, to those who have gone before. I began to ask myself was it a fragment of Druid worship that had come down even to our own day. But this is what I said to my kinsman :

" You did what was right, and no one would be better pleased than the woman who was gone ! "

" That is the way I felt myself at the first going off," he agreed : " but soon I began to question myself : When I did the right thing, that the neighbours gave me full credit for, was I thinking more of what was expected from the living or what was due to the dead ? Was I thinking of myself, and the great name I'd be getting from the self-same neighbours, or of the woman going into the clay, who only wanted their prayers ? Many's the long night this thought kept me on the rack till I was nigh gone astray in the head. In my mind I saw her, and her brown habit down to her feet, and she looking to me for help, and it my sin of human respect, as I felt, that kept her so long from walking on the sunny hills of Glory ! Funeral after funeral went the way, for people have to die ; but not a one but passed the rusty gate of Gort na Marbh as a poor woman of the roads might give the go-by to a stricken house.

" At length and at last, I could stand it no longer, and one night I got up from my bed and made my way to the graveyard. 'Twas in the dark hour before the crowing of the cocks, when wandering spirits are warned home to their house of clay."

" And did you half expect to see the Watcher o' the Dead ? " I asked.

" Did I ? And why not ? " he asked in turn, by way of reply.

" With your mind disturbed that way," I went on, " the wonder is you didn't see her, if only in fancy."

I meant to be kind. He faced me testily.

" I did see her, as sure as I'm a living man ! " he declared.

I had not the heart to urge my view that it was only a brain-born figure.

" I no sooner crossed the stile," he said softly, " than I got clear sight of herself. She was moving through the graves she guarded, and a kindly look in her two eyes. The dead image I thought her

of the Nuns you see in the sick ward of the poorhouse in Bally-
brosna, and she taking a look at the beds in their little rows, and
fearing to waken the tired sleepers in her charge. There she was,
in truth, as I had seen her a thousand times in my own mind."

"In your own mind!" I said after him. "It was on your eyes,
so to speak, and you merely saw what was in your mind already.
Was it not more natural to see the figment that never left your
sight than not to see it at all?"

It was all very clear to me, and I felt this was sound talk; and
isn't it a caution the way the rage of battle will rise in a body and
set the tongue loose! But Tim's reply put a stop to any dispute
or war of words.

"It was in my mind, for sure," he said. "But tell me, you who
have the book learning, why was it in my mind? When a man's
brain begins to work, what gives it the start, or sets it going—or
does it start to go of itself?"

I had to give in that I always left such vexed questions to wiser
heads, adding, whimsically enough as it seems to me now, that
I was not such a great fool as to attempt an answer where they
failed. In a way I was put out by the reflection that this old man,
who "didn't know his letters," was making a mockery of me on the
head of my few books and my small store of book learning.

"There is nothing hard about the case I am after putting before
you," he said. "It was on my mind because the thing was taking
place in Gort na Marbh night after night, was taking place in the
Field of the Dead, though there was no living eye to see it!"

I had no reply to that, whether it was a head-made ghost or not.
Where was the use of starting to argue that nothing really takes
place if not within the knowledge of man? I told myself weakly
that such visions were due to the queer strain in the old man the
neighbours spoke about this day. It might be that, in his present
state, all this had only come into his head as the two of us talked
together. It did not occur to me then, and I have too much
respect for the dead to credit it now, that he was "taking a rise"
out of me, as the plain saying is.

Tim became a little rambling in his speech and asked me to
let him lie flat in the bed. I gathered from the words he mumbled
and jumbled that he made a promise to the departed spirit to take
her place till his own time came in real earnest: that he had bid
her go to her rest, in the Name of God, much, I could not help but
think, as one might banish an evil spirit to the "red sea" to make

ropes of the sand ; that he had kept his word, which brought great peace to his breast : and that he never set eyes on her again from that hour, there or there else.

I had no doubt he had but laid the ghost of his own troubled thoughts. It is not every poor mortal can do that same, even by dint of hard sacrifice. Tim was growing worse. I tried hard to cheer him. It was all to no use. I talked of his son, Michael, who was far away on the fishing grounds. We had already sent word for him to come home, and he might be here any stroke, if it was a long ways off, itself.

" Michael will never be here in time ! " the father groaned. " That is my great trouble. I never could ask another to do it. It would be again' reason."

" There is nothing you could name I would not gladly do ! " I declared ; and, in all fair speaking, I meant it.

" There are things no man should ask of his friend," he said to that, with a slight shake of the head.

" And who else should he ask but his friend ? " I laughed, trying to rouse him. " But, first, I'll send for the Doctor——"

" The Doctor, how are ye ! " he broke in on me. " That is not what I want. What can the like of himself do for a body who has seen the Watcher o' the Dead ? "

" What harm if you did itself ? " I asked. " The sign of a long life it is, as likely as not. It would be another story, entirely, one's ' fetch ' to be seen in the late hours of the day. An early death that would signify."

" The man," he made answer, " the man who lays eyes on the Watcher o' the Dead, late or early, if the like could come to pass at all before dark, that man will soon be only a shadow himself. I am saying, he will soon be among the silent company. The time I took the woman's place, the woman who held my heart for years, I knew rightly, it would not be for long. It is for that reason and no other I am after telling you my secret sorrow. I will never be able to put out this night, if I live through this night of the nights, or any night for the future ; and if it was a thing I failed her, sure herself would be disturbed in her rest."

I took a grip of his hand and looked down steadily into his eyes.

" Put your trust in me ! " I said. " I'll take your place till such time as you are laid in the clay ! "

Who is it, though he might throw doubt on the very stars above his head, would not try to humour an old man or a little child ?

" God sent you for a friend," he said, " praised be His holy
Name ! For all I know, I may not want you to do so much : I may
want you to do a little more, but in another way. I want you to
take my place till Michael comes, and not an hour more ; I want
you, as well as that, to tell him all I have told you and to give
him my dying wish, if it is a thing he does not come before I go
for ever. Whisper ! You'll tell Michael, in case I'm too far
through myself, that I am dying happy knowing he will not
refuse a last favour to the father who reared him. It is this :
That he will become the Watcher o' the Dead, though a living
man, like myself, and let me, after so much fret and torment,
go straight to herself, to his mother, in Heaven. Tell him I
know he will do this, for the rest of his mortal days, if it
comes to that. Tell him I know that, after that again, if he
gets no release he will have his bones laid in Gort na Marbh
and wait his own turn. I have done my share of watching, God
knows ! "

Some kind neighbours gathered during the course of the day,
and the priest of the parish was sent for. Father Malachy was
a man of the world, without being worldly. It is not for the knowing, and never will be in this world, whether Tim told him about
the Watcher o' the Dead. As a man, his reverence knew all the
customs and beliefs of the people, for he was one of them himself.
Deep in his nature a body might expect to find a kindly toleration
for the harmless " superstitions," as some would call them, lingering from the pagan days of Firbolg or Tuatha de Danaan. As a
priest, he had, no doubt, full knowledge of the rites of the Church
for dealing with " appearances " from the other world, which
shows it to be no harm to give heed to such things.

Tim kept quiet till the night wore on. Then he got restless and
began to mutter to himself. The use of his speech was wellnigh
gone. I caught such words as " Gort na Marbh," and " Herself,"
and " the Watcher o' the Dead." His grip was tight on my fist
when I said in his ear that I would not fail him, dead or alive, till
Michael came. The kind neighbours did not let on to hear the
pair of us, and I left him in their charge while I set out for the
strange duty I had taken on myself so lightly, taken on, indeed,
with a certain zest, in the vague hope of enlarging my experience.
It was clear from Tim's behaviour that the hour of the night had
come when he felt the " call " to the graveyard, and still there was
no sign of Michael. The moon was in the sky. The night was cold.

There was no stir. The place held no terrors for me. I set little store by Tim's story, except as a " study " in delusion. The old man was much in my thoughts, for he was passing rapidly away. I saw him in my mind, as he used to say, and he walking here and there through the graves that now held nothing but cold clay, passing by fallen stones, broken and moss-grown. I tried hard to banish such airy pictures, for I did not want to begin seeing sights.

What was that story Tim told me a few days ago as we stood before a headstone in Gort na Marbh ? It was a true tale of revenge, revenge both on the living and the dead, and it was a poor sort of revenge at that. Before long I would be seeing again the spot where the dead man he spoke about was laid in the clay. His relations, in blood and law, hoped to benefit largely by his death. But he left all to his son. The boy was an only child whose mother died the hour he came into the world. He came home, a likely youth, to be at the father's funeral. For the first time in his young life he saw the place that was now to be his own. It was natural for him to ask why the usual black plumes did not wave above the hearse instead of white. The errors of the past, if any, should have been covered by charity. Feuds are forgiven, if not forgotten, in the hour of death. It is what they told him, with wild malice, that black plumes were only for people who were lawfully joined in wedlock.

Here I found the elements of tragedy, but the story only helped to keep the figure of Tim before me. I was stepping over the stile and thinking of the nights he spent walking about in the dreary waste, for, after so much neglect, that is what it had by now sunk to. I felt the nettles rank and dank as I set foot on the ground ; and then—if it was not wild phantasy !—I got sight of Tim moving in the moonlight among the shadows of the headstones and the trees.

" In the Name of God ! " I cried, profanely, I am half afraid, " leave the place at once, and let me keep my promise in peace."

I was furious with the neighbours for letting him rise and he in a fever. But were they to be blamed ? I crossed hastily and found myself alone ! This gave me a start, and I began to wonder whether in that strange ground—for, surely, the place was not " right " !—I, in my turn, saw what was on my eyes only ! Had Tim been there in the flesh or was it that I, in my turn, had laid but the ghost of a deranged imagination ? Could it be that the queer strain of the family, if there is such a thing, runs in my own blood? Or does a sane man put such a question to himself? Without waiting for the crowing of the cocks, I made haste back to the house. My heart was beating loudly.

" We were going to call after you," the neighbours said to me. " Hardly was your back turned when the end came ! "

Tim was stretched there in his long sleep, his features set free by the kindly touch of death !

Last night at the same hour we dug his grave. I was heartened by the presence of the neighbours and lingered over the work till the dawn broke, walking about from time to time, " by way of no harm," trying to keep my promise to the dead man. More than once the shadows, moving with the shifting lanthorn, took a start out of me. There were a few of the neighbours would not put out with us. One was the strong young man who was so free of the tongue this day.

" Why do you want to choose such an unreasonable hour? " they grumbled. " It is not lucky to turn up the sod in the dead of the night."

" As likely as not," I heard another make answer, " he was waiting to see would Michael come on the long car."

I did not put him right. If we were waiting for Michael only the work could have been left over till morning. It is the long wait we would have, for the same Michael, God rest the poor boy ! God rest him ! I say, for before Tim was taken out this day word came that the hardy young fisherman had been lost a week ago in the depths of the salt water. The hungry, angry sea did not give up its dead. And now his death comes home to me ! Michael's bones will never be laid in Gort na Marbh. Michael will never, never, either in life or death, become the Watcher o' the Dead ! And I have pledged my word to the man who is gone, the father, to take his place till such time as Michael should come home ! That will be never, never !

What way can I break my word to the dead, whether I credit his story or doubt it ? It was part of his own belief, part of himself. What odds does it make even if he was out of his mind, or if I am a madman myself ? A promise, a promise to one passed away, is sacred.

Where is the good of talking of common sense ? Half the world is stupid with common sense, if there is any such quality. But I see a dismal prospect before me, till the end of my days, as likely

as not, let alone, for all I know, till the Day of Judgment itself !
Already I feel there is a stir in my blood, the time has come for me
to get up and make my lonely vigil : for I have been putting this
down in black and white for many hours. It is a true word for
Tim ; every man has his own story, his own agony. But I set out
to tell of his troubles, which, for sure, are at an end, and not of my
own, which, for all a body can see, are only in their birth throes.

———

E. and H. Heron

THE STORY OF KONNOR
OLD HOUSE

from " Real Ghost Stories" (Second Series), PEARSON'S
MAGAZINE, *April 1899*

" I hold," Mr. Flaxman Low, the eminent psychologist, was
saying, " that there are no other laws in what we term the realm
of the supernatural but those which are the projections or exten-
sions of natural laws."

" Very likely that's so," returned Naripse, with suspicious
humility. " But, all the same, Konnor Old House presents problems that won't work in with any natural laws I'm acquainted
with. I almost hesitate to give voice to them, they sound so impossible and—and absurd."

" Let's judge of them," said Low.

" It is said," said Naripse, standing up with his back to the fire,
" it is said that a Shining Man haunts the place. Also a light is
frequently seen in the library—I've watched it myself of a night
from here—yet the dust there, which happens to lie very thick
over the floor and the furniture, has afterwards shown no sign
of disturbance."

" Have you satisfactory evidence of the presence of the Shining
Man ? "

" I think so," replied Naripse shortly. " I saw him myself the
night before I wrote asking you to come up to see me. I went into

the house after dusk, and was on the stairs when I saw him : the tall figure of a man, absolutely white and shining. His back was towards me, but the sullen, raised shoulders and sidelong head expressed a degree of sinister animosity that exceeded anything I've ever met with. So I left him in possession, for it's a fact that anyone who has tried to leave his card at Konnor Old House has left his wits with it."

" It certainly sounds rather absurd," said Mr. Low, " but I suppose we have not heard all about it yet ? "

" No, there is a tragedy connected with the house, but it's quite a commonplace sort of story and in no way accounts for the Shining Man."

Naripse was a young man of means, who spent most of his time abroad, but the above conversation took place at the spot to which he always referred as home—a shooting-lodge connected with his big grouse-moor on the West Coast of Scotland. The lodge was a small new house built in a damp valley, with a trout-stream running just beyond the garden-hedge.

From the high ground above, where the moor stretched out towards the Solway Firth, it was possible on a fine day to see the dark cone of Ailsa Crag rising above the shimmering ripples. But Mr. Low happened to arrive in a spell of bad weather, when nothing was visible about the lodge but a few roods of sodden lowland, and a curve of the yellow tumbling little river, and beyond a mirky outline of shouldering hills blurred by the ever-falling rain. It may have been eleven o'clock on a depressing, muggy night, when Naripse began to talk about Konnor Old House as he sat with his guests over a crackling flaming fire of pinewood.

" Konnor Old House stands on a spur of the ridge opposite— one of the finest sites possible, and it belongs to me. Yet I am obliged to live in this damp little boghole, for the man who would pass a night in Konnor is not to be met with in this county ! "

Sullivan, the third man present, replied he was, perhaps—with a glance at Low—there were two, which stung Naripse, who turned his words into a deliberate challenge.

" Is it a bet ? " asked Sullivan, rising. He was a tallish man, dark, and clean-shaven, whose features were well-known to the public in connection with the emerald green jersey of the Rugby International Football Team of Ireland. " If it is, it's a bet I'm going to win ! Good-night. In the morning, Naripse, I'll trouble you for the difference."

" The affair is much more in Low's line than in yours," said Naripse. " But you're not really going ? "

" You may take it I am though ! "

" Don't be a fool, Jack ! Low, tell him not to go, tell him there are things no man ought to meddle with——" he broke off.

" There are things no man can meddle with," replied Sullivan, obstinately fixing his cap on his head, " and my backing out of this bet would stand in as one of them ! "

Naripse was strangely urgent.

" Low, speak to him ! You know——"

Flaxman Low saw that the big Irishman's one vanity had got upon its legs ; he also saw that Naripse was very much in earnest.

" Sullivan's big enough to take care of himself," he said laughing. " At the same time, if he doesn't object, we might as well hear the story before he starts."

Sullivan hesitated, then flung his cap into a corner.

" That's so," he said.

It was a warm night for the time of the year, and they could hear, through the open window, the splashing downpour of the rain.

" There's nothing so lonely as the drip of heavy rain ! " began Naripse, " I always associate it with Konnor Old House. The place has stood empty for ten years or more, and this is the story they tell about it. It was last inhabited by a Sir James Mackian, who had been a merchant of sorts in Sierra Leone. When the baronetcy fell to him, he came to England and settled down in this place with a pretty daughter and a lot of servants, including a nigger, named Jake, whose life he was said to have saved in Africa. Everything went on well for nearly two years, when Sir James had occasion to go to Edinburgh for a few days. During his absence his daughter was found dead in her bed, having taken an overdose of some sleeping draught. The shock proved too great for her father. He tried travelling, but, on his return home, he fell into a settled melancholy, and died some months later a dumb imbecile at the asylum."

" Well, I shan't object to meeting the girl as she's so pretty," remarked Sullivan with a laugh. " But there's not much in the story."

" Of course," added Naripse, " countryside gossip adds a good deal of colour to the plain facts of the case. It is said that terrible details connected with Miss Mackian's death were suppressed at the inquest, and people recollected afterwards that for months the girl had worn an unhappy, frightened look. It seemed she disliked the negro, and had been heard to beg her father to send him away, but the old man would not listen to her."

"What became of the negro in the end?" asked Flaxman Low.

"In the end Sir James kicked him out after a violent scene, in the course of which he appears to have accused Jake of having some hand in causing the girl's death. The nigger swore he'd be revenged on him, but, as a matter of fact, he left the place almost immediately, and has never been heard of since—which disposes of the nigger. A short time after the old man went mad ; he was found lying on a couch in the library—a hopeless imbecile." Saying this, Naripse went to the window, and looked out into the rainy darkness. "Konnor Old House stands on the ridge opposite, and a part of the building, including the library window, where the light is sometimes seen, is visible through the trees from here. There is no light there to-night, though."

Sullivan laughed his big, full laugh.

"How about your shining man ? I hope we may have the luck to meet. I suspect some canny Scots tramp knows where to get a snug roost rent free."

"That may be so," replied Naripse, with a slow patience. "I can only say that after seeing the light of a night, I have more than once gone up in the morning to have a look at the library, and never found the thick dust in the least disturbed."

"Have you noticed if the light appears at regular intervals ? " said Low.

"No ; it's there on and off. I generally see it in rainy weather."

"What sort of people have gone crazy in Konnor Old House ? " asked Sullivan.

"One was a tramp. He must have lived pleasantly in the kitchen for days. Then he took to the library, which didn't agree with him apparently. He was found in a dying state lying upon Sir James's couch, with horrible black patches on his face. He was too far gone to speak, so nothing was gleaned from him."

"He probably had a dirty face, and, having caught cold in the rain, went into Konnor Old House and died quietly there of pneumonia or something of the kind, just as you or I might have done, tucked up in our own little beds at home," commented Sullivan.

" The last man to try his luck with the ghosts," went on Naripse, without noticing this remark, " was a young fellow, called Bowie, a nephew of Sir James. He was a student at Edinburgh University and he wanted to clear up the mystery. I was not at home, but my factor allow him to pass a night in the house. As he did not appear next day, they went to look for him. He was found lying on the couch—and he has not spoken a rational word since."

" Sheer—mere physical fright, acting on an overwrought brain ! " Sullivan summed up the case scornfully. " And now I'm off. The rain has stopped, and I'll get up to the house before midnight. You may expect me at dawn to tell you what I've seen."

" What do you intend to do when you get there ? " asked Flaxman Low.

" I'll pass the night on the ghostly couch which I suppose I shall find in the library. Take my word for it, madness is in Sir James's family ; father and daughter and nephew all gave proof of it in different ways. The tramp, who was perhaps in there for a couple of days, died a natural death. It only needs a healthy man to run the gauntlet and set all this foolish talk at rest."

Naripse was plainly much disturbed though he made no further objection, but when Sullivan was gone, he moved restlessly about the room looking out of the window from time to time. Suddenly he spoke :

" There it is ! The light I mentioned to you."

Mr. Low went to the window. Away on the opposite ridge a faint light glimmered out through the thick gloom. Then he glanced at his watch.

" Rather over an hour since he started," he remarked. " Well, now, Naripse, if you will be so good as to hand me *Human Origins* from the shelf behind you, I think we may settle down to wait for dawn. Sullivan's just the man to give a good account of himself—under most circumstances."

" Heaven send there may be no black side to this business ! " said Naripse. " Of course I was a fool to say what I did about the Old House, but nobody except an ass like Jack would think I meant it. I wish the night was well over ! That light is due to go out in two hours anyway."

Even to Mr. Low the night seemed unbearably long ; but at the first streak of dawn he tossed his book on to the sofa, stretched himself, and said : " We may as well be moving ; let's go and see what Sullivan is doing."

The rain began to fall again, and was coming down in close straight lines as the two men drove up the avenue to Konnor Old House. As they ascended, the trees grew thicker on the banks of the cutting which led them in curves to the terrace on which stood the house. Although it was a modern red-brick building, rather picturesque with its gables and sharply-pitched overhanging roofs, it looked desolate and forbidding enough in the grey daybreak. To the left lay lawns and gardens, to the right the cliff fell away steeply to where the burn roared in spate some three hundred feet below. They drove round to the empty stables, and then hurried back to the house on foot by a path that debouched directly under the library window. Naripse stopped under it, and shouted : " Hullo ! Jack, where are you ? "

But no answer came, and they went on to the hall door. The gloom of the wet dawning and the heavy smell of stagnant air filled the big hall as they looked round at its dreary emptiness. The silence within the house itself was oppressive. Again Naripse shouted, and the noise echoed harshly through the passages, jarring on the stillness. Then he led the way to the library at a run.

As they came in sight of the doorway a wave of some nauseating odour met them, and at the same moment they saw Sullivan lying just outside the threshold, his body twisted and rigid like a man in the extremity of pain, his contorted profile ivory-pale against the dark oak flooring. As they stooped to raise him, Mr. Low had just time to notice the big gloomy room beyond, with its heaped and trampled layers of accumulated dust. There was no time for more than a glance, for the indescribable, fetid odour almost overpowered them as they hastened to carry Sullivan into the open air.

" We must get him home as soon as we can," said Mr. Low, " for we have a very sick man on our hands."

This proved to be true. But in a few days, thanks to Mr. Low's treatment and untiring care, the severe physical symptoms became less urgent, and in due time Sullivan's mind cleared.

The following account is taken from the written statement of his experience in Konnor Old House :

" On reaching the house he entered as noiselessly as possible, and made for the library, finding his way by the help of a series of matches to Sir James's couch, upon which he lay down. He was conscious at once of an acrid taste in his mouth, which he accounted for by the clouds of dust he had raised in crossing the room.

" First he began to think about the approaching football match with Scotland, for which he was already in training. He was still in his mood of derisive incredulity. The house seemed vastly empty, and wrapped in an uneasy silence, a silence which made each of his comfortable movements an omen of significance. Presently the sense of a presence in the room was borne in upon him. He sat up, and spoke softly. He almost expected someone to answer him, and so strong did this feeling become that he called out : ' Who's there ? ' No reply came, and he sat on amidst the oppressive silence. He says the slightest noise would have been a relief. It was the listening in the silence that bred in him so intense a longing to grapple with some solid opponent.

" Fear ! He, who had denied the very existence of cause for fear, found himself shivering with an untranslatable terror ! This was fear ! He realised it with an infinite recoil of anger.

" Presently he became aware that the darkness about him was clearing. A feeble light filtered slowly through it from above. Looking up at the ceiling, he perceived directly above his head an irregular patch of pale phosphorescent luminance, which grew gradually brighter. How long he sat with his head thrown back, staring at the light, he does not know. It seemed years. Then he spoke to himself plainly. With an immense effort, he forced his eyes away from the light and got upon his feet to drag his limbs round the room. The phosphorescence was of a greenish tint, and as strong as moonlight, but the dust rose like vapour at the slightest movement, and somewhat obscured its power. He moved about, but not for long. A clogging weight, such as one feels in nightmare, pressed upon him, and his exhaustion was intensified by the overpowering physical disgust bred in him by the repulsive odour which passed across his face as he staggered back to the couch.

" For a few moments he would not look up. He says he had an impression that someone was watching him through the radiance as through a window. The atmosphere about him was thickening and cloaking the walls with drowsy horror, while his senses revolted and choked at the growing odour. Then followed a state of semi-sleep, for he recollects no more until he found himself staring again at the luminous patch on the ceiling.

" By this time the brightness was beginning to dim ; dark smears showed through it here and there, which ran slowly together till out of them grew and protruded a fat, black, evil face. A second later Sullivan was aware that the horrible face was sinking down nearer and nearer to his own, while all about it the light changed to black, dripping fluid, that formed great drops and fell.

" It seemed as if he could not save himself ; he could not move ! The fighting blood in him had died out. Then fear, mad fear and strong loathing gave him the strength to act. He saw his own hand working savagely, it passed through and through the impending face, yet he swears that he felt a slight impact and that he saw the fat, glazed skin quiver ! Then, with a final struggle, he tore it himself from the couch, and, rushing to the door, he wrenched open, and plunged forward into a red vacancy, down—down—— After that he remembered no more."

While Sullivan still lay ill and unable to give an account of himself or of what had happened at Konnor Old House, Mr. Flaxman Low expressed his intention of paying a visit to the asylum for the purpose of seeing young Bowie. But on arrival at the asylum, he found that Bowie had died during the previous night. A weary-eyed assistant doctor took Mr. Low to see the body. Bowie had evidently been of a gaunt, but powerful build. The features, though harsh, were noble, the face being somewhat disfigured by a rough, raised discoloration, which extended from the centre of the forehead to behind the right ear.

Mr. Low asked a question.

" Yes, it is a very obscure case," observed the assistant, " but it is the disease he died of. When he was brought here some months ago he had a small dark spot on his forehead, but it spread rapidly, and there are now similar large patches over the whole of his body. I take it to be of a cancerous character, likely to occur in a scrofulous subject after a shock and severe mental strain, such as Bowie chose to subject himself to by passing a night in Konnor Old House. The first result of the shock was the imbecility, an increasing lethargic condition of the body supervened and finally coma."

While the doctor was speaking, Mr. Low bent over the dead man and closely examined the mark upon the face.

" This mark appears to be the result of a fungoid growth, perhaps akin to the Indian disease known as *mycetoma* ? " he said at length.

" It may be so. The case is very obscure, but the disease, whatever we may call it, appears to be in Bowie's family, for I believe his uncle, Sir James Mackian, had precisely similar symptoms during his last illness. He also died in this institution, but that was before my time," replied the assistant.

After a further examination of the body Mr. Low took his leave, and during the following day or two was busily engaged in a spare empty room placed at his disposal by Naripse. A deal table and chair were all he required, Mr. Low explained, and to these he added a microscope, an apparatus for producing a moist heat, and the coat worn by Sullivan on the night of his adventure. At the end of the third day, as Sullivan was already on the road to recovery, Mr. Low, accompanied by Naripse, paid a second visit to Konnor Old House, during which Low mentioned some of his conclusions about the strange events which had occurred there. It will be an easy task to compare Mr. Flaxman Low's theory with the experience detailed by Sullivan, and with the one or two subsequent discoveries that added something like confirmation to his conclusions.

Mr. Low and his host drove up as on the previous occasion, and stabled the horse as before. The day was dry, but grey, and the time the early afternoon. As they ascended the path leading to the house, Mr. Low remarked, after gazing up for a few seconds at the library window :

" That room has the air of being occupied."

" Why ?—What makes you think so ? " asked Naripse nervously.

" It is hard to say, but it produces that impression."

Naripse shook his head despondently.

" I've always noticed it myself," he returned, " I wish Sullivan were all right again and able to tell us what he saw in there. Whatever it was it has nearly cost him his life. I don't suppose we shall ever know anything more definite about the matter."

" I fancy I can tell you," replied Low, " but let us get on into the library, and see what it looks like before we enter into the subject any further. By the way, I should advise you to tie your handkerchief over your mouth and nose before we go into the room."

Naripse, upon whom the events of the last few days had had a very strong effect, was in a state of scarcely-controllable excitement.

" What do you mean, Low ?—you can't have any idea——"

" Yes, I believe the dust in the house to be simply poisonous. Sullivan inhaled any amount of it—hence his condition."

The same suggestion of loneliness and stagnation hung about the house as they passed through the hall and entered the library. They halted at the door and looked in. The amount of greenish dust in the room was extraordinary ; it lay in little drifts and mounds over the floor, but most abundantly just about the couch. Immediately above this spot, they perceived on the ceiling a long, discoloured stain. Naripse pointed to it.

" Do you see that ? It is a bloodstain, and, I give you my word, it grows larger and larger every year ! " He finished the sentence in a low voice, and shuddered.

" Ah, so I should have expected," observed Flaxman Low, who was looking at the stained ceiling with much interest. " That, of course, explains everything."

" Low, tell me what you mean ? A bloodstain that grows year by year explains everything ? " Naripse broke off and pointed to the couch. " Look there ! a cat's been walking over that sofa."

Mr. Low put his hand on his friend's shoulder and smiled.

" My dear fellow ! That stain on the ceiling is simply a patch of mould and fungi. Now come in carefully without raising the dust, and let us examine the cat's footsteps, as you call them."

Naripse advanced to the couch and considered the marks gravely.

" They are not the footmarks of any animal, they are something much more unaccountable. They are raindrops. And why should raindrops be here in this perfectly watertight room, and even then only in one small part of it ? You can't very well explain that, and you certainly can't have expected it ? "

" Look round and follow my points," replied Mr. Low. " When we came to fetch Sullivan, I noticed the dust which far exceeds the ordinary accumulation even in the most neglected places. You may also notice that it is of a greenish colour and of extreme fineness. This dust is of the same nature as the powder you find in a puff-ball, and is composed of minute sporuloid bodies. I found that Sullivan's coat was covered with this fine dust, and also about the collar and upper portion of the sleeve I found one or two gummy drops which correspond to these raindrops, as you call them. I naturally concluded from their position that they had fallen from above. From the dust, or rather spores, which I found on Sullivan's coat, I have since cultivated no fewer than four specimens of fungi, of which three belong to known African species ; but the fourth, so far as I know, has never been described, but it approximates most closely to one of the *phalliodei*."

" But how about the raindrops, or whatever they are ? I believe they drop from that horrible stain."

" They are drops from the stain, and are caused by the unnamed fungus I have just alluded to. It matures very rapidly, and absolutely decays as it matures, liquefying into a sort of dark mucilage, full of spores, which drips down, and diffuses a most repulsive odour. In time the mucilage dries, leaving the dust of the spores."

" I don't know much about these things myself," replied Naripse dubiously, " and it strikes me you know more than enough. But look here, how about the light ? You saw it last night yourself."

" It happens that the three species of African fungi possess well known phosphorescent properties, which are manifested not only during decomposition, but also during the period of growth. The light is only visible from time to time ; probably climatic and atmospheric conditions only admit of occasional efflorescence."

" But," object Naripse, " supposing it to be a case of poisoning by fungi as you say, how is it that Sullivan, though exposed to precisely the same sources of danger as the others who have passed a night here, has escaped ? He has been very ill, but his mind has already regained its balance, whereas, in the three other cases, the mind was wholly destroyed."

Mr. Low looked very grave.

" My dear fellow, you are such an excitable and superstitious person that I hesitate to put your nerves to any further test."

" Oh, go on ! "

" I hesitate for two reasons. The one I have mentioned, and also because in my answer I must speak of curious and unpleasant things, some of which are proved facts, others only more or less well-founded assumptions. It is acknowledged that fungi exert an important influence in certain diseases, a few being directly attributable to fungi as a primary cause. Also it is an historical fact that poisonous fungi have more than once been used to alter the fate of nations. From the evidence before us and the condition of Bowie's body, I can but conclude that the unknown fungus I have alluded to is of a singularly malignant nature, and acts through the skin upon the brain with terrible rapidity, afterwards gradually inter-penetrating all the tissues of the body, and eventually causing death. In Sullivan's case, luckily, the falling drops only touched his clothing, not his skin."

" But wait a minute, Low, how did these fungi come here ? And how can we rid the house of them ? Upon my word, it is enough to make a man go off his head to hear about it. What are you going to do now ? "

" In the first place we will go upstairs and examine the flooring just above that stained patch of ceiling."

" You can't do that I'm afraid. The room above this happens to be divided into two portions by a hollow partition between 2ft. and 3ft. thick," said Naripse, " the interior of which may originally have been meant for a cupboard, but I don't think it has ever been used."

" Then let us examine the cupboard ; there must be some way of getting into it."

Upon this Naripse led the way upstairs, but, as he gained the top, he leant back, and grasping Mr. Low by the arm thrust him violently forward.

" Look ! the light—did you see the light ? " he said.

For a second or two it seemed as if a light, like the elusive light thrown by a rotating reflector, quivered on the four walls of the landing, then disappeared almost before one could be certain of having seen it.

" Can you point me out the precise spot where you saw the shin-ing figure you told us of ? " asked Low.

Naripse pointed to a dark corner of the landing.

" Just there in front of that panel between the two doors. Now that I come to think of it, I fancy there is some means of opening the upper part of that panel. The idea was to ventilate the cup-board-like space I mentioned just now."

Naripse walked across the landing and felt round the panel, till he found a small metal knob. On turning this, the upper part of the panel fell back like a shutter, disclosing a narrow space of darkness beyond. Naripse thrust his head into the opening and peered into the gloom, but immediately started back with a gasp.

" The shining man ! " he cried. " He's there ! "

Mr. Flaxman Low, hardly knowing what to expect, looked over his shoulder ; then, exerting his strength, pulled away some of the lower boarding. For within, at arm's length, stood a dimly shining figure ! A tall man, with his back towards them, leaning against the left side of the partition, and shrouded from head to foot in faintly luminous white mould.

The figure remained quite motionless while they stared at it in surprise ; then Mr. Flaxman Low pulled on his glove, and, leaning forward, touched the man's head. A portion of the white mass came away in his fingers, the lower surface of which showed a bunch of frizzled negroid hair.

" Good Heavens, Low, what do you make of this ? " asked Naripse. " It must be the body of Jake. But what is this shining stuff ? "

Low stood under the wide skylight and examined what he held in his fingers.

" Fungus," he said at last. " And it appears to have some property allied to the mouldy fungus which attacks the common house-fly. Have you not seen them dead upon window-panes, stiffly fixed upon their legs, and covered with a white mould ? Something of the same kind has taken place here."

" But what had Jake to do with the fungus ? And how did he come here ? "

" All that, of course, we can only surmise," replied Mr. Low. " There is little doubt that secrets of nature hidden from us are well known to the various African tribes. It is possible that the negro possessed some of these deadly spores, but how or why he made use of them are questions that can never be cleared up now."

" But what was he doing here ? " asked Naripse.

" As I said before we can only guess the answer to that question, but I should suppose that the negro made use of this cupboard as a place where he could be free from interruption ; that he here cultivated the spores is proved by the condition of his body and of the ceiling immediately below. Such an occupation is by no means free from danger, especially in an airless and inclosed space such as this. It is evident that either by design or accident he became infected by the fungus poison, which in time covered his whole body as you now see. The subject of obeah," Flaxman Low went on reflectively, " is one to the study of which I intend to devote myself at some future period. I have, indeed, already made some arrangements for an expedition in connection with the subject into the interior of Africa."

" And how is the horrible thing to be got rid of? Nothing short of burning the place down would be of any radical use," remarked Naripse.

Low, who by this time was deeply engrossed in considering the strange facts with which he had just become acquainted, answered abstractedly : " I suppose not."

Naripse said no more, and the words were only recalled to Mr. Low's mind a day or two later, when he received by post a copy of the *West Coast Advertiser*. It was addressed in the handwriting of Naripse, and the following extract was lightly scored :

" Konnor Old House, the property of Thomas Naripse, Esquire, of Konnor Lodge, was, we regret to say, destroyed by fire last night. We are sorry to add that the loss to the owner will be considerable, as no insurance policy had been effected with regard to the property."

W. B. Seabrook

TOUSSEL'S PALE BRIDE

from THE MAGIC ISLAND

George G. Harrap, 1929

An elderly and respected Haitian gentleman whose wife was French had a young niece, by name Camille, a fair-skinned octoroon girl whom they introduced and sponsored in Port-au-Prince society, where she became popular, and for whom they hoped to arrange a brilliant marriage.

Her own family, however, was poor ; her uncle, it was understood, could scarcely be expected to dower her—he was prosperous, but not wealthy, and had a family of his own—and the French *dot* system prevails in Haiti, so that while the young beaux of the *élite* crowded to fill her dance-cards, it became gradually evident that none of them had serious intentions.

When she was nearing the age of twenty, Matthieu Toussel, a rich coffee-grower from Morne Hôpital, became a suitor, and presently asked her hand in marriage. He was dark and more than twice her age, but rich, suave, and well educated. The principal house of the Toussel habitation, on the mountainside almost overlooking Port-au-Prince, was not thatched, mud-walled, but a fine wooden bungalow, slate-roofed, with wide verandahs, set in a garden among gay poinsettias, palms, and Bougainvillæa vines. He had built a road there, kept his own big motor-car, and was often seen in the fashionable cafés and clubs.

There was an old rumour that he was affiliated in some way with Voodoo or sorcery, but such rumours are current concerning almost every Haitian who has acquired power in the mountains, and in the case of men like Toussel are seldom taken seriously. He asked no *dot*, he promised to be generous, both to her and her straitened family, and the family persuaded her into the marriage.

The black planter took his pale girl-bride back with him to the mountain, and for almost a year, it appears, she was not unhappy, or at least gave no signs of it. They still came down to Port-au-Prince, appeared occasionally at the club *soirées*. Toussel permitted her to visit her family whenever she liked, lent her father money, and arranged to send her young brother to a school in France.

But gradually her family, and her friends as well, began to suspect that all was not going so happily up yonder as it seemed. They began to notice that she was nervous in her husband's presence, that she seemed to have acquired a vague, growing dread of him. They wondered if Toussel were ill-treating or neglecting her. The mother sought to gain her daughter's confidence, and the girl gradually opened her heart. No, her husband had never ill-treated her, never a harsh word ; he was always kindly and considerate, but there were nights when he seemed strangely preoccupied, and on such nights he would saddle his horse and ride away into the hills, sometimes not returning until after dawn, when he seemed even stranger and more lost in his own thoughts than on the night before. And there was something in the way he sometimes sat staring at her which made her feel that she was in some way connected with those secret thoughts. She was afraid of his thoughts and afraid of him. She knew intuitively, as women know, that no other woman was involved in these nocturnal excursions. She was not jealous. She was in the grip of an unreasoning fear. One morning when she thought he had been away all night in the hills, chancing to look out of a window, so she told her mother, she had seen him emerging from the door of a low frame building in their own big garden, set at some distance from the others and which he had told her was his office where he kept his accounts, his business papers, and the door always locked. . . . "So, therefore," said the mother, relieved and reassured, "what does this all amount to ? Business troubles, those secret thoughts of his, probably . . . some coffee combination he is planning and which is perhaps going wrong, so that he sits up all night at his desk figuring and devising, or rides off to sit up half the night consulting with others. Men are like that. It explains itself. The rest of it is nothing but your nervous imagining."

And this was the last rational talk the mother and daughter ever had. What subsequently occurred up there on the fatal night of the first wedding anniversary they pieced together from the half-lucid intervals of a terrorised, cowering, hysterical creature, who finally went stark, raving mad. But what she had gone through was indelibly stamped on her brain ; there were early periods when she seemed quite sane, and the sequential tragedy was gradually evolved.

On the evening of their anniversary Toussel had ridden away, telling her not to sit up for him, and she had assumed that in his preoccupation he had forgotten the date, which hurt her and made her silent. She went away to bed early, and finally fell asleep.

Near midnight she was awakened by her husband, who stood by the bedside, holding a lamp. He must have been some time returned, for he was fully dressed now in formal evening clothes.

"Put on your wedding dress and make yourself beautiful," he said ; " we are going to a party." She was sleepy and dazed, but innocently pleased, imagining that a belated recollection of the date had caused him to plan a surprise for her. She supposed he was taking her to a late supper-dance down at the club by the seaside, where people often appeared long after midnight. " Take your time," he said, " and make yourself as beautiful as you can— there is no hurry."

An hour later when she joined him on the verandah, she said, " But where is the car ? "

" No," he replied, " the party is to take place here," and she noticed that there were lights in the outbuilding, the " office " across the garden. He gave her no time to question or protest. He seized her arm, led her through the dark garden, and opened the door. The office, if it had ever been one, was transformed into a dining-room, softly lighted with tall candles. There was a big old-fashioned buffet with a mirror and cut-glass bowls, plates of cold meats and salads, bottles of wine and decanters of rum.

In the centre of the room was an elegantly set table with damask cloth, flowers, glittering silver. Four men, also in evening clothes, but badly fitting, were already seated at this table. There were two vacant chairs at its head and foot. The seated men did not rise when the girl in her bride-clothes entered on her husband's arm. They sat slumped down in their chairs and did not even turn their heads to greet her. There were wine-glasses partly filled before them, and she thought they were already drunk.

As she sat down mechanically in the chair to which Toussel led her, seating himself facing her, with the four guests ranged between them, two on either side, he said, in an unnatural strained way, the stress increasing as he spoke :

" I beg you . . . to forgive my guests their . . . seeming rudeness. It has been a long time . . . since . . . they have . . . tasted wine . . . sat like this at table . . . with . . . with so fair a hostess. . . . But, ah, presently . . . they will drink with you, yes . . . lift . . . their arms, as I lift mine . . . clink glasses with you . . . more . . . they will arise and . . . dance with you . . . more . . . they will . . ."

Near her, the black fingers of one silent guest were clutched rigidly around the fragile stem of a wine-glass, tilted, spilling. The horror pent up in her overflowed. She seized a candle, thrust it close to the slumped, bowed face, and saw the man was dead. She was sitting at a banquet table with four propped-up corpses.

Breathless for an intsant, then screaming, she leaped to her feet and ran. Toussel reached the door too late to seize her. He was heavy and more than twice her age. She ran still screaming across the dark garden, flashing white among the trees, out through the gate. Youth and utter terror lent wings to her feet, and she escaped. . . .

A procession of early market-women, with their laden baskets and donkeys, winding down the mountainside at dawn, found her lying unconscious far below, at the point where the jungle trail emerged into the road. Her filmy dress was ripped and torn, her little white satin bride-slippers were scuffed and stained, one of the high heels ripped off where she had caught it in a vine and fallen.

They bathed her face to revive her, bundled her on a pack-donkey, walking beside her, holding her. She was only half conscious, incoherent, and they began disputing among themselves as peasants do. Some thought she was a French lady who had been thrown or fallen from a motor-car ; others thought she was a *Dominicaine*, which has been synonymous in creole from earliest colonial days with " fancy prostitute." None recognised her as Madame Toussel ; perhaps none of them had ever seen her. They were discussing and disputing whether to leave her at a hospital of Catholic sisters on the outskirts of the city, which they were approaching, or whether it would be safer—for them—to take her directly to police headquarters and tell their story. Their loud disputing seemed to rouse her ; she seemed partially to recover her senses and understand what they were saying. She told them her name, her maiden family name, and begged them to take her to her father's house.

There, put to bed and with doctors summoned, the family were able to gather from the girl's hysterical utterances a partial comprehension of what had happened. They sent up that same day to confront Toussel if they could—to search his habitation. But Toussel was gone, and all the servants were gone except one old man, who said that Toussel was in Santo Domingo. They broke into the so-called office, and found there the table still set for six people, wine spilled on the table-cloth, a bottle overturned, chairs knocked over, the platters of food still untouched on the sideboard, but beyond that they found nothing.

Toussel never returned to Haiti. It is said that he is living now in Cuba. Criminal pursuit was useless. What reasonable hope could they have had of convicting him on the unsupported evidence of a wife of unsound mind ?

And there, as it was related to me, the story trailed off to a shrugging of the shoulders, to mysterious inconclusion.

What had this Toussel been planning—what sinister, perhaps criminal necromancy in which his bride was to be the victim or the instrument ? What would have happened if she had not escaped ?

I asked these questions, but got no convincing explanation or even theory in reply. There are tales of rather ghastly abominations, unprintable, practised by certain sorcerers who claim to raise the dead, but so far as I know they are only tales. And as for what actually did happen that night, credibility depends on the evidence of a demented girl.

So what is left?

What is left may be stated in a single sentence:

Matthieu Toussel arranged a wedding anniversary supper for his bride at which six plates were laid, and when she looked into the faces of his four other guests, she went mad.

THE END